A Theological Introduction to the Old Testament

Mark W. Hamilton

OXFORD
UNIVERSITY PRESS

OXFORD
UNIVERSITY PRESS

Oxford University Press is a department of the University of Oxford. It furthers
the University's objective of excellence in research, scholarship, and education
by publishing worldwide. Oxford is a registered trade mark of Oxford University
Press in the UK and certain other countries.

Published in the United States of America by Oxford University Press
198 Madison Avenue, New York, NY 10016, United States of America.

Library of Congress Cataloging-in-Publication Data
Names: Hamilton, Mark W., author.
Title: A theological introduction to the Old Testament / Mark W. Hamilton.
Description: New York : Oxford University Press USA, 2018. | Includes index.
Identifiers: LCCN 2017032763 (print) | LCCN 2018005571 (ebook) |
ISBN 9780190203139 (updf) | ISBN 9780190865160 (epub) |
ISBN 9780190203115 (hardcover : alk. paper)
Subjects: LCSH: Bible. Old Testament—Theology. | Bible.
Old Testament—Introductions.
Classification: LCC BS1192.5 (ebook) | LCC BS1192.5 .H35 2018 (print) | DDC 221.6/1—dc23
LC record available at https://lccn.loc.gov/2017032763

9 8 7 6 5 4 3 2 1

Printed by Sheridan Books, Inc., United States of America

For Samjung, Nathan, and Hannah

Yosi son of Yoezer, the man from Saredah, says,
"Let your house be an assembly point for the wise. Powder yourself with
the dust of their feet and drink their words in gulps."
(Pirqe Abot 1:4)

Contents

Acknowledgments

MANY MINDS PLAY a role in writing a book of this sort, and many deserve thanks. First, I wish to thank the many students who have discussed the texts of the Old Testament with me over the past two decades. Their names are too numerous to list, but their faces run through my brain, and I recall them with affection and gratitude. The numerous anonymous reviewers of the book in its various stages also contributed much to its clarity and usefulness. Robert Miller and Steve Wiggins of Oxford University Press enabled the publication of this project and encouraged its completion. Josiah Peeler has read and commented on successive versions of the book, always to good effect and with cheerfulness. My children, Nathan Hamilton and Hannah Hamilton have not only suffered through their father's obsessions with teaching old texts to young people but have also read large parts of this book with an eye toward its improvement. They have unstintingly given of their knowledge of music and science far exceeding that of their father, often with results that improve this book, and more importantly my life. Most of all, I thank my wife and partner, Dr. Samjung Kang-Hamilton, who believed in this work even through difficult patches in writing it.

Abbreviations

Romans	Rom	Jude	Jude
1–2 Corinthians	1–2 Cor	Revelation	Rev
Galatians	Gal		
Ephesians	Eph		
Philippians	Phil	**GENERAL ABBREVIATIONS**	
Colossians	Col	BCE	Before the Common Era
1–2 Thessalonians	1–2 Thess	CE	Common Era
1–2 Timothy	1–2 Tim	CH	Chronistic History
Titus	Tit	DH	Deuteronomistic History
Philemon	Phlm	ET	English Translation
Hebrews	Heb	LXX	The Septuagint or ancient Greek
James	Jas		translation of the Hebrew Bible
1–2 Peter	1–2 Pet	MT	Masoretic Text, the standard text
1–3 John	1–3 John		of the Hebrew Bible

1 Introduction

WHILE MOST PEOPLE skip over the introductions to books, you have chosen to be better than your peers and read the beginning. Congratulations on your intelligent decision! There is an old Israelite aphorism that appears in the book of Ecclesiastes (also known as Qoheleth), "Of making many books, there is no end. And much study wearies the flesh" (Eccl 12:12). The author (or editor) of the ancient book makes an ironic comment on the work as a whole, as if to say "there are too many books in the world, and here's another one." Not that there is anything wrong with either wearying the flesh in a good cause or publishing another book, as long as it helps the reader in some way. How should this book help you while not wearing you out?

WHY SO MANY BIBLE TRANSLATIONS? AND HOW TO CHOOSE ONE

All or part of the Bible has been translated into almost three thousand languages, far more than any other book. Christians began translating it into English beginning in the ninth century or even earlier, and that work has only grown over time, so that English versions are more numerous than in any other language. For several centuries, the dominant translation was the King James Version (published 1611), which has had an enormous influence on American and Commonwealth culture. If you've ever been saved by the "skin of your teeth" or seen the "handwriting on the wall," you can thank the wordsmiths who made that great translation four hundred years ago. Today's readers of English have many options, from easy-to-read versions to the midlevel literacy versions like the New International Version or English Revised Version to more complex renderings such as the New Revised Standard Version. Each has strengths and weaknesses, and several different theories of translation inform them, but each strives to render the biblical text as faithfully as possible.

To begin, consider what this book is not. It is not a substitute for the Bible itself. Nothing can equal the experience of sustained, careful, reasoned, and thoughtful study of the sacred book shared by Jews and Christians (and honored by Muslims, but that's another story). Rather, this work invites the reader to examine the biblical text itself. Consider this a sort of guidebook. No guidebook can be a substitute for seeing the Grand Canyon or the Aurora Borealis, but learning a little geology or astronomy can enhance the experience. No textbook can substitute for the original biblical text, with its gorgeous poetry, gripping prophetic critique, and thrilling or bewildering stories.

To continue, then, what is this book? It is a handbook on the literary, historical, and especially theological dimensions of the biblical text. It is designed to provoke conversation, perhaps even dissent or dismay, and thereby make us better readers and, one hopes, better persons. And because the Bible is most of all a collection of texts about the deepest concerns humans have—who is God? Who are we? How do we relate, if we can? How should we live?—reading it presents a demand upon the reader not easily reduced to mere understanding of ancient data. All literature, properly approached, makes demands on the reader. The Bible does so most of all.

Read this book, then, with your Bible open. Choose a good translation (or more than one). All the translations in this book are the author's own, so yours may differ from it in various ways.

Things to Watch For

Now for a little housekeeping. Each chapter of this book tries to situate a particular biblical book in its historical setting or settings, to consider how it works as literature, and what it says about key theological commitments of ancient Israel and modern Christian (and to some extent, Jewish) readers. The book is intended to have an ecumenical flavor: it considers the text from several angles, both drawing on the long history of interpretation of the Old Testament in the church and synagogue, and trying to address the most crucial questions that the text raises about the nature of God, humankind, religion, creation, politics, and, in short, the things contemporary readers most care about. The key is not to silence the voice of the biblical text but to interrogate it in the deepest possible ways.

Along with these large-scale features, a few terms deserve to be named at this point

- The Old Testament calls God by a range of names, in part because the Bible merges different ancient traditions with varying understandings of God, and in part because the creators of the Bible wished to emphasize the ultimate inability of human beings to define God straightforwardly in terms of one name or attribute or another. The proper name is Yhwh, represented in ancient Hebrew manuscripts by the four letters *yodh-he-vav-he* (יהוה), also called the Tetragrammaton, and probably originally pronounced "yahveh." English translations often render this name as "the LORD," following a very ancient practice (at least as early as the third century BCE) that sought to prevent blasphemy by avoiding the divine name. This textbook tries to honor both the Hebrew original and the long-standing practice of reading a substitute for it by printing the divine name as Yhwh. The Hebrew Bible also uses the name Elohim about 2,600 times, El about 237 times, and various other names occasionally. This textbook prints Yhwh for the Tetragrammaton and the traditional English word "God" elsewhere except when making a special point, in which case the original Hebrew name appears.

- Hebrew words appear occasionally in the text when their appearance helps give a flavor of the biblical text. The system of transliteration works this way:

aleph	ʾ	*bet*	*b*	*gimel*	*g*	*he*	*h*	*vav*	*w*
zayin	*z*	*khet*	*ḥ*	*dalet*	*d*	*yodh*	*y*	*kaph*	*k*
lamed	*l*	*mem*	*m*	*tet*	*ṭ*	*samek*	*s*	*ayin*	ʿ
pe	*p*	*tsade*	*ṣ*	*nun*	*n*	*resh*	*r*	*sin*	*ś*
shin	*š*	*tav*	*t*	*qoph*	*q*				

Long vowels are marked with a macron, so *ā, ē, ī,* and *ō* represent the vowels in "f*a*ther," "th*e*y," "mach*i*ne," and "th*o*ugh." (Think about how vowels work in French or Spanish, and you'll be close!). The Hebrew letter *khet* (*ḥ*) is hard, as in the "ch" "*ch*orus," and *shin* (*š*) represents the "sh" sound, while *tsade* (*ṣ*) has the *ts* sound (as in "ca*ts*").

- BCE and CE—dates in this book follow the most current scholarly convention "Before the Common Era" and "Common Era." Note that the years themselves are the same in the older system BC and AD ("Before Christ" and "Anno Domini" or "In the year of the LORD").
- Pullout boxes appear throughout the text to pursue topics of historical or literary interest.
- Footnotes are kept to a minimum, but suggestions for further reading at the end of each chapter should benefit students who are writing papers or who simply want to learn more. They may also help professors at times.
- Each chapter includes a few sources for further reading. Some will be more technical than others.

Some Key Terms and Ideas

Before tracing the Bible's story and considering the arguments it makes, one must first clarify some of the key concepts about it. What is the Bible, first of all? Answering that deceptively simple question depends on other considerations, and in part, the clarification of other terms, such as canon and Scripture, which are not identical but still overlapping.

CANON

The first term, *canon*, is perhaps the most complex, because any discussion of it must consider texts as both "an authoritative voice in written or oral form that was read and received as having the authority of God in it" and "a perpetual fixation or standardization, namely, when the books of the Bible were fixed or stabilized."[1] The collection of sacred texts has authority—it shapes behavior of individuals and groups—in the religious communities using it, whether Jewish or Christian (or Muslim, for the Qur'an). Even this last formulation is ambiguous, because it could refer to the stabilization of a single book or to the fixing of a collection with clear boundaries. For our purposes, the term *canon* denotes the collection itself, not the exact form of a given text within it, since manuscripts copied by hand inevitably contain slight (or sometimes not so slight) variations from one another. To recognize the Bible as a canon is to acknowledge that the various parts of it interact with each other and color how readers interpret each part.

What does one call this collection of sacred texts, then? The answer to that depends on who is doing the calling. Jews often speak of the *Miqra* ("what is called out or spoken") or *Tanak*. Most Christians speak of the Old and New Testaments, the former being the collection they share with Judaism. Modern scholars speak of the Hebrew and Greek Bibles or the First and Second Testaments or the Former or Latter Testaments in order to acknowledge that the various collections in play overlap and also that each group using them deserves respect. This volume uses these terms more or less interchangeably and without prejudice.

Yet there is a conceptual problem here because different groups that use these collections include different texts within it. Not only do Jews and Christians differ about what goes into the collection, but Samaritans, for example, venerate only the first five books (the Pentateuch), while Christians disagree among themselves as to whether the Apocrypha or Deuterocanonical books belong in or out. The Ethiopian Church, uniquely, uses the ancient work 1 Enoch (written in several stages from 200 BCE to 200 CE or even later) and other ancient texts. So canon cannot be a straightforward concept. Moreover, the variation in content leads to some variation in belief and practice. For example, whether a person believes in purgatory or not depends in part on which texts he or she thinks have canonical status.

At the same time, however, the existence of variety should not obscure an important level of agreement. Both Jews and Christians have regarded the vast majority of other books as noncanonical, not necessarily bad but definitely less important. And they have agreed on the basic ideas that fit within the canon (the unity and oneness of God, the election of Israel, the emphasis on justice as the root of piety, and so on). The surface pluralism underscores a deeper unity. And so one must take account of both factors—diversity and unity—without overemphasizing one or the other. To overemphasize diversity can cause one to lose a sense of the crucial ideas of the Bible and their development. To overemphasize unity can lead to fanatical support of positions that, again, lose perspective.

Moreover, in addition to the theological issues surrounding the idea of canon, historical issues must be considered. While many details of the development of the biblical canon remain obscure, a few things are clear enough. Until the second or third century CE, when Christians and others began using a newfangled invention called a codex (a book bound as ours are today), a "bible," then, was simply a cabinet full of scrolls that a worshiping community, a synagogue or, later, a church, used in worship, meditated upon, and wrote commentaries, sermons, and prayers about. Different cabinets held different books (Table 1.1).

Some Jewish communities also included additional works in their cabinet of scrolls, such later works as 1–4 Maccabees, Wisdom of Solomon, and Tobit. These documents, discussed more fully in Chapter 30, became part of most Christian collections of sacred texts as well. Because many (most?) early Christians after the first century CE were Greek-speaking gentiles, they used the ancient Jewish texts that had been translated into Greek, including this larger collection. Thus the earliest Christian lists of sacred books that have survived—from Origen in the early third century CE and Eusebius about a century later—include the books that modern Western Christians usually speak of as the Apocrypha or the Deuterocanonical books.

Amid all this complexity, we should recall an important fact. Finding the limits of the canon has historically been less important than ensuring healthy teaching in the church's or synagogue's life. The primary theological and moral concerns of these communities did not revolve around determining precisely which books came in and which stayed out, but around the overall theological picture or what Christians often call a "rule of faith": a basic pattern of belief and practice rooted in the Bible but not dependent on a literal, restrictive reading of it.

The need for precision became most acute during times of crisis. For Jews, it meant rejecting the Old Greek translation (the Septuagint or LXX) for the synagogue and a growing emphasis on the Masoretic Text (MT), the Hebrew text standardized in the first century CE and preserved to the present, as well as translations derived from it. For Christians, defining the boundaries of the Old Testament, or rather defending its importance to their faith, took on urgency in the second century CE because of internal disputes surrounding an eccentric Roman church theologian, Marcion of Sinope. A convert to Christianity, Marcion apparently sought to free his new faith from its Jewish past by accepting the widespread gentile critique of the Old Testament's portrayal of God as a morally defective, ignorant being who could not be the good creator of the universe worshiped by Jesus Christ. Law and grace, he believed, could not coexist. At least

TABLE 1.1

| Old Testament Canonical Lists | |
Masoretic Text	Septuagint
Genesis	Genesis
Exodus	Exodus
Leviticus	Leviticus
Numbers	Numbers
Deuteronomy	Deuteronomy
Joshua	Joshua
Judges	Judges
1–2 Samuel	Ruth
1–2 Kings	1–4 Kingdoms
Isaiah	1–2 Chronicles
Jeremiah	1–2 Esdras[1]
Ezekiel	Esther
12 Minor Prophets	Judith
	Tobit
	1–4 Maccabees
Psalms	Psalms
Job	Odes
Proverbs	Proverbs
Ruth	Ecclesiastes
Song of Songs	Song of Songs
Ecclesiastes	Job
Lamentations	Wisdom of Solomon
Esther	Ben Sira (or Ecclesiasticus)
Daniel	Psalms of Solomon
Ezra-Nehemiah	12 Minor Prophets
1–2 Chronicles	Isaiah
	Jeremiah
	Baruch
	Lamentations
	Epistle of Jeremiah
	Ezekiel
	Daniel
	Susanna
	Bel and the Dragon

[1] 2 Esdras = a revision Ezra and Nehemiah.

CAPTION: Greek and Hebrew biblical manuscripts before the Middle Ages arrange the books in different ways except in the Pentateuch, which always takes the same order.

according to his opponents, Marcion rejected not only the Hebrew scriptures that other Christians venerated but also most of what became the New Testament as well (since the latter quotes the former on virtually every page), leading him to honor Paul as the only true apostle and an expurgated version of Luke as the only true gospel. Nor was his work the last time that some Christians sought to dissociate themselves from Judaism and the Hebrew Bible: the German Christian movement of Nazi Germany is the most notorious and extreme example of an unfortunate trend on the margins of Christianity. Even today, many people wrongly believe that the God of the Old Testament differs radically from the God of the New.

The Christian Church in general has gone another direction, agreeing with the earliest followers of Jesus—all Jewish adherents of a Jewish messiah, after all—that the earlier texts of Israel belonged in the church and, indeed, were indispensable to its spiritual health. The early Christians' retention of a connection to Israel has shaped both faiths to this day. Even if the boundaries of the Jewish and Christian canons differ, both collections function as scripture (sometimes "Scripture,") that is, as written texts performed orally and studied (in many media) in religious settings in ways that shape communities and their beliefs and practices.

SCRIPTURE

Now to a second term: *scripture*. From the Latin verb *scribere* ("to write"—hence the English words "scribble," "script," and "scribe"), the term simply denotes something written, especially a sacred text. In the great monotheistic religions that derive ultimately Israel—Judaism, Christianity, Islam, and Baha'i—key sacred texts have a unique authority in their parts and as collections. True, the understandings of the origins and content of these texts vary considerably, but the notion that the followers of these faiths are Peoples of the Book (to use the Muslim expression) is an important insight into their workings. Attention to the Qur'an (for Islam) or the Kitab-i-Iqan (for Baha'i) lies well beyond the scope of this book, but suffice it to say that the phenomenon of a book religion, a religion for which a single text carries unparalleled authority in faith and morals, is not unique to Christianity or Judaism. The idea that the one God would communicate fairly clearly with human beings through the medium of prophets, whose words could be preserved in writing, is a corollary of a belief that God has a profound interest in the well-being of human beings in every aspect of their lives. Thus the sacred texts do not function primarily as talismans that work on the divine realm, but as documents that human beings must understand and somehow implement. The question is, how?

The Bible as an Interpreted Document

How does one understand a text? It depends on both the text and the reader. Consider an elementary example from contemporary life:

"MARK STRUCK OUT AT HOME"

Assuming I know English (and recognize that the text is in English), I quickly realize that it has a subject ("Mark") and a verb ("struck out"), as well as a reference to a location ("at home"). But what does the text mean? Since it seems fragmentary, I want to know about the larger conversation of which it is a part. Does the sentence come from a report of a baseball game (*Mark, a batter, missed contacting the ball safely three times in a row and thus was put out*)? A romance novel (*Mark, a frustrated lover, failed to impress his wife sufficiently to receive an amorous response*)? A crime report (*Mark, a deranged person, beat on his house with a crowbar*)? Is Mark a person in history, a fictional character, an ancient deity? No text exists by itself but only in association with other moments of communication, thickly layered in an interpreter's experiences.

Interpretation becomes more complex when the text we are encountering comes to us only in written form, and in a dead language to boot. Customs, beliefs, and practices that the text assumes without much explanation have grown obscure. Even the act of translating the text from, in our example, Hebrew or Aramaic to English or another modern tongue, requires a great deal of knowledge, not just of grammar and vocabulary but of literary forms and techniques. When the text is an extremely complex one, such as the Bible, the work becomes all the more difficult, as well as all the more rewarding.

The academic discipline of interpretation is called hermeneutics. It relates closely to the task of exegesis, which is the attempt to explain what a text said in its earliest discernible context. However, hermeneutics goes beyond that fundamental task, or as Antony Thiselton puts it,

> whereas exegesis and interpretation denote the actual processes of interpreting texts, hermeneutics also includes the second-order discipline of asking critically what exactly we are doing when we read, understand, or apply texts.[2]

Sometimes scholars speak of the "hermeneutical circle" or "hermeneutical spiral," which is simply the recognition that anyone reading a text brings to it his or her own presuppositions, experiences, memories, and imagination. The act of interpreting a text involves a sort of dance of the readers with the text. The dance has three dimensions, so to speak.

First, the "ideal reader" of the Bible, for whom the texts were created, is not the solitary individual "objectively" reading a text. (Such a reader is imaginary anyway, an unfortunate by-product of the Enlightenment's admirable attempts to eliminate prejudice and ignorance.) Rather, the best reader of these texts is the one who attends to them with great care, engaging them with a critical eye and also with some degree of willingness to hear what they seek to say. At one level, such a requirement would be true of the reader of any great work of literary art, yet it is doubly true of religious texts like the Bible because they insist on trying to form their readers in particular ways. Something happens to us when we read them.

Second, the most brilliant readers of the Bible through the centuries have understood it to engage the profoundest questions human beings ask, and indeed, to point to God. As the great New Testament scholar Rudolf Bultmann (1884–1976) stated:

> The Bible does not approach us at all like other books . . . . We come to know it through the Christian church, which put it before us with its authoritative claim. The church's preaching, founded on the Scriptures, passes on the word of the Scriptures. It says: God speaks to you *here*![3]

Today one might qualify Bultmann's statement in various ways in part because the pressure on religious claims he responds to does not always rise to the level he experienced under the Nazis, the time at which he said this. Yet the basic insight that the collection we call the Bible survives because Jews and Christians read it for meaning in the lives of their communities is relevant to its interpretation. Critical scholarship can, and often does, go hand in hand with an attitude of reverence and attentive listening for the key claims of the text, not only claims *about* the nature of reality but claims *upon* the commitments of readers.

Third, contemporary readers of the Bible may operate as precritical, critical, or postcritical interpreters. Most Jews and Christians before the eighteenth century could be called precritical, not because they were not intellectually serious, for they often were, but because they did not question the basic veracity of the biblical text. Or if they did question its literal sense (a move very common among some interpreters such as the ancient Christian school of Alexandria), they did so in order to find a deeper spiritual sense. However, beginning in the sixteenth century with such thinkers as Baruch (a.k.a. Benedict) Spinoza (1632–1677), scholars asked whether the historical and scientific claims that a literal reading of the Bible would stand up to careful scrutiny. A major insight of this approach has been the recognition that the Bible is, whatever else it may be, a human work making arguments and reflecting ideas that have a location in time and space. In more recent times, a postcritical reading has become possible. In such a strategy, of which there are many variations, the interpreter recognizes that the Bible has a history and that many of the historical motivations of its creators can be identified within the stream of human experience (it did not drop out of heaven). Yet she also seeks a deeper theological truth, a "nevertheless," according to which the biblical text speaks to some deeper reality shaped by God and available to human beings through the medium of the text itself, properly read.

A Theological Introduction to the Old Testament—the very book that you are reading— attempts a postcritical approach. On the one hand, it takes seriously the findings of modern research and seeks to understand how and why the various biblical books came into being. On the other hand, it seeks to interpret those books in terms of a hermeneutics of sympathy, that is, from a point of view that wishes to understand the theological arguments that those books make on their own terms, with an eye toward the sort of readers they endeavor to create.

Two basic hermeneutical lines of inquiry shape much of this textbook. The first is the relationship between tradition and imagination. The biblical texts are highly imaginative as they employ numerous literary genres and techniques, often in surprising ways. The level of artistry is ordinarily of the highest sort. At the same time, the ancient Israelite writers did not set the same premium on originality that has become indispensable since the Romantic movements of the late eighteenth and early nineteenth centuries. Rather, all ancient authors (Israelite or not) felt themselves answerable to a public that expected certain things. The goal was not to be novel but to be creative within the bounds of existing practices. They did not confuse the new with the good. The biblical texts thus come out of what one might call traditioned imaginations: their creators followed the rules of the time while creating great art, much as Shakespeare borrowed plot lines and structures while writing his plays, or Michelangelo sculpted within the context of Renaissance conventions while transforming them from the inside out. The interplay of tradition and imagination will appear time and again in this work.

The second hermeneutical lens can be called divine-human synchrony. The Bible says things about God and humans that reflect a coherent and accurate view of both. To be clear, one may acknowledge that various statements in the Bible about facts of human history or natural science need not be taken as fact in a strict sense, often because they were not intended to be. The real world does not have a storehouse for hail (Job 38:22), and daylight does not exist independently of the sun (Gen 1:3–5), for example. A very literal-minded reading of the Bible will thus often mistake its poetic register and seriously misunderstand it. Yet when it speaks of human sinfulness and divine love, of the relationship of covenant with its obligations and affections, among other topics, it speaks of the deepest things humans can know. At least this is the thesis that this book will test. Welcome to the conversation!

Notes

1. Lee McDonald, *The Biblical Canon* (Peabody, MA: Hendrickson, 2006), 55.

2. Antony C. Thiselton, *Hermeneutics: An Introduction* (Grand Rapids: Eerdmans, 2009), 4.

3. Rudolf Bultmann, *Existence and Faith: Shorter Writings of Rudolf Bultmann*, ed. and trans. Schubert M. Ogden (New York: Living Age/Meridian, 1960), 168.

For Further Reading

Barth, Karl. *Church Dogmatics.* 13 vols. Edinburgh: T. & T. Clark, 1949–1962.

Graf Reventlow, Henning. *History of Biblical Interpretation.* 4 vols. Translated by Leo G. Perdue and James O. Duke. Atlanta: Society of Biblical Literature, 2009–2010.

Ricoeur, Paul. *Memory, History, Forgetting.* Translated by Kathleen Blamey and David Pellauer. Chicago: University of Chicago Press, 2004.

Taylor, Charles. *Sources of the Self: The Making of the Modern Identity.* Cambridge: Oxford University Press, 1989.

2 The Pentateuch in Brief

IMAGINE AGAIN THE cabinet in the synagogues of the first century CE. In every Jewish and Samaritan community the core texts for worship and study were the five scrolls of Torah, usually known by their Greek name the Pentateuch (Genesis–Deuteronomy). Early interpreters of these texts attributed them to their major character Moses (often calling them the Books of Moses) even though the books themselves do not explicitly claim him as their author. (Exod 17:14 and 24:4 refer to shorter works by him.) By the first century, Jews and Christians spoke of the Pentateuch as the books of Moses or the law of Moses (see Mark 12:26; Luke 24:44) without worrying about the great prophet's precise role in composing the books.

Early on, however, careful readers of the Pentateuch noticed certain problems with the assumption that Moses had written all of it. Thus the Babylonian Talmud, a vast collection of Jewish law and lore compiled from earlier sources in the sixth century CE, reports rabbis who wondered how Moses could have written the story of his own death in Deut 34.[1] (Answer 1: he wrote it through prophecy, weeping. Answer 2: he did not write it, but rather Joshua picked up the pen where Moses had left off in Deut 33.) Several centuries later, the Spanish rabbi Abraham ibn Ezra (1092–1167) observed anachronisms in the Pentateuch such as "The Canaanite was then in the land" (Gen 12:6) and "Og's bed is still in Rabbath-Ammon" (Deut 3:11). However, neither he nor anyone else tried to work out the implications of such facts because their interests lay with reading the Bible for its ideas about God and human behavior.

During the early modern period careful readers concluded that the Pentateuch contains many statements that seem in tension with each other. Who created the world, for example? Is the deity's name Yhwh or Elohim or Yhwh Elohim? Whom did Cain marry (Gen 4:17) if his family were the sum of the human race? Did Noah bring into the ark a pair of each animal (6:19; 7:9) or seven pairs of some animals (7:2–3), and did the flood last 40 (7:4, 17), 150 (7:24), or 375 days? And why, after the Flood, did the mountains appear in the middle of the season that Israel would celebrate as the Feast of Tabernacles (Gen 8:5; see Lev 23:39–43; Num 29:12–38)? If Gen 36:31 lists Edomite kings who predated Israelite kings, does this statement imply that Israelites already had kings? And so on it goes.

At the same time, in spite of all these minor difficulties, the Pentateuch is not just a hodgepodge of stories, laws, and poems. Rather, the five books contain a clearly structured story that begins with the whole human race and zooms in on one family that soon becomes a nation. The episodes of the story fit together, not like a modern novel with prolonged explorations of the motives and values of the individual characters, but through a process often called gapping, in which each vignette offers just enough detail to help it make sense and leaves enough unexplained to make it interesting and worth reading. There is a highly cultured narrative art at work in the Pentateuch that is different from modern expectations but sophisticated on its own terms. The Pentateuch combines many sorts of genres together into an integrated whole.

Since the seventeenth century, many scholars have tried to identify both the coherence and incoherence of Genesis–Deuteronomy by referring to sources of some sort. Since ancient people had no notion of copyright or plagiarism, the ancient authors could sometimes quote those sources or allude to them or simply incorporate them en masse. And this is what modern scholars concluded had, in fact, occurred in the Pentateuch. In some ways, such a hypothesis should not be very surprising. All literary works use sources, and most authors have in their heads a great many books that they have read. That is why modern people invented the footnote as a way of honoring their sources (as well as bedeviling unsuspecting university students!). Modern scholars have typically thought of the sources of the Pentateuch in two ways.

One idea, called the Documentary Hypothesis (DH), combines at least two, and more likely three or four, fully worked out documents recounting Israel's earliest history. The sources were usually identified as J for the Yahwist (Jahwist in German), E for the Elohist, D for the Deuteronomist, and P for the Priestly Source. According to the Documentary Hypothesis, the Pentateuch's duplicate stories, different viewpoints, and changes in literary style derived from the disparate origins of different sections of the book.

Other scholars, meanwhile, have argued for something more like a Fragmentary Hypothesis, according to which different texts come from many locations and coalesce only late in the evolution of the book. In this view, there are still two major layers of the Pentateuch, a Priestly layer (P) and a nonpriestly layer (non-P, or everything else). These two layers interacted with each other until they were combined into one grand work sometime during the fifth or fourth century BCE.

It would be hard to know how many contemporary scholars hold each view, and in some ways the dispute always involves assumptions that are hard to test. Remember the old optical illusions from introductory psychology classes? Is the object a duck or a rabbit? A vase or two people facing each other? These hypotheses are a bit like that.

What we know for sure is that much of the Pentateuch has a strong interest in the sacrificial worship in sanctuaries (so it's priestly), and much does not (so it's probably not priestly). Yet the stories in Genesis–Deuteronomy, not to mention the laws, come from different times and places, and thus reflect different viewpoints on a range of issues.

At the same time, the creator(s) of the first five books of the Bible worked to place these materials together in a coherent whole that made sense. The process of composition was conservative in that it allowed the tensions between various texts to survive rather than smoothing things out. (Hence all the minor problems pointed out earlier.) Yet it was also highly creative, because it fashioned a theological world out of all the disparate raw material with which it worked. The Pentateuch is an authorizing story, a text that both explains how Israel came to be and argues for a way of life that it should adopt, preserve, and celebrate.

The Pentateuch works by juxtaposing stories and laws, so that the thoughtful reader could use each to interpret the other. Consider first the stories: biblical narrative, in the Pentateuch and elsewhere, consists primarily of short vignettes woven together to form a comprehensive story. Unlike other literatures, Israel's does not emphasize the interior state of the character, but rather reveals the character through action and brief speech, usually with just enough conversation happening to reveal the characters' inner world. How does one read such stories, then?

J.P. Fokkelman suggests ten productive questions to ask of any narrative texts:

1. Who is the hero?
2. What is the quest in which the hero engages?
3. Who are the helpers and opponents?
4. Where does the narrator intrude in the text?
5. Does the narrator keep to the chronology of events or alter it in some way?
6. Where is time skipped?
7. Is there a plot?
8. Where are the speeches, and what do they say?
9. What surprising choice of words appear in the text?
10. Where does the unit start and stop, and how are the divisions indicated?

This list opens up an understanding of the Bible as a literary creation, and will be useful to us throughout this book. But we should also add some deeper questions that illuminate the Bible as a theological work:

1. What are the moral values of the characters? Of the narrator?
2. What vision of God is in play? Are there several visions? How do these cohere with other views within Scripture?
3. Where does the narrator challenge our own views of reality? How do we respond to that challenge?
4. How does the interplay of values within a text shape our own conversation about values?

Questions such as these allow the reader or hearer of a given biblical story or of the narrative as a whole to place the text in dialogue with his or her deepest understandings of reality.

Narrative, and now law. As the discussion of Exodus–Deuteronomy will show, the legal traditions of Israel take a very particular shape when the Pentateuch situates them within a narrative context. Instead of being just a set of rules about human interactions—already necessary and valuable in their own right—the laws of the Pentateuch become part of Yhwh's story of redeeming Israel. Torah—divine instruction or law—becomes a vehicle for perpetuating the deity's grace in the structures, habits, commitments, and values of a people. This combination of norm and story, of what has been and what should be, constitutes the generative dynamic, the capacity for survival and flourishing that characterizes Israel's life in the past and today. Now to enter into these texts.

Note

1. *B.Baba Bathra* 15a.

For Further Reading

Baden, Joel S. *The Composition of the Pentateuch: Renewing the Documentary Hypothesis*. New Haven: Yale University Press, 2012.

Fokkelman, J. P. *Reading Biblical Narrative: An Introductory Guide* (Louisville: Westminster John Knox, 1999).

3 "In the Beginning"
THE BOOK OF GENESIS

> **Key Text**: *And Yhwh said to Abram, "Go from your land and your birthplace and your family to the land that I will show you. And I will make you a great nation and bless you. And I will make your name great [i.e., make your reputation outstanding], and it will be a blessing. I will also bless those blessing you and curse those denigrating you. In you, all the families of the earth will be blessed."* (Gen 12:1–3)

In reading any book, one of the first questions to ask is, "what's it all about?" In asking this about the first book of the Bible, Genesis, or in Hebrew "In the Beginning" (*běrē'šît*), the answer reveals the main subjects of the first five books of the Bible, the Pentateuch. At one level, Genesis concerns the migration of a single family (with an extended introduction of their forebears), the ancestors of the people of Israel, as they moved from Mesopotamia to Canaan to Egypt. The story concerns their adventures and misadventures, and offers a colorful panorama of polygamous families as they encounter internal and external challenges. At that level alone, Genesis is a great story worthy of the countless retellings it has undergone through the centuries in art, music, and literature.

But there is something of significance here, for Israel understood its own story as a theological exploration of its place in a larger world. Genesis serves both as a background story for the events of Exodus and settlement that follow in Exodus–Joshua, and offers a justification for Israel's possession of its land (Canaan its older name, and Palestine the one the Romans gave it much later, naming it after the Philistines).

THE PRIMEVAL STORY IN OUTLINE

A. Creation of the world and the human race (1:1–2:25)
B. The loss of paradise (3:1–24)
C. The expansion of humanity (4:1–26)
D. Genealogy of the antediluvians (5:1–32)
E. Extraordinary humans (6:1–4)
F. The flood: humanity destroyed (6:5–8:22)
G. Blessings and curses (9:1–29)
  1. Blessing Noah and humankind (9:1–17, 28–29)
  2. Curses on problematic people (9:18–27)
H. Genealogy of the postdiluvians (10:1–32)
I. The Tower of Babel (11:1–9)
J. Genealogy of Shem (11:10–26)

Some of the main theological ideas of the text are expressed in the blessing that Yhwh gives Abram in Gen 12:1–3:

And Yhwh said to Abram, "Go from your land and your birthplace and your family to the land that I will show you. And I will make you a great nation and bless you. And I will make your name great [i.e., make your reputation outstanding], and it will be a blessing. I will also bless those blessing you and curse those denigrating you. In you, all the families of the earth will be blessed."

The divine promise sets forth most of the major themes in Genesis: migration, family and its preservation, blessing, conflict and convergence with outsiders, and the inheritance of the promised land. The interplay of these elements will shape most of the stories that follow. Genesis thus depicts men and women struggling to find themselves and God, often in a world in which others, with other motives and histories, pursue different goals.

Narrative Structure

The book of Genesis has two major sections, each with several subsections. The first major unit includes chs 1–11, often called the Primeval Story because it lays out Israel's understanding (or one of its understandings) of the origins of the world and many of the human cultural practices in it. Although the section includes a variety of stories and genealogies, it does have a logical flow.

Much of this material has parallels in other ancient Near Eastern cultures. However, Israel did not mindlessly borrow from its neighbors, nor, conversely, did it always seek to correct their viewpoints. In other words, Genesis and other biblical texts reveal Israel's ongoing attempts to work out a coherent worldview from the raw materials of the

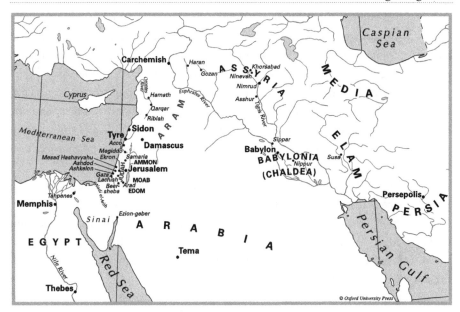

MAP 1 The Ancient Near East. From Michael D. Coogan, *The Old Testament: A Historical and Literary Introduction to the Hebrew Scriptures*, 3rd ed., p. 362.

broader ancient Near Eastern environment (see Map 1). Like all human beings everywhere, Israel shared ideas with others, borrowed ideas from others, developed their own ideas, and sought to relate all these layers of thought and meaning-making together in ways that made sense.

A good example of Genesis's creativity in using older material appears in the flood stories in chs 6–8. Similar stories have survived from ancient Mesopotamia (though not everywhere, as is often asserted—they were not universal). One version, the "Epic of Atrahasis," was definitively organized in the middle of the second millennium BCE in Babylon but drew on older sources. In this text, the gods (plural!), led by Anu (sky), Enlil (earth), and Enki (water), create humankind in order to employ creatures in the hard work of digging irrigation canals and tilling the soil. In other words, the text explains how human beings built a civilization in the inhospitable environment of southern Mesopotamia (today's Iraq), with its dryness, heat, and ever-present sand flies.

Over time, however, the humans get out of hand, overpopulating the world and making too much noise for the gods to bear. The cost-benefit ratio of creating humans becomes unacceptable, leading the chief god Enlil to command a flood to destroy humankind. Fortunately for humankind, not all the gods agreed, and one, Enki, warned Atra-hasis to escape, which he does by filling a large boat of his own devising with animals and people. The story ends with the gods accepting the survival of humanity but decreeing the existence of demons that cause death in childbirth.[1] Again, this is only one version of the story, and it is not clear whether all ancient Babylonians would have understood things in this way.

In any case, there are both striking differences and similarities to the biblical story. In both, a flood comes because humans annoy the divine realm. In both, humanity survives but with new limitations. Some versions of the Babylonian story even include the human hero releasing a dove and a raven from his boat in order to ascertain the possibility of docking somewhere, just as in Genesis. But the texts do show two major theological differences. The first is that Israel's story assumes the existence of only one deity and one whose motives and plans cannot be contested. The other is that in Israel's story, human wickedness motivates the flood, not just our excessive noisiness. These differences turn Genesis's story in directions that mark them as different.

What is more, the moral world that the primeval history imagines is the one in which patriarchs and matriarchs also lived. Their stories appear in chs 12–50.

This section revolves around the experiences of four generations of a single family: Generation 1, Abraham and Sarah; Generation 2, Isaac and Rebekah, Ishmael and his wives; Generation 3, Jacob and Esau, and the twelve tribes of Ishmaelites; Generation 4, the descendants of Jacob and Esau.

Each major character in the narrative has integrity, a distinguishing feature that appears repeatedly (Abraham the faithful, Jacob the trickster, Joseph the prodigy), perhaps because they were remembered this way in Israel's storytelling traditions.[2] Yet Genesis does not develop these characters fully but only gives enough detail to make the story work. By leaving the story open-ended, the Israelite narratives allow for a range of interpretations.

> The biblical figures appear elsewhere in the Bible, even in texts that may not have in mind precisely the stories we have in Genesis. In many cases, the list Abraham/Isaac/Jacob appears as a unit, much as modern Americans might speak of "The Founders" as the group of people who began the country (even though they were a very diverse lot). Sometimes, however, the figures appear either alone or at least with distinctive character traits. For example, Abraham appears as the one delivered by God (Isa 29:22; cf. Mic 7:20), the landholder (Ezek 33:24), the participant in a covenant with God (Ps 105:9, 42), and the symbol of God's rule of the whole world (Ps 47:10 [ET 47:9]). He also appears as a former polytheist in Josh 24:3. Isaac usually appears in a list with his father and his son (e.g. Lev 26:42; 2 Kgs 13:23; and many others), but sometimes shows up alone. So Amos makes him the ancestor of Israel's religion (Amos 7:9, 16). Jacob appears most often outside the Pentateuch often as a synonym of the national name Israel (e.g. see Isa 40–48 for many occurrences).

As we will see, Genesis is both the story of a people and the story of families, and so it must always be read on several levels. By choosing to paint on such a small canvas, which contrasts sharply with the much wider scope of the Primeval Story, the creators of Genesis make a statement about how human beings live in the world. The grand and the small, the universal and the local, the world-historical and the momentary and transient are all tangled up together.

Momentarily, we will consider the main ideas of the text, but since those ideas function within a narrative, understanding Genesis requires a sense of the plot of the book. Let us examine that plot in some detail.

THE PRIMEVAL HISTORY (GEN 1:1–11:32)

Genesis opens in a way that seems inevitable because it has become so familiar: "In the beginning Elohim created heaven and earth." In fact, however, this opening reflects a deliberate choice, for almost all ancient peoples believed that the world of humanity was simply part of a larger cosmos over which the gods presided, and they had no problem asking the question, "where did the gods come from?" Their stories of divine origins (cosmogonies) often began with a series of births leading eventually to the creator-god and current head of the pantheon. Other traditions think of an uncreated deity at the origin point. So, for example, the Egyptian priests in Memphis, writing in the thirteenth century BCE, described the god Amun creating "himself by himself" and speak of him as being unknowable in his true nature, even to the other gods, who are his offspring. Thus such ancient texts have things both ways: Deity is eternal, but individual deities may not be.³ Genesis takes a more direct approach: the creator and the God of Israel are the same eternal, unoriginated, uncreated being, and Israel need not interact with any other deity.

In order to allow for complex theological reflection, then, the creation story in Genesis appears in two versions, Gen 1:1–2:4a and 2:4b–25. The two differ in some respects, perhaps most importantly in that the first has Elohim simply decreeing the existence of everything, including the human beings in the divine image, while the second portrays Yhwh fashioning human beings from the ground. The first story emphasizes the creative divine word, while the second story underscores the more direct agency of Yhwh in meticulously fashioning the world as an artist would work in ceramic. The first story culminates in the religious act of observing Sabbath, which takes its legitimacy from the fact that God practiced it (see Exod 20:11). The second story culminates in the social act of marriage and family-making, again with divine sanction.

The twin opening of the book has prompted an enormous amount of discussion among readers over the past two millennia. Modern scholars often focus on the issues of sources and so underscore the differences in the two accounts. Classical Christian and Jewish sources tended to focus on the theological issues that the texts raise, for Christians most notably the question of the divine image (Hebrew: *ṣelem*) in humankind. This theme is not extensively developed in Genesis or even the rest of the Hebrew Bible, however. In general, a *ṣelem* denotes a sculpture or picture representing something or someone, and so in Genesis's theology, all human beings (not just males, nor just a particular ethnic group) resemble the deity in appearance. Yet Genesis also recognizes that the bodily appearance is only one aspect of a person, much less of deity, and so it is probable that Gen 1:27 has in mind a wide, but unspecified, range of characteristic capacities and behaviors in which God and humankind resemble each other.

GARDENS IN THE ANCIENT WORLD

Ancient societies were often fascinated by the creation of expansive parks, often as a way of demonstrating royal power, and sometimes as a way of recapturing the idyllic state of primeval times. By creating Eden, Elohim in Genesis demonstrates divine splendor. Similarly, by telling the story of Eden, Genesis invokes the idea that the world's present (arid, in the case of the ancient Near East) condition was not inevitable. The present is not the model for the future. Unlike the ancient royal parks, the most famous of which was Nebuchadnezzar's famous "Hanging Gardens," Eden housed all humanity (small as it was!), not just the powerful elites. Incidentally our word "paradise" comes from the Persian word for a royal park, via the Greek word *paradeisos*.

In any case, the story proceeds further in ch 3, in which humankind goes tragically astray. While later Christian theology often found in the story a description of a species-wide, or even cosmic "fall," Genesis itself does not use such language. Nor does the rest of the Old Testament, for that matter. As the final "curses" make clear, the story partly explains why humans do not live in Edenic splendor.

Yet one should observe the story closely and notice that it raises several issues: (1) Is Yhwh trustworthy? (the serpent says no); (2) Does knowledge of good and evil, the necessary condition of moral choice and accountability, belong only to the divine realm? (3) Does possession of such knowledge demand a set of formational practices that would make its use sustainable and beneficial? While many Western Christians, going back to St. Augustine, have understood the story to report a divine punishment for hubris, it is susceptible to other interpretations (and has often found them in Eastern Orthodox Christianity), according to which the expulsion from the garden protects humanity from knowledge's potential abuse. (Would it be a good thing to have immortal beings as gullible as poor Adam and Eve? Can the sufferings of childbirth and grueling farm labor also be redemptive somehow?) Most importantly, we should recognize that many of the effects of the so-called fall are reversed in Genesis itself, or at least by the end of the Pentateuch, at which point Israel stands poised to enter the "land flowing with milk and honey."[4]

The rest of the Primeval History follows the descendants of Adam and Eve. These chapters draw on the common traditions of the ancient Near East at several points. (1) The idea of a succession of superannuated humans in the past appears both here and in the Sumerian Dynastic Chronicle (where one Enmengalanna reigned 64,000 years, and his peers scarcely less astonishingly long), as well as in several Greek traditions that probably originated in the Near East; (2) The story of the great deluge (see above) and the survival of the human race through the divine rescue of a single family; (3) The construction of towers in the center of cities. Genesis 11 is set in Babylon ("Babel" is the Hebrew name for that city), and the great tower in question must be the ziggurat in the middle of the Esagila Temple dedicated to the chief Babylonian god Marduk. In contrast to Babylonians' self-image as the leaders of the center of the universe, Genesis wishes to propose a counternarrative in which the scattering of humankind is a positive good, because, by implication this great diversity reflects the divine will for all creation.

As in Gen 3, the Babel story reports Yhwh's preventing humans from taking actions that would lead to their unrestrained capacity to do whatever they wanted, surely a most dangerous eventuality to themselves (not to a deity who could send the flood or create the world by the way). In other words, all such stories explore the limits of human capacities and the dangers we pose to ourselves if we seek to transgress those limits. Such boundary-crossing does not result in self-empowerment or self-improvement but in strife and destruction. Or so most ancient people believed. Given the experiences of the past century, which Alexander Solzhenitsyn called the "century of the concentration camp," it is hard to disagree with them.

THE STORY OF THE PATRIARCHS AND MATRIARCHS (12:1–50:26)

Whatever the wider implications of these narratives, the story of the Tower of Babel comes as an answer to humanity's refusal to obey Yhwh's command to populate the planet (Gen 9:1; but see 11:4), which in turn rested on the divine promise not to undo the created order by flooding the world again (8:21–22). The divine change of mind comes, in part, because such destruction failed to repair the deep flaws in humankind, which seems always bent on self-destruction. Part of that scattering, and part of the mending of the flaws, comes from the election of the family of Abraham and Sarah, as well as their relatives and hangers-on.

The Stories of Matriarchs and Patriarchs
  A. The story of Abraham and Sarah (12:1–25:18)
    1. The election and call of Abraham's family (12:1–9)
    2. The matriarch in danger (12:10–20)
    3. Blessing Lot (13:1–18)
    4. Blessing the inhabitants of the land (14:1–24)
    5. Renewing the promise to Abraham (15:1–21)
    6. The Rescue of Hagar and Ishmael (16:1–16)
    7. A third blessing and call (17:1–27)
    8. Abraham's hospitality (18:1–16a)
    9. Abraham as intercessor (18:16b–33)
    10. Interlude: the destruction of Sodom and the fate of Lot's offspring (19:1–38)
    11. The matriarch in danger again (20:1–18)
    12. The birth of Isaac and expulsion of Ishmael (21:1–21)
    13. More conflicts (21:22–24)
    14. The binding of Isaac (22:1–19)
    15. Abraham's relatives (22:20–24)
    16. Sarah's death and burial (23:1–20)
    17. Finding a wife for Isaac (24:1–67)
    18. Conclusion of the Abraham and Sarah story (25:1–18)
  B. The story of Isaac and Rebekah (25:19–27:33)
  C. The story of Jacob and his wives (27:34–35:28)
    1. Jacob's departure to find a life (27:34–28:22)
    2. Jacob in Paddan-Aram (29:1–31:54)

3. Jacob's return to a new life (31:55–33:20)
4. Jacob in Palestine (34:1–35:29)
5. Appendix: the descendants of Esau (37:1–43)
D. The story of Joseph and his brothers (37:1–50:26)
   1. The brother's problems (37:1–36)
   2. Interlude: Judah and Tamar (38:1–30)
   3. Joseph the vulnerable slave in Egypt (39:1–40:23)
   4. Joseph the triumphant leader in Egypt (41:1–46:30)
   5. The reconciliation of the brothers (46:31–50:26)

The remainder of Genesis consists of a series of stories about the four generations of the descendants and relatives of Abraham and Sarah (also called Abram and Sarai). The sections do exhibit different narrative techniques, with the stories of the first three generations being much more episodic (or "gapped") than the life of Joseph, but there is enough continuity from chs 12–50 to speak of them as a continuous narrative. Many of these stories figure prominently in religious instruction for children in church and synagogue yet these stories are plainly not written for children. They contain adult themes and often surface deep ambiguities in readers' conceptions of God and human beings. Without trying to explore every story, let us consider three of the most problematic yet most theologically fruitful. The following section should illustrate ways of reading these texts that can be applied to many others.

Case 1—Genesis 18–19: The Destruction of Sodom and Gomorrah

One of the most famous stories of Genesis concerns the annihilation of Sodom, Gomorrah, and its neighbors. Popular preachers have often associated the "sin of Sodom" with homosexual practice, though nothing in the text itself supports such a reading. From a theological viewpoint, two elements of the story stand out instead. The first is the introduction. After eating with Abraham and Sarah (see the discussion of anthropomorphism), Yhwh announces to the former his intentions to investigate charges against Sodom lodged by those praying to heaven (Gen 18:20). The conversation takes on an educational dimension, which the text explains as a function of Abraham's future role as the progenitor of a group of people concerned with justice (Gen 18:19).

Abraham connects the dots in the divine speech, understanding that the proposed investigation of the evil cities will lead to their destruction. Horrified, he asks Yhwh to pay close attention to judicial process. His address is highly significant: "Far be it from you to do this thing, to kill the righteous with the wicked (so that the righteous would be like the wicked). Shall the judge of all the earth not carry out justice?" (Gen 18:26). Abraham's insistent question identifies a key element of Israel's understanding of God. Incapable of injustice, and not just on arbitrary grounds, Yhwh examines evidence to reach a fair conclusion. At the same time, including Abraham (and by implication, his descendants reading the book) in the discussion of justice has an educational purpose. By negotiating downward the number of righteous people required to save the cities (on the assumption that a tiny handful of such persons can justify the continued existence even of a deeply immoral community), Abraham learns that the pursuit of justice demands his full attention, as well as God's.

The story then moves forward to its second point. The destruction of the cities is justified because only four righteous persons live there, and even they do seem to deserve the label except on a very generous evaluation. The rejection of the heavenly messengers (and the people's attempts to rape them) simply confirms the charges lodged against the inhabitants of the cities by those praying to God in protest of their actions. Whatever its historical background, now lost but perhaps better known to Israel's oral tradition, the destruction of the cities in Genesis underscores Abraham's status as a prophet (uniquely Gen 20:7), to connect his family to events in Canaan before the rise of Israel as a nation, and most importantly, to evoke a view of the world in which divine justice was a foundational assumption.

Case 2—Genesis 22: The Binding of Isaac

The value of that assumption soon comes in for further examination in Genesis with the story of the Aqedah, or the binding of Isaac. One of the most widely discussed biblical stories over the past two-thousand-plus years, the Aqedah requires close reading if one is to hear its conclusions rather than the fruitful interpretations later assigned to it. Thus the story neither justifies nor excoriates human sacrifice (a known, if not necessarily common, practice in the ancient Near East), nor does it point to a notion of general resurrection (though later Jewish texts understood it that way; see Heb 11:19).

Two clear emphases do emerge from it, however. First, Genesis understands the event as a test (Hebrew: *nāsâ*) of Abraham's faith (Gen 22:1). Elohim tests Abraham, an act that allows for a confirmation of the righteous person's reputation for piety. While human beings ought not to *nāsâ* God (whose reputation is not up for grabs; see, e.g., Exod 17:2; Num 14:22; Deut 6:16), the reverse may occur in rare instances when the person in question is remarkable for piety (Ps 26:2; Dan 1:12) or when the consolidation of the people of Israel as a Torah-keeping community is at stake (Exod 16:4).

Second, however, the story ends with an etiology, or explanation of how some reality came to be. After the angel stills his hand, Abraham names the place "Yhwh Yir'eh" ("Yhwh sees"), and the narrator adds, "with respect to which it is said until this day, 'on Yhwh's mount it (or he?) is seen.'" In other words, Abraham's actions serve as the point of origin, and the ongoing rationale, for a theological claim about a holy site in Israel, probably the Temple Mount in Jerusalem. And the story of the binding of Isaac functions to explain why later Israelites visit that sanctuary (much as Jacob's dreams at Bethel in chs 28 and 35 validate the holy site there). From the narrator's point of view a series of meanings interconnect, because both the ancestors and their descendants reading this book expect Yhwh to see them in their hour of need.

To be sure, such an interpretation may grate on modern sensibilities. The mechanics of the narrative seem out of balance for our tastes. Why threaten a boy (albeit the text does not indicate Isaac's age) with death? Many scholars have argued that Gen 22 marks a transition in the overall narrative of the ancestors, with Isaac now becoming a full-fledged character in his own right. One may wonder if such an interpretation was in the author's mind. Perhaps it was, though binding someone on an altar is a strange rite of passage! More likely, the part of the story that troubles us most simply did not trouble the ancient storytellers as much, in part because the divine command to offer Isaac only made sense in the context of an assumption of divine deliverance in the final event.[5]

Case 3—Genesis 34: The Rape of Dinah

If it is possible to find a theological payoff in a text as difficult and upsetting as the Aqedah, the same is not easy to say for the story of the rape of Dinah in ch 34. The only named daughter of Jacob finds herself caught in the brutal world of male rivalry in which her sexuality belongs either to her family or to a husband. The precipitating event in this story, one of a number that the scholar Phyllis Trible famously called a "text of terror," is her rape by a Canaanite (or more properly, Hivite) aristocrat, one Shechem son of Hamor. The family of Jacob at first consents to Hamor's proposal that the two young people wed, provided that the Hivites undergo circumcision in order to unite the two groups. Jacob's family takes advantage of their postoperative vulnerability to kill the males of the city and plunder their property.

How did the narrator make sense of this story? It is obviously susceptible to many interpretations, from a thought-provoking modern feminist critique of male power to a more ancient one celebrating the cleverness of Jacob's sons and their willingness to engage in honor killing. (As Gen 34:31 seems to indicate, the narrator was aware of the latter interpretation but did not endorse it; the first one would undoubtedly have surprised ancient readers.) Some aspects of the story are revealing.

First the asides. The text offers several comments on the actions of the characters: "for he [Shechem] had done a disgraceful thing in Israel . . . such as should not be done" (34:7); "for he [Shechem again] was the most honored of all his extended family" (34:19); "and Jacob's sons came on the corpses and plundered the city because they [the Hivites] had polluted their sister" (34:27). For the author of the story, a matter of family honor is involved. The conundrum becomes how to deal with such a case.

This problem shapes the snippets of conversation among the characters in the narrative. Most notably, by recording the thoughts of the Hivites about the potential assimilation of Jacob's family (34:21–23), the narrator reminds the Israelite reader of the unsuitability of such an arrangement. For a minority group such as Jacob's family, absorption challenges identity, and the narrator warns against the hazards of carelessly drifting in such a direction.

There is more to the story, however, for the dialogue between Jacob and his sons at the tale's end presents two views of their murder: "you have brought me trouble" (Jacob's view; 34:30) and "will he make our sister like a whore?" (Simeon and Levi's view; 34:31).

Both arguments seem valid at some level, and both reflect the perspective of a small group that feels that its survival is at risk.

When did Israel feel such risk? Older scholars sometimes dated this story to the very earliest times of Israel's life, understanding it as a real historical event. More recently, many scholars have thought of the story as reflecting a time in Israel's life after its return from Babylonian exile, during which it was allegedly a minority group in its own land. Arguably, neither setting is entirely plausible. The late dating does not seem to reflect the best historical evidence, for the inhabitants of the land during the Persian Period (ca. 539–334 BCE) thought of themselves as Israelites (and no Hivites lived there at that late date). The early date is also difficult to establish because it would be difficult to imagine how the story could have been passed along for centuries in a form complete with internal dialogue and editorial comments. Perhaps the story reflects Israel's recurring anxiety surrounded by hostile neighbors. We simply do not know.

SUMMARY

These three texts, like many others, open some doors into Genesis. They demonstrate, if demonstration is needed, that the challenge for readers of Genesis is not to understand the obscure practices of ancient people. Recovering those practices requires serious historical investigation, but it is doable. No, the real challenge lies in stripping away the sentimental preconceptions that many readers bring to this text. Genesis is a much earthier text than popular readings make it out to be. Videos of dancing vegetables cannot do justice to its exploration of humanity as creatures before God.

Basic Ideas

Someone once said that reading Tolstoy's *War and Peace* always made him feel that his own house "were all full of people."[6] That is certainly true of Genesis. However, it helps to know that the book revolves around a few very basic ideas that inform almost every story in it. Let us consider some of them.

WORLD GEOGRAPHY

One important aspect of Genesis is its geographical imagination. The book meticulously situates its stories in place. This strategy begins with the mental map of Eden, which is said to be the source of four rivers:

> The name of the first is Pishon (it surrounds the land of Havilah [perhaps Oman?], where there is gold—and that gold of that land is good; there is also bdellium and onyx stone there!). The name of the second is river is Gihon (it surrounds all the land of Cush [today's Sudan]). And the name of the third river is Hiddeqel [the Tigris], which flows east of Assyria, while the fourth river is the Euphrates. (Gen 2:11–14)

It's not easy to see how such a geographical view could fit on a real map—the hydrology simply does not work. But Genesis wishes its readers to imagine Eden as a place both remote in time and locale and impossibly splendid. And in doing so, the book draws on ancient ideas of faraway wealth (since gems were imported from as far away the Baltic and Afghanistan) as well as of deities living in splendid parks surrounding a palace.

The book's geographical descriptions become more real-world by ch 10, which lists the nations of the known world, and then in the stories of the patriarchs and matriarchs. In chs 12–50, the ancestors of Israel visit places of which every ancient reader knew the location. Even the characters in the story form part of the book's mental geography, for Esau was the ancestor of the Edomites, Lot of the Ammonites and Moabites, and Jacob lived for awhile in northern Syria, in Paddan-Aram. In other words, the biblical stories are acted out on a gigantic stage embracing many nations, friendly or not. Genesis wishes not only to show that Israel rightly lives in its land but also that Yhwh shows concern for everyone else. Genesis does not serve up a crude nationalism but a complex view of the world in which many human populations can coexist if the terms are right.

All human beings have in our heads a map that provides one of the major ways in which we understand the relationships among the various components of our world. When Genesis maps out the world that ancient Israel knew, it both makes the land of Canaan the imagined center of that world and reminds readers that not everything of importance happens there.

FAMILY

Moreover, the text's fascination with geography intersects with some of its other ideas, including such abiding realities as the importance of family (and the values of fertility, harmony, and prosperity), the nature of God, the sanctity of the land of Israel, the harmony among the tribes, and so on. Families are extremely important in Genesis, and many stories revolve around tensions in them. The book takes an interest in the family in various forms (nuclear families; polygamous, multigenerational families; slave families dependent on their masters; and others) without imagining that any one of them is ideal. In every case, the stories reflect at least three major values, which David Petersen has described as "(1) the value of defining family in expansive terms; (2) the value of family continuity; (3) and the value of nonviolent resolution of conflict within the family."[7] The need to preserve the family and solve its problems while minimizing violence explains Cain's escape from "justice" (4:8–16), Esau's "forgiveness" of Jacob (33:1–17), and the strained scene between Joseph and his brothers after their father's death (50:15–21).

Sibling rivalry is a major subtheme, with conflicts dividing such figures as Cain and Abel, Isaac and Ishmael, Jacob and Esau, and Joseph and his brothers. Yet rivalry is not the only way generational peers relate. Each story of conflict, except that of Cain and Abel, which is foreshortened by murder, has a complementary story of sibling reconciliation.

Thus Ishmael and Isaac bury their father together (Gen 25:9–10), Jacob and Esau reconcile and live apart (Gen 33:1–17; cf. 36:7; similarly, Lot leaves the land in Gen 13), and Joseph and his brothers resolve their differences not once, but twice (Gen 45:1–15; 50:15–21). At one level, these stories of sibling conflict and cooperation both evoke a world of family in which the competition for scarce resources can engender both moral and immoral behavior. Yet at another level, the stories also have a political dimension on the level of whole cultures, for the various members of Abraham's family stand in for entire peoples and their interrelationships.

On a related note, one of the literary devices of the book, and of many other parts of the Bible, is the genealogy. Ancient people of many cultures used genealogies to show relationships among groups, to stake out legal or moral claims to land or social privileges, and to elevate reputations of groups or individuals named, among other reasons. So the lists of names in Genesis do not merely pass on a lot of data in a condensed form. They offer a mental map of Israel's world, one in which neighbors are cousins, however distantly removed, and so share a common history and, perhaps, a common future.[8] Although most of the names in the genealogical lists of names in Genesis are male—it was after all a patriarchal world—the key ancestors for the main family of the story are the matriarchs. Sarah's son, not those of Abraham's other wives, is the heir of the promise. Rebekah's co-wives, if any, do not even receive a mention in the text at all.

A closely related literary device in the book is called the "Toledot Formula," from the Hebrew word for "generations" (*tôlĕdôt*). "These are the generations" announces either a new genealogy or a story about a new family member in Gen 2:4; 5:2; 6:9; 10:1, 32; 11:10, 27; 25:12, 13, 19; 36:1, 9; 37:2. In Genesis the formula is a device for advancing the story without writing a full-blown episode about transitions. The "generations" move through time, but they do not break with what came before them.

THE ONE GOD

The importance of family in Genesis is closely related to the importance of the deity. Israel's one God bears several names: Yhwh, Elohim, El, El Elyon ("God Most High"), El Shaddai ("God Almighty"), El Roi ("God Who Sees or Is Seen"), among other titles. Some of these names appeared outside Israel. So, for example, El is the standard Semitic name for deity as well as the personal name of the supreme deity (= Akkadian Ilu or Arabic Allah). Elyon is a divine name widely attested throughout Syria and Palestine centuries before Israel appeared on the scene. And even Yhwh, the distinctive name of Israel's God, may have a connection to the land in the border areas of today's Saudi Arabia and Jordan, which the Egyptians of the second millennium BCE called "the land of Yau."

Yet names are one thing and personalities are another, and Genesis fairly obsesses over the nature of its deity. To understand Genesis's portrayal of the deity, perhaps a good place to start is with Jacob's declaration on his deathbed in Gen 48:15–16:

Then he blessed Joseph and said, "the Elohim before whom my ancestors Abraham and Isaac walked, the Elohim who shepherded me through my life until today, the Angel/Messenger (Hebrew: *mal'āk*) who rescued me from all evil–may he bless the young men" [i.e., Joseph's sons Ephraim and Manasseh].

Genesis portrays God as the personal deity of the ancestors. So, this God can appear in visions to Abraham (Gen 12:1–3; 15:1–20; 17:1–22; and 18:22–33) and Jacob (Gen 28:10–17; 32:1–2, 22–32), with the content of the visions revolving around the family's survival and success. This God also ensures successful childbirth (Gen 21:1–2; 25:21; 29:31–35), and the survival of children (Gen 21:20–21). The "god of the ancestors," as Jacob calls him, is one interested in the ordinary events of life.[9]

At the same time, this God appears as the creator of the world. To modern people, the combination of these ideas may seem unremarkable, just as the idea of there being only one deity seems obvious. For ancient people, however, both ideas must have seemed strange because they thought of the hierarchy of multiple gods as closely resembling the hierarchies of human societies. Thus, when Gilgamesh or Achilles—to take heroes from two different times and places—want to talk with the supreme deities, they approach them through lesser "personal gods." How much more inaccessible were the high gods to ordinary mortals! Yet Genesis attributes various divine names to one being, who can create the entire cosmos while also worrying about childbearing in one family.

This combination of ideas about deity created a theological revolution that is still playing out. For example, a major issue raised by Genesis is that of election. Is it just for the divine sovereign to select one group among others for a special purpose? The answer to this depends, at least in part, on what the purpose is, which is why Genesis takes pains to insist that Israel's election leads to the blessing of "all the nations."

Another problem: How limited in time and space can the deity be? In the book's first creation story (Gen 1:1–2:4), Elohim appears as a cosmic creator who can speak everything into existence—no holds barred. Similarly, Abraham can call Yhwh "the judge of all the earth" (Gen 18:26) and so expect that such a title implies certain divine behaviors and excludes others. Yet Yhwh also seems to learn new things from humans (Gen 22:12) and to regret creating human beings (Gen 6:6). Most shockingly to modern sensibilities, Gen 32 contains the story of Jacob wrestling with a being in the valley of the River Jabbok. After an all-night contest, the two combatants reach an impasse, resulting in Jacob receiving the new name Israel, the future name of the entire nation. His superhuman opponent explains the new name by means of a Hebrew pun, "You have striven [*śārîtā*—the two principal consonants *ś* and *r* also appear in "Israel"] with Elohim and with human beings and have prevailed," while Jacob names the place Peniel (Hebrew for "face of El"). In other words, both speakers identify Jacob's opponents as a deity or at any rate what we would call an angel, without being more precise.

Most readers over the past two thousand years would simply dismiss these examples as cases of anthropomorphism or anthropopathy (attributing human characteristics or emotions to nonhuman entities). Perhaps so. Rather, by allowing a view of Israel's God to survive that other parts of the Pentateuch will question or even discard (see the discussion of Leviticus below), Genesis notes that Israel's God cannot be measured or controlled but can elicit wonder. No language about God can be problem-free simply because of the inadequacy of the human discourse for its divine subject. All language about God is metaphorical. The challenge is to find language that speaks truly of God. That quest the Bible undertakes at many points.

THE LAND OF ISRAEL

Another conceptual issue in Genesis is that of the status of the land of Canaan, which had become for Genesis's earliest readers "the land of Israel." As already noted, the book does not denigrate any other part of the world, all of which it sees as the creation of Yhwh/Elohim. Moreover, unlike some biblical (and many other ancient Near Eastern) texts that think of departure from the homeland as a terrible thing, Genesis acknowledges that such travel can have the legitimate purpose of saving life, and that the sojourning Israelite may find friendship and meaning—even God—elsewhere. Yet at the same time the promised land itself is part of the offer of divine blessing on the people, and even Eden itself seems to have been situated there, or at least the two locales became associated in Israel's imagination (see Ps 24 [possibly]; 46:5 [ET 46:4]; Isa 51:3; Ezek 47:1–12).

In the family stories in Gen 12–50, then, the land plays a major role in several ways. First, the text recognizes that the ancestors owned almost none of it, except the burial cave of Machpelah in Hebron (Gen 23:1–20) and land near Shechem (Gen 33:19; cf. John 4:12; but contrast Acts 7:16 [which reflects an alternative Samaritan tradition]).

However, the ancestors did lay the groundwork for the nation of Israel's ownership of the land in two ways. First, and most obviously, they received the divine promise of the land (see Gen 12:1–3; 35:9–15). Second, they sacralized the land by erecting field-stone altars at various locations. So we read of Abraham building altars at Shechem (Gen 12:7), Hebron (13:18), and Moriah (22:9; later tradition, perhaps correctly, associates the location with Jerusalem), Isaac doing the same at Beersheba (Gen 26:25), and Jacob likewise at Shechem (Gen 33:20) and Bethel (Gen 35:1, 3, 7). Why? Although later Israelite law forbade the offering of sacrifices to Yhwh anywhere but in Jerusalem (see Chapter 7, "Deuteronomy"), the older traditions of the ancestors (and of Moses) saw things differently. Altars in open-air sanctuaries allowed a community or a family (see 1 Sam 20:6) to worship together. The land itself took on a sacred quality because the connection between God and humankind remained unsevered.

The most dramatic example of the sanctification of the land comes from the paired stories of Jacob's encounters with Yhwh at Bethel in Gen 28:10–17 and 35:1–4. (The place name means "the house of El," indicating that Genesis is equating El with Yhwh [see 35:1].) Bethel was a major sanctuary in the later kingdom of Israel, and Genesis reflects a tradition that predates the condemnation of that site in texts like 2 Kgs 12. In the first episode, Jacob dreams of angels climbing back and forth between heaven and earth and hears a voice promising him deliverance. The second vision, upon his return home, repeats the promise and in addition calls upon the returnees to cease worshiping foreign gods. The story reflects a view of the land of Israel that sees it as the land of Yhwh/El and therefore the land of the people who serve this God.

THE TRIBES

The final major idea to consider at this point is that Genesis assumes the division of the world into many nations, all somehow related, and also the division of Israel into twelve tribes or extended lineages. While tribes often coexist with states (and can even be formed by states),[10] the earliest organization of Israel as a people was in the form of a loose affiliation of tribes that sometimes united for self-defense (see Judg 5), when not fighting among themselves. These units were part of a nested hierarchy of family structures, beginning with the smallest unit, the two or three generations of a family living together (Hebrew: *bêt ʾab*) continuing to the clan (*mišpāḥâ*) and to the largest family unit, the tribe (*maṭṭeh* or *šēbet*).

Gen 49, in particular, contains an ancient hymn about the tribes. It assumes that the two major ones were Judah and Joseph, the central tribes of the later kingdoms of Israel and Judah. Although the tribes bore the names of the sons of Jacob, the stories about those sons should not be read simply as a symbolic way of talking about the tribes, for the stories of Jacob's family are primarily family stories, not tribal ones.

SUMMARY

All of these themes in Genesis create a rich mosaic of stories into which a reader may enter with empathy. The house really is full of people. And not just any people, but the flawed human beings whose descendants became the people of Israel. By telling the story of their people's origins through the lives of such realistic characters, Israelite authors explored the implications of living out the Abrahamic blessing in a world to which it might prove meaningful.

Implications

Modern readers of Genesis stand in great company. One of the most influential interpreters of Genesis's exposure of both human and divine pathos was the early Christian missionary Paul. His reading of Genesis still bears fruit today. Like his Jewish contemporaries—and Paul always considered himself a Jew committed to following the Jewish messiah, Jesus of Nazareth—he thought of the book as an organic whole, a story in which the God of Israel worked to redeem the world. So creation seemed to him a model for God's ongoing work of redeeming all of humankind, and Abraham became the ancestor of all who trust

Yhwh. He talks about this latter point in several ways, but perhaps his most integrated reading of the story comes in Rom 4. Paul quotes Gen 15:6, which says that "Abraham believed [trusted?] God, and it was reckoned to him as justice." He then goes on to frame the patriarch's actions as contrasting strongly to a reliance on Torah obedience, noting that since Abraham had done nothing at all to merit divine approval, the divine-human relationship could not rest on human achievements, however noble.

Paul's reading of the text has, again, exerted enormous influence on Christian readings of Genesis, with almost every word on the subject in Romans and Galatians provoking interpretation and even controversy. What is clear, however, is that Paul did not advocate moral sloth. Nor did he denigrate Torah itself or Jewish observance of it. He sought to see beneath contemporary interpretations of the Abraham story, which often saw him as a model of monotheistic obedience (Jubilees 12:16–24; Apocalypse of Abraham 1–8) and find a story about divine grace. At that level, his interpretation lay well within the Jewish mainstream. The ancient figures were seen as models, as in the first century BCE "Prayer of Manasseh" (see Chapter 30, "Secondary Canon"), which contrasts the penitent king's deep awareness of his own sin with the lives of the ancestors, "who did not sin against you" (v. 8). The stories of Genesis seemed to its earliest interpreters to be case studies in moral decision-making and spiritual discipline. Though many of the ancient interpretations of Genesis may strike modern readers as improbably pious, the instinct that the book contained more than a soap opera exploring human failure is correct. For "In the Beginning" also seeks to investigate not merely how things came to be, but how they might progress in Israel's future.

Notes

1. For the whole story, see the translation of Benjamin R. Foster in *Contexts of Scripture*, ed. William W. Hallo and K. Lawson Younger (Leiden/Boston: Brill, 2003), 1.130, 450–452.

2. On Abraham outside Genesis, see Thomas Römer, "Abraham Traditions in the Hebrew Bible Outside the Book of Genesis," in *The Book of Genesis: Composition, Reception, and Interpretation*, ed. Craig A. Evans, Joel N. Lohr, and David L. Petersen (Leiden/Boston: Brill, 2012), 159–180.

3. For the text and a discussion of this, see the translation of James P. Allen in *Contexts of Scripture*, ed. William W. Hallo and K. Lawson Younger (Leiden/Boston: Brill, 2003), 1.16 (23–26).

4. For the history of Christian viewpoints on the "fall," see Gary A. Anderson, *The Genesis of Perfection: Adam and Eve in Jewish and Christian Imagination* (Louisville: Westminster John Knox, 2001).

5. For a full analysis of the story and the history of its interpretation, see Jon Levenson, *The Death and Resurrection of the Beloved Son: The Transformation of Child Sacrifice in Judaism and Christianity* (New Haven: Yale University Press, 1993).

6. Edmund Wilson, *Letters on Literature and Politics, 1912–1972*, ed. Elena Wilson (New York: Farrar, Straus and Giroux, 1977), 284.

7. David Petersen, "Genesis and Family Values," *Journal of Biblical Literature* 124 (2005): 22.

8. See the useful cross-cultural discussion in Thomas Hieke, "Genealogy as a Means of Historical Representation in the Torah and the Role of Women in Genealogical System," in *Torah,* ed. Irmtraud Fischer and Mercedes Navarro Puerto, with Andrea Taschl-Erber (Atlanta: SBL, 2011), 151–192.

9. On Israelite family religion before the monarchy, see Karel van der Toorn, *Family Religion in Babylonia, Syria and Israel: Continuity and Change in the Forms of Religious Life* (Leiden: Brill, 1996), esp. 236–265.

10. For a handy introduction to the issues of tribes and states, see Philip S. Khoury and Joseph Kostiner, eds., *Tribes and State Formation in the Middle East* (Berkeley: University of California Press, 1990).

For Further Reading

Schmid, Konrad. *Genesis and the Moses Story: Israel's Dual Origins in the Hebrew Bible.* Winona Lake, IN: Eisenbrauns, 2010.
Ska, Jean-Louis. *Introduction to Reading the Pentateuch.* Winona Lake, IN: Eisenbrauns, 2006.
Westermann, Claus. *Genesis,* 3 vols. Minneapolis: Fortress, 1994–2002.

4 Rescue and Renewal
THE BOOK OF EXODUS

Key Text: *And God spoke to Moses and said to him, "I am Yhwh. And I appeared to Abraham, to Isaac, and to Jacob as El Shaddai. I was not known to them as Yhwh. Also, I instituted a covenant with them, agreeing to give them the land of Canaan (the land of their sojourning—where they sojourned). And also I have heard the distress of the children of Israel by means of which Egypt has enslaved them, and I remembered my covenant."* (Exod 6:2–5)

If Genesis longs for the future, Exodus embraces it with both hands. Its story of deliverance from bondage remains one of the most famous in the world, the subject of movies and music, from DeMille's two versions of *The Ten Commandments* to Handel's *Israel in Egypt.*

To understand Exodus, one may begin with the war poem found in chapter 15:1–18. The oldest part of the book, and possibly the oldest text in the whole Bible, sets forth the key themes of the entire story. (Its opening line appears at the end of the 1990s movie, *The Prince of Egypt:* ʾāšîrâ laʾdōnay kî gāʾō gāʾâ—"let me sing to Yhwh, for he has triumphed gloriously.") These ideas include Yhwh's work as deliverer, the migration of Israel to the holy mountain, and the reputation of Yhwh among the nations. The poem reads, in part,

> Let me sing to Yhwh, for he has triumphed gloriously.
> Horse and its rider he has hurled into the sea.
> Yah is my strength and song, my salvation. . . !

The enemy said, "I will pursue, overtake, divide spoil, fill my every desire . . .
You blew with your wind, moved the sea.
They sank like lead in the noble waters . . . .
The peoples heard and trembled . . . .
You brought and planted them on your mountainous estate, your freehold.

Israel's life as a people in covenant with Yhwh is a major presupposition of the book, which seeks to explain how that reality came about. Exodus both continues the story of Genesis and presents a parallel account of the origins of Israel as a community sustained by its ongoing practice of reflecting theologically on its story of deliverance. The two books refer to each other in several ways, with stories of both Abraham (Gen 15:12–21) and Joseph (Gen 50:24–26) foreshadowing the deliverance from Egypt and the book of Exodus often referring to the stories of the patriarchs and matriarchs.

Vladimir Propp offers a list of plot elements shaping folktales. Many of these elements appear in Exodus and other biblical narratives, probably indicating that these stories were shaped by oral storytelling, not just the free invention of the biblical authors. Propp's elements include

1. a family member is away from home;
2. an interdiction is addressed to the hero;
3. the interdiction is violated;
4. the villain makes an attempt at reconnaissance;
5. the villain receives information about his victim;
6. the villain attempts to deceive the victim in order to take possession of his or her belongings;
7. the victim falls for the deception and thus unwittingly helps the villain;
8. the villain harms a member of a family, or (8a) one family member lacks or desire to have something;
9. misfortune or lack is made known, and the hero is dispatched to do something about it;
10. the seeker agrees to or decides upon counteraction;
11. the hero leaves home;
12. the hero is tested, interrogated, or attacked, which prepares the way for the introduction of a magical helper;
13. the hero reacts to the actions of the future donor;
14. the hero acquires the use of a magical agent;
15. the hero is transferred, delivered, or led to an object of search;
16. the hero and villain join in direct combat;
17. the hero is branded;
18. the villain is defeated;
19. the initial misfortune or lack is remedied;
20. the hero returns;
21. the hero is pursued;
22. the hero is rescued;
23. the hero, unrecognized, arrives home or in another country;
24. a false hero presents unfounded claims;
25. a difficult task is proposed to the hero;

26. the task is resolved;
27. the hero is recognized;
28. the false hero or villain is exposed;
29. the hero receives a new appearance;
30. the villain is punished; and
31. the hero is married and ascends the throne.

See Vladimir Propp, *Morphology of the Folktale,* trans. Laurence Scott; rev. Louis Wagner (Bloomington: University of Indiana Press, 1968; repr. Austin: University of Texas, 1994).

The book of Exodus consists of three major parts, which are marked by geographic movement. Chapters 1–15 occur with Egypt as the backdrop. Even when Moses resides in Midian, Egypt is not far away; chapters 19–40 take place at Mount Horeb, more famously called Sinai. Egypt is the place of tyranny, Sinai of law. Egypt marks the absence of Yhwh, Sinai of Yhwh's abiding presence. Egypt means slavery, Sinai freedom.

A bridge section consists of chapters 16–18, which is set in the wilderness. This section anticipates much of the material in Numbers, and shares with the later book a sense that all was not well during Israel's forty-year sojourn in the desert between its departure from Egypt and its arrival in the promised land. (This pessimistic view was not universally shared in Israel, as a comparison with Jer 2:1–11 and Hos 2:16 [ET 2:15] shows.) However, the full-blown mutinies of the book of Numbers do not appear in Exodus, where Israel's complaints are the understandable response to hunger, thirst, and a gnawing uncertainty about the character of the liberator God, who seems capable of destruction, but whose capacities for sustained leadership remains in question. Interestingly, the book of Exodus does not offer the only version of the ancient stories (see, e.g., Pss 78; 80; 105; 106; 136; Hos 11), but it is the definitive, most theologically loaded version.

In any case, this basic structure (Egypt → Wilderness → Holy Mountain) derives from the Song of the Sea in chapter 15 and is thus deeply embedded in Israel's collective memory of its past. All the key ingredients of the story's plot appear at the earliest known stage, even if many elements of the Exodus deliverance narrative accreted around the central story as Israelites told and reenacted it over and over. Just as it does not mention Moses, the Song does not specify where the mountain is, and its original referent may have been the land of Israel as a whole, but in Exodus at least (and very early in Israel's historical existence), the destination became at least partially identified with Sinai. Exodus 15's vagueness in identifying the mountain's location allowed the image of "God's mountain" to take on more than one association.

The Narrative Structure of Exodus

Like any good story, then, Exodus has a clear plot. The geographical setting creates the space (real and imagined) for the actions of characters solving problems and working toward a dénouement. The emplotment of the book reveals a gradual empowering of the weak (Moses and Israel) and disempowerment of the strong (Pharaoh and Egypt).

PLOT STRUCTURE OF EXODUS

I. Israel in Egypt (1:1–15:21)
  A. The problem of names and namelessness (1:1–7:7)
  B. The obliteration of Egypt: The ten blows (7:8–11:10, 12:29–32)
  C. The salvation of Israel (12:1–28; 12:33–15:21)
II. Israel in the Wilderness (15:22–18:27)
  A. New places (15:22–27)
  B. Bread and water (15:22–17:7)
  C. New enemies (17:8–16)
  D. A new Judicial Structure (18:1–27)
III. Israel at Sinai (19:1–40:38)
  A. Torah from Sinai (19:1–24:18)
    1. Israel prepares to meet Yhwh (19:1–25)
    2. Torah from Sinai (20:1–24)
    3. The ten words (20:1–21)
    4. The altar law (20:22–26)
    5. The Covenant Code (21:1–23:19)
    6. Supplement to the Covenant Code (23:20–33)
    7. Israel meets Yhwh again (24:1–18)
  B. The Tabernacle blueprint (take 1) (25:1–31:18)
  C. The Golden Calf episode and its aftermath (32:1–34:35)
  D. The Tabernacle blueprint (take 2) and its dedication (35:1–40:38)

The book's plot carries along the theological agenda of the book, which seems to be stated well at a critical juncture:

> And God spoke to Moses and said to him, "I am Yhwh. And I appeared to Abraham, to Isaac, and to Jacob as El Shaddai. I was not known to them as Yhwh. Also, I instituted a covenant with them, agreeing to give them the land of Canaan (the land of their sojourning—where they sojourned). And also I have heard the distress of the children of Israel by means of which Egypt has enslaved them, and I remembered my covenant." (Exod 6:2–5)

The book does not concern merely the adventures of a people. It is not just a tale of political or social liberation, though it does include those elements. Because its primary actor is a deity, the story cannot be understood except as a religious document, first and foremost.

EL SHADDAI AND YHWH

The Pentateuch uses several names for Israel's deity: Exod 6:2–5 proposes a chronological relationship among the names, with El Shaddai ("God the Almighty") being the ancient name used by the ancestors and Yhwh being the more appropriate name for the liberated people. In truth, both names were used in the later period, but Exodus may be pointing to a historical awareness of the fact that Yhwh was not a divine name shared with other peoples and therefore not as deeply rooted in the religious landscape of Canaan and neighboring countries.

To explore how the book works as a religious narrative, one might consider a series of episodes that advance the plot.

PLOT POINT I: NAMES AND NAMELESSNESS (EXOD 1:1–7:7)

The first section of the book is framed by two genealogies, that of the whole nation of Israel in its first few generations (1:1–7) and what looks like a fragment of an expanded genealogy with more names, those of the major clans of certain tribes. The climax of the second one comes with Moses and Aaron, who, the narrator assures us, are "the Aaron and Moses to whom Yhwh said, 'bring forth the children of Israel from the land of Egypt'" (Exod 6:26). This reminder seems gratuitous—what other Moses or Aaron was there to talk about?—but it provides an important clue for understanding the narrative. In a culture that prized genealogies as a way of organizing a mental picture of the world, using the lists of names as a framing device or inclusio signals the fact that the new story of the exodus, with its extraordinary heroes, connected to Israel's everyday life. Moses was no demigod, no hero like Gilgamesh or Achilles, but a man with a background among his people. And that people will be the subject of its own story.

The emphasis on names and namelessness continues as Pharaoh appears (unnamed) and "forgets" (i.e., does not know about) Joseph (Exod 1:8), leading to the enslavement of Israel. The narrative then introduces the hero, who receives the name Moshe (possibly related to the Egyptian name Mose ["son of"], but this is debatable)[1] with a story similar to that of the birth of the even more ancient king of Agade in southern Mesopotamia, Sargon the Great (twenty-third century BCE). According to stories of their births, the parents of both men placed them as babies in reed baskets and floated them down a river to their rescue. In contrast to Sargon's lifetime spent as a conqueror, however, Moses lived as a liberator.[2]

Whatever the connection between the two birth stories, the Exodus narrative continues by dissociating Moses from Egyptian power structures and their built-in violence. This phase of the story raises, but then rejects, the possibility that Israel's deliverance will come through violent revolution. Accordingly, Exod 2:11–15 offers a false start, in which Moses kills and Egyptian slave driver in order to protect an Israelite, leading the reader, who of course knows about Moses from Israel's oral traditions, at first to expect the launch of a liberation movement. A second false start appears later in the chapter, as Moses defends the Midianite women at the well from the abuse of nomads. In the Exodus story proper, however, only Yhwh may kill so that humans will not solve one pattern of injustice by creating another.

The crucial turning point in this first section of Exodus occurs in Exod 3–4, the story of Moses's prophetic call. Moses the shepherd in Midian, an urbanized zone in the Transjordan, climbs Mount Horeb (a.k.a. Sinai) to investigate a burning thicket that seems not to be consumed. There he meets Yhwh, the deity who self-identifies as the God worshiped by the ancestors of Israel and the one who has witnessed the cruel sufferings of their descendants in Egyptian bondage. Yhwh then calls Moses to the task of announcing divine salvation to both the Israelites themselves and to their overlord, the anonymous Pharaoh. As in other prophetic call or commissioning narratives (see Isa 6; Jer 1; cf. Jonah 1), the designated prophet expostulates at length, attempting to convince Yhwh of his unsuitability to this onerous task. Moses, being the greatest prophet, offers the most detailed reasoning for his unworthiness for the task: "What is your name?" "suppose they don't believe me" and most ironically (since he makes a powerful speech about his inability to make speeches) "Lord, I am not a man of words, neither in the past nor the present" (Exod 3:13; 4:1, 10). As in other prophetic call stories, the designated prophet must accept the call in the end despite his incapacities.

The most remarked-upon part of this story is probably the announcement of the divine name in 3:14–15:

> Then Elohim said to Moses, "I am who I am." Then he said, "You should tell Israel's Children[3] that 'I am sent me to you.'" Moreover, Elohim said to Moses, "You should tell Israel's Children, 'Yhwh, the God of your ancestors, the God of Abraham, the God of Isaac, and the God of Jacob sent me to you.' This is my name forever and this is my memorial [or perhaps, reputation] from generation to generation."

That is, the revelation of the divine name both links the imminent liberation with the ancient promises. The God who appears to Moses is both the deity worshiped by the ancestors and a being with capacities newly revealed. The text thus connects the two traditions of Israel's origins—the ancestral stories and the exodus story—by subordinating both to the traditions about divine activity.

As part of this depiction of Moses as emergent leader, the final episodes in this plot point involve his difficult relationships with first Israel and then Pharaoh. In both cases, he worries that his audience will not know the identity (name) of Yhwh. He therefore asks for a miraculous capacity that will demonstrate his connection to the deity, though curiously the ability to transform staffs into snakes or make one's skin "leprous" ultimately persuade no one but Moses. Pharaoh says, "Who is Yhwh" (Exod 5:2), a state of ignorance that prompts him to impose still harsher burdens on the Israelite slaves. (In other words, as Exodus conceives of things, not knowing the identity of Israel's God leads to oppression.) Then, dramatically, Yhwh announces to Moses, "I am Yhwh," the climactic moment in this first great section of the book. The self-revelation of the deity sets in motion the rest of the book's action.

PLOT POINT 2: THE TEN BLOWS (EXOD 7:8–11:10; 12:29–32)

Exod 7–12 recount a series of "blows" (the Hebrew term) or "plagues" (the equivalent offered by the ancient Greek translation or Septuagint [LXX]). These terrible calamities wreak havoc on the Egyptian economy and society, systematically destroying the agricultural and governmental systems of the nations, while exempting the Israelites from the suffering. The "blows" figured in the story of the exodus even in Israel's liturgical traditions (see Pss 78:44–52; 105:26–36; the order of the plagues varies in these texts, for the sequence was not crucial to the story), indicating that at some point the disasters came to assume a theological weight of their own.

What was that weight? Many commentators have tried to connect individual plagues to Egyptian deities (e.g., darkness assaults Re, the sun god or the bloody Nile assaults the river god), and some of these proposals make sense in the context of ancient views of divine combat. But because the Bible itself does not name these gods and because the proposals vary among themselves as to which Egyptian deity is under attack, this overall approach does not seem to explain the Bible's own viewpoint fully.[4]

Exodus's own understanding of the events comes through at the recommissioning of Moses and Aaron as spokespersons in Exod 7:1–7:

> Now Yhwh said to Moses, "Look, I am appointing you as Elohim to Pharaoh, and Aaron your brother will be your prophet. You will say everything I command you, and Aaron your brother will tell Pharaoh that he should release Israel's Children from his land. And I will harden the heart of Pharaoh, and I will multiply my signs and my miracles in the land of Egypt. But Pharaoh will not listen to you, so I will put my hand upon [i.e., strike] Egypt and bring my armies, my people, Israel's Children from the land of Egypt with great judgments. Then Egypt will know that I am Yhwh, when I stretch out my hand against Egypt, and I will bring Israel's Children from their midst. So Moses and Aaron did what Yhwh commanded them—that's what they did. Moses was eighty years old (and Aaron was eighty-three years old) when they spoke to Pharaoh.

This text, which shows strong priestly sensibilities such as the emphasis on Aaron (the first high priest), reveals several notable features. First, the communication with Pharaoh, who stands in for his entire nation, is a prophetic act. True, it is an unparalleled prophetic communication. Instead of the usual God → prophet → audience sequence, the pattern is God → Moses → prophet (Aaron) → audience. While promoting Aaron, the text also elevates both Moses and Yhwh by distancing them from Pharaoh in the communicative act. The narrator thus manages to exalt the founder of the priesthood Aaron without diminishing the importance of Moses.

Second, the words of the speakers relate closely to their deeds, making them what scholars often call prophetic sign acts (cf. e.g., Jer 13:1–11; 19:1–15). These are actions that speak a message in a memorable and dramatic way that mimics the events taking place in history. The prophetic words uttered after the sign acts interpret that message in more understandable ways or, rather, exclude some possible but undesired interpretations.

Third, the interpretation of the acts revolves around Yhwh's work as deliverer of Israel. The "blows" are not just terrible disasters, but "my [Yhwh's] signs" (Hebrew: 'ōtōtay) pointing to impending deliverance and "wonders" or "miracles" (Hebrew: *môpĕtay*) dramatically demonstrate Yhwh's presence.

Fourth, and most controversially, the events of these chapters confront Pharaoh with a difficult set of choices. To save his nation, he must remove one of the major sources of its power, the mass of Hebrew slaves. He can win only by losing. There is no possible compromise. He opts, as tyrants often do, to see his people die rather than free their human chattel. Exodus understands Pharaoh's moral crisis in terms of the hardening of his heart, which does not mean simply that he lacks compassion (as we would mean by the phrase in English), but that he lacks comprehension or judgment. In fact, the text uses several terms for this process. Sometimes Pharaoh's heart "grows heavy" (Hebrew: *kābad*; Exod 7:14; 8:11, 28 [ET 15, 32]; 9:7, 34), meaning it grows less capable of functioning. In these texts, Pharaoh impairs his own mental faculties. Sometimes, however, his heart "grows strong" (Hebrew: *ḥāzaq*; Exod 9:12; 11:10; 14:4, 8, 17). In these cases, Yhwh is an agent of his stubborn refusal to see sense.

In the text just cited (Exod 7:3), the Hebrew verb is *qāšâ* ("to harden"), and again Yhwh does something to Pharaoh. But what, exactly? Most scholars have recognized that the change of vocabulary corresponds to different layers of the story. One literary layer understands Pharaoh as being in control of his actions, while the other sees Israel's God as fully in charge of human affairs.[5] What happens when we read the layers together? Exod 7 puts it well: (a) Yhwh will harden Pharaoh's heart, but (b) Pharaoh will not listen to Moses and Aaron. Pharaoh is not an innocent victim, as chs 1 and 6 have already made clear: he is a savage tyrant. In the final form of the book, therefore, the agency of both Pharaoh and Yhwh are preserved in a delicate balance in which both exercise judgment. Pharaoh is neither a puppet on a string nor the master of his own destiny. Contrary to his presuppositions, he is interdependent with Israel's God. By failing to recognize the true nature of his relationship with the deity, Pharaoh has lost control of his own destiny.

PLOT POINT 3: PASSOVER AND LIBERATION (EXOD 12:1–28; 12:32–15:21)

The next unit consists of two major parts centered on Israel's liberation and the religious festival designed to preserve its memory. First, strategically located within the narrative of the so-called plagues or "blows" are the instructions for keeping the festival of Passover/Unleavened Bread (Exod 12:1–28). The placement of the instructions serves a dramatic function—slowing the action just before the climax is a widely used technique in storytelling for building suspense and underscoring the significance of the story's climax, in this case the destruction of the Egyptian firstborn and the release of the Israelites. But there is more at stake as the narrative points beyond itself to the readers' ongoing life.

ISRAEL'S FESTIVALS

Like all religious communities, ancient Israel organized the year around a series of major festivals, some tied to agricultural cycles, but all eventually engaging the remembered story of the nation's faith. The festivals originally included Passover/Unleavened Bread (March–April), Shavuot or Pentecost (fifty days later), and Sukkot or Tabernacles, in September–October. Over the centuries other festivals were added, including two more just before Sukkot (Rosh HaShanah and Yom Kippur or the Day of Atonement). Still later, Jews celebrated Purim a month before Passover and Hanukkah in December. Both were festivals commemorating liberation from gentile rulers (see Esth and 1–2 Macc for more details).

The festival of Passover coincides with the turn of the year (see the discussion on the Israelite calendar in Chapter 5 on Leviticus). Possibly the ritual early on had an association with the agricultural year as well as the spring equinox. That would hardly be surprising given the prevalence of both lunar and agricultural festivals in many cultures, both ancient and modern. Yet in Exodus, the key point is not the coinciding of the festival with the agricultural year but its status as a commemoration of the founding moment of Israel, the deliverance from Egypt. Like all major rituals, this one concerns a community's understanding of its history, aspirations, and commitments.

The instructions for the Passover in Exod 12–13 spell out its practice in its original setting in Egypt (where it marked the end of slavery, albeit through the tragic death of the firstborn Egyptian males, a sort of poetic justice balancing out the oppression of Yhwh's "firstborn," Israel). The text also calls for the perpetuation of the festival, even under changing circumstances (Exod 13:1–10). Perhaps most importantly, the text interprets the festival by reminding the reader to avoid leavened food (since most festivals have special food rules), and enjoining him or her:

> And you should tell your child on that day, "because Yhwh did this for me when I came from Egypt . . . ." And it will be to you a sign [Hebrew: *'ôt*] on your hand and a memorial [Hebrew: *zikkārôn*] between your eyes so that you will speak of Yhwh's law. For he brought you from the land of Egypt with a strong hand. (Exod 13:8–9)

First, in lines highly reminiscent of Deuteronomy, the instructions in Exodus expect that each generation will pass on the exodus story and will understand it as a "sign" of divine action to be memorialized through ritual. This remembrance involves the whole community, and it takes some concrete form. (Later interpreters assumed that "on your hand" and "between your eyes" referred to phylacteries worn in worship, but this interpretation is probably anachronistic.)[6]

Second, the story of Passover gives way to the dramatic turn in Exodus's narrative, the departure from Egypt. Leaving, perhaps via the Wadi Tumilat connecting the Nile Delta with the lakes lying along what is now the Suez Canal, Israel heads for Canaan. Curiously, Exodus tells the story twice, once as prose (Exod 14:1–31) and then as poetry (15:1–18). The linguistic features of the two versions indicate that the poetic one is much older, probably dating back to the twelfth or eleventh centuries BCE, and thus being an early witness to Israel's theological reflections on its own history. Interestingly, again, this older version does not mention Moses. As in other biblical texts, the creator of Exodus has told the story twice in order to emphasize its importance. (This same technique of following the prose version with an older poetic version, possibly known from the oral traditions of singers reciting Israel's story, also appears in Judg 4–5, Num 22–24, and 1 Sam 31–2 Sam 1.) The two versions of the crossing of the Reed Sea work together to emphasize both the importance of the event and the importance of commemorating it.

RED SEA OR REED SEA? WHICH BODY OF WATER DID ISRAEL CROSS?

The Bible designates the body of water that the Israelites crossed as the Yam Suph, usually translated as "sea of reeds" and associated with the shallow lakes lying near the current route of the Suez Canal north of the Gulf of Suez. There is no basis for popular ideas that they crossed the Gulf itself. However, the biblical references sometimes seem to place the Yam Suph near the Gulf of Aqaba, further east (Num 21:4; Deut 1:40; 2:1; 1 Kgs 9:26; and possibly other texts).

PLOT POINT 4: ISRAEL IN THE WILDERNESS (EXOD 15:22–18:27)

After the song the narrative takes a frightening turn. Israel heads into the wilderness of the Sinai Peninsula, the Arabah and the western part of the Arabian Desert. One of the bleakest and most inhospitable regions on earth, the area is nevertheless graced by oases in strategic locations. (See Num 1 for a possible list of some of them, as well as other sites on the path to Mount Sinai.) Israel recalls its story as a group who wandered through this region.

The story in Exodus does not, however, focus on the aridity of the region or the people's suffering. Those realities are presupposed. Its focus, instead, lies upon the interaction between Israel and Yhwh regarding the lack of food and water. The stories in Exod 15:22–18:27 function as part of a larger complex of murmuring stories that also appear in Num 11–20. All these stories note the ongoing complaints of the people and Yhwh's provision of food or water. Yet there is a difference in tone between Exodus and Numbers. The frustration of all the parties escalates over time. "How much proof do you need?" seems to be the question Moses and Yhwh ask of the people. As Num 14:20–25 sums up the movement of these stories, Israel's constant complaining lead Yhwh to allow the initial generation of liberated people to die off in the wilderness so as to preserve the community as a whole. That is, the text repeatedly considers the relationship between the present generation of Israelites (the readers) and those who preceded them, some of whom failed to understand the implications of their status. Israel does not remember its origins as a time of glorious success, but as one of human failure amid divine deliverance.

The unit in Exodus, in any case, includes several elements:

A. The initial searches for water (15:22–27)
B. The provision of manna (16:1–36)

C. A complaint against Moses (17:1–7)

D. The ambush by the Amalekites (17:8–16)

E. The establishment of the Israelite judiciary (18:1–27)

These seemingly randomly arranged miracle stories, in fact, demonstrate both deep theological reflection on the part of their storytellers and careful integration into their current context.

A clue to understanding how Exodus thinks about the stories comes from near the middle of the section: "And he called the name of the place Massah (Testing) and Meribah (Conflict) because of the conflict of Israel's Children and their testing of Yhwh when they said, 'Is Yhwh among us or not?'" Does the liberator God still live among us? That indeed is the question. Exodus understands the stories as demonstrations of the divine presence rather than Israel's failure of nerve or radical ingratitude.

The theological shaping of these texts emphasizes several themes: Yhwh as healer (Exod 15:27), provider of water and food (repeatedly), the giver of Sabbath rest (Exod 16:29), and the deity whose actions have gained international fame (Exod 18:1, 8). Perhaps most significantly, Exodus thinks that a major institution in Israelite life, its judicial system sans monarch, dates to the period of wandering through the wilderness. Exodus tells the story in ch 18 because behind the story lies a conversation, of which we see traces in many Pentateuchal stories. The conversation concerns the question, what practices shall we engage in that will maximize justice and beneficial orderliness in our land, without the dubious benefit of a monarch? (See further the discussion of monarchy in 1 Samuel in Chapter 12 "God, King, and People".) Exodus draws here on old traditions to make its point. If even Moses needed to respect the wisdom of lesser judges and the customs of his people, how much more do all subsequent leaders need to do so? This attempt to build a culture of respect, situated in a world in which one assumes the constant presence of divine benevolence, underlies the rest of the narrative of the book.

PLOT POINT 5: TORAH FROM SINAI (EXOD 19:1–24:18)

How does the story proceed, then? Arguably, the most theologically rich part of Exodus, and perhaps even of the entire Bible, occurs in the giving of Torah (law, instruction) at Sinai. In fact, Exod 19–Num 10 is a large unit of material set at Sinai. Here the priestly contributors to the Pentateuch placed most of their work, in order to emphasize that the liberator God also gave norms to a people sorely needing them. These norms came to Israel as a gift, completing the promise of Exod 3:12 ("and this shall be the sign that I am sending you, when you bring this people from Egypt: you shall serve Elohim on this mountain"). The deliverance will reach completion when Israel comes to the mountain to encounter its deliverer God. Torah, in short, functions to preserve the achievements of the exodus. It is the seedbed in which the original life of Israel may bloom.

LAW CODES IN THE BIBLE AND THE ANCIENT NEAR EAST

Compilations of laws in the ancient Near East significantly predate the Bible, with Mesopotamian kings beginning the practice by about 2100 BCE. These documents include the "codes" of

Ur-Nammu 2100 BCE
Eshnunna 1800 BCE
Lipit-Ishtar 1930 BCE
Hammurabi 1750 BCE
Middle Assyrian laws ca. 1300 BCE

These collections were not comprehensive, and so it is a little misleading to speak of them as "codes." But they all sought to provide a baseline for justice, which the king essayed to establish. As the Code of Hammurabi's prologue puts it, "It was then that Anu and Enlil ordained Hammurabi, a devout prince who fears the gods, to demonstrate justice within the land, to destroy evil and wickedness, to stop the might exploiting the weak, to rise like Shamash over the mass of humanity, illuminating the land; they ordained me to improve the welfare of my people."

The Pentateuch itself contains seven distinguishable legal collections, totaling, according to the rabbinic count, 613 laws. See the discussion in Chapter 5, Leviticus, for more detail.

It is important to understand this basic conception of the Torah as a gift because many readers of the Hebrew Bible or Old Testament take an exaggeratedly negative view of law. This view has a history, of course. Early Christians such as the Apostle Paul critiqued an overreliance of Torah-adherence in letters to Galatia and Rome. His corrections of abuses, or often of the straight-out misapplication of Torah to gentiles, to whom Yhwh did not give it, took on a life of its own that the apostle could not have intended. Luther's sixteenth-century critique of late medieval practices that sought to ground God's acceptance in human achievement, and his sharp contrast between law and gospel, reinforced misreadings of Paul. And then again, the general process of oversimplification that besets many intellectual movements, religious or otherwise, sets in, leading to a situation in which many Christian and secular readers misunderstand the Pentateuch's own conception of Torah or Law as a sign of grace, not its antithesis.

How does the idea of Torah as gift play out in Exodus, then? At least three things are important. First, Exodus includes two law codes that relate but are separable. The first is the Ten Commandments or Decalogue (Exod 20:1–17 = Deut 5:1–21). To be sure, different traditions count the units of the Decalogue differently. (Is the prohibition of idolatry one or two commands—one against worshiping other gods and the other against making images for worship? Is the prohibition of coveting one or two injunctions—one against coveting a spouse and the other against craving someone else's property?) Multiple cases exist for each arrangement. But what is clear is that the Decalogue does not comprehend all possible crimes. They give a basic set of commitments that even a child can memorize—one commandment for each finger!

Second, those commitments imply significant patterns of behaviors in groups and individuals. The first unit of the Decalogue bans idol-making in imitation of any creature in any of the planet's three habitats as the priests saw them: the ground, the air, and the water (cf. the classification of creatures in Gen 1:1–2:4). The text calls for an aniconic religion in which ideas of the deity cannot be frozen in stone but must be subjected to the uncertainty—and creativity—of words. Moreover, the prohibition of "taking Yhwh's name in vain," which means involving God in anything nefarious or morally flawed (e.g., a false oath), makes the ban on idolatry all-encompassing. The religion becomes still more concrete in a practice without real parallels in the ancient Near East, the weekly observance of a day of rest, the Sabbath. This law, because it is innovative in Israel's environment, requires the most detailed warrant (Exod 20:8–11). Because Yhwh stamped the created order with a blessing and declared it holy (cf. Gen 2:2–3), all humans and animals within the ambit of Israel ought to imitate the deity and rest. The Sabbath law's radical reordering of time and economic life cascades through the structures of Israel's life.

The latter part of the Decalogue concerns human interactions with each other. The bridge commandment, "Honor your father and mother, so it may go well with you," presumes the continuity of religious culture by seeking to create a culture of respect within the most basic human relationships, those of family. The next commandments continue this fundamental outlook by fostering a culture of respect among the next most proximate relationships, those of neighbors. Climaxing with the prohibition of crass materialism and greed, the Decalogue offers a starting point for Israel's ethical reflection.

Because such a short list of norms can offer only a starting point, the narrative immediately continues with a second code of law, the Covenant Code (Exod 21:1–23:33). Many of these laws have parallels in other ancient Near Eastern law codes, a fact that is hardly surprising since legal traditions reflect the ways people live,[7] including their lives' environmental, economic, and familial aspects. Some of these laws seem to make sense in an economy of small villages engaging in subsistence agriculture. At the same time, the law code does not mindlessly integrate the rules of Israel's neighbors. Rather, the Covenant Code places a theological Yahwistic stamp on this material. Deep thought has occurred.

This latter point becomes clear in a law like that in Exod 21:28–32, which states rules for dealing with the practicalities of out-of-control oxen. The revealing line occurs in v. 30: "If a monetary compensation is substituted for it [the death penalty prescribed in v. 29] then one [the defendant] should pay a settlement of whatever is assessed him." In other words, the law itself shows some flexibility at least in the penalty stage. In a case of negligent homicide (an ox's owner has not properly secured an animal prone to gore people), a legal process ensues in which the community decides on a proper penalty by carefully weighing the rights and obligations of the various parties. Far from being an inflexible instrument, law always reflects the complexities of circumstances on the ground.

This case is just one example of how the legal collections in the Pentateuch assume the existence of a legal community—a set of customary practices and designated persons responsible for maintaining a culture of law. That is, the legal system presupposes human capacity for decision making through drawing analogies ("Case 1 is like Case 2") and differentiation ("Case 3 is not the same as Case 4"). While the laws of the Pentateuch seem at first glance to be clear-cut divine decrees, this understanding of them is incorrect, or at least inadequate. Torah assumes Torah-keepers.

The complexity and theological significance of the law codes becomes more evident in laws within the Covenant Code that assume religious warrants. Consider the series of prohibitions of oppressing vulnerable people in Exod 22:20–26 [ET 21–27].

> You shall not harass a resident alien or wrong them because you were aliens in the land of Egypt. You shall not oppress any widow or orphan. If you should oppress them, when they urgently cry out to me, I will carefully listen to their cry. Then I will be fiercely angry, and I will kill you by the sword. And your wives will be widows and your children orphans. If you lend money to a poor member of my people, you should not act like a moneylender, exacting usury from him. If you take your neighbor's cloak as collateral, you must return it by sundown, because he would otherwise lack a garment to sleep in, garb for his skin. In what will he lie down? And if he cries out to me, I will listen because I am gracious.

These laws assume a close-knit community of people who should help each other in times of need. This community includes both Israelites and non-Israelites, the married and the widowed, the prosperous and the destitute. The laws ground their views of a culture of respect in their views of Yhwh's character. Notice, then, the appeals to Israel's history ("you were aliens in Egypt"), as well as to Yhwh's proclivities toward hearing earnest prayers ("I will listen"), righteous indignation ("I will be angry and kill you"—not a particularly subtle clarification of consequences!), and compassion toward the vulnerable ("I am gracious"; cf. 34:6; Jonah 4:2). In significant ways, then, the Torah presupposes the narrative of Israel's deliverance in the exodus. The creators of the Pentateuch have situated the legal tradition, which of course enjoyed a complex life of its own as legal traditions always do, within the story of the people.

Now we come to the third point regarding Torah at Sinai. Exodus 19–24 surrounds the legal material with stories of a particular kind—they relate to ritual, or rather of Israel carrying out ritual. The ceremony of lawgiving requires forty days, though the duration seems almost lost in the telling. It begins with the ritual purification of the people and the cordoning off of much of the mountain, making it a sort of sanctuary. (The Temple in Jerusalem similarly had a series of nested courtyards that became progressively more exclusive the closer one drew to the Holy of Holies, into which only the high priest could go, and that only once a year.) After the Decalogue, Exod 20:22–26 offers an altar law that differed from any subsequent Israelite practice and which the narrative implies applied only to the moment of lawgiving at Sinai. The altar law appears where it does in the narrative in order to emphasize the fact that the Torah was a gift from Yhwh to which Israel should respond with thankfulness.

Then, finally, the section closes with one of the most extraordinary stories of divine encounter. In Exod 24, Moses, Aaron and his sons, and the key leaders of the people share a meal somewhere on the mountain and, according to Exod 24:10, "they saw the God of Israel, beneath whose feet was a pavement of lapis lazuli, pure as the sky itself." This vision of God or theophany came to the leaders of Israel as a special favor, and as a prelude to Moses's still more dramatic (and completely solitary) encounter with the deity even higher up the mountain. The larger group sees God standing atop the blue dome of the sky—a curious thing in itself, since the deity is usually understood to be invisible, but see Isa 6:1. The fact that the narrative says so little about the vision is perhaps the most remarkable thing about it, however. The reader's overwhelming natural curiosity remains unsatisfied because the story rushes ahead to its key point, the giving of the next element of Torah, the instructions for the Tabernacle.

SEVEN LAW CODES IN THE PENTATEUCH

The Pentateuch contains seven distinct collections of laws:

The Ten Commandments (Exod 20; Deut 5)
The Covenant Code (Exod 21–23)
The Ritual Decalogue (Exod 34)
The Priestly Code (Lev 1–16)
The Holiness Code (Lev 17–27)
The Deuteronomic Code (Deut 12–26)
The Curses Code (Deut 27)

PLOT POINT 6: BUILDING YHWH'S PORTABLE TENT SHRINE
(EXOD 25:1–31:18; 35:1–40:38)

Many modern readers find this long section of Exodus, a third of the book more or less, to be almost excruciatingly boring. Why does the text go on about the carpentry of a building that Israel replaced as soon as it could with a permanent temple? No clearer example of the radical difference between ancient and modern sensibilities could exist.

Consider an alternative strategy of reading. Imagine a place dear to you and your community. Think about the materials from which it is built, its floor plan and ornamentation, and the uses to which those who love it put it. Give yourself time to imagine every cranny, every texture and smell. Think about the people who have used it, and how it has come to symbolize values, beliefs, and commitments important to you and others. If you do all that, you may have some inkling of the significance that the priests and people of Israel attributed to the Tabernacle.

Like many ancient Near Eastern temples, this structure consisted of two rooms inside a large courtyard (see the discussion of 1 Kgs). The space symbolized the elusive presence of Yhwh. "Elusive" because not everyone could gain access to the space, with many persons circulating up to the courtyard entrance and bringing their offering to the point, the priests proceeding to the outdoor altar of burnt offering and then inside for aspects of the sacrificial ritual, and finally only the high priest proceeding to the innermost sanctum in which the Ark of the Covenant, a symbol of Yhwh's heavenly throne, resided. "Presence" because to come to the Tabernacle was always to come *lipnê Yhwh* ("before Yhwh") in a way qualitatively different from the divine presence anywhere else on earth. The Tabernacle was a spot on the *axis mundi* or orbital center of the cosmos.

Granting all this, why does Exodus describe the Tabernacle and its furnishings not once, but twice? In large measure, the needs of the narrative dictate repetition because the catastrophe of the Golden Calf episode necessitates a rebooting (so to speak) of the covenantal relationship between Yhwh and Israel. The dramatic conclusion of Exodus, in which Yhwh enters the Tabernacle to signal the perpetual, concrete, institutionalized presence of deity with humanity, needs a proper buildup if the reader is to get the full effect.

In short, then, the Pentateuch conceives of the Tabernacle as a symbol-rich, socially complex space in which important practices of Israel's religion take place.[8] While the "meaning" of individual elements of what he calls the building's "spatial practice" may remain elusive to modern readers (or ancient ones, for that matter), the overall effect of the literary description of the building is unmistakable. The book of Exodus begins with a state in which Yhwh seems absent—so absent that the Israelites do not know his name (a state corresponding to the oblivion of slavery). The book ends with a divine presence so palpable that human beings can scarcely bear it. This transition is the one to which the creators of Exodus were pointing.

PLOT POINT 7: THE GOLDEN CALF AND ITS CONSEQUENCES
(EXOD 32:1–34:35)

To reach that climax, however, requires a detour, and not just for dramatic effect. The detour is the story of the Golden Calf and the reaffirmation of the Torah in the so-called Ritual Decalogue of Exod 34. A number of items stand out in this unit.

First, the text offers a critique of a set of symbols that many Israelites found both acceptable and holy. The use of the calf as a symbol of Yhwh enjoyed the sanction of major temples in Dan and Bethel (see 1 Kgs 12).

Exod 32–34 has to be understood, then, as an intra-Israelite discussion of the appropriate use of symbols in relationship to God. No one, as far as we know, thought that Yhwh actually looked like a calf or was, somehow, a calf (though in texts from the Late Bronze Age city of Ugarit, the God Ilu, or El in Hebrew, is called "Bull Ilu," probably a similar image, though the relationship between calf and bull symbols of deity remains obscure and debatable). Some Israelites thought that either the calf symbolized the divine pedestal on which Yhwh stood in majesty, or that the animal somehow evoked Yhwh's presence. Their texts and their ideas have not survived except in a form refracted through the views of their critics, and so their precise ideas (assuming they had precise ideas) are now lost.

What is not lost, though, is Exodus's understanding of the use of a calf as part of Yahwistic iconography. The creators of the book (and for other biblical books such as 1 and 2 Kgs), thought the calf iconography inappropriate. They espoused a radical aniconism and understood the worship of the Golden Calf in the wilderness as an act of straight-up idolatry. By creating a cultic system unlike that being revealed on Sinai (the Tabernacle and its accoutrements), the Israelites in Exod 32 construct a different religion divorced, or so Exodus argues, from the core story of deliverance from Egypt. This in spite of the Israelites' claim that the calf represented "your Gods, O Israel, who brought you from the land of Egypt" (Exod 32:5; cf. 1 Kgs 12:28). At stake is a central idea in Israel's theology and liturgy, the capacity of the physical to represent the divine. While bodily *descriptions* of God in words are acceptable, bodily *representations* of God (however indirect or allusive) are not.

Still more is at stake in this story. That is the very survival of Israel as a people. In a brilliantly written dialogue between Yhwh and Moses, the narrator frames the issue starkly. Moses out-argues Yhwh, dissuading the deity from annihilating an ungrateful people:

> Why, Yhwh, are you so angry with your people whom you brought from the land of Egypt by great power and with a strong hand? Why should Egypt say, "for an evil cause he brought them out, to kill them in the mountains, to finish them off from the world"? Let go of your fierce anger and relent from the evil plan against your people. Remember Abraham, Isaac, and Israel, your servants, to whom you promised by yourself, "I will multiply your offspring like the stars of the sky, all this land that I am referring to I will give to your offspring, so they will possess it forever. (Exod 32:11–13)

Notice the identification of Israel as "your people" and the repeated reference to the exodus. Yhwh, as Moses and the narrator maintain, has taken on the responsibility of preserving the nation of Israel in spite of the people's recalcitrance and ignorance. By this display of rhetorical savvy, Moses persuades the deity to reaffirm the covenant, even if, as ch 33 makes clear, some negative consequences for Israel's actions occur.

This reaffirmation, again, occupies ch 34, which restates many laws that appear elsewhere in the Pentateuch, though with a decidedly cultic emphasis. The most decisive part of the reaffirmation of Torah comes in at the very beginning of ch 34. Here Yhwh borrows language that apparently comes from the cult for it is the sort of thing the priests must have intoned in prayer and song. "Yhwh, Yhwh, a God [El] merciful and gracious, slow to be angry, and full of steadfast love and loyalty" (Exod 34:6). He goes on to explain that he shows mercy to thousands of generations while still holding people accountable for three or four generations, a balance of mercy to justice that heavily favors the former.

This opening liturgical act by Yhwh sets the tone for everything that follows. The laws in ch 34 should be understood as examples of the infinite reach of divine mercy.

The Cast List of Exodus

How do the characters in Exodus experience this mercy? The book of Exodus ("exit"; the Hebrew name is *Šĕmôt* or "names," from the first words, "these are the names"), recounts the story of Israel's liberation from slavery in Egypt and its reception of a sanctuary, the Tabernacle, as a place for ongoing communication with the liberator God. In telling that story, it fashions characters whose interactions determine the book's overall meaning and significance. The most significant characters are Yhwh, Moses, Pharaoh (standing in for Egypt), and Israel as a people. Supporting figures appear in some corners of the book, include Moses's family of origin, especially Aaron his brother and the first high priest, and Moses's Midianite wife Zipporah and her family. The secondary characters often advance the plot of the story by offering some insight or corrective to the major character, as when Moses's father-in-law advises him on the proper state of a new Israelite judiciary (Exod 18).

THE MORAL VISION

In describing the interactions of its characters, Exodus consistently offers subtle views of motivations, values, and therefore actions. It might seem at first that the characters of the book are simply cardboard cutouts: bad Pharaoh, heroic Moses, almighty Yhwh. But such a reading would work only on a very superficial level of reading the text. In fact, the characters develop over time, and, while Exodus employs the same minimalist technique of storytelling that appeared in Genesis (gapping), careful attention to the details of the text reveals a highly sophisticated view of the nature of human systems and the people that occupy them.

> Modern critics often begin with Exod 3–4 as a parade example of the different layers of material present in the Pentateuch. This instinct is correct, as far as it goes. The claim of Exodus that the ancestors had not known the deity under the name Yhwh is difficult to reconcile with the fact that Genesis uses the divine name well over 100 times. Ordinarily, scholars argue that the Priestly Writer (see the discussion in Genesis) understood the full awareness of the identity of Israel's God to begin with Moses. Other sources of the Pentateuch thought of that knowledge as something older. By putting both perspectives together, the Pentateuch (which includes Genesis and Exodus) signals that the story of Israel's relationship with Yhwh has many dimensions and is not easily reduced to a single story or idea.

Consider the least complex character here, Pharaoh. Several aspects of his story are curious. He does not appear here as someone who experiences self-doubt or political pressures, but as a brutal tyrant who can understand the legitimate protests of an enslaved people only as a sign of their lack of enough to do (Exod 5:17). Paradoxically, in a book whose Hebrew name is "Names" (*Šĕmôt*), this ruler has no name (though already in antiquity he was identified with Ramesses II [r. 1279–1213 BCE] on the basis of Exod 1:11). His anonymity contrasts strongly with the emphasis on the names of the "children of Israel," the list of which opens and closes the first major section of the book (Exod 1:1–5; 6:14–25). It is as if the book wishes to erase Pharaoh from history, thereby disavowing his view of the world, in which some are slaves and some free on account of their birth or place in a political system. Exodus continues to portray Pharaoh as a treacherous liar, who repeatedly reneges on his promises.

The contrast to Pharaoh lies in the person of Yhwh, whom the narrative introduces in the prophetic call story of chs 3–4. As with the later prophets Samuel (1 Sam 3:10–14), Isaiah (Isa 6:1–13), and Jeremiah (Jer 1:4–10), the Bible recounts a narrative in which a human being is called to the task of prophecy, primarily with a view toward the announcement of doom on account of human sinfulness. Like Isaiah and Jeremiah, Moses protests his call, objecting that he is unworthy of the dubious honor of being a prophet! Yet the conversation does not really focus on Moses. Rather, it is the moment at which the character of Israel's God is established.

Yhwh appears to Moses as creator ("did not I make the human mouth?") and a warrior competent to take on the mightiest empire of the world. However, the book of Exodus must also show that the deity of Israel is not merely a bearer of plague but a beneficent and gracious God. How to do this in the story? The book accomplishes the demanding task by portraying Yhwh as the lawgiver who inspires human goodness.

In Exodus, the first divine command given to Israel (other than "leave Egypt") comes in the Wilderness, in ch 16, before the Ten Commandments in Exod 20:1–17. It is the command to collect manna, a food of unknown nature (the very name means "what?") which the Israelite tradition eventually came to call the "bread of angels" or of "heaven" (Ps 78:25; 105:40; cf. John 6:22–59), but a sweet goo that sustained people in the desert (see Exod 16:14–35). Exodus 16 is clearly a miracle story, for apparently the chemical properties of manna changed on the Sabbath, when it did not rot as on other days (or to put it more whimsically, the resident bacteria took a break, too!). While such a story may elicit many responses in modern scientifically oriented readers, Exodus highlights the gracious provision of Yhwh. This sense of divine grace appears in the other legal material of the book, a point to which we will return.

The other thickly developed character in Exodus is, of course, Moses. The text introduces him as a member of the priestly tribe of Levi, and he occasionally presides at offerings (Exod 24:1–8). It then portrays him as a prophet who speaks against the power of Pharaoh, but finally shifts to the unprophetic role of national leader (administrator, general, lawgiver). He is both the critic of power and its embodiment. Deuteronomy shows awareness of the problem created by these overlapping roles when it speaks of Moses as the model prophet (Deut 18:15–22), and Exodus similarly thinks of him as a one-of-a-kind figure. Yet Exodus does more than other biblical portrayals of Moses by exploring him as a rounded character with a psychological makeup—a moral compass, interior struggles, and growing steadiness of touch in dealing with both his divine conversation partner and the people of Israel.

The development of Moses as a character of deep moral sensibility appears in the story of the Golden Calf in ch 32. Confronted by a people who violated the Ten Commandments' ban on idol-making and Yhwh's determination to terminate the covenant with them on grounds of infidelity, Moses offers a series of arguments for mercy:

> Why, O Yhwh, does your wrath burn against your people, whom you brought from the land of Egypt by great strength and an outstretched hand? Why should Egypt say that you brought them out for evil reasons—to kill them in the mountains and to finish them off from the surface of the earth . . . ? Remember Abraham, Isaac, and Israel your servants, to whom you swore on your own authority, quote, "I will multiply your offspring like the stars of the heavens and all this land about which I spoke, I shall give to your offspring so that they might own it forever. Relent, O Yhwh, from the evil that you plan to do to your people. (Exod 32:11–14)

The first argument is one of identity: Israel belongs to Yhwh. The second argument appeals to the international reputation of Yhwh (remember the theme from the Song of the Sea?), on the unstated assumption that the actions of the divine realm ought to be moral and seen as such by human beings. The third argument appeals to the people's stories of origin: the ancestors received a promise, and the exodus underscored its security. But the key point derives not from the content of the arguments, though that is fascinating enough. The fact that Moses argues with Yhwh at all reveals a basic assumption of the book, namely, that the justice of God is a topic for serious, sustained conversation. We will see how that conversation develops throughout the rest of the biblical canon.

Implications

To conclude, what does Exodus mean to contemporary readers? To answer that, consider two dominant ways of interpreting it. Traditional Jews often emphasize the importance of Torah from Sinai, the sure evidence that Yhwh lives among the people of Israel. Many Christians and especially Protestants, on the other hand, often emphasize the aspect of liberation from bondage, a theme that appears already in the New Testament. Who is right? Does it matter?

The answers are that both are right; and yes, it matters. Exodus seems to say that freedom and obligation do not oppose each other. They connect because they both exist within a relationship between a liberated people and a liberating God. Obedience to God is simply giving God what is appropriate. As the contemporary philosopher Nicholas Wolterstorff has recently put it, "Given that Yhwh has the standing right to issue commands to Israel, when Yhwh does in fact issue commands, Israel is under obligation to obey those commands . . . . If obedience is not forthcoming, Yhwh is wronged, treated unjustly."[9] The rightness of these assumptions is part of the subject of the rest of the Pentateuch, for the exodus story lies at the foundation of Israel's entire self-understanding and thus the shape of the Bible as a whole.

Notes

1. For this fairly technical issue, see Yoshiyuki Muchiki, *Egyptian Proper Names and Loanwords in North-West Semitic* (Atlanta: SBL, 1999), 216–217.

2. For the text of the story of Sargon's birth, see the translation by Benjamin R. Foster in *Contexts of Scripture* 1.133 (461).

3. Throughout this book, the phrase "Israel's Children" appears instead of the standard English translation "children of Israel."

4. See the discussion in William H. C. Propp, *Exodus 1–18*, Anchor Bible 2 (New York: Doubleday, 1998), 347–352.

5. An excellent analysis from this perspective is that of Robert R. Wilson, "The Hardening of Pharaoh's Heart," *Catholic Biblical Quarterly* 41 (1979): 18–36.

6. As argued by Propp (*Exodus 1–18*), 423–424, based on similar expressions in Prov 1:9; 3:3, 22, and other passages enjoining children to remember their parents' counsel.

7. For a fairly maximalist view of the connections, see David P. Wright, *Inventing God's Law: How the Covenant Code of the Bible Used and Revised Hammurabi's Laws* (New York/ Oxford: Oxford University Press, 2009).

8. As argued by Mark K. George, *Israel's Tabernacle as Social Space* (Atlanta: SBL, 2009). For a history of tent shrines in the ancient Near East, see Michael M. Homan, *To Your Tents, O Israel! The Terminology, Function, Form, and Symbolism of Tents in the Hebrew Bible and the Ancient Near East* (Leiden: Brill, 2002).

9. Nicholas Wolterstorff, *Justice in Love* (Grand Rapids: Eerdmans, 2011), 107.

For Further Reading

Hillers, Delbert. *Covenant: The History of a Biblical Idea*. Baltimore: Johns Hopkins University Press, 1969.

Larsson, Göran. *Bound for Freedom: The Book of Exodus in Jewish and Christian Traditions*. Peabody, MA: Hendrickson, 1999.

Redford, Donald B. *Egypt, Canaan, and Israel in Ancient Times*. Princeton: Princeton University Press, 1992.

Richardson, M. E. J. *Hammurabi's Laws: Text, Translation and Glossary*. Sheffield: Sheffield Academic Press, 2000.

5 On Holiness and Life
THE BOOK OF LEVITICUS

Key Texts: *And he said to Moses, yes, Yhwh spoke to him from the Tent of Meeting: "Speak to Israel's children and say to them, 'anyone of you who brings a gift to Yhwh, if it's an animal, should bring your gift from the herd or from the flock.'"* (Lev 1:1–2)

You should not bear a grudge against your people's children; rather, you should love your neighbor as yourself. I am Yhwh. (Lev 19:18)

In contrast to the common reaction to the drama of Exodus, many people find the book of Leviticus boring or incomprehensible or, at best, a relic of past ways of thinking about the world. After all, it speaks of sacrificial animals, rituals for skin diseases, food laws far removed from the practices of most people, and so on. It seems to be a combination of barbecue recipes and rules for personal and household hygiene, topped off with improbable political solutions to the long-standing human problem of the poor distribution of wealth. Why read such a weird book?

Or it would be a weird book if, in fact, these things were what it was about. Part of the popular conception of the book seems, however, to reflect a xenophobic lack of self-awareness on the part of modern readers. All cultures have rituals—they are part of what make us human beings—and skin diseases are irrelevant unless you happen to itch yourself! And while we often use the word "sacrifice" to describe the surrender of something desired in the interest of a noble cause, we might also recognize a deeper aspect to it. The English word, which comes from the Latin *sacrificium*, relates to the word "sacred," and so even for us the term evokes actions connecting human beings to the holy. (In Hebrew, the word's [*zebaḥ*] etymology connects it to communal meals.) This is why all religions have a notion of sacrifice, including Christianity, in which the practice became one way of describing the central event of cosmic history, the death and resurrection of Jesus. Part of the modern Western response to Leviticus must also reflect a legacy of latent (and often overt) anti-Semitism, according to which Judaism and Jews were considered a problem because they were "other."

Not all negative reactions to the book come from such sources, of course. Yet they do play their role, and they combine with our common modern tendency to underestimate the value of anything outside our own experience. Is there another way to understand the book, then? Might it have a theological weight both for Torah-observing Jews and for Christians (or others, for that matter)?

The Shape and Flow of the Book

Let's be clearer. If the Tabernacle described in Exodus is a stage on which the Israelites might act out a great drama, then how would that drama be acted out? Not just in words but in choreographed gestures and words, through movement and sounds and smells. So think of Leviticus as the "script" for the play carried out on the stage that Exodus describes. Leviticus continues the discussion of the Tabernacle that begins in Exod 20, indicating that the same priestly circles bore responsibility for both works. In fact, Leviticus seems at first to be part of a larger work, with the current division into books being somewhat arbitrary.

However, things are not so simple. A large section of Leviticus, chs 17–27, does not directly concern the Tabernacle. More importantly, the books of the Pentateuch show clear transitions and literary shaping that support the standard divisions of them. The end of Exodus has the feel of a climax, while the opening of Numbers restarts the narrative after the long series of laws in Leviticus. Therefore, while Leviticus sits at the center of the Pentateuch and lacks an obvious introduction or conclusion, it also has its own integrity as a book.

So a precise outline of the book is in order:

A. The location of sacrifice (Exod 25–31, 35–40)
B. The sacrificial system (Lev 1:1–10:20)
  1. Introduction (1:1–2)
  2. The burnt offering (1:3–17)
  3. The cereal offering (2:1–16)
  4. The well-being or "peace" offering (3:1–17)
  5. The purification or "sin" offerings (4:1–5:13)
  6. The reparation or "guilt" offering (5:14–26)

7. The order of sacrifices (6:1–7:38)
8. Preparing the priests for their work (8:1–10:20)

C. Discussion of things that defile the sanctuary and worshipers, and their remedies (Lev 11:1–15:33)

1. The laws of kashrut (11:1–47)
2. Rituals for childbirth (12:1–8)
3. Skin diseases (13:1–59)
4. Purification from skin diseases and fungous houses (14:1–57)
5. Genital discharges (15:1–33)

D. A key ritual: the scapegoat and Yom Kippur (Lev 16:1–34)
E. The Holiness Code (17:1–27:34)

The Key Ideas of Lev 1–16

The first major section of Leviticus is part of a layer of the Pentateuch usually called the Priestly Code. This material directly impinges on the work of the priests in Israel's sanctuary. It is not a technical manual for every aspect of the priest's work—many of those details were undoubtedly passed down orally from father to son (since all of Israel's priests were male). But neither is it a popular-level tract. These chapters offer inside-the-guild discussions for priests who must know how to operate at the altar of Yhwh and how to instruct nonpriests to play their part there as well. While the precise original audience of this material remains unclear, it does seem to fit somewhere between the technical and popular poles.

What is it about, then? The complexity of these chapters really revolves around a few key ideas: sacrifice, purity and impurity, and the relationship between the priests and the rest of the Israelites. These topics intertwine in the chapters at hand in ways that are difficult to unravel, but still comprehensible.

SACRIFICE

Take sacrifice, to begin. If we accept Roy Rappaport's definition of ritual as "the performance of more or less invariant sequences of formal acts and utterances not entirely encoded by the performers,"[1] then the nature of sacrifice becomes a little clearer. In each sacrificial act, an Israelite individual or family or community brings an animal to the sanctuary for sacrifice. The offerer places his (or her?) hand on the beast and utters words transferring it to the environment of the sacrifice. The animal now belongs to Yhwh to be used for new purposes. The priest slaughters the animal, cleans its carcass, pours or sprinkles its blood in prescribed ways at prescribed places, and then roasts the animal on the altar. The carcass may be disposed of in several ways: some sacrifices are food for the offerers, and some are incinerated. Some of the meat can be food, while the suet, bones, and entrails must be burned. The priests must dispose of the skin and contents of the digestive system in a specially reserved, or in Leviticus's terminology, a "clean" place outside the sanctuary. All the sacrificial rituals follow this basic structure, even if details vary depending on the type of sacrifice, the occasion, and the offerer.

To be more specific, Leviticus describes five types of sacrifices:

(1) The burnt offering (1:3–17) or *ōlâ* involves the incineration of the animal (minus its hide). The complete destruction of the animal underscores the seriousness of the offering, which can accompany a prayer to God about some critical emergency in the community (as Jacob Milgrom points out for 1 Sam 13:12; 2 Sam 24:21–25; Jer 14:12, and other texts).[2] This offering has many purposes and can consist of any appropriate sacrificial animal.

(2) The cereal offering for poorer Israelites (Lev 2:1–16) bears a name that in other texts applied to a range of sacrifices. It is called the *minḥâ*, a word that just means "a gift" or "tribute" (see, e.g., Gen 4:3–4) and can also include animals in other contexts. For Leviticus, the *minḥâ* reconciles humans to God when the humans in question simply cannot afford to give an animal.

(3) The offerer and the priests ate the well-being or "peace" offering (Hebrew: *šĕlāmîm*, related to the well-known word *shalom*; Lev 3:1–17) in the sanctuary, symbolizing the harmony to which Israelites aspired, since eating together often cements friendship.

(4) The purification offerings (Lev 4:1–5:13) are of two types. The Hebrew word for them, *ḥaṭṭāʾt*, is related to the verb for "to sin," and so this offering is often translated as a "sin offering." However, that label is misleading, for the purpose of the offering is not simply to cancel out moral failures but to mark a number of life transitions such as childbirth (Lev 12), the completion of a Nazirite vow (Num 6), and the dedication of altars, among other things.[3] None of those latter events involves "sin" strictly speaking. Rather, the offering purifies the sanctuary itself. The law for the *ḥaṭṭāʾt* arranges the instructions in order of the power and wealth of the offerer—the more powerful you are, and the more your accidental errors or life transitions make an impact on the larger community, the larger your offering must be.

And (5) the reparation or "guilt" (Hebrew: *ʾāšām*) offering (Lev 5:14–26) marks the repentance of someone who has earlier either desecrated holy objects in the sanctuary or harmed another human being, through deliberate action or neglect.

Much of the material on sacrifice in these chapters involves intricate descriptions of the "more or less invariant sequences of formal acts" of the priests. What the priests or worshipers said during the sacrifice remains unknown, though the practice at some point came to involve singing the Psalms (see 1 Chron 25 for early hints in this direction). Yet the overall point comes through clearly enough. Leviticus describes a system of regular, understandable actions through which human beings could approach God and receive forgiveness, healing, and restoration. Just as Yhwh claimed in his first encounter with Moses at Mount Horeb to have "seen, heard, and known" the plight of Israel in Egypt (Exod 3:7), so now an institution existed for ongoing communication between God and Israel, the sacrificial system.

Hence the dramatic movement in the next section, Lev 8–10. Here the priests inaugurate the sacrificial cult at Moses's behest. The key to understanding these chapters, and the creative nature of the sacrificial system itself, lies in the story in Lev 10. Actually, there are two scenes in one act. In the first, Nadab and Abihu, Aaron's oldest sons, make a serious error in their work and are incinerated by heavenly fire (lightning?) for their actions. Then their younger brothers, Eliezer and Ithamar, make a mistake in the ritual and receive a scolding from their uncle, Moses. Why the different consequences for what seem to be similar errors?

Several parts of the story matter. First, the two mistakes are not similar. The first pair of priests offer "strange fire," that is, they fueled their incense burners with coals taken from the wrong part of the sanctuary (or maybe outside it). Within the ritual system's internal world, they have broken a major symbolic chain. (Bizarre Christian examples might be using food other than bread or wine in the Eucharist or baptizing someone in soda pop rather than water.) Perhaps the text has in mind the widespread practice of offering incense outside the sanctuary, or perhaps it simply wishes to portray them as intensely disrespectful of Yhwh because they could not distinguish between holy objects within the sanctuary and ordinary objects outside it. This cavalier attitude on their part existed in spite of the fact that they had received detailed instruction from Moses in the previous chapters of Exodus and Leviticus.

In contrast to the first brothers, the second pair fail to eat the meat sacrificed. Again, their mistake is real, as Moses points out. But Aaron's defense of his sons is significant: "Today, they brought their purification and burnt offerings before Yhwh, and things like these happened to me! Would Yhwh be happy if I ate the purification offering today?" (Lev 10:19) His point is this: "eating the sacrifice implies a celebratory attitude. Though I cannot mourn inside the Tabernacle (see Lev 10:6), I also cannot celebrate." The storyteller approves of the argument, noting that Moses accepted it. In short, then, Leviticus does not conceive of the sacrificial system as rules that the priests robotically followed. Thinking is required, and sometimes difference of interpretation is both possible and beneficial.

PURITY AND IMPURITY

If careful thought informs the laws of the sacrifice, the same is also true of Lev 11–16, which concern ways of ordering the Israelite body for a proper orientation to the divine realm. The material in these chapters may seem randomly arranged, as well as alien to most modern people's experience, but they all concern issues of purity and impurity as an aspect of bodily existence.

Consider both aspects of this claim, beginning with "bodily existence." Many modern religious people believe that spirituality is solely a mental practice. They accept a basically Greek idea of a soul accidentally, and irrelevantly, encased in a physical body. But such is not the biblical view. The body matters, and the proper care for, and display of, the body has profound moral and spiritual significance. Most of us know this if we think about it, which is why some people today are vegan or worry about carbon footprints, while others concentrate on the morality and spirituality of the body. How does Leviticus address such concerns?

It does so by discussing several things: (1) the laws of *kašrût* (11:1–47)—most people know the related adjective *kosher*. The food laws prohibit eating predatory and scavenging animals as well as animals that seem somehow anomalous (such as fish without scales). The prohibition of pork is the best known rule to non-Jews, and it is attested archaeologically for Israel's earliest period by the absence of pig bones from villages in the hill country of Israel during the Iron Age I period (before 1000 BCE). (2) Rules for the quarantine and cure of skin diseases and fungus-covered houses (13:1–14:57). Most of us would not place growths on our skin and growths on the walls of buildings in the same category, though of course both may involve related microorganisms, nor would we ask a priest to address either psoriasis or mildew. Yet in many ancient cultures, the priest functioned as both a doctor and a source of knowledge about all sorts of things that could be treated by the chemistry known at the time. So it would not have seemed strange to Israelites to combine these practices or to connect them to the Tabernacle. And (3) rituals for genital discharges by men or women (15:1–33). For both men and women, rituals existed to make sure that they could reenter ordinary life and function as full-fledged members of the community. While modern practices (assuming that they enjoy some sort of uniformity) might differ from ancient Israel's, the concern about the body that these laws show has many parallels around the world.

How does one understand the theology of the rules in these chapters, then? At a general level, the priesthood's interest in actions both inside and outside the tabernacle reflected a commitment to building a world in which human beings ordered their lives for piety toward Yhwh. The rules do not exist for their own sakes, much less to restrict or repress people. Quite to the contrary, they attempt to bring about a world in which forgiveness, reconciliation, orderliness, and health prevail. Such a world does not begin to exist, the priests thought, simply through a focus on interiority and careful thinking. Rather, they wanted human beings to regulate themselves in community.

But one can, and should, be more specific. On a few occasions in these chapters, the text breaks the flow of the instructions to offer a warrant for them. The most notable example of this practice comes at the end of the food laws in Lev 11:44–47:

> For I am Yhwh your God. So you should sanctify yourselves and be holy, for I am holy. And you will not pollute yourselves with any sort of vermin swarming on the ground. For I, Yhwh, brought you up from the land of Egypt to be your God. So you should be holy just as I am holy. This is the instruction [*tôrâ*] for beasts, birds, and life swarming in the water, as well as for everything swarming on the

ground—to divide between the impure and the pure, and between the edible creatures and the inedible ones.

Three distinct sets of warrants underwrite the law of kashrut. The first is an appeal to God's holiness, that is, to God's nature as divine. The second explains the first more specifically by referring to Israel's core story, the exodus from Egypt. Yhwh's "holiness" consists of his record as a deliverer of a distinct people. The third warrant refers to a habit of mind in which Israel can distinguish various sorts of animals by habitat (just as in the creation story in Gen 1:1–2:4 and the Ten Commandments in Exod 20:4). The uneaten creatures are not somehow inferior or "ungodly," just not for the Israelite table.

These ideas speak to an ideal for which Israel's everyday life somehow reflects their history as a people whom Yhwh has saved and to whom Yhwh has given important tasks. So there is nothing "necessary" to the various rules given—other principles might have been in play. (For example, there's nothing morally superior in beef as opposed to pork, or washing for some skin conditions but not others.) But neither are the rules merely arbitrary. They fit together in a way that allows Israel to consider its role in relationship to the Tabernacle. Just as skin diseases and the wrong sorts of animals and bodily emissions can render a priest ritually impure for the sacrificial cult, so these same conditions can impair the ordinary Israelite's ability to think of the world in a priestly way ("distinguish") or acknowledge God's special character or remember the exodus.

THE SCAPEGOAT AND YOM KIPPUR

This "priestly way" of thinking comes through in Lev 16, the instructions for the celebration of Yom Kippur or the "Day of Atonement." This holiday comes just after the autumn harvest and just before the great celebration of the Feast of Tabernacles (Sukkot). Yom Kippur is a fast day, in which Israel remembers its sins and seeks reconciliation with Yhwh. While the ritual for the day eventually (after the Roman destruction of the Temple in 70 CE) came to focus on some very beautiful prayers, in Leviticus the focus lies on a strange quasi-sacrificial ritual in which a goat is sent "to Azazel" (Lev 16:10). Technically, the goat is not a sacrifice, for it bears all the impurity of Israel and the priesthood into the wilderness. Moreover, Azazel was probably originally the name of a demon, a version of the Canaanite god of death, Môt, but in Leviticus the erstwhile demon has no function. He neither receives the goat nor menaces it. (So the phrase "to Azazel" is a frozen expression, much as when Christians sing "We're Marching to Zion" they neither march nor travel to Jerusalem, or, to take a more offensive example, when someone is told to "go to hell," he or she does not start traveling in search of a lake of fire into which to jump.) Rather, the whole ritual symbolizes the departure of human impurity of all sorts from the sanctuary "into the wilderness," that is, away from the world in which Israel lives and interacts with God. In this way, all of Israel participates in the life of the Tabernacle.

If Lev 1–16 calls Israel both to carry out the sacrificial system accurately and to extrapolate from it to ways of living other aspects of life, the second major section of Leviticus operates at a different level. The intended audience of these chapters, often called the Holiness Code, consists of laypeople, not just the priests. This is why each section in chs 1–16 begins with Yhwh telling Moses to speak to the priests, while in chs 17–27, the announced audience includes all the people (as well as the priests).

The laws of these later chapters address many areas of ordinary life, beginning with a more popular-level law of sacrifice (Lev 17), then proceeding to rules against incest (Lev 18), miscellaneous laws (Lev 19–20), a story about blasphemy (24:10–23), and instructions for the Sabbatical Year and Jubilee (Lev 25), both of which are attempts at reordering economic life in Israel so as to prevent greed and sharp divisions between haves and have-nots. Sandwiched between these rules for the laity were an entire set of regulations for the priesthood in their interactions with the rest of the community (Lev 21:1–24:9), including a calendar for the religious year (Lev 23).

DOES THE HOLINESS CODE PROHIBIT SAME-SEX SEXUAL RELATIONS?

Lev 18:22 says literally, "with a male you shall not lie in the same way as the lying with a woman. It is a disgrace." This verse is often used as a prooftext for the claim that the Bible bans all sorts of homosexual encounters. Read in a strict way, however, the text appears to prohibit sexual penetration, and therefore presumably anal sex. Yet the much larger conversation about sexual ethics in Jewish or Christian traditions cannot rest on a single text or set of texts but must consider more central theological ideas underlying norms for conduct within the communities espousing those norms.

The Holiness Code proper seems to conclude with blessings and curses similar to the end of the law code in Deuteronomy (Deut 28). Then Lev 27 seems to be an appendix, a final set of rules about vow-making and vow-keeping with a view toward the economic implications of piety (Lev 27). (Or perhaps the chapter reminds the readers of the seriousness of keeping Torah, which is an expression of Israel's relationship with its divine Redeemer, Yhwh.) The entire book of Leviticus ends with a comment on itself, "These are the commandments that Yhwh commanded Moses with respect to Israel's Children on Mount Sinai" (Lev 27:34), showing the book's consciousness of the integrated nature of the rules, disparate though they are, and of their role in constructing the entire life of an Israelite person.

How should one understand this material? Most of it revolves around three major aspects of life in the body: food, sex, and property. As in the earlier part of Leviticus, and in much of the rest of the Bible, the Holiness Code assumes that the spiritual and the physical closely interrelate (in fact, the distinction is almost completely alien to its way of thinking). Consider each element, then.

FOOD

The initiation of the sacrificial system in ch 17 both calls upon Israelites to stop worshiping satyrs (Lev 17:7) and instructs them to eat only animals that they have sacrificed at the central sanctuary. This text differs in an important respect from the rule for slaughtering animals seen in Deut 12:1–31. Deuteronomy argues that only one sanctuary is legitimate, and therefore animals killed and eaten elsewhere are not sacrifices. Leviticus, however, thinks of meat eaten as a sacrifice (following an older model that Deuteronomy was changing) and tries to eliminate offerings to deities other than Yhwh. The two books thus share a similar underlying theology with respect to Israel's relationship to its God, but each differs on the application of that theology in the practical world of menus. (This topic will receive further consideration in the chapter on Deuteronomy.)

SEX

Leviticus 18 famously prohibits a series of sexual practices within prohibited degrees of consanguinity (in other words, incest). Unlike Egyptian culture, which permitted brother-sister marriage, especially in polygamous families, Israel limits sexual expression. The text offers a series of strong warrants: such behaviors characterized the Canaanites (18:24–27), defile the land (18:28), and ignore the nature of a moral God (18:30). Abstinence from them, on the other hand, made space for the development of other aspects of the moral life.

PROPERTY

Leviticus does not assume an absolute right to private property. At a very practical level, it instructs its readers to leave parts of their harvest for the poor to gather (19:9–10; cf. Exod 23:11; Ruth 2). Such a rule fits the book's overall interest in protecting the most vulnerable of the people, and even resident aliens (Hebrew: *gēr*), from the worst suffering brought on by economic inefficiency or natural disaster.

Aside from down-to-earth rules observable in the course of everyday life, Leviticus calls for a utopian group of practices, the Sabbatical and Jubilee years. The older law in the Covenant Code (Exod 23:10–11) had said, "You shall sow your land for six years, and you may gather its produce. But during the seventh it should lie fallow, and the poor of your people may eat of it, and you should eat what's left of the living things of the field (and you should do the same for your vineyards and olive groves)." That law does not state that all fields should lie fallow at the same time—rotation of crops would be possible. Moreover, the law assumes a level of fertility for the land that would allow both the storage of food and the productivity of fallow land covered with volunteer food plants.

Leviticus 25 expands this older law (which it quotes in v. 3) first by reconceiving of the "resting of the land" as an event closely resembling Sabbath as humans practice it, and then by calling for two concrete procedures. The first is the Sabbath year, during which all agriculture should cease (Lev 25:1–7). The second and more elaborate is the Jubilee, occurring every fifty years. During the Jubilee, farming should cease, debts should be remitted and indentured servants freed, and all land sold since the last Jubilee should return, for a fair price, to the family of its original owners (Lev 25:8–55). Although various forms of land reform and debt remission have occurred in many ancient and modern societies, the difficulty of implementing a policy as radical as the Jubilee provoked a series of considerations in Lev 25 itself. Hence the law's prohibition of withholding short-term loans to the needy (25:35–38) and regulations for prorating prices for debt slaves and other indentured servants (25:29–55). Leviticus seeks to prevent anyone from gaming the system.

No evidence exists that the ancient Israelites ever observed the Jubilee (though the reference to the transfer of ancestral land in Jer 32 may have such a festival in mind). In fact, the second-century BCE pseudepigraphic Book of Jubilees assumes that they did not.[4] One wonders if the author of the law intended its actual implementation or offered it as a sort of ideal, much like Thomas More's *Utopia* or Plato's *Republic*. But one thing is certain: Leviticus seeks to build a national community that does not take the pursuit of wealth as an end in itself. As always, beneath the seemingly alien laws lies a bold view of the world in which sanity prevails.

Implications

What should modern readers make of Leviticus? In a recent study of ritual in the Bible, Gerald Klingbeil concluded that "Rituals are the 'Sistine Chapels' of communication. They form intricately tuned, meaning-loaded masterpieces of inter-communication, on both an interpersonal and societal level."[5] Although many religious people in the West have internalized a critique of ritual that gathered steam during the Protestant Reformation, human groups simply cannot survive without ritual (or angels either, if the vision of Isa 6 is correct!) because they—rituals—do things that cannot be done by other forms of communication. Without ritual, we have only the hyperindividuality of the modern lonely soul.

Following the destruction of the Second Temple by the Romans in 70 CE, both Jews and Christians have been compelled by the end of the sacrificial system, or rather its sublimation under other rituals (prayer and Eucharist respectively), to read Leviticus in a way that extrapolated from its concerns to theirs. Sometimes this rereading of the book has degenerated into crude allegory or, more often, into utter neglect. But perhaps a note from one of its earliest readers, the third-century Christian scholar Origen (l. 185–254 CE in Alexandria and Caesarea) would help. He writes in his Homilies on Leviticus,

> we who read or hear these things should . . . be pure in body, and upright in mind, pure in heart, reformed in habits. We should strive to make progress in deeds, be vigilant in knowledge, faith, and actions, and be perfect in deeds and understanding in order that we may be worthy to be conformed to the likeness of Christ's offering."[6]

Similarly, the great early Jewish commentary on Leviticus, *Sifra* (written in stages before 500 CE), speaks of the opening lines of the book as a divine revelation comparable to that majestic encounter in Exod 3–4. It wonders why Yhwh gave Torah in intervals to Moses, rather than all at once:

> What purposes did the pauses serve? To give Moses an interval for reflection . . . . If one (as Moses), who hears (words) from the mouth of the Holy One, blessed be He, and who speaks with the help of divine inspiration, must be given time to consider . . . how much more should an ordinary person require time to consider?[7]

In other words, both Jews and Christians see Leviticus as a window onto the nature of God and God's relationship to human beings. Despite their radically different appropriations of the book, the two religious traditions agree on the basic need to understand it as something other than just a dead letter.

Notes

1. Roy Rappaport, *Ritual and Religion in the Making of Humanity* (Cambridge: Cambridge University Press, 1999), 24.

2. Jacob Milgrom, *Leviticus 1–16*, Anchor Bible 3 (New York: Doubleday, 1991), 175.

3. See ibid., 253.

4. For an argument for this viewpoint, see Milgrom, *Leviticus 23–27*, 2263.

5. Gerald Klingbeil, *Bridging the Gap: Ritual and Ritual Texts in the Bible* (Winona Lake, IN: Eisenbrauns, 2007), 241.

6. Origen, *Homilies on Leviticus*, trans. Gary Wayne Barkley, Fathers of the Church 83 (Washington, DC: Catholic University of America Press, 1990), Homily 1.5.3 (38).

7. *Sifra: With Translation and Commentary*, ed. and trans. Morris Ginsberg, South Florida Studies in the History of Judaism 194 (Atlanta: Scholars Press, 1994), 1.9 (8).

For Further Reading

Hamerton-Kelly, Robert, ed. *Violent Origins: Ritual Killing and Cultural Formation*. Stanford, CA: Stanford University Press, 1987.

Klingbeil, Gerald. *Bridging the Gap: Ritual and Ritual Texts in the Bible*. Winona Lake, IN: Eisenbrauns, 2007.

Watts, James W. "The Torah as the Rhetoric of Priesthood." In *The Pentateuch as Torah: New Models for Understanding Its Promulgation and Acceptance*, edited by Gary N. Knoppers and Bernard M. Levinson, 319–331. Winona Lake, IN: Eisenbrauns, 2007.

6 In the Desert
THE BOOK OF NUMBERS

Key Text: *Say to Aaron and to his sons, "In this way, you shall bless Israel's children, saying to them, 'May Yhwh bless you and keep you. May Yhwh smile at you and be gracious to you. May Yhwh turn toward you and give you peace.' So shall they place my name upon Israel's children so that I may bless you."* (Num 6:23–27)

If Leviticus seems foreign at first, it at least has a fairly obvious organization. Not so with Numbers. Even the name of the book may put off less math-obsessed people. As if that's not bad enough, in fact, the fourth book of the Pentateuch goes by two different names: the Greek translators of the Septuagint called it *arithmoi* ("numbers") after the tabulations of tribes and clans in the first few chapters, and this name passed down through the Latin Vulgate to most modern English translations. The Hebrew name, however, is *bĕmidbār* ("in the desert") because the book consists of a series of episodes occurring in the wilderness between Israel's departure from Mount Sinai/Horeb and its arrival in the promised land. Both names make sense, but there is something to be said in favor of the Hebrew name, for the book discusses far more than census figures. Instead, it tries to describe an ideal Israelite community, not primarily through law imaginatively laid out (as in Leviticus and Deuteronomy) but through narratives about successes and failures in the first generation of postexilic Israelites. Those ancestors, from the point of view of the final editors of Numbers, offer a model for the future, even if the model is often an example of how not to act.

NUMBERS IN OUTLINE

A. Preparing for the Wilderness migration (1:1–10:10)
   1. Israel's outer camp: the Twelve Tribes (1:1–2:34)
   2. Israel's inner camp: the Priests and Levites (3:1–4:49)
   3. Rules for the outer camp (5:1–6:27)
   4. Rules for the inner camp (7:1–10:10)
B. Events on the desert road (10:11–36:13)
   1. A failed attempt to enter the promised land, with conflict stories (10:11–14:45)
   2. The Migration proper (15:1–36:13)
      a. The demise of the exodus generation (15:1–20:29)
      b. Early settlement (21:1–35)
      c. The Balaam stories (22:1–24:25)
      d. Baal Peor (25:1–18)
      e. Distributions of the promised land (25:19–36:13)

On a first reading, again, Numbers seems chaotic, or at least episodic. On closer examination, though, some major themes occur repeatedly, many of them set forth in the most famous text of the book, the priestly blessing in Num 6:23–27 ("May Yhwh bless you and keep you."). The idea that Yhwh blesses the people, often through the mediation of the priests, is a central idea of the book. Hence the story of the professional curser Balaam (Num 22–24), whose misadventures result in the blessing of Israel in spite of his and his employer's plans. And so the allocation of lands for the various tribes and the emphasis on the priesthood and its work. A small set of primary concerns holds this book together.

An outline of the book shows that it addresses several key issues: Who are the Israelites? Who will lead them and how? How will they interact with their non-Israelite neighbors? And how will they settle their new land, or better, which tribe and clan will end up where, and how does the mental map that Numbers lays out help the reader understand the relationships among constituent groups within Israel? Some texts respond to these questions only indirectly, but most of the material here, which comes from many different sources and points of origin, addresses these key questions in one way or another.

As Won W. Lee recently argued,[1] the story of Israel's failure in the wilderness empha-sizes both (1) the human capacity for defying God and fouling up the divine plan to redeem Israel and (2) the ability of the priestly institutions (Tabernacle/temple, priest-hood, sacrifice, moral formation) to overcome the human desire to go one's own way. While Lee tends to understand the agenda of Numbers in mostly sociopolitical terms, the biblical book itself also makes a strong theological case. Israel, it says, can be saved, in spite of itself, if it will adhere to Torah.

To explore the text in greater detail, we should consider each major point in its narra-tive plot. The overall story of events "in the desert" has a coherence that points to a group of theological claims.

The first section of Numbers, chs 1:1–10:10, picks up where Leviticus left off. Israel remains at Mount Sinai/Horeb awaiting divine instructions to depart. Having received Torah and, in response to it, built the Tabernacle and instituted sacrifice, the community now must embark on a journey that will lead it to its eventual home. This section of the book, then, depicts its community's inner workings to prompt readers to think of their own environment. However, the interest in the priesthood and its relationship to the rest of the people does not lie far in the background, for, like Leviticus, Numbers aims at helping its readers learn the ways of Yhwh.

THE CENSUS (NUM 1:1–4:49)

The opening subsection details the makeup of the people by tribe. Numbers simply lists each of the twelve tribes of Israel, as well as their constituent clans and their leaders, and then lists the number of males available for military service. While parallels to this sort of text did exist in the ancient Near East, most similar texts involve much smaller populations. Modern scholars have questioned the high numbers involved here, for they seem to assume a population much larger than Palestine supported either during the Iron Age or any other period before the twentieth century. That historical problem has been solved in either of two ways: either by (1) recognizing that the word Hebrew word *ʾelep* used here may denote either "1,000" or simply "the military unit of the clan," meaning a much smaller but indeterminate number, or (2) by simply arguing that the numbers involved are not to be taken literally, but like other ancient numberings in literature (for example, the one million troops that Herodotus attributes to Xerxes's army during the Persian War) simply indicates a large collection of people. In other words, by the second line of reasoning, modern readers accustomed to numbers precisely arrived at and reported, say in a text on accounting or finance or statistics, make a literary-genre mistake by assuming that ancient writers used such numbers in the same way we do. Both interpretations have strengths and weaknesses, but the second one is probably the more accurate.

The first section of Numbers may put off modern readers in other ways, too, but something important is happening in the text. Notice that it moves from the nation as a whole (the tribes; Num 1:1–2:34) to the tribe of Levi (Num 3:1–4:49), both the priests and their more distant relatives who attended to the Tabernacle's worship but did not offer sacrifice. In a sense, the text thinks in terms of binary oppositions as illustrated by the chart: Israel vs. the nations; within Israel the Levites vs. the other tribes; within the foreign nations, friendly vs. unfriendly powers.

Yet like all binary oppositions, and all sophisticated texts working with them, the one with which Numbers begins soon becomes much more complex. Many boundary-crossing examples occur, such that the reader soon realizes that simple binariness is not quite the right way to think about things. People can leave the box to which we assign them. (For, after all, the world is either binary or it's not.)

WHAT IS A TRIBE?

Like other ancient Near Eastern societies, and many others in human history, Israel understood its highest level of family-based society to be the tribe. Tribes are quasi-familial social structures that often coexist with a state structure, sometimes offering a central government support and sometimes opposition. Often, as in the Israelite case, tribes are localized to a bounded area. The Israelite tribes, or at least some of them, are attested in ancient records outside the Bible, and they seem to have persisted for centuries. However, the idea of the "Ten Lost Tribes" is an urban legend based on a misunderstanding of the biblical text.

The book's deeper theological attitude comes to the fore in at least two ways, then. First, notice that Numbers associates all the tribes together by arranging them around the Tabernacle in sets of three tribes each.

East Side: Judah, Issachar, Zebulun
South Side: Reuben, Simeon, Gad
West Side: Ephraim, Manasseh, Benjamin
North Side: Dan, Asher, Naphtali

The two tribes that historically had the most influence, Judah and Ephraim, receive the most prominent positions (cf. Gen 49), with Judah taking the lead in the nation's movements (Num 2:3), just as it would under the Davidic monarchy. More interestingly, the tribes partially cluster by the geographic proximity they enjoyed long years after the Mosaic period, during their history in their own land.

But there is an exception. The Judah group also includes two northern tribes, Issachar and Zebulun. Why? If we remember that the book of Numbers was probably finished during the period after the Babylonian conquest of the land (586 BCE), even if much of the material in it is older, then the book would be thinking about a situation in which the unity and even survival of the people of Israel seemed doubtful to many people. (The same would be true at a somewhat earlier period, as well, for Israel and Judah experienced a string of invasions between the eighth and sixth centuries BCE.) The text therefore emphasizes the unity and might of the people, the integrity of their leadership structures, and their capacity for survival even without a human monarch (notice that there is no king here, another fact that may point to a later rather than an earlier date). The idea of "all Israel" is important to Numbers, even if at some level its most prominent tribe remains Judah. Regionalism, tribal rivalries, and self-serving renditions of history all must go out the window so that the people may survive as a unified whole.

There is a second theme in Num 1–4: the role of the priestly tribe of Levi. Unlike the other tribes, Levi provides no soldiers to the national militia. The census does not count its males, because the census has primarily a military function. Nor does the tribe of Levi own a settled location in the promised land. One might say that it resembles a caste more than a tribe. Notice the key theological point that appears in Num 3:11–13:

Then Yhwh said to Moses, "As for me, I will take the Levites from the midst of Israel's children in the place of every firstborn that opens the womb (from Israel's children). Then the Levites will be mine. For every firstborn is mine. When I killed all the firstborn of Egypt, I sanctified to myself every firstborn Israelite, whether human or beast. They are mine. I am Yhwh.

This multilayered and strange text proposes a form of substitution. The Levites will stand in for everyone else with respect to Yhwh. But what does it mean?

To understand its meaning, one must know three things: (1) Firstborn children, especially males, in many cultures play a special role in caring for parents both in life and even after their deaths (with mortuary meals and commemorations). Their status had to be signified by means of ritual. Thus the Pentateuch contains several examples of ritual relating to the firstborn children (Exod 13:11–16; Deut 15:19–23; cf. 1 Sam 2:24–28). The firstborn offspring betokened the promise of ongoing fertility, meaning that Israelites could trust Yhwh to care for them and could signify that trust by offering the firstborn person or animal to God, though in different ways. (2) The prominence and special role of the firstborn of Israel ties into the Pentateuch's understanding of the exodus itself, during which Yhwh rescued the firstborn child Israel by slaying the firstborn of the Egyptians (Exod 11–12; cf. Hos 11:1). The ongoing practice of consecrating firstborn people and animals reminds Israel of its foundation story. And (3) the text recognizes that the special status of the firstborn somehow mirrors the special status of the Levites. Both have a responsibility to care for those around them and both demonstrate Yhwh's presence. Although the tribe's eponymous founder, Levi, was not the firstborn child, still the tribe functioned symbolically for the nation as a firstborn child would for the family.

As odd as such a parallelism may seem to modern readers, it plays out in Numbers in important ways. In the first instance, Num 4:40–51 amplifies the law by asking exactly how the substitution of Levites for everyone else must take place, and suggests that the primary means is through the offering of goods and funds, especially money that would facilitate the movements of animals for sacrifice. (Since it was not always practical to bring your own animal for sacrifice, a way of purchasing appropriate animals had to be available). In Num 8:14–19, moreover, the priests stand in for the people during sacrifice itself in order to avert the possibility of plague erupting should the rituals in the Tabernacle go awry.

RULES FOR THE CAMP (NUM 5:1–10:10)

The next section of Numbers discusses a series of laws regarding personal purity and religious commitment for all Israelites, not just the Levites. The topics in the first unit in this section (Num 5:1–6:27) include quarantine for skin diseases (Num 5:1–4), the disposition of fines when the wronged person or his or her heir cannot be located (Num 5:5–10), the rules for settling accusations of adultery (Num 5:11–31), and the rules for a nazirite (Num 6:1–21), all topped off by the priestly blessing (Num 6:22–27). The second unit in this section, applying to the Tabernacle itself (Num 6:1–10:10), describes the gifts to the Tabernacle from each tribe (Num 7:1–89), the inauguration of the Tabernacle worship (Num 8:1–26), exceptions to the general rules for Passover (Num 9:1–14), the function of the cloud over the Tabernacle (Num 9:15–23), and the final order to leave Mount Sinai (Num 10:1–10). All of this material, like chs 1–4, reflects a strong priestly sensibility, which sought to ensure the bodily purity of the people as well as their attachment to principles of justice. In fact, these chapters offer a sort of mental map of the community, especially of its members who do not fit into tidy categories.

Several of the laws deserve some explanation. Take the law of the woman accused of adultery (Hebrew: *šōtâ*) in Num 5:11–31, to begin. In a world without DNA paternity tests or private investigators, a patriarchal society could allow a suspicious husband to kill a wife or daughter on flimsy grounds. Such so-called honor killing still occurs in parts of the world. However, the ritual of the *šōtâ* creates a structure that would save a woman's life (if not necessarily her honor). The husband making the accusation escorts the wife to the sanctuary, where the priest administers a nauseating liquid compounded of dust and ink from a curse written on papyrus. Drinking the liquid could apparently induce vaginal bleeding or perhaps even a miscarriage (though the language is ambiguous on this point) or, alternatively, could do nothing at all. Such a trial by ordeal, common in many societies until the modern period, assumes the active intervention of the deity and the belief in that intervention on the part of all concerned. By carrying out the ritual, the priesthood transferred a matter often kept within the family to the larger world of the community, thus insuring some level of protection for all concerned. In other words, a husband could not harm his wife on the basis of mere suspicion. However alien to our own thinking and practice (though perhaps not as alien as we would wish to pretend), the law does try to prevent the worst sorts of violent abuses.

Numbers then continues with a law for the nazirite (6:1–21). These persons were holy people whose actions reminded Israel of the presence of their divine lord. The very oddness of their behavior invited comment and reflection on the uncanniness of the presence of Yhwh among the people. Thus the prophet Amos paired nazirites with prophets: "Yet I elevated some of your children to be prophets and your young people to be nazirites—isn't it so, Israel's Children? An oracle of Yhwh. Yet you made the nazirites drink wine and commanded the prophets 'do not prophesy'" (Amos 2:11–12). In other words, both groups of people helped the communication between the divine and human realms, and both could be suborned by unscrupulous people. Numbers 6 specifies a lifestyle for the nazirites (abstinence from alcohol and haircuts, as well as contact with dead bodies), as well as a ritual for helping them exit that state by means of a sacrifice. Numbers does not explain why someone would become a nazirite. Unlike the prophetic office, it seems to have been purely voluntary. The most famous nazirite, though hardly typical or morally commendable, was Samson (Judg 13–16), whose military achievements only partially compensate for his remarkable lack of self-control. In normal situations, in any case, the status of nazirite seems to have been a sort of initiatory state, comparable in some ways to the vows taken in many societies at the entrance into adulthood or marriage or some other major transition in life. Perhaps one could take on the role at several different points in life and remain in it only long enough to become ready for the next phase of life, whatever it was.

The rule for the nazirite, like the preceding rule for the *sôtâ*, attempts to regularize a practice that might easily fall outside the purview of the priesthood in the central sanctuary (the Tabernacle in the Pentateuch, the Temple in most of Israel's history). By doing so, Numbers makes a group at the margins of society into a model for the community as a whole. In some ways, then, the nazirites were like the monks or hermits of the European Middle Ages or in Buddhist countries of East Asia today, who followed different life rules in order to symbolize to their neighbors the possibilities of escaping ordinary life, at least temporarily.

THE KETEF HINNOM AMULETS

The only biblical text preserved in a copy from the period of the Israelite monarchy is found in the small amulets from Ketef Hinnom near Jerusalem. These tiny texts were rolled up and buried with the dead. The texts themselves consist of a slightly modified version of the priestly blessing in Num 6:24–26.

In any case, Num 7–10 concerns items related to the sanctuary and its priests, thus rounding out the discussion of life in and around the Tabernacle that began back in Exod 25. The chiefs of the tribes initiate the communal sacrifices, a story that Num 7:1–89 reports at length in order to picture a unified, religiously oriented nation that future generations of leaders and followers could imitate. Numbers 8:1–4 offers another dramatic moment with the lighting of the menorah, or golden seven-branched lampstand that has become one the primary symbols of Jewish life.

The section continues by announcing the ritual purification of the Levites, the major part of the Tabernacle's staff, who were responsible for janitorial and maintenance activities (a high prestige job, in spite of the messiness). This section also includes instructions for emergency Passover-observance in the event of a problem during the normal times (9:1–14; cf. 2 Chron 30:1–5). In the event of an emergency, a given Israelite or a family (or in 2 Chron, the entire country) could keep the Passover one month late. Thus the main point of the ritual could be preserved even when life intervened to disrupt the customary patterns of worship. The section concludes with the command for Israel to leave Sinai, a transition that both advances the narrative (every plot requires change to keep it interesting) and offers closure on the moment of lawgiving at Sinai. It is as if the book of Numbers wishes to say that the revelation of Torah occurred at one time and place—Mount Sinai immediately after the exodus—but forever afterward, Israel must strive to live out the implications of the gift it has received.

The rest of the book adopts a series of perspectives, both priestly and nonpriestly, or rather both focused on the ritual life of Israel and not. Even more than the first major section of the book, Num 10:11–36:13 gives the impression of jumbledness, but this state of affairs seems appropriate in a book called "in the desert," for a migratory campaign of thirty-eight years would have consisted of many variegated episodes.

In fact, Numbers does have a structure and a narrative flow that brings the reader to the verge of the promised land while investigating aspects of ongoing life within it. It does the latter surreptitiously, without explicitly saying what it is doing. These chapters talk about such questions as leadership, the status of the Mosaic law and its relationship to other sources of divine revelation (especially prophecy), the relationships between Israel and its neighbors, proper practices for landholding and inheritance, and other items. In doing so, it is working out its thoughts on how to live in the promised land. In other words, Numbers is thinking politically and theologically about how the community of its ideals should operate.

CONFLICT AND FAILURE (NUM 10:11–14:45)

What should leadership look like in the community of Israel? One way the book of Numbers addresses this question is by reporting stories of conflict about leadership between Moses and the whole people (11:1–35) and various possible rivals, including his own family (12:1–16). The story of the spies in chs 13–14 carries on the same theme. Moses here appears as a once-in-history sort of leader, the founder of the nation (but not a king) and its chief lawgiver, who must still face adversity in leading a people, including their fear of the unknown and their excessive focus on immediate survival. But if all this section did was talk about the role of Moses, it would be a mere historical curiosity, even for the ancient Israelites. Instead, the creators of Numbers used these stories to work out some basic understandings of the role of Torah itself as a guide for leaders.

This larger role of the story becomes clear at with two points. First, Num 11:26–30 reports two otherwise unknown characters named Eldad and Medad prophesying in the camp. "My master, Moses, stop them," said his assistant Joshua. "Are you worked up because of me?" said Moses. "Would that Yhwh made all the people prophets, for Yhwh has put his spirit on them!" (Num 11:28–29). Why does the text report this story? Not just to show Moses's lack of insecurity, surely an important trait in successful leaders. The more important point is that even though Moses is a great prophet, he is not the only one (cf. Deut 18:15–22). The social role of prophets as messengers of the divine reflects Yhwh's choices, not the whims of political leaders. Not even Moses can suppress prophecy (contrast the attempts of various kings do so in 1–2 Kgs). However, Moses's role surpasses that of prophecy as a source of divinely inspired knowledge and therefore as a warrant for appropriate action. Like the prophet Joel, who envisioned the day when

"I [Yhwh] will pour out my spirit on all flesh so that your sons and your daughters may prophesy" (Joel 2:28–29 [Hebrew 3:1–2]; quoted in Acts 2:17–18), Numbers imagines a world in which prophecy is radically democratized, even if that possibility seems remote.

Another way to understand this story is to recognize that it relativizes prophecy not by dismissing it as a genuine source of divine revelation, but by subordinating it to the words of Moses, which survive in the written Torah. The texts of the Pentateuch (and for that matter, the texts of the prophetic books, as will become clear in chs 23–29) both preserve the prophetic word so that it can be useful to the community for all time and limit the effects of new prophetic words by forcing them to pass the test of coherence with the Torah. A lot is happening in this story.

The second relevant episode is in Num 12, in which both Aaron and Miriam hear Yhwh say in no uncertain terms that even though their roles are important (she is a prophet and he the first high priest), Moses's role surpasses them in that he speaks with God "face to face as with a friend" (Num 12:8). Again, the role of the giver of Torah, and therefore the role of Torah itself, surpasses even those of the priest or the prophet.

> Why does Miriam contract a skin disease while Aaron goes unpunished when both have challenged Moses unjustly (Num 12)? While it is tempting to read the different experiences of the two ancestors as a simple case of male bias and patriarchy run amok, the more socio-logically and literarily congruent explanation is that Aaron, as the high priest, cannot contract such a disease since that would jeopardize the entire sacrificial system. A priest cannot participate in the worship in the Tabernacle while tainted with such a condition. On the other hand, Miriam's condition requires the ministrations of a priest to declare the outbreak of a disease (perhaps some form of psoriasis?) to be in remission (see Lev 13–14). Also, note that English translations may be somewhat misleading when the render the Hebrew word *ṣaraʿat* as "leprosy." Any skin disease could be in view.

In the middle of this section on leadership conflicts comes the story of the spies (Num 13:1–14:45; see also Deut 1:19–46), one representing each tribe. The basic story is simple enough: Israelite spies scout the land of Canaan and return after forty days (an important symbolic number, surely) to report their findings. The majority report sends a mixed message: "the place is nice, but its inhabitants are too militarily successful and physically imposing for us to take on." A minority of two, the famous military heroes Joshua and Caleb as it happens, argue that in view of the nation's previous experiences with Yhwh, conquering the land should not pose insuperable problems. The people believe the majority report, however, and begin to blame Yhwh and by association Moses for their plight: stuck in the wilderness with no place to go.

All of this sounds like a typical murmuring story, which appears also in Exodus, with the crisis triggered by a failure of the people's faith in Yhwh. However, Numbers deepens the oft-told tale through the speeches of the characters. First, the people function as a single character, one that is argumentative, whiney, and querulous: "O that we had died in the land of Egypt or in this desert. O that we had died. Why did Yhwh bring us to this land? To die by the sword along with our wives and our children? To be plunder? Wouldn't it be better for us to return to Egypt?" (Num 14:2–3). That is, they attribute to Yhwh the worst possible motives and actually wax nostalgic for the time of their oppression. Second, the opposite character in the drama is Yhwh, who shows extraordinary disgust with them, offering Moses a second chance to become the ancestor of a chosen people (Num 14:12; cf. Exod 32:10), and finally agreeing to allow Israel to survive through its second postexilic generation, with the adult escapees dying along the road. By contrasting Yhwh's gracious signs and wonders, and proper indignation at fecklessness, on the one hand, with the irrational ingratitude of the Israelites, and on the other, the authors of this material (both P and non-P, as it happens) characterize the moral issues at stake in this story as ones of loyalty, gratitude, and courage, all basic human values. They accentuate this contrast by portraying the third character, Moses, as a mediator between Yhwh and his people, hence as a man who both struggles with the same fears as others but who manages to overcome them and even to remind the enraged deity that compassion, to be real, must extend to those most unreceptive to it. Hence Moses's conciliatory speech in Num 14:13–19, which quotes fairly closely both Exod 32 and Exod 34 to the effect that destroying the people would (1) induce the foreign powers to believe that Yhwh was a destructive being only, (2) betray promises made to the people of Israel, and (3) give the lie to the proclamation of Yhwh as the one who is "slow to anger and full of loyalty, removing iniquity and transgression (though not acquitting wrongly but punishing the iniquity of the ancestors upon the children to the third or fourth generations)" (Num 14:18). Based on these succinctly stated but impressively imaginative arguments, Moses implores Yhwh to "forgive this people commensurately with the greatness of your loyalty, just as you raised this up from Egypt until this day" (Num 14:19). The final resolution of the conflict, in which Yhwh decides to punish the people by allowing them to wander in the desert for thirty-eight more years, must be seen as the affirmative answer to Moses's request.

How does a story as pregnant with meaning as this one fit with those preceding it? Numbers reports the story of the spies to illustrate the superior character of Moses (and thus of the Torah of Moses). Its postexilic audience can draw from Moses's example and Moses's Torah inspiration for the future. As with many charismatic leaders, not everyone accepted that primacy, just as not everyone accepted the Torah set forth in the Pentateuch, and so the next section of Numbers continues the theme of internal conflict in order to make matters clearer still.

THE DEMISE OF THE EXODUS GENERATION (NUM 15:1–20:29)

The next section develops the theme of the demise of the exodus generation but in an unexpected way. It focuses upon conflicts within the priestly circles themselves and articulates a set of purposes for the priesthood. Though some of the stories' details are fairly lurid—the ground swallowing various malcontents or Moses angrily striking a rock to bring forth water—the section as a whole concentrates on matters that seem esoteric at first, that is, the role of the priesthood and terms of membership in it. For most modern Western readers, such concerns seem extremely remote. However, it helps to remember that in ancient societies, most occupation roles were inherited. Yet in a hereditary society in which families might contest positions, and in which therefore the traditions of the entire group become at risk, it becomes important to clarify who is a priest and what that position entails.

Num 15–20 set out to answer these questions by combining instructions for sacrificing (Num 15:1–41; 19:1–22) with stories of rivalry (16:1–50 [Hebrew16:1–17:15]) and complaint (20:1–13); a report of the selection of the priestly family (17:1–13 [Hebrew 17:16–28]) and heir to the high priesthood (20:22–29); and a discussion of priestly mediation on behalf of the people (18:1–32). The piece that seems at first not to fit appears in Num 20:14–21, a story of an embassage to the king of Edom, but this story sets up events to follow in chs 15–20.

The key stories here revolve around the attempted ouster of Moses and Aaron by their rivals, Dathan and Abiram, and especially the Levite Korah. The question at stake in chs 16 and 17 is just who should be high priest and therefore who should superintendent both sacrifice and the teaching of Moses's Torah. This Korah seems to have been related to the Levitical family otherwise known as Temple (or Levitical) singers in other biblical texts (1 Chron 6:7, 22; 9:19; the superscriptions to Pss 42, 44–49, 84–85, 87–88 [see the discussion of the superscriptions in Chapter 19 (Psalms), and so most scholars understand the story to concern a rivalry within the priesthood about the primacy of the family of Aaron and its claims to hold the priesthood in perpetuity.

This sort of struggle may well be the background of the story. In Numbers, however, the conflict has a different drift, the question of how Israel sorts out problems. The story of Korah and his allies, who seek to gain leadership of various levels of society, not just explicitly religious ones, ends with a decisive verdict. The ground (or perhaps underworld, for the Hebrew word *'ereṣ* can mean either) swallows up the insurgents and their families (since ancient people believed in group responsibility), and Yhwh thereby vindicates Moses's and Aaron's leadership. Then in Num 17:16–26, a miracle occurs whereby only Aaron's staff demonstrates the unusual capacity of blooming when cut off from a source of plant nutrients. End of story. No ambiguity here.

Or is there? The book of Numbers uses this story to explore what it means to function as a leader in the Israelite tradition. Like Samuel in 1 Samuel 12, who was similarly criticized for his leadership, Moses offers a remarkable defense of his administration in a prayer to Yhwh (who must judge the whole affair): "Not one donkey have I taken from them; I have not mistreated even one of them" (Num 16:15). He does not bother to deny the critics' charges that he has failed to bring them to the promised land, for the reader of the text already knows why this failure has occurred, despite Moses's best efforts. In other words, the story picks up the motif of Israel's ingratitude and self-indulgent carping and places it in the mouths of the priestly and nonpriestly critics of Moses and Aaron. For Numbers, their attitudes alone would render Korah and his associates unworthy bearers of the nation's traditions and stories, even if Yhwh had not already chosen other leaders.

The nature of this choice becomes clear in the material surrounding the story of the rebel's unscheduled trip to the underworld. The priesthood bears the obligation of offering the sacrifices that express gratitude or, in the event of some error of judgment, reconcile Israel to God and each other (Num 15 and 18). Thus the priesthood must bear carefully the role of mediator between Israel and its divine lord. And this is why these chapters in Numbers take such pains to describe the role of Eliezer, Aaron's son and successor, the principal sacrifices (already discussed, though with minor differences, in Leviticus), and, perhaps most interestingly, the attitude that the mediator must take.

On this score, note the response of Moses and Aaron to Yhwh's threat to destroy the people who still complained after the death of Korah and his coconspirators:

> And Moses said to Aaron, "take the censer and put fire from the altar on it so as to produce smoke and then go quickly to the congregation and atone for them, for wrath has come from Yhwh's presence. A plague has started." So Aaron took [the equipment] just as Moses had said and ran to the midst of the congregation, for a plague had indeed started among the people. So he spread the smoke and atoned for the people. (Num 16:46–47 [Hebrew Num 17:11–12])

A modern reader of this vignette may be most impressed by the seemingly out-of-control divine anger, but the story concentrates most upon the lengths to which the priests, here embodied in their ancestor Aaron, should go to protect Israel from any misfortune. The incense functions as a sort of prayer *for* the people and a symbol *of* the divine protection, as well as an appeal to the deity to make that protection tangible. And in this way, despite its ambiguity, these stories of conflict and its resolution play out on a major theological idea: the role of the priesthood in defending both God from charges of malfeasance and cruelty, and Israel from the consequences of its sins.

EARLY SETTLEMENT (NUM 21:1–35)

This brief section combines two stories by the simple mechanism of a travel notice, "and Israel's children traveled" (21:10). The first story concerns yet another episode of complaining, one which led to a plague of fiery serpents (Hebrew: *nĕḥāšîm haśśĕrāpîm*). The text may have in mind the sort of winged cobras that often appear on Egyptian seals rather than a known animal species, or perhaps "fiery" is just a metaphor for the snakes' venom or their coloring.

In any case, Moses stills the plague by the erection of a bronze serpent as an apotropaic object signifying the disease or problem from which persons are cured, much like the innumerable eye amulets that survived from ancient temples. In any case, this bronze object had a long afterlife before its final destruction in the late eighth century BCE (several centuries after Moses) by King Hezekiah, because it had become an object of illegitimate veneration in its own right (2 Kgs 18:4).

The second story in this "meanwhile, on the road" section that connects two larger units in Numbers concerns Israel's encounters with two kings in the Transjordan, Sihon and Og. The conquest story itself is unremarkable, for Israel readily defeats these monarchs. What is more interesting is that the story of their defeat became a fixture in Israel's oral poetry, the songs of the past that they sang at various occasions. So references to the paired kings Sihon and Og occur many other times in the Bible, twenty-eight times for Sihon and nineteen for Og. Thus we see that more traditions about them circulated than Numbers reports.

Even more interestingly, Num 21 does include some parts of these oral songs, some of it from a cycle of war poetry which it calls, "the book of the Wars of Yhwh" (Num 21:14). The poetry in Num 21:17 is a lovely work song, "Rise up, O well," celebrating the community's collaboration in producing usable water (a major achievement, as those who dig wells in the economically developing world know very well).

Meanwhile, the poetry in Num 21:27–30 tells of the heroism of great warriors, not Israelites but rather their soon-to-be-vanquished enemies:

Therefore the tellers of tales say,

"Go to Heshbon. It is built
Established is Sihon's city.
For fire comes from Heshbon, a flame from Sihon's burg.
It devours Ar-Moab,
the lords of the Arnon Heights."

It would be interesting to know whether this bit of saga, which must come from a much longer poem of war and victory, reflects the songs sung by the Bashanites themselves, or if it was simply a composition by an Israelite bard who then turned to the story of the ultimate defeat of the great king Sihon. It is interesting that the place names in the song also appear in the only extensive Moabite text that survives, the stele, or monument, of King Mesha, from the late ninth century BCE, although Numbers and Mesha take different views of the desirability of Moabite victory and defeat. One wonders if there is some connection between the two texts.

THE BALAAM STORIES (NUM 22:1–24:25)

However this may be, the Moabite connection shows up in the following unit of Numbers. In the middle of the stories of wanderings and defeats comes a tale of a wizard or professional curser named Balaam. Mostly likely, these chapters were written as a single block of material before the editor of Numbers took them over because they tell the story with a focus on the Moabites without mentioning Moses or the Israelite leadership.

The Balaam stories have a different literary prehistory from the stories around them. Moreover, they also connect to a text outside the Bible, the story of Balaam from a site in Transjordan called Deir Alla. In 1967, archaeologists discovered there a text written in ink on plaster from about 800 BCE. The text was written in a language previously unknown to modern scholarship but related to Aramaic, and it concerned the visions of a prophet named Balaam son of Beor, the same figure who appears in the Bible. Interestingly, however, the Balaam here worships a set of gods called the Shaddayin, and the text itself is apparently not Israelite. In other words, the figure of Balaam was well known east of the Jordan River, where the Bible sets him. He had a reputation as a seer whose frightening visions foretold radical changes in the world as people knew it. So, according to the plaster text, Balaam's vision portrayed the gods agreeing to "Sew up, bolt up the heavens . . . ordaining darkness instead of eternal light," a sad reversal of fortune that leads preyed-upon animals to hunt their predators and humans to experience pestilence and death. In other words, both the biblical and the nonbiblical texts portray Balaam in essentially the same way, as one who had access to the divine realm and warned humans of coming catastrophes.

The biblical story of Balaam depicts him as a wizard for hire, and portraying him much more negatively than the non-Israelite text (which may have seen him as a sort of hero). In Numbers, the Moabite king Balak, terrified for his throne and his people, invites Balaam to pronounce a curse on Israel. He, his people, Balaam himself, and apparently the Israelite readers of the story all assumed that such a curse could work, and it thus became important for the narrative that Balaam not pronounce it. At first, therefore, Yhwh refuses Balaam permission to accompany Balak's emissaries. When Balaam goes anyway, after misunderstanding Yhwh's "go" as real permission rather than the exasperated statement it was, the jenny he rode off to Moab rebels against him. In a brilliant parody of prophetic visionary experience—the donkey sees what Balaam cannot!—Balaam must at last confront the implications of his actions. An angel threatens to kill him unless he agrees to bless Israel instead of curse it, and the jenny saves his life. Again, this part of the story has a highly comic element. Talking donkeys and frustrated prophets are things to laugh at, and Numbers certainly intends the reader to laugh. Yet it also makes a serious point: it is not just that only a very poor seer could be more obtuse than the donkey he mounts, but also that the world of magic, which was pervasive in the ancient world, could not thwart the plans of Yhwh.

The story then continues with a series of poems that Numbers calls *mĕšālîm* (Num 23:7–10, 18–24; and 24:3–9) the word that usually means "proverbs" or "sayings," but must here mean something like "oracles" or even "saga" or "epic" (as in 21:27). Each poem speaks of the successes that Israel will enjoy in the future. Naturally, these blessings infuriate Balaam's Moabite employer, King Balak, who had expected praise but paid for curses instead. And thus the comedy of Balaam comes to an end, with the unfortunate wizard losing his client and his reputation, and Israel walking away from trouble owing to the protection of Yhwh.

BAAL PEOR (NUM 25:1–18)

This brief episode concerns sexual encounters between Midianites and Israelites. The problem does not seem to be the potential of intermarriage per se, for after all, Moses's own wife was the Midianite Zipporah. Rather, the problem lies in the realm of religion, with the Midianites teaching the Israelites to worship a local manifestation of the god Baal, one Baal Peor. Later Jewish tradition, and therefore Christian readers so dependent on the earliest readers of the Bible, connected Balaam to the sexual exploits of this chapter (see, e.g., Rev 2:14), though the connection appears only later and incidentally in Numbers itself (Num 31:16).

DISTRIBUTION OF THE PROMISED LAND (NUM 25:19–36:13)

Before getting to that point and to the significant problems it raises, one should consider the last large section of the book, Num 25:19–36:13. Some of this material retraces ground covered in Leviticus (the calendar in Num 28–29 is closely related to that in Lev 23), some of it recounts the names of clans that appear earlier in the book (so Num 26 connects to Num 1), and some of it consists of lists of stops in the wilderness wanderings that may connect to a shorter list in Deut 1 (Num 33). Several bits of the narrative are new, however.

The first is the framing device in Num 27:1–11 and Num 36:1–13, the story of the daughters of Zelophehad. According to this story, Zelophehad died without male offspring. His daughters, in order to preserve his memory and their family inheritance, asked Moses whether they could inherit in their own right, although the norm in theirs and most other ancient cultures did not allow female inheritance of land. They appealed to Moses as the final arbiter of difficult legal matters (cf. Exod 18), and he received from Yhwh the verdict that the women could, in fact, inherit. This story seems designed to demonstrate both the remarkable commitment to family honor on the part of these women and the flexibility of Israelite law, which allowed women to inherit under some circumstances (usually in the absence of male heirs, but see Job 42:15, which offers at least one exception to the cultural rule). The use of this story as a bookend around other material regarding Israel's settlement of land in the Transjordan seems calculated to emphasize the blessing of land ownership through Yhwh's mercy.

The second new topic occurs in ch 30, which gives rights to women to keep oaths they had made freely without their being annulled by their husbands or fathers. We know from archaeology that ancient Israelite women sometimes owned seals held on necklaces or signet rings, with which they could seal a document and thus transact business in their own name. It also appears that Torah considers them free agents for at least some purposes, even in a society that was still patriarchal in many respects. Again, Numbers explores the options available for women, preferring to assume their moral agency rather than the opposite.

The third new topic occurs in ch 31, in which Israel decimates the older civilization of the Midianites (though not quite, for the same group appears in the book of Judges). The crisis in the story occurs when Israelite men take Midianite women as captives, or rather as potential sexual partners. This ancient version of sex trafficking meets Moses's disapproval, but not for the reasons one might expect. Rather, he says, "Have you let every female live? Surely, they're the ones connected to Israel's children during the Peor affair to draw us away from Yhwh by the word of Balaam, so that the plague fell on Yhwh's community" (Num 31:15–16). He then commands their execution.

Now any thoughtful reader of this story must find it troubling. True, Moses assigns to women a high degree of agency and self-determination in carrying out evil (just as story of Zelophehad's daughters commend women for choosing good), and the earlier story in ch 25 made the culpability of the Israelite males clear too. Yet, the solution seems unsettling for all sorts of obvious reasons, in part because no trial or assessment of evidence occurs. Nor can the story be understood as part of the later alleged massacres of Canaanites found in Joshua and Judges, for the Midianites do not fall under the category of "peoples of the land" or "Canaanites" to be dispossessed (a topic to be taken up later). Rather, the text expects the reader to accept its own moral vision in which the sin of idolatry is so heinous that the only response to it is death. It was one thing for the Midianites to worship Baal Peor—the Bible often assumes that non-Israelites cannot help themselves—and quite another to lead Israelites, the beneficiaries of Yhwh's gracious actions, to do so.

In any case, the fourth new element appears throughout these chapters, the settlement of the land proper. Numbers 32 and 34 tell the story of the lodgment of Israelite tribes in Transjordan, thereby explaining to the readers of the book (1) why their people settled where they did, (2) the actual boundaries of the promised land, including territory also claimed by the Moabites and Ammonites, and (3) reasons validating the choice of the tribes of Reuben, Gad, and Manasseh (in part) to live where they did. In other words, the book ends with a vision of an entire people, an especially compelling conclusion for readers whose experiences were different. If the book was finished, as most scholars believe, in the era after the so-called Babylonian exile of the sixth century BCE, or even if parts of it are a century or two earlier (as is probable), then it must be that readers would have considered the fate of their deported compatriots. Numbers offers a hopeful picture for such readers.

Implications

To conclude, then, how should a modern reader of Numbers assess it? One might compare it to a large room full of all sorts of furniture and knickknacks from many periods and in many styles—jumbled, dusty, and disordered. But a closer look reveals careful planning, even if the sheer diversity of the furniture makes tidiness difficult.

Numbers expresses three major concerns. First, it wishes to place the stories of Israel's complaints and wilderness wanderings into a moral context to create a warning for future readers (a theme already understood by Paul in 1 Cor 10:1–13; cf. Ps 95:8–10). Second, it seeks to connect the Transjordanian population to their fellow Israelites west of the river, thus making one nation. And third, and most importantly, it elevates the Aaronide priesthood by placing them under the Torah of Moses, making them responsible for teaching it and sacrificing according to it, and thus provides for the nation's continuity in the absence of charismatic leaders such as Moses. By making the miracle of Torah normal, even routine, it makes ordinary life meaningful. And that may be its greatest contribution to the Bible as a whole. Certainly it is a meritorious one.

Note

1. Won W. Lee, *Punishment and Forgiveness in Israel's Migratory Campaign* (Grand Rapids: Eerdmans, 2003).

For Further Reading

Achenbach, Reinhard. *Die Vollendung der Tora: Studien zur Redaktionsgeschichte des Numeribuches im Kontext von Pentateuch und Hexateuch.* BZAR 3. Wiesbaden: Harrassowitz, 2003.

Lee, Won W. *Punishment and Forgiveness in Israel's Migratory Campaign.* Grand Rapids: Eerdmans, 2003.

Leveen, Adriane. *Memory and Tradition in the Book of Numbers.* Cambridge: Cambridge University Press, 2008.

7 On Memory and Action
THE BOOK OF DEUTERONOMY

> **Key Text**: *For this command that I am commanding you today is not too splendid for you, nor is it too distant. It is not in the sky, prompting one to say, "who will ascend to the sky for us and bring it to us, and make us hear it so we will do it?" It is not across the sea, prompting one to say "who will traverse the sea for us and take it to us, and make us hear it so we will do it?" For the word is very near you, in your mouth and in your heart, in order to (make it possible) to do it.* (Deut 30:11–14)

The book of Deuteronomy, a farewell speech attributed to Moses, both concludes the story of Israel's origins (the Pentateuch) and opens the story of its life in the promised land (Josh–2 Kgs or the Deuteronomistic History). This great biblical book, one of the most influential in the history of Judaism and Christianity, combines laws, poems, and narratives, all with an aim of inviting the reader to reflect on the nature of Yhwh's work with the elect people, Israel. Moses's speech as a whole lays out for Israel the options of life and death, as its climax in ch 30 puts it. All of the types of material of the book fit together to foster the book's view of life lived well.

By placing the laws of the book's core within a narrative context (Deut 1–11, 29–31), Deuteronomy proposes an interpretation of the norms it presents. As the opening chapters reflect on Israel's past story, these norms take on the character of a response to human rebellion. Deuteronomy calls Israel to a high standard of personal and group ethics. Because, for all human beings, the past profoundly shapes the future, the recovery of the past as a resource for the future is an important theme in the Bible. Deuteronomy seeks to create what Georg Braulik has felicitously called a "commemorative culture,"[1] that is, the deliberate cultivation of a set of experiences that will make Israel's awareness of its own past—hence its own identity—an inescapable reality. Careful attention to that past profoundly shapes how Deuteronomy thinks about the world. Israel cannot speak of itself without reference to the mighty saving deeds of God.

In part, the book's efforts at reexamining the past in order to create a usable future reflect the experiences of the book's creators. A large section of Deuteronomy was apparently the "book of the Torah" discovered in the Jerusalem Temple during the reign of Josiah (ca. 627 BCE), and thus the basis of that king's reforms of Judah's religion (2 Kgs 22:8–23:23). Although some of the laws in Deuteronomy, and much of its basic outlook on the world are extremely ancient, much of the text we have now seems to come from the late eighth or seventh century BCE and to reflect the experience of Assyrian domination over Israel and Judah during that period.[2] On the other hand, Deut 30 seems to presuppose widespread deportations of Israelites and their potential return, a date that may point to a date of writing a few decades after the destruction of Jerusalem in 586 BCE (though it could also conceivably refer to the widespread dislocation of Israelites following the Assyrian invasions more than a century earlier). In other words, Deuteronomy presupposes several generations of both good and bad experiences in its readers' past, and it uses those experiences to craft a moral vision of the future.

Part of this vision involves the laws, especially in chs 12–26. While modern Americans, religious or otherwise, often think of religious "law" as restrictive and impersonal, the Bible does not think of the category in this way. For example, Ps 1 imagines the wise person as one who "meditates on Yhwh's Torah day and night," taking "delight" in it. Because the law, or norms, of God becomes internalized in Deuteronomy's ideal world, Israel can follow it with one of Deuteronomy's favorite words, "joy" (Deut 12:7, 12, 18; 16:15; 24:5; 33:18). Now, this internalization requires biblical law to address many aspects of life, not just the "religious" side of it, because each of us lives one life, not several at once. Accordingly, the laws in chs 5 and 12–26 cover many topics, from the sublime to the mundane. As a whole, these laws aim to create a new society in which justice, freedom, joy, and piety will reign. The norms of human existence in which one's economic value triumphs over all else do not apply in Israel.

OUTLINE OF DEUTERONOMY

Introduction (the time and place of the book) (1:1–5)
The first speech, a summary of the origins of Israel with theological commentary (1:6–4:40)
A note on the three cities of refuge (4:41–43)
A bridge between the first and second discourses of the book (4:44–49)
The second speech, the laying out of the laws for Israel (5:1–11:32)
The code of laws (12:1–26:19)
The founding of Israel before the entry into the promised land (27:1–26)

Blessings and cursings (28:1–69)
More on the covenant (29:1–28)
A promise of return after repentance (30:1–20)
The charge to Joshua and the nation (31:1–30)
The "Song of Moses" (32:1–43)
An epilogue to the "Song of Moses" (32:44–47)
God's command to Moses to climb the mountain (32:48–52)
The blessing of Moses (33:1–29)
Moses's death (34:1–12)

Following the laws is a second sermon section (chs 29–31) and two beautiful poems (chs 32–33) that describe the future of Israel as it lives under the blessing of God. These two sections, both written in a gorgeously elevated way designed to challenge and inspire, invite the book's readers into a deeper relationship with Yhwh and thus each other.

The book's final narrative is the death scene of Moses. The emphasis here is not so much on his demise as on the fact that Israel's history goes on, now under Joshua.

From a theological point of view, Deuteronomy both draws together older legal and narrative traditions and interprets them in light of core theological ideas so as to make them usable for a new day. The key ideas of the book are clear: Israel, the redeemed people, should serve the one God, Yhwh, and in doing so will enjoy a life of joy and plenty in its own land and thus will witness to other nations of the goodness of the redeemer God.

At another level, however, it is difficult to reduce Deuteronomy to a set of discrete ideas. Rather, the book offers a totalizing picture of the redeemed people. Thus, for example, law serves to better individuals, families, and the nation because, as Terence Fretheim puts it, "God is concerned about the best possible life for all of God's creatures." The law does not serve its own ends but gives shape to Israel's vocation as a people finishing God's creation.

The Sermonic Framework (Deut 1:6–11:32; 29:1–31:30)

The key to understanding how Deuteronomy thought of its laws lies in the "sermonic" framework surrounding them. The book presents itself as a speech by Moses, in which he introduces a new summary of Israel's law (in Greek *deuteros* = "second," and *nomos* = "law"). The law code differs from other codes in the Pentateuch in some respects, hence the need to set it in a context that explains it.

Deut 1–11 consist of a pair of speeches (basically chs 1–4 and 5–11) attributed to Moses in the setting of a nationwide meeting in Moab (east of the Dead Sea) just prior to the entry into the promised land. The speeches mingle historical recitation with exhortation to embrace the values and norms extolled by the book. Chs 5 and 7 comprise specific laws (in the former the Ten Commandments; cf. Exod 20), forming a prelude to the more extensive set of laws that function as the book's core (chs 12–26).

To understand how these chapters work rhetorically—that is, how they try to persuade their audience to embrace the Torah as Deuteronomy sets it forth—remember that any rhetorical event consists of at least four parts. These are a speaker, an audience, an occasion or reason for the communication taking place, and a set of conventions for speaking as well as arguments that go together to make the speech.

1) Since Deuteronomy was written later than the time of Moses and probably much of it comes from the seventh century BCE or later, the figure of Moses here is a literary device. That is, the book is not a literal transcript of a speech that he gave. But it does reflect Israel's most cherished beliefs and values in a way that profoundly respects the Mosaic tradition.

(2) Like every text, Deut 1–11 has in mind an audience, or in fact multiple audiences. It constructs this audience as a group with a history of ingratitude toward, and rebellion against, Yhwh. Consider for example the reinterpretation of the story of the spies in Num 13–14: "But you were not willing to go up; rather you were bitterly opposed to Yhwh your God, and you griped in your tents and said, 'Because Yhwh hates us, he brought us from the land of Egypt to give us into the clutches of the Amorites, so they could destroy us'" (Deut 1:26–27). Given everything that Deuteronomy says about the compassion and justice of Yhwh, such an accusation on the Israelites' part could only appear folly. And by portraying their attitude as one of indefensible ingratitude, the text raises the possibility that their viewpoints cannot be trusted.

At the same time, the audience is the recipient of divine care on account of the promises to the ancestors, who figure repeatedly in these chapters. (The Hebrew word *ʾab*, "father, ancestor" appears about seventy times in the book, usually in the plural [*ʾābôt*] with references to ancestors in general.) For example, Deut 1:8 states a major theme for the first time: "Look, I have set the land before you. Go and possess the land that Yhwh promised to give your ancestors—Abraham, Isaac, and Jacob—and to their offspring after them." And Deut 30:20 calls for an emotive response to this generations-long story of promise and fulfillment by reminding Israel "to love Yhwh your God, to listen to his voice, and to cling to him. For that is your life and duration [literally: length of days], so that you may live on the land that Yhwh promised to give your ancestors—Abraham, Isaac, and Jacob." The book repeats these sentiments often.

Still, things are not quite this simple. The ancestors provided both positive and negative models (cf. Josh 24:2, a text deeply influenced by Deuteronomy), and each subsequent generation must choose how to live within the divine promise. Deuteronomy nuances the idea of the promise to the ancestors by calling upon its readers in each generation to reaffirm the commitment to following Yhwh. And Deut 5:2–5 puts it this way: "Yhwh our God made a covenant with us at Horeb. Yhwh did not make this covenant with our ancestors, but with us, those of us here today—all of us who are alive. Yhwh spoke face to face with you in the mountain from the middle of the fire. I was standing between Yhwh and you at that time to tell you Yhwh's word, for you feared the fire and did not ascend the mountain."

In the logic of the Pentateuch's own narrative, this text is not literally correct. The people hearing Moses at Mount Nebo are the descendants of those at Horeb (also called Sinai), and the people did not actually hear Yhwh's words but required Moses's mediation. But pointing out these so-called discrepancies misses the point. For the audience of Deuteronomy, the experience at Horeb remains part of their collective memory. Every generation of Israelites stands at Horeb receiving Torah. Each must reaffirm it by living out its code of conduct in intelligent and emotionally satisfying ways.

A useful term for this way of viewing a people's history is anamnesis, which means "reenactment" or memorial in a very broad sense. By reliving the experiences of Torah-giving at Horeb, Deuteronomy's intended audience can begin to understand itself as a covenant-keeping people. They can pass on this idea to their children. They can be, in short, a people.

Constructing peoplehood is the aim of the sermonic framework of the book, as becomes clear in the outer frame, chs 29–31. Deuteronomy follows its law code (Deut 12–26) with a call to decision along with promises and threats (Deut 27–28). As the book reflects on Israel's history, it recognizes the fatefulness of the decisions made in each generation regarding whether the community would adhere to the ethical and religious standards of the God of Israel, or not. The center of the outward frame, and in some ways the most important section of the book, Deut 30, asks a simple question: What happens if the Israelites abandon their faith and fall into the terrible situations that the covenantal curses in ch 28 envision? Is there life after death?

Deut 30 works toward a positive answer to the question in three moves. First, vv. 1–10 make an offer of reconciliation. While acknowledging Israel's failure of nerve in pursuing the life of Torah, the text asserts that all can be forgiven. Because humans naturally exist in association with one another, both sin and repentance exist in a communal setting.

Second, vv. 11–14 expand the idea of reconciliation by describing what is on offer. The choices facing Israel are "life" and "death," perhaps literally in many cases, but certainly at an existential level. By describing the way of Torah as life and the opposite as death, and by emphasizing that no heroism is required of the life of faith ("it is not in the sky... nor across the sea"; Deut 30:12–13), Deuteronomy makes clear its assumption that the laws of chs 12–26 are easier to keep than to break. At the same time, this section also emphasizes the nearness of Yhwh to the nation even in its state of punishment. Distance from the redeeming God is never a matter of physical space, but of moral and spiritual disposition.

Third, vv. 15–20 summarize the preceding offer, and as in Josh 24 and 1 Sam 8, state clearly the choices confronting the nation. Although this section does not describe a specific mechanism for keeping the covenant, it does assume that each generation of Israelites must accept the consequences of their actions.

The chapter ends by inviting its audience " to love Yahweh your God, to hear his voice, and to cling to him—for he is your life." It then promises the restoration of the land as a token of God's generous love. The relationship between Yhwh and Israel is not one of bought loyalty, but of love and longing, of clinging and communicating face to face.

The sermonic framework of Deuteronomy espouses a view of Israel's life well expressed by the Latin phrase later used to describe certain views of the Christian church, *semper reformanda*, "always to be reformed." By acknowledging that Israel's sin was both avoidable because humans choose between good and evil, but inevitable because humans often make the wrong choice, Deuteronomy offers its readers freedom to choose the norms of Torah. Rather than being consumed by shame or despair, they can move to something better.

The Torah of Deuteronomy (Deut 12:1–26:19)

The core of Deuteronomy explicates details of the covenantal norms on offer. This section of the book consists of a series of laws that order communal worship (Deut 12:2–16:17), communal leadership roles (Deut 16:18–18:22), the judiciary and military (Deut 19:1–21:9), and civil and family life (Deut 21:10–25:19). The laws take up some of the same topics seen in other law codes (especially Exod 20 + 21–23; Lev 17–27), indicating that ancient Israelites shared a basic way of thinking about how to organize a law code. Deuteronomy's set of laws concludes in ch 26 with liturgical notes, just as the Covenant Code ends in Exod 23. Consider each subsection in turn.

KNOWN ISRAELITE TEMPLES AND ALTARS

Mentioned in the Bible
Shiloh, Bethel, Shechem, Samaria, Gilgal, Mahanaim, Sinai/Horeb,
Known from Archaeology or ancient texts besides the Bible
Megiddo, Samaria, Arad, Kuntillet Ajrud (?), Beth Shemesh, Mount Gerizim/Ebal
The fact that Deuteronomy does not explicitly name Jerusalem as the locale for the one national shrine, but speaks instead of "the place where Yhwh will choose to 'put his name,'" meant that some Israelites preferred a central location on Mount Gerizim. The group that built a major temple there later came to be known as the Samaritans. But that is another story.

THE SINGLE SANCTUARY AND ITS USES (DEUT 12:2–16:17)

The most distinctive theological idea in Deuteronomy, and among its most important, is the notion that Israel should worship Yhwh in only one place. While, according to Genesis, the ancestors erected altars at many locations, Deuteronomy calls for the closing of open-air "high places" (Hebrew: *bāmôt*), which were local shrines dedicated to Yhwh or other deities. While the open-air sanctuaries used the iconography of wooden poles (Hebrew: *ʾăšērâ*, also sometimes the name of a Canaanite goddess) such as uncut or rough-cut standing stones (Hebrew: *maṣṣēbôt*) to symbolize the divine presence at a site, Deuteronomy sought a system in which the only symbols of Yhwh would be a temple, and more importantly, the people itself as it kept the covenant.

The exaltation of a single sanctuary in Jerusalem apparently met some resistance in the Judaean countryside, and the implementation of Deuteronomy's viewpoints by King Josiah (2 Kgs 22:1–23:20) did not ultimately succeed. His successors undid his work.

Deuteronomy 12 itself takes pains to justify the centralization of the cult, first by associating the open-air sanctuaries with foreign deities (even though some were also sites of the worship of Yhwh), and by criticizing their iconography (even though the patriarchs and Moses also erected "standing stones" [Hebrew: *maṣṣēbôt*] around altars; see Gen 28:18–22; 31:51; 35:15; Exod 24:4). But the most concrete problem that Deut 12 must solve involves the slaughtering and eating of animals. The most ancient practice, known throughout the Near East, was to offer a part of every animal (or at least every domesticated animal) as a sacrifice to one's god. However, just as Lev 17 presented the priestly law of sacrifice, so Deut 12 discusses a new option for ordinary Israelites. Since one cannot bring an animal to the temple for slaughter every time meat is on the menu, Deuteronomy allows a different ritual. From now on, Israelites may eat any clean animal, domesticated or wild, as long as they pour its blood on the ground (as one would do in a sacrifice).

Deuteronomy inherited a conception of animal life with several categories: animals in the human food chain vs. those not, and in each of those larger categories animals domesticated and those not. In this way of seeing the world, which revolves around a set of binary oppositions, domesticated animals in the human food chain (cows, sheep, goats, some birds) were also sacrifices, while wild animals (deer, antelopes, gazelles) were not. Deuteronomy simply splits the category of edible domesticated animals into two: animals that are sacrifices at the central sanctuary, and those that are not sacrifices because they were eaten elsewhere. By making this move, it neatly solves the most obvious practical problem created by its theology. Henceforth, Israelites should treat all animals slaughtered for food as nonsacrificial animals (i.e., wild) unless they were actually sacrificed at the central sanctuary.

At the same time, this neatness is almost too easy. Deuteronomy must also account for the feelings and memories that its audience associated with age-old practices at their holy sites. Thus it commends an attitude of "joy" (Deut 12:12), and it retains part of the old rituals of slaughter, namely, the pouring out of the animal's blood. (It is thus somewhat inappropriate to label its prescribed practice as "secular slaughter," as is often done.)

The remainder of the first legal unit, Deut 12:2–16:17, explores a series of other practical issues. These include distinctions between true and false prophecy (Deut 13:1–18); a rule against body rituals designed to appease the dead (Deut 14:1–2); the law of *kašrût* (Deut 14:3–21; cf. Lev 11); rules for tithing, debt remission, term limits on indentured servitude, and other social practices designed to care for the poor (Deut 14:22–15:18); the redemption of firstborn animals (Deut 15:19–23); and the celebration of the three major festivals of Passover, Pentecost, and Tabernacles (Deut 16:1–17; cf. Exod 23:14–17). For the most part, this material simply explicates or further develops the basic norms of the Covenant Code.

However, Deuteronomy makes its own way on two significant points. The first concerns the identification and silencing of false prophets. Deuteronomy, like the prophets whose words appear in the Bible (see notably Jer 23:9–40; 28:5–17), recognized the importance of discerning whether a given self-proclaimed prophet accurately represented the divine word in his or her speeches. They propose a series of tests. A screening test revolves around prophetic verification: if the words of the prophet do not come true, they are probably not divine in origin. This test is not foolproof because Yhwh may have a change of mind, and because prophetic speech is susceptible to multiple nonliteral interpretations.

Deuteronomy 13 therefore proposes another test. Any prophetic speech that violates the basic theological tenets of Israel's faith, notably the notion of worshiping Yhwh the redeeming God of the exodus to the exclusion of other deities, by definition cannot be authentic prophetic speech. Such speech, no matter by whom, is a capital offense in Deuteronomy's view of things. (One should remember, however, that even capital offenses in the biblical tradition could receive lesser penalties under certain circumstances; see the discussion of the law of the goring ox in this book's chapter on Exodus.) All sorts of theological discussion can happen within the boundaries of a monolatrous commitment to Yhwh, Deuteronomy seems to say.

The second space for innovation occurs at the end of this unit, when Deuteronomy rethinks the practicalities of the three major festivals (not yet as long a list as in Lev 23 and Num 28–29). The Passover lamb no longer functions as a sacrifice except in the city of the chosen sanctuary (Deut 16:5–6). Yet neither is lamb an ordinary meal, for the rules for choosing it, laid out in Exod 12, still apply. Deuteronomy thus has things both ways: the Passover remains an important ritual, but since it is now disconnected from the central sanctuary, its consumption in ordinary households makes them miniature sanctuaries of sorts. Moreover, the unleavened bread, which according to Exod 12:11 Israel ate in their haste to escape from Egypt, becomes in Deut 16:3 "the bread of suffering," a reference to the suffering and oppression Israel experienced in Egypt. In other words, the ritual food takes on a new meaning as part of the commemorative culture of Deuteronomy. Slavery and suffering figure prominently in the collective self-image that Deuteronomy tries to foster for all its readers.

COMMUNAL LEADERSHIP ROLES (16:18–18:22)

This collective memory also shapes the book's understanding of political and religious leadership, as the next section of the law code makes clear. Opening with Israel's traditional practice of local elders arbitrating disputes and punishing criminal behavior (cf.

Exod 18:1–27), Deut 16:18–18:22 assumes that only the cases involving the most serious offenses or the least clear-cut evidence reach higher courts. In Deuteronomy, the higher court consists of both elders and priests living in Jerusalem (notably, not the Israelite king, contrary to the custom of other nations of the time). Much of this legal system sounds familiar to modern ears, given our own multilayered judiciary, and the rest makes sense within an ancient agrarian culture.

More interesting is the way in which Deuteronomy sandwiches between its two descriptions of the judiciary (16:18–20 and 17:8–13) rules against erecting a cult pole or stele (Hebrew: *ʾăšērâ* and *maṣṣēbôt*; 16:21–22), sacrificing defective animals (17:1), and idolatry (17:2–7). Why stick these laws in the middle of this discussion? The answer seems to be that the text includes some of the most difficult cases that judges might face. The first and last are capital offenses, while the second is at least highly offensive because it is sacrilegious. Deuteronomy includes these laws here in its description of the legal structures because it tries to connect the pursuit of justice to the veneration of Yhwh, the God of justice. It also wishes to ensure appropriate judicial procedure, hence the requirement that at least two witnesses must support the charges in a capital case.

TWO OR THREE WITNESSES?

Biblical law requires multiple witnesses in a capital case in order to protect the rights of the accused. Yet even such a requirement can be circumvented. The suborning of witnesses is the theme of the story of Susanna, which appears in the Greek version of the book of Daniel, as well as the story of the adulterous woman that appears in late manuscripts of the Gospel of John (John 7:53–8:11) and, most relevantly, the show trial of Naboth (1 Kgs 21). On the other hand, a capital sentence could result from a confession by the defendant, as in the case of the Amalekite in 2 Sam 1.

A similar desire for balancing order and justice appears in the "law of the king" in Deut 17:14–20. While the Deuteronomistic History (Josh–2 Kgs) expresses anxiety about the capacity of monarchs for abuse of power and corruption, Deuteronomy itself permits kingship, with important restrictions. The ideal king must be Israelite and must avoid acquiring a large military apparatus, an extensive treasury (hence, tax collection system), and a large harem (hence, diplomatic ties to many states and local notables). He must also take an oath of office at his coronation, which involved writing down the law in the presence of the priests. Much of the attraction of the job, at least for those of questionable of moral rectitude, disappears in Deuteronomy's rendition of it. Given the hazards of kingship, the book seems to say, Israel should subordinate the monarchy to religion.

This section closes, then, with instructions for priests and prophets. The priests may reside anywhere in the nation, and they may receive a salary from their community. Before the centralization of the cult in Jerusalem, this salary would have been their share of the sacrifices and whatever they could grow. After the cult centralization, the local priests would face impoverishment, were it not that the biblical text provides an alternative method of supporting them. Since it is speaking of the priesthood, the text offers another subject sandwiched into its discussion, the prohibition of idolatrous practices for discerning the will of the divine realm.

Finally, Deut 18:15–22 speaks of the survival of prophecy in the Mosaic manner. While many ancient societies sought the will of the gods through reading the entrails of sacrificial animals or through stargazing or the examination of other omens, Deuteronomy imagines a sole form of communication with Yhwh, namely prophecy. For Deuteronomy, it is a method of warning human beings of danger, moral or physical. Its very ambiguity and lack of susceptibility to human control makes it an important form of communication, because engaging it requires that listeners pay close attention to the words offered as prophecy and their moral and spiritual implications.

THE JUDICIARY AND MILITARY (DEUT 19:1–21:9)

If a community must consider the characteristics of its leaders, it must also learn to control violence. Since no one has ever found a way of eliminating human violence on a large scale, any realistic legal system must deal with the problems that arise from homicide. Deuteronomy, like the other law codes in the Pentateuch, is nothing if not realistic. Thus the next section of its laws.

Deuteronomy 19 expands the Covenant Code's basic law on asylum (see Exod 21:12–14). While the original law allowed for asylum at "a place where I [Yhwh] will make for you," meaning any place that had an altar and sanctuary, Deuteronomy rethinks the law in light of its main theological idea of cult centralization. In many ancient Near Eastern cultures, temples offered asylum for someone fleeing a blood feud triggered by his or her accidental killing of a member of someone else's family. The original Israelite law simply carries on that custom. Deuteronomy, however, calls for three cities (and then six if the size of the nation's territory warrants the expansion) to be cities (not temples) of asylum. In other words, Deut 19 disconnects asylum from an altar, and an altar from asylum. Those wrongly accused of murder may find an escape from a feud without having to go to Jerusalem, while the temple remains free to be a shrine for the prayer and sacrifices of the entire people. Interestingly, the book does not forbid blood feud, perhaps because in the ancient world, where effective police forces did not exist and governments rarely intervened in family affairs, such a prohibition simply would not have worked. A similar law appears in Num 35.

The same process of revision also appears in ch 20, which offers a law for warfare. Like other biblical reflections on warfare, the law attempts to impose limits of actions undertaken in battle. The most important distinction it makes is between war within the promised land with the Canaanites and war outside it with other groups. In the former case, the rules of the *ḥerem* or so-called holy war apply, and everything must be destroyed. (See the more extended discussion in Chapter 9 on Joshua). In the latter case, and thus in the vast majority of situations, the law imposes restrictions on the execution of prisoners and destruction of property. The rule against cutting trees (Deut 20:19) is especially telling because it opposes a practice of the Assyrians. Since the core of Deuteronomy, at least as it exists today, seems to come from the Assyrian period, this reference is unsurprising.

How to make sense of this law? If we understand it as a conclusive statement on the problems of warfare, it seems easy to dismiss it as insufficient or primitive. But if we understand it more as a beginning point in a millennia-long process of reflection, culminating in laws of war distinguishing between civilians and combatants, then Deuteronomy takes its rightful place as the first step away from unrestrained savagery.

The final part of this section, Deut 21:1–9, deals with a problem that all legal systems face: the shortage of clear evidence in the event of a violent death. It provides for a ritual (not a sacrifice, because that can occur only in Jerusalem) by which a community absolves itself of responsibility. This curious little ritual, seemingly so out of place in its context, actually reveals a great deal about Deuteronomy's conception of legal responsibility. While individuals bear responsibility for crimes they commit, their communities do as well. The book thus tries to balance levels of accountability for moral failures without playing them off against each other.

CIVIL AND FAMILY LIFE (DEUT 21:10–25:19)

The same need to balance ideals with real-world possibilities shapes the next section of law, which takes up in turn a wide range of issues in everyday life. The issues seem to revolve around three major topics (as well as several minor ones): marriage, business dealings and care for the poor and vulnerable (especially widows and orphans), and bodily purity and wholeness. While many of the laws reflect life in a rural, agrarian society, the principles driving them have wider applicability, as later Jewish and Christian reflections have demonstrated. Consider each major category.

First, love and marriage. Deuteronomy includes a series of laws that prohibit husbands from humiliating their wives, whether they are captives of war (Deut 21:10–14) or simply unloved (Deut 21:15–17; 22:13–22). It allows divorce but seeks to prevent capricious exchanges of marital partners (Deut 24:1–4; cf. Matt 19:1–12; Mark 10:1–12). And it provides for the institution of the levirate marriage, a system in which a childless widow marries her dead husband's nearest relative (not his father) in order to perpetuate the dead person's lineage in an honorable way (Deut 25:5–10). Many of these rules seem deeply rooted in a patriarchal system of male privilege and female subordination. At the same time, however, the laws show some effort to take the edge off that system. For example, a false accusation of unchastity in a wife results in a staggering fine of 100 pieces of silver (cf. Deut 22:19). Such a fine would be beyond the reach of all but a handful of people, thus constituting a strong barrier to such arbitrary mistreatment of wives. Similarly, Deut 21:15–17 insists that the firstborn son, even if from an unfavored wife in a polygamous household, has the right to inherit as his birth order would otherwise dictate. In summary, Deuteronomy tries to regulate a less than ideal system. Later Jewish and Christian thinking would forbid polygamy and otherwise mitigate restrictions on the lives of women.

Second, business and money. Deuteronomy takes an uncompromising attitude toward neglecting another person's endangered animal (Deut 22:1–3), withholding small loans to a neighbor in need (Deut 23:20–21 [ET 19–20]), or using dishonest weights for measuring items in the marketplace (Deut 25:13–16). Even more centrally, the law forbids collecting a garment as collateral (Deut 24:17; cf. Amos 2:8) or the gathering of all the food in field or vineyard, both ways of insuring that the poor have basic food and protection from the elements. The warrants for the commands are especially striking and theologically significant: Israel should connect the story of its redemption from oppression in the exodus to its ongoing life. Far from being a society of winners and losers, it must aspire to something more.

The something more, from Deuteronomy's point of view, includes attention to the body and its functionality. Unlike some modern societies with their strong bias toward physical wholeness and beauty, ancient Israel's interests in bodily purity were confined to issues of sexuality and fitness for participation in worship. The two concerns intersect in rules against admitting those with genital mutilation (i.e., eunuchs; but see Isa 56) to the sanctuary (Deut 23:1),[3] as well as something as basic as building sanitary latrines (Deut 23:13–15 [ET 12–14]). It also includes rules for washing after a nocturnal emission of semen (Deut 23:11–12 [ET 12–13]). While Deuteronomy lacks Leviticus's obsession with purity of body—the distinction comes because one book concerns the life of mostly laypersons, while the other sees the life of the priests as a model for everyone else—it does try to clean up the world.

CONCLUDING LITURGICAL NOTES (DEUT 26:1–19)

To conclude the law code, Deut 12–26 moves from laws about the practical lives of people to a sketch of a ritual inaugurating life in the promised land. The ritual includes gifts of food, confession of both Israel's wrongdoing and Yhwh's gracious redemption, commitments for care for the vulnerable (including non-Israelites living with the people), and a process for perpetuating the ceremony. This end for Deuteronomy's law code says a great deal about its creators' overall sensibility. The Deuteronomists aimed to create a society marked by order, to be sure, but order that made space for human qualities of gratitude, generosity, and truth-telling. This higher aim sometimes makes the specifics of their laws seem less than adequate, creating the tension necessary for later interpretations to be generative of new meanings for the text that transcend the particularities of the society in which it originated. Was the creation of this tension deliberate? Perhaps so. Surely the various layers of Deuteronomy show an awareness that Israel could not always keep even the Torah that made concessions to human failures, as ch 30 makes clear.

Enacting the Covenant (27:1–28:69)

The law code of Deut 12–26 gives way to the first framing device for it. (The second is the sermonic framework already discussed.) The work as we have it seeks to understand the laws of chs 12–26 not just as a collection of instructions regulating the lives of people but as part of an ongoing relationship with a deity, Yhwh. This relationship, in turn, depends for its meaning on the ongoing story of that deity's world-changing redemptive work in the exodus and continued willingness to engage a human community in the messiness of its life. Therefore, chs 27–28 interpret the law as an aspect of a covenant.

One of the most disconcerting laws for modern readers is Deut 25:11–12, which prescribes mutilation as a penalty for a woman grabbing a man's genitals during a fight. The law seems out of place because ordinarily such a penalty would be reserved for causing a loss of limb in another person. Medieval Jewish commentators were also puzzled by the law and explained it as referring to extreme cases of attempting to kill or at least humiliate the man caught in such an embarrassing way. The best explanation seems to be that the law assumes an act designed to eliminate the man's ability to have children. Hence the preceding law regarding a childless dead man. (Laws were often arranged by related topics.) Later interpretations of the law assumed that a monetary fine could substitute for removal of a hand, much as in other laws (see the discussion of the goring ox in Exodus).

The term "covenant" (Hebrew: *běrît*) appears in Deuteronomy many times (Deut 4:13, 23, 31; 5:2, 3; 7:2, 9, 12; 8:18; 17:2; 9:9, 11, 15; 10:8; 28:69; 29:8, 11, 13, 20, 24; 31:9, 16, 20, 25, 26; 33:9), and in every major section. Curiously, however, it appears in the legal material itself only once, in Deut 17:2, where violation of the covenant happens during an act of idolatry. For the most part, the references to the covenant occur in the framing material as a way of understanding the law code as a whole.

But what is a covenant? In ancient Near Eastern politics, states made treaties between themselves in which an overlord or suzerain imposed a set of obligations on a weaker power. The weaker king called the more powerful one "father" and promised to "love" him (meaning that the weaker king would not rebel or forget to pay tribute). Violating the suzerainty treaty could lead to severe penalties and was regarded as a morally reprehensible act (see 2 Kgs 17:1–4). Deuteronomy picks up this literary form but radically transforms it. No longer were the covenant partners two states with the gods as witnesses, but a deity and a people. The combination of curses and blessings shapes the Deuteronomic view of the relationship between Israel and Yhwh. Their relationship is asymmetrical in that the deity is much more powerful, and therefore much more responsible, than the human collective.

A Rolling Epilogue (Deut 32:1–34:12)

The book concludes with two poems, both older than the rest of the work, and with the death scene of Moses, probably the latest part of the book. However, the conclusion fits together as a carefully worked-together whole. It forms a final valediction of a great hero, comparable to those for Jacob (Gen 49), Joshua (Josh 23–24), Samuel (1 Sam 12), and David (2 Sam 22). Therefore it constitutes not just an end to Deuteronomy but to the

Pentateuch as a whole, and to an entire era in Israel's history as the people remembered it. The first poem calls upon the heavenly bodies to bear witness to Yhwh's ongoing dealings with Israel, a relationship marked by human sin, divine punishment, and ultimate deliverance. Like many texts in the prophetic books, Deut 32 uses the idea of transcendental realities as witness to the divine action because it wants to say that the story of Israel deserves commemoration and reflection without being subject to the fragility of human memory and human perspective. While older scholars tended to think of this text as a "covenant lawsuit," the arguments for this hypothesis are not very strong. It is an old poem, probably from the time before the foundation of the monarchy (though it assumes the settlement in the land as a past event, not a future one), as indicated by the archaic nature of its Hebrew. The poem, called in Jewish circles *Ha'azinu* ("let us hear," after its opening line), tries to interpret Israel's history after the time of Moses. So, in the context of Deuteronomy, the poem is a foreshadowing of things to come.

> The most famous textual variant in Deut 32, and maybe in the whole book, occurs in v. 8. The Masoretic Text, the standard medieval Hebrew text, speaks of the division of the world according to the "number of Israel's children," a reading that makes very little sense. The Septuagint or LXX, the ancient Greek translation of the Hebrew Bible, reads "according to the children of Elohim," which would mean that Yhwh created the world and then assigned to various deities or heavenly beings each a portion of it. The MT reading is almost certainly an editorial correction of an older reading that now survives in the LXX but was originally in Hebrew manuscripts as well. Probably, the later scribes responsible for the MT thought of the alternative reading as opening the door to polytheism, and so they altered it.

Meanwhile, Deut 33 offers an alternative view of Israel's potential. It is a blessing, and appears here to complement and counterbalance the more morally bracing text of ch 32. The combination of these poems, so different in tone and intent, create a message that is richer than either part alone could be. That message fits well with the overall tone of the rest of the book, which calls Israel to decision—will your story be one of judgment and failure or one of blessing and success?

The final scene, then, involves Moses's death. Deuteronomy forestalls any notion of finding the great man's tomb and creating a funerary cult around a shrine for him. The lawgiver's only legacy must remain the law itself and the redemptive relationship with Yhwh on which it rests. So ends one of the great masterpieces of biblical theology.

Implications

What makes Deuteronomy such a masterpiece? Perhaps a better way is to ask what ideas does it emphasize and why are they important? The key ideas of the book include the "choice" of the single sanctuary, the importance of "keeping" and "doing" Torah, the obligation of covenant-keeping, the shaping of the human-divine relationship in terms of forgiveness and obligation, and the unshakeable conviction that Yhwh alone is the one God. Yet, again, it is not possible to reduce Deuteronomy to a collection of ideas because the book seeks to foster in its readers a set of attitudes, values, commitments, and behaviors that transcend merely intellectual pursuits.

Notes

1. Georg Braulik, *The Theology of Deuteronomy*, trans. Ulrika Lindblad (North Richland Hills, TX: BIBAL, 1994).

2. Just how much is a matter of considerable dispute. A good case can be made for a form of the book that includes chs 5–26 + 28, more or less. Such a work would have made sense to a king as a basis for religious reform. The sermonic material in chs 1–4 and 29–31 would then have been added sometime later. But this is not the only possibility. For an excellent and accessible treatment of the issues, see Ziony Zevit, "Deuteronomy in the Temple: An Exercise in Historical Imagining," in *Mishneh Todah: Studies in Deuteronomy and Its Cultural Environment in Honor of Jeffrey H. Tigay*, ed. Nili Sacher Fox, David A. Glatt-Gilad, and Michael J. Williams (Winona Lake, IN: Eisenbrauns, 2009), 201–218.

3. Isa 56 interacts with both Deut 23 and Ezek 44, in effect rewriting the law to allow gentiles to enter the Temple provided that they come there to pray. Some foreshadowing of this broader attitude also appears in at least one text influenced by Deuteronomy, namely 1 Kgs 8:41–43, though that text applies to foreigners from "far away," that is, people with no background of neighborly betrayal. For a discussion of the techniques of interbiblical exegesis in Isa 56, see Joachim Schaper, "Rereading the Law: Inner-Biblical Exegesis of Divine Oracles in Ezekiel 44 and Isaiah 56," in *Recht und Ethik im Alten Testament*, ed. Bernard M. Levinson, Eckart Otto, and Walter Dietrich (Münster: LIT, 2004), 125–144.

For Further Reading

Braulik, Georg. *The Theology of Deuteronomy*. Translated by Ulrika Lindblad. North Richland Hills, TX: BIBAL, 1994.

Plant, Ian M. "The Influence of Forensic Oratory on Thucydides' Principles of Method." *Classical Quarterly* (NS) 49 (1999): 62–73.

Tigay, Jeffrey H. *Deuteronomy*, JPS Torah Commentary. Philadelphia: Jewish Publication Society, 1996.

8 Israelite Historiography

> History, which interprets the past to understand the present and confront the future, is the
> least rewarding discipline for a dying species.
>
> —P. D. JAMES, The Children of Men

THERE IS NO universally accepted way of writing history, in part because historians attempt to explain things, unlike antiquarians who simply collect facts and repeat them often without understanding their significance. As Henry Steele Commager stated, "history . . . collects and organizes such facts [about the past] as are available and relevant, provides some kind of framework for them, and lays down the guidelines for the presentation. It supplies order, harmony, direction, for what might otherwise be a chaotic assemblage of miscellaneous facts."[1] Moreover, Commager notes that the historical record is full of biases and lacunae. This does not mean that history is what we make it—far from it, since some things happened and others did not. But it does mean that our understanding of the past needs ongoing revision.

For the Old Testament, there are two major historiographic works. Each "collects and organizes" information from a range of sources and "provides some kind of framework for them." Modern scholars call the first work the Deuteronomistic History (Josh, Judg, 1–2 Sam, and 1–2 Kgs) and the second the Chronistic History (1–2 Chron, with Ezra and Neh being related but independent). While other parts of the Hebrew Bible recount Israel's past, these two major works carry the weight of the task.

They do differ from each other in many ways, as will become clear. But perhaps the greatest difference lies in an overall attitude toward the past. For the Deuteronomistic History, or DH, Israel's past consists of disconcerting misadventures (with a few bright spots), culminating in the disasters of the ends of the states of Israel and Judah in 722 and 586 BCE respectively. Even great figures such as David and Solomon come off in this work as troubled men whose very talent contains within it the seeds of their failure. Like the heroes of Greek tragedies, all the characters in the DH are flawed. For the Chronicler, or CH, however, some parts of that history seem rosier. David and Solomon, as well as some other figures in the DH appear in the CH as more pious, less violent, more self-aware and more admirable figures.

This overall difference in understanding of the past profoundly shapes how each work is written, meaning which facts are selected for presentation, which stories are omitted, and so on. Why? In part, the difference arises from the different needs of the creators of these great works. Put simply, the DH asks on behalf of Israelites experiencing the devastation of their culture: "How did we reach this state?" The CH, written later and using the DH as one of its primary sources, asks a different question: "Have we any precedents that will allow us to flourish now that we have found ourselves back home?" With many qualifications and nuances, these questions help a reader understand many of the details of these books.

History behind the History-Writing

If these writers and their sources were reconstructing a history of their people, one should ask what can be known about that history. To answer that, one might investigate several dimensions of history.

ISRAEL'S ENVIRONMENT

One should start with the longest terms of history, at which human life is an ongoing response to the physical environment. To be specific, the land of Israel lies along the Mediterranean coast near the intersection of Asia and Africa. As such, it is situated at a major crossroads for human migration going back many millennia. The land itself lies within several geological and climatic zones. The coastal plain, like most of the Mediterranean coast, is fertile for a few miles inland, dotted (before modern drainage) with swamps and hospitable to olives, grapes, and a range of fruit-bearing trees and vegetables. Running parallel to the plain lies a range of steep hills and narrow valleys, the Central Hill Country. Running again north to south dissecting the hilly flanks of the Mediterranean coast, the Jordan River waters a deep valley, itself part of a group of related though distinct faults extending south as far as Mozambique. The fault in Syria-Palestine contained a series of lakes connected by the Jordan River. Two of these lakes figure prominently in the Bible, the Lake of Kinneret in the north (better known as the Sea of Galilee) and the Dead Sea in the south. The first is fresh water and has hosted fishing for millennia. The Dead Sea, meanwhile, has earned that somber name owing to its hypersalinity (more than eight times that of the oceans). Only microscopic creatures can live in it. Because it lies more than 1,200 feet below sea level, and is thus the lowest spot on the Earth's surface, the southern lake has no drainage. Only evaporation keeps it from overflowing. The Jordan Valley was a single lake as recently as the end of the last Ice Age (ca. 12,000 years ago), but in the historical period it has become a zone of alternating semidesert, thickets (north of the Dead Sea), and farmland. East of the valley lies the hill country of biblical Ammon and Moab.

In historical times, the rainfall map of the land of Israel essentially shows increasing drying as one moves south and west. Thus farmers in the Galilee and as far south as Jerusalem can practice terraced agriculture on the hillsides, relying on a combination of rainfall and water stored in cisterns to make do. Farther south in the Negev, the desert conditions make farming possible only through extensive irrigation, a practice that existed on a sustained basis during the Byzantine period (prior to the seventh century CE) and after the foundation of the modern state of Israel. Both there and in rainier parts of the land, the husbanding of goats and sheep became a primary source of meat, fiber, milk, and fuel (dung).

A life revolving around the agricultural year repeats many actions. Days began with the drawing of water from the spring or well and eating a simple meal of bread, baked on a hot stone or in a small clay oven, coupled with available fruits or vegetables. Farmers continued with the work of the seasons, plowing, hoeing, harvesting, storing. And while some tasks may have followed old patterns assigned by gender or age (young girls hauling water, as does Rebekah for Abraham's servant in Gen 24:15–27, or teenage boys hunting for lost donkeys as does Saul in 1 Sam 9), others involved everyone physically capable of carrying them out, as with Ruth's harvesting of the grain alongside the young men (Ruth 2).

Even those living in cities engaged in similar patterns of life, though there the occupations available were more diverse, including the roles of potters (the small changes of whose artisanship allows archaeologists to date sites), jewelers, leatherworkers, and other crafts, including the craft of government with its scribes keeping records, soldiers collecting taxes or defending the ramparts, or kings building their harems or dreaming of war or peace. Goods and services moved long and short distances without the benefit of money or bills of credit. Yet in the cities the opportunities for diversion were perhaps wider and the subjects of conversation more interesting. Much of this life continued in the same patterns for centuries.

Like all people before the invention of the railroad and the steamship in the nineteenth century, ancient citizens of Canaan, later Israel, moved only as fast as foot or sail could move them. In some periods, such as the Persian Empire with its well-made roads for couriers and especially in the later Roman Empire with paved roads and bridges, some of which are still in use after two millennia, transportation overland could be at least predictable, if not fast. But overland travel was a difficult way to move goods more than fairly short distances (except as tribute), although trade by caravan did exist at least as early as 2000 BCE with the movement of wool and tin between Anatolia and Mesopotamia. Other goods traveled by sea, whether bronze ingots from the Near East to the west, or with cedars from Lebanon to Egypt (already in the third millennium or even earlier). Shipwrecks from the second and first millennia contain cargoes not only of metal but also of wine and opiates.

There is no way to measure the relative amount of the ancient economies that revolved around trade, especially international, long-distance trade, and most of the movement must have involved high-end luxury goods. And ideas, of course, such as the alphabet that Phoenician traders brought to the Greeks by 1200 BCE or thereabouts. The patterns of movement created by the currents of the Mediterranean and the shapes of mountain ranges and rivers profoundly influenced Israel and its neighbors, even if most people never moved more than a few dozen miles from the village in which they were born.

HISTORY IN THE MIDDLE TERM

None of this should lead one to think, however, that history did not move for the ancients. It simply means that history moves at several paces all at once. The middle pace is one of social organization, that of tribes and kingdoms, family structures, and religious practices. Ancient Israel began its existence as a series of kinship groups, sometime around 1250 BCE or earlier, and acquired a state only in the tenth century. Individuals lived as parts of families, which were themselves part of larger kinship groups sometimes conventionally called clans and still larger groups called tribes.

For most of a person's life, the primary reference point was the small kinship group, the one to three generation family living in a single house or small cluster of houses. The larger clan assembled at holidays or life transition events (births, marriages, deaths), and clans were localized to one or a few villages or cities. Tribal identity was evidently less central and may not have existed in many ancient Near Eastern cultures at all, especially those in which the city (or city-state in Mesopotamia) became a sort of substitute kinship reference point. Tribal groups began as all the kinship units in a given area and who claimed a single ancestor as part of their self-understanding (but even if genetic testing, were it available, would have shown a very different history). These groups do exist for ancient Israel (the famous twelve tribes), for second-millennium Mari (Tell Ḥariri), a city on the Middle Euphrates, and for Babylonia in the first millennium, among other places. These larger units came into play during warfare (Judg 19–20; 1 Sam 10–11) and perhaps in religious festivals. They formed part of the self-identity of individuals vis-à-vis others (see 1 Sam 10:20–21; cf. Judg 5:13–18; 6:15).

Atop this family structure, or rather alongside it, lay the apparatus of the state. The term "state" means the governmental structures larger than a kinship unit that collected taxes (in precious metals, grain, or even days of public labor or corvée) and redistributed wealth either directly to its key officials or less directly in the form of monumental architecture such as palaces, fortresses, city walls, or in irrigation and drainage canals in Mesopotamia or Egypt. States arose certainly by the end of the fourth millennium BCE, and probably earlier, though the absence of writing before about 3200 BCE makes the politics of the time uncertain. States coexisted with tribes and clans, often using the older form of social organization as mediators for the needs of the whole.

History of Events

At the most rapidly moving level of history flows the stream of events, around which people structure their lives. The most dramatic events relate to warfare, and the prevalence of stories of battle and the struggle of peoples in ancient and modern literature reflects that fact. The Bible, in particular, arose in response to a few key sieges and battles that made their mark. Yet its ancient authors marked time by other events, so, for example, the book of Amos is dated in reference to a now unknown earthquake (Amos 1:1).

We will discuss the many historical events to which the Bible refers in appropriate places later, but for now a few reference points deserve attention.

Several key military events turned the course of history such as the battles of Qarqar (853), Megiddo (609), and Carchemish (605), and the sieges of Samaria (722) and Jerusalem (701, unsuccessfully, but 586 all too so). In particular, the destruction of Judah and the deportation of some of its population by the Babylonians in the early 580s, which led to the so-called Babylonian exile, made an impact on Israelite history still reverberating today. It would be difficult to exaggerate the impact of that single event on biblical literature, and thus on the practices and beliefs of Jews and Christians even now.

The Deuteronomistic History (DH)

The next few chapters will discuss the first work of Israel's history writing, the DH. This work includes Joshua, Judges, 1–2 Samuel, and 1–2 Kings. Although it includes many sources of various dates, this work draws heavily for its final shaping on the book of Deuteronomy, whose basic ideas it reflects. Like Deuteronomy, the DH interprets Israel's history as a struggle to keep covenant with the God who liberated Israel in the exodus. This viewpoint is clearest in the parts of the work written largely by the Deuteronomistic historians themselves rather than their sources, especially in such speeches as in 1 Kgs 8 and Josh 24.

The basic architecture of the book is clear enough: Joshua tells the story of the settlement of Israel in the promised land; Judges recounts the decades of conflict and confusion before the monarchy; Samuel the rise of kingship in the persons of Saul and especially David, and Kings of the division of Israel into two entities (the kingdoms of Israel in the north and Judah in the south). In other words, the storyline moves from an entrance into Canaan to an exit from it, from the destruction of the autochthonous settlers to the destruction of their successors. For the DH, all of this movement, spanning perhaps six centuries, results from Israel's success and then failure at observing the covenant proposed in Deuteronomy (see table 8.1).

TABLE 8.1

Chronology (all dates BCE)	The larger world	Israelite events	Selected inscriptional evidence
1300–1000	End of Egyptian New Kingdom; collapse of Late Bronze state system	Formation of Tribes in land	Merneptah stele
1000–850 or slightly later	Formation of new states in Syria, Phoenicia, and Anatolia	Creation of Israelite state(s)	Dan Inscription
850–722	Rise of Assyria to dominance in Near East	Rise, decline, and fall of Israel, rise of Judah	Many Israelite, Moabite, Mesopotamian, and Aramaean texts
722–586	Assyrian dominance and after 605 Babylonian Empire	Judah as client state and then its destruction	Lachish and Arad ostraca, Kuntillet Ajrud graffiti
586–late 500s	Collapse of Babylonia and Rise of Persian Empire	Judah/Yehud and Israel/Samerina part of larger empires	Babylonian texts
539–334	Persian Empire	Several small sub-provinces inhabited by Israelites	Elephantine and Wadi Daliyeh Papyri
334–165	Alexander and successors	Provincial status continues in new empires	Coins, earliest Dead Sea Scrolls
165–63	Seleucid and Ptolemaic empires vie for control of Near East; Roman rise	Independent Jewish state	Same

The time of the DH's origin is debated. The final version postdates the year 562 BCE, which is the date of the last recorded event in the work. The reality of the deportations of the early sixth century BCE informs the work at many points. At the same time, not only are many of the sources of the work earlier (or even much earlier) but its overall structure does not necessarily point to an exilic or postexilic context. Accordingly, many scholars have argued that an earlier edition of Joshua–Kings (or Deuteronomy–Kings), including most of the material in it, dates from the reign of Josiah (ca. 640–610 BCE) and reflects the optimism of that era as Assyria passed from the scene and Judah's future seemed more secure. For these scholars, the references to the nation's demise come from a second edition of the work. Other scholars are more skeptical of this Josianic edition, while recognizing that the final creators of the work employed extensive sources available to them.

The Chronicler's History (CH)

As Chapter 14 makes clear, 1–2 Chronicles abridges and revises the DH with an aim at reclaiming the sordid picture of the older work for a new time. The newer work celebrates the achievements of David and Solomon, downplaying their failures and thereby present-ing them as new, more pious and admirable characters. This recharacterization of the past extends farther into the CH's almost complete erasure of the Northern Kingdom of Israel (except to note its corrupting influence on the Southern Kingdom and then its demise), and its expansion of the DH's stories of good kings such as Hezekiah. Through many subtle changes, the CH presents a cleaner view of the past than the DH, emphasiz-ing less the sins of leaders than their capacities for repentance.

It might seem strange that the Bible would include two works covering much the same ground, with one citing the other verbatim in many places. A revision of a work implies two things: that the work deserves attention and respect, and, conversely, that it does not deserve so much respect as to make it unchangeable. If imitation is the sincerest form of flattery, revision may be a close second.

Other Historiographical Works

In addition to these major works, the Hebrew Bible also includes Ezra and Nehemiah, books that continue the story of the community centered in Jerusalem and its immediate environs (the subprovince of Yehud) into the fifth century BCE. While closely associ-ated with the CH in some ways, these shorter works seem to have originated separately from it.

The LXX also includes other historical books, notably 1–4 Maccabees (or at least some of those works, depending on which Greek manuscript one considers). These works, written between the second century BCE and, in their latest stages, the first century CE, describe events leading up to and resulting from the Maccabean revolt against Hellenistic rule in the 160s BCE (see Chapter 30).

Conclusions

The biblical books to be examined in the next few chapters thus arose over a period of centuries, through successive crises in Israel's relationships with its neighbors. Like all intellectually significant works, they sought to influence that history in their own ways, and they did so by fashioning a usable narrative out of their oral and written sources.

The creators of these texts did not write simply because they found the past interesting (even though it is). They wrote because they thought doing so mattered in a world in which their people was a small, vulnerable group whose past seemed problematic even to itself. By relating that past, even in its least attractive moments, the creators of these texts sought to find rewards for a species they wished to keep from dying.

Note

1. Henry Steele Commager, *The Study of History* (Columbus: Merrill, 1980), 3.

For Further Reading

Aḥituv, Shmuel. *Echoes from the Past: Hebrew and Cognate Inscriptions from the Biblical Period*. Jerusalem: Carta, 2008.

Cohen, Susan. "Cores, Peripheries, and Ports of Power: Theories of Canaanite Development in the Early Second Millennium B.C.E." In *Exploring the* Longue Durée: *Essays in Honor of Lawrence E. Stager*, edited by J. David Schloen, 69–75. Winona Lake, IN: Eisenbrauns, 2009.

Hallo, William W., ed. *The Context of Scripture*. Vol. 1: *Canonical Compositions from the Biblical World*. Leiden: Brill, 2003.

Iggers, Georg. *Historiography in the Twentieth Century: From Scientific Objectivity to the Postmodern Challenge*. 2nd ed. Middletown, CT: Wesleyan University Press, 2005.

Leprohon, Ronald J. "What Wenamun could Have Bought: The Value of His Stolen Goods." In *Egypt, Israel, and the Ancient Mediterranean World: Studies in Honor of Donald B. Redford*, edited by Gary N. Knoppers and Antoine Hirsch, 167–177. Leiden: Brill, 2004.

Smith, Mark S. *The Early History of God: Yahweh and the Other Deities in Ancient Israel*. 2nd ed. Grand Rapids, MI: W. B. Eerdmans, 2002.

9 A New Land and a New People
THE BOOK OF JOSHUA

Key Text: *"Then Joshua built an altar for Yhwh Israel's God at Mount Ebal, just as Moses, Yhwh's servant, had commanded Israel's children, according to the writing of the book of Moses's Torah. It was an altar of stones unhewn by iron, and they placed on it whole burnt offerings to Yhwh (and they also sacrificed offerings of well-being). Then he wrote there on the stones the copy of Moses's law, which he [i.e., Moses] had written before Israel's children. And all Israel, its elders and attendants and judges, both aliens and citizens, were standing here and there around the Ark [of the Covenant] before the priests and Levites, the bearers of the Ark of the Covenant. Half of them were on Mount Gerizim and half on Mount Ebal, just as Moses, Yhwh's servant, had commanded. This was in order to bless the people of Israel at the beginning. Later, [Joshua] called all the words of the Torah, the blessings and the curses, everything written in the Book of the Torah. Joshua did not fail to read before the entire community—women, children, and everyone approaching them—of Israel a single word from everything that Moses had commanded."* (Josh 8:30–35)[1]

Is the past really done, or can it sometimes also provide a model for the future? This question occupies the book of Joshua. As Charlton Heston put it in the old movie, *The Ten Commandments*, "It would take more than a man to lead the slaves from Egypt. It would take a god." In the narrative world of Joshua, Yhwh has led the slaves from Egypt, and now they must come to the promised land. Yet their leader, Moses, has died (at the end of Deuteronomy, and so a new arrangement for mediating divine activity must appear. His name is Joshua.

The book of Joshua opens the DH with the story of the post-Mosaic age, the settlement of Israel in the promised land and their commitment to keeping the covenant recorded in "the book of Moses's [or God's] Torah" (Josh 1:7, 8; 8:31–34; 23:6; 24:26). The book both gathers together the basic theological ideas of Deuteronomy and anticipates those worked out in the historical work that follows. Joshua, in short, anticipates much of what follows in Joshua–2 Kings.

ON THE ORIGINS OF THE DEUTERONOMISTIC HISTORY

It has long been obvious that Genesis–2 Kings tells a continuous story, sometimes called the Primary History. A subset of that history tells the story of Israel's life as a nation in its own land. This work, comprising the books of Joshua, Judges, 1–2 Samuel, and 1–2 Kings, contains stories, lists, songs, and speeches describing the people's history over perhaps six centuries.

How did this work come together? Since the 1940s, scholars have noted that at key points, Joshua–2 Kings resorts to language that sounds much like Deuteronomy. The conclusion to be drawn from that fact is that at some point, one or more persons deeply influenced by Deuteronomy had edited the material together in a more or less coherent way. Most of these works do not sound like Deuteronomy and thus seem to be older than the final version of the material. And because the characters in the stories do not always behave as Deuteronomy would recommend, even when the text itself commends them, indicates that the stories took shape earlier than the time of this revision. In other words, the Deuteronomistic creators of the work used their sources conservatively, preserving viewpoints they did not themselves accept fully.

There are at least two basic ways of understanding the literary history of the work. In one view, a major edition of Joshua–Kings dates to the reign of Josiah, while a second and more negative revision occurred after the debacle of the destruction of Jerusalem in 586 BCE. A second explanation thinks of a single moment of editing, probably later in the sixth century and probably with a freer hand in reworking stories or creating them more or less out of whole cloth. The book you are reading does not take a stand on this question but simply notes throughout when the Deuteronomistic voice is heard and when it is not.

For example, while the character Joshua appears in this work as the successor of Moses and not as a monarch, he does take on several roles usually associated with kings: conquering warrior, builder of altars for nationwide worship, and enforcer of laws. By emphasizing his practice of all these kingly roles, the book casts Joshua as the forebear of its great heroes, David and Josiah. At the same time, however, Joshua is manifestly not a king, and so the DH is setting up a contrast that it will work through at various points in 1–2 Samuel and 1–2 Kings as well. Like David and Josiah, but unlike most other rulers, Joshua defeats the enemies of Israel, while also worshiping Yhwh in ways of which the DH approves.[2]

MOSES IN THE BOOK OF JOSHUA

The book of Joshua mentions Moses about forty-eight times, often in connection with his role as a lawgiver and especially in his plan for the settlement of the tribes in their various homelands (see Josh 1:2–17; 3:7; 4:10–14; 8:31–35; 9:24: 11:12–23; 12:6; 13:8–33; 14:3–11; 17:4; 18:7; 22:2–7; 24:5). By mentioning the now deceased hero, whom the DH and perhaps its sources see as the very model of a prophet revealing the key truths of faith in Yhwh, the book of Joshua wishes to connect its portrayal of an ideal Israel to its understanding of Torah. In other words, it seems to say that, yes, the Torah can function in the real world. The emphasis does not fall so much on the personality of Moses, or of Joshua for that matter, but on the crucial nature of the law of Moses and the commitment to keeping that law that underlies the DH's understanding of what Israel should be.

The book itself, like all of Israel's historical works, incorporates large stretches of older material into its narrative, adding occasional statements that connect those sources both to Deuteronomy and to later stories. In the form that has come down through time, the book follows a clear outline:

A. Initial events of Israel's settlement in Canaan (Josh 1:1–12:24)
B. The distribution of the land among the tribes (13:1–22:45)
C. Concluding speeches by Joshua (23:1–24:28)
D. Joshua's Death (24:29–33)

Each of these parts has its own purpose and method of working up source material. In Part A, most of the stories predate the Deuteronomists and seem to reflect old traditions about the initial relationships of Israel to surrounding cultures. Part B, meanwhile, seems to contain both early and later material, not easily sorted out. It also includes stories that connect Joshua to the book of Numbers, indicating some sort of interest in priestly traditions about how Israel and its Canaanite neighbors interacted. The two major speeches in Part C (Josh 23:1–16; 24:1–28) both include elements that sound like Deuteronomy, but both also include both pre- and post-Deuteronomistic elements as well. In short, then, sorting out the history of the development of Joshua as a book is no easy matter. This fact may not matter much for its interpretation except when we come to the problem of the book's interest in the elimination of Canaanite culture. That the book seems to take more than one view probably reflects the complex way in which it came together.

Initial Events of Israel's Settlement in Canaan (Josh 1:1–12:24)

Joshua picks up where Deuteronomy left off, with the death of Moses. Yet, for the DH, a new chapter in history has begun, with the old promises of Yhwh to Israel now taking the form not of unfulfilled commitments but of impending realities.

The opening verses make the DH's sense of periodization clear:

After Moses, Yhwh's servant, died, Yhwh said to Joshua son of Nun, Moses's assistant, "Moses my servant is dead. So now, get up, cross this Jordan, you and all this people, to a land that I am giving to them [i.e., Israel's children]. Every place that the soles of your feet touch I will give you, just as I said to Moses." (Josh 1:1–3)

The key elements of the book's theology of history appear in these opening lines: divine guidance of the leader, a divinely designated succession of leaders, the completeness of Israel's investment in the promised land, and the continuity of the past with the future. By couching the entire period of settlement as an errand out of the wilderness, the DH creates a baseline for understanding all of Israel's subsequent history. Since the DH as a work came together during the late monarchy through the so-called exilic period, that is, during a period of intense political and military struggle and the constant presence of foreign invaders, with the ultimate loss of Israel's political independence and the accompanying crisis in religion resulting from the challenge to Yhwh's rule of the cosmos. In short, by reminding the readers of a glorious past that preceded a terrible decline, the DH poses the possibility of a glorious future based on the same terms.

This past that could be a future takes the form of a series of stories about battles and worship events. The first segments of the overall unit describe a campaign in the middle of Canaan, at the border zone between what later became the kingdoms of Israel and Judah. The text then turns farther south and, in a brief report in ch 11, to the north. The following outline charts the plot line of these chapters:

1. Preparations for entering the land (1:1–18)
2. Rahab insinuates herself into Israelite protection (2:1–24)
3. The miraculous parting of the Jordan (3:1–17)
4. Commemorating the crossing (4:1–24)
5. Preparing the Israelite males for battle (5:1–15)
6. The battle of Jericho (6:1–27)
7. Aftermath of Jericho: Achan's sin (7:1–26)
8. The battle of Ai (8:1–29)
9. The reading of the law (8:30–35)
10. The Gibeonites insinuate themselves into Israelite protection (9:1–27)
11. Additional southern campaigns (10:1–43)
12. A northern campaign (11:1–15)
13. Summation of Joshua's campaigns (11:16–12:24)

Although it is difficult to discern a rigid structure to the sequence of these stories, the repetition of themes reflects a concerted attempt by the book's creators to build in a high degree of coherence among them. Thus various sections resemble each other (2 ≈ 10, 5 ≈ 9, 6 ≈ 8), thus forming a loose nesting of stories a bit like those small Russian dolls sold in airport shops. The overall story sounds less like an invasion than a sort of pilgrimage festival, with the fighting being almost incidental to the arrival of the Israelite horde in its divinely delegated land.

The stories themselves deserve some attention. To paraphrase: Joshua sends spies to Jericho, just west of the Jordan River, in order to ascertain proper ways of invading the country. They find hospitality in the house of a prostitute, one Rahab, who is perhaps accustomed to the visits of strange men and who shows a remarkable grasp of the situation. With a speech that allows the narrator to reflect on the core story of Israel's occupation of Canaan, Rahab says,

> I know that Yhwh has given you the land and that we are all frightened of you. Every inhabitant of the land is trembling before you. We heard that Yhwh has evaporated the waters of the Sea of Reeds before you when you came from Egypt, and also what you did to the two Amorite kings across the Jordan, Sihon and Og, when you massacred them. Yes, we heard and our hearts melted and not one of us could catch our breath because of you, because Yhwh your God is God in the sky above and the earth below. (Josh 2:9–11)

That is, she plays the age-old role of the wise woman who speaks the key lines in the narrative to shed light on its true meaning (cf. 1 Sam 14:1–20). That she is a gentile makes her theologically rich speech all the more remarkable as the book of Joshua seeks to avoid a merely parochial telling of its story.

In any case, the spies return to tell the tale and to commit their people to rescuing Rahab from the impending conflagration. The battle of Jericho will proceed not by siege but through a ritualized procession of the army around the beleaguered city, once a day for six days and then seven times on the Sabbath (Josh 6:1–27) . . . but not before the text has interrupted its story of warfare with a long discussion of the Israelite army's preparations for battle.

Joshua 3–5 explores the warlike preparations; chs 3–4 tell the story of a miraculous crossing of the Jordan and the commemoration of the parting of the river by the erection of a pile of stones, much in the vein of Deuteronomy's emphasis on memorial-making as a method of educating future generations. The procession of the Ark of the Covenant first with the priests and then with a representative of each of the twelve tribes creates a field-day atmosphere. Yet the party has a serious purpose. The occupation of the land, the narrative asserts, will not result from mere human tactical superiority or strategic insight but from divine activity. This superhuman dimension of the battle, which is in fact a widespread presupposition of many ancient cultures' conceptions of warfare, necessitates human preparation. Hence ch 5's description of the circumcision of all the males prior to battle. Israel must be prepared.

THE BOOK OF JOSHUA AND HISTORICAL ACCURACY

Joshua reports the destruction of Jericho and Hazor, among other sites, leaving the initial impression that Israel swooped into Canaan and conquered the land in a brief period of time. However, this picture does not fit the archaeological record. While the massive citadel of Hazor was destroyed around 1200 BCE, possibly but not necessarily by the Israelites,

Jericho was unfortified at that period. Other sites remained Canaanite well into the Iron I period (ca. 1200–1000 BCE). So one cannot read Joshua as a straightforward account of a massive horde overwhelming a native population. History simply did not unfold in this way.

The book of Joshua itself seems to reveal an awareness of the issue because it also tells stories of Canaanite survivors. It seems best, then, to understand its summary lists as a literary device, a way of telescoping periods of time, perhaps long periods of time at that. The intent of a list like that at the end of ch 12 is less to report a time period than to underscore the scope of Israel's occupation. Note, for example, that Josh 12's list of defeated kings includes the city-state rulers of Jerusalem and Gezer, which came under Israelite control during the reigns of David and Solomon respectively. That is, the text seems more interested in geographical comprehensiveness than temporal precision.

Unfortunately, the aftermath of the siege of Jericho is the defeat at the minor site of Ai (literally, "the ruin"), a disaster owing to the violation, by one Achan, of the taboo against taking booty. The rule of the *ḥērem* (sometimes misleadingly translated "holy war") demanded the complete destruction of all persons and objects in a conquered territory. Achan's violation of the rule by keeping precious metals and clothes for himself led to the defeat of the people, a defeat repaired by the execution of the perpetrator and appropriate penitential rites.

In any case, the story continues with other warlike events, including the conquest of several Canaanite city-states and the adoption of one group into Israel's ambit. This group, the citizens of Gibeon, pretend to "have come from a faraway land" and then request a treaty ("covenant") with the Israelites (Josh 9:6). This ruse succeeds to such a degree that even when the Israelites catch the Gibeonites out, the deal stands. The story typifies what must have been a much more common phenomenon of local (Canaanite) groups assimilating into Israel in various ways (cf. Josh 16:10; 17:12–13; cf. 1 Kgs 9:20–21), albeit in reduced circumstances. Love and trade often trump religious ideals.

In any case, all these stories of conflict and assimilation impress on the reader Israel's success at occupying much of its land thanks to Joshua's leadership. However, the book is not satisfied with mere annals of conquest in the manner of ancient royal inscriptions. Instead, it must think through its narrative from a theological point of view. Accordingly, interspersed throughout the narrative are prayers (e.g., Josh 7:6–9) and other theological reflections. The most extensive discussion occurs in Josh 8:30–35 and highlights the strong connection between Moses's (or rather, Yhwh's) promises to Israel and their fulfillment in the settlement in the land. The theological lens through which the Deuteronomistic editors look at their stories is one of promise and fulfillment, with human action being a necessary but far from sufficient component of the divine action.

THE CASE OF THE CANAANITES: DIVINE DECISION OR GENOCIDE?

Many readers today and in the past object to the moral values of Joshua, particularly its call for the elimination of the seven nations of the land of Canaan. What should readers make of such a viewpoint?

Modern reflections on Joshua and related texts seem to take one of three possible points of view: validation of the genocide ("whatever God says is right because God says it"), outright repudiation of it ("the God-talk must be political propaganda unless God is a monster"), or a historical-critical approach. The first seems morally problematic and indeed contradicts the Bible's own view of God as morally accountable, while the second inevitably discards the entire biblical tradition unless it resorts to arbitrary distinctions between acceptable and unacceptable texts. The third sort of approach, which leaves some problems unresolved, at least tries to understand the precise aims of the biblical text and the history of their interpretation.

Taking the third approach, what can one say? First, it seems clear that the call to extirpate the Canaanites sits uneasily within Joshua itself. Some texts presuppose their continued existence. For example Josh 22:6–8 says, "You should be resolute in observing everything written in the book of Moses's Torah, not deviating from it to the right or left. Do not interact with these nations remaining among you nor invoke the name of their gods nor swear by them nor serve them nor worship them. Instead, cling to Yhwh your God just as you have done until this day." In other words, the text assumes that the Canaanites will persist and that the danger from the concerns their religion. Idolatry is the principal concern of the text. Second, the instructions to eliminate the Canaanites concern them only. Other biblical texts propose a set of rules for dealing with warfare with other people, thus providing the roots of the later laws of war that have matured in the past few centuries (see, e.g., Deut 20–21). Third, the text describes several occasions on which Joshua destroyed an entire community, human and beast (Josh 2:10; 8:26; 10:1, 28, 35, 37, 39, 40; 11:11, 12, 20, 21), with most of the notices occurring in lists summarizing events (much like the lists of conquests in Neo-Assyrian royal summary inscriptions, that is, reflecting a way of telling about conquests without necessarily implying that the statement is to be taken entirely literally). Fourth, the commands to extirpate the peoples of the land of Canaan are fairly rare. The book describes a practice, known also from Moab (mentioned in the Mesha Stele) and possibly practiced in other southern Levantine states.

Does knowing the details of Joshua's description of a historical practice, limited to a single period and set of circumstances, solve the moral problem raised by the text? Of course not. But gaining greater clarity about the precise nature of the problem does help. Neither Joshua nor any other biblical text allows for ethnic cleansing as a practice outside the particular moment of the initial Israelite settlement in Canaan.

The Distribution of the Land Among the Tribes (Josh 13:1–22:45)

If the first half of Joshua answers the question of why the Canaanites lost their ancestral land, then the next ten chapters address the question of where the Israelite tribes and their constituent clans lived and why. In a world in which extended families might remain in a locale for generations or even centuries, establishing a sort of mental map of who lived where was both possible and necessary. Persons in such cultures might readily ask, "Are the people three valleys over friends or foes, relatives or strangers? How should we interact with them?" Joshua 13–22, like Num 26 and 1 Chron 1–9 in different ways, situates the tribes of Israel in their proper location with a view toward emphasizing the completeness of their occupation of their land. This focus on "all Israel" as a unity preceding and independent of the monarchic states that arose during the tenth and ninth centuries BCE allows the book of Joshua to emphasize the possibility of Israelite life irrespective of the forced migrations of persons that began in the eighth century and continued intermittently for more than 150 years. Whatever Israel's eventual history, its beginnings held out other possibilities.

Joshua 13–22 explores these possibilities in the form of several types of stories, providing a divinely sanctioned organization of the land before the origins of the state:

1. The command to divide the land (13:1–7)
2. The apportionment of tribal lands in Transjordan (Josh 13:8–33)
3. The dispositions of Eliezer and Caleb (14:1–15)
4. The apportionment of tribal lands in Cisjordan (Josh 15:1–17:18)
5. The tribal occupation of their territories (Josh 18:1–19:51)
6. The organization of asylum cities (Josh 20:1–9)
7. The allocation of property to the Levites (Josh 21:1–45)

Much of these chapters consists of lists of place names, some of which are currently identifiable, indicating a close attention to boundaries within the larger entity called Israel. While such attention to borders could imply a focus on keeping the groups separate, the more probable explanation is that the text seeks a comprehensive understanding of the arrangement of the nation's territory. This sort of close attention to place makes sense in a culture closely attached to the land from which it drew its life and deeply aware of the precariousness of its tenure of that land.

Amid the long lists of tribes and the settlements they occupied, a number of elements reveal ideas driving the text. Some of these features appear almost incidentally, while others are developed more fully.

First, Josh 13–22 portrays all the events of the settlement of the land in a compressed form that glosses over the complexity of a process that must have taken several generations (as becomes clear from reading the book of Judges). Sometimes this complexity shines through as in ch 18's description of a nationwide meeting in which Joshua chides the people for their hesitancy:

So Joshua said to Israel's children, "How long will you hesitate about going out to possess the land that Yhwh the God of your ancestors has given you? Designate for yourselves thirty men per tribe and I will send them and they will get up and go forth throughout the land and write down their property and then go to it." (Josh 18:3–4)

Stirring up a land rush requires energetic leadership, it would seem, and the narrative uses the literary device of hesitancy to indicate its awareness that Israel's conquest did not happen all at once.

Second, the text consistently portrays the occupation of the land as a process directed from the top by the kingly non-king Joshua speaking at divine behest. That is, in sharp contrast to the DH's later heroic figures with their flaws, the storyline here centers on an unproblematic character into whose interior life the reader has no access (unlike David or Jeroboam, say) but who acts strictly on the surface of the text. Joshua is a flat, if glorious, figure.

Third, accompanying this shimmering picture of Joshua is an equally uncritical one of his contemporaries Eliezer and Caleb (see Josh 14:1–15). By mentioning these figures seen also in Numbers, the text not only ties up loose ends in the narrative. (Recall that in Num 13–14, Caleb and Joshua alone among the spies offered an optimistic report about the potential for conquering Canaan. For Joshua, this report explains the survival of the Calebites as a distinct group within the territory of Judah and near that tribe's traditional center in Hebron.) The book of Joshua uses these stories to give color to a drama that seems almost too triumphant to be interesting (rather like a long passage in a Wagner opera or some other hyperpatriotic, overblown work).

Fourth, the narrative deals with some other problems in Israel's ongoing life. The final arrangements of the tribes do not occur without ritual moments, especially in chs 13 and 18, during which the nation hears a divine decree to settle the land. This interest in ritual extends further into the final chapters of this unit, which discuss the creation of cities of asylum (Josh 20:1–9; see the discussion of Deut 19 in Chapter 7 on Deuteronomy) and the distribution of cities to the tribe of Levi (since the priests had no contiguous territory of their own; Josh 21:1–45). These Levitical cities existed within the territories of the other tribes in order to create a priestly presence everywhere in the land, not just in a single sanctuary. Thus the book of Joshua both sums up older traditions and practices and constructs them in a way that will make sense in the final Deuteronomistic vision of Israel centered on Jerusalem's Temple but sanctified in every corner as well.

Concluding Speeches by Joshua (Josh 23:1–24:28)

Aside from the brief appendix about the deaths and burials of Joshua and others, the book of Joshua ends with two testamentary speeches by its hero in his old age. Since the use of such end-of-life speeches is a recurring feature of the DH (Deuteronomy itself by Moses; 1 Sam 12 by Samuel; 2 Sam 22–23 by David) and since Deuteronomistic phraseology abounds in Josh 23–24, these parting words by Joshua are best seen as a sort of editorial commentary on Israel's history and potential future on the part of the book's editors. Like Deut 30, Josh 23–24 sees moments of transition as occasions for decision, for or against Yhwh, for or against the covenantal commitments, for or against life itself.

Having said that, the two speeches in Josh 23–24 differ from each other. Joshua 23 makes the sort of rhetorical moves one might expect from a Deuteronomistic speech: an appeal to past experience ("You have seen all that Yhwh your God did to all these nations" [23:3]), calls for further appropriate uses of sense impressions to gather relevant information and draw appropriate conclusions ("see" [23:4]), calls for courage ("be strong" [23:6], "watch carefully" [23:11]), "if you cling to Yhwh" [23:8, 11]), promises of rewards for faithfulness ("Yhwh will let you inherit" [23:9]), and validation of the divine word ("all this good word that Yhwh your god spoke to you" [23:15]), among other elements. With its repetitive emphasis on Israel's faithfulness as a response to Yhwh's fidelity, the first concluding speech breathes the air of the book of Deuteronomy in all its particulars. It appears where it does in order to situate the story of Joshua within the larger DH.

The second speech introduces new elements, leading many scholars to believe that parts of it must be older than the DH itself (though how much older is difficult to say). The speech is rhetorically interesting as Joshua first recites the story of the people and then calls for their acceptance of Yhwh's covenant in perpetuity (Josh 24:2–15). When they accept it (Josh 24:16–18), he questions whether their answer is not too glib, "You are not able to serve Yhwh, for he is a holy God, a radically committed God. He will not remove your [deliberate] transgressions and sins" (Josh 24:19). By refusing to take yes for an answer, the text compels the people within and beyond the text to consider carefully their commitments to faith in Yhwh. Religious language is easily used but not easily meant. Thus the call to careful consideration, since once made, a covenant can be unmade only by introducing the violent punishments that Deut 28 lays out (again, see the discussion in Chapter 7).

Within this large-scale rhetorical strategy of drawing out real commitment, the text tells the story of Israel's past in a way that questions any grand interpretation of it:

> Thus says Israel, Yhwh's God: "your ancestors dwelt across the River [Euphrates] from time immemorial—Terah the father of Abraham and Nahor. And they served other gods. But I took your ancestor Abraham from across the River and brought him to the entire land of Canaan and multiplied his offspring and gave him Isaac. Then I gave Isaac Jacob and Esau, and I gave Esau the hill country of Seir to inhabit, but Jacob and his children went down to Egypt." (Josh 24:2–4)

The narrative goes on to recount Israel's deliverance from Egypt, not to introduce new information but to insist on Yhwh's gracious action and Israel's utter helplessness before its oppressors. The covenant between Israel and Yhwh, Joshua insists, rests in the first place on divine mercy. Yet the text calls for more than mere gratitude on Israel's part. Gift-giving (in this case, rescue from certain death) creates a new relationship which each generation must renew and value. Like the remote ancestors, the readers of Joshua can return from a place where foreign gods are worshiped (whether in or out of the promised land) and find new purpose in adherence to the Torah that Deuteronomy set forth and Joshua now tries to make work in the bounds of history.

Joshua's Death and Three Burials (Josh 24:29–33)

The conclusion of the book seems anticlimactic, but it serves to mark not just the death of a major character in the DH but the end of one era and the beginning of another. In contrast to the end of Deuteronomy, which insists that Moses's grave is unmarked and therefore not a possible place for veneration of the dead, the end of Joshua gives three burial traditions:

> And after these things, Joshua son of Nun, Yhwh's servant, died at the age of 110. They buried him on his estate in Timnath-serah in the Ephraimite hill country north of Mount Gaaš. So Israel served Yhwh all Joshua's days and all the days of the elders who succeeded Joshua who knew all Yhwh's work that He did for Israel. Moreover, they buried Joseph's bones, which Israel's children had brought from Egypt, in Shechem on the agricultural property that Jacob had bought from the children of Hamor, Shechem's father for 100 *qesitah*s. So they belonged to Joseph's children as an inheritance. As for Eliezer son of Aaron, after he died, they buried him at the Hill of Phineas his son, which was given to him in the hill country of Ephraim.

These short notices not only presuppose a knowledge of earlier traditions, including some in Genesis, but also an interest in these locations. The graves of all ancestors were sacred places, none more so than the burial places of such exalted figures as a military leader and a priest (Joshua and Eliezer), and especially the great ancestor Joseph. The commemoration of the past (that theme again!) allows the readers of the book to recall the possibilities of an equally glorious future.

Implications

To conclude, Joshua makes most sense within the plot line of the DH. While the text includes many older narratives, and much of its current shape and content especially in chs 1–12 must predate the Deuteronomists, it is instructive to consider how the book as a whole would have sounded to readers who knew how the story ended in 2 Kgs. A reader during the reign of Josiah might well have thought of the story of Joshua as a glorious foreshadowing of a revival of Israel impending in that king's reign. A couple of generations later, someone who knew of or had experienced the destruction of Jerusalem would have read Joshua very differently. In the latter case, the stories of conquest and settlement must have seemed bitterly ironic, or at any rate a haunting reminder of the fragility of human obedience to Yhwh.

Is the book of Joshua then a precursor of tragedy? Perhaps. Yet the answer to this question is not easy, for it depends on how one understands Israel's overall story. Certainly all must appear tragic to anyone who believes that the end arrived with the cataclysm of 586 BCE, with the destruction of Temple and kingship and the devastation of an entire land, calamities so poignantly commemorated in Lamentations, Ezekiel, and Jeremiah. Yet that was not the end, for out of deaths sometimes resurrections emerge. The book of Joshua seems to be a book haunted by death and eager for something after it.

Notes

1. It will seem strange to some scholars to select this text as a window onto the book of Joshua as a whole because there is some doubt about its correct location and its origins. The MT places it at the end of ch 8, while the Old Greek layer of the LXX places a slightly different version of the same text in ch 9, and 4QJosh[a] apparently situates it after ch 4. See the discussion in Eugene Ulrich et al., eds., *Qumran Cave 4*, vol. 9: *Deuteronomy, Joshua, Judges, Kings*, Discoveries in the Judaean Desert 14 (Oxford: Clarendon, 1995), 143; similarly Émile Puech, "Les copies du livre de *Josué* dans les manuscrits de la mer Morte: 4Q47, 4Q48, 4Q123 et X*Josué*," *Revue Biblique* 122 (2015): 481–506. A floating passage like this usually indicates a late addition to the book of which it is part. However, the variation between MT and LXX is quite minor, and so we may have to do here with a deliberate rearrangement of the material. Whenever and however the text made its way into Joshua, it seems to summarize the basic points of the book and thus offer a commentary on many other passages in the work.

2. For the layers of relationships between the beginning and end of the DH, see Richard Nelson, "Josiah in the Book of Joshua," *Journal of Biblical Literature* 100 (1981): 531–540; but cf. Gregory Goswell, "Joshua and Kingship," *Bulletin for Biblical Research* 23 (2013): 29–42.

For Further Reading

Campbell, Antony F., and Mark A. O'Brien. *Unfolding the Deuteronomistic History: Origins, Upgrades, Present Text*. Minneapolis: Fortress, 2000.

Earl, Douglas S. *Reading Joshua as Christian Scripture*. Winona Lake, IN: Eisenbrauns, 2010.

van der Meer, Michaël N. *Formation and Reformulation: The Redaction of the Book of Joshua in the Light of the Oldest Textual Witnesses*. Leiden: Brill, 2004.

Nelson, Richard. *Joshua: A Commentary*. Louisville: Westminster/John Knox, 1997.

10 Seeking Order Amid Chaos
THE BOOK OF JUDGES

> **Key Text**: *Israel's children did what Yhwh deemed evil—they served the Baals, and they abandoned Yhwh their ancestors' God, who had brought them from the land of Egypt and went after other gods (the gods of the peoples surrounding them) and worshiped them, thereby annoying Yhwh. Yes, they abandoned Yhwh and served Baal and the Ashtorot. Yhwh became incensed with Israel and gave them over to the plunderers (who plundered them). He also sold them to their foes all around so that they could not stand up to their foes. Whatever they did, Yhwh opposed them just as Yhwh had spoken and sworn to them. Great trouble befell them. Then Yhwh raised up defenders who rescued them from their plunderers. But they did not even listen to their defenders. Instead, they whored after other gods and worshiped them. They turned quickly from the path on which their ancestors walked with respect to listening to Yhwh's commands. They simply did not do as they should.*
>
> *Yet Yhwh raised up defenders, and Yhwh was with each defender and rescued them from their foes all the days of the defender. For Yhwh had compassion on their outcry before their tormentors and oppressors. Then, after the death of the defender, they turned away and acted more corruptly than their ancestors in going after other gods in order to serve and worship them. They did not fail to measure up to their [evil] deeds and their hard way.* (Judg 2:11–19)

The death of great leaders can create a crisis in the communities they head. At such moments the internal contradictions of the system, the old rivalries barely suppressed, and the new aspirations previously unarticulated or only dimly felt all come to the surface. Sometimes chaos ensues, and sometimes it continues for a long time until a new and more stable system arises.

This vision of politics is exactly the one that the book of Judges projects for Israel during the Iron Age I (ca. 1200–1000 BCE). The DH presents a view of the past in which the great period of Joshua leads to the messiness of the (so-called) judges. From the perspective of later centuries in which monarchy both eliminated chaos and replaced it with various forms of tyranny, the period before the rise of the state seemed anarchic. Without a king, a standing army, a systematic tax collection and redistribution system, public works, or the other features of an ancient state, the earliest form of Israel seemed to its descendants to be a fascinating time, but not an especially enviable one.

As it stands, Judges contains a series of stories that fit loosely together, with only the slenderest sense of their proper chronological sequence being apparent. The origins of some of them are obscure, though presumably they originated near the geographical points they describe (with the stories of Deborah or the Danites coming from the north, and of Samson from the south). At times they reveal a great deal of local color, as when the Song of Deborah lists tribes that do not appear (at least under the same names) in other texts, or when Samson operates in the Sorek Valley, a region known from archaeology to be heavily populated by Philistines during the eleventh century BCE (while David operates farther north in the valley of Elah, which seems to have been more Philistine later). In other words, the stories of Judges contain memories of persons, places, and events long predating the monarchy.

If we consider not just its constituent stories but the book as a whole, we recognize that it connects closely with the books on either side of it and also that it stands on its own as a depiction of a certain period of time with all its challenges and opportunities. As part of a larger work, Judges opens with stories of Israelite conquest, leaning backward to the book of Joshua. Judges 19–21, on the other hand, lean forward into 1–2 Samuel. Even the book's last line, "In those days there was no king in Israel [so] everybody did whatever seemed right to him or her" (Judg 21:24), foreshadows later developments. Yet on its own, it follows a clear historiographic conception.[1]

The book follows a clear outline:

A. Early successors of Joshua (1:1–3:31)
B. Deborah and Barak (4:1–5:31)
C. Gideon vs. the Midianites (6:1–8:35)
D. Abimelek (9:1–57)
E. Minor judges, Tola and Jair (10:1–5)
F. Jephthah vs. the Ammonites (10:6–12:7)
G. Minor judges, Ibzan, Elon, Abdon (12:8–15)
H. Samson (13:1–16:31)
I. Micah and the Danites (17:1–18:31)
J. The Benjaminite war (19:1–21:25)

The basic structure comes from the arrangement of discrete stories that apparently long antedate the book's final editing by the Deuteronomists.

However, someone had to put these stories together according to a plan. The historiographic and theological assumptions behind that plan come to light at several places in which the language of Deuteronomy and the DH emerge. The clearest statement of these themes appears in Judg 2:11–22 (part of which is cited earlier). This sermon (from an anonymous "messenger of Yhwh") picks up all the Deuteronomic ideas of listening to divine instruction, respecting the proper commitments of the ancestors, and worshiping Yhwh alone. It also introduces a new theme, a historiographic pattern through which to understand the period between the settlement in the land and the rise of the monarchy two or more centuries later. According to this pattern, Israel's history before the monarchy takes a cyclical form: deliverance, idolatry, punishment, and repentance. The constant repetition of this cycle drives the book of Judges forward.

The book fits the stories it records into this simple scheme, emphasizing at each turn of the wheel of time the contrast between human contrariness and divine mercy.

The power of this conception appears in the way the book marks the passage of time: the formula "and Israel's children did evil in Yhwh's eyes" or "and Israel's children kept on doing evil in the eyes of Yhwh" appears at most transitional moments (Judg 3:7; 4:1; 6:1; 10:6; and 13:1) during the first three-fourths of the book, while the final section marks transitions with a line that augurs developments in 1 Samuel: "in those days, there was no king in Israel" (Judg 18:1; 19:1; 21:25). This latter refrain introduces a tension within the book, as we will see. No friend of kingship in general, the book of Judges also sees a flaw in a culture lacking kingship, encapsulated in the book's last line, "so everyone did whatever he or she wanted."

WHY IS IT CALLED THE BOOK OF JUDGES?

In modern English, the word "judge" conjures up images of a legally trained man or woman in a black robe rendering a decision about a court case. Sometimes in the Bible, the Hebrew word usually translated "judge" (*šōpēṭ*) bears such a meaning. But in this book, all of the "judges" are in fact military leaders and "defenders" of the people. Some seem almost like warlords (though the "Book of Warlords" has an unwelcome ring to it!). The Greek-speaking translators of the LXX called the book *Kritai* ("deciders" or "umpires"), which became the Latin Vulgate's *Iudices* and English "Judges."

For Judges, tyranny and anarchy both present problems, often closely related ones. The absence of kingship makes a civil war possible, and yet the perpetrators of the war, the tribe of Benjamin, end up producing the first king, Saul. The DH's strong antipathy toward that king is foreshadowed even in its presentation of the period before the monarchy.

With all of these aspects of the editors' major ideas in mind, it becomes possible to read the stories, at least to some degree, as the book's first readers might have encountered them, not merely as stories of adventure and derring-do but as bits of evidence in the book's overall brief, its case for Yhwh and against Israel.

Early Successors of Joshua (Judg 1:1–3:31)

To repeat, the opening section of Judges picks up where Joshua left off, with the conquest of the land. In response to a divine oracle, "Judah shall go up, and I will put the land under its control" (Judg 1:2), the tribe of Judah leads the conquest of the area west of the Jordan River. Why Judah, especially given that tribe's relatively small role in the rest of Judges? Answer: Judah takes the lead in the story as a foreshadowing of its central role in a later part of the Deuteronomistic History, the life of David. That is, the reader should recognize that Judges looks forward to future developments.

This foreshadowing at the book's beginning complements a similar leaning forward in its final story, the decimation of the tribe of Benjamin (Judg 19–21). While Judah gave the nation its great king David, Benjamin produced its first king, Saul. The intertwining careers of David and Saul will take center stage in 1 Sam, especially chs 13–31. Again, the persons responsible for aggregating all this material draw the readers' attention to this later literary development. Since Judg 1–3 and 19–21 contain relatively little Deuteronomistic language, their connection probably came from an earlier stage in the book's development, but this is hard to be certain about and not crucial to an understanding of the work as a whole.

How does Judges wish its overarching narrative to be understood? According to the opening sections, the various "defenders" who now appear continue the role of the divinely ordained leader that appears in the lives of Moses and Joshua. Accordingly, Judg 2 addresses this question by telling the story of a "messenger" (whether celestial or human) who recites the story of the exodus and draws the implication that a covenant (Hebrew: *bĕrît*) with Yhwh renders a treaty of friendship (again, *bĕrît*) with the local Canaanites unthinkable (Judg 2:1–2). The text explains this rapprochement with the locals as one in which Israel comes to worship their gods, indicating that the text's real concern is less ethnic or political than religious. Thus, Judg 2 flashes back to the age of Joshua to recall the pristine early days, preceding the later crises.

The age of crisis begins in Judg 2:11–12. As this text puts it,

> Israel's children did evil in Yhwh's view by serving the Baal gods. Yes, they forsook Yhwh their ancestral god, who had brought them from Egypt's land. They pursued other gods, the gods of the peoples around them. They worshiped them and annoyed Yhwh.

This generalized statement triggers the cycle of sin/punishment/repentance/redemption that informs the rest of the book through ch 16. For the book of Judges, Israel's behavior appears gratuitous, rooted in a blatant disregard for their responsibilities and even self-interest.

The first story about a deliverer comes in Judg 3:10–11 with reference to one Othniel, who receives little press. A longer story comes next, with one Ehud (Judg 3:16–31), who rescued Israel from an invasion of Moabites led by their morbidly obese king Eglon (whose name means "little calf"). Ehud, a left-handed man and therefore suspect in an ancient society, tricks the foreign king into believing that he had "a message from Elohim for you" (Judg 3:20). After convincing Eglon's guards to leave the room, Ehud delivers the message: a sword to the gut. In the grotesque story, the assassin disembowels the king and escapes the locked room, apparently through the drainpipe. The story plays upon the grotesque nature of the foreign ruler and emphasizes the cleverness of a member of an oppressed group. Not a pretty tale, the story at least has the merit of energetically narrated a brave act by a resourceful, if not perhaps spiritually inspiring, leader.

THE DELIVERERS AND GEOGRAPHY

The book of Judges shows an interest in geographical coverage in its choice of deliverer stories. The leaders thus appear from various parts of the land of Israel:

Transjordan—Jephthah
The north and central hill country—Ehud, Deborah and Barak, Gideon, Abimelek, Elon, Abdon

The south and Shephelah—Ibzan, Samson
This geographical spread demonstrates the book's ecumenical sensibility according to which all of Israel's history deserved attention, and all Israel experiences Yhwh's deliverance. The list is thus a merismus. On the other hand, the plurality of stories from the north-central hill country shows a bias in the traditions' preservation. The core Israelite tribes preserved the stories that reached, in time, the editors of the DH.

Deborah and Barak (Judg 4:1–5:31)

The next cycle operates at an arguably higher level but with the same celebration of the resilience of key Israelite leaders even amid the failures of the people at large. Judges 4–5 consists of first a prose description of the event in question, and then a much older poem celebrating that event. As already noted, this practice of embedding old oral poetry in younger prose narrative also appears in the stories of Jacob's death scene (Gen 48–49), the crossing of the Reed Sea (Exod 14–15), the funeral of King Saul (2 Sam 1), and other places. That is, the author of the prose had access to traditional oral poetry from which to draw, even while creating a new version of the story.

The story is simple enough: the ruler of the major Canaanite city of Hazor (the largest city in Canaan during the Iron I period) seeks to subjugate the village-dwelling Israelites. His general Sisera, whose name probably originated in the Aegean world and who thus may have been related to the Sea Peoples (the emigrants from that region that included the Philistines and other groups), finds his plans thwarted by a deliverer named Deborah and her sidekick Baraq. The prose narrative tells the story of Sisera's defeat in battle, against all odds, and his timely assassination by another woman, one Jael.

The poem in Judg 5 offers the oldest version of the story known, probably dating to the period before the monarchy and thus close to the events it recounts. It includes various poetic prompts to characters singing it ("bless Yhwh," "I will sing," "wake up, wake up Deborah") which, again, point to a world of oral poetry sung to commemorate great deeds. It also tells a story, one that differs only slightly from the prose narrative.

The song opens by setting the scene as one of contrast between Israel's courage ("when women leaders led in Israel and the people volunteered"; v. 2) and the desperate circumstances they confronted. "The peasants ceased, ceased in Israel . . . . No shield nor spear was seen among forty thousand in Israel." (vv. 7, 8). Hunted and harried, Israel turned to the female hero Deborah and her colleague Baraq, who mustered the armies of some of the tribes, but not all of them.

THE TRIBES IN THE SONG OF DEBORAH

Much evidence suggests that Judg 5 predates, probably by centuries, the prose narrative around it. The use of archaic linguistic forms and the references to Israelite groups that later had other names points in such direction.

As an old war song that predates the prose material around it, the Song of Deborah contains some ethnographic information about an early stage of Israel's life. Its tribal list (Judg 5:14–18) lists the tribes Ephraim, Benjamin, Makir, Zebulon, Issachar, Reuben, Gilead, Dan, Asher, Zebulon, and Naphtali, all tribes in the middle and northern hill country. Judah is conspicuously absent, and Makir and Gilead replace Manasseh and Gad respectively (presumably the names of tribes can change over time). Dan also appears on the sea coast, prior to its move inland (see Judg 18). There are two interesting things about these tribes: (1) they seem to function primarily during times of warfare, when it became necessary for groups larger than a single village to cooperate; and (2) they operate in relationship to a state, in this case the city-state of Hazor. These two behaviors fit tribal practices in many other cultures and times as well.

In the song, the victory over Sisera at the Wadi Kishon occurs through direct divine intervention:

> The kings came, fought, yes the kings of Canaan fought
> At Taanach by the waters of Megiddo, taking no silver as plunder.
> The stars fought from the sky, fought with Sisera from their paths. (Judg 5:19–20)

That is, the poem places the battle in the cosmic realm, not understanding it as merely an against-the-odds triumph by a peasant army over their better-equipped overlords.

The drama of the poem continues in the final two scenes. In the first, Sisera flees the battlefield and meets his doom while a fugitive in the tent of his erstwhile ally. Jael, the wife of a Kenite ally of Sisera (the Kenites being a local ethnic group), gives him a comforting bowl of milk curds and then, as he dozes off, strikes him in the head with a tent peg:

> Between her feet he knelt, fell, lay. Between her feet he knelt, fell.
> Where he knelt, there he fell – destroyed! (Judg 5:27)

An elegant poetic progression for such a violent act! Yet the violence surfaces an important reality in warfare, its gendered nature. Often the victims of warfare, in this poem women take the initiative and bring about the demise of the males who oppress Israel.

However, the binary opposition man:woman does not function in a simple way in the poem, for the last scene introduces Sisera's mother as someone awaiting his return, explaining the delay to herself as his using time to find "a womb or two" (Judg 5:30). Here an elite woman expresses her group's depersonalizing understanding of Israel's women as mere bearers of children for their overlords. In other words, social rank plays a major role in the story, too. And so the poem involves the inversion of social relationships, with the weak becoming strong and the strong utterly destroyed. This inversion explains the fascination with which readers have long greeted this story of Israel's resilience during a time of adversity.

Gideon vs. the Midianites (Judg 6:1–8:35)

The following section turns to the next hero, Gideon (also known as Jerubbaal, probably in variant traditions). In contrast to traditional stories of warriors who cannot wait to fight (like Samson or, in Mesopotamia, Gilgamesh), the stories of Gideon describe a reluctant general. The longish section dedicated to his career begins with the editor's notice of Israel's sin and punishment (Judg 6:1–10) and then commences a cluster of stories about Gideon's call by an angel and desecration of Baal's altar (Judg 6:11–32), his test of the call with fleece (6:33–40), his tactically unorthodox battle against the Midianite invaders (7:1–25), the pursuit of the fleeing Midianite lords (8:1–21), and the Israelites' offer of kingship to him with his refusal and assumption of other forms of leadership (8:22–35).

The story explores themes of heroism, much as in other stories in Judges, but introduces several new themes. First, after returning to the theme of the angelic messenger (as in Judg 2), the story states Gideon's reluctance in the form of a lament to that messenger, "If Yhwh is really with us, then why does all this trouble find us, and where are all his miracles that our ancestors recounted to us when they said, 'Didn't Yhwh bring us up from Egypt?' Yet, now Yhwh has abandoned us and given us into our enemies' control" (Judg 6:13). This protest is reminiscent of lines in various psalms (see Chapter 19, "The Book of Psalms"). Corresponding to this human reluctance is the divine willingness to demonstrate commitment to rescuing Israel, as seen in the odd exchange of dew-covered and dry fleece, and more significantly in the victory over the Midianites by means of trickery.

The third theme is the contest between Yhwh and Baal, reminiscent of similar contests in the story of Elijah (see 1 Kgs 18:20–40). In the Gideon story, he must destroy Baal's altar and the Asherah pole next to it as proof of his loyalty to Yhwh alone. This theme of monolatry, the worship of only one deity, which this story has in common with both the prophetic stories of 1–2 Kgs and the later Deuteronomists reusing those stories, places the Gideon stories in a different light than some of the other hero stories of the book.

The telltale theological point of the story comes from the mouth of Gideon's father, who must defend him from the lynch mob seeking his life after the destruction of their holy site. Joash says, "Will you argue Baal's case? Will you rescue him? . . . If he is a god, he will defend himself because it was his altar that was destroyed" (Judg 6:31). Apparently, the argument that a god can protect itself convinced Israelites, an interesting fact in its own right.

RETELLING THE STORY OF GIDEON'S DESTRUCTION OF THE ALTAR

Later postbiblical traditions used the idea of the hero destroying the altar. The story migrated to Abraham, who became the model convert from idolatry to monotheism. And so in in Jubilees 11–12 (second century BCE), Apocalypse of Abraham (first or second century CE), and Genesis Rabba 38 (mid-first millennium CE), Abraham became the altar-destroyer, and his father Terah the priest of the false god. As so often in ancient texts, a story illustrating a major value of the community (in this case, courage in the service of Yhwh) migrated from a relatively minor character to a more famous one.

On the other hand, Hebrews 11:32 in the New Testament mentions Gideon in a list of heroes from the books of Judges and 1 Samuel, all of whom succeeded against the odds. And so his story also survived in the tradition as a model of pious behavior.

The fourth theme is that of kingship. Gideon defeats the Midianites by famously refusing to assemble a large army but instead reducing his horde to a mere three hundred men who could lap water like dogs (an odd test of military ability, surely!) and thus showed familiarity with life in the rough. After a series of adventures chasing the invaders out of Israel (and persuading all the Israelite groups to help him), he meets a delegation of leaders who offer him the crown. Their proposal states clearly the dynastic principle: "Rule over us, you and your son and your grandson, for you have rescued us from the control of Midian" (Judg 8:22). Successful generalship leads to permanent power. However, Gideon rejects both the proposal and the great-man-of-history Bonapartism underlying it by insisting that "Yhwh will rule you" (8:23), thus picking up the same sharp contrast between human and divine kingship that appears as an option in other texts (notably 1 Sam 8), even though it is often rejected by those same texts in favor of a more nuanced, "both-and" sort of solution.

Abimelek (Judg 9:1–57)

If Gideon rejected kingship in favor of accepting payment in gold, the next hero in the chain actively sought dynastic rule. Abimelek's very name means "my father is king, and he sought to live up to his name by trawling for the throne. Judges 9 introduces him as "son of Jerubbaal," perhaps indicating the origin of this story in an early stage of the development of the Gideon narrative (before it was clear that Gideon and Jerubbaal were, in fact, the same person). Yet as it stands in the present book of Judges, the story of Abimelek stands in contrast to the story of Gideon. The younger man operates from his base in Shechem, a major early Israelite city, and works from there to extend his rule across the country. Unlike the other major figures in Judges, he does not rise to power after delivering the people from foreign invaders but simply by persuading the local leaders that he is the man for the job.

Abimelek's career succeeded for awhile until it met its sudden end during a siege of Migdal (literally, a "tower"). A woman hurled down on him a grinding stone, probably a basalt object the size of a small loaf of bread and of course fatal when dropped from a height. The woman's test of gravity marked an ignominious end to both the man and the attempt at monarchy shorn of divine sanction.

Embedded within this tragicomic tale, however, is an interesting early poem, called by modern readers, "Jotham's Fable." Standing atop Mount Gerizim, which soars 2,890 feet (881 m) above Shechem, Jotham offered his comment on kingship (Judg 9:7–15):

> Listen to me, rulers of Shechem, and Elohim will listen to you.
> The trees assembled to anoint themselves a king.
> So they said to olive tree, "be our king."
> And the olive tree said to them, "Should I stop my growing, which
> benefits gods and people? Should I go out waving over the trees?"

The trees repeat the attempt with the fig tree and the vine, Palestine's other two principal large food-bearing flora, but with the same negative results. Finally, desperate for a ruler, they ask the thorn bush, whose ironic answer states Jotham's contempt for monarchy. The thorn says,

> If you are really anointing me as king over you, then go, rest in my shadow.
> And if not, then fire will come out from the thorn and devour the cedars of Lebanon.

Far from attracting the best and the brightest, kingship draws the worst and the most stupid. As elsewhere in biblical narrative, Judges uses the poetry of a minor character to comment on the actions of the major ones (comparable perhaps to how Shakespeare uses Polonius and Ophelia to put Hamlet's ravings into context).

Minor Judges, Tola and Jair (Judg 10:1–5) and Ibzan, Elon, Abdon (Judg 12:8–15)

The book of Judges inserts at several points references to deliverers about whom it has little information. Often spoken of as "minor judges," these figures advance the narrative by allowing the story to skip time without delving deeply into new episodes, thus keeping the focus tightly on other stories, which the book uses to explore the major themes it wishes to address.

Jephthah vs. the Ammonites (Judg 10:6–12:7)

Sandwiched between these two lists of less well-known deliverers, Judges tells the story of Jephthah. Born to a prostitute after casual sex with Gilead, Jephthah's father, he struggles to find a place in a home with the children of his father's legitimate wife. On reaching adulthood, Jephthah flees and finds a home in the "Land of Tob" outside the normal patterns of settlements in the Transjordan. As the country falls to Ammonite invaders, Jephthah's fellow Gileadites invite him to assume the leadership of their militia. This he does with some reluctance, but with ultimate success.

Two elements of the Jephthah story deserve closer attention. The first is the diplomatic jockeying for legitimacy between the Israelites and the Ammonites around the question of boundaries (Judg 11:12–28). Jephthah contests Ammonite claims that Israel had stolen their territory by reciting much of the material narrated also in the book of Numbers:

> Israel did not take the land of Moab or the land of the Ammonites. In fact, when they came from Egypt, Israel traveled via the wilderness up to the Sea of Reeds and came to Qadesh. Then Israel sent envoys to the king of Edom with the message, "Please let me pass through your land." But the king of Edom did not listen, but rather sent a message to the king of Moab not to agree. So Israel remained at Qadesh. Later, (Israel) went through the steppe and skirted the lands of Edom and Moab and went east of the land of Moab and encamped on the Arnon River. They did not cross the border of Moab, for the Arnon is the Moabite border. (Judg 11:15–18)

The text goes along in this vein reporting well-known Israelite conquest traditions (well-known to the Israelites, for sure, but also at least plausible to outsiders). It is hard to say whether Jephthah expects the Ammonites to accept his version of their history or simply states a negotiating position.

WOMEN IN THE BOOK OF JUDGES

A curious feature of Judges is that, while at first it seems to concern primarily male warriors, in fact many women populate its tales. These range from Achsah to Deborah and Jael to anonymous women such as Samson's mother and various partners, the Levite's murdered concubine, and the women left for the Benjaminites to "capture." And of course Jephthah's daughter, a victim of child sacrifice like Isaac (almost) and Mesha's son (not almost—see 2 Kgs 3). This parade of female characters, whether casualties of male bellicosity or actors in their own right, illustrates both the complexity of Israelite society and the narrator's sense that perhaps all is not well. These women are neither queens nor whores, nor do they easily fit stereotypes, whether of ancient readers or ourselves.

The communication is interesting because it seeks a warrant for political behavior in history. Jephthah (or rather, the storyteller) recognizes that states may not simply steal each other's land. In this narrative, Ammon did not yet exist as a state during the Iron Age I, and the predecessor states exerted their rights, which Israel respected. The international diplomatic system had worked, more or less, and the new Ammonite claims marked a break with precedent and thus were illegitimate. So Jephthah's diplomatic missives claim. Arguably, this entire discussion reflects less the era of a Jephthah in the Iron Age I (when, in fact, Ammon had apparently not yet emerged as a state) than a date during the Israelite monarchy. Perhaps the story uses "Ammon" the way textbooks speak of the history of "France" before the country was called that. But in any case, the story's exploration of the rules of diplomacy and its efforts at anchoring Israelite statecraft in its core story of divine redemption. This is a remarkable text on the ethics of politics.

Alas, Jephthah's skill as a diplomat does not extend to his parenting. His story ends with the tragic vow he makes to guarantee victory. He promises to incinerate a whole burnt offering of whatever first leaves his house. The victim turns out to be his only daughter. While the story does not explicitly describe her sacrifice, there can be little doubt that the text intends as much but pulls a curtain over the scene, in part as a technique of literary mastery but also to protect the reader from the full force of the story. Jephthah's anonymous daughter must "mourn for her virginity" (Judg 11:38), becoming the heroine of a cultural practice (in Transjordan?) of a young girl separating herself from the community as a rite of passage into adulthood. An irresistible story, this final tale of woe cures any illusions on the reader's part of Jephthah's story as one of unqualified success.

Samson (Judg 13:1–16:31)

Equally tragic is the story of Samson. Here, Judges' deconstruction of the idea of the hero reaches its full force. Far from being a deliverer, Samson falls victim to his own lack of discipline. Though the most famous part of the story comes at the end with his pulling down the temple of Dagon upon himself and his foes, the Samson narrative does more than explore the personal failings of one person. It explores the failures of a system that looks again and again for a charismatic leader who will rise from the people and conquer the odds in order to save them. The ideal of the strong man of history does not find favor here.

The Samson story consists of five major subsections:

1. Introduction (Judg 13:1)
2. His birth announced by a divine messenger (13:2–25)
3. His marriage to a Philistine and first conflicts (14:1–19)
4. Conflicts with the Philistines (15:1–20)
5. The betrayal of Delilah and Samson's death (16:1–31)

In many ways, these stories resemble the traditions of heroes prevalent around the ancient Near East and Mediterranean. The rash warrior who grabs what he wants figures in the tales of Gilgamesh and Herakles, to take the two most famous examples, and such traditions have influenced how Judges tells the story of Samson. All of these stories involve the hero's wildness and attempts to domesticate him (outside vs. homebound), the theme of male restlessness and desire for adventure and danger, and the complex relationships between the hero and women to whom he may or may not have a permanent, social sanctioned relationship (i.e., marriage).[2] All of these stories find the hero simultaneously attractive and repulsive. The audience of the story can admire the courage while being appalled by the irresponsibility that makes the courage possible.

A window into his character appears in his love of the *bon mot*. For example, Samson regales his wedding guests with the riddle "From the eater comes something eaten, and from the strong comes the sweet" (Judg 14:14), a reference to his finding honey in a lion carcass. The guests threaten his wife into drawing out the answer from him, and then surprise the betrayed husband with "What is sweeter than honey or stronger than a lion" (Judg 14:18), to which Samson can reply only with another (not very playful) witticism, "If you had not plowed with my heifer, you would not have discovered my riddle" (Judg 14:18). It's all very clever, this Shakespearesque touch by which the characters reveal a major flaw in Samson's character: his lack of understanding of social relationships and the superior thickness of blood to a recently contracted marriage. The theme of male violence extorting information from vulnerable women returns in Judg 19 and 21 (see The Benjaminite War), but the tables are turned in Judg 16 as Delilah gets Samson to reveal his hair as the source of his strength. The point here is not the untrustworthiness of women (as sometimes modern readers assume), but the fragility of the hero's command of himself and his social environment when brief spurts of superhuman violence are not involved. In such a world, the hero model falls short of providing a sustainable political environment for Israel.

Micah and the Danites (Judg 17:1–18:31)

With the Samson story, the core part of Judges as the story of rescuers comes to an end. The final two units of the book constitute a sort of appendix, or rather another layer (possibly added later) that constitutes an implicit commentary on the warrior stories preceding them. The previous tales seem, at least to some of the editors responsible for Judges, to illustrate the serious flaws of a system that must rely on the periodic rise of deliverers to rescue Israel from the consequences of its infidelity to Yhwh. Hence the refrain in the final chapters "there was no king in Israel, so everyone did whatever he or she wanted" (Judg 21:25; cf. 17:6; 18:1; 19:1).

The story of Micah, the Levite, and the Danites seems to be a weaving together of two or more distinct stories. In the first, a prosperous person named Micah creates a sanctuary for himself, complete with a cult statue (Hebrew: *pesel massēkâ*), and then recruits a Levite to carry on the work of sacrifice. In time, a group from the tribe of Dan, harried by the Philistines in their settlements along the coast, decides to migrate inland and northward. To set up a proper establishment in their new situation, they recruit (coerce?) the Levite to accompany them as the head of a new sanctuary.

As Judg 18:27–28 summarizes the story, "They took what Micah had made and the priest that he employed, and brought them to Laish to a quiet and trusting people. Then they put them to the sword and burned the city. No one could rescue them because it was too far to Sidon, and nobody carried the news because it was in an isolated valley. Then they rebuilt the city and inhabited it." Far from seeing this conquest as a glorious event, the narrator sees it as an ignoble act of a predatory group. More to the point, the narrator makes a significant theological point.

As it happens, Dan was a major cultic site during the period of the Israelite monarchy (see the discussion on 1 Kgs 12 in Chapter 13). The narrative of Judg 17–18 offers a strong polemic against the worship there. Though addressed to Yhwh, this worship appears in the Deuteronomistic History as (1) idolatrous because not aniconic, and (2) rooted in illicit violence or indeed straight-up thuggery (remember the "quiet and trusting people").

The Benjaminite War (Judg 19:1–21:25)

The descent into pointless violence continues in the final story of Judges, the sordid tale of the civil war between Benjamin and the other Israelite tribes. The story depicts escalating ferocity caused by a lack of appropriate communication systems among the tribes. A single event triggered the war, indicating the preexistence of underlying causes, no doubt. But the presenting cause was terrible enough. A traveling Levite found himself confronted in a Benjaminite village with a mob that could only be placated by allowing them to gang rape and murder his secondary wife, traveling with him. (The story of violated hospitality immediately calls to mind the Sodom story of Lot and his angelic visitors in Genesis.) Demanding justice from the Benjaminites, the other tribes find themselves stonewalled as that tribe decides to defend its own rather than seek a reasonable solution. The result is the near extermination of the tribe of Benjamin.

This terrible calamity can only be averted by the expedient of allowing the surviving Benjaminite males to marry the women of Jabesh-gilead (a town that will figure in later stories) and then by leaving young women in the open field where they can be "found" by the still unmarried Benjaminites. The story has some superficial similarities to the famous Roman story of the rape of the Samnite women, also set during the early period of that nation's history. Perhaps such stories of marriage outside the normal social structures gave a cheap thrill to ancient audiences.

Certain, however, is the point that Judges seeks to make from this grisly story. Judges 21:1–4 describes a scene at the temple of Bethel in which the people seek a clarification of values and therefore of correction actions. As this text puts it:

> Each Israelite man swore at Mizpah, "none of us will give his daughter to Benjamin as a wife." Then the people went to Bethel and remained there until evening before

Elohim. They shouted and wept loudly. They said, "O Yhwh God of Israel, why has this happened in Israel, the destruction today of a tribe from Israel?" The next day, the people got up early and erected there an altar and offered whole burnt offerings and offerings of well-being.

That is, the group (or at least its males) experiences a conflict between protecting their daughters from marrying such persons and the need to preserve lineages as fully as possible. The unthinking entrance into civil war has led to a negative double bind. They seek a way out of it by oppressing the women of Jabesh-gilead, but even this lamentable action does not solve the larger problem. Thus the book of Judges reaches an impasse, in part resolved by the selection of a Benjaminite king in 1 Samuel, but indeed also accentuated by that choice.

Implications

As already mentioned, the book of Judges exists within a larger work. While its beginning and end demarcate it as a coherent phase in Israel's history (as understood by the DH), this period seems in the overall work to have the nature of an interlude, a period of accelerating social decay. Many of the themes that appear in 1–2 Sam and 1–2 Kgs appear for the first time in Judges, notably the alteration of good and bad rulers, the dangers from foreign invasions, and the need for community-wide, not just individual, religious commitment to the worship of Yhwh alone.

If, then, Judges offers a warning to readers of the realities of chaos, it also illustrates the resilience of Israel, not just in its ability to raise up the occasional deliverer but of the entire people to cry out for help, that is, to repent. By interpreting the history of the Iron Age I through the lens of its theological cycle of sin/repentance/deliverance/rest, the Deuteronomists (and to some extent their sources) created a text that also offers an odd sort of hope. Whatever the affective resonances of the book, it seeks to retrieve stories of heroes, situate them in a pan-Israelite narrative, accentuate their potential for illustrating moral (or immoral) qualities, and in short make them usable for later readers. The fascination with which we still read them demonstrates the success of this effort.

Notes

1. But see also the cautions of Serge Frolov on Judges' integrity as a single work in Serge Frolov, "Rethinking Judges," *Catholic Biblical Quarterly* 71 (2009): 24–41. He notes that the beginning and end of the book connect it to prior and following material (as I have said), but concludes from that fact that we should be very careful about thinking of Judges as a freestanding work. In part, the problem arises because the creators of the work are trying to wrestle older material into shape, to make it "fit" when it already has its own fit.

2. A succinct discussion of these themes appears in Gregory Mobley, *Samson and the Liminal Hero in the Ancient Near East* (New York: T. & T. Clark, 2006).

For Further Reading

Ackerman, Susan. *Warrior, Dancer, Seductress, Queen: Women in Judges and Biblical Israel.* New York: Doubleday, 1998).

Brettler, Marc Zvi. *The Book of Judges.* London: Routledge, 2002.

Mobley, Gregory. *The Empty Men: The Heroic Tradition of Ancient Israel.* New York: Doubleday, 2005.

11 The Model Convert
THE BOOK OF RUTH

> **Key Text:** *All the people in the gateway, as well as the elders of the city, said, "May Yhwh make the woman who has come to your house like Rachel and Leah, the two who built up Israel's house and strengthened Ephratah and renamed it Bethlehem. And may your house be like Pharez's house, the one whom Tamar bore to Judah. So may your offspring that Yhwh gives you from this young woman be."* (Ruth 4:11–12)

A resilient community remains flexible, though realistic, about its boundaries. So the book of Ruth asks, what if a gentile wanted to enter the Israelite community? And what if that gentile were a woman, widowed, but caring for her mother-in-law? This small work, a sort of ancient novella probably written in the late Second Temple period but set much earlier, presents a charming picture of domestic life in ancient Israel, especially involving women and therefore issues of fertility, relationships among in-laws, and practices of courtship.

In English Bibles, which follow the LXX on this point, Ruth appears just after Judges, reflecting the shorter book's setting during the period of the longer one. In Hebrew Bibles, however, Ruth appears after Proverbs because the Moabite woman was a "strong woman" (Hebrew: *ʾēšet ḥayil*) an embodiment of the idealized "strong woman" of Prov 31 (also *ʾēšet ḥayil*). The Hebrew Bible's sequence reflects the fact that Ruth originated separately from, and later than, the DH, while the Greek Bible's order reflects a more widespread attitude of attempting to place things in their nominal historical context.

Ruth, then, is a clearly organized story consisting of a series of scenes that lead to a happy conclusion. One may outline the book this way:

A. Why Ruth entered the family (1:1–5)
B. Ruth commits to Israel's life (1:6–18)
C. The return to Bethlehem (1:19–22)
D. Farming in Bethlehem (2:1–23)
E. Courting in Bethlehem (3:1–18)
F. Negotiating a marriage (4:1–6)
G. The wedding of Ruth and Boaz (4:7–12)
H. The birth of a baby (4:13–17)
I. A genealogy (4:18–22)

Like other ancient Israelite courtship tales, the story of Ruth and Boaz involves conversations of mutual respect and prolonged discussion, especially, of the woman's work ethic and commitment to a dignified life. Perhaps the closest comparisons are the descriptions of Sarah in the book of Tobit and Judith in the book bearing her name, both later works that reflect the deep interests in personal piety that animated authors in the late Second Temple period. Ruth seems to be an earlier example of this later emphasis on female morality, though here the heroine is not Jewish before her conversion. Unlike some older courtship stories (e.g., Gen 24; 29; 34; Exod 2:16–22), there seems to have been no parental involvement in Ruth and Boaz's courtship, simply because Ruth was a migrant with whom no family-based relationships could be worked out.

Modern readers rightly ask whether texts from a patriarchal setting can offer anything to our allegedly more egalitarian society. While Ruth is a love story in which the characters show great respect for each other, they also operate within a set of cultural assumptions that they must either accept, reject, or bend in some way. In ancient Israel (and most premodern societies), males often made major decisions about mating and reproduction, often in their own self-interest. At the same time, such systems were not then, and are not now, monolithic. Like all social structures, they have rules and standard customs, which are not necessarily the same. Persons may maneuver within them. For example, Genesis's many stories of women controlling their own reproduction (Sarah, Rachel, Tamar, Potiphar's wife). Some of these maneuvers met approval, and some did not. In other words, morality had to be worked out in the messiness of life, then as now. Is Ruth patriarchal in some sense? Perhaps. But it also shows women making choices that seemed sensible to them given the challenges of their own lives.

Why Ruth Entered the Family (Ruth 1:1–5)

This story of female social creativity opens with a famine (as in various stories in Genesis). A family from Bethlehem find themselves in Moab seeking a livelihood, a strange move since Moab is poorer and more arid than Judah. The book gives these characters symbolic names: Elimelek ("my God is king"), Naomi ("pleasant"), Mahlon ("sickly"), and Kilyon ("terminal"). The boys' unusual names may have other etymological explanations, and of course it is difficult to imagine real persons with names of such predictive power. The narrator winks at the reader here as if to say, "remember that this is a work of fiction."

The death of the father and two brothers creates the narrative problem that the rest of the book must work to solve. In Israelite culture, a childless widow married her deceased husband's nearest kinsman (preferably brother) in order to produce a child in honor of the deceased husband as well as, of course, making a long-term commitment of marriage. In this story, no male marital candidates survive, and none are in prospect since Elimelek also dies. Hence the problem.

Ruth Commits to Israel's Life (Ruth 1:6–18)

In the second, highly poignant scene, Naomi attempts to solve this problem for her daughters-in-law by severing her family ties with them. Her sensible proposal to free Ruth and Orpah from any obligations to her family meets the two possible responses possible: Orpah understandably returns to her family (and the text passes no moral judgment on her decision), while Ruth opts for the riskier choice of accompanying Naomi home to Bethlehem, which the earliest readers knew as the home of King David.

Ruth's famous statement of loyalty in 1:16–17 works at two levels: as a commitment to Naomi and as an oath of loyalty to Israel's religion and life. It is thus the speech of a model convert. She says, "Do not press me to abandon you, to turn away from you. For I will go where you go, lodge where you lodge. Your people will be my people, and your God my God. Wherever you die, I will die and be buried. So may Yhwh do to me and more so . . . if even death intervenes between me and you." (Strangely, this touching promise of one woman to another often figures in modern heterosexual weddings.)

Ruth's statement reflects a considered desire not just to remain in association with Naomi but to accept major aspects of Israelite life: family commitments, burial in a family tomb, and especially worship of Yhwh. Ruth thus stands in marked contrast to women who married Jewish men but did not convert to Judaism (see the discussion of Ezra and Nehemiah in Chapter 15).

The Return to Bethlehem (Ruth 1:19–22)

With nothing left to do in Moab, then, the two protagonists head to Bethlehem. When her old friends welcome her home, Naomi comments upon her experiences of loss by telling those women "do not call me 'Pleasant.' Instead, call me 'Bitterness' because Shaddai has profoundly embittered me" (Ruth 1:20). Returning to the pattern of symbol-laden names, the story gives Naomi a brief line that reveals both her internal state and her analysis of the trials she has faced. Famine and forced migration and the loss of family, common enough occurrences in the ancient world, exact a toll on a person's body and spirit. Naomi does not hide this fact, nor does the text itself. Yet there is another turn to take.

Farming in Bethlehem (Ruth 2:1–23)

The next act in the drama introduces the male lead, a prosperous farmer named Boaz, who invites Ruth to work on his land and offers her appropriate protection. The exchange between the two of them sets the stage for what follows:

> BOAZ : "My daughter, won't you listen? Don't go glean on another farm or leave this
> one. Just stay my young women. Focus on the field where they're harvesting and
> follow them. Haven't I told the young men not to harass you? If you're thirsty, go
> to the drinking pots and drink what the young men have drawn."
> RUTH (BOWING ON THE GROUND) : "Why have I met your approval so that you
> should notice me, a foreigner?
> BOAZ : "Everything you did for your mother-in-law after your husband's death was
> told me. You recently left your father, mother, and ancestral land and came to a
> people you didn't previously know. May Yhwh make your action worthwhile,
> and may you have an appropriate reward from Yhwh the God of Israel under
> whose wings you have come to seek shelter." (Ruth 2:8–12)

Since Ruth is a "Moabite woman," as the characters keep reminding each other, she needs protection from over-eager young men who might take advantage of her isolation, and Boaz protects his female employees. Yet more comes out here: despite her strangeness, Ruth has practiced the key Israelite virtues of care for parents (or an in-law in her case), diligent work, and respect for God. Boaz responds with a blessing.

Part of the comedy of this scene appears in its slightly over-the-top statements of respect. Ruth commits a faux pas by bowing to an employer—outsiders to a culture frequently make such well-intentioned social mistakes. And Boaz concludes his heartfelt commendation of Ruth's behavior with a benediction more at home in a temple than an open field. Yet this mixing of linguistic and behavioral registers endears the characters to the readers and to each other. The storyteller has moved us one step closer to the inevitable wedding.

Courting in Bethlehem (Ruth 3:1–18)

The next scene comes a few days later, at the conclusion of the harvest. The male workers are asleep on the threshing floor, a large plaza of exposed bedrock or beaten earth on which grain could be separated from stalk through beating (threshing). In the middle of the night, at Naomi's instructions, Ruth jostles the tired Boaz awake and joins him at the floor, uncovering his feet to offer herself as a potential wife to him. It is often alleged that the reference to Ruth uncovering Boaz's "legs" is a euphemism for a more intimate male body part, but this claim is not provable (since euphemisms are not always easy to spot). In the story itself, Naomi instructs Ruth on how to approach Boaz, concluding that "he will tell you what you should do" (Ruth 3:4). When he tells her what to do, the instructions do not include sexual activity. In any case, as a widow, Ruth probably needed no such instruction. So, again, we simply do not know what they did, but whatever happened on the threshing floor, Ruth and Boaz agreed to marry as soon as possible because of both mutual respect (and attraction) and the fact that he was her nearest kinsman and thus the primary candidate for her husband.

Negotiating a Marriage (Ruth 4:1–6)

Yet not quite the nearest relative, as they discover the next day. So Boaz must negotiate a settlement for Ruth's hand, which he does by astutely remind the nearer relative that while Naomi's field may be for sale, it comes with a major string attached, a young Moabite woman. Since a man upon his death must divide his estate among his surviving sons, and since it is likely that he will have sons by Ruth if he marries her (who could resist?), the other relative decides to forgo both the field and the wife. Boaz is free to marry her, and does so.

This fascinating story reveals much about the practice of marriage (levirate) law in ancient Israel. An exchange of goods takes place in a marriage, as in both economic transactions and nonmarket-driven gift exchanges. This system conceives of women as a special category not to be bought and sold by males like property, but also not free to contract marriages at will without regard for larger family commitments and relationships. It is tempting to see the transaction involving Ruth as something on the analogy of buying land or cattle, but this conclusion is too hasty. A related but different category of transaction is in view here.

The Wedding of Ruth and Boaz (Ruth 4:7–12)

The next unit, the climax of the story, also contains interesting ethnographic data. The narrator reminds the reader of an old practice, apparently extinct during the days of the book's composition, of exchanging sandals during transactions within families involving rights to land or wives. Witnesses sign the documents (a practice widely attested through the ancient Near East and elsewhere). And most significantly, a blessing occurs, with the entire community invoking the memory of both honored and more "problematic" ancestral women, Rachel and Leah and Tamar, and connecting the foreigner Ruth to that line of women who "built up Israel's house."

The Birth of a Baby (4:13–17)

Inevitably, with such a blessing, marriage led to pregnancy and the birth of a son. Curiously, both the father and the mother fail to get the last word, for this belongs to Naomi, the grandmother, who receives at last a child to complete circle of life broken by the death of her own.

A Genealogy (Ruth 4:18–22)

The final unit of the book feels like a sort of footnote, but the author apparently wished to situate the story within a much larger and more important one, that of the Davidic monarchy. By insisting that David descended from a foreign woman, the author flies in the face of Deut 23:3–6's prohibition of even tenth-generation descendants of Moabites and Ammonites entering the sanctuary. (In any case, that law would be unenforceable absent genetic testing and seems a case of hyperbole used in making a point about community boundaries.) It is impossible to know whether the author knew that text or worried about the apparent contradiction set up, or merely considered David an exception to the rule (since presumably Yhwh can make exceptions to Yhwh's own rules). Given the genre of Ruth as a pleasant tale of marriage and affection, perhaps such theological niceties simply did not matter.

Implications

What to do with such a story? George Gordon, Lord Byron once remarked that

> All tragedies are finish'd by a death,
> All comedies are ended by a marriage.[1]

Ruth is a comedy in the most basic sense that it has a happy ending. Modern readers may rest uneasy with the arrangement of the marriage in a way that seems, at first, to privilege the already privileged male over the impoverished alien female. But given the many alternative paths the story might have taken, it is difficult to understand this as anything other than a relatively happy ending. This text, like Song of Songs and Esther, portrays strong and pious women who find dignity in world dominated by men. That alone makes it worth reading.

Something else is also important. The text insists that, in Israel, biological descent is less crucial that behavior. The life well lived counts for more than one's personal history, for one may enter Israel's story of ethical living in the ordinary routines of life, as did Ruth. So argues this story.

Note

1. *Don Juan*, Canto 3, Stanza 9.

For Further Reading

Brenner, Athalya, ed. *Ruth and Esther: A Feminist Companion to the Bible*. Sheffield: Sheffield Academic Press, 1999.

Sasson, Jack M. *Ruth: A New Translation with a Philological Commentary and a Formalist-Folklorist Interpretation*. 2nd ed. Sheffield: Sheffield Academic Press, 1989.

12 God, King, and People
1–2 SAMUEL

Key Text: *And Yhwh said to Samuel, "How long will you make a lament over Saul, since I have repudiated his kingship over Israel. Fill your horn with oil and go. I will send you to Jesse the Bethlehemite because I have selected one of his sons to as my king." Then Yhwh said to Samuel, "Do not look at his [i.e., David's brother Eliab's] appearance or his height because I have rejected him. It's not about what people see. People look with the eyes, but Yhwh looks with the heart [or, people look at the eyes, but Yhwh looks at the heart]." (1 Sam 16:1, 7)*

After the book of Ruth, not originally part of the DH or Former Prophets spanning Joshua–2 Kings, English Bibles resume the original work of the Deuteronomistic History with 1–2 Samuel. These two books recount the rise of the monarchy in ancient Israel, offering a multilayered reflection on the implications of that institution for the religious life of the nation. While most of this material predates the creation of the DH and probably shaped its overall view of Israel's history, 1–2 Samuel also shows a singular, if complex, point of view, according to which monarchy may be a vehicle for divine activity, but only under certain conditions.

First and Second Samuel weave together stories and poems from several sources (not all now identifiable) in order to create a picture of Israel's life during the eleventh and tenth centuries BCE, a time of transition from a village-based society organized by clans and tribes to a more urban one with a central government. By telling of three great leaders—Samuel, Saul, and David—these books open a window onto larger cultural, including theological, concerns.

The books of 1–2 Samuel are closely linked in theme and style, breaking in the middle of the story of King Saul's death (1 Sam 31–2 Sam 1). Most of the stories concern the three majors figures Samuel, Saul, and David, as well as their various hangers-on and enemies. The intertwining of their lives allows the narrative to address the transition from a loosely affiliated collection of clans and tribes to a territorial state. In telling this story, 1–2 Samuel follow a six-part organization:

A. The story of Samuel (1 Sam 1:1–7:17)
B. The rise of King Saul (1 Sam 8:1–15:34)
C. The fall of Saul and rise of David (1 Sam 15:35–31:13)
D. David's successes (2 Sam 1:1–10:19)
E. David's failures (2 Sam 11:1–20:22)
F. Supplemental information about David (2 Sam 20:23–24:25)

THE TEXTUAL CRITICISM OF SAMUEL

The books of 1–2 Samuel survive in the Hebrew and Greek manuscript traditions with significant differences. The oldest Hebrew manuscripts from Qumran, including 4QSama-c, often show more similarities in specific readings to the LXX tradition than to the MT. The latter seems to have suffered many small mistakes in the course of its transmission. In some cases, moreover, the LXX reflects not just a better version of the text (fewer mistakes made by copyists over the years) but a different edition of it. For example, the LXX story of Goliath includes material not present in the MT, indicating deliberate revision.

The Story of Samuel (1 Sam 1:1–7:17)

First Samuel opens where the book of Judges left off, with stories about festivals involving inhabitants of the land of Benjamin. However, whereas the end of Judges describes a half-baked solution to a tragedy involving the near-destruction of a tribe, the opening of Samuel speaks of divine blessing of an infertile woman and her family. It then progresses through a series of events in the life of Samuel, the last person said to "judge" Israel as a non-monarch (1 Sam 7:15) and the reluctant creator of the monarchy. The story of his life before the creation of kingship consists of five interrelated episodes that together describe the failure of the priestly clan of Eli and the last success of the charismatic, nonhereditary style of leadership prior to the rise of the monarchy (1 Sam 1:1–2:21; 2:22–36; 3:1–21; 4:1–7:2; and 7:3–17).

The story of Samuel opens in 1 Sam 1–2 as a tale about one Elqanah but really more directly his sterile wife Hannah. This polygamous family lives in the hill country of Ephraim, the central ridge of the land of Israel on which the tribes of Benjamin and Ephraim were located. Like the stories of Jacob and his wives and children (Gen 29–50), the tale of Elqanah, Hannah, and Peninnah plays on the dynamics of polygamy, in which the male may choose which wife and children to value. Elqanah looks beyond the economic importance of a wife who can bear children (workers in the field and proofs of male prowess) to see his beloved woman. Even so, the lack of a child drives her to seek divine aid at the sanctuary of Shiloh.

Hannah's prayers elicit the narrator's interest. Her first prayer (1 Sam 1:11) makes a vow to Yhwh, asking for a divine grant of fertility (ancient Israelites believed that God could ensure or prevent conception at will), in exchange for the gift of the firstborn son. The story thus addresses a deep and perennial human concern (fertility and child-rearing) within the context of an Israelite religious practice. Israelites, according to some biblical texts, thought of the firstborn child as belonging to Yhwh in a special way. Such a child must be redeemed with a sacrifice (see Exod 22:28; 34:20; Num 18:15–17). Hannah offers her firstborn son as an attendant in the sanctuary in Shiloh.

Her second prayer, 1 Sam 2:1–10, is a typical psalm of praise, probably composed for another setting later than the historical Hannah since it speaks of the monarchy but fitly representing the feelings of a new mother. (It is also the model for the Magnificat in Luke 1:46–55.) The poem uses the traditional language of rejoicing:

> My heart exults in Yhwh, my horn is elevated in Yhwh,
> My mouth smiles at my enemies for I rejoice in my deliverance.
> No one is as holy as Yhwh—no one is like you—no rock is like our God.

The text proceeds to describe the reversal of fortune experienced by many poor Israelites as they encounter the God "who raises the poor from the dust." And perhaps most tellingly, the poem ends by noting that "Yhwh judges the ends of the earth and gives strength to his king, raising up the horn of his anointed one."

As so often with poetry embedded in Israelite prose, this poem works on several levels. Not only does it concretize the feelings of a character who credits Yhwh with a turn in her fortunes as a wife and now mother, but it also both reaffirms the old theme of divine care for vulnerable Israel and takes that theme in a new direction by foreshadowing the imminent rise of kingship. Security, the text claims, lies in a well-functioning ruler under divine protection. The search for that ruler will occupy the rest of 1–2 Sam.

But not yet. The next episodes in the story of Samuel must also introduce new characters, the sons of Eli, priests of Shiloh. In 1 Sam 2:22–36, these priests appear as corrupt leaders who extorted too much food from families offering at the sanctuary in Shiloh and sexual predators to boot. Their abuse of power led to twin divine oracles of condemnation, first in the mouth of a "man of God" or prophet (1 Sam 2:27–36) and then via the young boy Samuel in the story of his call to the office of prophet (1 Sam 3:1–18).

The first indictment is particularly interesting because it lays out the duties of the priesthood, their history, and rules whose violation could lead to their overthrow. According to the prophet,

I was revealed to your ancestral family when they were in Egypt in Pharaoh's house. I chose it out of all Israel's tribes as my priests, to make offerings on my altar, to burn incense and to carry the ephod before me. I also gave your ancestral house all the fire offerings of Israel's children. So why have you abused my altar, my gifts that I commanded you by respecting your children more than me in order to misappropriate the best parts of every gift of Israel pertaining to my people? (1 Sam 2:27–29)

By anchoring the critique of the Elides in the story of the exodus, the "man of God" frames their abuse of power as both an act of ingratitude and disrespect toward Yhwh and as a betrayal of the solidarity between priest and people that should underscore leadership in Israel more generally. The rhetorical power of such an appeal to the reader (not just to Eli, whom it did not rouse to action) should be clear as part of the long-standing discussion in the DH and its sources of the importance of personal probity and structural transparency among powerful institutions.

This abuse of power by the Elides led, according to the narrative, to their defeat by the Philistines, during which they lost custody of the key symbol of Yhwh's presence, the Ark of the Covenant (1 Sam 4:1–22). The stories of 1 Sam 4:1–7:2 report the Philistine expansion into Israelite territory in the late eleventh century BCE, which eventuated in the destruction of Shiloh and threatened the existence of several Israelite tribes. Although the Elide family survived in the village of Anathoth north of Jerusalem, and its traditions were passed down several centuries down to their possible descendant the prophet Jeremiah (1 Kgs 2:26; Jer 7:12–15), 1 Samuel uses their story to highlight what can happen when religious leaders see their jobs as opportunities for gain.

More than that, 1 Sam contrasts the family of Eli with Samuel, investing him with the role of prophet, war leader, and priest in order to explore what it might mean to have well-functioning leadership. The decisive feature of such leadership is that Yhwh designates it as such. First Samuel 3:1–21 is a prophetic call narrative (cf. Exod 3–4; Isa 6; Jer 1), in which the prophet-elect misunderstands or tries to avoid his call only to receive a command to warn and challenge those in authority. The boy Samuel must challenge Eli in an oracle reminiscent of later ones against Saul (1 Sam 15:22–23), David (2 Sam 12:1–10), Jeroboam (1 Kgs 13:1–10), and Ahab (1 Kgs 22:1–23). His criticism (1 Sam 3:17–18) and Eli's acceptance of it foreshadow the following failures and successes of Israel. Thus the prophetic call serves as a narrative trigger for what follows.

Again, what follows is the worst imaginable disaster for ancient people, the loss of the main symbol of deity, in this case the Ark of the Covenant. The books of 1–2 Samuel will return to the theme of the Ark, exploring to what degree it is a fitting symbol for Yhwh and how it should be treated. For those who remember it in association with Indiana Jones, perhaps it will be useful to recognize that the Ark was a gorgeous gold-plated box topped with two terrifying sphinxlike creatures, the cherubim. The Ark symbolized the throne of Yhwh. Eventually, it would reside in the innermost room of the Temple, where it would signify the notion that Yhwh owned an earthly palace that resembled the heavenly one. The Ark was thus a reminder of the presence of God, and its loss of God's absence. The gallows humor surrounding its return (1 Sam 5:1–12), preceding which the Philistines experienced a series of humiliations including an epidemic of a tumorous disease (possibly bubonic plague) and the toppling of statutes of the chief Philistine god Dagon (a patron of grain-growing, since his name is the standard Canaanite/Hebrew word for "grain"), witnesses to the sophistication of the narrative.

ON PHILISTINE RELIGION

The Philistines entered the southern Levant as one of a group of peoples collectively called the Sea Peoples. Their origins seem to have lain in the Aegean region, and while they must have spoken a non-Semitic language originally, the few texts from their cities are later than the tenth century and written in a Canaanite dialect close to Phoenician (and Hebrew). So the original name of the god of grain, Dagon, must have been something else. From the Bible itself, we learn only the unsurprising facts that the Philistines worshiped various deities similar to the Canaanite gods, built temples, and engaged in sacrifice. Naturally, the Bible had less interest in describing Philistine religion than in challenging its claims vis-à-vis Yhwh.

The conclusion of this opening section of 1 Sam reports its hero's success in battle as well as his bona fides as a religious reformer much in the manner of the later kings Hezekiah and Josiah, two heroes (albeit flawed ones) of the DH. Samuel's invitation to "remove the gods of the foreigner from your midst" so that Yhwh "may rescue you" (1 Sam 7:3) and other aspects of the story sound reminiscent of Deuteronomy and thus must come from the Deuteronomistic editors as they position Samuel within a chain of pious military leaders, the last one not to wear a crown. With his successes against the Philistines, the pre-monarchic period comes to an end, as the text's creators see it.

The Rise of King Saul (1 Sam 8:1–15:35)

Endings also mark beginnings, and such is the case here. The second section of 1–2 Samuel recounts the rise of the monarchy during the tenth century BCE. Weaving together several disparate stories about Saul, the heir of a noble Benjaminite family, the narrator creates a picture of a monarch in whose successes lie the seeds of failure. The section has two large subsections, a cycle of stories about Saul's rise to power (1 Sam 8:1–12:25) and a further series about his successes and ultimate failure (1 Sam 13:1–15:35).

Here, chs 8–12 form a single complex of stories revolving around the question of whether Israel needs a king, and if so, of what sort. The story opens with a confrontation between Samuel, now old and, like Eli, unable to control his corrupt children, and the leaders of the nation, who desire a king to lead the nation's armies in place of the earlier system of tribal militias. At Yhwh's instruction, Samuel warns the people that such a ruler will almost inevitably be a tyrant who misappropriates the nation's resources. The people will have none of it, however, insisting that they only want the king to be a war leader, and that they mean no disrespect to Yhwh. The conversation in 1 Sam 8 resolves the conflict (for the moment) and allows the search for the proper sort of king to go forward.

First Samuel 8 is often misunderstood as a blanket denunciation of kingship as inescapably tyrannical. Scholars have commonly identified it as coming from an anti-monarchic source different from the "pro-monarchic" source presupposed by chs 9–10. While it is probable that the various parts of 1 Sam 8–12 come from different oral traditions since they have such diverse literary characteristics, they fit nicely together into a coherent story, none of which is straightforwardly pro- or anti-monarchic. Rather, the narrative has stated the possible abuses of kingship in the starkest ways in order to offer a solution to the problem, namely, a king who does not fit the bill of autocrat.

The "custom of the king" (Hebrew: *mišpaṭ ham-melek*) includes a series of abuses of power such as appropriating land and parceling it out to his clients, compelling subjects to work in luxury goods manufacture or general services to the court, and raising taxes to support a larger standing army (1 Sam 8:10–18). While such a description fits many kings, it conspicuously does not fit the first one, for Saul's great failing is indecisiveness in the face of popular pressure, not an abuse of power. The narrative takes pains to portray him as the very opposite of the feared ruler.

Awareness of this literary strategy of defanging Saul, so to speak, puts the whole conversation in 1 Sam 8 in a different light than first meets the eye. Upon hearing of the people's demands for a king, an incensed Samuel reports the request to Yhwh, who in turn insists, "they have not rejected you but rather have rejected me from being king over them" (1 Sam 8:7). This binary view—either Yhwh or a human king—becomes more complex when the people insist that they want a ruler only to lead them in battle, not the warned-against despot. Yhwh accedes to their request, apparently moderating the either-or of the original assessment of their request. Later texts in 1–2 Sam, notably 2 Sam 7, insist that God and king may coexist in harmony without any necessary conflict.

Then, chs 9–12 tell stories that explain in several ways how Saul was not the sort of despot that Samuel feared. According to 9:1–10:16, Saul sought, not the throne but merely his father's donkeys. Samuel, the seer at Ramah, brought up the subject of kingship to the surprised young man. The humorous story of the clueless Saul, guided by his servant and stumbling accidentally into power, must have elicited laughter from an Israelite audience, but it also makes a serious point that will become clearer later in the book. While the lack of desire for power on the part of a potential ruler has merit, there must be more qualifications, notably resolve in pursuit of duty.

After this tellingly comic interlude, 1 Sam 10:17–27 tells the story of the election of the king. Here Saul protests his unfitness for the job because he has no family power base (from which all ancient leaders would have operated). The episode ends with a story of a few "scoundrels" who refuse support the new monarch (the Hebrew term *běnê běliyaʿal* is essentially a curse word, a deeply insulting term). Against such opposition, the new king shows proper restraint, refusing to divide his new subjects over small issues.

In a related vein, the next story (1 Sam 11:1–13) reveals Saul to be not only a great warlord but one capable of restraining himself from vengeance on the "scoundrels." The saga of Saul's rise to power ends at the old and storied sanctuary of Gilgal (1 Sam 11:14–12:25), at which Samuel gives a farewell address charging Israel to remain faithful. They have purchased a loaded gun called the monarchy, and they must beware lest it go off in their faces. As the story ends, Samuel allows for the possibility that monarchy will work, if the people will obey God.

The final scene of the appointment of the monarch in 1 Sam 12 completes its efforts at quarantining the king and embedding him within a social system that can control his power. Here Samuel, in a story reminiscent of that of Moses in Num 16 (see the discussion in Chapter 6), makes an impassioned defense of his handling of affairs, claiming never to have appropriated anyone's property, and then appealing (in good Deuteronomistic style) to the past stories of Yhwh's defense of the ancestors. This apologia for leadership is the perfect counterweight to 1 Sam 8, offering a sharp contrast between the good and the bad leader, and defending again the necessity of proper checks and balances in society.

IS SAUL AMONG THE PROPHETS?

On two occasions, Saul experiences some sort of trace and out-of-control physical behavior (1 Sam 10:10–13; 19:23–24). In the first instance, his former associates express surprise at his participation in such a socially marginal (or at least rare) phenomenon, but the experience seems to confirm his new status as king-designate. In the second instance, however, the experience concludes with his lying naked, an indication of a more degraded state and thus a sign of his loss of kingship. The conception of prophecy in play here differs from that of later texts (such as the prophetic books or even the prophetic stories in 1–2 Kings) in that the behavior seems out of the realm of ordinary speech, and not just in terms of content. What Saul said was less important than the fact that he said it in an unusual, though unexplained, way.

At this point, chs 13–15 turn the story of Saul in a new and tragic direction; chs 13–14 describe battles with the Philistines, who inhabited the coastal regions of Palestine and repeatedly raided the hill country, where Israel was based. The stories of male bravado and national victory make for exciting reading, which the narrator summarizes in 1 Sam 14:47 with the passing line, "after Saul had secured his kingship over Israel ... " Like any successful ruler, Saul defeated foreign foes and then settled down to siring a dynasty.

These stories also introduce a new character, Saul's adult son Jonathan. (Evidently, the narrative has skipped a number of years or has simply incorporated variant sources out of sequence without solving the apparent chronological inconsistency.) During battle, Saul has foolishly taken an oath to kill anyone who stopped fighting to eat. The one person doing so was Jonathan, the greatest soldier in the army, whose quick repast of honey gave him enough calories to continue. The rash Saul must be talked out of killing his own son (1 Sam 14:45), a discussion that illustrates a serious flaw in the king's character. Impulsiveness can lead to disaster.

On the other hand, so can a stubborn attachment to improvisation mixed with impatience. This flaw comes to the fore in the tragedy of ch 15, the turning point of Saul's reign. There, Saul fights the Amalekites, Israel's hereditary enemy living in the arid steppe of the Negev (see Exod 17:8–16), and defeats them. However, instead of eradicating them in conformity with the then standard practice of holy war (Hebrew: *ḥērem*), Saul spares animals and the king, Agag, preferring to make sacrifices to Yhwh. Samuel criticizes that decision and pronounces the end of Yhwh's support for Saul.

The discussion between king and prophet is often quoted out of context to illustrate more general points about piety. But the context is significant. Samuel had instructed Saul to annihilate the Amalekites. Rather than arguing against such an action or, conversely, carrying it out, Saul simply changes the rules by sparing the monarch and animals for sacrifice, thus rendering the *ḥērem* an ordinary war. After blaming the people for this lapse, Saul must hear the stinging response of Samuel:

> Is it a small thing to you to be head of Israel's tribes? Yhwh anointed you as king over Israel. And Yhwh sent you on the path you should go on, telling you to repay the sins of the Amalekites and fight against them to their utter destruction. So why didn't you listen to Yhwh's voice instead of capturing plunder and doing evil in Yhwh's eyes? (1 Sam 15: 17–19)

This criticism of failure to annihilate the Amalekites, a marauding group against Israel had a long and understandable grievance, annoyed Samuel. Hence the most famous lines from later in the conversation:

> More pleasing to Yhwh than offerings and sacrifices is listening to Yhwh's voice,
>   Listening more than a nice sacrifice, attentiveness than the fat of rams.
>   For rebellion equals the sin of divination and disobedience is like the lying of small idols (Hebrew: *tĕrāpîm*).
>   Because you rejected Yhwh's words, he has rejected you as king (1 Sam 15:22–23).

Far from being a set of platitudes about the necessity of obedience to God, this short poem (arranged as it is in parallel couplets) blames Saul for failure to eliminate an enemy.

Modern readers undoubtedly find the story shocking since none of the characters (God, least of all) object to ethnic cleansing on principle but assume that such a practice, at least in this case, would conform to the will of the deity protecting Israel. However, for the narrator, the point is that Saul did not obey the divine command but attempted to exercise his own judgment in ways that might place the nation in peril. As discussed in Chapter 9 on Joshua, the so-called "holy war" in Israel and its environs followed different rules form other forms of warfare both then and now.

At the close of this section, then, Israel has a problem. Its king is no longer legitimate, not because of tyranny but because of his indecisiveness and propensity to blame his subjects for his own failures (a theme that crops up repeatedly in ch 15). How to solve the problem?

The Fall of Saul and Rise of David (1 Sam 15:35–31:13)

The next major section of the book, sometimes called the Story of David's Rise, introduces David and plays him off against Saul until the latter's death. In part, the narrative attempts to vindicate David of possible charges of treason and banditry by explaining how in each of case when he benefits from the death or defeat of someone else, circumstances extenuate his actions. At another level, the stories explore a major political question (what is the proper role of a king?) and a theological one (what does Yhwh want from the king on behalf of Israel?). Therefore, it is possible to read the stories at several levels while recognizing their extraordinary literary artistry.

DAVID AND HIS WIVES

A subtext of the David story involves his interactions with his wives. In addition to the princess Michal, daughter of Saul, he also married Ahinoam the Jezreelite (a northerner), Abigail (formerly the wife of Nabal and apparently a southerner), Maakah a princess from the neighboring kingdom of Geshur, Haggit, Abital, and Eglah (the last three of uncertain origin (2 Sam 3:2–5). He later acquired other wives while in Jerusalem (2 Sam 5:13).

The politics of the harem and its children plays a major role in the stories about David, from his off-again, on-again marriage to Michal to the rivalry between Absalom and Amnon. In several cases, the women exert significant influence on David and others, sometimes changing the course of affairs by their actions.

This large literary unit carefully weaves together different scenes of conflict between the once and future king. As David rises, Saul declines. Often scenes alternate in a sort of sandwich style. For example, 1 Sam 24:2–23 and 26:1–25 each recount a surprise encounter between Saul and David in which the latter spares the former's life. First Samuel 25 tells a story about David's acquisition of a major wife, Abigail. Similarly, 1 Sam 27:1–12 and 29:1–30:31 recount David's interactions with his Philistine overlords, while ch 28 puts Saul at Endor consulting a necromancer. Again, a sort of sandwich is formed, with the outside stories highlighting a contrasting story between them. Interestingly, in these two cases, the sandwich "filling" concerns the major male's characters' interactions with women. Whatever the origins of these various stories, it is impossible to see their organization as anything other than intentional and skillful.

To begin, 1 Sam 16 and 17 introduce David, not once but twice. The first story tells of his skill as a singer at Saul's court, where he provides a partial cure for the king's growing madness. In the Goliath episode of 1 Sam 17:1–18:5, however, Saul seems not to know David, and David must prove himself as a warrior. The inconsistencies in the stories derive from their being from different sources, which the narrator/editor of 1 Samuel has not tried to reconcile. Yet taken together, the stories portray David as a complex character, a man humble enough to play for an increasingly erratic king yet skilled enough a warrior to defeat a giant (slingers were important specialist troops in ancient armies, and so David was not overmatched in the field).

Here David appears as the fierce opponent of Israel's chief competitors, the Philistines. In contrast to Saul's supine approach to Goliath, David can win in single combat (due in part to a technologically superior weapon) and then lead an army in pursuit of a fleeing enemy.

The continuation of the story, however, explores how male rivalry leads to a jealous king seeking the life of his most successful courtier. The remainder of the section tells this story by arranging episodes in part according to a geographical scheme. So, 1 Sam 18:6–20:42 places David at court, where he can receive help from two of Saul's children, the crown prince Jonathan and David's own wife, and Saul's daughter, Michal. Meanwhile 1 Sam 21:1–26:25 locates David the fugitive in Judah and Moab, or in other words in the thinly populated zone south or east of Saul's kingdom and probably outside his consistent control. And 1 Sam 27:1–30:31 puts David outside the Israelite sphere of influence altogether, in the coastal areas controlled by the Philistines. This geographical arrangement is signaled in various ways, perhaps most interestingly by the threefold use of the wartime ditty "Saul has killed his thousands and David his tens of thousands," which appears in a strategic location in each of the sections (1 Sam 18:7; 21:12; and 29:5), each time as a telling statement on both David's prowess and also his ultimately pacific intentions toward Saul (but not the Philistines). More details are in order, then.

Following on, chs 18–20 depict David as Saul's successful general. He defeats the Philistines, marries the princess Michal (after bringing in a grisly dowry of Philistine foreskins), befriends the crown prince Jonathan, and otherwise shows himself to be a loyal member of the royal court.

His actions do not, however, endear him to Saul, who interprets the ambiguous song "Saul has slain his thousands and David his tens of thousands" (1 Sam 18:7; cf. 21:12; 29:5) in the most negative possible way. (The song is open to interpretation, however, because its two lines could be interpreted as synonymous parallelism, that is, as two ways of saying the same thing.) Saul decides to assassinate David, setting in motion the latter's flight to the wilderness (21:1–16; 23:1–28), the cruel murder of the priests aiding him (22:1–23), and various adventures including missed chances to kill Saul (24:1–26:25). Through skillful use of dialogue, the narrator systematically exonerates David. All the characters except Saul and his henchmen know his innocence. Although Nabal dies and David wins his wife Abigail (25:2–42), though David gathers a harem and an army, and though he consorts with the Philistines (27:1–29:11), the narrator exonerates him of all possible charges against him. While Saul has exceeded the worst nightmares of kingship stated by Samuel in ch 8, David shows himself to be a man of compassion, loyalty, and good sense.

This comparison cannot be accidental. In David's own time and probably long afterwards, his legacy was controversial. Was he a loyal follower of Yhwh who reached the throne almost effortlessly? Or was he a traitor, a shrewd exploiter of the misery of others, who worked his way to the throne through the most underhanded means? Was he a usurper or the rightful heir (though not through birth)? Was he a collaborator with the Philistines or their most implacable foe? Or was he perhaps all of these things at once? Certainly such disputes would have interested Israelites for a long time, and most acutely during his own lifetime and shortly thereafter. Finally, 1 Sam tries to answer them by telling stories that respond to the worst charges while acknowledging the factual basis behind them.

This section closes, then, with the death of Saul. Despite his own ban of divination and sorcery, he consults a necromancer at Endor (28:1–24; not a "witch" but one who probably used the Anatolian custom of digging a hole in the ground, placing in it objects that would lure the ghosts of the dead to reenter the world of the living). This event marks his complete downfall from his status as king, a pathetic end to a promising reign. In contrast to his inability to defend the nation, David defeats Amalekite raiders (30:1–30). And in contrast to Saul's treachery, David manages both to honor his agreement with Achish of Gath and to avoid fighting Saul, his erstwhile overlord. Saul then dies by his own hands at the battle of Mount Gilboa, at a location far from the Philistine homeland and deep in Israelite territory. In a brilliant bit of storytelling, the narrator removes David from an ethical dilemma: if he fights with the Philistines, then he betrays his own people, while if he fights against the Philistines, he shows ingratitude to his rescuers. David escapes the dilemma when the Philistine chiefs dismiss him from the battle (fearing his betrayal). Again, the storyteller takes pains to explain why the greatest Israelite king's intermittent alliance with the Philistine city-states did not blot his reputation.

The book of 1 Sam ends with the death of Saul in battle at Mount Gilboa. More precisely, 1–2 Sam reports three versions of the death scene, first in the voice of a third-person omniscient narrator (1 Sam 31:1–13), then in the report of an Amalekite (2 Sam 1:1–16), and then in a funeral dirge by David (2 Sam 1:17–27). The ancient scribes who divided the entire work at this point did so for valid reasons, although a division at the end of 2 Sam 1 would also have made sense.

In any case, the death scene powerfully portrays Saul's final descent into despair, and the final end of a reign characterized by poor choices of friends and enemies, unwarranted paranoia, abuse of family members, and other tokens of the madness that seems to have unraveled this king's mind. His death by suicide—one of two such stories in 1–2 Sam (see esp. 2 Sam 17:23)—led to the disgraceful display of his body on the walls of Philistine cities as a trophy of war until the brave rescue operation by his former subjects. The hunter became the hunted and haunted king as Samuel's curse in 1 Sam 15 reached its inexorable conclusion.

If the reign of Saul ended in tragedy, it also marked a transition in Israel's history. Before Saul, Israel was a loose confederation of tribes, uniting only during war, if then. After him, the monarchy was a presupposition of Israel's life. For the DH and its sources, that was his lasting legacy.

David's Successes (2 Sam 1:1–10:19)

Again, 2 Sam 1 opens with the second and third accounts of Saul's death, one from an Amalekite (by definition an unreliable witness and an unsympathetic character), and one from David (his funeral song in 1:17–27). The dirge pulls back the curtain again on the warrior culture, in which one male must mourn the loss of another:

> How the mighty ones have fallen!
> Do not tell nor recount it in Ashkelon's plazas,
> Lest the Philistines' daughters rejoice, lest the daughters of the uncircumcised exult . . .
> Saul and Jonathan, beloved and delighted in during their lives
> And not neglected in their death. (2 Sam 1:20, 23)

Here the song speaks of contests among males celebrated by women. The song shows the new king as the rightful mourner in chief for the old one, as well as an innocent party in Saul's death.

The next subjection, 2 Sam 2:1–5:25, recounts David's consolidation of power. The interwoven stories follow a careful pattern with an introduction underscoring David's search for Yhwh's guidance (2 Sam 2:1–7), followed by tales of conflict between the remnants of Saul's family and leadership structure (2 Sam 2:8–3:39), the death of Saul's last son (2 Sam 4:1–12), and the consolidation of David's power at home (2 Sam 5:1–10) and abroad (2 Sam 5:11–25).

Ishbosheth (or probably, originally, Ish-baal, "man of Baal") builds a power base in the Transjordan at the old site of Mahanaim (see Gen 32). However, his reliance on his general (and uncle) Abner leads to his undoing, for Ishbosheth proves an incompetent and indecisive ruler. Abner, the real power behind the throne, decides to throw in his lot with David. Before he can achieve the shift in power, however, Abner dies at the hands of David's own chief general Joab (again, David is innocent!).

The political maneuvering concludes when the northern tribes' leaders ask David to assume the throne (2 Sam 5:1–3). According to the summary of his reign in 2 Sam 5:4–25, David solidified his rule by building a new capital in territory outside the traditional tribal regions (Jerusalem), constructing a new palace, assembling a notable harem, and fathering numerous sons, all signs of his kingly success. For ancient cultures, the king was one of the primary symbols of cosmic order and the favor of the divine realm. The successful king, as measured by the sorts of achievements characteristic of David, could guarantee the well-being of the nation as a whole. The summary in 2 Sam 5 thus presents David as a model monarch.

The most important mark of royal success for ancient societies was the building of temples. Chs 6–7 present David as attempting to do so as he first brings the most important symbol of Yhwh, the Ark of the Covenant, to his newly conquered capital. David apparently wished to connect his dynasty to the ancient priesthood of Shiloh, and its symbols thus connected new successes to ancient verities. The effort goes awry, however, when a priest named Uzzah touched the Ark. His infraction of cult rules (not a moral violation but a ritual one) leads to his death. A nervous David declines to go forward, leaving the Ark for a while with a nearby supporter. The Ark finally reaches Jerusalem when David decides that its arrival poses no danger to him or his capital. Still, the story does not end well, for the celebration attending the Ark's arrival affronts David's wife, Michal, who finds his dancing humiliating (and perhaps sexually provocative). She articulates the opposition to David that many of his subjects, especially those with fond memories of Saul (Michal's father), must have felt.

THE ARK NARRATIVE OF 1–2 SAMUEL

The stories of Samuel and David (interestingly, not Saul) contain stories about the Ark of the Covenant (1 Sam 5:1–7:2; 2 Sam 6:1–23), its loss and then recovery. This Ark narrative is older than the narrative in which it is embedded and thus reflects very ancient traditions. The monarchy's appropriation of a pre-monarchic tradition was part of David's (and his successors') efforts to connect their rule to Israel's core religious understandings of Yhwh as the deliverer and patron of the people. By moving the Ark to his new capital of Jerusalem, previously not an Israelite site at all, David both gained legitimacy for his rule and earned a reputation for piety. That is, we should understand his motives as complex, not simply as a power play.

The story of David's success continues in 2 Sam 7, and as in 2 Sam 6, it introduces a note of uncertainty. Whereas most ancient Near Eastern kings built or refurbished temples as key acts demonstrating their fitness to rule, David is forbidden to do so. Instead, he receives from Yhwh a promise of an eternal dynasty, even without the building of a temple. The story plays on the Hebrew word *bayit*, literally "house" or "household," and by extension "temple" (when the house belongs to God) and "dynasty" (when the household is the king's). That is, David will not build Yhwh a *bayit* but rather the reverse. Yhwh promises to defend the Davidic dynasty, even if particular kings misbehave in such a way as to merit their removal. This promise served as the basis of a great deal of later theological reflection (see 1 Kgs 8:16–21; 11:9–13; Ps 89), ultimately leading to the messianism of Second Temple Judaism and early Christianity.

David's prayer (2 Sam 7:18–29) in response to Yhwh's promise of a dynasty models the piety that the narrator of the Story of David's Rise commends in a ruler:

Who am I Lord Yhwh, and who is my family that you bring me to this point? It was a minor thing to you, Lord Yhwh, when you spoke to your servant's family at some remove .... Because of your word and your heart, you have done all this great thing, to make your servant know. Therefore, you are great, Lord Yhwh. For there is no one like you and no God except you in all that we have heard about with our ears. (2 Sam 7:18–19, 21–22)

The prayer uses deferential language ("your servant" instead of "me"), emphasizing the human king's dependence on the much greater divine ruler. David acknowledges that the promise to protect the dynasty was a gift, not a reward for meritorious action, and that like all gifts in the ancient world, it implied a relationship of reciprocal obligations and commitments.

The promise of divine blessing is fulfilled in 2 Sam 8, which resembles the summaries of royal achievements in Assyrian inscriptions from just after the time of David, and in 2 Sam 10, a story of an Israelite victory that forms a pair with 1 Sam 11 (just as Saul defeated the Ammonites, so must David). The story in the middle (2 Sam 9:1–13), recounting David's mercy to Mephibosheth, a grandson of Saul, displays the king as a generous benefactor. David can impress his subjects with his kindness while taking no political risks because Mephibosheth is a semi-invalid.

David's Failures (2 Sam 11:1–20:22)

The portrayal of David's success in the first half of 2 Sam makes the next section all the more painful to read. Often called the Court History for its gossipy tales of intrigue that only David's courtiers could have known, 2 Sam 11:1–20:22 recounts a story of adultery and murder so criminal in its betrayal and humiliating in its outcome that the earliest reviser of Samuel, the author of 1 Chron, cannot bear to repeat it (see the discussion in Chapter 14, "1–2 Chronicles"). David's adultery with Bathsheba and murder of her husband, Uriah, one of David's most trusted soldiers, incensed Yhwh to such an extent that the very existence of the dynasty was at stake.

JERUSALEM AS THE CITY OF DAVID

According to 2 Sam 5:6–10, David captured the fortified city of Jebus, which was known as Jerusalem in Egyptian texts of the second millennium BCE, by entering the water system somehow. The means of entry is unclear, since Jerusalem of David's time was supplied both by tunnels under a heavily fortified tower on the city's eastern slope (built about five hundred years earlier) and by other tunnels, all predating the tunnel dug at the inspiration of Hezekiah during the late eighth century BCE. It was probably impossible for human beings, no matter how intrepid, to have climbed the cavity called Warren's Shaft, as is sometimes argued. Whatever entry point David's men took, their actions demonstrate resourcefulness as David captured a city thought impregnable.

But why Jerusalem? The attraction of a city that was not part of any Israelite tribe but had strategic importance because of its location on a significant east-west road, is obvious. David made it his capital and his personal property, hence the new name "City of David." From the small Canaanite core of about five hectares (12 acres) grew arguably the most famous city on earth.

This royal soap opera is comprised of several episodes revolving around clusters of major characters (with minor ones floating in and out as needed): David, Bathsheba, and

Uriah (2 Sam 11:2–27); David, Nathan, and Bathsheba's baby (2 Sam 12:1–25); Absalom, Amnon, and Tamar (2 Sam 13:1–39); David, Joab, and Absalom (2 Sam 14:1–16:19); Absalom, Ahithophel, and Hushai (2 Sam 16:20–17:23); again David, Joab, and Absalom (2 Sam 17:24–20:25). In other words, the stories are organized around the interactions of three major characters, which overlap from unit to unit. The first two stories sit within the framing device of stories about war against the Ammonites (2 Sam 11:2; 12:26–31), also indicating a highly intentional method of composition.

Admittedly, some stories in 2 Sam 11–20 fit a little less snugly into the overarching plot line. Still, the storyteller's art is on exhibit here at a very high standard. Now to examine things more deeply.

Second Samuel 11 opens with the tale of a war, but the focus does not lie here so much as on the king's adultery. Still, the military setting again surfaces the ethic of the warrior culture. While David's staying at home probably does not indicate any real dereliction of duty (kings need not always go to war), his cuckolding of Uriah does. In the story, he stands atop his palace balcony, no doubt at the highest point of the little City of David/Jerusalem, and gazes upon an attractive young woman bathing. Since the Peeping Tom is also king, a sexual encounter ensues, leading to pregnancy, leading to the recall of Uriah from war, leading to his refusal to sleep with his wife (sex at home would have violated the warrior's code), leading to David's decision to have him murdered in battle.

The response comes in Nathan's little parable in 2 Sam 12:1–4:

> There were two men in a city, one rich and the other poor. The rich one had numerous flocks and herds. But the poor man owned nothing but one little female lamb, which he had bought. He kept it alive and it grew alongside his children, ate his food and drank from his cup. It slept at his side and was like a daughter to him. Yet when a traveler visited the rich man, he did not take an animal from his own flock or herd to make a meal for his visitor. Instead, he took the lamb of the poor man. So what should be done to the man who came to him?

The parable plays on the pathos of the situation it describes, appealing to the sense of justice that a king must embody (cf. Ps 101). Yet, of course, the lamb-stealer turns out to be David himself, whom the prophet has now shocked into self-awareness.

David's self-sentence of death for murder seems just, yet it presents a major problem. Since Yhwh had promised to preserve the dynasty, and since David's heirs are even less honorable than he is (as the stories of Absalom and Amnon illustrate), imposing a death sentence on David is out of the question. Thus Yhwh opts for a curse on David's family, announced by Nathan, and carried out by David's sons themselves. Then, ch 12 begins the chain of tragedies by recounting David's petitions on behalf of his dying (illegitimate) son. His servants mistake his prayers for laments for his son, but they in fact are prayers of repentance. This is why they end when the boy dies. The story ends by emphasizing that Solomon, David's eventual successor, was not the child of adultery, allowing the story also to legitimize Solomon's doubtlessly controversial rule. But in a larger sense, the story of the dead baby illustrates the unfailing commitment of Yhwh to bring about justice even when no palatable solution presents itself.

The playing out of the curse begins in earnest in 2 Sam 13:1–39, in which the harem politics begins again as the oldest son Amnon rapes his half-sister Tamar. A particularly painful moment occurs in 2 Sam 13:13, in which a desperate sister pleads, "How could I escape my disgrace? And you would be like one of the fools in Israel. So, now, speak to the king. For he will not keep me from you." It is hard to assess her argument, since marriage between half-siblings was not customary in Israel (and prohibited by some, probably later, legal texts such as Lev 18), though it did occur in the royal family of Egypt. Is Tamar grasping at straws, then? Or does she know David's cavalier attitude toward women's fates? Or is such a marriage possible? All of these interpretations have been proposed, and it is hard to settle on one, although it is striking that Tamar thinks that such an appeal to male honor might work. Not with Amnon, however.

But the question of honor is a tricky one, as Tamar's brother Absalom knows. He waits two years before avenging his sister's honor and then does so dramatically by murdering Amnon in the presence of the other royal princes. This murder leads to his flight to his grandfather's kingdom Geshur (a small state located northeast of the Sea of Galilee but south of Damascus) and subsequent return at the behest of Joab.

The following chapters of the story recount Absalom's coup d'état, which fails as David brilliantly plays for time. Tension builds in ch 14 as a wise woman persuades David to invite Absalom back home from exile. This understandable act of family reconciliation proves to be a major political mistake. Any hope of peace disappears in 2 Sam 15:1–6 as Absalom takes on the trappings of a would-be king. Playing on latent tensions within Israel, Absalom seizes power, even going so far as to engage in prominent displays of sexuality with David's concubines, proof of his desire to be king and his male prowess as a potential sire of a dynasty.

In contrast to the foolish indecisiveness of Absalom, the narrator paints David as a pious man who declines to remove the Ark from the city (thus refusing to hijack the sacred for his political ends) and acknowledges Yhwh's right to decide his fate (15:23–31). His flight proves successful as a part of a campaign of attrition. In a brilliantly drawn scene of espionage (17:1–23), the narrator shows the double agent Hushai persuading Absalom to delay acting, a sure sign that he is not ready to be king. His delay costs him his life, giving David time to rally supporters and split the forces behind the insurrection.

The death of Absalom takes on tragic dimensions as he is caught in the flowing hair symbolizing his masculinity. The report of his death reveals another side the story: David's prominent display of grief—"Absalom my son, my son Absalom! I wish I could have died instead of you, Absalom, my son, my son!" (2 Sam 19:1)—reveals a father's inconsolable state. By this, the narrator again exonerates David of the death of an enemy and shows him not as a calculating political leader but as a leader caught up in events beyond his control.

At the same time, 2 Sam is not naïve about the political realities. Hence the speech of David's cousin, general, and problem-solver in chief, Joab:

> Today you are humiliating all your servants, the very ones who rescued your life today (as well as your sons, daughters, wives, and concubines). You seem to love your enemies and hate your friends! (2 Sam 19:6–7)

Joab insists that David has allowed his emotions to trump his political sense (as shown by his well-timed and disciplined mourning for Saul and Abner among many other occasions). Here the text explores an important dimension of kingship, the relationship between the personal and the public lives of the ruler. Joab reminds the king of his obligations to his loyal subjects who have suffered alongside him during a major crisis. The king's private grief must remain private.

The text's overall sensitivity to the nuances of political life in Israel continues in ch 20, which though possibly derived from different sources, continues the Court History's juicy story about resistance to David with stories about old leaders avoiding the blandishments of the court and new, but less successful, rebel leaders. Thus the entire unit of 2 Sam 11:1–22:22 trails off into the undramatic last years of David's reign. Curses do not carry on forever.

Supplemental Information About David (2 Sam 20:23–24:25)

The final section of 2 Sam constitutes a sort of appendix, breaking the narrative flow of the book by repeating some material and adding others. However, the entire section is structured chiastically (ABCCBA). Opening with a list of David's officials (2 Sam 20:23–26), it moves quickly to a story of a famine and the grisly cure for it, the execution of Saul's descendants for their grandfather's mistreatment of the Gibeonites (2 Sam 21:1–14).

Meanwhile, 2 Sam 22 reports a song that exists in a slightly different version as Ps 18. This psalm of thanksgiving offers a sort of concluding verdict on David's reign, which has been characterized by repeated instances of divine deliverance. A second song, David's valedictory address, appears in 23:1–7 as a second verdict on his reign. Together, the two songs serve the same narrative function performed by the songs in Deut 32–33 for Moses's biography or the speeches of Joshua in Josh 23–24. Among other options, Israelite storytellers concluded their narratives by having their heroes speak to the next generation of the most important insights they had gained.

Complicating this narrative technique, however, are the final chapters, which include several lists of David's greatest warriors (23:8–38) and a story of a plague (24:1–25). The book's concluding episode may raise issues about Yhwh's character for modern readers—why would Yhwh punish the nation for what seems like a harmless mistake on David's part?—but the editor of 1–2 Sam and his readers would have understood the story as an attempt to explain why the Temple was located where it was (see also the discussion in

Chapter 14). Solomon built it just north of the old Jebusite city of Jerusalem (renamed the "City of David") because there Yhwh had stilled the plague. The Temple was to be a place of healing and refuge.

Implications

To conclude, then, Israel's search for security, so intimately connected to kingship and temple, ultimately failed because the nation forgot that behind those symbols of divine power and care lay Yhwh. God was more important than the symbols of God. Or so the Deuteronomistic editors of Joshua–Kings wished to argue. History, of course, never lends itself to monocausal explanations, even theological ones. This is why 1–2 Sam seems at times to contain agendas at cross purposes with one another, and why the gorgeously drawn characters in the work exhibit motives, beliefs, and actions that differ widely from those the narrator might have wished for them. Yet the book does offer several theologically weighty lessons.

First, though kingship and temple can be appropriate vehicles for the gracious work of Yhwh, the symbols can take on lives of their own unless Israel remembers its central stories about divine deliverance and calling. Second, leaders bear special responsibility for insuring the continuity of the nation's faithfulness. Power can corrupt, but it can also be a tool for a higher cause. Third, trust in divine providence should lead to an ethical life for individuals and the community as a whole. This trust should lead the people to penitent, obedient, and generous lives. And fourth, Israel must recognize their inability to manage, coerce, trick, or otherwise control their God. Yhwh seems mercurial, even arbitrary, to those who do not seek the sort of integrity to which the experiences of exodus and settlement lead.

For Further Reading

Cross, Frank Moore, Donald W. Parry, Richard J. Saley, and Eugene Ulrich. *Qumran Cave 4, XII: 1–2 Samuel*. Discoveries in the Judaean Desert 17. Oxford: Clarendon, 2005.

Halpern, Baruch. *David's Secret Demons: Messiah, Murderer, Traitor, King*. Grand Rapids: Eerdmans, 2001.

McKenzie, Steven L. *King David: A Biography*. Oxford: Oxford University Press, 2000.

13 The Triumph and Tragedy of Monarchy
1–2 KINGS

Key Text: *If they sin against you—for there is no one who doesn't sin—*
and you become angry with them and hand them over to an enemy,
and then they are deported to the enemy's land, whether far or near,
and they change their mind in the land to which they have been deported (i.e., they repent
and seek your mercy in the land of their exile),
and say, "we have sinned and gone astray and done evil,"
and they turn to you with their entire mind and very being in the land of their enemies to which
they deported them,
and then they pray to you in the manner of their land (which you gave to their ancestors) toward
the city that you choose and the temple that I have built for your name,
then you in heaven, your dwelling place, should listen to their prayer and their petition for mercy
and take up their cause and forgive your people (who sinned against you of all their transgres-
sions that they transgressed against you and give to them mercies before their captors so they can
be merciful to them. (1 Kgs 8:46–50).

The final stage in the DH's presentation of Israel's history involves the development of kingship and the evolution and fall of the Israelite states. The books of 1–2 Kings open with the reign of Solomon, David's successor, and then catalogue the rulers of the two states that emerged after Solomon's reign. The demise of Israel (in the north) and Judah (in the south) followed their collision with the great empires of their era, Assyria and Babylonia respectively. Yet, for the DH, the progressive ripping apart of the Israelite kingdoms resulted less from the disparities of power involved than from a lack of religious commitment. That is, 1–2 Kings seeks to squeeze history into the mold of religion.

This squeezing involves several important processes and presuppositions. First, the act of narrating the lives of two sets of kings simultaneously was itself an innovation. Earlier chronicles of rulers from Mesopotamia had tracked king lists and select military or political events for one city state at a time, or a list of them in succession. To move beyond such a simple form of chronicle to more elaborate storytelling techniques interlinking two related states marked an innovation in the craft of history writing.

Second, and on a related note, by insisting that Israel and Judah belonged together as one people, 1–2 Kings defied what one might argue was the lesson of their history, that is, that they belonged apart. Unity under Yhwh became the ideal for the Deuteronomistic History, not only as a framework for understanding the past but also as a model for constructing the future.

Third, if the unity of Israel is a theological idea for the Deuteronomistic History—and it is—then other ideas underwrite that idea. These include the centrality of the Temple in Jerusalem (not elsewhere), the importance of aniconic worship of Yhwh alone, the centrality of the exodus as a touchstone for ethical reflection, and the value of collective memory. All of these themes come from Deuteronomy, and they all appear in the editorial material that sews together the various sources of 1–2 Kings.

In pursuit of these goals, the books of Kings follow a clear organization:

A. The rise and reign of Solomon (1 Kgs 1:1–11:43)
B. The intertwining histories of Israel and Judah (1 Kgs 12:1–2 Kgs 17:41)
C. Judah's century alone and demise (2 Kgs 18:1–25:30)

This organization reflects both the nature of the sources of 1–2 Kings, including apparently extensive chronicles of the reigns of at least some kings of Israel and Judah, and also a historical and theological conception (see table 13.1). Just as the Deuteronomistic History thinks of the Iron Age I (ca. 1200–1000 BCE or slightly later) as a period of charismatic deliverers following a more pristine era of settlement, it sees the era of the monarchy as a succession of rulers of varying qualities. That is, 1–2 Kings is the *Doppelgänger* of Judges, resembling it in the listing of one leader after another, differing from it in being a exposé not of anarchy but of tyranny.

The stories of the monarchs form the spine of the book. Each story opens with the formula "in the year X of King Y of Israel/Judah, N became king of Judah/Israel," and each story ends by noting that the "rest of the deeds of N are available in such and such a source." Most reports of reigns describe battles or temple-building, the usual stuff of royal chronicles, but the narratives that extend the description of a given reign almost always do so by adding material about prophets, thus laying out a second dominant theme of the work.

So important are the prophetic stories that one might almost wish that the names of the books were "1–2 Kings and Prophets." Most of the prophetic stories are set in the north, with these divine spokespersons criticizing the rulers of Israel. Some stories are also set in Judah, however.

TABLE 13.1

| The Kings of Israel and Judah in 1–2 Kings | |
Israel	Judah
Jeroboam (1 Kgs 12:1–14:20)	
	Rehoboam (1 Kgs 14:21–30)
	Abiyam (15:1–8)
	Asa (15:9–24)
Nadab (15:25–32)	
Baasha (15:33–16:7)	
Elah (16:8–14)	
Zimri (16:15–20)	
Tibni (16:21–22)	
Omri (16:23–28)	
Ahab (16:29–22:40)	
	Jehoshaphat (22:41–47)
Ahaziah (1 Kgs 22:52–2 Kgs 1:18)	
Jehoram (3:1–8:15)	
	Jehoram (2 Kgs 8:16–24)
	Ahaziah (8:25–??)
Jehu (9:1–10:36)	
	Athaliah (11:1–20)
	Joash (12:1–22)
Jehoahaz (13:1–9)	
Jehoash (13:20–25)	
	Amaziah (14:1–22)
Jeroboam II (14:23–29)	
	Azariah (15:1–7)
Zechariah (15:8–12)	
Shallum (15:13–16)	
Menahem (15:17–22)	
Pekahiah (15:23–26)	
Pekah (15:27–31)	
	Ahaz (16:1–20)
Hoshea (17:1–41)	
	Hezekiah (18:1–20:21)
	Manasseh (21:1–18)
	Amon (21:19–26)
	Josiah (22:1–23:30)
	Jehoahaz (23:31–35)
	Jehoiaqim (23:36–24:7)
	Jehoiakin (24:8–17)
	Zedekiah (24:18–25:22)
	Gedaliah the Governor (25:23–26)

Preceding all this backing and forthing of monarchies comes the story of the so-called United Monarchy, the reign of Solomon. Whatever the historical realities of the pre-division period, the Solomon narrative offers a nuanced view of a ruler capable of both good and evil.

The Rise and Reign of Solomon (1 Kgs 1:1–11:43)

First Kings 1–11, then, constructs this story of Solomon out of various kinds of material, including annalistic reports of royal deeds, architectural descriptions, prayers, and court stories. Woven together, these stories present both positive and negative aspects of his reign. This balancing act stems from the Deuteronomistic editors' desire to present both the challenges and opportunities of kingship in the person of a figure who, unlike his father, was not principally a warrior but a statesman of peace.

The Solomon narrative opens with stories about his accession to the throne during a crisis in the Davidic royal family. The first two chapters (1 Kgs: 1–2) properly belong with the Succession Narrative material in 2 Sam 11–20, with the same characters (David, Bathsheba, and Solomon) and the same political problem (the securing of a viable heir) driving both sets of stories. In 1 Kgs 1–2, the crisis arises when an aged and apparently impotent David, who must draw body heat from an attractive young concubine with whom he can nevertheless not engage in intercourse, finds his two sons Adonijah and Solomon competing for the throne. Adonijah enlists the support of David's old officials Joab and Abiathar, while Nathan backs Solomon (despite his condemnation of the marriage between his parents as reported in 2 Sam 12:1–12). In this case, harem politics trumps the more public face of power, as Adonijah's large-scale feasting of his admirers fails to win the only vote that matters, David's.

The historical nature of this material presents challenges. The brutality of Solomon's purges as reported in 1 Kgs 2:1–38 seems to reflect a real memory, since the text is unlikely to have invented a story so unflattering to the temple-building ruler. He systematically eliminated many of his father's old advisors (Abiathar, Benaiah, and especially Joab), as well as his own brother Adonijah and his father's old enemy Shimei. The text attempts to defend these executions as the response of a dutiful son to his father's advice (1 Kgs 2:1–6). It also masks the self-serving nature of these acts in the pious language of the principals. Hence David's counsel:

> You should keep a commitment to Yhwh your God, to go in his ways, to keep his statutes, his commands, and his judgments, and his testimonies, just as it is written in the Torah of Moses, so that you will succeed at all that you do. (1 Kgs 2:3)

as well as the repeated use of oath formulae by Solomon ("as Yhwh lives"). And yet this masking is not all it seems. Some of the language here comes from the Deuteronomistic editor (as the quotation above shows, with its repeated synonyms drawn straight from

Deuteronomy), and some is older. In other words, the incorporation of this story into the larger text of 1 Kings demanded a certain amount of scrubbing, and yet not so much as to resolve the moral challenge presented by the story. Quite the opposite in fact—the pious language highlights the problematic nature of the deeds. And yet one can hardly feel very sorry for most of the dead, whose misdeeds had caught up with them.

In any case, 1 Kgs 3–8 takes a different tack, presenting a much more positive side of Solomon. The narrative consists of a series of episodes: (1) a dream at the high place (Hebrew: *bāmâ*) of Gibeon during which Solomon receives a promise of divine wisdom (1 Kgs 3:4–15); (2) an immediate fulfillment of that promise in which he decides to give a live child to the mother who will care for it regardless of its true biological parentage (1 Kgs 3:16–28); (3) a description of his newly imposed governmental structure, including a standardized bureaucracy of department heads with distinguishable assignments and a list of administrative districts that cut across tribal boundaries, as well as diplomatic relations and systems for provisioning the government (1 Kgs 4:1–5:32); and (4) the building and dedication of the Temple (6:1–8:66). This disparate material apparently comes from different sorts of sources, including archives (lists of names and places), court stories, and Temple records. Scholars debate the historical accuracy of some details, since the archaeological remains of the tenth century BCE are difficult to date and do not, in any case, seem to reflect the mighty empire to which a superficial reading of these chapters would point. On the other hand, the most recent archaeological work at Jerusalem does indicate the presence of monumental architecture for this period. Nor is it easy to discern a motivation for inventing centuries later such things as lists of royal officials. Moreover, the fact that the tradition attributes the building of the Temple in Jerusalem not to Israel's greatest king, David, but to his son seems to argue for some sort of historical kernel to this material.

SOLOMON AND MARK TWAIN

In *Huckleberry Finn*, Jim the escaped slave and Huckleberry himself discuss the story of Solomon and the prostitutes. As Jim observantly puts it, "Blame de point! I reck'n I knows what I knows. En mine you, de *real* pint is down furder—it's down deeper. It lays in de way Sollermun was raised. You take a man dat's got on'y one or two chillen; is dat man gwyne to be waseful o' chillen. No, he ain't; he can't 'ford it. He knows how to value 'em. But you take a man dat's go 'bout five million chillen runnin' roun' de house, en it's diffunt. *He* as soon chop a chile in two as a cat. Dey's plenty mo'. A chile er two, mo' er less, warn't no consekens to Sollermun, dad fatch him!" Whether 1 Kings intended to question Solomon's wisdom in this way or not, intelligent readers do recognize the complex portrayal of the king, as Twain's Jim points out. The common sense of the slave accustomed to the ways of the powerful speaks a kind of truth about the casualness with which a ruler may risk the lives of the most vulnerable subjects.

The most crucial part of the Solomon story describes the building of the Temple as part of the palace complex in Jerusalem. Like some temples in Syria, this one consisted of three chambers aligned on a single axis, each room holier than the one before it as one moved inward from the single entrance. According to 1 Kgs 6, the building measured about 30 × 10 meters (98 × 32 ft.), with the innermost room, the Most Holy Place, being a perfect cube.

Perhaps more significant than the floor plan of the Temple, the iconography and furnishings work together to create an environment reminiscent of ideas about the heavenly realm. So the decorations of the walls consisted of recurring images of sphinxes (Hebrew: *kĕrûbîm*), palm trees, and lotus blossoms, all imagery from the garden of God (1 Kgs 6:29; cf. Ezek 28). In front of the Temple was a major altar for burnt offerings and, more surprisingly, a giant cast bronze pool atop twelve bronze oxen. (1 Kgs 7:23–26) This "sea," apparently symbolizing the cosmos itself, would have been a technological marvel of metalworking.

The theological payoff of the temple-building story comes in 1 Kgs 8. This text depicts the dedication of the Temple as a seven-stage ritual, with (1) the gathering of the people (8:1–2); (2) the procession of the Ark of the Covenant into the building (8:3–9; cf. Ps 24); (3) a divine intervention in the ceremony through the presence of a thick cloud preventing priestly activity (8:10–11; cf. Exod 40:34–38); (4) an initial prayer by Solomon (8:11–21); (5) a much longer prayer, again by Solomon (8:22–53); (6) a blessing of the congregation (8:54–61); and (7) sacrifice on a massive scale (8:62–66).

The clearest statements of the theology of this material comes from the two prayers. While no good reason exists to believe that the prayers represent a transcript of Solomon's precise words, they do capture the key ideas of Israel's convictions about the Temple as a sign of Yhwh's presence and favor. The first, which seems to be earlier in terms of its composition, links the monarchy with the deity:

> Yhwh spoke about dwelling in darkness. Today I have built you a noble house, a place to dwell in eternally. (1 Kgs 8:12–13)

Behind such a simple statement lies the notion that the king bore a duty to provide a temple for his divine patron, an idea widespread in the ancient Near East. Also, it reflects a conception about the architecture of the building itself, for the innermost room, in which the Ark stood, was an unlighted room, inaccessible and forbidding. The following lines make connections explicit as Solomon connects his work to Yhwh's selection of David as king. That is, the text links three major theological ideas, kingship, Temple, and the exodus (Israel's core story).

The much longer prayer that follows, which is chockablock with Deuteronomistic phrases and conceptions (1 Kgs 8:17–53), partially corrects any false impressions that might arise about the Temple and then adds more significant issues that point beyond the time frame of the book itself. As a matter of correction, Solomon is made to say, "Will Elohim really dwell on the earth? Truly, the sky and the sky above the sky cannot contain you. So how could this house that I have built?" (1 Kgs 8:27). Then begins a series of petitions addressed to Yhwh seeking in advance forgiveness for Israel when it repents.

The prayer considers a series of scenarios, including the ultimate expulsion of the people of Israel from their land (see the quotation cited at the beginning of this chapter [1 Kgs 8:46–50]) and seeks beyond all possible calamities the mercy of Yhwh.

One of the most extraordinary requests appears in 8:41–43, which requests that Yhwh treat a foreigner, otherwise a feared category of people in parts of this book, just like an Israelite:

> Moreover, with respect to a foreigner, someone not of your people Israel—if such a person comes from a faraway land on account of your name [i.e., reputation], having heard of your great name and your strong hand and your outstretched arm, and in coming prays in the direction of this temple, then you should hear from heaven, your dwelling place and do all that which the foreigner asks of you.

In the context of the book as a whole, which knows of the Babylonian destruction of the Temple and near annihilation of Israelite life, such a request appears audaciously broad-minded. By timing this prayer during the dedication of what the DH argues should be Israel's only shrine, the book breaks the bonds of narrow national conceit and embraces a larger viewpoint.

SOLOMON AND THE QUEEN OF SHEBA

Saba was an important kingdom in the southern Arabian peninsula (roughly, Yemen and Hejaz), gaining part of its power from its access to an international trade in spices. This significant power has left behind remains of dams and waterworks, as well as the city of Marib/Maryab. Kings of Saba show up in Assyrian records from the eighth century BCE on, though archaeological remains are older. The Queen of Sheba story took on new life in Ethiopia about seven hundred years ago as it became part of the legitimation strategy of the self-designated Solomonic Dynasty (which ended only in 1975). The new rulers of Ethiopia claimed descent from Menelik, the love-child of Solomon and the Queen of Sheba. While no historical reality lies behind this legend, it does show the abiding significance of the story, and it reflects a distantly refracted memory of a historical reality, that is, the cultural and possibly political connections between the Sabaeans and Ethiopia as areas both fronting the southern end of the Red Sea.

Unfortunately, this high point of Solomon's career as depicted in 1 Kings cannot last. The final three chapters of the story present decline, not a precipitous fall, to be sure, but a downward trajectory nonetheless. While 1 Kgs 9:1–9 returns to the promise of wisdom and protection given at Gibeon in chapter 3, and then follows that oracle report with a list of major foreign and domestic policy accomplishments (notably, relations with the Phoenician city-states and the construction of a port on the Gulf of Aqaba), and chapter 10 reports the famous visit of the queen of Sheba to Solomon and his extraordinary wealth, all of this is overshadowed by his success at loving "many foreign women, including Pharaoh's daughter" (1 Kgs 11:1).

For 1 Kings, this intermarriage of Solomon resulted from religious problems, not just from the inevitable commitments of ancient great power politics, for which the accumulation of a large harem was the inevitable consequence of relationships with foreign kings. The text does not blame his idolatry on these women, for the choice remained with him. But it does understand the state-sponsored sanctuaries of gods other than Yhwh to be "foreign," something outside the Israelite norm, a direct violation of Yhwh's command not "to go among them or let them go among you, since they will surely lead your mind after their gods" (1 Kgs 11:2). Even though the Deuteronomistic History knows that the worship of some deities other than Yhwh had a long history in Israel (see Josh 24 and all of Judges), it attributed to Solomon egregious polytheism. This practice, along with his oppressive taxation policies supporting the luxury of Jerusalem, led to the collapse of his state, not during his lifetime but after his death. Thus 1 Kings understands this history, offering an explanation of the ensuing division of the nation as something inorganic to Israel, not as the result of the long-standing cultural differences between north and south, which show up in both the archaeological record and, albeit tucked away in quiet corners, the biblical text itself.

The Intertwining Histories of Israel and Judah (1 Kgs 12:1–2 Kgs 17:41)

The center section of 1–2 Kings details the reigns of successive rulers of the larger Northern Kingdom of Israel and the smaller and poorer Southern Kingdom of Judah. After considering the historical context of this material and the main plot points of the narrative, it should be possible to identify some key themes that appear throughout it.

THE HISTORICAL CONTEXT

The narrative of the so-called Divided Monarchy begins in the 920s BCE, even though no firm history anchor points (at least in writing) exist outside the Bible itself for this time period. Such points do begin with the ruler Omri, for Assyrian texts from the ninth century on refer to the land of Israel as the "house of Omri" (Akkadian: *bīt Ḥumri*), while the king himself is named in the Mesha Stele from Moab, also from the ninth century. Several northern rulers are also mentioned in Assyrian texts of the ninth and eighth centuries. The end of the state came in 722 BCE, when Sargon II sacked Samaria and deported much of its population to other parts of the Assyrian Empire, an event that both Israelite and Assyrian texts recorded. Moreover, the Aramaic inscription from Tel Dan from the ninth century BCE speaks of an Aramaean king's defeat of the king of Israel and the king of the "house of David" (i.e., Judah), again giving some control to our understanding of the biblical text as historical material.

The ninth century BCE is also well known archaeologically. Major building projects occurred at Megiddo, Samaria, Dan, and other northern sites during the Omride Dynasty (ninth century), probably including the so-called Solomonic stables and gates (which may, however, rest upon tenth-century foundations in some cases). In Judah, also,

MAP 2 Israel and its neighbors. From the *New Oxford Annotated Bible*, 4th ed., p. 1285.

some monumental architecture dates to this period at Lachish. The north especially was not a backwater but a flourishing society. No wonder, then, that at the battle of Qarqar in 853 BCE, the coalition of western states facing down Assyrian aggressors, included as its largest military contingent the army of Israel led by Ahab.

It is striking how little of the historical backdrop draws the attention of the narrative of 1–2 Kings. Here, the focus lies on the smaller scale, the conversations of rulers and prophets, the day-to-day getting and holding of power. For example, the ruler who may have had the most power of all, Omri receives almost no press, while his son Ahab's is highly negative despite his successes on a geopolitical scale. Assyria shows up merely at the end, and then only as necessary. In other words, the historical reportage of 1–2 Kings seems selective (as always for all historiographic works), but more than that, interested in topics that illustrate larger theological points.

As it stands, the literary framework into which all the reports of northern royal doings are inserted contains a refrain (with some variations) that signifies much of the editors' view of their sources: "King X committed/did not turn from the sins of Jeroboam son of Nebat" (1 Kgs 16:31; 2 Kgs 3:3; 10:31; 13:2, 11; 14:24; 15:9, 18, 24, 28). That is, the story of the Northern Kingdom is the story of national apostasy. For the Deuteronomistic editor(s), apostasy consisted of worshiping Yhwh through the mediation of calf statues in Dan and Bethel, rather than aniconically in Jerusalem. Other sins flowed from this primordial one.

This conception of the north's history relates to another feature of 1–2 Kings, namely, the presence of a massive expansion of many stories of Israel's kings by means of prophetic stories. Without these additional stories, the books of Kings would lack much of their flavor, falling into a regular rhythm of stories of rulers, begun and concluded in the predictable same ways. The prophetic narratives thus add depth and excitement to the overall effect. The relative scarcity of such stories for the south not only reflects the nature of the sources underlying 1–2 Kings (maybe fewer such stories existed?), but more importantly a basic conception of prophecy shared by many biblical writers. In such a view, prophecy existed primarily to correct the abuses of rulers. And so the episodes involving prophets such as the anonymous predictor of the rise of Josiah (1 Kgs 13), the crusty Ahijah (1 Kgs 14), Micaiah ben Imlah (1 Kgs 22), and especially the redoubtable Elijah and his disciple Elisha, all signal a strong trust in Yhwh's demands for justice and an equally strong contempt for human corruption. This sensibility, which predates the Deuteronomists but certainly informs their outlook, infuses the whole work as it now stands.

MAJOR PLOT POINTS

While the skeleton of these stories of kings and prophets follows the same sort of outline (name and relative date of the king, one or more stories of his achievements, concluding summary and death announcement), some kings receive perfunctory treatment, and others much more. The narrative of 1 Kgs 12–2 Kgs 17 highlights five reigns in particular, those of the northern kings Jeroboam I (late tenth century BCE), Ahab (mid-ninth century), his son Jehoram, Jehoram's replacement through a coup d'état Jehu (later that century), and the southern ruler Joash (along with his grandmother and sometime regent Athaliah). Two of these rulers were members of the Omride Dynasty, and two of them its opponents, indicating the storytellers' obsession with a line of rulers to which they strenuously objected on both theological and social-justice grounds. Many themes recur throughout these skillfully told stories. The final plot point in this larger section concerns the fall of the Northern Kingdom of Israel itself.

CHRONOLOGY IN THE BOOKS OF KINGS

At first glance, 1–2 Kings seems to present a clear chronology of the rulers it lists. However, on closer examination, it turns out that the numbers of years for the reigns do not quite add up. This apparent discrepancy arises from the ancient practice of counting part of a year as a year of a reign and, possibly, the presence of overlapping reigns (a father might associate his son with him as co-king, for example). Therefore, instead of offering unjustifiably precise dates for the various kings, it makes sense to suggest general ranges.

On the other hand, some chronological anchors do exist for the rulers of Israel and Judah, especially from the 800s on. For example, Assyrian texts place Ahab at the battle of Qarqar in 853 BCE, while the contemporary Mesha Stele (from Moab) mentions "the son of Omri" (which might be Ahab or one of his sons; cf. 2 Kgs 3) as a ruler from whom Mesha freed his new kingdom. Assyrian records also mention Jehu, Menahem, and Hoshea, down to the final destruction of the Northern Kingdom in 722 BCE by Sargon II. So excessive skepticism about the Bible's general chronology is misplaced.

Plot Point 1: Jeroboam I (1 Kgs 12:1–14:20)

The first of these reigns is that of Jeroboam I, an erstwhile official in Solomon's bureaucracy who returns from involuntary exile in Egypt to find himself ruler of the northern tribes (minus Judah and perhaps Benjamin; contrast 1 Kgs 12:20 with 12:23). The Jeroboam story introduces two new themes that will play throughout the rest of the book: (1) the dispersed vs. the central place of sacrifice, and (2) the role of prophets in the making and breaking of kings.

The first theme appears as the aftermath of the breakup of the unified kingdom. The scene opens with a nationwide assembly at Shechem, an ancient Israelite center in the north, at which the people request an abatement of taxes from Solomon's heir Rehoboam. After taking counsel with both his father's mature advisors and his own younger cronies, Rehoboam decides on the latter's advice to assert his authority in the most insulting way possible. Using the imagery of cattle or at least slaves pulling a heavy burden, he says, "My father imposed on you a heavy yoke, but I will add more (weight) to your yoke. My father punished you with whips, but I will punish you with scorpions" (1 Kgs 12:11). A king who regards his subjects as mere slaves subject to his whim courts insurrection, and Rehoboam received immediate and overwhelming rejection of his legitimacy. Almost without a fight, he lost most of his kingdom, thanks to this crass violation of Israel's conceptions of the integrity and basic dignity of all the people.

Stepping into the breach caused by the Davidide dynasty's failure to secure its power by securing its legitimacy, Jeroboam receives the throne from the gathered national assembly (thus legitimating his rule on the basis of popular assent) and also receives additional confirmation when a prophetic oracle instructs Rehoboam not to "fight against your siblings, Israel's children—return home, each of you" (1 Kgs 12:24). So far so good.

However, Jeroboam's third effort at legitimating his rule falls flat, as far as the narrator is concerned, when he installs worship of Yhwh through the medium of a gold (-plated) calf in the sanctuaries of Dan and Bethel. For the storyteller, his motivation, though kept secret "in his heart" was a cold, if paranoid, political calculation ("Now the kingdom will return to the family of David. If this people goes up to make sacrifices in Yhwh's temple in Jerusalem, the heart of this people will turn to their lords, to Rehoboam the king of Judah, and they will kill me" [1 Kgs 12:26–27]). The installation of the calves themselves drew on older practice, and even a ritual cry known also from Exod 32:8, "Israel, these are your gods, who brought you from Egypt's land" (1 Kgs 12:28). It is difficult to know how an author could have had access to the king's motivations, though the storyteller's art allows for such things, and the apparently traditional character of worship of Yhwh in Bethel and Dan (see Gen 28:10–22; Judg 18) also points to other possible explanations for Jeroboam's actions. Certainly the ideas of royal patronage of temples and the use of images bothered no one else in ancient Near Eastern societies, except the theologians of Israel. Even a text like Amos 4:4—"Go to Bethel and sin, to Gilgal and multiply sinning, and bring your sacrifices each morning—does not criticize the sanctuary in Bethel per se, but only those ways in which religion papered over social injustice, at times with royal support. In short, then, the critique of Jeroboam's sanctuary-building comes from the Deuteronomistic circles who believed that worship of the one God entailed sacrifice only in Jerusalem and therefore the separation of other aspects of worship (prayer, feasting) from sacrifice.

Moreover, the second major theme that begins with Jeroboam's reign is the oppositional nature of prophecy. Prophets resist kings, at least sometimes. In the Jeroboam story, the resistance begins with a traveling prophet who stands up in Bethel and predicts the coming of a future great king (Josiah) who will desecrate that very sanctuary. That is, 1 Kgs 13:1–10's story foreshadows the much later episode of the pathbreaking rule of the very ruler whose work brought the Deuteronomistic theology to the fore. The prophetic emphasis continues in 1 Kgs 14:1–20 in which a prophet named Ahijah, whom the queen consulted during the illness of her son, the crown prince. Ahijah detects his royal visitor in spite of her disguise, thanks to Yhwh, and then gives her an oracle:

> Thus says Yhwh Israel's God, "Because I elevated you from among the people and made you prince over my people Israel and tore kingship from the family of David and gave it to you—yet you have not been like my servant David (who kept my commands and sought with his whole heart to do only what I approved of), but instead you did all the evil you could and made for yourself other gods and images in order to irritate me, and pursued your desires—therefore, I am bringing calamity to Jeroboam's family and will eliminate Jeroboam's wall-pisser,[1] whether kept or let go in Israel. (1 Kgs 14:7–10)

The rest of the curse on the Jeroboam dynasty becomes even more colorful. The prophetic ideal reflects some attachment to David as a model, not to the Davidic dynasty as an instantiation of that model.

Sandwiched between these two episodes is a more troubling one, in which the prophet who went to Bethel to announce a future ruler's destruction of that sanctuary finds himself tricked by an older prophet into taking another road home and then ends up inside a lion that frequented that very road. At some level, this tragicomedy warns against trusting the prophetic word completely, especially if one has direct access to Yhwh's voice. So, while the story troubles readers (and for good reason), it must function as part of a larger Israelite discussion on the need to confirm the individual prophet's words by other prophetic speech (see the discussion on Deut 13 in Chapter 7).

Plot Point 2: Ahab (1 Kgs 16:29–22:40)

Ahab and his wife Jezebel may be the most notorious biblical couple who ever lived, famous for pointless cruelty in their persecution of the prophet Elijah, theft of property from Naboth, and general self-absorption. Yet the morality tale masks a more complicated reality. Ahab seems to have been one of Israel's most successful rulers, the leader of the largest military contingent against Assyria and probably the builder of major fortifications and other monumental architecture at Samaria, Megiddo, and other sites. From a certain point of view, his reign must go down as a triumph.

The biblical traditions about him do not share that point of view but instead regard him as a tyrant. Why? While simply accepting or rejecting the critique of his reign (according to one's preconceptions) always tempts readers, understanding the critique requires greater care and offers more insights.

The Ahab narrative intertwines with stories about the doughty prophet Elijah and the almost equally formidable Micaiah son of Imlah. These stories begin and end in the usual way of 1–2 Kings, with a synchronism to a king of Judah, a comment on Ahab's evil deeds, and (at the end) a summary of his reign. Within the editorial framework, however, appear a series of stories of royal conflicts with prophets. A minor historical problem arises in the apparent conflict between 1 Kgs 22:40 ("and Ahab lay with his ancestors," i.e., was buried in his ancestral tomb), a formula that usually implies death by natural causes, and 1 Kgs 22:34–37, which describes the death of the anonymous "king of Israel" in battle. The text in 1 Kgs 22 consistently refers to an unnamed "king of Israel," leading many scholars to argue that the story originally belonged to a later king and was somehow transferred to Ahab. That scenario is possible, and certainly the story of a royal death comes from a different oral source than the preceding stories about Ahab. Yet it is also possible that "lying with one's ancestors" need not always have implied slipping this mortal coil in one's own bed.

ELIJAH AND THE HISTORY OF ISRAELITE PROPHECY

Israelite prophecy seems to have taken several forms, including (1) prophets in royal employ (much as in other ancient Near Eastern societies), (2) miracle-workers at the social margins, and (3) critics of the system whose followers preserved their words orally and in writing (a later stage of prophecy). Without doubt, the sociology of prophecy was more complicated, with individuals performing the role of prophet in different ways, depending on their circumstances, personality, and purposes. Elijah and his successor Elisha fit into the second category. While their oracles have largely gotten lost, their actions (and miracles) occupy the center of their story.

Consider the prophetic conflict stories, then. First Kings 17–19 portrays Elijah, a Transjordanian prophet, as miracle worker and critic. In the first scene (1 Kgs 17:1–24), he resurrects a dead boy whose mother has shown him hospitality.

The second scene (1 Kgs 18:1–46) famously describes a conflict between Elijah and hundreds of prophets of the god Baal, all in royal employ, taking place on Mount Carmel. This promontory soars about 525 meters (ca. 1700 ft.) above the Mediterranean coast (near modern Haifa, but more relevantly, near the major coastal roads of antiquity), and provides the most dramatic possible backdrop for a moment of divine intervention. The story is familiar: to demonstrate the superiority of their deities, Elijah and the other prophets build competing altars and wait for fire to reign down from heaven. Naturally,

Baal's pyrotechnic skills are found wanting, and Yhwh's incineration of the waterlogged altar and the sacrifice convinces the audience of the need to worship their ancestral god alone.

In its polemic against worship of gods other than Yhwh, the story resorts to satire, with Elijah egging on the prophets of Baal: "shout loudly, for he is a god—maybe he is thinking or relieving himself or on a trip or asleep and about to wake up" (1 Kgs 18:27). While some biblical texts do conceive of Yhwh as sleeping (e.g., Ps 44:24 [ET 44:23]), only to dismiss the idea, the picture of Baal here clearly dismisses his divinity as a mask for humanlike frailty.

More to the point, the aftermath of the story makes clear its political overtones: Jezebel puts in motion the royal power apparatus to crush Elijah. While the text wishes to mark the worship of Baal as "un-Israelite" and foreign-backed (even though at least some Israelites undoubtedly worshiped Baal before Jezebel arrived on the scene), this aspect of the anti-Baal polemic is subdued. The problem lies not the cult's alleged foreign origins but in its existence in Israel and with royal support.

The third Elijah story in this section concerns his flight to Mount Horeb, the traditional site of the reception of the Torah and of encounter between Yhwh and Israel (1 Kgs 19:1–21). Elijah flees there, believing himself to be the only Yhwh prophet remaining, only to hear the divine counsel to the contrary. The divine word comes as part of a theophany during which "Yhwh passed by. There was a fierce wind that ripped up the mountain and shattered rocks before Yhwh, but Yhwh was not in the wind. After the wind was an earthquake, but Yhwh was not in the earthquake. And after the earthquake came a fire, but Yhwh was not in the fire. And after the fire a quiet, subdued voice" (1 Kgs 19:11–12). Unlike the display of Yhwh's might in the theophany to Moses and Israel in Exod 19 (on the same mountain), here the destructive accoutrements of nature revealed no new decree but simply questioned Elijah's actions ("what pertains to you here?" [1 Kgs 19:13]). His answer, pointing to the Israelites' desecration of altars and other disrespectful acts—notice that this story assumes the validity of multiple altars to Yhwh, contrary to the Deuteronomistic theology—ought not overdetermine Elijah's actions. "Go back," Yhwh tells him, as if to say that his mission as a prophet does not depend on his popularity but solely on the power of the divine word.

Following the Elijah stories, the Ahab cycle recounts a conflict with the coalition of Aramaean states led by Damascus (1 Kgs 20:1–43), the king's theft of Naboth's vineyard (1 Kgs 21:1–29), and his final defeat in battle at Ramoth-gilead. (1 Kgs 22:1–38). Each story involves a prophetic component, and each develops the character of Ahab and his reign as marked by irresolution entangled with cruelty.

The first story depicts a war between Israel and an Aramaean coalition, which Ahab repeatedly defeats but does not destroy. The story highlights competing theological ideas, with the invaders wrongly assuming that Israel's "gods were mountain gods" (1 Kgs 20:23) and therefore seeking battle on the plains where the Israelites would be more vulnerable. As it happened, making military decisions on flimsy theological grounds proved unwise, with Ahab winning a major victory. The story ends with a prophetic oracle criticizing him for not finishing off the Aramaeans: "So says Yhwh, 'Because you the one I designated for slaughter, your life will be exchanged for his, and your people for his people'" (1 Kgs 20:42). The same sort of theology according to which the king must capitalize on his opportunities for victory operates in the story of Saul and the Amalekites, for example (1 Sam 15).

In any case, royal failure continues with the infamous story of Naboth's vineyard. Ahab covets a beautiful vineyard, but according to Israelite law its owner Naboth cannot alienate his property but must pass it on to his family. That is, private property rules were not absolute. Ahab, egged on by his wife Jezebel, refuses to accept a refusal. The queen suborns the judges of the town of Jezreel (a secondary capital and significant city in the Jezreel Valley in the northern part of Israel), leading to Naboth's arrest, death, and loss of property. This gross abuse of power elicits a prophetic curse by Elijah on both Ahab and his dynasty. In words reminiscent of the curse on Jeroboam I, the Omrides receive the divine sentence, "Indeed, I am bringing on you calamity and I will destroy your offspring and cut off Ahab's wall-pissers whether kept or let go in Israel" (1 Kgs 21:22).

The third conflict between crown and prophet comes in the final chapter of 1 Kings. The "king of Israel" and king Jehoshaphat of Judah (apparently a vassal of the Northern Kingdom) seek prophetic guidance before going to battle against their common enemy. Consulting the divine realm before battle was standard practice in ancient Near Eastern cultures, and seeking multiple voices, as in this case, ensured an accurate assessment of the future. Finding all the prophets agreed on the kings' success but suspicious of such glowing reports, the rulers consult a final prophet, Micaiah ben Imlah, even though (or perhaps because) the king of Israel notes that, "there is one more man for seeking Yhwh, but I hate him because he never prophesies good for me, but rather evil" (1 Kgs 22:8).

LYING PROPHETS AND LARGER TRUTHS

The story of Micaiah ben Imlah disturbs some readers because it seems to make God lie to human beings. A more sophisticated way to read the story, however, would point out that one can lie successfully only when (1) the hearer of the lie cannot suspect it, and (2) the teller of the lie does not reveal its deceptive nature. Neither of these conditions is met in this story. As one humorist put it, "if I'm lying to you, and you know I'm lying to you, and I know that you know that I'm lying to you, it's not lying. It's politics!" In this story, it *is* politics.

Perhaps more significantly, the political lie surfaces the larger philosophical problem of when one owes someone else the truth. For example, when the midwives lie to Pharaoh about the vitality of Israelite mothers in childbirth (Exod 1:19–20), their lie receives commendation because it protects lives of innocent people from a brutal tyrant. That is, a lie is more virtuous when truth-telling would lead to unjustified violence. In its avoidance of Victorian prudery, the biblical traditions deal in a realistic fashion with real-world ethical issues.

When Micaiah offers a hopeful oracle, the king becomes all the more suspicious, suspecting duplicity. His suspicions prove correct, for Micaiah reveals that "I saw Yhwh sitting on his throne and all the army of heaven standing before him left and right. And Yhwh said, 'Who will deceive Ahab so he will go up and fall at Ramoth Gilead?'" (1 Kgs 22:19–20). That is, the words of hope coming from the other prophets represent deliberate deception of the king by Yhwh, a due punishment for his repeated abuse of power. Again, the prophet points the narrative toward the divine will for justice, including the defeat of evil rulers.

Plot Point 3: Jehoram (2 Kgs 3:1–8:15)

The next reign demonstrates similar themes. After an interlude in which Elijah ascends to heaven in a fiery chariot and passes on the torch of prophecy to his disciple Elisha, the story passes to the final rulers of the Omride dynasty. However, the personality of the king fades into the background before the stories of prophecy and national crisis.

ELIJAH AND ELISHA

Both 1–2 Kings deliberately construct the Elijah and Elisha stories in parallel, with the important difference between their final scenes, an ascent to heaven versus a death. The stories include

	Elijah	Elisha
Famine in the land	1 Kgs 17	2 Kgs 4:38
Feeding a widow and resurrecting her son	1 Kgs 17	2 Kgs 4
Fighting Aram/Damascus	1 Kgs 20	2 Kgs 5, 7

At the same time, the two prophets' cycles of stories differ, with the miraculous aspect of Elisha's career being greatly accentuated, including stories of healing a foreign general, causing an iron ax head to float, and revealing the angelic army to an unperceptive servant. That is, 1–2 Kings connect the stories but make no effort to impose a rigid uniformity on them.

The miraculous aspects of the Elisha story come to the fore. By highlighting the wonder-working capacities of the prophet, the narrative also underscores Yhwh's willingness to accept the devotion even of foreigners, as is illustrated in the story of the general Naaman of Damascus. Just as the Deuteronomistic prayer of Solomon at the Temple dedication allowed for gentile piety toward Yhwh, the story of Naaman's miraculous healing in the Jordan culminates in a reflection on his gratitude for deliverance from a deleterious skin disease. As he puts it:

Please allow you servant to be given a load of earth for two mules to carry, because your servant can never again make a whole burnt offering or sacrifice to other gods except to Yhwh. In a certain case, please let Yhwh forgive your servant when my lord [i.e., King Ben-Hadad] goes into the temple of Rimmon to worship there, and I am his assistant and [as such] I worship in the temple of Rimmon—when

I worship in the temple of Rimmon, please let Yhwh forgive your servant in this case. (2 Kgs 5:17–18)

Here, Naaman seeks an exemption from the rules about monolatry, worship of one deity alone, owing to his status as the one "on whose hand the king leans." Elisha grants him the exemption, indicating a pragmatic approach to the problem, for while Israelites could expect no legitimate exception to the rule, gentiles were another matter. At the same time, the exception proves the rule, for those who receive Yhwh's mercy must respond by giving honor and gratitude, acts that bind them together in a community of thankfulness. Naaman finds a creative way to enter that community while remaining outside it when he carts of loads of Israelite dirt for his own devotions.

Plot Point 4: Jehu (2 Kgs 9:1–10:36)

The supine rule of the last Omrides, who could neither help when Naaman sought healing nor resist him when he came as a conqueror, led to their replacement with a new dynasty, founded by Jehu. Although Jehu has the dubious distinction of being the only Israelite king whose likeness has come down to us in contemporary art—the Assyrian monument called the Black Obelisk portrays him prostrating himself before the emperor Shalmaneser III—he appears in the Bible as a resolute general whom prophets prompt to stage a coup d'état.

In the story, Elisha commissions one of the "sons of the prophets," the band following him and (earlier) Elijah, to anoint two generals, Jehu in Israel and Hazael in Aram. Both generals overthrow their masters and seize power. Both generals are also known from Assyrian (and in Hazael's case, Aramaic) texts outside the Bible. That is, Elisha plays kingmaker not only in his own land but also in its most powerful neighbor.

The appointment of Jehu leads to his violent overthrow of the Omride dynasty, in direct fulfillment of earlier curses by Elijah and in direct parallel to the end of Jeroboam I's dynasty (2 Kgs 9:8–10). Jehu destroys the entire Omride family, including the by-now-aged Jezebel. The reign of Jehu, whatever its interests in its own right, serves primarily in 1–2 Kings to illustrate the end of his predecessors' style of rule and in particular their devotion to the god Baal, whose temple, cult, and priestly establishment Jehu destroys (2 Kgs 10:18–31). This religious purge gains the support of prophetic circles around Elisha, but it does not negate the Deuteronomistic circles' ultimately negative view of Jehu and all other rulers of the Northern Kingdom.

Plot Point 5: Joash and Athaliah (2 Kgs 11:1–12:22)

Amid all these stories of the Omrides and their enemies appears a pendant tale, this time relating events in Judah. An Israelite princess named Athaliah had eliminated her own family (much in the mode of a Greek tragedy) except for her infant grandson Joash, whom the priests hide. When the boy reaches the age of seven, the priest Jehoiada reveals him to the public, invests him with David's "spears and quivers" and the crown jewels (2 Kgs 11:10–11), and proclaims him king in the Temple courtyard. The counter–coup d'état ousts Athaliah, who has managed to survive the destruction of her family in the north but cannot resist local sentiment for the Davidides.

The story exhibits the qualities of family strife that one would expect in ancient story-telling, complete with the folkloric elements of the hidden king, the dramatic overthrow of foreign oppression, and (later) the restoration of the Temple at the new king's behest. However, there is no particular reason to dismiss it as merely a fiction justifying the tight-ening of the Temple priesthood's grip on power in Jerusalem, as is sometimes argued. Rather, the story shares with other texts in Samuel–Kings a conviction about the neces-sary connection between legitimate dynasty and properly functioning temple. In that sense, the story looks both backward to the promises to David and then forward to their actualization in more famous reformer kings, Hezekiah and Josiah.

This connection comes through in various theological observations made in these chapters. Note, for example, sentences such as "And Jehoiada made a covenant among Yhwh, the king and the people for the people to be Yhwh's (as well as one between the king and the people)" (2 Kgs 11:17). The Deuteronomistic editors assess his reign posi-tively "except that he did not eliminate the 'high places' [i.e., open-air sanctuaries] or stop the people from sacrificing or burning incense at the 'high places'" (2 Kgs 12:4)—a problem but not a fatal one, given the long tradition of operating such sanctuaries. More to the point, 2 Kgs 12 portrays Joash carrying out a traditional ancient Near Eastern task of kings, the refurbishing of his kingdom's main temple.

Plot Point 6: The Fall of Israel (2 Kgs 17:1–41)

While the story of Joash presages themes that will appear later for kings of Judah, the story of the Northern Kingdom slides to its demise. In a repetitive text that shows signs of repeated reworking, 2 Kgs 17 reports the Assyrian destruction of Samaria and the Northern Kingdom in 722 BCE, which it blames on Israel's unrelenting commitment to polytheism and rejection of the Deuteronomic theology. Sargon II, who had come to the Assyrian throne during the war against Israel reports deporting over 27,000 persons, not to mention those who died in the war. Moreover, at least one letter from his reign reports the work of craftspeople from Samaria in the Assyrian homeland.[2]

Second Kings reports little of life in the north after the Assyrian conquest when Israel was divided into several provinces (Samerina, Duru, Magidu, and Gal'adda), and the occupying power constructed governmental buildings in key locations. The single story about that time concerns the settling of foreigners in the land (as per Assyrian practice). When the new populations found themselves preyed upon by lions (whose population perhaps grew after the decline of the only competing top predator, human beings), they sought help from the government. So, "the king of Assyria commanded, 'send there one of the priests exiled from there, and let them go and dwell there and teach them the custom of the gods of the land" (2 Kgs 17:27). Typically of ancient peoples, he saw lions as a problem for theologians as well as hunters (a view no longer common, alas). This command led to the new arrivals worshiping Yhwh along with their own gods, whom the text names in detail out of an awareness of the counter-theologies against which the Deuteronomic revisers and their sources all argue. As the text concludes, "These nations were honoring Yhwh as well as serving their idols. Also, their children and grandchildren did just like their ancestors until this day" (2 Kgs 17:41). That is, from the point of view of the narrator, the unfortunate mix of Israelite and foreign religious practices continued to mar life in the north.

Judah's Century Alone and Demise (2 Kgs 18:1–25:30)

If the north disappears from the DH at this point, the attention to the south becomes still more important. The last section of the entire work considers the last century of Judah, focusing on two heroes and a villain, whose careers offer models for the positive and negative possibilities of kingship.

The first positive figure, Hezekiah, reigned at the end of the eighth century BCE and experienced Assyrian invasion. As Sennacherib (reigned 705–681 BCE) puts it in his own annals,

> As for Hezekiah the Judahite, who did not submit to my yoke, 46 of his strong walled cities as well as the small towns in their environs, which were without number—I besieged and took those towns . . . . Him I shut up in Jerusalem, his royal city, like a caged bird.[3]

Second Kings 18–20 (equals Isa 36–39) recounts the same event and with similarly grim acknowledgement of the destruction of Judah wrought by Sennacherib. However, the biblical account also underscores the deliverance of Jerusalem from the foreign hordes.

Moreover, the Hezekiah story highlights his piety at several points, with the narrative depicting him as a model king in the vein of Deuteronomic ideals, if not from other points of view. Although his sponsorship of public works still shows itself to tourists in Jerusalem who walk through his tunnel there today, 2 Kgs does not emphasize his work as a builder, in part because the destruction of his kingdom by the Assyrians in 701 BCE made any building projects almost superfluous.

During the siege of Jerusalem, when a high-ranking Assyrian official made a speech criticizing Hezekiah's closing of open-air sanctuaries (part of a proto-Deuteronomic approach to religious centralization), Hezekiah prays for divine deliverance. His prayer hits the key theological notes:

> Yhwh God of Israel, dweller upon the cherubim, you are the only God over all the earth's kingdoms. You have made the heavens and the earth. Yhwh, listen carefully and hear. Yhwh, open your eyes and see. Hear the words of Sennacherib which he sent forth to taunt the living God. (2 Kgs 19:15–16)

The prayer goes on to refer to the various gods defeated by the Assyrians (possibly referring to their practice of collecting statues and other sacred objects from conquered temples). Drawing on the ancient claims about Yhwh's nature and power, the prayer contrasts the core theological values of Israel with the dire present reality, appealing to divine honor for resolution of a problem.

The response to the prayer, a divine oracle, asks the invading emperor (at least in the narrator's imagination), "will you look haughtily [literally, lift your eyes high up] upon the Holy One of Israel?" (2 Kgs 19:22 = Isa 37:23). It concludes by threatening the invaders with a taste of their own medicine: "I will put my hook in your nose ... I will make you return by the road you came in on" (2 Kgs 19:28 = Isa 37:29). And so it happened, with Sennacherib withdrawing before eliminating Judah altogether, even though its postwar condition could hardly inspire enthusiasm.

Another instance of Hezekiah's piety occurs during a near-fatal illness. On requesting of Yhwh an extension on his life, he receives the hopeful reply, "Thus says Yhwh the God of your ancestor David, 'I have heard your prayer and seen your tears. Yes, I am healing you within three days. You should go up to Yhwh's temple. I will add to your days fifteen years and rescue you and this city from the power of the king of Assyria'" (2 Kgs 20:5–6 = Isa 33:5–6). The chronology is vague here ("in those days" [2 Kgs 20:1 = Isa 38:1]), but the most natural reading of the text as it stands would connect it to the siege of Sennacherib. At the same time, 2 Kgs 19 and 20 as occurring simultaneously creates problems with understanding the energy level of the king at the various points of the story. Yet in any case, the point remains clear: a pious king may seek help from a generous deity.

Not so with a notoriously evil one. Hezekiah's son Manasseh (reigned about fifty-five years) provides the Deuteronomistic editors with a counter-argument to any naïve advocacy of the Davidic dynasty. They portray him as a heinous ruler who "rebuilt the open-air sanctuaries that Hezekiah had destroyed and erected altars to Baal and made an Asherah like the one Ahab king of Israel made, so that they [the people?] worshiped the heavenly hosts and served them ... " (2 Kgs 21:3–4) culminating in human sacrifice in the valleys west of Jerusalem, and rousing prophetic opposition. Second Kings attributes the fall of Judah itself to Manasseh's savage reign (2 Kgs 24:3), branding his half-century of rule as a distillation of the entire negative history of the two Israelite kingdoms.

After a brief reign by Amon, his eight-year-old son Josiah became king. For the creators of 1–2 Kings, Josiah stands as the most exemplary king of Judah, even though his reign ended tragically. This fact, as noted in Chapter 8 ("Israelite Historiography"), has led many scholars to think of his reign as the time of the composition of the first edition of the DH.

MANASSEH IN HISTORY AND TRADITION

Manasseh appears in both the Bible and Assyrian inscriptions. Yet the Bible itself portrays him in two different ways: 2 Chron 33 repeats much of the material in 2 Kgs 21 but adds a further episode. After being deported to Babylon for malfeasance by his Assyrian over-lords, Manasseh repents of his sins. He then reclaims his throne. For Chronicles, he also escapes blame for the ultimate demise of Judah, blame for which transfers elsewhere. Still later, around the first century BCE, the Prayer of Manasseh describes him as praying such things as, "So now I bow the knees of my heart, entreating your compassion. I have sinned, Lord. I have sinned, and I know my lawless deeds. I ask, beg you, forgive me, O Lord, forgive me" (PrMan 11–13). This remarkable transformation of a ruler's reputation speaks more of the later Jewish emphasis on repentance and forgiveness than anything about the historical Manasseh, even as it also demonstrates the abiding interest in the ancient rulers as models for the entire people in other times.

In any case, Josiah's reign centers on an important event, the discovery of the "scroll of the Torah" during renovations of the Temple. This book (also called "the scroll of Moses's Torah") served as the basis of Josiah's reforms of Judahite worship, including the centralizing of all sacrifice in the Jerusalem temple and thus the closing of rural open-air sanctuaries as well as other (urban) temples. Most scholars since the early nineteenth century have under-stood this "scroll" to be some version of the book of Deuteronomy (probably chapters 12–26 with or without parts of chapters 5–11). The reforms, in any case, displaced the age-old and honored practices of the countryside in favor of crown-sponsored worship in one loca-tion. While the reform did not comply with all aspects of Deuteronomy's theology (such as restrictions on royal power!)—a fact that has led some to deny the links between Josiah and Deuteronomy, though unconvincingly so—the prevalence of Deuteronomic theology throughout 1–2 Kings and the high valuation of Josiah in the latter books makes most sense if one understands the story to refer to the discovery of the more ancient work.

Unexpectedly, however, Josiah's reign did not usher in a golden age. As the Assyrian Empire collapsed in the 610s BCE, Josiah sought to block an Egyptian army headed north to aid the Assyrians against their Babylonian, Scythian, and Median opponents. At the crossroads of Megiddo, Josiah met the superior Egyptian army led by Pharaoh Necho, and in losing the hopeless battle, he also lost his life. This event in (probably) 610 BCE ushered in the final phase of Judah's existence, almost a quarter century of repeated Babylonian intervention (since Babylon temporarily replaced Assyria as the political center of the Near East). The last kings of Judah reigned only at the sufferance of their mightier neighbors, who repeatedly intervened in the politics of the land and trooped off herds of deportees in about 605–604 and 597 BCE. Finally, the summer of 586 BCE brought Babylonian invasion, the sack of Jerusalem, and the end of Judah as a state.

This final blow, unsurprisingly, elicits considerable reflection by the Deuteronomistic circles. Since much of the movement of the narrative from 1 Samuel on has involved the movement of the Ark of the Covenant to Jerusalem and the building of the Temple around it, the elimination of that building and its content shocks everyone. Nonetheless, 2 Kgs 25 narrates this tragedy in a dispassionate way, its very flatness underscoring the brutality of the event. As the story goes,

In the ninth year of his [i.e., Zedekiah's] reign, on the tenth day of the tenth month, Nebuchadnezzar king of Babylon and his army came upon Jerusalem and besieged it and built siegeworks around it. The city was beleaguered until the eleventh year of King Zedekiah. During the ninth month, famine gripped the city. There was no food for the refugees. Then the city was breached, but all the warriors escaped at night via the street near the gate between the two ramparts which were near the king's garden. Then the Chaldeans surrounded the city and closed the road to the Arabah. All the Chaldeans pursued the king and overtook him near the wilderness around Jericho while his entire army was dispersed around him. They captured the king and brought him up to the king of Babylon at Riblah, but spoke respectfully to him. However, they executed Zedekiah's children in his presence and blinded Zedekiah himself. They shackled him in bronze fetters and took him to Babylon. (2 Kgs 25:2–7)

This matter-of-fact report, which also appears almost verbatim in Jer 52, describes the end of Davidic rule of Judah. Yet the heartbreak does not end there, for the text goes on to describe in the same dispassionate way the destruction of the Temple itself. It catalogues the contents of the building with the same sort of painstaking love that 1 Kgs 6–7 had used to describe their creation. Full closure—that's the aim.

And yet the story does not quite end here, for the DH concludes with a tiny appendix, a faint note of hope added in the style of ancient chronicles, one more datum that nevertheless portends a possible future. As 2 Kgs 25:27–30 reports, "in the thirty-seventh of the exile of Jehoiakin king of Judah, on the seventh day of the twelfth month, Amel-marduk king of Babylon lifted up the head [i.e., showed favoritism toward] Jehoiakin king of Judah in his place of confinement." That is, the Babylonians improved treatment of a discredited ruler.

It would be easy to exaggerate the importance of this ending. The glimmer of hope remains almost imperceptible. Yet Deuteronomy–Kings does not celebrate catastrophe, no matter how justly deserved (as it argues). The larger DH seeks instead to find meaning in history, even when that meaning unsettles easy answers and comfortable habits. It finds that meaning, in some ways, not in the course of human events but in the sovereign decisions of the God who rules over them, dynamically engaging with human actors to shape a drama that is neither tragedy nor comedy, but something else again.

Implications

As part of the larger DH, 1–2 Kings tells the story of Israel's monarchic period. Yet the work does not merely report events or even seek to understand their causes simply as matters of economic or political forces. Rather, by concentrating on the relationships of kings to Temple worship and to the treatment of subjects—both age-old themes of Near Eastern kingship—these books argue that the demise of the two states of Israel and Judah came about because kings neglected their duties, and the people as a whole abandoned the "proper" worship of Yhwh for more manageable religious practices through which they could access divine power for less than transcendent ends.

It is tempting to read 1–2 Kings as a sort of obituary for Israel, but in this case, an obituary that includes hope for a resurrection. Israel's life has not necessarily ended, but the creators of this text seek to find in its history both explanations for the devastation wrought by the Mesopotamian empires and glimmers of hope for the future. They find both in the covenant with Yhwh set forth in Deuteronomy.

Notes

1. Excuse the literal translation, since the Bible is much less prudish than many of its readers. The phrase is a dismissive way of speaking of males.

2. Text 280 in Andreas Fuchs and Simo Parpola, eds., *The Correspondence of Sargon II, Part III: Letters from Babylonia and the Eastern Provinces* (Helsinki: Helsinki University Press, 2001), 176.

3. Column 3, lines 18–28. Translations modified from the edition of Daniel David Luckenbill, *The Annals of Sennacherib* (Chicago: University of Chicago Press, 1924), 32–33.

For Further Reading

Barrick, W. Boyd. *The King and the Cemeteries: Toward a New Understanding of Josiah's Reform.* Leiden: Brill, 2002.

Hamilton, Mark W. *The Body Royal: The Social Poetics of Kingship in Ancient Israel.* Leiden: Brill, 2005. Reprint, Atlanta: Society of Biblical Literature, 2008.

Lemaire, André, and Baruch Halpern, eds. *The Books of Kings: Sources, Composition, Historiography and Reception.* Leiden: Brill, 2010.

Leuchter, Mark, and Klaus-Peter Adam, eds. *Soundings in Kings: Perspectives and Methods in Contemporary Scholarship.* Minneapolis: Fortress, 2010.

14 Rethinking Israel's History
1–2 CHRONICLES

> **Key Text**: *So all Israel was genealogized as written down in the book of the kings of Israel and Judah. They were deported to Babylon for their unfaithfulness. However, the first dwelling [afterwards] on their property in their cities were some Israelites—priests, Levites, and temple servants. Also, some of Judahites and Benjaminites and Ephraimites and Manassites dwelt in Jerusalem.* (1 Chron 9:1–3)

Human beings constantly make history and just as often rewrite it. New generations of historians find in the past new material for the future, sometimes by discovering fresh evidence and sometimes by reexamining well-known data. As one recent scholar has put it in regards to history writing, "Indeed, the very variety of exemplars may confuse as much as illuminate. Selection is inevitable and there is no algorithm for success."[1]

So it is not surprising that the Hebrew Bible contains two large works recounting Israel's history, with one being the direct source of the other. Large parts of 1–2 Chronicles come more or less verbatim from Samuel–Kings (with some material from the Pentateuch as well), indicating that the later work revised the earlier one, probably during the Persian period (after 539 BCE but before Alexander the Great). That is, 1–2 Chronicles does not simply abbreviate Samuel–Kings but rethinks its story in light of a new situation. Both works recount Israel's life under the monarchy, including the destruction of Jerusalem by the Babylonians, but 2 Chronicles ends with a brief mention of the decree by Cyrus the

Great to restore the deportees to their homeland. Both works underscore the activities of kings, but 2 Chronicles omits the rulers of the Northern Kingdom almost entirely, concentrating on Judah and especially royal patronage of the Jerusalem Temple. This later historiographic work is thus a sort of "remake" of the older story. Much as a brand-new movie can retell the story of Batman or Sherlock Holmes for the umpteenth time, so too the composer(s) of Chronicles chose to "reshoot" their story, sometimes scene by scene, and sometimes much more freely.

What principles drive the remake then?

1. Chronicles accepts the basic narrative of Samuel–Kings, and apparently of the narrative going back to Genesis.
2. However, it abandons the attempt in 1–2 Kgs to correlate the histories of Israel and Judah, in part for technical reasons of storytelling.
3. It massively expands descriptions of events in the Jerusalem temple, not only making David into its guiding genius, but greatly enlarging stories about the Passovers sponsored by Hezekiah and Josiah.
4. It alters the reputations of both David (who does not seduce Bathsheba in 1 Chron or face revolt from Absalom) and Manasseh (who does commit atrocities but later repents). That is, it presents the kings of the past as more commendable figures than Samuel–Kings does.
5. It emphasizes the role of prayer.
6. It makes Yhwh act through mediators, as during the story of the plague after David's census.
7. It eliminates some of the Deuteronomistic comments on rulers that underscore their culpability in Israel's fate, while shifting blame onto other rulers at times. That is, it rethinks the Deuteronomistic conceptions of historical causality for certain events.

In short, then, Chronicles stands on its own as a new work, albeit one that draws on a revered source that it at once preserves and alters. Both preservation and alteration are important features of the work.

As it stands, 1–2 Chron (divided into two volumes simply because it was too long to fit on a single scroll) breaks into three major sections:

A. Israel prior to David (1 Chron 1:1–9:44)
B. The reigns of David and Solomon (1 Chron 10:1–2 Chron 9:31)
C. The reigns of Judah's subsequent kings and their fall and rise (2 Chron 10:1–36:23)

Each of these sections advances the book's movements toward its open-ended conclusion. The final lines, 2 Chron 36:22–23 hint at the book's horizons:

In the first year of Cyrus king of Persia, in order to fulfill Yhwh's word via Jeremiah, Yhwh roused up Cyrus king of Persia so that he issued an announcement to all his empire (actually a written decree): "Thus says Cyrus king of Persia, 'Yhwh God of the Heavens has given all the earth's kingdoms to me and suggested that I should build a temple for him in Jerusalem, which is in Judah. Whoever of you, from all his people—may Yhwh his [or her] God be with him [or her], and let them go up [to Judah].'"

The text looks backward to Jeremiah's prophecies of return from exile, forward to the rebuilding of the Temple, outward to the entire known world (now the Persian Empire), and inward to the Israelite community deported and now returned. Most of all, it situates geopolitical events within the realm of the deity's care for the world, with Cyrus and the structures he leads signifying both the fulfillment of prophecy and Yhwh's ongoing superintendence of Israel's welfare. All of the rest of the book points forward to this return from exile. Whereas Joshua–Kings justifies Yhwh's destruction of Israel and Judah as a response to their idolatry and utter lack of moral rectitude, Chronicles points to a different moral vision. The algorithm for success may be missing, but the formula insists that death gives way to resurrection.

Israel Prior to David (1 Chron 1:1–9:44)

The first part of the book hardly seems a promising opening for a story of renewal. Many readers give up in despair after a few lines of the genealogies filling these chapters. What could be more tedious than a list of unfamiliar names (unless you're editing a telephone book or trying to trying to hack a computer via possible passwords)? Yet this strange beginning masks two important points: (1) genealogies describe interrelationships among people over time and in a single moment, and (2) the presence of these names signals Israel's survival after the calamities of the Assyrian and Babylonian invasions. Just as modern museums of the Holocaust or similar genocides often includes pictures of victims and survivors, so too does 1 Chron 1–9 portray both the living relationships of Israelites and their intertwined ancestries over time.

GENEALOGIES IN CHRONICLES AND BEYOND

As noted in the discussion of Genesis in Chapter 3 of this book, ancient people used genealogies to describe, in a compressed way, relationships among individuals and groups. These lists served a literary purpose of reducing the complexity of those relationships to a comprehensible and usable form. For 1 Chron, in particular, the genealogies serve a rhetorical purpose. They argue loud and clear, "we are still here—all of us." Far from being obscure or unexciting, then, the genealogies celebrate the hope and challenge of survival.

The first nine chapters of 1 Chron employ these lists in a skillful way that allows them to retread the ground of Gen 1–1 Sam 31 without going into detail. "Compression as evocation" is one way to summarize this literary strategy. This highly intellectual literary technique can either excite or put off a readership depending on their willingness to understand and engage with the book's modus operandi.

The opening lists (1 Chron 1:1–2:2) lifts material from Genesis, moving from Adam to Judah and Esau (the kings of Edom). Then come the tribes proper but in a different order from the various sequences in Genesis and Exodus:

Judah, including the family of David (2:3–4:23)
Simeon (4:24–43)
Reuben (5:1–10)
Gad (5:11–17)
Reuben, Gad, and Half-Manasseh (5:18–22)
Half of Manasseh (5:23–26)
Levi (6:1-66 [ET 6:1–81])
Issachar (7:1–5)
Benjamin (7:6–12)
Naphtali (7:13)
The Other Half of Manasseh (7:14–19)
Ephraim (7:20–29)
Asher (7:30–40)
Benjamin Again (8:1–40)
The Temple Leaders (9:1–44)

The sequence does not follow an obvious overall structure by geography or ancestral birth order or geopolitical significance with the obvious exception that Judah comes first, and Levi and Benjamin, along with Judah, receive far more coverage than the other tribes. In other words, the list emphasizes those groups that were central to the Persian-era community of Yehud and Jerusalem, without completely erasing the other tribes, who were also part of the Chronicler's concept of a reunited Israel. (For the history of this period and the politics of Yehud, the subprovince centered on Jerusalem, see the discussion of Ezra-Nehemiah in Chapter 15).

Now, in compiling these lists from the Pentateuch and other sources (since some names postdate the period of that text), 1 Chron does more than simply list people. All sorts of details about life past and present lie embedded among the endless parade of names of persons and places.

For example, 1 Chron 3:10–23 enumerates the descendants of David, not only rulers but also those lines that led to the family members living during and leading the restoration of life in Jerusalem after Cyrus's decree permitting their return from Babylonia, and for several generations beyond (thus into the fifth century BCE). This little list indicates the continuing relevance of the Davidide family in the postexilic community.

Or again, 1 Chron 5:23–26 enumerates the clans of the part of the tribe of Manasseh living in the Transjordan, noting that "they were unfaithful to the God of their ancestors, prostituting themselves to the gods of the peoples of the land whom God had dispossessed before them." Their bad theology (in the Chronicler's view) led "Israel's God to rouse up the spirit of Pul, king of Assyria, one Tiglath-pileser [III, r. 745–727 BCE] king of Assyria" to the degree that "he deported" the Transjordanian tribes to other parts of his empire. In other words, the unimposing list tucks away a theological reflection on a major historical catastrophe centuries earlier than the Chronicler's composition itself.

Numerous other such tidbits lie within these texts, all revealing the concerns of the creator(s) of the book and/or its sources. In short, 1 Chron 1–9 does not give us the Jerusalemite telephone book of a certain period, but a much more thoughtful and elaborate attempt to work out a sort of mental geography for the reader. In this mind-map, Israelite groups populate the entire land owing to God's merciful dispensation to them, even when, in historical reality, their presence lies in the past.

The Reigns of David and Solomon (1 Chron 10:1–2 Chron 9:30)

After the parade of names spread over centuries, 1 Chron turns from preface to its central plot, the construction of the Temple by David and Solomon. The narrative traces much the same ground as in 2 Sam 1–2 Kgs 11, but with important omissions and additions. Gone from Chronicles are the stories of David's amorous advances to Bathsheba and the revolt of Absalom. Gone is the story of coup and counter-coup at Solomon's succession, gone too the father's instructions on political purges for his naïve son. In short, the David and Solomon of Chronicles lack the hard edge of the Deuteronomistic portraits. Whether these omissions reflect a deliberate sanitizing of the older stories or simply the Chronicler's use of versions of Samuel–Kings lacking them (both defensible positions), the end result is a depiction of the great Israelite kings as exemplars of piety and peacefulness.

CHRONICLES AS A PERSIAN PERIOD BOOK

In addition to the positive references to Persian rule at the end of 2 Chronicles, the book sometimes uses Persian terms for items long predating the empire. For example, 1 Chron 29:7 has David collect money for the Temple denominated in darics (Hebrew: 'ǎdarkôn or darkĕmôn; see also Ezra 2:69; 8:27; Neh 7:69–71 for less anachronistic uses of the term), the gold coin introduced by Darius the Great at the end of the sixth century BCE (i.e., four and a half centuries after David). This is a bit like saying the Dutch paid $24 for Manhattan Island, a straight-up anachronism. But the terminology also updates the David story and helps solidify his image as a mighty emperor, a peer of the Persian rulers who now governed David's people and land.

THE REIGN OF DAVID (I CHRON 10:1–29:30)

To paint such a picture, 1 Chron also adds a great deal of information to the Samuel–Kings story, drawing on a range of sources, especially from the priesthood. The additional material includes several types of information:

Lists of names
David's old friends from Ziklag (1 Chron 12:1–23)
Conscription units and their leaders (1 Chron 12:24–41)
Levitical groups (courses) for fortnightly Temple service (1 Chron 23:2–24:31)
Members of the principal Temple singer families (1 Chron 25:1–31)
Temple gatekeepers and maintenance staff (1 Chron 26:1–32)
Royal administrators (1 Chron 27:1–34)

Stories about Ritual Structures or Actions
A location for the Ark of the Covenant (1 Chron 13:1–4)
Reconsecration of the Ark (1 Chron 15:1–24)
Assignment of the Asaphites to the Ark and the Zadokites to Gibeon (1 Chron 16:37–42)
A sacrifice at the Ark's new location (1 Chron 21:28–22:1)
Materials gathered for the Temple (1 Chron 22:2–23:1)

Speeches and Prayers
A psalm medley (1 Chron 16:7–36)
David's farewell address to the people (1 Chron 28:1–29:9)
David's final prayer and benediction (1 Chron 29:10–19)

This insertion of new material within the Samuel-based (pre-Deuteronomistic) story of David creates two related effects. First, the remade story shifts the key achievements of his reign from military conquest to religious building projects, and second, it invests all the practices of the Temple and its personnel with the sanctity of antiquity. That is, the stories argue that the earliest and greatest rulers of Israel created the system of worship, thus bringing new life to the community of returnees from Babylonia. The cagey warrior of 1–2 Sam becomes here a master builder, not just in stone and metal but in human social structures.

The most important new material relates, then, to the ongoing worship in the Temple that Solomon will build. Chronicles takes pains to connect the new building to the old Ark traditions (just as 1–2 Sam has done), adding further information about the situation of the Ark in Jerusalem on the threshing floor of Ornan (called Araunah in 2 Sam). It also cleans up a potential problem in 1 Kgs 3:4–15, according to which Solomon worships at a "high place" or open air sanctuary (Hebrew: *bāmâ*) not in the presence of the Ark. While the Deuteronomists saw no problem in such worship prior to (but not after) the building of the Temple, 1 Chron 16:37–42 connects even this location to the Temple worship by noting that while the Asaph family attended to the Ark in Jerusalem, the Zadoq family (along with other clans of singers) took care of sacrifices at Gibeon. That is, the various groups that would serve together in Jerusalem first served separately in order to maintain the continuity of cultic practice. An obscure point, perhaps, but the story shows the pains that the Chronicler took to tie up loose ends.

A similar loose end from 1 Kgs concerns the staffing of the Temple itself. Apparently drawing on priestly traditions (of what age, it is hard to say), 1 Chron 23:2–26:32 sets out the biweekly rotations of priestly families who will carry out the sacrifices, as well as the Levitical crews responsible for the temple's upkeep and day-to-day operations. Moreover, three families of singers whose names also appear in the book of Psalms receive their appointments to the role of providing music for the services. Since this material does not appear in either the Pentateuch or 1 Kgs, most scholars believe it reflects more the practices of the Second Temple than of the First.

Perhaps most interesting is the ordination of the singers. According to 1 Chron 25:1, "David and the army generals designated Asaph, Heman, and Jeduthun as the ones prophesying by harps and lyres and cymbals." "*Prophesying* by harps and lyres and cymbals" introduces a startling conception of the work of the singers, namely that their songs carried the weight of divine inspiration in some way. The story goes on to designate them as "seers," as well.

The Chronicler's view of the performance of the psalms as a prophetic activity anticipates the later view, seen in the Dead Sea Scrolls, of David as the prophet composing psalms (11QPs[a]—see the discussion in Chapter 19). But in 1 Chron, which is earlier than the Qumran text, the prophetic activity applies to many singers, since Chronicles still knew that the Psalter had many authors. Indeed, these very names appear as composers: Asaph in Pss 50, 73–83, Heman in Ps 88, and Jeduthun in Pss 39, 62, and 77 (along with Asaph). Conspicuously absent from 1 Chron 25, however, is the name Korah, the ancestor of yet another family of singers whose oeuvre includes Pss 42, 44–49, 84–88 (the last with the Hemanites). Yet in 1 Chron 26:1, Korah appears as a gatekeeper, not a singer at all. Apparently, this difference of viewpoint reflects the evolving roles of the various temple groups, though more precise details are now lost.

What does remain, however, is the overwhelming presence of the Temple in the book. This presence makes itself felt, for example, in the prayer in 1 Chron 16:8–36, which is a pastiche of parts of Pss 105, 96, and 106 in that order. Some of the lines float about in Israelite hymnody from the Persian period, such as

> For Yhwh is great and very praiseworthy, awesome over all the gods (1 Chron 16:25; Ps 96:4; cf. Ps 48:2 [ET 48:1])

or

Let the sea and all in it thunder, the field and all in it exult.

Then shall the thicket's trees shout out before Yhwh when he comes to judge the earth. (1 Chron 16:32–33; Ps 96:11–13; 98: 7–9 [with slight changes])

In other words, during the Second Temple period, the words of poems (even older poems) could be recombined, redeployed for new purposes. The Chronicler, familiar with the ongoing worship practices of the Temple, uses them to describe David and his staff, here the Asaphites, as exemplary pious people.

CHRONICLES REWRITING SAMUEL–KINGS

As Isaac Kalimi has shown, the many changes that 1–2 Chronicles makes in its sources may have theological purposes, but more often they simply reflect historiographic or narrative concerns. Among the techniques used by the Chronicler, a number stand out as especially significant. It is instructive to try to identify these as one reads the text.

1. Literary-Chronological proximity—making adjoining texts more closely connected
2. Removing internal contradictions
3. Completing text from other texts
4. Omitting extraneous information (e.g., the names of foreigners, their gods, their relatives etc.)
5. Giving equivalent names for persons or places
6. Changing a problematic text to make sense of it
7. Harmonizations
8. Creating characters by renaming them or giving them speeches
9. Rendering characters less or more significant
10. Repetition of items to link different parts of an episode
11. Chiasmus
12. Repetition
13. Inclusio
14. Antithesis
15. Use of simile
16. Use of key words
17. Use of Numerical patterns (3/4, 6/7)
18. General to specific and specific to general

See Isaac Kalimi, *The Reshaping of Ancient Israelite History in Chronicles* (Winona Lake, IN: Eisenbrauns, 2005)

Part of this concern with recasting characters at least to some degree affects how Chronicles thinks about divine agency. In the book, God increasingly acts through mediators. For example, 1 Chron 21 rewrites 2 Sam 24, the story of the census. Some of the most important changes revolve around divine agency:

Yhwh was again angry with Israel and he incited David against them by saying, "Go count Israel and Judah." (2 Sam 24:1)

An adversary (Hebrew: *śāṭān*) stood against Israel and incited David to count Israel. (1 Chron 21:1)

and again

The angel positioned his hand to strike Jerusalem, but Yhwh relented from the calamity. (2 Sam 24:15)

And God sent the angel to Jerusalem to destroy it but relented from the calamity. (1 Chron 21:15)

These small alterations of its source illustrate the Chronicler's concern to fine-tune the older story's notions of divine causality. In 1 Chron, the command to count the people does not come directly from God and has nothing to do with divine anger. Yet God also keeps control of events by dispatching angelic messengers to act, just as in the older story. Some have argued that the replacement of Yhwh with *śāṭān* as the provocateur makes a radical break between source and revised story, but this is not correct since the *śāṭān* figure here is not the full-blown evil genius of the later rabbinic and Christian traditions but more like the irritating figure of Job and Zechariah.[2] God's activity becomes less direct though still crucial.

If, finally, God's action takes on a different color, so too does David's, and this becomes clearest at the end of 1 Chron, as the dying king takes up the older practice of the patriarch passing on his legacy to the people and nation (see Gen 49 for Jacob; Deut 1–33 for Moses; Josh 23–24 for Joshua). Here David cements his place in history by calling the people to worship:

And David said to all the assembly, "Bless Yhwh your God." And all the assembly blessed Yhwh the God of their ancestors, bowed, and did obeisance to Yhwh and to the king. They made sacrifices and incinerated whole burnt offerings to Yhwh the next day, including 1,000 oxen, 1,000 rams, 1,000 sheep, and all the accompanying libations—sacrifices for all Israel's multitude. Then they ate and drank before Yhwh on that day with great celebration, and they repeated the coronation of Solomon, David's son, anointing him as ruler before Yhwh and Zadoq the priest. (1 Chron 29:20–22)

Thus the transition to Solomon's reign, during which David's many plans for the temple become reality.

THE REIGN OF SOLOMON (2 CHRON 1:1–9:31)

For the reign of Israel's third king, Solomon, 2 Chron follows 1 Kgs 1–11 closely, confining most of its changes to small details, with two significant exceptions. Second Chronicles omits the disturbing stories of the succession crisis of 1 Kgs 1–2 and the portrayal of Solomon as a sponsor of idolatry in 1 Kgs 11:1–40. Just as David becomes in 1 Chron a paragon of piety and virtue, so too does Solomon assume that role in 2 Chron. The deliberately complex picture of a rich king who can master wisdom and technology but not his own lusts vanishes after a few deft erasures, and the Solomon of the later tradition as a hero of wisdom emerges.

The Reigns of Judah's Kings and Their Fall and Rise (2 Chron 10:1–36:23)

The remainder of 2 Chron narrates the same succession of rulers as in 1–2 Kgs except that it abandons the latter's practice of alternating the Northern and Southern Kingdoms, preferring instead to focus almost entirely upon Judah. Chronicles knows, of course, the stories of Jeroboam I and his successors because 2 Chron 10 retraces the story of national division laid out in 1 Kgs 12. Apparently, the Chronicler found the story of the north less relevant, even if his postexilic community included various northerners. The strong preference for Judah, Benjamin, and Levi as opposed to the other tribes shows up throughout the work and probably reflects the origins of the book of Chronicles in Jerusalem as well as a concern for its past and future.

The kings of Judah, then. 2 Chron 10–36 expands the stories of several kings, almost always in order to magnify their positive achievements, both military and religious. When 1–2 Kgs depicts these rulers as wicked, 2 Chron explains their wickedness, or conversely when 1–2 Kgs announces some success of a wicked king, then 2 Chron both explains the wickedness and adds some sort of exculpatory act that explains the success as a divine reward. A good example of this complex maneuver appears in the stories of Rehoboam's occupation of parts of Benjamin (2 Chron 11:5–23) and his later failures (2 Chron 12:1–16), and again of Abijah's successful war against Jeroboam (2 Chron 13:1–21). In the latter case, a wicked king gains success when fighting an even worse one.

In general, however, the additions relate to kings already spoken of positively in 1–2 Kgs. These include Asa's military successes and piety (2 Chron 14:1–15:15), Jehoshaphat's victories (2 Chron 17:2–19; 20:1–30), Hezekiah's Passover (2 Chron 30:1–31:21), and Josiah's Passover (2 Chron 35:1–19). Military victories go to kings with at least some redeeming qualities, an indication that book's theology has shaped how it presents its story. Yhwh's control of the world involves the rewarding of virtue and punishment of vice, even on a national scale.

A number of discrete features reveal a great deal of the overall thinking underlying the book. Consider just three:

The first is the repeated reference to Torah as a guiding principle in royal administration. A good example appears in the extended discussion of the reign of Jehoshaphat (ninth century BCE). As 2 Chron 17:7–9 explains:

In the third year of his reign, he instructed his officials Ben-hayil, Obadiah, Zechariah, Nathaniel, and Mikaiah to instruct the cities of Judah. Accompanying them were the Levites Shemaiah, Nathaniah, Zebediah, Asahel, Shemiramot, Jonathan, Adonijah, Tobijah, and Tobadonijah (all Levites), as well as the priests Elishama and Jehoram. And they instructed Judah, and with them was the Torah of Yhwh.

The important point is not the list of names. The idea of royal officials as teachers is difficult to find in either the Pentateuch or the Deuteronomistic History. For Chronicles, however, the teaching of Torah goes back long before the great reform of Josiah. Indeed, references to the Torah (sometimes called "Torah of Moses" or "of Yhwh") abound in stories of the monarchs, especially in 2 Chron (1 Chron 16:40; 22:12; 2 Chron 12:1; 14:3; 15:3; 17:9; 19:10; 23:18; 25:4; 30:16; 31:3, 4, 21; 33:8; 34:14, 15, 19; 35:26).

Moreover, unlike 1–2 Kgs' understanding of written Torah as primarily Deuteronomy, the Chronicler has in mind most or all of the Pentateuch. On several occasions, for example, priests receive instructions on ritual performance, topics simply not within Deuteronomy's purview (2 Chron 23:18; 30:16) but central to Leviticus. That is, Chronicles knew the final form of the Pentateuch or something like it.

A second and related feature is the accentuation of communal ritual, especially Passover. Both Josiah and Hezekiah are said to have celebrated the Passover as a nation-wide festival, and both events receive extensive coverage. Communities that pray and eat together find in that solidarity meaning and solidarity. For the creators and readers of 1–2 Chron such events inevitably would signal a hopeful possibility for themselves. History provides a model for a believable future.

A third feature is the alteration of the stories of some kings to highlight a feature of their reign that impinged upon their religious roles, shifting the balance of praise and blame in some way. Three examples of this phenomenon are instructive. The first occurs during the reign of Uzziah (mid-eighth century BCE). Isaiah 6:1 mentions his death, and 2 Kgs 15:1–7 (which calls him by his alternative name Azariah) briefly describes his reign as one "upright in Yhwh's eyes." Second Chronicles 26:3–23 expands the story in a negative direction by noting that

As he grew strong, he became arrogant to his own detriment, faithless to Yhwh his God. So he went into Yhwh's temple to offer incense upon the incense altar. The priest Azariah followed him along with the eight strongest priests of Yhwh. They opposed king Uzziah and said to him, "It's not your place Uzziah to offer incense to Yhwh. That's the job for the priests, Aaron's sons, who have been consecrated to offer incense. Go from the sanctuary, for you have been faithless. It's not for you to be around the glory from Yhwh God.'" (2 Chron 23:16–18)

This priestly move to protect the sanctuary receives divine validation when Uzziah comes down suddenly with a skin disease, just as Miriam does in Num 12, an obvious disbarment from presence in the Temple. The story serves to highlight the superiority of the priest-hood to kingship, at least as far as sacrifice goes, though it is not immediately obvious why Uzziah became such an object lesson for the Chronicler. This revised version of the story primarily explains 2 Kgs 15:5's observation that Yhwh had afflicted Uzziah with a skin disease, without explaining why. The story in 2 Chron explains why.

A similar story occurs in 2 Chron 33, which picks up most of the material about the unusually corrupt ruler Manasseh found in 2 Kgs 21:1–8. Rather than simply damning his memory, the Chronicler adds an important twist. Finding himself exiled to Babylon for his many sins, Manasseh "implored Yhwh, prostrated himself repeatedly before the God of his ancestors" and consequently received Yhwh's reward in his return from exile. He went on to restore the proper worship of Yhwh in Jerusalem. He thus is transformed into a prototype for the readership of Chronicles as a whole.

This story of repentance and redemption forces 2 Chron to omit the claim of 2 Kgs 24:3 that the Babylonian destruction of the early sixth century was owing to the sins of Manasseh a half century earlier. Such a rewriting of Manasseh's reign also leads the Chronicler to rework the story of Josiah's death (the fourth story in our incomplete list), which in 2 Kgs 23:28–30 lacks any moral or theological reason, in order to assign one. According to 2 Chron 35:20–22, Josiah decided to oppose the pro-Assyrian expedition of Necho of Egypt—the two longtime enemies were temporary allies against the Babylonians and Medes. Josiah ignored Necho's messengers, who tried to brush him (and his army) off by reporting a divine oracle. According to Necho, "God ordered me to hurry up. You stop opposing God, who is with me, so you won't be destroyed." This comradely warning goes unheeded, leading to Josiah's death at the battle of Megiddo. In other words, he dies for opposing the divine will as expressed to a foreign king. Like Uzziah, his arrogance got the better of him.

To summarize, then, 2 Chron 10–36 reworks 1–2 Kgs, omitting most of the stories about the north (except where southern kings were directly involved), polishing up the reputations of some rulers, emphasizing their work in the Jerusalem Temple and their cultivation of nationwide practices of religion. In recasting the stories this way, often no doubt with information either unavailable to, or ignored by, the Deuteronomists, the Chronicler seeks to find amid the vicissitudes of history a set of models for the future of the community as it functioned within the Persian Empire but dreamed of as a different set of possibilities.

Implications

Even if 1–2 Chron should be understood as a remake of Samuel–Kings (or even Genesis–Kings), still, the re-creation has merit in its own right. The two books of Chronicles are not simply a cheap knockoff of the DH. Rather, they rethink the received traditions both in light of new realities and as a reflection on the old stories themselves. The DH barely avoided writing an obituary for Israel, immersed as it was in the tragedies of the Assyrian and Babylonian deportations for which it must find reasons and therefore must assign blame. The CH, on the other hand, could move beyond tragedy to a more hopeful present. It found ways to reclaim the interconnections among kings and priests (with prophets functioning primarily to foreshadow future successes at worship or failure at ruling). And in so doing, it helped its readers imagine a different sort of future, perhaps devoid of Israelite kings but not devoid of the divine presence.

Notes

1. G.E.R. Lloyd, "Epilogue," in *The Oxford History of Historical Writing*, vol. 1: *Beginnings to AD 600*, ed. Andrew Feldherr and Grant Hardy, 606 (Oxford: Oxford University Press, 2011).

2. See the discussion in Sara Japhet, *I & II Chronicles* (Louisville, KY: Westminster/John Knox, 1993), 374–375, who argues that the adversary is human. For a critique of this part of her position, see Ralph W. Klein, *1 Chronicles* (Minneapolis: Fortress, 2006), 418.

For Further Reading

Endres, John C., William R. Millar, and John Barclay Burns, eds. *Chronicles and Its Synoptic Parallels in Samuel, Kings, and Related Biblical Texts*. Collegeville, MN: Liturgical Press, 1998.

Japhet, Sara. *The Ideology of the Book of Chronicles and Its Place in Biblical Thought*. Winona Lake, IN: Eisenbrauns, 2009.

Kalimi, Isaac. *The Reshaping of Ancient Israelite History in Chronicles*. Winona Lake, IN: Eisenbrauns, 2005.

Sparks, James T. *The Chronicler's Genealogies: Towards an Understanding of 1 Chronicles 1–9*. Atlanta: SBL, 2008.

15 Ezra and Nehemiah
FINDING LIFE AFTER DEATH

> **Key Text:** *But now our God, the great and mighty and awesome God, the one keeping the covenant and steadfast love, do not minimize all the suffering that has befallen us, our kings, our princes, our priests, our prophets, our ancestors—all your people—from the days of the kings of Assyria until this day. For you are just with respect to all that has come upon us. You have acted trustworthily, and we have done evil. Our kings, princes priests, and ancestors failed to do your Torah, nor did they observe your commands and testimonies that you testified to them . . . . However, we are slaves today, and as for the land that you gave to our ancestors so that they could eat its pleasant fruit, we are slaves upon it! Its abundant produce goes to the kings whom you placed over us because of our sins, ruling as they please over our bodies and our beasts. So we are in great distress.* (Neh 9:32–34, 36–37)

In her poignant chronicle of the life and death of the Jewish community of her hometown Eishyshok, Lithuania, Yaffa Eliach tells of returning home to what was once a thriving place before it was annihilated by the Nazis during the Holocaust. As part of an American commission—as a girl, she had come to the United States after World War II—Dr. Eliach resolved not merely to report the tragic end of a group of people but to "recreate for readers the vanished Jewish market town I had once called home." "I decided," she says, "I would set out on a path of my own, to create a memorial to life, not to death."[1]

A memorial to life, not to death. There could be no better description of the books of Ezra and Nehemiah. Like the book of Chronicles, which retraces the story of Israel from its beginnings (literally, from Adam) to the rise of the Persian Empire in order to reclaim the past for a hopeful future, Ezra and Nehemiah pick up the thread of the story and show how that future worked itself out, at least in part. These two short books, or rather one work more properly called Ezra-Nehemiah, seem to come from a different author than 1–2 Chronicles, but they pick up where the longer history stopped and thus seem a deliberate continuation of the other story.

Ezra-Nehemiah contains various sorts of texts (letters, lists of names, prayers, apparent diary entries, and so on), all of which give the book a jumbled appearance at first glance. However, a clear ordering does appear on closer examination:

A. Early events after the return to Yehud (Ezra 1:1–6:22)
B. Biographical notes about Ezra (Ezra 7:1–10:44)
C. The "memoir" of Nehemiah (Neh 1:1–7:72a [ET 7:73a])
D. Ezra's reforms (Neh 7:72b [ET 7:73b]–10:40 [ET 10:39])
E. Assorted notes on Nehemiah and others (Neh 11:1–13:3)
F. Nehemiah's second term as governor (Neh 13:4–31)

That is, the book intertwines the careers of the priest/teacher Ezra and the political leader Nehemiah, using them as twin models of excellent leadership in the renewed community. This "memorial to life" focuses on two characters in order to address the complex interactions of the internal life of the people with its larger surroundings.

YEHUD WITHIN THE PERSIAN EMPIRE

During the Persian Empire (539–334 BCE), the land of Israel was part of the large province or satrapy called "Beyond the River," which included most or all of modern Syria, Lebanon, Israel, Palestine, and Jordan and parts of Iraq. The area around Jerusalem was called Yehud (a variant form of Judah or Yehudah), and separate subprovinces were headquartered at Samaria and Dor. Coins and other artifacts from this era show Jerusalem as a center focusing primarily on the Temple, with the high priest doubling as a major local political figure.

The name for a person from Yehud was *Yehudi*, the word that eventually came to describe those who practiced the religion of that place, that is, "Jew."

Ezra 7:1–6 introduces Ezra as both a sixteenth-generation descendant of Aaron the high priest and as a "speedy [i.e., expert] scribe in Moses's Torah, which Yhwh Israel's God gave." That is, the book's first protagonist comes from circles that value the Mosaic traditions, both written and performed through ritual. Meanwhile, the second protagonist, Nehemiah, appears in Neh 1 as a high-ranking official at the Persian imperial court who requests permission from the emperor Artaxerxes to go to his ancestral city of Jerusalem and rebuild its walls. This voluntary career demotion after considering the continued state of the city's denizens living "in great calamity and shame, after Jerusalem's wall was broken down and its gates consumed by fire" (Neh 1:3). Each of these introductions comes in memoir-like material that the editor(s) of Ezra-Nehemiah use to form the larger story.

The events of the book seem to date to the reign of Artaxerxes I (r. 465–424 BCE), though it is remotely possible that they occurred under Artaxerxes II (r. 404–358 BCE). Ezra 1–6 reports earlier events, dating to the reigns of Cyrus the Great and Darius the Great in the sixth century BCE at the beginning of the Persian Empire. The book as a whole thus uses older sources from different periods, finally coming together sometime in the late fifth century as a single work.

Ezra-Nehemiah, in short, depicts life at a crucial moment in Israel's history, the early stages of its rebirth as a people. Consider, then, each section of this memorial to life:

Early Events After the Return to Yehud (Ezra 1:1–6:22)

Along with letters from the royal court of Persia and brief narratives of late-sixth-century leaders such as Joshua and Zerubbabel (who also appear in Haggai and Zechariah), the first six chapters consist of a series of names, much as in 1 Chron 1–9. They appear in Ezra for much the same reason as in Chronicles. The names mark points of survival and renewal. (Perhaps a modern functional equivalent would be the use of photographs of family members in homes—the living and the dead remain ever present.)

Two scenes in the narrative stand out in importance. The first appears in Ezra 3:1–13, in which Zerubbabel the governor (and descendant of David) and his colleague the high priest Joshua lead the returning deportees (Hebrew: *gōlâ*) in the rebuilding of the Jerusalem Temple. Laid waste by Nebuchadnezzar several decades earlier, the Temple site had remained well known and perhaps even been the site of sacrifice in the interim, but its rebuilding decisively formed the community as one that sought to renew itself by connecting its past to its future. The work of reconstruction coincided with the feast of Sukkot or Tabernacles, which the community followed "as it is written" (Ezra 3:4), a phrase that recurs in the book as it speaks about key practices. In other words, the story introduces a major theme in the book—the community's identity markers as a group that worships in the Jerusalem Temple, bases its decisions on an emerging canon of Scripture, and preserves ethnic boundaries vis-à-vis other groups. These signs of group membership distinguished the Yehudian community and with some adjustments still shape Judaism until this day.

"AS IT IS WRITTEN"

At several points, the stories in Ezra and Nehemiah contain a subtle explanation of the reasons behind the actions of their heroes. The phrase "as it is written" or "as it is written in the Torah of Moses," or something similar, names a warrant for keeping the feast of Sukkot (Ezra 3:2, 4; Neh 8:14–15), supplying needed goods for the Temple (Neh 10:35), and making offerings on behalf of firstborn children (Neh 10:37). This emphasis on a written text underlying the community's decisions owes something to the earlier Deuteronomists' emphasis on texts, but Ezra-Nehemiah takes the idea to a new level. That is, these books bear witness to an early stage of the focus on sacred texts that has become central to most forms of Judaism, Christianity, and Islam in one way or another. The festival was apparently important because it connected the agricultural cycle to Israel's core story of divine deliverance, all in an atmosphere of celebration and fun.

In Ezra-Nehemiah, the Golah group (returnees and their descendants) practice a strong group togetherness, including endogamy, avoidance of cooperation with other Israelite groups, and reliance on the Persian government for help. Or at least the text sees them in this way, emphasizing their solidarity as a group (the word *gôlâ* designating them in Ezra 1:11; 2:1; 4:1; 6:19, 20, 21; 8:35; 9:4; 10:6, 7, 8, 16; Neh 7:6). While one may easily exaggerate their cohesion and uniformity of thought, for Ezra-Nehemiah the return of this group demonstrated Yhwh's mercy and superintendence of history.

On a related note, the second important factor underlying the narrative occurs in Ezra 4:1–6:22. This section, written in Aramaic rather than Hebrew, reports an ongoing correspondence between the imperial government and the members of the Golah, regarding the rebuilding of Jerusalem's city walls. (The text is in Aramaic probably because that was the language of the imperial bureaucracy, and any correspondence with the government would have required that language.) The controversy dates to the reign of Artaxerxes, about eighty years later than the events of Ezra 1–3. Such construction projects required government approval because fortifications could show an empire's might or merely give its enemies a safe haven.

The Golah's enemies rightly understood the construction as a bid for providing their group with a viable future by reclaiming its past. Hence their charges against Jerusalem as a hotbed of sedition (Ezra 4:12–16). The Golah leaders, on the other hand, appealed to past precedents, including the much earlier letter from Darius giving permission to rebuild the Temple (Ezra 6:8–10).

The book of Ezra emphasizes the building of the Temple and the city walls and the dispatch of Ezra and Nehemiah to Jerusalem. But this emphasis raises important questions. How involved was the Persian government in the religious life of post-return Yehud? Some scholars speak of the Persian authorization of that life, including even the formation and preservation of Torah. A few have even argued that the Pentateuch itself reached its final form and widespread usage as the result of governmental policy of encouraging local traditions and laws in their empire.

The evidence for such an expansive view is meager. For example, there are few if any words or expressions drawn from Persian in Genesis-Deuteronomy (in contrast to 1–2 Chronicles or Ezra-Nehemiah). Much of the material in the Pentateuch predates this period, and all of it focuses on creating a community independent of foreign control, hardly a viewpoint that the imperial government would have encouraged. Thus it seems that a more modest explanation is in order: the Golah community often found it expedient to cooperate with their Persian overlords, and they sometimes believed that Persian rulers followed Yhwh's instructions (as in Isa 44–45; 2 Chron 36:22–23). As one group among many within the vast empire, the Yehudians relied upon the empire's basic sense of justice to protect their rights.

Biographical Notes about Ezra (Ezra 7:1–10:44)

After laying out these large-scale communal problems, Ezra introduces its namesake, the scribe and priest Ezra ben Sarayah. He comes to Jerusalem bearing a royal warrant to gather resources for the Temple, thus coupling the authority of sacred knowledge with that of political power.

EZRA IN HISTORY AND TRADITION

After the book of Ezra-Nehemiah, Ezra remained a famous figure, becoming in time the primary teacher of Judaism after Moses. For example, according to some traditions, he was associated with the Great Synagogue, the semilegendary group of leaders who refashioned Judaism as a Torah-observant community. According to these stories, he even had a hand in the writing of Torah as a whole after it had been lost during repeated foreign invasions and Israel's negligence. Fourth Ezra, written around 100 CE, describes a discussion between him and the angel Uriel about the fate of Zion, presenting Ezra as a wise man seeking to understand God's activities in history and especially God's apparent neglect of the well-being of Jerusalem and Israel as a whole. While the historical person remains obscure, his role in these tales demonstrates his importance as a type of person idealized in Second Temple Judaism, the pious and wise teacher.

Ezra exercises this authority in two primary ways, (1) by reorganizing the service of the Temple (Ezra 8:24–30) and (2) by insisting that those men who had married foreign women divorce them and send off their children as well (Ezra 9:1–44). The second action seems shocking, and not just to modern sensibilities, because it would have exacerbated the hardships for all involved. Here it must be understood as a strategy of communal survival. As Ezra 9:2 puts it, "they have mixed the holy seed with the peoples of the lands." It would be anachronistic to read this line as a case of early racism as is sometimes done, however. In a small community surrounded by others with different values, histories, and aspirations, extensive intermarriage threatened the very survival of the group. So, while the text does not sit well with a modern reader who assumes that the love between individuals trumps all other considerations, it is at least intelligible.

Underwriting both acts of Ezra's leadership is the prayer that appears in Ezra 9:5–15. Like prayers in Nehemiah, this one expresses the book's overall theology.

At the evening sacrifice, I arose and mourned and tore my clothes and mantle, and bowed my knees and spread out my hands to Yhwh my God. Then I said, "O my God, I am ashamed and embarrassed to lift up my face to you, O my God. For our iniquities are numerous up to the top of the head. Also, I am greatly ashamed up to the sky. From the days of our ancestors we had great shame until this day, and for our transgressions we, our kings, and our priests were given to the kings of the lands, by sword and deportation, in ignominy and disgrace as on this day . . . . And now, what can we say after this, O our God? For we have forsaken your commandments that you commanded through your servants the prophets, who said 'the land that you are to inherit is a land of menstrual impurity because of the menstrual impurity of the peoples of the lands, i.e., their abominations fill it from border to border with their uncleanness.'"

This graphic (even intentionally disgusting) use of the language of shame underscores Ezra's discontent with the state of the people and in particular the ease with which they had married exogamously. The book seeks to communicate the urgency of preserving the community through preserving the family, since one without the other is unsustainable.

The "Memoir" of Nehemiah (Neh 1:1–7:72a [ET 7:73a])

Coupled with the story of Ezra is the narrative of Nehemiah. Arguably based on a memoir that speaks of him in the first person, the Nehemiah story revolves around his role as governor of Yehud. As it opens, he appears as cupbearer to the Persian emperor in the imperial capital of Susa (the same palace that is the backdrop of the book of Esther). As mentioned, Nehemiah moves to Jerusalem to take up the role of governor of the city, taking a significant demotion in order to carry out his religious duties. The narrative emphasizes several themes of his governorship, including his conflict with the leaders in Samaria (Sanballat) and Ammon (Tobiah), his successful efforts at rebuilding the Jerusalem city wall, and thus his consolidation of Jerusalem as a center of influence alternative to Samaria. While it is possible to see Nehemiah's work as part of Persian efforts at consolidating their empire and securing frontier regions such as the southern Levant, the book of Nehemiah itself sees this work from a more local level, as the logical outcome of several generations of the Golah's efforts are building life around Zion.

Ezra's Reforms (Neh 7:72b [ET 7:73b] –10:40 [ET 10:39])

This larger religious pattern becomes clearer in the following section, which returns to Ezra as a hero but seems also to incorporate material more proper to Nehemiah. The centerpiece of this section is the prayer and accompanying festival described in Neh 8:1–9:37. The scene opens with a summons to the people to the festival of Sukkot (or Tabernacles), which they celebrate by gathering tree limbs from the hillsides, following what may already have been an ancient tradition (cf. Lev 23:40). The emphasis in Nehemiah does not lie on the sacrifices of Sukkot (as in Lev 23:33–44 and even more so Num 29:12–38) but on the communal nature of the festival (as in Exod 23:16, though with some differences), the reading of sacred texts, and prayer.

These three elements intertwine. The communal nature of the festival shines through not only in the assembling of all the Yehudians (Neh 8:1–4) but also in their distribution of food from the festival to all unable to attend the party for various reasons (Neh 8:12).

The reading of the "Torah of Moses," which may mean Deuteronomy or perhaps a more extended part of the Pentateuch, takes place in the public assembly, requiring the Levites as the Torah's guardians to offer interpretation of the text (whether translating it from its original Hebrew to the more commonly spoken Aramaic, or simply repeating the words to make Ezra's reading more audible, or, less likely, offering running commentary). As before, the Golah community engages the Torah of Moses as an identity marker of its life.

The most expansive theological statement of the entire book of Ezra-Nehemiah comes in the prayer of Neh 9:5–37. This statement of national confession retraces Israel's history, marking it as one of repeated sin and punishment (cf. Deut 1–4; Ps 78). However, self-flagellation does not seem to be its ultimate goal. Rather, as the ending of the prayer makes clear, a dialectic exists between human admission of guilt and Yhwh's acceptance of responsibility for Israel's fate. As the prayer adroitly puts it:

> But now our God, the great and mighty and awesome God, the one keeping the covenant and steadfast love, do not minimize all the suffering that has befallen us, our kings, our princes, our priests, our prophets, our ancestors—all your people— from the days of the kings of Assyria until this day. For you are just with respect to all that has come upon us. You have acted trustworthily, and we have done evil. Our kings, princes, priests, and ancestors failed to do your Torah, nor did they observe your commands and testimonies that you testified to them . . . . However, we are slaves today, and as for the land that you gave to our ancestors so that they could eat its pleasant fruit, we are slaves upon it! Its abundant produce goes to the kings whom you placed over us because of our sins, ruling as they please over our bodies and our beasts. So we are in great distress. (Neh 9:32–34, 36–37)

In short, says the text, "Yes, we are guilty, but . . . " The appeal to divine mercy includes an honest admission of fault, an acceptance of the Deuteronomic and prophetic critiques of past generations, but also an implied questioning of the appropriateness of the divine activities in supporting the current situation of subjugation to Persian rule.

The last few lines are especially telling in a book that largely approves of the imperial center's actions with respect to Yehud. By describing foreign occupiers as tax-sucking leeches (cf. Eccl 5:7–8 [ET 5:8–9]), the prayer reveals the complexity of the authors' feelings about the empire. Occupation is a punishment, but some forms of it are preferable to others. The colonized may interact constructively with the system, even if they hope for its ultimate demise. In short, Ezra-Nehemiah adopts a flexible and nuanced political theology.

Assorted Notes on Nehemiah and Others (Neh 11:1–13:3)

Theology aside, a community's life requires flexibility and nuance in other ways, in this case seen not only in the notices of Neh 10 about the Yehudian community's commitment to supporting the Temple with a regular tax, but Neh 11–13's lists of groups filling up Jerusalem and surrounding areas. Certainly the population of Yehud did grow during the later Persian period, as archaeological excavations bear out (since it reached a millennia-long low early in that period, the upward direction was almost inevitable). But as in 1 Chronicles, again, the lists remind the reader of the interconnectedness of the newly consolidating community.

Nehemiah's Second Term as Governor (Neh 13:4–31)

Consolidation, of course, requires leadership. So the book ends with a final notice (again perhaps from Nehemiah's memoirs) about a new series of reforms around Sabbath and intermarriage. Arguably, the renewed attention to the latter proves the failure of earlier attempts to create a "pure" society banning exogamy. "Love conquers all" or at least "marriage conquers theology." And so ends this work, the best surviving window onto life in the environs of Jerusalem during the fifth century BCE or for some time afterwards. The end is anticlimactic, opening itself up to the future that always awaits any flourishing group.

Implications

What, then, does Ezra-Nehemiah contribute to the theological reflections of the Hebrew Bible or Old Testament? Like other narratives, this book writes a memorial of life. While not all Israelites left Babylon and returned to the land of Israel, and indeed a thriving Jewish community survived there until the twentieth century, the ones who did return created a new thing. Attentive to the old traditions then coalescing in the Pentateuch, the Golah community sought an identity based on monotheism, shared worship at the Jerusalem Temple, and structures of sharing resources for religious ends. The coinage and texts of Persian-period Yehud show the centrality of the Temple especially to their lives. In such a context, then, Ezra and Nehemiah figure as models of courageous leadership even in their most uncomfortably exclusivistic moments.

Note

1. Yaffa Eliach, *There Once Was a World: A Nine-Hundred-Year Chronicle of the Shtetl of Eishyshok* (Boston: Little, Brown, 1998), 4.

For Further Reading

Albertz, Rainer. *Israel in Exile: The History and Literature of the Sixth Century B.C.E.* Atlanta: SBL, 2003.

Gerstenberger, Erhard S. *Israel in the Persian Period: The Fifth and Fourth Centuries B.C.E.* Translated by Siegfried S. Schatzmann. Atlanta: SBL, 2011.

16 The Queen of Comedies
THE BOOK OF ESTHER

Key Text: *So Queen Esther the daughter of Abihayil and Mordecai the Jew . . . sent letters to all the Jews throughout the 127 provinces of Ahasuerus's empire—words of peace and trust. [They instructed them] to observe these days of Purim in their seasons just as Mordecai the Jew and Queen Esther observed them and just as they solemnized their lives and their offspring, with fasting and lament. And Esther kept exhorting to observe the deeds of these Purim. And so it was written in the book.* (Esth 9:29–32)

What makes a hero, and how does a community talk about heroism? Every society tells stories of women and men whose courage, fortitude, and wisdom help them win against seemingly invincible foes. The Old Testament is no exception to this rule.

One of the two biblical books bearing the name of a woman, the book of Esther, reports the goings-on in the royal court of Susa, the capital of the Persian Empire. Its story of court intrigue, attempted murder, trickery, and ultimate triumph would work nicely in a cable network costume drama, except that, in the end, a mostly unambiguous good overcomes overt evil.

In reading Esther, bear a few things in mind. To begin, no one is sure when the book of Esther was written. It is set in the reign of Ahasuerus, better known as Xerxes (r. 486–465 BCE) the king infamous among the Greeks for his invasion of their country. Yet the book does not present sober history. Quite the contrary—and pun intended—it relates tales of drunken decision-makers. It is a satire of life under Persian rule. Like a Shakespearean comedy, it explores serious issues by holding up the insane policies of an empire to close scrutiny. It was written either toward the end of the Persian Empire or the beginning of the Hellenistic period, and so probably in the fourth or early third centuries BCE.

THE LAWS OF THE MEDES AND PERSIANS

Esther 1:8 introduces a significant concept in the book, Persian law or strong social custom (Hebrew: *dāt*). *Dāt* in Esther takes on an absurd quality (in contrast to Israel's law; see Esth 3:8). In the opening scene of the book, *Dāt* is the standard by which one organizes drinking parties, whereas elsewhere it involves silly regulations for women (Esth 1:19; 2:8, 12) and the mass murder of Jews (Esth 3:14–15; 4:3, 8, 11, 16). Since the law cannot be altered, again an absurd feature of the system, the emperor can protect them only by making another law permitting them to resist (Esth 8:13–17), thus creating civil discord. This, then, is part of the satire. When a feature of human society as important as law becomes inflexible and subject to the whim of a few powerful people, only the worst results can ensue. The book of Esther wishes to say that the empire in which Jews live has many absurd qualities. Those who would survive must show intelligence and courage.

Moreover, the book exists in two versions, one in the original Hebrew language (the version translated in most English Bibles) and one now surviving in Greek. The Greek translation comes from an expanded version of the book. In some English Bibles, the expansions are printed separately as "Additions to Esther," but no such freestanding work existed in antiquity, just a longer text. For more on that, see the discussion in Chapter 30 ("Secondary Canon").

The Basic Story

Anyone reading Esther, especially in its Hebrew version, should remember that it is a dark comedy. It explores taboo subjects such as ethnic cleansing and sexual exploitation and deception in a comic vein. It is a sort of literary cousin of works like Jonathan Swift's *Model Proposal* (in which he proposed solving Ireland's social problems by having the rich eat the poor) or some of the scenes in Dostoyevsky's *Crime and Punishment*. This sort of literature deliberately makes the reader uncomfortable in order to trigger serious thought. The plot and characters of the book all contribute to that end.

SCENE I (ESTH 1:1–22)

The story opens in the royal palace in Susa, today in southwestern Iran. This already ancient city became one of the major centers of the Persian Empire, and the site of a massive ornate palace at which the great emperor could display the finest products of his sprawling empire. He could not, however, hide the fact that his greatest weakness lay within, in his inability to control himself or even his subjects. And so the book opens with what sounds like the opening of a royal inscription boasting of the king's deeds.

Instead of listing conquests or building projects, the satire turns the old literary convention on its head by announcing the king's great achievement as a six-month-long drinking party involving all the leaders of his empire. The reader immediately is left to wonder who is running the empire if all its leaders are drinking at the capital, and of course this is the point. In the first scene, the author wishes to situate the story in a world gone mad owing to the irresponsibility of the powerful.

The narrative goes on in Esth 1 to describe at length the royal palace and then to introduce the problem whose solution leads to the happy ending of the book. In a drunken state, Ahasuerus decides to invite his queen, Vashti, to the main palace in order to "show her beauty to the people and the princes, for she was good-looking" (Esth 1:11). Since royal women usually resided in the harem and were in any case not art for exhibition, Vashti refuses, triggering a major political crisis. The king and his equally drunken advisors conclude that if other women hear of the refusal, they will similarly fail to obey their husbands. Yet, rather than hushing up the matter, they publicize it by commanding women not do what Vashti did, again, not an act of rational people!

SCENE 2 (ESTH 2:1–23)

This crisis leads to the introduction of the major heroic characters of the book, Mordecai and his ward and cousin Esther (also called Hadassah). These two figures appear in response to the king's search for a new queen, with Esther winning the competition for the role. While a prudish, Victorian sort of reading of this might accuse Mordecai of pandering his beautiful young cousin off to a lecherous monarch, the text itself does not pass such judgment but continues with its attempt to contrast Jewish integrity with Persian ignorance. Thus the scene ends with the king unaware of Esther's Jewish origins or Mordecai's role in thwarting a coup d'état against him. The disclosure of both facts will come at just the right moments in the later narrative.

SCENE 3 (ESTH 3:1–15)

The third scene introduces the villain of the piece, one Haman the Agagite. A major royal official with direct access to the monarch, he appears as a conceited leader whose hatred of the Jews comes from a perceived snub of him by Mordecai. It goes without saying that such an overreaction as planning mass murder does not befit the personal offense, a fact that the text underscores by its portrayal of the moment in which the final solution to the Jewish "problem" was reached. Haman and Ahasuerus drink together *in camera* and agree to kill all the Jews in the empire.

Note how Haman makes his case: since even the most irresponsible king would be reluctant to kill his own peaceful, obedient subjects, Haman (Esth 3:8) must portray the Jews as a people (1) scattered among the other nations (true), (2) obeying different laws than other ethnic groups (true), and (3) not carrying out the king's law (partly true, but then consider what the king's law [*dāt*] entails). He appeals to the widespread ancient

Near Eastern assumption that while each community might have its own laws that honored local customs, it was essential for all people to respect law as an overarching concept that guaranteed divinely inspired justice, and to honor the king as its protector and enforcer.

In other words, Haman's charge works at several levels: he means one thing by the statements, and the author and readers must conclude something else. Yes, Jews followed different laws, but they were superior laws, not inferior ones. This double meaning reveals an important aspect of the book's view of the world, for it believes that the best way to honor the divine realm is to question the empire's legal practices because they did not pursue their stated goals.

SCENE 4 (ESTH 4:1–17)

On discovering the plot, Mordecai persuades Esther to intervene with the king, using her physical attractiveness as a means of appealing to him. He argues that she should not expect to escape the impending massacre simply because her Jewish identity temporarily remained a secret, and he utters perhaps the most talked-about line in the book (Esth 4:14): "who knows if perhaps for a time like this you have gained access to the monarchy?"

The line is often assumed to refer obliquely to divine providence's guidance of the selection of Esther as queen, and this is certainly a defensible interpretation, though how carefully Mordecai has thought through the theological implications is unclear. At a minimum, he does appeal to her sense of responsibility for her own people on the assumption that people with power must use it responsibly.

SCENE 5 (ESTH 5:1–8)

This pivotal scene in the middle of the book sets the trap for Haman. Esther adopts the popular court practice of having a party (as in chapter 1), extending an invitation to Haman and Ahasuerus. A brilliant turn on her (and the author's) part, the invitation reminds the reader of the commitments of the male characters in a seemingly off-handed way.

SCENE 6 (ESTH 5:9–14)

Another brilliantly cast scene in which Haman brags to his wife and guests about the invitation to the queen's salon, as well as his own sexual prowess (referred to euphemistically by reference to the number of his sons) and in general his importance in the government. His words reveal him as a small man, pretentious and self-important. The scene ends ominously with the erection of a gigantic gallows fifty cubits (about twenty-five meters/82 ft.) high, far larger than any practical requirement for execution would demand.

SCENE 7 (ESTH 6:1–13)

Now that all the elements of the story are in place, the narrator begins the reversal of fortune in favor of the heroes Mordecai, Esther, and the rest of the Jews. This scene brilliantly depicts the stupidity of the king and his advisor by (1) having an insomniac king seek sleep through having the record of his achievements read to him (a very funny joke at his expense); (2) allowing Haman to choose a proper way to honor a royal favorite, who turns out to be his mortal enemy Mordecai rather than himself; and (3) by ending with Haman's wife (Zeresh) advising him to abandon his plots against Mordecai (and thus the Jews in general). All of these elements are part of the dark comedy.

SCENE 8 (ESTH 6:14–7:10)

Zeresh's ominous prediction comes true when Esther turns the table on Haman at the dinner table. She outs him as the enemy of her people, the Jews. Fascinatingly, the king takes no responsibility for the plot against the Jews, abandoning Haman to his fate as the malevolent monster he is. At this point, the story moves into the world of farce, with the king misunderstanding Haman's pleas for mercy with the queen as an attempt to rape her in his very presence, and the ever-present eunuch offering the gallows intended for Mordecai as a fit ending for Haman instead.

SCENE 9 (ESTH 8:1–17)

The king, now come to his senses, issues a decree permitting the Jews to defend themselves from their enemies on the day appointed for the massacre. Again, the problem of a legal system in which no decree can be repealed becomes clear. The Persian Empire can only save itself from injustice by fostering civil unrest.

SCENE 10: (ESTH 9:1–17)

The final part of the narrative involves the actual day of conflict, in which the Jews defeated their enemies, including the family of Haman and other high officials who plotted against them.

CONCLUSION (ESTH 9:18–28)

The book ends with an explanation of the origins of the festival of Purim, connecting it to the faithful work of Mordecai and Esther. This conclusion appears almost as an afterthought, but in fact it reveals a major purpose of the book. Purim, celebrated every year a month before Passover, did not appear as a festival in the Pentateuch but as a later addition to Jewish religious life, so some explanation of the innovation had to exist. Hence this book. The festival arose during the Persian period (perhaps the fourth century BCE) among Jews in the diaspora as a sort of echo of Passover. In both festivals, Jews celebrate delivery from foreign oppressors through the agency of courageous leaders. While the book of Esther has a life of its own as a brilliantly told story, it also serves this larger explanatory purpose.

Implications

Many of the latest texts of the Old Testament, as well as other contemporary Jewish texts, spoke of the struggles of being faithful to Torah in a world controlled by often hostile gentiles. Some of those texts, such as the book of Daniel, offer pious heroes who suffer few inner doubts. Esther is different because this book, in its Hebrew version especially, describes heroes whose integrity is more hard-won, whose doubts are real, and yet whose ultimate triumphs of the spirit inspire the reader also to show courage and fidelity to their identity as people of Torah. Perhaps this very humanness makes the book of Esther all the more attractive for modern readers who also struggle to find integrity in an often hostile world.

For Further Reading

Levenson, Jon. *Esther*. Old Testament Library. Louisville: Westminster/John Knox, 1997.

Potts, D. T. *The Archaeology of Elam: Formation and Transformation of an Ancient Iranian State*. Cambridge: Cambridge University Press, 1999.

17 Poetic and Wisdom Texts

INTEGRITY IS A characteristic of a literary work, as well as a life. C. S. Lewis once remarked that "The first qualification for judging any workmanship from a corkscrew to a cathedral is to know what it is—what it is intended to do and how it is meant to be used."[1] With respect to the "workmanship" of poetry the phrase "what it is intended to do and how it is meant to be used" signals two important things: readers should not impose upon the text values or viewpoints or purposes the text cannot bear, but the reader may expect to gain something through the reading of the text. Poetry depends not merely on the arguments it makes or the appeal of its narrative but on the very ordering of the words, the artisanry of choosing the right word for the right spot to express the right feeling or thought.

The books of Job, Psalms, Proverbs, Ecclesiastes, and Song of Songs contain primarily poetry of various forms. While poetry appears also throughout the Bible, and especially in the prophetic books, these five lyrical texts have different purposes. In Christian Bibles, these five works figure together, while in Jewish Bibles they appear as part of a larger grouping called the Writings. Several of the books also share a strong commitment to the necessary pursuit of wisdom (Job, Proverbs, and Ecclesiastes, and to some extent Psalms), while the Song of Songs offers a joyful exploration of the still deeper human need for love. The next few chapters will explore these works in detail.

For now, a few observations about Hebrew poetry are in order. What is it, and what is it not? Lacking rhyme, regular meter, or set numbers of lines, Hebrew poetry differs from more formal types of English poetry such as the sonnet or the villanelle. In Hebrew poetry, lines usually consist of two (or sometimes three) sublines (cola), each of eight to twelve syllables and usually roughly equally balanced (but many exceptions exist). That is, a line stretches out to cover a single thought, usually in a paired relationship (Part A and Part B), though frequently also enjambed lines, i.e., lines in which the thought simply keeps going, appear.

As Chapter 19 will explain in much more detail, this pairing has long gone under the name of parallelism since Robert Lowth so named it in the mid-1700s. Lowth thought that Hebrew poetry usually paired the A and B parts of the line in one of three ways: synonymous, antithetic, and synthetic parallelism. For example, Song of Songs 8:1 has the female lover say, "Who will make you like my brother, the one sucking on my mother's breasts?" A poet simply substitutes one phrase for its equivalent in the previous part. Or at the other end of the spectrum, "I will exalt you, O Yhwh, for you have drawn me up; you did not make my enemies rejoice over me" (Ps 30:2 [ET 30:1]). God's rescue of the person created a state of being radically opposed to one in which the poet's enemies could exult in his or her suffering. Or again, some parallelism seems to be neither restating an idea nor positing its opposite but rather doing something else, as in Ps 56:4 (ET 56:3]), where a psalmist avers, "I trust Yhwh. I will not fear. What can flesh do for/to me?" Trusting Yhwh may lead to fearlessness (synonymous parallelism), but the following question adds another layer of meaning, or rather a range of possible meanings. The question may ask, "How can human beings help me?" (in contrast to Yhwh's capacities) or "How can human beings harm me" (since they cannot, I need not fear them). This sort of "parallelism" is not simple at all. In such cases, Part B adds a new layer of meaning to Part A, enriching it in often unexpected ways.

As it happens, there are many other forms of parallelism in biblical poetry, and the phenomenon may extend to several lines. Lowth's basic start of the analysis was just that—a start.

The complexity of the poetry has led some scholars to question the value of the term "parallelism," a proper precaution surely. Hebrew poetry does value certain kinds of repetition, sometimes to a considerable degree. A good example of this appears in Jonah's prayer of thanksgiving inside his leviathanic transport:

From Sheol's womb I cried, and you heard my voice.
Though you cast me into the ocean's depths and the River overwhelmed me,
All your breakers and your waves surged over me,
Still I said, "I am out of your view—
How can I ever see again your holy temple?"
The water swelled neck deep, the abyss surrounded me.
The seaweed was draped around my head at the mountains' bases.
I descended to the underworld. Its gate-bars enclosed me forever. (Jon 2:3–7)

The watery abyssal imagery of the descent to the underworld and the confrontation there with the forces hostile to the creator God comes from ancient, pre-Israelite sources, evoking the darkest fears of the ancient Israelite reader (not to mention writers of textbooks and many of their readers). Jonah's "parallelism" underscores those anxieties lying within human minds by repeating itself, but each repetition adds something new, something richer to the evocation of death confronted and yet escaped. The basic unit of the line is extended across a larger cluster of lines. In short, then, the reader of Hebrew poetry must be aware of this technique of turning one image in ever-new directions to allow it to open new doors of meaning, yet without becoming too wooden in our understanding of that poetic practice.

In a more radical vein, James Kugel has observed not only that "parallelistic lines" also appear in prose (and in common speech), but that the very idea of the Bible as poetry comes from the earliest Greek-speaking readers of the Bible, not from the rabbis. (By the way, this different reading style explains why Matthew, in that Gospel's story of the Triumphal Entry on "Palm Sunday" (Matt 21:5–11) can interpret Zech 9:9's parallelistic couple "Your king comes, gently riding a donkey, and en-saddled on a foal" as referring to two different animals providing a ride (in contrast to the parallels in Mark 11:1–11; Luke 19:28–38; and John 12:12–19). Part A did not always seem to these ancient readers to be repeated in Part B.)

Kugel questions the legitimacy of using the word "poetry" for these texts since our modern use of that term, as with the Greeks from whom we inherited it, relies on assumptions of individual creativity, the emphasis on novelty (sometimes), and a close connection between the poet's emotional state and the poem's artifice that ancient people simply did not assume. And granted, modern readers must try to get behind the legacy of the nineteenth-century Romantics in their understanding of how poetry worked. In other words, we must remember what sort of "workmanship" lies before us.

Nonetheless, it seems difficult to abandon the word "poetry" (or "prose" as its *Doppelgänger*, for that matter) because these texts so emphasize the kind of close attention to wording that one associates with that term (as Kugel himself emphasizes). But one should be cautious here in not imposing upon the ancient works assumptions more appropriate for more recent ones. The psychology of a writer of a given psalm is not available to the modern reader. How it makes us feel is a function of the structure and use of the text, not something "inherent" within it, and not in any case crucial to its interpretation.

So now to Job, Psalms, Proverbs, Ecclesiastes, and Song of Songs. These works explore the exigencies of life with and without Yhwh. They fashion out of human experience pictures of life well and joyfully lived, even in the face of the ever-present sorrow that also befalls us. Their corkscrews and cathedrals still fascinate and inspire.

Note

1. C. S. Lewis, *Preface to Paradise Lost* (Oxford: Oxford University Press, 1942), 1.

For Further Reading

Couey, J. Blake. *Reading the Poetry of First Isaiah: The Most Perfect Model of the Prophetic Poetry.* Oxford: Oxford University Press, 2015.

Kugel, James. *The Idea of Biblical Poetry: Parallelism and Its History.* New Haven: Yale University Press, 1981.

18 God as Defendant and Plaintiff
THE BOOK OF JOB

> **Key Text:** *If I should call and he answered me, I do not believe he would hear my voice.... If it's about strength, he is the powerful one, and if it's about justice, then who will make him answer for anything?* (Job 9:16, 19)

In his charming poetic drama, *"A Masque of Reason,"* Robert Frost portrays a comedic conversation among God, Job, and Mrs. Job in a resort to which they have all retired. As they reminisce about their savage encounter earlier in life, Job asks why the trials he experienced had to be his. "It had to be at someone's expense," God says. "Society can never think things out: it has to see them acted out by actors." The biblical book becomes, for Frost and for many other modern readers, a drama exploring divine justice (or injustice?) and the limits of human endurance.

The author of Job probably understood the book in a slightly different way, yet Frost is right to see the story as a mental experiment, not just a clever tale. Drawing on older stories about an ancient heroic figure who interceded for others (see Ezek 14:14), the book of Job addresses several key theological questions. The first is whether God uses power justly to benefit the creation or treats human beings as playthings or even as prey. The second revolves around the question of language: what sort of language should human beings use to describe their relationships with God, and thus the nature of religious beliefs and practices? Unlike modern thinkers and a few Greek precursors, the book does not question the existence or power of God. Rather, it raises questions by means of a multilayered dialogue embedded in a simple story. Or, as Frost's God has it, society "has to see them acted out by actors." The book of Job acts out a set of ideas.

THE DATE OF CIRCUMSTANCES OF THE BOOK'S ORIGIN

Commentators have assigned Job to a wide range of dates. The Babylonian Talmud (*b. Baba Bathra* 15a), for example, implies that the work comes from the pre-Mosaic Patriarchal Age, apparently a deduction from the fact that its hero, Job, was a gentile who knew nothing of the Israelite tradition and its understanding of deity. The idea of an early date goes back at least to an addition to the LXX translation of Job, the end of which connects him to the Edomite king Jobab in Gen 36:33–34. However, this date commands no serious consideration today. Most scholars date the book to the Persian period (539–334 BCE) because the Hebrew of the prose framework (1:1–2:13; 42:7–17) best fits that era and because of the reference in 1:17 to the Chaldeans, the tribe that dominated Babylonian society in the seventh and sixth centuries BCE, assumes the Babylonian invasion of the southern Levant in the early sixth century.

At the same time, however, chs 3–31 and 38–41 do contain many unusual words and phrases that seem to reflect the author's extraordinary command of Hebrew poetry but also an origin for the work outside the main centers of Hebrew writing. Archaic or archaizing speech—distinguishing the two is not always easy—appears throughout these chapters, possibly indicating either that some of the book predates the Persian period or that the author wished to make it appear so.

Whether the prose framework dates earlier or later than the poetry is also debated, though it is difficult to imagine one without the other since 3:1 could not be a plausible beginning of the book (though, admittedly, 42:6 or even 41:26 [ET 41:34]) might make a suitable ending). In other words, the speeches as they stand presuppose something like the opening of the book as a narrative device for staging the conversation in which the audience can see the ideas of the book acted out.

Job tells this story through an easily recognizable structure

A. Prose prologue: setting the stage (Job 1:1–2:13)
B. Poetic dialogues: Job and his interlocutors (Job 3:1–42:6)
   1. Job's interchanges with his friends (Job 3:1–31:31)
      a. cycle 1 (Job, Eliphaz, Bildad, and Zophar; Job 3:1–11:20)
      b. cycle 2 (Job, Eliphaz, Bildad, and Zophar; Job 12:1–20:29)
      c. cycle 3 (Job, Eliphaz, Bildad; Job 21:1–25:6)
      d. Job's soliloquy, part 1 (Job 26:1–27:23)
      e. A paean to Wisdom (Job 28:1–28)
      f. Job's soliloquy, part 2 (Job 29:1–31:31)
   2. Elihu's speeches (Job 32:1–37:24)
   3. Yhwh's responses to Job's and Job's surrejoinders (Job 38:1–42:6)
      a. Yhwh's first speech (Job 38:1–40:2)

      b. Job's response (Job 40:3–5)

      c. Yhwh's second speech (Job 40:6–41:26 [ET 41:34])

      d. Job's second response (Job 42:1–6)

  C. Prose epilogue: denouement (Job 42:7–17)

In constructing this elaborate structure, the author or authors uses several literary genres: courtroom and plague stories, poetic disputation, proverbs, laments, and hymns, entangling them in a work of art unparalleled in the ancient world. For example, although the disputation was a recognizable form in ancient Mesopotamia, as seen for example in the "Dialogue of Pessimism," which questions the meaning/futility of life, the scale of the Joban dialogues has no obvious parallel.

The laments of the character Job have some of their closest parallels in the ancient Babylonian hymn "Let me praise the Lord of Wisdom" (named for its Akkadian first line, *ludlul bēl nēmeqi*). For example, both texts speak of a supreme deity capable of both good and ill, both lament human suffering and insist upon the sufferer's innocence, and both are interested in the limits of human knowledge about sin and the ways of the divine realm. While any direct literary dependence is improbable, both texts witness to a pan–Near Eastern intellectual discussion about the nature and destiny of humankind.

The Prose Framework (Job 1:1–2:17; 42:7–17)

As it stands, then, the story of Job takes the form of a prose tale in which a massive poetic dialogue has been embedded. The prose tale shares with the folk story of Job known by the prophet Ezekiel (Ezek 14:14, 20) the portrayal of the character Job as a righteous intercessor for others, first for his own family (Job 1:5) and then for his so-called friends (Job 42:7–8). As Ezekiel puts it, "If these three men were in its [i.e., Israel's] midst—Noah, Dan'el, and Job—they in their righteousness would only rescue their own lives," meaning that unlike the ancient sinful communities barely rescued by such notables, his own times would have no chance at all. Ezekiel, that is, assumes that these ancient persons such as Job have a special righteousness that allows them to intercede for an otherwise deeply corrupt society. The book of Job assumes something similar about its protagonist.

And so the book opens by drawing the main characters: Job as a remarkably pious and wealthy man, and a gentile from Transjordan (Uz); Yhwh as a distant monarch whose gaze falls upon Job as an exceptional creature; and the *śāṭān* (the Hebrew word for adversary or foe or possibly accuser), who is here not a cosmic diabolic figure.

The narrative works by juxtaposing two planes of discourse, earth and heaven, with the knowledge of the two realms confined to the heavenly beings gathered at Yhwh's court. Minor characters include the *bĕnê 'ĕlōhîm* (literally, "children of Elohim" or "sons of God," but roughly equivalent to what later texts would call "angels") and Job's family and friends (also Transjordanian figures from known cities).

The storyteller has made several important narratival choices. First, in casting Job as a gentile, the book not only picks up an older tradition portraying him as a non-Israelite sage but more importantly distances the discussion from the particulars of Israelite theology. The themes of exile and cultural destruction that lie in the book's background hide behind the surface discussion of the hiddenness and even possible tyranny of Yhwh. The gentile Job is not Everyperson, but he appears to be a substitute for Israel in its alienation from Yhwh.

Second, the use of the *śāṭān* character does not make him a villain. Merely an agent of Yhwh, he always works under divine control. His speeches serve as a narrative device to begin the trial that follows. Yhwh always bears responsibility for Job's sufferings, which is why the conclusion of the book drops the *śāṭān* character altogether.

Third, Job is a rich man, and that fact matters. Since chs 1–2 offer a sort of mental experiment—at what point will the righteous person break down and blame God?— Job must gradually lose all desirable things. Yhwh has gambled that a truly righteous human being is not a fictional character but a real possibility. Contrariwise, the *śāṭān* has wagered that certain losses will lead to moral failure as well. The righteous poor will not serve in such a test since ancient people, almost all of whom were poor, would not have thought their losses noteworthy. Job passes the first test (loss of wealth and children) by uttering the pious platitude about Yhwh's ability to give good and evil (Job 1:21), and the second test by responding to his wife enigmatic "bless God and die" with a resigned statement that God's gifts balance out. So far, the wager has shown a heroic figure whose integrity does not depend on the accoutrements of success.

> Job 2:9 is often translated as "curse God and die" on the assumption that the author wrote the verb *bārak* ["to bless"] as a euphemism to avoid writing blasphemy; but Job's wife may have simply wished him to say his prayers and be done with his suffering. There is no obvious way to know, and in any case, she disappears from the story except implicitly, since he has new children at the end.

The final unit of the book (Job 42:7–17) returns to a prose style in order to tie together the narratival loose ends, returning to the opening claim that Job, despite appearances, was blameless and thus that his accusers were not. The author seeks to salvage the reputation of both Yhwh and Job, a difficult task that requires both an acceptance of Job's charges and a refutation of them. This is so because if Job is right to charge God with injustice, then the whole universe's governance becomes suspect, while if Job seems unjust himself, then Yhwh has lost the wager made with the *śāṭān* in ch 1 and humankind has proven inadequate to the test of its righteousness. The trap that the narrator has set for the book's author has only one way of escape, and Yhwh's speech in Job 42:7–8 offers it:

> Then Yhwh said to Eliphaz the Temanite, "I am extremely angry with you and your two compatriots because you did not speak correctly about me [or, "to me"] regarding my servant Job. So now, take for yourselves seven bulls and seven rams and go to my servant Job so that you can immolate a whole burnt offering for yourselves, and

my servant Job will pray for you, and I will honor him without dealing with your stupidity. For you did not speak about me correctly as my servant Job did."

The divine judgment vindicates Job's overall tone, if not every detail of Job's speech (an impossibility since he contradicts himself at times). The friends did not do what righteous people should have done in response to the distress of a righteous sufferer. For intercession and empathy, they substituted accusation, treating Job not as an innocent person but as one of the wicked under God's judgment. They thus misunderstood the nature of the dialogue they were having with Job, which Yhwh interprets as the cry of the righteous sufferer, at least here.

The book ends in the MT with the restoration of Job to his former estate. Yhwh recompenses him twice over for his suffering, an act resembling the settling out of court favored in cases of wrongful alienation of property (see Exod 22:3, 6 [ET 22:4, 7]). Job also receives seven new children, not as replacements for the previous ones (since ancient people did not think of children so cold-bloodedly), but as a token of renewed blessing. Curiously, Job gives his daughters unusual names (Yemimah, Qeṣi'ah, and Qeren Happuk, i.e., Dove, Cinnamon or Cassia, and Mascara Palette), signifying the unusual status as heirs that he also accorded them. Thus the prose framework ends with restoration. The LXX augments this basic ending with a historical note describing Job's locale and his relationship to Israel, apparently responding to the question of how Jewish readers should situate Job's story within their own.

The "Friendly" Dialogue (3:1–31:31)

Before reaching this happy conclusion, however, the core of the book offers a series of speeches by Job and his three interlocutors, Transjordanian sages named Eliphaz, Bildad, and Zophar. The section works by alternating voices of Job and his friend, and then in Job 26:1 moving into soliloquy (though a number of scholars have argued that chs 26–27 may belong to the friends, with some sort of disruption in the process of copying them in antiquity having mistakenly shifted them to Job). The speakers, all sages capable of brilliant Hebrew poetry (though gentiles!), play with arguments around several key themes, notably the nature of revelation, human sin and self-interest, and especially the character of the deity (usually called Eloah, El, or Shaddai, all names common to the cultures of the southern Levant, as in the Deir Alla inscriptions discussed in Chapter 6, "The Book of Numbers"). The book never asks whether God can exercise raw power (since by definition a deity enjoys great power), but whether God is just.

An example of how the author proceeds occurs in chs 8–9. In ch 8, Bildad describes the fate of the wicked in a series of metaphors for transience (spiders' webs, shadows, dried up plants, and the like), concluding with a valedictory (Job 8:20–22):

El will not reject the perfect nor take the hand of the malefactor.
He will fill your mouth with laughter, your lips with exultation.
Those hating you will wear shame, and the tent of the evil ones will cease to be.

For Bildad, humans may find divine approval through repentance (a view he negates in ch 25 in arguing for irremediable human depravity). Job, however, rejects this view in his response by seeming to take up the friends' arguments with his opening, "But how can a human being be just(ified) before El?" (Job 9:2). The next few verses make clear, however, that Job does not mean that humans are incapable of justice. Indeed, his whole defense depends on the assumption that they can be just, as he argues in chs 29–31, and as the narrator (and Yhwh) assume in ch 1.

Job 9, however, argues that human failure to be just derives from a flaw in the divine governance of the universe:

> If one is pleased to sue [or dispute with; Hebrew *rîb*] him [i.e., El], one could not answer him one time in a thousand.
> Wise in heart and powerful in strength—who can dispute him and succeed? (Job 9:3–4)

The speech goes on to cite ancient hymnic language about the deity's ability to alter the landscape and culminates in a decisive statement of Job's dilemma in dealing with such a powerful foe:

> If it is about strength, he is the powerful one. But if it is about justice, who can make him answer? (Job 9:19)

Here the author considers two possible ways of understanding Job's treatment at the hands of God: the deity has either assaulted a greatly inferior foe (a possibility the book often frames in hunting metaphors; e.g., Job 7:12–21; cf. 20:20–29; 27:7–23), or has interfered with due process in the cosmic courtroom. In either case God is a tyrant.

The friends' attempts to defend the deity of such serious charges fail because they do not reframe divine action—God need not be either a lawyer in court or an Olympic level hunter. Instead, they choose to accuse humans falsely. This proves to be a serious mistake because it destroys the very thing that is supposed to characterize humanity—the capacity for justness. Unlike many modern apologists for God, especially in the Calvinist mode, the book of Job believes that justice is explicitly a human quality, as well as a divine one (albeit in a different way).

As a close reading of Job makes clear, the author sought to acquit both Yhwh and Job of charges of injustice. Part of the acquittal lies in the nature of the argument, including both Job's brilliant self-defense in chs 29–31, one of the most extensive descriptions of the ethical commitments of a powerful person in the Bible and perhaps all ancient literature, and Yhwh's equally brilliant self-defense in chs 38–41.

In the former text, Job attempts to restart the increasingly hopeless argument with his friends by comparing his own life to the best ideals for human existence. He contrasts the ordered existence of his past (Job 29) with the chaos of the presence

(Job 30) and the standards by which one should live always (Job 31). His brief summary of basic ethics, especially the conduct of people with power over others bears examination:

> I made a covenant with my eyes—how can I stare at a virgin?
> What portion would I have with Eloah above,
> or inheritance with Shadddai on high?

He then enumerates his obligations to various classes of people, including slaves and the poor, the assumption of his own greater power fitting with the book's portrayal of him as a great magnate. (That is, far from being an attempt to retain or recapture his privileged position, the chapter simply operates from the assumption that the alternative to corrupt elites consists of responsible elites.) As he argues, he should share his food with the hungry and treat the dependent with respect because otherwise,

> What would I do when El arose,
> and when he demanded payment, what could I give back?
> Is not the making me in the womb the same as the one making another person?
> Didn't one being constitute us both in the uterus? (Job 31:14–15)

The book does not adopt a democratic viewpoint, but it does argue for social responsibility across the boundaries of status, power, and wealth.

Such responsibility also extends to God. This point is one to which the rest of the book is moving.

JOB 28

Job 28 is an apostrophe to wisdom, considered as an abstraction. The elusiveness of wisdom befits its preciousness. Many scholars consider this poem a later addition to the book because it seems to fit its context loosely. However, in the final form of Job, the poem serves rhetorically to reframe the argumentative structure of chs 3–27, cleansing the intellectual palette, so to speak, and making room for the final speeches of self-defense by Job and Yhwh. Whether added later or not, the chapter thus plays a role in the overall book by stating what "everyone" should know, that is, the older wisdom platitude, "Indeed, awe before Adonai is wisdom, and repentance from evil is understanding" (cf. Prov 1:7). This means that wisdom has a fundamentally ethical dimension, and human reflection on our place in the world begins with a sense of limit and obligation.

Elihu's Speeches (Job 32:1–37:24)

This pursuit of human and divine responsibility also informs the intervening speeches by Elihu. Job 32:1 introduces a new character, Elihu the Buzite (cf. Gen 22:21; Jer 25:23), who states the implied readers' concerns that the friends' case against Job has failed, while the charges against the deity have gone unrefuted. He seeks success where his elders have failed. Whether he finds it is another matter.

Scholars have often argued that the Elihu speeches are a later addition to the book because (1) Elihu does not figure in the list of friends in 2:11–13, (2) his arguments essentially repeat those made earlier while adding little new, and (3) most significantly, the literary style of his speeches lack the edgy sophistication of the earlier orations of Job and the friends. The last argument, while probably correct is not irrefutable, however. Conceivably, an author capable of the literary mastery of Job could have written a character whose youthful lack of linguistic mastery would come to the fore. Perhaps this has happened here. Still, the speeches probably reflect an early modification of the book, not so much to sanitize it (since the earlier problems are left intact), as to state a series of objections that devout people might make. Elihu's claims about the deity's complete unavailability to humans—"As for Shaddai, we cannot find him. Staggeringly powerful and just, replete with righteousness, he cannot be answered" (37:23)—flatly contradict the divine speeches themselves. In other words, the book as it exists now portrays Elihu as wrongheaded (though very much like some modern "defenders of the faith").

Still, Elihu does consider an important theme of the book from a new angle: divine knowledge and human access to it. The book sets up the problem in its very construction, by placing the trigger of the action, the divine wager, on a plane of existence to which the book's characters never have access. Various speakers, meanwhile, name the popular ancient means of divine revelation, including dreams (3:12–16) and the dissemination of traditional sayings in the form of proverbs (many occurrences). Elihu's focus on antiquity (15:7) shares the assumption, widespread throughout the ancient Near East, that the earliest humans knew everything worth knowing and that subsequent generations must play catch-up. Elihu, however, inverts the last idea, exploring the possibility that youth might know best because they see through their elders' mistakes. Ultimately, however, he concludes that the divine is unknowable and for that reason to be held in awe (Job 37:24).

The Divine Speeches and Job's Responses (38:1–42:6)

Still, awe is one thing, but understanding is another. The book of Job seeks some sort of understanding, and in the divine speeches it gets it. The climactic scene of the book of Job, which opens with Yhwh's inquiry, "who is this who darkens counsel without knowledge" has long puzzled interpreters. Yhwh's answers to Job's questions seems at best dodgy and at worst stated with a cold condescension, as if to say, "what do you amount to anyway?" So many scholars, not to speak of amateur readers, take the divine speeches. Even as great a commentator as the medieval theologian Thomas Aquinas (1225–1274 CE) felt compelled to direct the query about Yhwh's obviously incompetent interlocutor to the garrulous and vapid phrase-monger Elihu (as Aquinas saw him), while reserving the substantive questions to Job himself.

Such an interpretation, though common, badly misses the point because, while an ancient writer might charge a given deity with injustice, as the Mesopotamian "Erra Epic" does its eponymous antihero, or the *Iliad* does Hera, or Aeschylus does Zeus in *Prometheus Bound*, to charge the entire divine realm with injustice would have seemed deeply problematic. In other words, such readings reflect modern sensibilities more than ancient ones.

But there are more profound reasons for rethinking the ending of Job than mere generalities of this sort. To discover them, let us put the divine speeches in some sort of rhetorical context. The book of Job often subtly transforms the reader's expectations through misdirection. A key example appears in the intertextual connection between Job 9:3, in which the character Job complained that "If one is pleased to sue [or dispute with; Hebrew *rîb*] him [i.e., El], one could not answer him one time in a thousand," so anticipating the terrifying first words of Yhwh's pronouncements in 38:1–3. Here Yhwh (appearing with that name for the first time since the opening prose narrative) thunders out,

> Who is this darkening deliberation with ignorant words?
> Clothe your thighs like a human being.
> Then I will ask you, and you will answer me!

Yhwh then asks Job a series of unanswerable questions about the non-human world and Job's ability to understand its interrelatedness and the sharply defined limits of humanity's ability to control its myriad inhabitants.

Yet, crucially, the confoundment and humiliation that Job 9 expects from the divine encounter does not materialize. The divine speech leaves room for a human response. Thus the foreshadowing is indirect, off-center. The brilliance of the author's literary technique can hardly be overestimated. The author has set a trap for the reader, but then offers and escape.

The escape comes through Yhwh's two speeches (38:1–39:30 and 40:6–41:26 [ET 41:34]) do at least three things: (1) they introduce Yhwh as a character in communication with human beings, fearsome of course, but also able to engage in a dialogue; (2) they make arguments for overall divine care for the creation, seeking to refute Job's charges of divine tyranny, though indirectly; and (3) they leave many things unsaid, giving credence to the literary critic Frank Kermode's observations about novels, a different but not dissimilar literary genre:

> Secrets, in short, are at odds with sequence, which is considered an aspect of propriety; and a passion for sequence may result in the suppression of the secret. But it is there, and one way we can find the secret is to look out for evidence of suppression, which will sometimes tell us where the suppressed secret is located . . . . To read a novel expecting the satisfactions of closure and the receipt of a message is what most people find enough to do . . . because it resembles the one that works for ordinary acts of communication. In this way the gap is closed between what is sent and

what is received, which is why it seems to many people perverse to deny the author possession of an authentic and normative sense of what he has said.[1]

Communication, then. The encounter between Job and Yhwh is the meeting of two famous characters. The book reveals both. The prose prologue opens with a description of Job as a truly exotic creature, a blameless human being. So rare is such a person that he is famous enough to be talked about in the divine council. On earth, meanwhile, the humans know enough about God to be dangerous, a realization Job finally has in his concluding confession of the difference between his prior and his current knowledge of the deity. Yet unlike the goddess Ishtar, whose proposal of marriage Gilgamesh rejects as impossibly dangerous and disingenuous (*Gilgamesh Epic*, Tablet VI), or Prometheus's horrifying conflict with Zeus in the plays of Aeschylus, Yhwh's encounter with Job does not elicit greater fear, but rather deference and reconciliation.

Admittedly, some modern scholars have understood Job's silence in his first and second responses to Yhwh (40:1–5; 42:1–6) as ironic rejections of Yhwh's sovereignty. Such an understanding, however, seems highly anachronistic. Job has spoken of silence and deference as the proper attitudes of the less wise toward the more wise in his self-defense (29:7–9):

When I went out to the town gate and took my seat in the plaza,
The young saw me and left, the aged rose and stood,
Princes withheld words and put their hands on their mouth.

In the ancient world, students remained silent before the great sages, and so Job defers to Yhwh's greater wisdom as signaled by the series of questions with which the divine sage begins his speeches.

By creating the ethos of the divine speaker as a king who can use the most gorgeous poetry and speaks out of the storm (as with Moses on Sinai), the speeches bring clarity to the book's conversations, which have hitherto spoken of the absent deity in most unknowing ways (hence Job's line in 42:5: "I heard about you by the ear, but now my eyes have seen you"). The speeches themselves do not explain Job's situation or even the human experience of gratuitous suffering. Rather, they seem to respond to Job's repeated charges of divine malfeasance without, however, erasing human dignity or pointing to human sin, as the friends have done. The rhetorical strategy adopted takes several turns:

- Yhwh has created a gorgeous world filled with the praise of angels and beasts;
- There is an order to the world, though it does not revolve around human needs, but rather a more ecologically interconnected one described in the final questions of ch 38: "Do you stalk the lion's prey or sate the young lion's hunger? Who gives the raven its food when its hatchlings cry out to El?" (Job 38:39; cf. Ps 147:9). In other words, Yhwh hears the prayers even of the beasts and feeds them—with other animals. The world order is still red in tooth and claw;
- This order does is not subject to human control (ch 39).

However, the end of the first speech could easily leave the impression that humans exist in a hostile environment or that they live as merely one animal among others. The first possible objection is dispensed with in the discussions of the great beasts Behemoth and Leviathan in chs 40–41. As in many ancient Near Eastern depictions of terrifying supernatural animals, these mythological creatures symbolize the dangers of the world, its potential for chaos. But they live in Yhwh's menagerie and under Yhwh's control. The second collapses under consideration of the entire conversation, in which Yhwh invites Job to converse, something other beings cannot do.

Implications

If Frost is right that ideas require plot and character to make themselves real to people, then the book of Job must go down as a theological masterpiece addressing with the greatest intellectual problems facing monotheism. Since the divine realm has only one occupant, Yhwh, a dualistic solution to the problem of evil is impossible. Job does not answer the question of why the innocent suffer (though it does explore the possibility that some suffering is a test, as in Gen 22), but it does set forth the major questions of revelation, sin, limitation, and divine providence, all of which have figured prominently in Jewish, Christian, and Muslim theologies ever since. Perhaps more significant for what it asks than for what it answers, the book presents a set of brilliant characters that live out, not merely talk about, things that matter.

Note

1. Frank Kermode, *Pieces of My Mind* (New York: Farrar, Straus and Giroux, 2003), 165–166.

For Further Reading

Aeschylus. *Prometheus Bound.* Translated by James Scully and C. John Herington. Oxford: Oxford University Press, 1975.

Aquinas, Thomas. *The Literal Exposition on Job: A Scriptural Commentary Concerning Providence.* Translated by Anthony Damico. Introduction by Martin D. Yaffe. Atlanta: Scholars Press, 1988.

Eisen, Robert. *The Book of Job in Medieval Jewish Philosophy.* Oxford: Oxford University Press, 2004.

Foster, Benjamin F., trans. and ed. *The Epic of Gilgamesh.* New York: W. W. Norton, 2001.

Lambert, W. G. *Babylonian Wisdom Literature.* Oxford: Oxford University Press, 1960; reprint ed. Winona Lake, IN: Eisenbrauns, 1960.

Newsom, Carol. *The Book of Job: A Contest of Moral Imaginations.* Oxford: Oxford University Press, 2003.

19 The Praises and Laments of Israel
THE BOOK OF PSALMS

Key Texts: *Blessed is Yhwh, Israel's God, from eternity to eternity. Amen* (Ps 41:14 [ET 41:13]).
*Blessed is Yhwh Elohim, Israel's God, the unique doer of miracles. And blessed is his glorious
name forever, for his glory fills all the earth. Amen and amen* (Ps 72:18–19). *Blessed is Yhwh
forever. Amen and amen* (Ps 89:53 [ET 89:52]). *Blessed is Yhwh, Israel's God, from eternity to
eternity. And all the people said, "Amen. Hallelujah"* (Ps 106:48).

Like Job, Psalms explores the depths of humankind's attempts to relate to God, not however through storytelling but through song. Joy and sorrow, fear and courage, ecstasy
and boredom—all of these experiences connect in some way to music as ways of expressing the depths of human existence. Songs do not, of course, express emotion directly.
Rather, they "repackage" it so others can understand, appreciate, and empathize with
the experiences about which the singer sings. We can sing along because we too either
have experienced something similar to what the song relates, or can imagine doing so.

Ordinarily, the songs we sing are in poetic form (no one would make an opera libretto
of the telephone book or an accounting spreadsheet!). Great artists can combine words
and music in ways that explore the depths of existence.

In the book of Psalms, the verse numbers often differ between the Hebrew and English
texts. Some Psalms in the English translation print a superscription or introduction to the

Psalm in tiny type, not counting it in the verse enumeration. However, the Hebrew editions count the superscription as v. 1 (and sometimes vv. 1–2). In this chapter, therefore, the Hebrew verse number is printed first, and if it differs from the English one, that follows, prefaced by ET for English Translation.

The largest collection of music lyrics in the Bible appears in the book of Psalms, most of which were originally words sung in the Temple in Jerusalem (and perhaps in other temples in ancient Israel). This collection of 150 poems, written over several centuries and compiled from earlier collections probably around 300 BCE, do not just recollect the emotions a poet felt at some encounter with nature or the sublime or God. Instead, they craft a conversation between human beings and God that aims at building a sense of common purpose and shared identity for them.

There are different ways to engage in a scholarly study of the Psalms, either as individual poems or as a whole collection. Here the approach will be to start with the largest scale of the book and move to individual psalms and then to individual poetic devices and themes. It would, conversely, also make sense to proceed in the opposite direction.

The Psalter as a Book

The Psalter (another name for the book of Psalms) printed in English Bibles is a translation of the Hebrew text that became canonical in antiquity, with adjustments made when the preserved Hebrew text seems incorrect, as when the LXX preserves a better reading than the MT. It contains 150 psalms of varying genres.

This version of the Psalter is not the only one that exists, however. The LXX version also contains 150 psalms (or 151 in some manuscripts) and in the same order, but it combines and splits some texts differently. So, for example, the LXX combines Ps 9 with Ps 10 and Ps 114 with Ps 115, as well as splitting some Psalms that are combined in the MT. The two versions compare in this way (see table 19.1):

TABLE 19.1

MT and ET	LXX
1–10	1–9
11–113	10–112
114–115	113
116:1–9	114
116:10–19	115
117–146	116–145
147:1–11	146
147:12–20	147
148–150	148–150

In fact, things are still more complex because the Hebrew texts in the Dead Sea Scrolls also seem to recombine or split certain psalms. This means, then, that the ancient scribes agreed that there should be 150 psalms in the collection, but the exact dividing line among them varied from one manuscript tradition to another in slight ways.

A more complex problem arises from one of these Dead Sea Scrolls manuscripts, 11QPs^a. This manuscript, which was copied during the late first century BCE or early first century CE, contains parts of several psalms, but not in the order they appear in the MT. It also includes several other poems known from other compositions. Perhaps most interestingly, it includes near the end a learned note about the composition of the Psalter as a whole:

> David . . . wrote 3,600 psalms and songs to sing before the altar over the burnt-offering, the daily regular burnt-offering, for all the days of the year 364; and for the Sabbath offerings 52 songs; and for the offering of the new moons and for all the days of the assembles and for the day of atonement 30 songs. And all the psalms which he spoke were 446, and songs to make music over the afflicted, 4. And the total was 4,050. All of these he spoke through prophecy which was given to him from before the Most High.

This extremely large number is, of course, fictional, but the passage as a whole indicates the view of the creators of this version of the Psalms. They believed that the poetic texts they were copying (1) originated from David, (2) constituted only a small part of his literary output, (3) originated through prophecy (divinely inspired in some way), and (4) played roles in the worship in the Temple and so were keyed to the major holidays.

DID DAVID WRITE THE PSALMS?

Traditional biblical interpretation generally assumed that David wrote the Psalms. Even the New Testament refers to individual psalms in this connection (see, e.g., Acts 2:25). However, since the nineteenth century, most scholars have argued that the book of Psalms actually dates to several different centuries and thus could not have come from David.

Several arguments support this view. First, the Psalms themselves differ in style and linguistic profile. Some contain more ancient forms of Hebrew than others (just as a modern English speaker knows that "thou wouldst" is older than "you would"). Second, several psalms refer to events after the time of David, as in Ps 137's mention of the Babylonian Captivity or in Ps 83's allusion to the eighth-century BCE Assyrian invasion. Third, a number of the ancient Psalm superscriptions themselves refer to other figures: the Korahites (42–49, 84–85, 87–88), Asaphites (50, 73–83), Solomon (72, 127), Heman (88), Ethan (89), Moses (90), and Jeduthun (39, 62). These names do not indicate the various psalms' authors, but rather some unspecified association with them. And fourth, the Hebrew phrase sometimes translated "by David" (*lĕ-Dāwīd*) can also mean "for David" or "with reference to David." Far from being a unified composition by one person, then, the Psalter is the songbook of a whole people.

Now, there are several issues to consider here. Was 11QPs^a a different version of the book of Psalms than the one in the biblical canon, or was it a secondary creation, a sort of "greatest hits" versions? If it had an independent life of its own, did it precede or follow the 150-psalm collection? Could it have been, for example, based on a shorter collection of psalms out of which the 150-psalm version grew? These questions are hard to answer with surviving evidence, but two things are clear: the Psalms were a lively part of the worship life of Jews during the Second Temple period, and the scribes who copied these texts found it useful to organize and reorganize them for purposes of communal worship and individual meditation as seemed to fit a variety of circumstances.

How far back did this scribal activity in the collection of Psalms go, then? Fairly far, in fact. This extent of scribal activity, or better, learned annotation of the Psalms becomes visible in several ways. First, there are the superscriptions, which are of several types (some of which also get combined):

- Notes connecting a psalm to an event in David's life, usually before his reign (Pss 34, 52, 53, 54, 56, 57, 59, and possibly 18 and 63), but sometimes during it (Pss 3, 51, and 60)
- Ascriptions of the Psalm to a person such as David, the family of Asaph, the family of Korah, Ethan the Ezrahite, Moses, and Solomon
- Performance notes such as "to the choirmaster" or the type of song (using the Hebrew words *maskîl* or *mizmôr*, whose exact meanings are unknown) or even the name of the tune to which it was sung, such as "Sheminith" (the eighth) in Ps 6 or "Gittite" in Ps 8

These learned annotations apparently came from different sources and were probably added at different times. So the references to "Asaph" (Pss 50, 73–83) or the "children of Korah" (Pss 42, 44–49, 84–85, 87–88) name the group of Temple singers (certainly in the Second Temple and possibly earlier) responsible for that cluster of psalms (see 1 Chron 25:1–7; 2 Chron 5:11–14; 20:19 for their roles as singers). The notes on tune names or particular melodies may indicate a performance tradition but of an uncertain time period. (After all, the same words can be sung to several tunes.) The notes linking a psalm to David's life seem to have been emerging about the time the LXX was translated because the Greek notes differ from the Hebrew ones in at least two places (the beginnings of Pss 18 and 34), indicating that an unfinished process of commenting on the Psalms was underway. The biographical details are highly speculative, since nothing in the psalms themselves indicate a biographical point of reference. The point, however, is that whoever wrote them thought otherwise, and so we see here an example of early biblical interpretation. The scribes copying the Psalms thought of the stories of David as part of an authoritative (canonical) text to which the material they were copying also connected somehow.

Second, in addition to the superscriptions, there is evidence for attempts to organize the various psalms in meaningful patterns so that they conveyed an overall message. So, for example, probably at a late stage of forming the 150-psalm collection, the scribes creating it divided it into five books (MT and ET Pss 1–41, 42–72, 73–89, 90–106, 107–150), each ending with a doxology, or short statement of praise to God. These four doxologies appear at the beginning of this chapter.

The insertion of these lines, which do not easily fit with the psalms of which they are now part, helps frame the entire book as one of praise, even if much of it includes complaining and protest. And, not incidentally, the division into five "books" mimics the organization of the Pentateuch.

Even more elaborately, the arrangers of the 150-psalm collection ensured that the last five psalms were all hymns of praise, creating a grand finale for the work by ending it in one triumphant, exuberant psalm after another. Each one of Pss 146–150 begins with the command "praise Yah" (Hebrew: *hallĕlûyâ*, with Yah being a variant of the normal divine name Yhwh). The placement of these psalms at the end can hardly be accidental. The collectors of the Psalter intended it to be a book of celebration.

Again, if the organization of the anthology of psalms was important at certain strategic points, it makes sense to ask how far one can press this. How organized is the Psalter? There is no short answer to this question. On the one hand, like all anthologies of poetry, in places one could rearrange the psalms and come up with an equally meaningful sequence. On the other hand, some psalms clearly do belong in a sequence, as with the Psalms of Ascent in Pss 120–134 or the Psalms of Asaph or Korah, already mentioned, or the "Yhwh reigns" psalms in Pss 93–99. Psalms 1 and 2 also seem strategically located to introduce the reader of the book as a character to be taken seriously: "wise people pray this book and seek to understand and embrace its meaning," the opening seems to say. Moreover, royal psalms appear near the end of some of the so-called "books" (so Pss 72, 89), possibly indicating a royal connection.

To summarize the discussion so far: The book of Psalms is not just a hodgepodge of randomly thrown-together texts. The organization is loose but still meaningful. And the final organization is designed to make this a book of praise to God, a celebration of the divine care for Israel and, indeed, all creation.

The Question of Genre

If this is true of the book as a whole, what about the many poems that make it up? Since the late nineteenth century, a number of scholars have engaged in what is called form criticism, an approach to primarily oral texts (such as songs or stories) that seeks to classify them by type (or form), to clarify their structure, and to understand the sort of setting from which they might come. To take a contemporary example, a speech that includes "Do you take this man to be your lawfully wedded husband" obviously comes from a wedding, or "We, the jury, find the defendant not guilty" comes from a trial. These sorts of texts tend to be predictable and uttered somewhat independently of the persons speaking them or the subject matter they address. (In other words, most weddings are alike.)

The most influential form critic, a German scholar named Hermann Gunkel, identified a series of genres of psalms, including laments of the individual (Pss 3, 5, 6, 7,
13, 17, 22, 25, 26, 27, 28, 31, 35, 38, 39, 42, 43, 51, 54, 55, 56, 57, 59, 61, 63, 64, 69, 70, 71,
86, 88, 102, 109, 120, 130, 140, 141, 142, 143); laments of the people (Pss 44, 58, 74,
79, 80, 83, 106, 125; Lam 5); hymns (Pss 8, 19, 29, 33, 65, 67, 68, 96, 98, 100, 103, 104,
105, 111, 113, 117, 135, 136, 145, 146, 147, 148, 149); royal psalms (Pss 2, 18, 20, 21, 45, 73,
89, 101, 110, 132, 144), and so on.[1] Indeed, many of the texts in each category strongly
resemble each other in structure and outlook, and so probably in the ways in which
Israelites used them. For example, many (but not all) laments have the same basic elements: address and introductory petition, a complaint, a confession of trust in God,
a request for help, and either a word of praise or a promise to praise once deliverance
comes. The form critical approach to these texts cannot become a straightjacket for
understanding them because creative artists can use a rigorous form but do many different things with it. (Think, for example, about how both Shakespeare and Petrarch
wrote sonnets, an especially rigid form, but with different, though equally beautiful,
results.)

For our purposes, we should define genre as simply a category of literary works, written
or oral, instances of which share common structures, subject matter, and literary devices
as recognized by a community of readers or hearers. Our modern genre categories may
not be (in fact, are not) identical to those that ancient people used. However, we use
these categories as a way of classifying texts that makes sense of their content, structure,
and apparent usage. But one should not press these labels too far.

With that caution in mind, one should observe that the fact that psalms show both
variety and predictable form means that we need an additional way of understanding them. One way might be to understand that most psalms try to balance four elements: praise of God, blame of self, blame of God, and justification of self. The differing
balances explain why hymns differ from laments, but also include some of the same literary devices and ideas.

Psalms that focus on complaint and blame especially external foes are laments. If
they mostly blame the psalmist, that is, they confess sin, they are penitential psalms.
Conversely, psalms that praise God and criticize various forces of evil are hymns. Yet the
point is that many psalms include several of the elements, and what differentiates them is
the balance of those elements.

THE MAIN GENRES: LAMENT AND HYMN.

Consider two examples, then, one a lament and the other a hymn, both relatively straightforward examples of their art. It is possible to examine each one from a form critical
point of view and then make wider points. Readers may apply some of the questions and
approaches taken with these two examples to other psalms, as well. So consider these
cases as models for further application.

EXAMPLE 1: To begin, Ps 3 reads (with form critical units indicated in small capital letters)

ADDRESS

Yhwh,

COMPLAINT

how numerous are my foes. Many are those rising up against me.

Many are those saying about my life, "there is no salvation in God for him!"

EXPRESSION OF TRUST

But you, Yhwh, are a shield on me, my glory, the one lifting my head (i.e., honoring me).

With my voice I cry to Yhwh, and he answered me from his holy mountain.

I can lie down and sleep and then awake, for Yhwh sustains me.

I will not fear mobs of people who surround me.

REQUEST FOR HELP

Arise, Yhwh. Save me, my God.

For you have struck all your enemies' cheeks.

You have shattered the teeth of the evil people.

FINAL PRAISE

Salvation belongs to Yhwh. Let your blessing be upon your people.

Now, Israelites knew a lament when they heard one, and part of the social expectations for how to perform a lament is revealed by its structure. A proper lament oscillates between complaint about the ills of life and expressions of trust in God's providential care. The performer of the psalm must distinguish the roles of the psalm's three primary characters, God, the one praying, and the various foes of both the psalmist and God. The form of the psalm—its structure and flow—remain relatively stable. In this sense, the ancient Hebrew lament is a highly traditional form of poetry whose structural conservatism allows the poet to concentrate creativity on the imagery and content of the poetry. This mix of conservatism and innovation is the secret of the great poetry in the Psalter.

Yet, at the same time, attention to purely formal aspects of the poem does not really capture its beauty. Notice three aspects of the poem, at least. First, the poem creates characters and a plot. That is, it tells a story. In this story, a benevolent God protects an innocent (or at least penitent) sufferer from unnamed enemies. This underlying narrative idea creates the tension in the psalm, a tension that must be resolved both at the literary level (hence the movement of the lament toward praise in the last lines) and in the real-life experiences of the poet.

Second, the poem uses various images to tell its tale of woe and joy. So the enemies speak blasphemies ("God won't save this person"), the psalmist sleeps, and God breaks teeth as a divine warrior crushing foes (literal or otherwise). These graphic images carry the weight of the drama as the tensions that the psalmist names dissipate. That is, catharsis occurs.

And third, the content of the theology of the poem is important. The psalmist does not simply emote; he or she prays. The addressee is not anyone willing to listen, but Israel's God. And the attitude of the psalmist is not paranoia but a pious attitude of ultimate trust. Almost all laments express this sort of trust in God's care at some level. (An exception might be Ps 88, but even that text addresses "Yhwh God of my salvation.")

EXAMPLE 2: these aspects of the lament show up, though in different balances and expressions in hymns. Consider a famous example, then, Ps 8:

ADDRESS
Yhwh our LORD, who noble is your name in all the earth,
for he has put his name over the heavens.

WORDS OF PRAISE: THE CREATOR/KING
From the mouth of infants and sucking babies you have established power,
On account of your foes, to defeat the enemy and the vengeful.
For I see your heavens, the works of your fingers—
The moon and stars that you have made secure.

WORDS OF PRAISE: THE HUMAN VICEROY
What is the human being that you remember it,
    the person that you attend to it?
You fashioned it as something a little less than Elohim,
    crowned it with glory and splendor.
You made it ruler over your handiwork;
    you put everything under its feet—
flock and cattle—all of them—as well as wild beasts,
    the birds of the sky and fish of the sea (which travel the sea's
    roads).

ADDRESS
Yhwh our LORD, how noble is your name in all the earth.

Here, as in most hymns, the structure is less rigid than in some laments. (In fact, hymns vary widely among themselves in terms of structure.) But the psalm is unmistakably a hymn of praise because it praises God and faults evil, being convinced that that evil falls under divine control. The most obvious structuring device is the repetition of the first line in the last, a literary technique called inclusio. This bookending process tells the reader of the psalm precisely what it is about: Yhwh's surpassing greatness and human awareness thereof.

If the structure of the psalm is unremarkable, the same is not true of its content and the devices through which that content takes shape. As with the lament in Ps 3, Ps 8 creates a sort of narrative, with Yhwh as the creator of the world and the patron of human interaction with the rest of the created world. The psalmist marvels at this narrative, including himself or herself with the humans to whom such great responsibilities have been delegated, but still finding the story almost unbelievable given human fragility.

Here the imagery lends itself to a sort of mental map of an orderly cosmos inhabited by both sentient and non-sentient beings, all of whom, somehow, offer their praises to God (cf. Ps 19; Job 38:7). Humanity sits in a key position, but the psalmist is quick to point to the limits of human resemblance to God: the heavens and earth themselves do not come within the scope of human control, and even the fish of the sea have a habit of wandering about, well outside our control. Far from being a license for human domination of our ecosystem, Ps 8 assumes that humans will, within our limits, care for the world in the same way its benevolent creator does, because we serve as his delegates, not as owners in fee simple.

OTHER GENRES

In addition to the major genres, lament and hymn, the book of Psalms contains other types of poems. First of all, for example, several psalms extol wisdom and the wise person. Probably the most famous of these is the enormous Ps 119, whose 176 verses make it the longest chapter in the Bible. Its author worked with the literary form of the acrostic, which in the Hebrew Bible consists of each successive line starting with the next letter of the Hebrew alphabet (see other acrostics in Pss 9–10, 25, 34, 37, 111, 112, 145; Lam 1, 2, 3, 4). The artist behind Ps 119 started each of eight lines in a group with the same letter (so with 22 letters in the Hebrew alphabet, *aleph* through *tav*, one arrives at 176 verses), in order to create a comprehensive vision of the life of the wise Torah-observant person. This psalm's interest in wisdom also appears in such texts as Pss 1 and 19, both of which distinguish sharply between the intelligent life and the foolish one.

Second, a related genre is the historical recitation. As already noted, many psalms think about a sort of imagined past for individuals and the community as a whole. Some texts explicitly list events of the nation's past, often with a didactic purpose. So, for example, Ps 78 recounts various failures on the part of the first post-exodus generation of Israelites, offering their story as a warning to the present. Pss 105, 106, 135, and 136, conversely, tell of the same events, but from a more celebratory point of view, underscoring both Yhwh's graciousness to the people and their willingness to accept divine grace.

At times, moreover, the psalms reciting national history take on a higher-level artistry, and they intermingle with other types of psalms. For example, Ps 80 is a communal lament that assumes historical awareness on the singers' part. It opens with an appeal to the "Shepherd of Israel," whom it asks for relief from various enemies, and then mourns the disaster befalling the people. It ends with a final turning to God and a promise to praise God for deliverance. At strategic turning points in the flow of ideas, it inserts the appeal for God's attention ("turn") and illumination ("enlighten us"), and the expectation of ultimate deliverance ("we will be saved").

The text as a whole reads (with sections indicated)

Section One

O shepherd of Israel, listen, you who lead Joseph like a flock.
Shine forth, O one dwelling among the cherubim.

Section Two

Rouse your strength before Ephraim, Benjamin, and Manasseh, and come to save us.
O God, return us, and let your face shine so that we may be saved.

Section Three

O Lord God of Hosts, how long will you fume over the prayer of your people?
You have stuffed them with tears as bread and made them drink tears till they choked.
You made us the derision of our neighbors,
so that our enemies laugh scornfully among themselves.
O God of Hosts, return us, and let your face shine so that we may be saved.

Section Four

You hauled a vine from Egypt and expelled nations so as to plant it.
You worked the field for it and established its roots so that it filled the earth.
The very mountains shaded it, and its branches were veritable cedars of God.
It sent its branches to the sea, and its runners to the river.
So, why have you broken its walls so that everyone walking the path picks its fruit?
Yes, the boar from the woods uproots it, and the wild animals devour it.
O God of Hosts, please turn. Look down from heaven and see, and attend to this vine.

Section Five

Yes, attend to what your right hand has planted, to the child you made strong for yourself.
It is burned in the fire like sawdust. May the culprits perish when they see your angry
   countenance!
Place your hand on the person at your right hand, on the human being you have
   strengthened for yourself.
Then we will not desert you. We will live, and we will call on your name.
O Lord God of Hosts, return us. Let your face shine so that we may be saved.

Within the confines of a straightforward poetic structure, the psalmist soars to spiritual heights. He or she recognizes that God has previously saved Israel and can do so again.

The reference to the exodus in v. 8—"You brought a vine from Egypt"—simultaneously reminds the audience (and God!) of past deeds and expresses hope for similar actions in the future; vv. 14–16 continue the vine metaphor by tying it to present harsh realities. These verses probably refer to the destruction of the Northern Kingdom of Israel by the Assyrians in 721 BCE, as indicated by the mention of exclusively northern tribes in v. 2. Present reality and past reality thus blend into one arena of the activity of God, the shepherd of Israel.

In seems, then, that both the wisdom and the recitational psalms explore the life of integrity either by the Israelite community as a whole or by individual members of it. But there is a third literary group that Gunkel and most subsequent scholars have identified, that of the royal psalms. These psalms do not fit a single genre in that they include hymns (Pss 2, 21, 72, 144) and laments (Ps 89), as well as more minor genres that do not easily fit either category, such as a wedding song or epithalamium in Ps 45 and war songs such as Ps 20. But modern scholars often speak of them as a group because they fit a particular social setting, the worship in the Temple associated with the king. Later, when they were incorporated in the Psalter, they came to be understood to apply either to the whole people or to the messiah, but this was a later development, after the period of the Hebrew Bible's formation.

Lines and Themes

Moving to smaller scales, we now proceed to the smallest recognizable unit of the poetry of the Psalms, the line. Studies of Hebrew poetry often begin at this point, thanks to the pioneering work of Robert Lowth, an eighteenth-century scholar and bishop. Lowth's 1754 Latin volume whose translated title *Lectures on the Sacred Poetry of the Hebrews* first introduced some of the basic ideas of reading biblical poetry with which scholars still work. Lowth described Hebrew poetry, especially in the Psalms, this way:

> The Hebrew poets frequently express a sentiment with the utmost brevity and simplicity, illustrated by no circumstances, adorned by no epithets (which in truth they seldom use); they afterwards call in the aid of ornament; they repeat, they vary, they amplify the same sentiment; and adding one or more sentences which run parallel to each other, they express the same or a similar, and often a contrary sentiment, in nearly the same form of words. Of these three modes of ornament, at least, they make the most frequent use, namely, the amplification of the same ideas, the accumulation of others, and the opposition or antithesis of such as are contrary to each other.[2]

In other words, he describes the key way in which Hebrew poetry structures a line, namely, parallelism. Hebrew poetry rarely exhibits a regular meter or deliberate rhyme, though it often uses alliteration and assonance, or the repetition of consonants and vowels for effect. Yet it does use lines written in parallel form. As already noted, more recent scholars have shown that Lowth's conceptions of parallelism are too rigid in some cases, for the repetition of an idea often adds new layers of meaning to the original statement. Still, his overall conception is useful even today.

In fact, his conception of poetry goes further than this, because he does not see parallelism as merely a structuring device, but as a form of "ornamentation." We should consider this idea. Poetry is characterized by the heightened use of language. We recognize that words can convey literal meaning as well as figurative meaning through elements such as simile, metaphor, personification, or irony. Since poetry evokes aspects of life in multiple dimensions, it helps both poet and audience imagine new, unexpected connections among things, people, and ideas. Hebrew poetry often creates parallelism based on similar sounds or word associations through linguistic, semantic, or other sorts of factors suggest new, and often inventive, connections.

In other words, as the great American poet Robert Penn Warren put it,

> poetry is a way of life, ultimately—not a kind of performance, not something you do on Saturday or Easter morning or Christmas morning or something like that. It's a way of being open to the world, a way of being open to experience. I would say, open to *your* experience, insofar as you can see it or at least feel it as a unit with all its contradictions and confusions. Poetry, for me, is not something you do after you get it fixed in your mind. Poetry is a way of thinking or a way of feeling; a way of exploring.[3]

Poetry is a way of exploring.

To proceed then: as Lowth noted two centuries ago, the Hebrew poetic sentence consists of two parts, conveniently labeled Part A and Part B, which in some way balance out or complement each other. Lowth understood this practice as a form of ornamentation, an idea indirectly related to Warren's notion of "exploring," that is, a way of making memorable and striking the ideas or emotions expressed by the psalm in question. This view in some ways is preferable to the way many later scholars understood parallelism, more as a simple structuring device, a fairly mechanical method of writing poetry. In truth, many psalms show great creativity in fashioning lines even within this simple two-part structure. (And, by the way, some lines have three or occasionally even four parts.)

Consider, among hundreds of possible example of synonymous parallelism, Ps 80:6–7 (ET 80:5–6),

> <u>You have fed them tears for bread</u>; you have given them a full complement of tears to drink.
> <u>You have made us a laughingstock to our neighbors</u>; our enemies snicker among themselves.

The A line and the B line in each case says essentially the same thing, but the repetition adds a slight nuance, perhaps an explanation of an ambiguous idea or an intensification of an emotional response. The task of the poet is to be creative, rather than mechanical, within the limits imposed by the form of the line.

This is why sometimes the parallelism extends beyond a single line, such as in the case of Ps 15:1–2, which ways

> <u>Yhwh, who can sojourn in your tent?</u> Who can dwell in your holy mountain?
> <u>The one walking perfectly</u> and doing righteousness and speaking truth in his heart.

Verse 1 poses two similar questions, with the second half clarifying the first; v. 2, meanwhile, answers the question with three parallel clauses (participles in Hebrew). All five clauses describe the same sort of person, the one whose life has qualities of excellence. And all five implicitly locate that person's life in the Jerusalem Temple and thus associate him or her with the worship that occurs there. So the parallelism cannot only have a complex literary shape; it can make a complex moral point.

Or think about some examples antithetic parallelism:

> <u>For Yhwh knows the way of the righteous ones</u>, but the way of the wicked ones will perish (Ps 1:6)
> <u>Though my father and mother have abandoned me</u>, Yhwh has gathered me up (Ps 27:10)

> <u>Many are the pains for the evil person</u>. But righteousness surrounds the one trusting Yhwh (Ps 32:10)
> <u>Many are the evils befalling the righteous person</u>, but Yhwh rescues him from all of them (Ps 34:20 [ET 19])

In these cases (and many others like them), the B part contrasts with some aspect of the A part, but again not in a mechanical way. One rarely finds lines like "I like lemons; I do not hate them" though they may occur ("I have loved Jacob and hated Esau"). Ordinarily, the antithesis is more complex and surprising.

For example, Ps 34:20 might have said, "Many are the evils befalling the wicked, and many are the good things coming to the righteous." But that would have been much less interesting than the line as it actually appears. What does Part A mean when it says that the righteous experience evil? Surely this claim raises many problems or at least it worries the reader. So Part B offers a surprising turn, an antithesis to be sure, but also a resolution of an unstated problem (i.e., if the righteous experience evil, why be righteous?).

And then there are the cases that Lowth called synthetic parallelism, i.e., neither almost synonymous nor almost antithetical. These are lines such as

> <u>Yhwh sits above the flood</u>; Yhwh sits as king forever (Ps 29:10)

In this case, the B line is really the simpler idea, and the A line depicts one aspect of Yhwh's kingship, its eternity, while also developing the idea in a way that does not simply repeat the basic idea of the B line. Or another example,

<u>And he will be like a tree planted on watery ditches,</u>
which bears its fruit in its time, whose leaves do not wither
and all he does prospers (Ps 1:3)

Here the A line introduces a simile that the B line expands upon (does not simply repeat), while the C line explains the simile in a more "literal" way by moving from the world of well-watered trees to the world of ethical behavior.

Or one last example, Ps 19:5–6 (ET 19:4–5):
<u>Their voice goes into all the earth,</u>
their words to the ends of the dry land,
To the sun, which has a tent among them.
And it is like a bridegroom coming from his nuptial chamber.
He rejoices like a warrior running his race.

This one is surely more complicated. The first two lines are obviously in synonymous parallelism (voice = words; earth = dry land). But the third line answers an unstated question: How far can the praises of God be heard? Answer: To the place where the sun sets and then rises. Then line 4 (v. 6 [ET 5]) thinks about another unstated idea, the sunrise, and compares it to the enthusiastic bridegroom bursting forth after his first intimate encounter with his new bride. And speaking of raciness, line 5 picks up the idea of excitement and skilled running and connects it to imagery of sprinting. Now this sequence of lines makes sense as a sort of disciplined association of ideas in a sequence in which each element builds on the previous one. There is parallelism in Lowth's sense, but it is not built on either the repetition of ideas or the posing of antitheses, but on a more complex principle of association, or to use his word, the ornamentation of ideas. By combining all these ideas, the psalmist makes a point that is not explicitly stated: the cosmos proclaims God's glory not as a matter of obligation or grudging acceptance, but with joy. And so a serious theological point can emerge from the form of the poetry, as well as its explicitly stated content.

To conclude this brief discussion of the poetic line in Psalms, it is important to note that other forms of parallelism exist.

Musical Language

Most, and perhaps all, psalms were composed for singing, often as the libretto for staged performances that also included orchestral playing, dance, and procession. Yet the workings of Israelite music remain only partially understandable. For example, the list of instruments in Pss 149, 150, and elsewhere includes several types of string, percussion, and wind instruments. The audience of a good Israelite band would have heard lyres, lutes, trumpets, sistra, hand drums, kettledrums, large and small cymbals, ocarinas, and flutes, among other things.[4] Numerous pictures of such instrument survive from Israelite seals and from other ancient Near Eastern sources.

In a few cases, parts of instruments have also survived, especially bone flutes or scrapers and metal percussion instruments.

While reconstructing the instruments is possible, the complete absence of musical notation for them makes reconstructing the sound of the music more or less a guessing-game. There is some evidence from Mesopotamia that the strings on lyres were tuned to a pentatonic scale with the tone, minor third, just fourth, minor sixth, and minor seventh.[5] But even this is very uncertain and may not apply to all times and places. Certainly, the system of tonic and dominant that emerged in European music in the late medieval or early modern period would have seemed very strange to ancient people.

In the Psalter, some traces of performance practice do survive. These include (1) the names of tunes such as "deer of dawn" (Ps 22), "on the lilies" (Pss 45, 69, 80), "on the Gittite" (Pss 81, 84), and perhaps others; (2) consignment of the psalm to the "direc-tor" of the Temple choir (Pss 4, 5, 6, 8–9, 11–14, 18–22, 31, 36, 39–42, 44, 46, 49, 51–62, 64–70, 75–77, 80–81, 84–85, 109, and 139–140); and (3) names of types of songs such as the now mysterious, but once clearly understood, labels *mizmôr, nĕgînâ, šiggāyôn*, and (4) the famous and ubiquitous term *selah* whose meaning is completely lost, though its presence in the middle of various psalms must indicate some transition in performance. Many psalms include several music terms, indicating that the classifi-cation system included a principle of nesting. For example, a *mizmôr* (psalm) could be for the "director" or not.

Moreover, a psalm like Ps 150 shows that the performance of the psalms in the Second Temple (and probably its predecessor) at least sometimes included choirs, orchestras, and often dancers. So in reading them, we should imagine them as dramatic performances, not as words mumbled without emotion or understanding.

Words as Images: The Building Blocks of Poetry

If we think about the performance of the psalms as something following rules that are no longer entirely comprehensible (although they must have been originally), a more direct route to understanding the psalms does appear through studying the imagery that the poets who wrote these great works used. This is because poetry is all about the nouns and verbs, the more concrete and evocative the better. Ancient Hebrew lends itself to such concreteness because it shows a real shortage of adjectives and adverbs, as well as abstract verbs, when compared to modern languages and even to many ancient ones. The Israelite poets who wrote the psalms could draw on an old poetic tradition that specialized in the memorable use of imagery.

A detailed list of all the images in the Psalms would take up a great deal of space, and a student of these texts would be well advised simply to read through a few psalms and highlight each one that appears. It may be useful to try to categorize the images somehow.

One way is this: since the imagery of the Psalms relies upon the senses, one may speak of visual, auditory, olfactory, gustatory, and tactile imagery. The poetry often works by starting with one sort of controlling image and then adding related ones to it to create an overall effect. For example, Ps 23 starts with two basic images, sheepherding and banqueting, and both play out each one separately and then connects them:

SHEEPHERDING
Yhwh is my shepherd → He makes me lie down in green pastures/by still waters→I can walk safely through a gloomy valley→

BANQUETING
Yhwh prepares a table →my cup runs over

Or another example appears in Ps 42:2 [ET 1], "like a deer pants for streams of water, so my soul pants for you, Elohim." An auditory image concretizes the experience of feeling the absence of God.

Or yet another: Ps 19:11 [ET 10] speaks of wisdom as being "sweeter than honey," clearly an image related to the sense of taste. In fact, this example is even more interesting, because it follows another item inferior to wisdom, that is, gold (Hebrew: *zāhāb*) and much fine gold (Hebrew: *pāz*). Honey and gold have in common their color, indicating that the composer of Ps 19 can associate visual images and then connect one of them to another sense altogether.

One might extend this list to thousands of items, but perhaps these few examples make the point. The poets of the Psalter had the capacity to marshal various kinds of imagery almost at will to create their texts.

A last point on imagery, then: whenever a person from one culture reads the poetry of another, a certain amount of confusion may ensue from the imagery being considered. At times, English translators of the Psalms may obscure the original images by seeking an equivalent in English. One might, for example, translate Ps 23's "he makes me lie down in green pastures" as "he provides for me," or something equally pedestrian and boring. Good translations, however, let the poetry speak for itself whenever possible. Still, some images clearly do need explanation.

For example, consider the familiar, but still obscure Ps 133:

How good and pleasant it is for siblings to dwell together.
It's like good oil on the head, running down the beard,
  Aaron's beard.
Which flows down his collar.
It's like Hermon's dew
Which flows down Zion's mountains.
For there, Yhwh commands his blessing,
Life forevermore.

The first and last sentences are clear, as well as profound. Yet the sentences in the middle seem quite strange. Even if one knows that Hermon is a mountain in the far north of Israel, the connection between it and Zion must be symbolic, since dew does not usually travel long distances. And why oil on Aaron's beard? Even if we remember that Aaron was the high priest and that this psalm (like all the Psalms of Ascent) was sung in or near the Temple during a festival procession, as well as the use of oil to anoint priests (and anyone else) as a sign of celebration, still the image would probably not occur to a modern poet. We can "understand" it, but its alienness still arrests us.

The very strangeness of the imagery forces a modern reader to investigate the cultural practices and presuppositions behind the imagery, revealing something about both the ancient text and our modern selves. To avoid the bigoted (but unfortunately widespread) assumption that anything outside our cultural experience is bad, we must remain open to the very strangeness of the imagery as a way of challenging our own conceptions about lived experience, religious or otherwise.

Theological Ideas

Until this point, then, the discussion has focused primarily upon the psalms' methods of composition, use of imagery and structure, as well as the uses to which their audiences put them. Attention to such details is important reflecting Robert Penn Warren's point: "Poetry is a way of thinking or a way of feeling; a way of exploring." Reading poetry simply for its ideas is like talking about food without eating any.

However, that is not to say that the book of Psalms lacks ideas. To the contrary, the book contains rich insights into the interactions between God and human beings, and it reveals evidence of the conversations about religion that Israelites had among themselves and with their neighbors over a period of several centuries.

Although the 150 psalms differ among themselves on various points, they show a remarkably consistent set of assumptions. First, they confess the kingship of Yhwh as the creator and sustainer of the cosmos. Many psalms think of Yhwh as surrounded by other, lesser deities (e.g., Pss 29, 82, 89), but the difference between them is so great as to allow one to speak of a practical monotheism in the Psalter. Even if other deities exist, they exert no power in Israel and therefore deserve no consideration. Yhwh's kingship spans Israel's history (Ps 78, 99, 105, 106, 135, 136) and embraces all the human world (Ps 97) and indeed the whole cosmos (Ps 19).

Second, Yhwh's kingship is expressed in Israel, and especially in Jerusalem/Zion. The earliest Israelite traditions, in which sacrifice to Yhwh could occur in several roughly equivalent places, gave way by the time of the collection of the Psalms to an idea that the Jerusalem Temple enjoyed a unique status. The Psalter as we have it (though not all the psalms in it) must have come from that Temple. But in any case, the Psalms think of Zion as the pivot around which the world revolves (the *axis mundi*). Thus Yhwh is called the "one dwelling in Zion" (Pss 9:12 [ET 11]; cf. 99:2; 132:13), who builds the city's walls (Ps 51:20 [ET 18]: cf. 69:36 [ET 35]; 102:17 [ET 16]), and is also the one "loving" Zion (Ps 78:68; 87:2). Jerusalem is called "Mount Zion at the far ends of the north, the city of the great king" (Ps 48:3 [ET 2]; cf. 74:2; 133:3). All these images pick up the old Canaanite idea of the gods living on a mountain up north (which Jerusalem was not, in a literal sense) but then transform that idea by making Jerusalem the home of the divine king (cf. Ps 20:3 [ET 2]; 110:2; 128:5). The emphasis on Zion later had a profound influence on both Judaism and Christianity.

A third theme is the centrality of the Temple. Famously, Ps 23:6 expresses the wish to dwell "in Yhwh's house forever," that is, a desire always to be close to the altars at which Yhwh provides for Israel's needs. Or Ps 96:6 speaks of the splendors of Yhwh's sanctuary (Hebrew: *miqdāš*), and Ps 68:36 [ET 35] speaks of the sanctuary as the point from which divine power emanates. For modern Western readers of the psalm, this notion of sacred space may seem alien. Yet, as the discussion in Leviticus in Chapter 5 showed, the idea of one locale in which God's presence was more manifest than elsewhere is a common assumption of the majority of other cultures in human history, and in Israel in particular. Ancient people often thought of a temple as a copy of the deity's palace in heaven, and as a sort of model for the entire cosmos. So being in that place and participating in its rites inspired ancient poets with a sense of the sublime.

A fourth theme is the relationship between Yhwh and the "praying I" or "we," that is, the implied speaker of each psalm. In any given psalm, whether the speaker is imagined as an individual, the king, or the entire people, the relationship between speaker and deity is one of dependence and support. The petitioner either seeks help or gives thanks for help received. Lying behind the laments and praise are the further ideas of God's overwhelming compassion for people who seek good (and wrath against people who seek evil) and humanity's overwhelming need for help. This idea appears in every psalm in one sense or another.

A fifth theme is the reality of gentile opposition and potential friendship. Psalm 129:5 speaks of "those hating Zion," while other psalms speak of foes from the distant past (such as Og and Sihon from the Pentateuchal tradition) or from the present (e.g., Ps 83). In other words, these psalms realistically assess the hostility of some of Israel's neighbors and seek Yhwh's protection from it. Conversely, other psalms speak of the entire world rejoicing in Yhwh's kingship (e.g., Ps 97:2), indicating a desire for peaceful relationships with outsiders.

To summarize this much too brief survey of the theology of the Psalms, let us return to Warren's claim that poetry is a way of exploring the world. The same is also true of theology, and doubly so of the Psalter's poetic theology or theological poetry. The texts are searching for a way of relating to God, for expressing an interior identification with the desires of God. This means that from a rhetorical point of view, the Psalms work to build bridges between Yhwh and humans, and among the humans themselves.

Implications

The book of Psalms, to conclude, offers many openings for study of issues historical, linguistic, poetic, and cultural. Yet at its most fundamental level of meaning, this collection of 150 poems is a book of piety, a resource for a praying community seeking to discern the ways of Yhwh and their own place in the created order. Not everyone who reads them today, of course, uses them in the same way. For practicing Jews and Christians, these are texts encountered in communal worship as well as private devotion. For others, they still offer windows onto a prolonged exploration of the depths of the human soul as it expresses its longing for a more just and beautiful world and, most of all, its longing for a relationship to the creator of everything. The existential depth of the Psalter and the individual poems within it still inspire and still provoke more reflection.

Notes

1. Hermann Gunkel, *Einleitung in die Psalmen: die Gattungen der religiösen Lyrik Israels,* ed. Joachim Begrich (Göttingen: Vandenhoeck & Ruprecht, 1933).

2. Robert Lowth, *Lectures on the Sacred Poetry of the Hebrews*, trans. G. Gregory, 4th ed. (London: Tegg, 1839), 48–49.

3. Robert Penn Warren, *Talking with Robert Penn Warren*, ed. Floyd Watkins, John Hiers, and Mary Louise Weaks (Athens, GA: University of Georgia Press, 1990), 370.

4. An excellent survey of the available evidence appears in Joachim Braun, *Music in Ancient Israel/Palestine: Archaeological, Written, and Comparative Sources*, trans. Douglas W. Scott (Grand Rapids: Eerdmans, 2002). For the entire Near East, see Richard J. Dumbrill, *The Archaeomusicology of the Ancient Near East*, illustrated by Yumiko Hogan (Victoria, BC: Trafford, 2005).

5. Dumbrill, *Archaeomusicology*, 32.

For Further Reading

Brown, William P. *Seeing the Psalms: A Theology of Metaphor*. Louisville: Westminster John Knox, 2002.

Eaton, John. *The Psalms: A Historical and Spiritual Commentary with an Introduction and New Translation*. London/New York: Continuum, 2005.

Holladay, William L. *The Psalms Through Three Thousand Years*. Minneapolis: Fortress, 1996.

Kugel, James L. *The Great Poems of the Bible*. New York: Free Press, 1999.

Murphy, Roland. *The Gift of the Psalms*. Peabody, MA: Hendrickson, 2000.

20 Proverbs

WISDOM AND THE ORDER OF THE WORLD

Key Texts: *The proverbs of Solomon, David's son, king of Israel. [These are] for knowing wisdom and discipline; for understanding discerning words; for successfully acquiring discipline, righteousness, justice, and equity; for giving insight to the naïve, knowledge and awareness to the young—and also let the sage hear and gain more perception, and let the understanding person acquire still more acuity—for understanding a proverb and a saying, the words of sages and their riddles. Awe before Yhwh is the starting point of knowledge. Wisdom and discipline come from shunning evil things.* (Prov 1:1–7)

In contrast to the beauty of the Psalms, the book of Proverbs may seem at first glance to be a giant collection of fortune cookie adages, both trite and tedious. Yet this first impression, often reinforced by the way the book's popular interpreters talk about it, reveals more about the readers than the book itself. Far from being a mind-crushing assemblage of unrelated sayings, the book shows considerable artistry and insight into the human condition. While many individual sayings stand on their own, the whole is greater than the sum of the parts.

The book consists of subcollections of sayings. Some of these apparently come from the period of the Israelite monarchy, though the final editing of the book may date to the Persian period. It is difficult to date these texts with any precision because they refer so rarely to specific events or short-term processes in the external world, and because their language is often so elliptical, getting a grammatical or semantic profile on them proves difficult. Proverbial language in other languages often preserves older grammatical forms, so again, dating this work is difficult.

Consider, then, the humble proverb. Many cultures employ such sayings: Americans like to say "a stitch in time saves nine" or "the early bird gets the worm" (both commending diligence), as well as "fools rush in where angels fear to tread" and "a bird in the hand is worth two in the bush" (both questioning the value of excessive diligence). Koreans like to say, "an empty cart rattles loudly" (i.e., stupid people make lots of noise). And on it goes. All of these truisms approve of some behaviors and criticize others. So it is with the proverbs of the biblical book, which collects such sayings and thereby becomes something of its own. We should consider both proverbs and collections of proverbs as genres.

First, individual proverbs: It is not clear how many of the sayings in Proverbs were "in the air" in ancient Israel and how many were literary compositions by learned people. Since the book attributes them to Solomon (Prov 1:1; 25:1), the "sages" (Prov 22:17), Agur (Prov 30:1), and Lemuel and his mother (Prov 31:1), and since there are so many of these sayings, most probably arose through deliberate artistry, not the accident of folk culture.

In the Bible, proverbs tend to consist of a single line, with two parts (A and B). Part A often describes a commonly observed occurrence, and Part B draws a lesson, makes a comparison, or otherwise triggers an association that leads to meaning making. Sometimes the proverb is very simple:

> The remembrance of the righteous person is a blessing, but the name of evil people rots. (Prov 10:7)

In this case, B is the opposite of A. A more elaborate proverb is one like Prov 20:15:

> There is gold and there are many pieces of coral, but the most precious object is the lips of [i.e., speaking] knowledge.

The aphorism begins by listing valuable objects but then compares them unfavorably to lips that speak wise things. But notice the second item in part A, coral. Coral, like lips, is often red, and this pigmentary similarity links the two parts of the parable together, even though the text nowhere states it explicitly. Underneath the words lies a world of sight and sound.

PROVERBS AND PROVISIONAL TRUTHS

Individual proverbs do not aim at absolute truth but only at observations of truths in particular domains of life. "Usually" more accurately describes their claims than "always" or "never." The collectors of proverbs are well aware of this limitation, as becomes clear from two proverbs sitting side by side in Prov 26:4–5:

Do not answer a stupid person according to his folly, lest you also be like him.
Answer a stupid person according to his folly, lest he think of himself as a sage.

Which is it? The wording of the proverbs creates space for wisdom to dawn: the two say-ings employ the same words for "answer," "stupid person," and "folly," signaling the paradox whose resolution requires discernment. However, the contrast plays upon the range of pos-sible meanings of the Hebrew preposition *kě-* ("according to," "in the manner of," "like"), subtleties not readily available in English translation. The wise person must not answer "in the manner of" the fool, but must answer "in response to" that person.

More elaborate still are proverbs like those of Prov 30. For example, Prov 30:24–28 reads:
There are four small things in the earth, but they are sages among those acquiring wisdom:

The ants are powerless people, but they collect their food in the summer.
The badgers are a weak people, but they make their home among rocks.
The locusts lack a king, but they move about organized.
The gecko is grabbed by hands,[1] but it lives in kings' palaces.

The list of creepy-crawlies might elicit disgust in some ancient readers, but admiration shines through instead. These creatures succeed by tenacity, not perhaps as individuals but surely as collectives. Their unconventional "wisdom" deserves commendation and perhaps imitation by human beings, whose capacity for wisdom so often exceeds its realization.

Second, in addition to the individual proverb as a genre, one must also consider the proverb collection as something else entirely. The book of Proverbs resembles other collections from the ancient Near East, such as the roughly contemporary book of Ahiqar, an Aramaic collection prefaced by a story of its eponymous hero (see also the discussion on Tobit in Chapter 30). More significantly, Prov 22:17–24:34 draw on the Egyptian text "The Sayings of Amenemope," indicating an international connection between sages and the works they produced, copied, circulated, and studied. All of these ancient collections functioned as scribal exercises for teaching students, intel-lectual tracts for more advanced thinkers interested in wisdom, and life manuals for a range of readers.

The book as it stands, then, is a carefully organized whole, consisting of several subcol-lections prefaced by a long discourse by a parent/teacher trying to lead learners into a world of wisdom. The book follows a clearly recognizable outline:

A. Introduction and thesis statement (Prov 1:1–7)
B. Instructions of a child by a parent (Prov 1:8–9:18)
C. The first "Solomonic" collection (Prov 10:1–22:16)
D. Words of the sages (Prov 22:17–24:22)

E. Additional words of the sages (Prov 24:23–34)

F. The second "Solomonic" collection (Prov 25:1–29:27)

G. The sayings of Agur (Prov 30:1–33)

H. The sayings of Lemuel (Prov 31:1–9)

I. Concluding poem praising Ms. Wisdom (Prov 31:10–31)

The shifts from section to section are indicated by editorial notes introducing the succeeding material's origins (e.g., "Solomon's proverbs" or "the words of the sages"). Parts A and I form an envelope into which the subcollections are fitted, though not in an obvious order, except that two shorter collections follow each "Solomonic" one. Finally, the concluding poem praising the wise woman concretizes an image from chs 1 through 9, which personifies wisdom as a brilliant woman whose counsels benefit both God and humankind. Proverbs 31:10–31 also complements the emphasis on the male learner in chs 1–9 with a female learner and model. At the end, the personified Wisdom becomes a wisdomized person (so to speak).

Introduction and thesis statement (Prov 1:1–7)

The opening of the book sets the stage for the book's ever-present intertwining of abstract wisdom and the formation of persons. Like other creators of wisdom texts, the voices responsible for Proverbs assumed that "wisdom" was both external to the human person (part of the fabric of the universe) and internal to those who pursue it. Hence the opening of the book, which seeks to move the "naïve" toward knowledge and to continue the instruction of those more advanced.

WHAT IS "WISDOM"?

The word wisdom (Hebrew: ḥōkmâ) means many things in modern cultures, but in biblical studies it describes three distinct but related things:

1. A literature that focuses upon the acquisition and development of ḥōkmâ
2. The content of ḥōkmâ, that is, the software that runs the universe and the basic structure of human virtue
3. Human social circles responsible for the creation and preservation of ḥōkmâ

In the Bible itself, ḥōkmâ can refer to skill at particular crafts or at life itself. This range of meanings is revealing: Israelites thought of life as a sort of craft to be mastered through practice of skills tested over time for their merit or worth. Such a viewpoint values both tradition and the ability of an individual to "perform" the tradition skillfully.

The opening lines speak of the learners (both initiates and aficionados), the content learned (wisdom and its synonyms), and the medium of instruction (proverbs, riddles).

In this pithy opening, then, the book both identifies its audience and describes the methods by which readers will acquire wisdom.

Instructions of a Child by a Parent (Prov 1:8 ḥōkmâ 9:18)

After the introduction, including the book's motto ("Honor [or "fear"] of Yhwh is the beginning of knowledge"), Proverbs moves into a long monologue of a father/teacher instructing a son/student. While the "mother" appears occasionally in these chapters, and the principles underlying the discourse apply more or less equally to all persons, the text frames the discussion in male terms, reflecting the realities of education in the ancient Near East. Even the advice to the student adopts the gendered perspective of the male, with warnings against "loose" women and (obviously commendable) counsel to cling to the wife of one's youth. That is, the text aims to rein in male self-assertion and aggression by disciplining the mind and attitudes in more socially constructive ways.

The basic organization of this section is simple. It consists of ten short lectures each beginning with "my son" (Hebrew: *běnî*), a word that appears at Prov 1:8; 2:1; 3:1, 21; 4:1, 10, 20; 5:1; 6:20; and 7:1. Also, five "interludes" or "orations" interrupt the lectures, digressing onto other topics (1:20–33; 3:13–20; 6:1–19; 8:1–36; and 9:1–38), with the middle of these also beginning with "my son," but the rest speaking either through the voice of personified wisdom or about her.[2]

The dialogue counsels readers against oppressing others, criticizing privileged young men who join gangs to "swallow up living things like Sheol does" (Prov 1:12) or who arouse a cuckolded husband's violent anger by stupidly "committing adultery" (Prov 6:32–33) or who laze about living on borrowed money (Prov 6:1–11). Practical advice for functional adults seems to be the goal.

Yet two aspects of this advice deserve more comment—their partial grounding in religion and their conception in gendered terms—two themes that in fact intersect. First, while many scholars speak of Proverbs as a secular text, and in truth it does say little about major theological ideas or cultic practices (or even prayer), the book does speak frequently of Yhwh as a reference point for its moral reflection. Most significantly, the third lecture (3:1–12) focuses entirely upon piety as a presupposition of wisdom. It enjoins the audience to

> abandon neither loyalty nor trustworthiness;
> bind them on your neck and write them on your mind's tablet;
> thereby find favor and insight before God and humankind;
> trust Yhwh with your entire mind and do not rely on your own comprehension. (Prov 3:3–5)

While it is possible to over-sentimentalize such a call to commitment, and indeed the text lacks any specific instruction about religious practice or belief other than a vague trust in

God, it can hardly be read as merely window dressing for an essentially secular pursuit. For Prov 1–9, piety comes from a sense of human limitation and the need to discipline humanity's (especially males') dangerous impulses.

As with piety, so with the second and much more extensive theme in Prov 1–9: the gendered nature of its conceptions of wisdom. Since the primary audience is male, the dialogue enjoins its readers to exercise caution in dealing with women, acknowledging that both men and women experience sexual desires that, if unchanneled, threaten to disrupt social harmony and corrupt the individual pursuit of wisdom. Since the primary audience (again) is male, the text risks stereotyping women (from a modern point of view) but does so in order to foster male self-discipline. The rhetoric of the text also underscores the authority of the father (i.e., the speaker of the discourse) in ordering his potentially out-of-control male heirs, all for the sake of familial order. Thus the text should be read as an attempt to limit the potential abuses of a patriarchal society in which male agency has greater "freedom" than female agency.[3]

The most dramatic way in which gender enters into the discussion is the depiction of wisdom itself as a woman, Ms. Wisdom, (and her foe, the less publicized Ms. Folly). In Hebrew, all nouns are either masculine or feminine, and since ḥōkmâ ("wisdom") is feminine, the poetic device of personification of wisdom as female presents itself as a path for creative exploration. The parental discourse creates the character of Ms. Wisdom as an orator most fully in the "interlude" of Prov 8:1–36, in which she stands up to speak (in the public assembly of the community) and to invite all hearers to join her in the banquet of knowledge. Her call, "Understand prudence O naïve ones, understand O stupid people" (Prov 8:5) hardly flatters the audience, but it does remind it of its true position as human beings both needing and lacking real insight. At the same time, the speech addresses all humans equally by challenging distinctions rooted in status or wealth.

Ms. Wisdom's self-understanding situates her as a paragon of virtue—only truthful speaking for her (Prov 8:8–9)—and also as a functionary in the divine realm. Indeed, with her help, Yhwh made the world after "forming me as the first of his way, the beginning of his deeds of yore" (Prov 8:22). Thus Wisdom influences both humanity and God, not being the sole province of either but a shared experience.

The cosmos reflects the underlying divine wisdom, or conversely a correlation exists between the universe's order and the human mind's ability to discipline itself for understanding that order. Wisdom is not purely a human construct, Proverbs avers, but it does make itself available to human beings who prepare themselves to receive it.

The First "Solomonic" Collection (Prov 10:1–22:16)

How does one receive it, then? The postexilic dialogue in Prov 1–9 introduces the older collections of sayings, which are arranged loosely or seemingly not at all. While the collection in Prov 10:1–22:16 may seem almost random in nature, it does show organization on smallish scales: groups of similarly themed proverbs tend to cluster together, and several proverbs are repeated almost verbatim, though often widely separated in the text. Consider, for example, a run of aphorisms such as Prov 17:1–5, which combines seemingly unrelated thoughts that prove more closely connected on deeper reflection:

> A dry morsel with calmness is better than a banquet house full of conflict.
> An intelligent slave will rule over a shameless heir and may share the inheritance alongside the children.
> As a crucible works for silver and a smelter for gold, so does Yhwh test minds.
> An evil person regards lying lips, and a lie feeds upon a deceptive tongue.[4]
> The one mocking the poor insults their Maker; the one rejoicing in calamity will not be acquitted.

The first two sayings underscore the superiority of dignified poverty to undignified wealth, and the last one turns that theme in a different direction by criticizing the arrogant rich who mock the poor and thereby insult God, their protector. The third and fourth seem unrelated to that set of contrasts and to each other, and yet on closer examination, the logic of the chain appears: the lying person lives out of an unrealistic and immoral view of reality, one that the celebration of wealth for its own sake exemplifies. In contrast to that dishonest view of reality stands the truth-telling God, Yhwh, who tests hearts. The testing of hearts, in turn, allows for intelligent discrimination between reality and appearance. So, far from being random statements accidentally jammed together, the chain of sayings lays out a moral vision that no single proverb could do.

This sort of concatenation appears all over Prov 10:1–22:16. Ordinarily, the chain breaks after a few verses, but the associative logic that led to the creation of this work operates throughout it and invites the reader to draw his or her own deductions. Key themes of these texts include sloth versus industry, the value of truth-telling, the centrality of family, the danger of violence, and especially the strong contrast between the sage and the fool. In their pithiness, these sayings invite the reader to think broadly about his or her own life and so to fashion out of human insights new and deeper meanings.

Words of the Sages (Prov 22:17–24:22)

A similar attitude appears in the second subcollection in the book. Proverbs 22:17–24:22 bills itself as "words of sages" and "my knowledge," referring apparently to the speaker as a person who draws upon the lore of others for inspiration. In truth, this two-sided authorship claim accurately reflects the origins of the material, which go back to an older Egyptian collection of proverbs called the "Sayings of Amenemope," a text created in the twelfth or eleventh centuries BCE.[5] Since Egypt was the high status culture in the minds of Israelites during the early first millennium BCE (as evidenced by the numerous Egyptian-influenced works of art from Israel dating to that period), it seems probable that the Egyptian text made its way to Israelite circles either in (Aramaic?) translation or in the Egyptian original, probably later in the period of the Israelite monarchy. Since no culture can monopolize wisdom (or stupidity, for that matter), no necessary theological obstacle prevented Israelite thinkers drawing on foreign material, as long as they removed overtly polytheistic elements (which in any case are rare in "Amenemope").

Prov 22:17–24:22 consists of thirty units (Prov 22:20) more or less mirroring the "thirty chapters" of "Amenemope." The "sages" warn their readers against oppressing the poor or ignoring the discoveries of their predecessors. They seek to create a world in which people exercise their own agency for the common good, while also producing happiness for themselves. Perhaps the approach is summed up in Prov 22:29's rhetorical question, "Have you seen a person skilled at his work? He will spend time with kings. He will not spend time with the lowly." True, "standing before kings" presents dangers to a would-be courtier, as these chapters note, yet career success coupled with personal virtue commends itself to most people and certainly to the implied readers of these texts.

At the same time, these instructions do not value mere wealth or even other marks of success as ends in themselves. Quite to the contrary, the sages enjoin the reader "not to reach out for wealth—stop your thinking about it! Your eye lights upon it, but then it vanishes as though it had wings like an eagle, a bird in the sky" (Prov 23:4–5). No mere self-help text, the collections of sayings try to cultivate a self-disciplined, skilled, and socially responsible elite that can live with moderation in an age of excess (as most ages are). In this sense, then, the "Sayings of Amenemope" in their Israelite dress (as well as in their original Egyptian) bespeak a view of the world in which the only alternative to responsible elites involves irresponsibility and self-promotion. That outcome it seeks to avoid.

PROVERB COLLECTIONS OUTSIDE THE BIBLE

In addition to the biblical book of Proverbs and works that imitate it more or less directly (such as Ecclesiasticus/Ben Sira or the Wisdom of Solomon (see Chapter 30), collections of sayings exist from several ancient Near Eastern cultures. For example, Ahiqar was written in northern Syria in Aramaic sometime before 500 BCE. Egyptian texts include the "Instructions of Merikare" as well as those of Amenemope, while Akkadian dialogues also include sayings. In short, then, Proverbs fits into a larger literary tradition that crossed cultural boundaries over long periods of time.

Additional Words of the Sages (Prov 24:23–34)

Following the Amenemope-like sayings comes a shorter collection of only eight sayings counseling against abuse of others (whether in court or in taking revenge) and neglect of one's work. As so often in Proverbs, laziness comes under fire based on the observation that "A little sleeping and little snoozing, a little folding of hands while lying down, and then poverty will come on you like a vagrant, and need like a warrior" (Prov 24:34). The cluster of sayings adds little new, but its inclusion allows the editor of Proverbs to preserve words already present in the prior traditions of the sages.

The Second "Solomonic" Collection (Prov 25:1–29:27)

The same aim of preserving the wisdom of the past motivates the incorporation of the second "Solomonic" collection as well. Proverbs 25:1 claims that the succeeding unit contains Solomonic proverbs that "the men of King Hezekiah of Judah transcribed." In other words, the royal court preserved this material and passed it on to complement the earlier Solomonic collection in Prov 10:1–22:16.

This second "Solomonic" collection contains aphorisms on language, industry, deference to authority (but also the superiority of wisdom to power), and other topics that populate the rest of the book, and indeed nonbiblical wisdom collections. Some strings of proverbs seem particularly instructive. For example, in common with the sayings in Ahiqar, Prov 25:2–6 explores the nature of kingship (and therefore power and submission) in contrast to both God's sovereignty and the vulnerability of weaker human beings. The collocated proverbs read, in three pairings:

> (Pair 1) God's honor comes from concealing a matter, kings' honor from discerning a matter.
> The heavens are above and the earth is below, but the mind of kings is inscrutable.
> (Pair 2) Extract dross from silver, and it comes into the crucible.
> Extract evil from the king's presence, and his throne is established on justice.
> (Pair 3) Do not promote yourself in front of a king nor stand in the spot of the powerful.
> It's better that he says, "Come up here," than that he embarrass you in front of the courtiers.

Each saying stands on its own well enough, but the combination of them sketches a picture of life at a royal court, ideally one pursuing justice by managing authority in legitimate ways. Moreover, the first pair sets the political world within a larger horizon, making politics at the topmost levels an act of discerning the hidden wisdom through tenacious observation and thus a godlike activity.

This notion of wisdom's accessibility to the persistent leads the collector of these sayings to include advice about life on an interpersonal scale, including lines famous from elsewhere:

> If your enemy hungers, feed him bread, and if he thirsts, give him water to drink.
> For you will thereby heap flaming coals on his head, and Yhwh will reward you (Prov 25:21–22).

The text appears in the New Testament in Rom 12:20, interpreted as counsel against revenge and an invitation to "overcome evil with good," arguably a broader application than Proverbs itself intended. But no matter, for wisdom texts invite wide and narrow interpretations.

The remainder of these sayings similarly advise restraint in such sayings as "It's not good to eat too much honey" (Prov 25:27), or point to the incongruity of honoring the wrong people ("Like snow in summer or rain at harvest time, so honor does not befit a stupid person" [Prov 26:1]), or even the jolt that comes from mixing incompatible things ("Vinegar on natron[6] is what singing songs to a sad heart is like" [Prov 25:20]). The collection ends with a series of proverbs counseling trust in Yhwh, as well as with the disconcerting truism, "The evil person is abhorrent to the righteous ones, and the straight path is abhorrent to the evil" (Prov 29:27). That is, the wisdom-seeker does not aim at popularity or comfort. Evil remains in the world and must be managed, for it cannot be removed.

The Sayings of Agur (Prov 30:1–33)

This sober ending makes a nice transition to the sayings of Agur, an otherwise unknown sage. Proverbs 30:1 describes this text as an "oracle" (Hebrew: *maśśā'*; literally, "burden"), though it does not seem very "prophetic" and in fact cites commonplace ideas. In some ways, the text seems almost an anti-oracle, or a sort of parody of the world.

After describing himself as hopelessly ignorant, the author asks for neither wealth nor poverty but instead the capacity for truth-telling (Prov 30:8) and proper self-evaluation. Commendable, perhaps, but hardly an ambitious program of wisdom-seeking. Yet the text describes in melancholy fashion a word in which "Three things are never satisfied, four never say, 'enough': Sheol and the infertile womb, the earth that never has enough water, and fire—these never say 'enough'" (Prov 30:15–16). Agur further characterizes the world as full of disobedient children and other misfits.

Some of his puzzles, worked out with the number parallelism device "three things/yes four" that other biblical and nonbiblical writers also employed, underscore this negativity. So Prov 30:20 culminates a series of comparisons involving movement of one object across another (flying birds, slithering snakes, sailing ships, and amorous lovers) with reference to the sexually unrestrained woman (and implicitly, the man). Similarly, Prov 30:21–23 takes the reader to a world in which up is down, and the reversal of fortune so often celebrated in biblical traditions has led not to utopia but to tyranny or anarchy. Ruling slaves and young wives ousting older ones are not marks of a well-run society but rather its opposite. In short, then, Agur's world is dystopian, and he struggles to find meaning within it.

The Sayings of Lemuel (Prov 31:1–9)

The words of Lemuel take a different tack, however. This last collection of sayings in the book presents itself as the advice of a queen mother to her son, a non-Israelite (or perhaps fictional) ruler who needs to learn self-restraint. Here Proverbs returns to the motif of the (potentially) wise ruler, counseling Lemuel and any would-be readers to avoid excess in all forms and to seek justice through that restraint.

Concluding Poem Praising Ms. Wisdom (31:10–31)

And finally, the book returns to the personification of wisdom already articulated in Prov 1–9. Like that discourse, the final poem probably comes from the latest hands in the book, hands that seek to wrap around the various anthologies of proverbs a more comprehensive view of things. Proverbs 1–9 and 31:10–31 frame the middle sections in order to highlight their usage in the formation of wise people, whether male or female.

The final poem is an acrostic, with the inevitable succession of initial letters creating not rigidity but a comprehensiveness of approach. The deft poem describes an ordered world in which industry, family respect and love, and the public celebration of virtue count. The "woman of strength" (Hebrew: *ʾēšet ḥayil*) functions not as a rigid law for what all women must be but as a model of what all wise persons might be. Wisdom can assume flesh, and this eventuality demands all the efforts that the book makes.

Implications

To summarize, then, the book of Proverbs assembles observations aiming at bringing order to human affairs. The reader of the book must enter into the maelstrom of life and seek some bearings, not absolute certainty but reliable truths that allow for stable social relationships and individual happiness.

In such a pursuit, when teaching in his illegal seminary during the Nazi period, Dietrich Bonhoeffer once gave a lecture on Prov 3:27–33. He remarked to his students, who risked their lives during the period of tyranny, "Wisdom is the gift of being able to discern the will of God in the concrete tasks of life . . . . It orders the relationship of the human being to his neighbor, of the man to his wife, the friend to a friend, the father to a child, the teacher to the pupil, to the poor, to the enemy, to possessions, to desires."[7] The gendered language aside, the advice seems sound and appropriate to Proverbs. The book finds the transcendent in the everyday, and therein lies its value.

Notes

1. Or, "the gecko grabs with [its] 'hands.'"

2. On this structure, see Michael V. Fox, *Proverbs 1–9* (New York: Doubleday, 2000). There are different ways of understanding the structure, but this one seems the most economical.

3. See the excellent discussion of the multiple layers of these warnings as worked out by Christl Maier, *Die "fremde Frau" in Proverbien 1–9: Eine exegetische und sozialgeschichtliche Studie* (Göttingen: Vandenhoeck & Ruprecht, 1995).

4. The translation is debatable, with many scholars emending the MT in various ways. The basic idea, however, is clear enough: liars like lying.

5. A translation of Amenemope by Miriam Lichtheim appears in William W. Hallo and K. Lawson Younger, eds., *The Context of Scripture* (Leiden: Brill, 2003), 1:115–122.

6. Natron is an alkaline mixture containing sodium carbonate decahydrate, so the combination of natron and vinegar has the same effect as combining the latter with baking soda. All fizz, but with uncertain results.

7. Dietrich Bonhoeffer, *Theological Education at Finkenwalde: 1935–1937*, Dietrich Bonhoeffer Works in English 14, trans. Douglas W. Stott (Minneapolis: Fortress, 2013), 861.

For Further Reading

Brenner, Athalya, and Carole Fontaine, eds. *The Feminist Companion to Wisdom and Psalms*. London: Bloomsbury, 1998.

Brown, William P. *The Ethos of the Cosmos: The Genesis of Moral Imagination in the Bible*. Grand Rapids: Eerdmans, 1999.

Fox, Michael V. *Proverbs 1–9*. Anchor Bible 18A. New York: Doubleday, 2000.

Fox, Michael V. *Proverbs 10–31*. Anchor Bible 18B. New Haven: Yale University Press, 2009.

Snell, Daniel. *Twice-Told Proverbs and the Composition of the Book of Proverbs*. Winona Lake, IN: Eisenbrauns, 1993.

21 Ecclesiastes
DOUBT AS AN ORDER OF FAITH

Key Text: *In summary, Qohelet was a sage. He taught the people knowledge, attentiveness, and discernment. He organized many proverbs. Qohelet tried to find attractive words, properly written, true words. The words of sages are like goads, and like sticks studded with prongs are those of the masters of [proverb?] collections. As for the rest of these things, pay attention my child. There is no end to making many books, and a lot of study wearies the flesh.* (Eccl 12:9–12)

If the book of Proverbs collects fragments of wisdom in order to fashion a mosaic displaying the underlying order of the world, Ecclesiastes exposes the patchiness of that very world. Far from being a place of transparent purpose, Ecclesiastes's universe has not only an ugly side but several confounding ones. Its author values limits over expansiveness, self-awareness over aspiration, restraint over exuberance. Yet a joy amid sorrow remains, as an act of the will, to be sure, but also as a proper response to God's inscrutable benevolence.

The book of Ecclesiastes goes by this and another name, Qohelet. The Hebrew noun *qōhelet*, which the book gives as the name or title of its author, refers to someone calling together an assembly. Even though the noun is feminine, the book refers to its author as a male.[1] The Greek noun *ekklēsiastēs* denotes a member of the Hellenistic city assembly or *ekklēsia*, and this became the book's name in the LXX. Although ancient tradition associates the book with Solomon, the adoption of the royal persona in chs 1–2 is a literary device, one of several "voices" that the narrator assumes while considering the limits of human knowledge.

The Hebrew of the book is among the latest in the Old Testament, from some time in the Second Temple period. More precise dating depends on one's view of the book's relationship to Greek philosophy. Many scholars have compared its view of fate or pleasure as a source of meaning to views from Epicureanism. If correct, such a connection would necessitate a date after about 300 BCE. Many others date the book earlier, to the Persian period, arguing that the absence of Greek words in the book and the very generalized parallels to Greek thought do not convincingly point to a time after the coming of Alexander to the Near East. Either way, the book does lie outside the mainstream of biblical texts, offering a viewpoint that challenges overly comfortable interpretations of the traditions of Torah, Temple, and community.

How does Ecclesiastes do its work? The epilogue to the book (Eccl 12:9–12), cited earlier, describes its creator and his work in a way that fitly depicts the ideals of the wisdom teacher. While acknowledging the tiresomeness of study and writing (as every university student knows), the text emphasizes (1) the importance of wisdom embodied in a teacher, (2) the aesthetic dimension of wisdom teachings as something "attractive" as well as true, and (3) the provocative nature of the words themselves. But perhaps the key clause is "he arranged many proverbs," for that describes the book of Ecclesiastes to a T. It consists of many sayings clustered around a theme and then juxtaposed with other clusters. "While X is true, so also is not-X or not-quite-X" captures the book's overall approach as it seizes upon the aspectual features of proverbial language.

The book concerns itself with a few main ideas: the repetitiveness of life and therefore its lack of progress over time, the limits of knowledge, the need for appropriate pleasures as antidotes to despair, the failure of social ties (however necessary and good in themselves) to provide ultimate meaning, and even the limits of piety. Qohelet asserts, "When people say, 'look, this is something new' in reality it's always been like that before us—there's no memory of the former things, nor later will there be (memory) of things that will be." (Eccl 1:10–11). In doing so, the book questions the expectation of innovation that makes up one of the most exciting elements of prophetic speech, which envisions Yhwh's innovations in human history (see, e.g., Isa 40; Jer 31). Qohelet does not embrace cynicism or fatalism, but does accept a view of reality deeply skeptical about grandiose theories or wild enthusiasms. This book is a country for old men, if any in the Bible is.

Impressed by the circularity of life, the book reflects that circularity in its own structure, which seems deliberately fractured (unsurprisingly for a collection of jostling sayings). An outline that seems at least plausible would be something like this:

A. Title (Eccl 1:1)
B. Meditations on life's ephemeral nature (Eccl 1:2–6:9)
C. Meditations on the limits of wisdom (Eccl 6:10–8:17)
D. Meditations on life and death as limit and opportunity (Eccl 9:1–12:8)
E. Epilogue (Eccl 12:9–14)

While the subdivisions within each unit (especially B) are debatable, the overall flow leads toward the book's conclusions about the inevitability of death and therefore the need for self-awareness and the pursuit of attainable levels of happiness.

How does one know these things? Qohelet speaks often of his experiences of "seeing" life, as opposed to passing on tradition derived from the testimony of the ancestors. The verb *rā'à* ("to see") occurs forty-eight times in the book, including fourteen times as "I saw" (Eccl 2:13, 24; 3:10, 16, 22; 4:4, 15; 5:12, 17; 6:1; 7:15; 8:9, 10, 17), ordinarily prefacing an observation about the limits of life (and in Parts B and C of the book, which is building the case that the final part will draw to its inexorable conclusion). One "sees" the value of enjoying food and companionship, the simple things of life (Eccl 2:24; 5:17), as well as its injustices, which result from human envy or greed or contempt for life (Eccl 3:16; 4:4; 5:12; 6:1; 8:10). For Qohelet, the unbiased observer of life concludes that its limits are real but also that happiness within them also exists.

The Title (Eccl 1:1)

The opening of the book situates it within the emerging "Solomonic" literature from the Second Temple period, a body of work by different authors including not just the "canonical" books bearing the ancient king's name but also works from the secondary canon (see Chapter 30) such as "Wisdom of Solomon," "Psalms of Solomon," and later "Odes of Solomon." Ecclesiastes does not really make a claim for Solomon's authorship, since it soon begins referring to the author as Qohelet (Eccl 1:1, 2, 12; 7:27; 12:8, 9), a wisdom teacher. The literary device of Solomonic authorship serves, instead, to position the book as a wisdom book taking a broad, kinglike overview of life itself.

VANITY OR PUFFS OF WIND?

One of Qohelet's favorite words is *hebel*, which the traditional English translations (following the Latin Vulgate) render as "vanity," but in fact refers to a puff of air or perhaps the sound one makes when expressing moderate frustration. In its various appearances, the word denotes something transitory or futile (see Eccl 1:2, 14; 2:11, 17; 3:19; 6:2, 4, 11; 12:8). Life, for Qohelet, has a transient quality, with even its best aspects limited in duration and therefore meaningfulness.

Meditations on Life's Ephemeral Nature (Eccl 1:2–6:9)

The book opens this broad overview with a meditation on life's repetitiveness. In a world in which the "sun rises and sets" and "the wind goes round and round," human experiences also repeat, so that "what was will be, and what was done will be done—there is nothing new beneath the sun" (Eccl 1:5, 6, 9). By opening the book this way, Qohelet locates human limitations within the structure of the universe itself. These limitations need not imply loss, for the passage of the sun or the water cycle or even air movements creates life-sustaining patterns too. But they are confines, signaling the need for modesty.

Ecclesiastes 1:12–2:26 considers the alternative to such restraint, the untrammeled pursuit of power, status, and wealth. While the text has often attracted moralizers in the pulpit and beyond—criticisms of luxury always draw an audience!—Qohelet's point is deeper. The pursuit of such superlatives offers diminishing returns. A billionaire cannot be a thousand times happier than a mere millionaire.

On the other hand, the earth does not imprison people in suffering, since good things do exist. Therefore, the pursuit of pleasure should reflect the limits of the human condition. As the section concludes:

> There is nothing better for a person than to eat and drink and discern good in his life from his labor. Also, I have seen that this is from God's hand. For who can eat or take pleasure except me? To the person whom [God] approves, [God] gives wisdom, knowledge, and joy, but to the sinner [God] gives the trouble of gathering and collecting to put what's good before God. Also, this is breath and a puff of wind. (Eccl 2:24–26)

That is, God appoints boundaries for human existence but also allows freedom within those boundaries, a freedom to experience appropriate pleasure. Moreover, the ethical life leads to knowledge and joy, while the unethical life leads to the relentless pursuit of unsustainable experiences.

This sense of futility appears in the famous poem in Eccl 3:1–9 (at least famous to baby boomers as a song sung by the 1960s rock band The Birds, and Pete Seeger before them). "For everything there is a season," with its pairs of activities that cancel each other out, culminates in the wistful question, "So what profit does a person have under the sun?" Not much, it seems. All that activity, though valuable in itself, does not advance human life toward any ultimate goal.

For Qohelet, however, this lack of progress is morally neutral. Less neutral is an element that contributes to the presence of human evil. That is, the circularity of life does not simply derive from nature, as ch 1 might lead one to believe. Qohelet laments, "the tears of the oppressed have no one to comfort them" (Eccl 4:1), and this pervasive injustice becomes visible on observation. Qohelet analyzes the political structure of the empires of which Judah and Samaria were part by observing, "If you see someone oppressing the poor and perverting justice and righteousness in a given province, do not derive any pleasure from the realization, for the important person has someone even higher watching, and someone higher still over them. Then again, it benefits every land to have a king served for a field" (Eccl 5:7–8 [ET 5:8–9]). That is, abuse of power occurs even when, and sometimes because, a formidable state structure exists to bring about order. Power does not merely corrupt individuals, but it freezes in place their abuse of those unable to stand up to it.

And yet, such negativity sits side by side in this section with a much more positive view emphasizing the basic human capacity for friendship, taking pleasure in simple things, and persevering in the search for wisdom. By stating this alternative, Ecclesiastes prevents its readers from succumbing to despair, keeping a balance between the limits of life and their opportunities in view.

The Limits of Wisdom (Eccl 6:10–8:17)

The next section explores the need for balance, arguing for pursuing higher goods and enjoy life's opportunities. Yet amid these legitimate human pursuits, the nagging question of limits remains. While one should seek a good reputation throughout life (Eccl 7:1–2) and should use even painful occurrences as opportunities to mediate on the good life, one should also recognize "God's deeds, for who can straighten what [God] has made crooked?" (Eccl 7:13).

QOHELET AND EPICURUS?

Some scholars have compared Qohelet's ideas to those of Epicurus (341–270 BCE), for whom the highest good was pleasure, not debauchery or excess but the modest pleasures of life properly balanced so as to minimize pain of body or soul. Both men, for example, questioned conventional notions of deity or common fears and prejudices. While similarities between these two ancient thinkers do exist, Qohelet does not ground his ethics in pleasure in the same way, nor does he argue that avoidance of pain is a major goal, since such avoidance may impair the acquisition of wisdom. Epicurus's own works have survived only in fragments, but a systematic explanation of his philosophy complete with quotations from writings comes from Diogenes Laertius, a writer of the third century CE.

Beyond the pursuit of the goods persistently available to humans, Qohelet discusses the limits of pursuing wisdom (cf. Job 28:1–28), especially noting its relationship to power. As Eccl 8:1–9 puts it in a somewhat rambling way:

Who is like the sage? Who knows how to interpret a matter?
A person's wisdom makes him or her smile and softens wrinkles.[2]
Observe a king's mouth like a word of an oath from God.
Do not leave him quickly nor stand up for something bad,
for he does whatever he wants.
A king's word has power. Who can ever say to him, "What are you doing?"
[However], the one keeping the commandment knows nothing evil
and the sage's heart knows the time and the manner [of proper action].
For there is a time and a manner for everything worth doing,
because a person's evil greatly affects that person.
Indeed, we don't know what will be—how can anybody tell how it will be?

Just as nobody has power over the wind to control the wind, so also no one has power
over the day of one's death.
There is no demobilization from war, and no disaster can save its practitioners.
I saw all this and focused my mind on everything that is done under the sun. Whenever
someone has power over another, it is to that person's detriment.

The wise person, in other words, faces life with a knowing smile when recognizing the
inescapability of human power and its ability to impinge on even the best person's life.
Qohelet advises the aspiring official to avoid offending power. At one level, the attention
to the king is a standard theme in ancient Near Eastern wisdom literature. It appears in
the Bible in Proverbs and outside it in a contemporary Aramaic collection called Ahiqar,
among other places. So, even though Qohelet's audience may not have had access to anyone higher than a local ruler (who still sometimes wore the title "king"), ancient people
knew to protect themselves from those above them.

Qohelet, however, makes a slightly different point. Wise people know that happiness
sometimes eludes their grasp because of the constraints of political structures.

Life and Death as Limit and Opportunity (Eccl 9:1–12:8)

What remains then, if all the aspects of life fail to provide a secure basis for confidence in
human experience? The final section takes up this question by proposing a set of possible
actions for the wise person.

Ecclesiastes 9:1–12 opens the constructive portion of the book by noting that "a living
dog is better than a dead lion" (Eccl 9:4), and so the embrace of life makes more sense
than the fatalistic will to die. Moreover, the text continues, "the living know that they will
die, but the dead know nothing whatever" (Eccl 9:5). That is, while human beings confront the limits of our existence at all times, knowing this has its own value and certainly
surpasses the ignorance of the dead. Since Qohelet does not consider the idea of post-
mortem existence (whether the immortality of the soul or resurrection) as a concept that
can factor into his calculations, he attempts to reason solely with the evidence of lived
experience. Even such limitation of knowledge, he argues, leads one to an embrace of life.

Ecclesiastes 9:13–10:20 continues with another long speech, including a series of proverbs, all focused on political incongruities. As a citizen of an occupied, colonized country, Qohelet recognizes the evils built into a system of domination and subservience. He
does not resort merely to mockery or resignation, the eternal strategies of the weak. Nor
does he propose revolution, since he believes that such trouble taking leads nowhere.
(And popular revolutions did not occur in antiquity—they are a modern social innovation.) Rather, he insists on clear-sightedness as a strategy of survival. Claiming that "the
words of sages deserve to be heard more than the shouting of a ruler among fools" (Eccl
9:17), this speech goes on to lament waste and luxury, as well as to hold out hope that
"you are blessed, O land, when your king is a descendant of nobles and your princes eat at

the right time for strength and not for dissipation" (Eccl 10:17). That is, power need not always corrupt, and rulers who take their responsibilities seriously deserve approbation.

However, the constructive part of the book does not concentrate solely on politics. Ecclesiastes 11:1–12:8 turns to the deeper things of life, the contrasts between youth and age and between impiety and piety. Ecclesiastes 12 describes feeble old age in graphic terms as a time when hearing and sight and taste disappear, surely an observable fact for many people. And yet the larger subsection also invites the audience of the book to embrace piety in youth. While the book cautions against long-winded prayer and other forms of religious pomposity (Eccl 5:1–7), it also invites the young person who seeks wisdom to "remember your creator in the days of your youth" (Eccl 12:1). Without trying to over-interpret such a charge by making it overly pious, one must acknowledge the basic piety of the book at this and other points. Qohelet calls upon the reader to carry out the human side of religion and leave the divine side to God. Qohelet supports a religion without excessive speculation or unrealistic expectations.

Epilogue (Eccl 12:9–14)

The restraint of such a call coming at the end of the book underscores its overall message. Life has meaning, but on a human scale. Such a view risks sounding unorthodox, even if it appears in many other biblical texts in one way or another. Hence the epilogue.

The final section, as already noted, speaks of the author in the third person, situating him as a wisdom teacher who sought to make sense of the world on behalf of others. Most scholars conclude that this epilogue comes from a different hand than most of the rest of the book, since it does speak of Qohelet as someone living in the past, perhaps an editor's teacher or intellectual hero. If so, the editor aims to preserve Qohelet's reputation from the charge of heterodoxy, and instead portray him as one whose unconventional thoughts fit well within the broad outline of traditional wisdom, with proper skepticism of human pretensions as well as honor of God. Whether this defense succeeds is another matter.

Implications

It would be wrong, then, to think of Qohelet as an ancient cynic. Rather, like Voltaire or Shakespeare, he knew the limits of human freedom to make life in our own image. His skepticism is thus more about cutting through silly illusions than about a systematic rejection of God or the livability of the world. True cynicism demands a level of self-hatred and contempt for others that Qohelet does not accept. Rather, his struggle for modesty before God is more like that of the modern poet Paul Claudel (1868–1955), who wrote:

> If what you need, Lord, are virgins, if what you need are brave men beneath your standard . . .

Well then there's Dominic and Francis, Saint Lawrence and Saint Cecelia
  and plenty more!
But if by chance You should have need of a lazy and imbecilic bore,
If a prideful coward could prove useful to You, or perhaps a soiled ingrate,
Or the sort of man whose hard heart shows up in a hard face—
Well, anyway, You didn't come to save the just but that other type that abounds,
And if, miraculously, You run out of them elsewhere . . . Lord, I'm still around.[3]

Qohelet did not, perhaps think of himself so negatively, but the wry self-awareness of the "lazy and imbecilic bore" would have appealed to him as a genuine human type, and therefore one in whom a strange dignity resides. This strange book that fits so oddly in the Bible poses the question of whether humans can find dignity in this world. And the answer is yes.

Notes

1. Except in Eccl 7:27 MT, where the statement "says Qohelet," uses the feminine Hebrew verb *'āmĕrâ*, oddly enough. This may be simply a scribe's mistake: the final letter *he-* could go with "Qohelet" giving "says (masculine verb) *the* Qohelet," which is precisely the expression in Eccl 12:8. In other words, MT may simply have split the consonants incorrectly.

2. Or more literally, "wisdom lights up a person's face and changes his or her face's strength."

3. Paul Claudel, "The Day of Gifts," trans. Jonathan Monroe Geltner, *Poetry* 199 (2012): 532.

For Further Reading

Fox, Michael V. *A Time to Tear Down and a Time to Build Up: A Rereading of Ecclesiastes*. Grand Rapids: Eerdmans, 1999.
Krüger, Thomas. *Qoheleth*. Translated by O. C. Dean, Jr. Minneapolis: Fortress, 2004.

22 Love in the Air
THE SONG OF SONGS

> **Key Text:** *Place me like a seal on your heart, a seal on your right arm.*
> *For love is stronger than death,*
> *Passion harder than Sheol.*
> *Its flames are flames of fire,*
> *So are its blazes.* (Song 8:6–7)

The Song of Songs, also called the Song of Solomon, is a poem about longing. In this case, the longing occupies the space between a man and a woman, two lovers whose voices fill the page with their passion for each other. It is a love poem, full of the language of the body as a mirror of nature and nature as a model of the body. Frank and fresh, the poem celebrates human love, not merely human sex. Its love knows few boundaries, but it never finds complete fulfillment either, and this incompleteness makes the poetry speak to readers who also know what love is about.

Not surprisingly for a poetic dialogue among three speaking parts (the male lover, the female lover, and a chorus or circle of friends, much as in Greek dramas), the Song of Songs is very difficult to outline, and commentaries differ significantly among themselves. Perhaps it is best simply to see the book as an extended discussion among the dramatis personae as they move forward in time, expressing an increasing degree of frustration at the incompleteness of love. In other words, the poem is so tightly woven together and repetitive that sorting out its structure is quite difficult. While the narrative does progress toward consummation of love, the final act does not arrive.

Along with this issue of structure, the book as it stands has been variously dated. Traditional interpreters assigned it to Solomon, based largely on the opening verse, which connects it to him in some way. (The Hebrew phrase *li-Šĕlōmōh* is equivalent to *lĕ-Dāwīd* in the superscription of many Psalms—it is less a claim about authorship than about a sort of poetic association.) Solomon appears as a character in the book but not as the male lover and not, in fact, as a model worth emulating (see Song 3:6–11; 8:11). The language of the book points to a later era than the age of Solomon, although precision is impossible. The language of the book seems to be a dialect of northern (Israelian) Hebrew, indicating an origin somewhere north of Jerusalem, not in the kingdom of Judah.

What is the Book About?

In the long history of its interpretation, the Song has usually been understood as a poem about deep longing, but not always with the same object in mind. Ancient and medieval readers, Jewish and Christian, often read the book as an allegory of the mutual longing between God and Israel or the church or even the human soul. In this very powerful reading, the male lover was God and the female lover the human being, or sometimes the male lover was the wise human and the female lover was Wisdom or spiritual maturity. In this interpretation, the longing involved the deepest human capacities, with religion claiming the emotional depth often reserved for eros.

A good example of this overall interpretation occurs in the sermons on the Song of Songs by Gregory of Nyssa, the influential fourth-century CE Christian leader. He warns readers:

> If any bear a passionate and carnal habit of mind and lack that garment of conscience that is proper dress for the divine wedding feast, let such persons not be imprisoned by their own thoughts and draft the undefiled words of the Bridegroom and Bride down to the level of brutish, irrational passions.[1]

Similar warnings appear in such early Christian interpreters as Origen and Jewish rabbis such as the second-century CE martyr Rabbi Akiva. These and much later figures understood the book allegorically, not out of prudish distaste for love or sexuality, but because of a belief that religion at its heart drew upon the same human emotional depths as the erotic life. Therefore, the love poem could point to higher truths.

THE SPEAKING PARTS IN THE BOOK

Some English translations of Song of Songs print captions for the speaking parts of the book (the male and female lovers and the chorus). While not part of the original text, these captions have precedents going back to the fourth century CE. The Greek manuscript Codex Sinaiticus prints captions of the *nymphios* and *nymphē* (male and female lover) to clarify the identity of each speaker in the dialogue.

Such an interpretation certainly has exercised great power, and one feels a sense of disappointment at exchanging it for a more "natural" reading of the poem as one concerned with human love. At the same time, however, some elements in the book do suggest that its creator intended the male and female lover to be more than ordinary people, but rather symbols of an ideal of longing and love. For example, Song 5:10–16 compares the male lover to a statue with a golden head, facial features resembling fine woods and flowers, and an ivory belly. (Ancient statues were often of wood overlaid with various precious materials.) In other words, the poem resorts to the language of myth and symbol to cast its characters as somehow superlative. In short, while the figurative interpretation of the book does not reflect the original intentions of its creator, the reading does have a certain logic.

The Plot and Characters of the Poem

Again, the Song portrays two figures, a man and a woman, as equally beautiful and desirable, yet equally at pains to explain the intensity of their love to others. Other characters in the book include Solomon, the woman's brothers, and especially a chorus that comments on the other speakers' poems or perhaps interrogates them. The poetry of the book embraces a rich repertoire of images drawn from nature and including sight, sound, smell, touch, and taste. Like the Egyptian love poetry on which the book is at least partly modeled, the Song uses family language ("brother" and "sister") to speak of the lovers' intimacy. While for some modern readers this sort of language may sound incestuous, it seems unlikely that such was the poet's intention (even though brother-sister marriage did exist in Egypt at least for the aristocrats with polygamous households, and lovers in other languages, such as Korean, may call each other "brother" or "sister" to indicate intimacy and distinction by age). Rather, in the Song the sibling language simply expresses the radical intimacy and mutuality of the two primary characters.

Consider a few exchanges, then. Near the opening of the book, the male lover speaks of his companion by saying:

> My companion, I will compare you to a mare among Pharaoh's chariots.
> Your cheeks are beautifully decorated, your neck adorned with jewels.
> We will make you a gold torc inlaid with silver. (Song 1:9–11)

To this, the woman replies

> While the king lay on his couch, my perfume's scent wafted forth,
> My beloved to me is like a sachet of myrrh lodging between my breasts. (Song 1:12–13)

That is, the both speakers resort to metaphor to describe themselves as passive, even lazy, observers of beauty that comes to them. The horse imagery may seem strange, but a mare would certainly excite the mostly male chariot horses. Similarly, all lovers know the power of smell to signal the presence of the other person's body in a most intimate way.

Similarly luxuriant but static imagery appears throughout the book. Some images evoke motion, however. So we read of the male lover bounding like a gazelle and the female lover reflecting on a time when

> At night, I lay on my bed seeking the one my life loves.
> I sought him but did not find him.
> "Let me get up and wander about the city's alleys and plazas,
> Let me seek the one my life loves."
> I sought him but did not find him.
> The sentinels found me wandering about the city.
> "Have you seen the one my life loves?"
> Just after I left them, I found the one my life loves
> I grabbed him and did not let him go
> till I brought him to my mother's house,
> to the chamber of the one who gave me birth. (Song 3:1–4)

The poem does not explain where this Romeo had been or why the watchmen would care about the self-involved obsessions of this Juliet. It is enough to speak of love as the search for the other, of desire as a thirst not to be ignored, and of the need to draw the beloved into the relationships of family and home. Again, images of motion and stasis alternate throughout the book to create a sense of the search for love, which always seems to elude the two characters' grasp.

The close of the book circles one last time this understanding of love as a powerful compulsion that fulfills and does not fulfill at the same time. Thus in an enigmatic request, the woman asks the man to

> Place me like a seal on your heart, a seal on your right arm.
> For love is stronger than death,
> Passion harder than Sheol.
> Its flames are flames of fire,
> So are its blazes. (Song 8:6–7)

It is difficult to know the precise connection between love and death that the Song seeks to evoke. A few scholars have argued that the entire book relates to the cult of the dead in ancient Israel. This view is not as far-fetched as it may sound, for many texts and works of art do make such a connection. However, a more convincing reading may simply be that the poem recognizes that the greatest threat to love is death, which makes final consummation impossible. Or at least it seems to. The poem seeks the near-impossible, the defiance of death itself and the discovery of a force more powerful than it can be. Love.

SONG OF SONGS AND EGYPTIAN LOVE POETRY

Not surprisingly, ancient people liked love poetry about as much as modern people do. This poetry ranges in tone from the polite to the pornographic, much as it does today. In Egypt, for example, Papyrus Harris 500 is a dialogue between a male and a female protagonist, much as in Song of Songs. In one passage, the young woman says,

> My heart is not yet done with your love, my wolf cub!
> Your liquor is your lovemaking.

And later:

> The voice of the goose cries out,
> As he's trapped by the bait.

To this, the male makes appropriate responses. Song of Songs, then, stands in a long tradition of love poetry writing, much as one should expect from experience with human beings. For the texts, see the translations of Michael V. Fox in William W. Hallo and K. Lawson Younger, eds., *The Context of Scripture*, vol. 1, *Canonical Compositions from the Biblical World* (Leiden: Brill, 2003), 1:49–51.

Implications

This book's search for the most elusive thing in the world, a love that survives death, allowed its premodern readers to understand it as a profoundly religious text, however implausible such an interpretation might seem today. The desire to love and to be loved is a religious thing because it involves at a deep level the human pursuit of the good. Song of Songs crosses boundaries ensconcing men and women in predetermined gender roles. While some modern readers have thought the book expresses a male projection of what heterosexual love should be, there is no strong reason for such a jaundiced view. We do not know whether the author of the book was male or female, nor is it clear that male authorship need imply a misunderstanding of a woman's point of view (or vice versa). The Song of Songs opens the door to a world in which the traditional boundaries fall away or rather become useful in service of a mutual passion that celebrates the deepest qualities of human existence. No wonder the book has commended itself across the centuries.

Note

1. Gregory of Nyssa, "Homily 1, lines 21–24," in *Homilies on the Song of Songs*, ed. and trans. Richard A. Norris Jr. (Atlanta: Society of Biblical Literature, 2012), 15.

For Further Reading

Gregory of Nyssa. *Homilies on the Song of Songs*. Edited by Richard A. Norris Jr. Atlanta: Society of Biblical Literature, 2012.

Noegel, Scott B., and Gary A. Rendsburg. *Solomon's Vineyard: Literary and Linguistic Studies in the Song of Songs*. Atlanta: Society of Biblical Literature, 2009.

23 Introduction to the Prophetic Books

OTHER TEXTS WITH centuries-long reputations are the prophets. Every year at Easter time (or sometimes Christmas), English-speakers hear the George Frideric Handel's *Messiah*, an oratorio recounting the story of Jesus as the messiah. After a brief orchestral opening, a tenor voice sings the magnificent words "Comfort ye my people," followed by "Ev'ry valley" and, in the chorus this time, "And the glory of the Lord." All these words come from ch 40 of the book of Isaiah. Handel and his librettist Charles Jennens drew on a long tradition of interpretation of a set of biblical prophetic texts that inspired musicians, painters, preachers, scholars, and casual readers for twenty-five or so centuries. Not just the words of Isaiah but also the other prophetic texts have stimulated theological and artistic work in many times and places.

Yet these works present readers with the hardest interpretive challenges of any biblical books. This is true for several reasons. First, these texts often receive the most improbable interpretations, having been hijacked by modern interpreters who use them as grist for their own attempts to "read the signs of the times." Televangelism has done its best to discredit these works.

There is, however, a second and deeper reason. These books present genuine interpretive problems even for those trying to read them on their own terms. It is crucial to step back for a better perspective because these texts offer brilliant language for ongoing moral and spiritual reflection.

For a proper orientation, remember the cabinet in any given ancient synagogue. Several scrolls in it bore the names of prophets. These were the books called the Latter Prophets (as distinguished from the Former Prophets or what Christians usually think of as "historical books"). Four major scrolls of prophetic texts came under this rubric: Isaiah, Jeremiah, Ezekiel, and the Book of the Twelve Minor Prophets. These books are of similar length, with Jeremiah weighing in at about 22,000 words, Ezekiel at 19,000, Isaiah at 17,000, and the Twelve Minor Prophets at 14,000.[1] While each of these works has its own purpose, background, and theological objective, all belong to a single category because they begin similarly (by setting the named prophet in a historical context), employ similar literary strategies (weaving together short oracles into a larger whole), and argue for related (though not identical) theologies. They all came about through similar processes of literary development. This process began with oral speeches of prophets communicating with the divine realm, sometimes described as an encounter with the divine assembly (see 1 Kgs 22:19–23; Isa 6) and sometimes as direct communication with Yhwh alone (Num 12:6–8; Amos 7:7–9).

And it continued through a series of literary moments, of writing and rewriting the oracles until they formed the collections now called the prophetic books (a point to be considered further in a moment). Most importantly, all four books try to discern the ways of Yhwh in Israel's history and to offer language through which their audiences may begin the difficult task of reimagining their world after the debacles of Assyrian and Babylonian invasions and deportations.

In the Christian Bible, other works also appear among the prophets. Daniel, in either its long or short version, follows Ezekiel, while Jeremiah keeps company with Lamentations (and in the Secondary Canon, with Tobit and the Epistle of Jeremiah, on which see Chapter 30). Although these books developed differently from the main four prophetic works, it will be useful to treat them in the order in which they appear in the Protestant Bible, simply because most readers are familiar with that arrangement.

Moreover, connecting these works to the main four books illustrates the important fact that the category "prophetic book" does not have self-evident boundaries. As Israelite prophecy became more and more a literary phenomenon during the Second Temple period under Persian and then Hellenistic rulers, and as readers of the book increasingly applied them to their own times, a fondness for finding the secret meanings of cryptic texts set in. Daniel, in particular, exhibits this sensibility, as we will see.

All of these works share one additional quality: they are works of art by and for survivors. As such, they are the direct ancestors of the twentieth-century literatures commemorating and trying to make sense of such tragedies as the Holocaust or the various genocides in Rwanda and Armenia and Cambodia, among too many other places. How then, do we make sense of them?

The Prophets in their World

To understand a text—corkscrews and cathedrals again!—it is useful, first of all, to know something about its background, that is, the world in which it arose. Oftentimes only fragments of that world are recoverable, and such is the case with the prophetic books. Sometimes they refer to events or cultural practices from the world around them, and such data may reveal important layers of meaning in the texts themselves. (In other words, texts do not exist isolated from each other or the larger world.) For Isaiah, Jeremiah, Ezekiel, and the Twelve in particular, it is useful to consider how they reflect the nature of prophecy as an Israelite and pan–Near Eastern phenomenon.

To begin, these four books come at neither the beginning nor the end of a historical process of communication with the divine realm. Ancient prophets spoke on behalf of one or more deities about issues facing kings in several cultures from the sixteenth century BCE on. In Mari, a city-state on the Middle Euphrates, these prophets spoke about immediately pressing political issues. Closer to the time and location of Israel, an eighth-century BCE king of the neighboring kingdom of Hamath, one Zakkur, mentions in an inscription of his that when foreign powers invaded his kingdom, he "lifted up my hands to Ba'l-shamayin, and he answered me through the agency of seer and 'testifiers.' Yes Ba'l-shamayin said to me, 'Don't worry, for I made you king and I will raise up your people and rescue you from all these kings.'"[2]

Moreover, the very Assyrian rulers who dominated Israel and Judah also consulted their own prophets. For example, the seventh-century BCE king Assurbanipal received a message from a prophet of Ishtar:

> The Lady of Kidmuri [an avatar of Ishtar], who in her anger had left her cella and taken residence in a place unworthy of her, relented during my good reign which Assur had presented and, to make perfect her majestic divinity and glorify her precious rites, constantly sent me (orders) through dreams and prophetic messages.[3]

In short, Israel shared with other cultures basic ideas about prophetic communication with the divine realm, especially between deity and king regarding matters of state. The Bible itself says as much when it speaks of the prophets of the god Baal (1 Kgs 18:20–40).

The distinctiveness of the Bible lies elsewhere, then. Not only does the Bible take great pains to distinguish between true and false prophecy (see Deut 13), a need that other ancient persons must have felt to some degree, but it also shifts both the audience and the content of prophecy. That is, while early Israelite prophecy often addressed the king and his court regarding matters of war and administration (see, e.g., the stories of Nathan or Micaiah ben Imlah), the prophetic books add to this concern for high politics and the character of leaders a wider concern with the moral behavior of the entire people. This latter emphasis is almost completely absent from other prophetic traditions in the Near East, as far as the surviving evidence shows.

The Prophetic Books

Perhaps even more important than the shift of audience and content is that ancient Israel produced large prophetic books. While other ancient Near Easterners wrote down prophetic texts and kept track of them over time, nothing remotely as structurally complex, length, or artistically rich survives from elsewhere in Israel's environment.

Israel thus wrought an important change in prophecy. They transformed a context-specific phenomenon of transmitting short, time-sensitive oracles—either orally or in writing to interested parties at court—into a process of literary production involving careful preservation, editing, expansion, and interpretation of oracles for ever new situations. This major difference distinguishes the Israelite prophets from soothsayers and augurs, a distinction which at least some biblical texts also take pains to make (Lev 19:26, 31; Deut 18:9–14).

To think of the prophetic texts as books, as works of literature, raises important questions, though. For example, how did these books come together? A good example of how complex a biblical book's origins can be comes from Jer 36:27–32. In that narrative, after having a scroll of his writings burned by a disapproving King Jehoiakim, Jeremiah dictates another scroll containing his previous oracles, which he apparently remembered, and "added to them many other words" (v. 32). That is, the book contains a story about the prophet (not by him) and his literary activities (and by implication, those of the persons preserving his words) at a certain moment in his career.

What might one deduce from this brief story? Not only did the career of Jeremiah continue for several more decades (and thus his rewritten scroll could not possibly be the present book of Jeremiah), but also his later actions appear in the text as prose narrative told in the third person (and thus presumably not written by the prophet himself). The comment about "many other words" does not make clear whether Jeremiah and his scribe Baruch simply tacked on new material to the old or recast the now royally censored oracles, improving them in some way. Either is possible. Add also this another clue: Jer 51:64 says "until this point, the words of Jeremiah," which sounds like an ending, and yet the book concludes with ch 52. Still another clue lies in the fact that the MT and LXX versions of Jeremiah differ in both length and order of material (see the discussion of Jeremiah in Chapter 25).

In short, the book of Jeremiah grew in stages that can be partially recovered without speculation. At least these developments are clear:

Oral utterances → writing them down → adding new utterances and revising the oracles → telling the story in prose → final editing

Within the book itself, then, some words come from Jeremiah, some from those remembering his words, and some from the person or group responsible for compiling the book bearing his name. All the words, however, bear the authority of Yhwh's prophet. A similar process of gradual, but deliberate, augmentation of the prophet's words led to the creation of all the prophetic books, as will be clear in the discussions of each one below.

This process of literary growth over time did not result in hodgepodges of little speeches. Rather, each book possesses a coherence that marks it as a united work.

As will become clearer soon, many of the prophetic books show a strong connection among their parts, as the older texts lean into the later texts and vice versa. Themes and ideas occur repeatedly, with later texts revisiting earlier imagery and recasting it for new purposes. This process bears the French name *relecture*, the art of reading something again in a new way. For students of American history, an example of this practice is visible from a text like Martin Luther King Jr.'s "I Have a Dream" speech. He begins with the sentence "Five score years ago, the great American in whose symbolic shadow we stand . . .," an evocation of Abraham Lincoln (King was standing at the Lincoln Memorial as he spoke) not just in a general way but specifically of Lincoln's "Gettysburg Address." Lincoln had commemorated the "hallowed dead" by tracing their actions back "four score and seven years" to the Jefferson's "Declaration of Independence." So in this case, King conjures up Lincoln and Jefferson, not just to give a history lesson but to create new meaning that draws on hallowed tradition. Again, *relecture*.

The biblical prophetic books use just such a strategy of intertextual relationship not simply as a matter of technique but rather as a reflection of a basic theological assumption, namely, that the divine word given through the prophets is continuous, not discontinuous. This means that Yhwh speaks consistently even when the particularities of human history change. As perhaps the most famous example of this practice in a prophetic text puts it, "The grass withers, the bloom drops when Yhwh's wind blows on it. Surely the people is grass. The grass withers, the bloom drops. But our God's word remains forever" (Isa 40:7–8).

Conclusion

In conclusion, the prophetic books vary among themselves in the date of their composition, their interpretations of historical events, and their theological approaches to the future of their implied audiences. Yet they also share common approaches to problems. The later texts, especially in the Book of the Twelve, quote earlier ones, sometimes at length. And most of all, these works share a common conviction that the tragedies of the past need not define the future.

Perhaps most significantly, these texts have enjoyed a long afterlife of interpretation. In Christian circles, the prophetic texts came to be understood as witnesses to Jesus's work as the suffering servant (as in Isaiah) who brings in the new era (as in Jeremiah) for those who trust God (as in Habakkuk). For Jews, too, the prophets speak of Yhwh's desire for the people's well-being in an often hostile world. As will become clearer in the next few chapters, the rich history of interpretation of these texts arises out of the texts themselves, for their suggestiveness, their open-ended hopefulness for their future, and their own habit of returning to old images with new associations of meanings, all of which make them the sort of texts that can be reused in new situations.

THE PROPHETS AS PEOPLE

Most scholarship on Israelite prophecy in the past few decades has bracketed the question of the prophets as either individuals or sociological types. This fact often surprises newcomers to biblical studies because of Western culture's fascination with individual lives (or put less charitably, our voyeurism) and with group psychology. The truth is, however, that evidence for individual prophets remains very sparse. Biography was not a primary interest of the biblical texts themselves, and no other evidence for ancient Israelite prophets exists. Still, a few things can be said:

1. Both men and women could be prophets. The fact that only male prophets have biblical books named for them should not mislead one into thinking that the role was gender-specific. It may be that the accumulation of disciples who wrote down oracles was a particularly male enterprise.
2. Some early prophets (Elijah, Elisha) were miracle workers, while later prophets were not.
3. Prophecy functions socially to revitalize the culture. Therefore, the prophets were often respected or even feared, but equally often opposed, especially by the powerful.
4. When the biblical texts do preserve biographical information, it always serves some larger theological purpose and therefore offers little psychological insight into the individual prophets concerned.
5. Prophecy became at some point a scribal phenomenon, involving writers producing books, and most of the evidence really concerns the attitudes of the circles producing these books, often several generations after the prophets they revere.

Notes

1. David Noel Freedman, *Divine Commitment and Human Obligation*, vol. 1: *Ancient Israelite History and Religion* (Grand Rapids: Eerdmans, 1997), 504.

2. Text in Herbert Donner and Wolfgang Röllig, *Kanaanäische und Aramäische Inschriften*, 5th ed. (Wiesbaden: Harrassowitz, 2002), 5, col. 1, lines 12–14 (author's translation).

3. Translation from Martti Nissinen, *References to Prophecy in Neo-Assyrian Sources* (Helsinki: Neo-Assyrian Text Corpus Project, 1998), 35.

For Further Reading

Barton, John. *Oracles of God: Perceptions of Ancient Prophecy in Israel after the Exile.* Oxford: Oxford University Press, 2007.
Day, John, ed. *Prophecy and the Prophets in Ancient Israel.* New York: T. & T. Clark, 2010.
Olyan, Saul, ed. *Social Theory and the Study of Israelite Religion.* Atlanta: SBL, 2012.
Overholt, Thomas. *Channels of Prophecy: The Social Dynamics of Prophetic Activity.* Minneapolis: Fortress, 1989.

24 Isaiah, the Prophet of Salvation

Key Text: *You will gaze upon the king in his beauty. You will see the land from far away.* (Isa 33:17)

The book of Isaiah contains some of the most famous prophetic texts in the Old Testament, and some of the most misunderstood. Its call to "beat swords into plowshares and spears into pruning hooks" (Isa 2:4), its promise that "every valley shall be exalted" (Isa 40:4), and its depiction of the Suffering Servant (Isa 52:13–53:12) have all entered the popular mind. Sometimes called the "Fifth Gospel," the book has inspired both Christian and Jewish readers for centuries with its visions of Yhwh's transformation of the world into a more verdant and peaceful place.

The book articulates this vision against the backdrop of sweeping historical change. The earliest events described in the book date to the 730s BCE, when the old system of small states in Syria-Palestine yielded to the regionwide Assyrian Empire. Other historical moments that appear in the book include Sennacherib's invasion of 701 BCE, the rise of the Babylonian Empire at the end of the seventh century, and the return of the deportees from Babylon in the 530s subsequent to Cyrus the Great's decree allowing such repatriations. In other words, the book wrestles with at least two centuries of political change: warfare, subjugation, intimations of renewed independence, and the dashing of such hopes or rather their transference to the more distant future. Broadly speaking, chs

1–39 speak of the eighth or seventh centuries, and 40–66 of the sixth and fifth centuries or later.

This fact immediately leads to the consideration of two closely related questions: When was the book written, and how do its interactions with history relate to one another and to the prophet for whom the book was named?

As already noted, dating prophetic texts is difficult because they all contain material from diverse sources, both from the named prophet and from his disciples and their disciples. Isaiah is particularly difficult, but since the late eighteenth century scholars have recognized that since the parts of the book discuss different eras, and that the texts do not speak of the later periods as events of the distant future but of the present, and that the book contains different literary styles, the most elegant solution is to think of Isaiah as coming from several hands. In the nineteenth century, scholars began to speak of First Isaiah (the eighth-century BCE prophet), Second Isaiah (from the mid- to late-sixth century BCE), and Third Isaiah (a few decades later, the late sixth through fifth/early fourth centuries BCE), and to assign to them chapters 1–39, 40–55, and 56–66 respectively. This basic division is usually associated with the German scholar Bernhard Duhm and his contemporaries.

A number of conservative scholars opposed this viewpoint, arguing that since Isa 1:1 seems to claim a single author for the book, and since the New Testament and early Jewish tradition assume a single author, and since nothing prevents a real prophet from predicting the future, there is no basis for attributing the book to three or more writers. This viewpoint does not, however, seem convincing because the theory of multiple authors does not depend on a theory of prophetic inspiration but on simple analysis of texts and the belief that they must have been intelligible to their earliest readers, not cryptic messages awaiting the proper spiritual code-breaking processes. The impasse between these two viewpoints might seem unbreakable because the two approaches depend on different assumptions.

In more recent scholarship, however, a way past the impasse has presented itself. While the more economical explanation of the evidence seems to be that Isaiah was written over a period of centuries, it is not a jumble of texts. Later authors interacted with earlier ones in detail, preserving the older words, commenting on them, augmenting them, and putting them to new uses. Similar images appear repeatedly as a way of ensuring that the prophetic texts remained relevant over time.

COHERENCE THROUGH RECURRING THEMES

A number of examples of reworking older texts or themes recur in Isaiah. For example, in its world predating the Industrial Revolution's radical degradation of the environment, the book of Isaiah can speak of the peace-filled human life in the context of the beauties of nature. The book is filled with nature imagery of several kinds. For example, Isa 5:1–7 offers a love song about a vineyard which Yhwh plants, but which goes awry:

Let me sing about my beloved, a song about my beloved's vineyard.
My beloved had a vineyard in Horn-of-Oil's Child.

He dug out the stones and planted it with vines,
Built a tower in the middle of it and hewed a wine press for it.
Then he waited for it to make grapes, but it made sour grapes.
The house of Israel is Yhwh's vineyard.

This creative adaptation of a love song for a purpose completely alien to the genre's normal purposes (which is after all, to celebrate love and maybe induce someone to love the singer) gives the reader a jolt. Why did nature fail the farmer? Why did Israel fail God?

Isa 27:2–5 picks up the imagery of the vineyard again by noting that

On that day—sing about a pleasant vineyard.
I, Yhwh, keep it, water it at the right times,
So no one can raid it, I watch it night and day.

The poem continues with an interpretation in v. 6: "Someday, Jacob will take root. Israel will bud and flower." Isa 27 thus marks a reversal of Isa 5, a clear case of a poet turning the older oracle on its head while still honoring the older material. The reader of both poems must recognize the choices facing both Yhwh and Israel, the alternatives of evil and good, of doom and hope.

The book has already prepared the reader for this alteration of the imagery in some ways, because it had already referred to vineyards nonmetaphorically in Isa 3:14's indictment, "Yhwh comes in judgment against the elders of his people and its nobles, 'you have burned the vineyard—the plunder from the poor is in your houses,'" a text critical of the abuse of power.

Yet the imagery does not stop here, for at the end of the book, a final resolution is reached as Isa 65:21 anticipates a day in which the future prosperity of the people means that "they have built houses and lived in them, planted vineyards and eaten their fruit." A similar image, used in a different, more hopeful way.

The web of nature imagery hardly ends there. Thus Isa 6:13 imagines a stump sprouting a new tree, which turns out to be Israel itself, or in a different interpretation in Isa 11:1, a future king. Isaiah 40–55 repeatedly uses images of water-loving plants growing in areas now desert (Isa 41:18–19; 44:3–4; 45:8; 51:3, 11), and such imagery continues also later in the book (Isa 58:11; 61:3; 66:14), as well as appearing earlier (e.g., Isa 35:1–2). It appears at climactic moments, such as in Isa 55:10–11, the dramatic conclusion of a major section of the book. Meditating on the power of the prophetic word,, the text says that

Just as the rain or snow fall from the sky
And does not return there [i.e., evaporate] without watering the ground,
And making it give life and sprout and produce seed for the sower and
    bread for food,
So it is with my word coming from my mouth. It will not return to me useless.
No, it will do what I want and succeed at what I have sent it for.

References to nature describe, then, both human flourishing and the divine work in the world. Yhwh's work is not static or easily predictable, but like the world of nature, it teems with life and offers Israel hope for rejuvenation—like a tree or a vineyard or a dry valley about to receive rain.

As it stands, the book of Isaiah consists of the following major sections:

A. A call to reform (Isa 1:1–12:6)
B. An announcement of Yhwh's judgment on the nations (Isa 13:1–23:18)
C. The aftermath of judgment: a reordering of the world (Isa 24:1–27:13)
D. Further calls to reform and promises of renewal (Isa 28:1–39:8)
E. Announcements of restoration (Isa 40:1–55:13)
F. Postrestoration challenges (Isa 56:1–66:24)

The book shows evidence of intentional organization and a clear plot movement. It places in tension depictions of two possible worlds, one of doom and the other of hope. The juxtaposition of these two potential realities creates a third dimension of the book, one evoking human response. Each section contributes to the plot's progression, as the drama of Israel's history unfolds.

THE CALL TO REFORM (ISA 1:1–12:6)

The first section of Isaiah contains extensive material from the eighth century BCE prophet himself, though the final shaping of the material may owe something to later hands. Like the works attributed to Isaiah's contemporaries Hosea, Amos, and Micah, this section of the book follows an identifiable literary pattern in which criticism of Israel and calls for its repentance give way in time to promises of national renewal. This pattern, doom to hope or threat to promise, did not arise by accident, nor was it simply a literary device. Rather, it reflected a basic conception of how prophetic speech should be presented. The reader or hearer of the text faces a choice between two courses of action, one a commitment to oppression and the other commitment to moral integrity. A theological conception thus underlies the literary structure.

And so it is with Isa 1–12, which lays out the major tension that must be resolved in the book: the contrast between obedience to Yhwh and disobedience. It does so by stating both the problem and the solution in epistemic terms:

The ox knows its owner and the donkey its master's trough.
Israel does not know, my people does not comprehend (Isa 1:3)

and

Listen to Yhwh's word, Sodom's leaders (Isa 1:10)

and

"Come, and let's decide," says Yhwh.
"However red your sins, they will be white as snow,
though they be dyed crimson, they will be fulled like wool. (Isa 1:18)

In other words, the prophetic text assumes bad faith on the part of its audience, but it also hopes for revived clear thinking and a moral life attentive to the "the Torah of our God" (Isa 1:10). Such a life avoids oppressing the poor, creating hypocritical religious practices, or following irresponsible leaders ("Your nobles are strayers, bands of thieves / all of them love a bribe and pursue graft" [Isa 1:23]). Isaiah 1 thus sets the problem of the book. It presents the entire work as a sort of warning whose minatory nature inspires the reader to seek relief.

> Isaiah 2:1 presents a new introduction—"the word that Isaiah son of Amoz saw regarding Judah and Jerusalem"—a phrase that may come from an earlier level of the book prior to the inclusion of ch 1 and parallel to the similar "visions" in Obadiah, Nahum, and Habakkuk (who use the same Hebrew root *ḥāzâ*).

Then, chs 2–12 move the reader toward that relief, but not in a simple way. In any case, these chapters show a clear progression from the doom oracles of Isa 2:2–5:30 (except 4:2–6, which seems to be a later expansion or any rate an aside from the main point) to the soaring promises of hope in Isa 9:1–12:6. The transition comes in the middle subsection, Isa 6:1–8:23, which contains biographical material about Isaiah and his family as well as extended meditations on the nature of the prophet's task.

Curiously, this middle section describes the earliest parts of Isaiah's work, his call and key encounters with reluctant recipients of his oracles. It would have made perfect sense for the book to have begun with ch 6, the story of Isaiah's call to prophesy, had the intention of the book's creator been primarily historical. Clearly, the intention was something else, namely, to create a web of oracles that would transition the reader's mood from despair to elation, without creating the illusion that all was well in the present.

So, chs 2–12 consists of three major subsections. The first opens with a beautiful oracle of hope:

In times to come, the mount of Yhwh's temple will be secure,
As the highest peak of the range, the highest hill,
And all nations will flow to it.
Yes, many peoples will come and say,
"Come, let us ascend Yhwh's mount, the temple of Jacob's God.
For we will walk his paths and go on his roads."
For from Zion comes instruction to many peoples,
Yhwh's word from Jerusalem.
Yes, he will judge among nations, decide among many peoples,
And so they will beat their swords into plowshares and their spears into pruning hooks.
Nations will not raise the sword against each other, nor learn war again. (Isa 2:2–4)

This stunning vision of the future must await a resolution of current crises, however. The rest of Isa 2–5 immediately turns away from the bright future to the gloomy present. Verse

5 introduces a call to repentance with the cry, "O house of Jacob, come and let us walk in Yhwh's light." The hope oracle thus functions ironically, not as a description of an easily realizable goal but as an indictment of the present.

After this opening salvo of criticism and call for reform, Isa 6:1–8:23 tells the story of the prophet's call and some characteristic speeches. This section is sometimes called the Isaiah Memoir or *Denkschrift* (really a sort of memo book, a name it acquired in the 1920s from the work of Karl Budde) because it contains almost the only biographical material on the eighth-century prophet. From this text, several parts of his life become clear: he had contacts at the top of Judah's society (King Ahaz), enjoyed access to the temple (as a priest?), was married to an unnamed woman who also was a prophet, and had several children to whom he gave symbolic names.

As part of this biographical sketch, Isa 6 reports a theophany during which Isaiah saw not only Yhwh but also the terrifying heavenly court (the seraphim apparently being something like the flying cobras that appear in Egyptian art). Though sensitive to his own inadequacy for the task of prophecy, like Moses and Jeremiah, he accepts the call. Protestation of unworthiness was apparently a primary proof of suitability for prophethood in such call narratives.

An important aspect of his call lay in its assumptions about the responses of the audience. No audience, no prophetic work! But Isa 6:9–10 indicate that his audience would "listen carefully but not comprehend, look intently but not know," while Isaiah himself would "fatten up this people's heart and weigh down its ears and paste over its eyes." As earlier in the book, an epistemic problem exists for Judah: they cannot discern the correct life path. But the prophet's immediate task is not to clarify matters but to obscure them. As in the story of Micaiah ben Imlah (1 Kgs 22), the recipients of the prophetic message have drifted so far into their rejection of Yhwh that here—for the book of Isaiah and its creators (and Yhwh!)—it no longer makes sense to communicate with them transparently.

This puzzling text makes more sense as a summary of the entire career of the prophet and a commentary on the early reception of the prophetic work. It points the reader to the later parts of the book, especially chs 40–55, in which a new generation encountering the prophetic message may hear what their ancestors did not.

The Isaiah Memoir does not wait for this later generation, however. It recounts an event during the Syro-Ephraimitic War (ca. 734–732 BCE), in which Israel and Aram (Damascus) attempted to overthrow Ahaz of Judah in order to secure their southern flank in a war against Assyria. Isaiah counsels Ahaz to be still and wait for divine deliverance, but the king decides instead to ally himself with the Mesopotamian superpower. This policy decision proves to be a tragic mistake in the long run, for it invited foreign domination, a theme that most of Isa 7–8 explores in detail.

IMMANUEL AND OTHER NAMES

Isaiah 7–8 contain several symbolic names that speak of Judah's future. Immanuel ("God is with us"), Shear-yashuv ("a remnant shall return"), and Maher-shalal-hash-baz ("hasten the loot, hurry the prey") are all names that bespeak Isaiah's outlook on his people's future. On the one hand destruction awaits, but on the other hand some will survive. As with Hosea's children (Hos 1–3), the naming of these boys is a prophetic sign act, an activity that conveys a message similar to those related in the prophet's oracles.

The most complex name is that of Immanuel. The Gospel of Matthew (Matt 1:23) relates Isa 7:14 to the birth of Jesus, which it sees as the quintessential token of God's presence with Israel. Then, Isa 8:4 understands Isa 7:15–17, the description of the childhood developmental stages of Immanuel, as a reference to the life of Isaiah's son Maher-shalal-hash-baz. For Matthew and his Jewish contemporaries, no prophecy had only one referent in the real world. It might have several because Yhwh's superintendence of the world, seen most dramatically in the work of the Messiah, operated consistently and repetitively, revealed sometimes through intimations of sublimity and sometimes right out in the open.

The third part of the opening unit of Isaiah, Isa 9:1–12:6, makes the turn toward a hopeful future, delayed though it must be by Judah's current unfaithfulness. These chapters contain a mix of two types of text. The first sort describes the calamities of Assyrian invasion in 701 BCE, when Sennacherib destroyed most of Judah (an event commemorated in his monumental reliefs of the siege of Lachish). These sections include Isa 9:7–10:19 (ET 9:8–10:19) and 10:28–34 (ET 10:27b–34).

Wrapping around these descriptions of tragic events are statements of hope. Isaiah 9:1–7, 10:20–27, and 11:1–16 all speak of renewal postinvasion. Isaiah 9 uses the language of the royal court, probably from the coronation ceremony itself if the similarities between this text and Egyptian parallels are any indication, to speak of a coming king who will bring about "endless peace on David's throne and over his kingdom" (Isa 9:6 [ET 9:7]) and exert control over the devastated provinces of the Northern Kingdom of Israel (Zebulon and Naphtali in Isa 8:23 [ET 9:1]). Isaiah 11 returns to the royal imagery by depicting a scion of the Davidic family as one who will rule wisely (Isa 11:1–2), revisiting older royal ideas about the ideal just ruler (cf. Pss 2; 101).

In Isa 11:6–9, this idyllic future age takes on the image of the "peaceable kingdom." Throwing all real-world experiences to the wind, the prophet expects a complete overhaul not just of politics but of the created order itself. In this new world,

> The wolf will sojourn with the lamb, the leopard will sprawl out with the kid,
> The calf and the lion cub and the fatling together, and a child shall lead them. (Isa 9:6–9)

The innocence of childhood combines with visions of newly vegetarian top predators to form a field of images in which "knowledge of Yhwh" leads to the complete absence of violence and suffering (hence the opposite of the reality faced by the survivors of the 701 BCE invasion).

This essay at survivor literature, some of the earliest in world history, concludes in ch 12 with a hymn to be sung after the return of exiles from the Assyrian deportations. By using language more at home in the book of Psalms and thus in the Temple in Jerusalem, Isa 12:1–6 forms a fitting conclusion for a work that like the constituent works in the Book of the Twelve Minor Prophets sought to move readers from awareness of their present danger hope for their future. "Praise Yhwh, invoke his name. Report his deeds among the peoples, extol his exalted name"—this call to praise addresses Isaiah's eighth-century audience, but it must have found fuller meaning for later readers of the book experiencing Judah's subservience to Assyria and, even later, its destruction by Babylonia. Isaiah 12 points forward to the moment of redemption celebrated by the poems of Isa 34–35 and 40–55, the so-called Second Isaiah.

AN ANNOUNCEMENT OF YHWH'S JUDGMENT ON THE NATIONS (ISA 13:1–23:18)

Before moving to such words of renewal, the book shifts into a unit of oracles against the nations. (Such texts also appear in Jer 46–51, Ezek 25–32, Amos 1–2, Zeph 2, and the entire books of Obadiah and Nahum.) Commenting on the evil ways and just deserts of Israel's neighbors was a standard part of the prophetic repertoire, or at least of the literary shaping of prophetic books. Nor should this be too surprising, since other ancient thinkers also placed political realities in a theological context (as in the Egyptian so-called Execration Texts from the early second millennium BCE and Assyrian royal reliefs a millennium later).

And yet, the oracles in Isa 13–23 have a different purpose from these parallels. The Isaiah texts do not exalt Israel or Judah vis-à-vis other societies. Rather, the oracles against the nations are part of the book's critique of the entire known human race and the ways in which social evils occur within power structures. The prophets see their world as an interrelated whole, subject to the rule of Yhwh.

This world consists of Babylon (Isa 13:1–22; 14:4–23; and 21:1–10), Assyria (Isa 14:24–27), Philistia (Isa 14:28–32), Moab (Isa 15:1–16:14), Damascus (Isa 17:1–14), Kush (i.e., Sudan; Isa 18:1–7), Egypt (Isa 19:1–25), Dumah (i.e., Edom; Isa 21:11–12), the Arava (now Jordan or northwest Saudi Arabia; Isa 21:13–17), Jerusalem and Judah (Isa 22:1–22), and Tyre (or Sidon, depending on how one sorts the evidence of the super-scription and the rest of the text; Isa 23:1–18). The details of the visions are interesting, but more striking is the sequence in which they are arranged. The order does not follow an obvious cartographic sequence, arranged as it is reads a bit like a military campaign (including the return to Babylon as a base of operations in Isa 21:1–10) since it follows the main north-south roads, the coastal road or Via Maris, and the interior road or Way of the King. Is this arrangement merely a coincidence, or does it reflect some purpose?

Also puzzling is the minimal attention to the most significant power in Isaiah's world, Assyria. While Isa 14:24–27 does expect Assyrian expulsion from Israel, the relative brevity of this oracle seems odd given Assyria's prominence in chs 2–12. Some scholars have argued that ch 14 may have originally denounced Assyria, with a later modification of the oracle updating it to reflect the rise of the Babylonian Empire. It is also possible to explain the oracles against the nations as a collection reaching its final form after fall of Assyria, hence later than Isaiah's time.

Whatever the precise origins of the individual oracles, from a theological point of view they meld two historical settings: the campaigns of Sennacherib against the southern Levant in 701 BCE, and the successive campaigns of Nebuchadnezzar a century or so later. Isaiah 21:2 might even refer to the destruction of Babylonia by Iranian groups (although it may refer to earlier struggles with the same groups).

The primarily theological viewpoint becomes clear in the way the oracles depict the characters in the drama they construct. In several cases, the ruler of the criticized state personifies his country, and this ruler always assumes the role of the enemy king, a stock character in ancient Near Eastern texts who is always impious, foolish, and ultimately unsuccessful. So the king of Babylon has "fallen from heaven like the Day Star" (Isa 14:12; this verse became the basis of the Lucifer figure in later interpretation), while the Pharaoh of Egypt is surrounded by foolish counselors pretentiously claiming to be "a wise man, scion of ancient kings" (Isa 19:11). In most cases these oracles simply describe the collapse of the state in question.

Yet there is another character here, and another horizon of history. Yhwh, for these oracles, not only superintends the tragedy but also reverses fortunes. Thus in one of the most startling texts in Isaiah or anywhere else in the Bible, Isa 19:18–25 anticipates the location of Canaanite-speakers (i.e., people from Palestine and its immediate environs) in cities in Egypt, the building of a Yhwh temple in Egypt, and the conjoining of Assyria, Egypt, and Israel as three entities coequal in Yhwh's site.

This vision seems to fit ill with a set of texts condemning foreign nations, yet it does match the overall theological profile of these chapters. All nations, including Israel—especially Israel—both fall under divine judgment and experience divine mercy. A just ruler, especially a just God, can do nothing else.

THE NATIONS IN THE BOOK OF ISAIAH

The book of Isaiah often refers to the "nations" (Hebrew: *gōyîm*). Sometimes the nations are friendly seekers of Israel's well-being or searchers for Yhwh's revelation (Isa 2:2, 4; 11:10; 43:9; 55:5; 60:3; 62:2). Sometimes they engage in hostile acts toward Israel (Isa 30:28; 40:15, 17; 60:12; 64:1; 66:18). And sometimes they suffer from the predations of other nations (Isa 10:7; 14:6; cf. 45:1). In short, the book finds complexity in the world and seeks a complex theological explanation for it.

THE AFTERMATH OF JUDGMENT: A REORDERING
OF THE WORLD (ISA 24:1–27:13)

This universalism takes concrete expression in the next section, which is closely related to the oracles against the nations. Isaiah 24–27 are often called the "Isaiah Apocalypse" because the text refers to a worldwide elimination of evil and a reversal of fortune for the oppressed captives of Israel. And, in truth, some of the language of these chapters does appear in later apocalyptic literature (e.g., Isa 25:8's "then shall the lord Yhwh wipe away the tear from every face and remove his people's disgrace from all the land, for Yhwh has spoken" is quoted in Rev 7:17 and 21:4). Yet the phrase "apocalyptic" is a bit misleading here, for these chapters do not speak of the end of time (whatever that is) but of a turning point in the present world, the dawning of a new era of peace.

Isaiah 24–27 envision a new era without the political abuse caused by the abandonment of Yhwh's instructions (Hebrew: *tôrôt*; Isa 24:5). At the crisis moment, Yhwh will "punish the army of the heights on the heights and the kings of the earth on the earth" (Isa 27:21) a reference to human rulers and their gods ("the army of the heights"), whom Yhwh will overthrow (cf. Ps 82). This shaking-up of the political world will take place on a cosmic scale, symbolized by the defeat of the ancient chaos monsters Leviathan (Isa 27:1 speaks of this creature in its several forms). That is, the book of Isaiah understands political change as more than merely a trading of one ruler or empire for another but as something deeper, a real sea change in how the world functions.

Replacing these old structures will be ones in which "all the peoples" gather for a party on Mount Zion (Isa 25:6), and in which "the ones who perished in the land of Assyria or driven off to the land of Egypt" (Isa 27:13) will be reunited in their ancestral homeland. In other words, Isa 24–27 anticipates a significant reordering of the ethnographic makeup of the Near East, a shift in its religion from the honor of the gods of empires to veneration of the deliverer deity Yhwh, and a shift from want to plenty.

On this last point, Isa 25:6 reveals an important dimension of the text's expectations for its audiences: "Yhwh of hosts will make a feast of rich [literally, fatty] foods for all the peoples on this mountain, a feast of fine wines and marrow-filled marbled meat and well-strained wine." This reference to rich food may seem odd to modern people accustomed to the wide selection of food in grocery stores. But the reference fits a different context, which can be well illustrated by a modern parallel. In the "foreword" to his great work, *The Gulag Archipelago*, Aleksandr Solzhenitsyn describes a newspaper report of a discovery of frozen prehistoric salamanders. According to the paper, the concentration camp inmates who found them "ate them with relish." He writes that while ordinary readers could not have understood the story, he and his fellow inmates, *zeks* in the memorable Russian vocabulary,

> . . . understood instantly. We could picture the scene right down to the smallest details: how those present broke up the ice in frenzied haste; how, flouting the higher claims of ichthyology and elbowing each other to be first, they tore off chunks of the prehistoric flesh and hauled them over to the bonfire to thaw them out and bolt them down.[1]

Hungry, tortured human beings cannot be indifferent to moments of plenty, even in the form of creatures frozen for millennia. And so it is here: the eschatological focus of

Isa 24–27 addresses a community of people for whom deprivation is normal. As a people that understands itself as marginalized, the Israel imagined in these chapters awaits Yhwh's initiative in reversing the sentences of the oracles against the nations in Isa 13–23.

FURTHER CALLS TO REFORM AND PROMISES OF RENEWAL (ISA 28:1–39:8)

The following major section is perhaps the most loosely integrated in Isaiah, but it does continue the overall approach of the final form of the book, the practice of balancing oracles of doom and despair with those of hope. In all likelihood, the loose structure reflects the way in which the various subunits came into the book, for at an earlier stage the book may have ended in ch 33, after a resolution of the tension between doom and hope with the announcement of Yhwh's kingship, hence the divine care for the world's history in general, and Israel's in particular:

> Your eyes shall behold the king in his loveliness; you will see a land from far
>   Away...
> For Yhwh has judged us, Yhwh has legislated for us,
> Yhwh is our king. Yhwh is our savior. (Isa 33:17, 22)

Isa 34–39 seem to have entered the book later, but at different times. Isaiah 36–39 are almost identical to 2 Kgs 18–20 (the story of the reign of Hezekiah) and contain the same reworkings of the story that occurred during the reign of Josiah, while chs 34–35 closely resemble Isa 40–55 and therefore come from an even later stage of the book. The crucial point is not the process through which the various oracles came to be part of the book of Isaiah, but how they function in its final form.

The overall unit has three subunits. The first, Isa 28:1–33:24, consists of (1) five "woe" oracles describing the fate of the people of Israel (each starting with "woe" or "alas" [28:1; 29:1; 29:15; 30:1; and 31:1]), plus (2) a brilliantly executed oracle hoping for a human king who will "reign in righteousness" alongside "nobles leading justly" (Isa 32:1), and then (3) the concluding announcement of Yhwh's kingship.

The second subunit, Isa 34–35, describes the destruction of the imperial structure oppressing Israel as "Yhwh's day of vengeance" (Isa 34:8), which paves the way for a post-catastrophe utopia in which "the steppe and the wasteland shall celebrate, and the desert rejoice and blossom" (Isa 35:1). As one scholar recently put it, "human regeneration is envisioned in vegetative terms."[2]

And the third subsection, Isa 36–39, again, recounts a series of events during the reign of Hezekiah at the end of the seventh century BCE, including most notoriously his collaboration with the Babylonians in their failed revolt against Assyria.

What do all these diverse literary materials have to do with each other? A key clue lies in chs 36–39, which mention both Assyria (the imperial foe in Isa 1–33) and Babylonia (the foe in Isa 40–55). In other words, the story of Hezekiah and the ambassadors of the Babylonian ruler Marduk-apla-iddina II (the biblical Merodach-baladan) in Isa 39 foreshadows the victories of a later king, Nebuchadnezzar, over Judah. Yet even more importantly, these chapters, and arguably all of Isa 28–39, tie up the first part of the book, which focuses upon the deafness of Israel to the prophetic message (as stated by the prophetic call narrative in Isa 6). This unit of the book justifies Yhwh's decision to allow the kingdoms of Israel and Judah to fall to successive Mesopotamian empires. In doing so, it portrays Yhwh as a sovereign whose decisions to judge or show mercy shape time and the fate of nations.[3]

ANNOUNCEMENTS OF RESTORATION (ISA 40:1–55:13)

If ch 39 ends on a gloomy note, the turn to scherzo in ch 40 comes as a dramatic turn. In some of the most gorgeous poetry in the entire Bible, the book of Isaiah introduces a series of voices announcing

> "Console, console my people," says your God.
> Speak to Jerusalem's heart and say to her
> That her enlistment is complete, her transgression paid off,
> That she has received from Yhwh the full price of all her sins.
> A voice cries, "In the steppe prepare Yhwh's road.
> Grade a highway in the desert for our God." (Isa 40:1–3)

The text then turns, first in one voice and then in another, to a discussion about the imminent appearance of divine salvation as a keeping of the ancient promises and an undoing of current tragic structures of being.

Isaiah 40 reintroduces the theme of the prophetic word, which "remains forever" (Isa 40:8), returning to an idea from the prophetic call narrative of ch 6. Now, however, the word finds a ready audience among those who have experienced the Babylonian deportations and the resulting cultural dislocation. The theme of the divine word also appears in Isa 55, forming with ch 40 an inclusio and thus demarcating a coherent literary unit. This unit resolves the tension between doom and hope, seen throughout chs 1–39, in favor of hope.

The speeches of these chapters repeat a group of themes including (1) the contrast between the dismal past and the bright future (Isa 41:4, 22; 44:6); (2) the role of Israel as servant (Isa 41:8; 42:19); (3) the return of the exiles (Isa 41:9; 43:16–28); (4) the joy of those returning (Isa 41:13–16; 42:10; 43:1, 21; 44:5, 21–22); (5) the transformation of nature as a sign of deliverance (Isa 41:18–20); (6) the creativity of God (Isa 42:5; 43:1; 44:23; 45:7, 11–12); (7) Israel's mission to the nations (Isa 42:6; 49:1–6); (8) the reliability of God (Isa 41:4; 42:18; 43:8–12; 45:6); (9) the folly of idolatry (Isa 40; 41; 44:9); and (10) the importance of collective memory in shaping the future (Isa 44:21). As always in the book of Isaiah, the various themes backstop each other. So, for example, it is not enough to speak of the obvious joy refugees would experience on returning home. These texts hear the swaying of tree branches as applause for the deliverance of a people recreated (Isa 55:12).

The intricate web of images and ideas begins and ends in much the same way. Isaiah 40 opens with a series of voices that speak of God's movement to forgive Israel and restart the story of their salvation by bringing about a new exodus. This new word (Isa 40:8), though countermanding the preceding words of condemnation, also closely relates to them. The God who speaks has consistently sought words that human beings need to hear so that they can grow as just, gracious people living in community with one another.

Isaiah 55 forms a bookend with this opening gambit. Here, the prophet boldly invites Israel to drink water in the desert, evoking the old stories of post-exodus wandering as a model for a new time of pioneering. He promises an "eternal covenant" (Isa 55:3) for all who "seek Yhwh while he may be found" (Isa 55:6). Then, using the analogy of life-giving rain that unfailingly refreshes the earth, he promises refreshment to a tired people. The clincher comes in Isa 55:11—God's word does not fail but brings life to all who listen. Thus the foreboding vision of a heedless people that we saw in ch 6 gives way to a new vision of a people who understand their own place in a new world.

Between these meditations on the ability of the prophetic word to transform a community lie many other poems. Consider, for example, Isa 43:22–28. After the stunning announcement that God has re-created Israel as a people, the prophet asks why would a God who wished to bring about justice in the world through a particular people, but then found those very people uncooperative, at last return to them as the vehicle of grace?

This question seems to have bothered the prophet, because many parts of Isa 40–55 spend time rehabilitating the image of Israel as the servant (e.g., Isa 41:8; 42:19; 49:1–6; 52:13–53:12). A humiliated people must learn a deeper way of understanding the divine-human relationship. Quoting God, the prophet insists

> You did not bring me a sheep for your holocaust offering, and you did not honor me with your sacrifice. Nor did I put you to work for the sake of a gift or trouble you for frankincense.... Rather, you put me to work by your sins and troubled me by your iniquities. (Isa 43:23–24)

This comment on Israel's past sums it up as a time in which religion could not mask the deep fault lines in the culture. In the back of the prophet's mind lurks the question: On what basis, then, could the relationship with God proceed?

The answer comes in v. 25: "I, I am the one who blots out your transgressions for my own sake; indeed, your sins I will not remember." That is, the God whom sacrifices by evil people could not placate is the same God who could turn in mercy to the suffering of Israel.

A text like this presupposes deep moral reflection on the relationship of Israel to other human beings, the competition that comes from other views of the divine-human relationship, and the psychology of men and women who wish to be spiritually and morally mature. On the first point, Isa 40–55 makes two moves: chs 44–45 give divine sanction for the Persian Empire to the extent that its founder, Cyrus the Great, relieves the suffering of vulnerable people, Israel in particular. Then, again, the prophet also reflects on the role of Israel as servant. The servant must be a "light to the nations" (Isa 49:6) and thus fulfill the goal of blessing the nations that was part of the promise to Abraham (see Gen 12:3) and of the ongoing reflection on the exodus event.

On the second point, these chapters speak repeatedly of the folly of idolatry, arguing that a deity who can be represented by a human artifact lacks the basic qualities of God. The prophet is not a cold rationalist who asks the simple question: How can wood be a god? Rather, he assumes that any being worthy of the name "God" must be able to act and to speak on behalf of human beings. A vaguely benign attitude toward humankind is not enough: God must act. Anything else would be a severe limit to such a being and would make it unworthy of worship.

On the third point, the prophet recognizes the audience's sorrow and fear. Years of living precariously on the edges of Babylonian society have scarred them. The apparent utter failure of their religion, destroyed by the invasion of the Babylonian superpower, has impoverished them spiritually as well. And so we have a text like ch 49 with its exhortations to courage or the meditation in ch 53 on the redemptive possibilities of suffering. Hence, also, the repeated calls to rejoicing (Isa 41:16), singing (Isa 42:10), and the old traditional injunction "do not be afraid" (Isa 41:13–14; 43:1). The prophet asks them not to be afraid precisely because they were afraid.

POSTRESTORATION CHALLENGES (ISA 56:1–66:24)

Yet fearlessness is not enough. The final part of Isaiah seeks to construct a nonutopian vision of the world by encasing the soaring ideals of Isa 40–55 in a sober analysis of the real challenges facing the postexilic community. It does so by constructing the three large clusters of oracles as a triptych. The subunits are Isa 56:1–59:21, 60:1–62:12, and 63:1–66:24, with the outside sections assembling poems either depicting the destruction of some problematic social or political reality or calling the audience to repentance, much in the manner of Isa 1–39. Meanwhile, the middle section contains hope oracles reminiscent of Isa 40–55.

Isa 56 opens with a call to righteousness, not just to the Israelite survivors of exile but also to foreigners who have joined them. Since Isa 2:2–4's hope that gentiles would come to Zion for instruction has come true in the postexilic community, the text here addresses the important question of communal identity. Membership in the community is determined, according to Isa 56, not by genetics alone but by a willingness to adhere to basic moral requirements and to observe the Sabbath and complete key sacrifices. The most surprising part of this text is not just the openness to gentiles, which appears in many parts of Isaiah, but the sense that eunuchs also have a place in the Temple. This in spite of Deut 23:1's prohibition of their presence in sacred space.

The larger discussion in Isa 56–59 involves the community's lack of social justice. We hear not only the lament that "the righteous perish and no one cares" (Isa 57:1) and the charge that "your sins divide you from your God" (Isa 59:2), but also detailed analysis of systematic cruelty:

> Your hands are covered in blood. You have sin up to your fingertips. Your lips speak a lie and your tongue utters wickedness. Nobody speaks righteously or renders a just decision. They trust nonsense and speak deception. They beget mischief and birth evil." (Isa 59:3–4)

In other words, the leaders of the people, who should defend the vulnerable, instead dodge their responsibilities.

It is tempting to dismiss this material as moralistic preaching or to reduce its moral arguments to a thin sociological analysis. In the latter scenario, one understands the situation described as the result of outside oppression (by the Persian overlords), a view that does appear in some biblical texts (e.g., Eccl 5:7–8 [ET 5:8–9]). But Isa 56–59 does not understand the problem as one at the imperial level.

Rather, these chapters argue, the moral problem lies in the behavior of the Israelite community, with its straitened circumstances offering no excuse for the violation of group solidarity. Utopia did not arrive with the return from Babylon, but to remain faithful to Yhwh the readers of the book must act in anticipation of its doing so.

The middle subunit, meanwhile, returns to the theme of the prophet as harbinger of a new era. With a rhetorical flavor reminiscent of chs 40–55, ch 60 invites the readers, personified as the feminine "you" (that is, the Hebrew pronoun is feminine and probably refers to Jerusalem) to "rise, shine, for your light has come and Yhwh's glory will shine upon you" (Isa 60:1). The dawning of Yhwh's light—a metaphor that draws on ancient Near Eastern images of the sun god as the protector of the weak, to be sure, but even more profoundly on the normal human fear of darkness and desire for light—attracts the gentiles to the reformed Israelite community and its manner of life.

To guarantee the efficacy of this turn to the light, ch 61 brings up yet again the role of the prophet as the bearer of Yhwh's word. Here, the spokesperson for the new era is one on whom Yhwh's spirit has fallen and who, therefore (always, therefore!) goes out to "proclaim parole to the captive, to dress the wounds of the heartbroken, to announce liberation to captives, to unfetter the prisoners, to announce the year of Yhwh's favor, and a day of settling accounts for our God, for having mercy on all who mourn" (Isa 61:1–2). This extraordinary proclamation of compassion "for Zion" (v. 3) states in brief the core vision of this last major part of Isaiah. The two bracketing subsections (chs 56–59 and 63–66) object so strenuously to the injustices of the moment because they envision an alternative world in which the oppressed enjoy basic dignity.

To round out this vision, the final section of the book (chs 63–66) returns to the vigorous challenges of the first part of the triptych (chs 56–59), including a condemnation of idolatry (Isa 65:1–16). But there is a difference. The final poems of the book announce the imminent arrival of a new era:

> Indeed, I am creating a new heaven and a new earth.
> The former things will not be remembered, nor taken to heart. (Isa 65:17)

The "former things" ordinarily in the book refer to the era before the Babylonian invasions, some of which continued even into the postexilic era. In other words, the deferral of the oft-promised glorious future will not continue indefinitely. Unlike later apocalyptic texts (such as the book of Revelation), the "new era" does not take place outside the realm of human history, but it does involve the change of normal human conditions, with extended lifespans (Isa 65:20) and a drop in childhood mortality (Isa 65:23).

As ch 66's criticism of some forms of Temple worship (i.e., the abuse of religion by divorcing it from moral commitments) makes clear, the hoped-for divine reordering of human affairs must await the future. It remains an aspiration, rather than a concrete reality.

Implications

To summarize, the book of Isaiah contains oracles written over several centuries but carefully integrated into a work dramatically emplotted to reflect both the course of Israel and Judah's history from the eighth to the fifth centuries BCE and a prophetic vision of alternative realities that Yhwh offered to a penitent, attentive people.

Throughout the book, in spite of many variations of literary genre, historical background, or even theological conceptions, several themes appear consistently. The most important of them is the book's radically theocentric viewpoint. As Israel's king and protector, Yhwh sends the prophetic spirit to analyze the flaws of human society, on a large or small scale, and to invite Israel to a better future. The book of Isaiah, which understands itself to preserve and transmit that prophetic legacy, offers this two-sided message of critique and invitation and preserves the creative tension between the two elements until its very end.

Perhaps an analogy from twentieth-century art is useful here. In 1937, as war clouds gathered over both Europe and eastern Asia, Frank Capra released a fantasy film called *Lost Horizon*. In it, James Conway, played by Ronald Colman, is kidnapped by the inhabitants of a paradise tucked away in the Himalayas. The inhabitants of the paradise, Shangri-la, live three times the normal human life expectancy and enjoy perfect health and happiness. They are served by happy local peasants while they pursue lives of contemplation and peace. Conway decides to leave behind his responsibilities at home in Britain, where he is slated to become foreign secretary, and become the leader of the paradise instead. There he will ride out the storm threatening civilization, awaiting the day when Shangri-la's wisdom will bless a chastened world.

Escape to such utopias always tempts people of conscience, like Conway. We do not wish to accept the mess of the world as the only possible option. Thus we seek a refuge from responsibilities we did not choose, persons we do not love, and choices we do not wish to make. Escape is tempting not just because life can be difficult but because our visions of the possible are so lofty that realizing them seems impossible. The book of Isaiah reminds its readers that escape never works because the darkness lies within. Patience during adversity, hope during tragedy, wisdom during changing times—these are the qualities that the book seeks to foster in its rich literary complexity.

Notes

1. Aleksandr Solzhenitsyn, *The Gulag Archipelago 1918–1956: An Experiment in Literary Investigation*, trans. Thomas P. Whitney. (New York: Harper & Row, 1973), ix.

2. Patricia Tull, "Persistent Vegetative States: People as Plants and Plants as People in Isaiah," in *The Desert Will Bloom: Poetic Visions in Isaiah*, ed. A. Joseph Everson and Hyun Chul Paul Kim (Atlanta: SBL, 2009), 27; for many other examples and their interrelationships, see Kirsten Nielsen, *There is Hope for a Tree: The Tree as Metaphor in Isaiah* (Sheffield: JSOT Press, 1989).

3. For a prolonged study of this material, especially chs 36–39, see Christopher R. Seitz, *Zion's Final Destiny: The Development of the Book of Isaiah, a Reassessment of Isaiah 36–39* (Minneapolis: Fortress, 1991).

For Further Reading

Berges, Ulrich F. *Isaiah: The Prophet and His Book*. Sheffield: Sheffield Phoenix, 2012.

Blenkinsopp, Joseph. *Opening the Sealed Book: Interpretations of the Book of Isaiah in Late Antiquity*. Grand Rapids: Eerdmans, 2006.

Childs, Brevard. *The Struggle to Understand Isaiah as Christian Scripture*. Grand Rapids: Eerdmans, 2004.

Everson, A. Joseph, and Hyun Chul Paul Kim, eds. *The Desert Will Bloom: Poetic Visions in Isaiah*. Atlanta: SBL, 2009.

25 Not Just a Weeping Prophet
JEREMIAH

> **Key Text:** *Yhwh extended his hand and touched my mouth. Then Yhwh said to me, "I am putting my word in your mouth. Notice, I am commissioning you to pluck, demolish, destroy, and damage, but also to build and plant.* (Jer 1:9–10)

If the darkness lies within, as the book of Isaiah seems to insist, then the exploration of that darkness poses challenges. The book of Jeremiah takes up just that task, committing itself both to observe the destruction of a society during the transition from the Assyrian to Babylonian Empires (late seventh and early sixth centuries BCE) and to lay out prospects of that society's renewal in time. The confusion of the period of Jeremiah and of the later decades in which the book bearing his name came together required a great effort at theological reflection.

No wonder, then, that the two words that come to mind for many readers of this book are "melancholy" and "jumbled." The prophet Jeremiah has gone down in history as the "weeping prophet," an unenviable reputation that emerges out of the book itself: it consists of a series of meditations on the doom of Judah at the hands of the Babylonians from the death of Josiah in 610 or 609 BCE to the years immediately after the destruction of Jerusalem by Nebuchadnezzar in 586 BCE. Its apparent jumbledness is a more complicated matter.

It is possible to outline the Hebrew (MT) book as follows:

Such an organization seems orderly enough, but it masks a greater degree of turbulence within the text itself. The book is, at times, difficult to follow, in part because readers have been conditioned to expect of it something it apparently was not intended to deliver.

For example, readers who expect a book that reports historical events to pay attention to chronology will be severely disappointed because Jeremiah does not report events sequentially. To take only a few examples, ch 25 reports events of 605 BCE, ch 26 a few years earlier, ch 27 a decade later. Similarly ch 35 takes place during the reign of Jehoiakim, more than a decade before the tragic events of chs 32–34, while chs 37–39 return to the later timeline. Flashback has run amok, so to speak. Or rather, it is clear that the creators of the book do not share modern readers', possibly naïve, preconceptions about how to marshal stories.

This turbulence in the text can be explained, at least in part, in one of two ways. The first way is to explore the origins and development of the book (mentioned already in Chapter 23). The book of Jeremiah arose in a series of stages over an unknown period of time. This process was not as orderly (or not orderly in the same way) as that which gave us the book of Isaiah, say. Several scholars have spoken of the literary history of Jeremiah as that of a "rolling corpus." That is, commentary and stories were inserted over time in the middle or end of smoothly worked-out collections of prophetic speeches in order to create a relationship between the earlier speech and its later commentary that would continue to generate new meanings.

THE ROLLING CORPUS IN ACTION: THE CASE OF THE TEMPLE SERMON (JER 7 AND 26)

A famous episode in the biography of Jeremiah was his sermon in the Jerusalem Temple opposing dishonest religion, which assumed that the presence of the symbols of Yhwh's grace guaranteed divine protection, no matter what the recipients of that grace did. Religion without morality was Jeremiah's target.

The story of his sermon appears in two widely separated chapters. Jeremiah 7 reports his denunciation of an over-reliance on "Yhwh's temple, Yhwh's temple, Yhwh's temple"

(Jer 7:4), which the prophet characterizes as "lying words." Meanwhile, ch 26 reports the aftermath of the controversial sermon. According to that postscript, the sermon offended the community's leaders, which they resolved in the prophet's favor by noting that earlier prophets (notably Micah of Moresheth) had similarly prophesied words of doom that had come true and were therefore divine in origin. So, they decide, lynching the prophet was not warranted since their ancestors had not done so under similar provocation.

Why do these stories appear in the book separated by a large amount of material? The separation seems to have something to do with the literary practices of the book's creators. Jeremiah 26 is a commentary on Jer 7, recommending a legitimate response to the prophetic words of doom, not just at one moment of Jeremiah's career, but whenever his oracles are read.

The complexity of this literary development is most visible in the fact that Jeremiah does not survive in only one ancient version, but in two. The Hebrew text (MT) has the outline traced (see p. 291), but the LXX translation (and the Hebrew text it translates) has a different organization, with the oracles against the nations (MT chs 46–51 but not their introduction in ch 45) appearing after 25:13a (MT) rather than at the end of the book. The oracles against the nations themselves appear in different orders in the two versions, while throughout the book, the LXX has a shorter and therefore probably superior text in many places.

The effects of this rearrangement of material can be seen, for example, in how the MT combines two verses that are separate in LXX. Jeremiah 25:13 MT reads "*And I shall bring upon that land all my words that I spoke against it, everything written in this book that Jeremiah prophesied against all the nations.*" In LXX, this verse is split in two: Jer 25:13 LXX reads "*And I shall bring upon that land all my words that I spoke against it, everything written in this book.*" Then follows all the oracles against the nations. This collection of oracles ends in Jer 32:13 LXX with "*that Jeremiah prophesied against all the nations,*" a fragmentary clause that also appears in Jer 46:1 MT as the introduction to the oracles against the nations in the MT arrangement! In other words, the LXX represents an original text which MT has split up and put to new purposes.

Now, at one level it matters very little to the overall interpretation of the book whether the oracles against the nations come at the center or the end of Jeremiah, except that MT seems to want to make them a final word that underscores the promises of deliverance which appear elsewhere in the work. But the fact of the rearrangement does show that, at some level, the apparent disarray of the book of Jeremiah was intentional, not an accident created by incompetent editors. (And, by the way, throughout this chapter, unless otherwise noted, references to passages within Jeremiah will cite the chapters and verses of the MT, which is the basis of most English translations.)

This point then leads to a second way of thinking about the book's counterintuitive organization. In an essay on secrets and sequence in modern novels, the literary Frank Kermode observed that readers of texts naturally seek in them a certain orderliness which they believe to be proper. Texts conform to this search for propriety, for order, to a greater or lesser degree. Some texts advertise themselves as hiding their true order, that is, of containing secrets (as we will see in the apocalyptic text of Daniel, which paradoxically speaks openly about not speaking openly!). Other texts hide their secrets better, but all texts exist on a continuum between maximum imaginable order (and therefore propriety) and maximum imaginable disorder (therefore, secrecy). As Kermode puts it, "Secrets, in short, are at odds with sequence, which is considered as an aspect of propriety; and a passion for sequence may result in the suppression of the secret. But it is there, and one way we can find the secret is to look out for evidence of suppression, which will sometimes tell us where the suppressed secret is located."[1] What does Jeremiah hide through its avoidance of a readily discernible sequencing of events?

The simplest way to answer this question is to consider what the book does not hide. It hides neither the collapse of Judah under the Babylonian onslaught nor Jeremiah's steadfast critique of Judah's kings and their policies before the destruction of their state nor even Jeremiah's flirtation with collaboration with the conquerors. Not even the prophet's deep agony at his culture's annihilation or his own part in undermining morale at critical moments escape examination, almost clinical in its exhaustiveness and clarity. The secret that the reader must discover is why: not simply the causes of the destruction, but the ends to which it can be put. What future does the book seek for its readers, if it is not to become merely their obituary?

The book itself does reveal this secret in the short section sometimes called the "Book of Consolation" (Jer 30–33). In contrast to the depressing texts of the rest of the book, this brief collection of oracles offers a possibility that a radically new future may come about through the transformation of human attitudes and lifeways, described as the giving of a "new covenant." How then does the book progress toward such a conclusion, even in its own indirect way?

The Scroll of Doom (Jer 1:1–25:38)

The first half of the book of Jeremiah contains alternating poems and prose narratives, all of which detail the prelude and aftermath of the Babylonian destruction of Jerusalem during the summer of 586 BCE. This literary work, therefore, marks a search for the causes and meaning of that event, for propriety in history. In some ways, the surface disorder of the texts—the aforementioned lack of obvious chronological, spatial, or even thematic progression—masks a deeper sense of order, which the book creates in two ways.

The first way is through the creation of characters. Throughout these chapters, the reader hears different voices and sees shifting perspectives regarding the calamities befalling Judah and Jerusalem. A third-person narrator reports events in Jeremiah's life and the broader historical context in which he and other actors play their roles. Yhwh also speaks, alternatively lambasting and cajoling and lamenting in the divine search for a rhetorical strategy that will provoke Judah's repentance. And Jeremiah speaks, reluctantly, haltingly in his assigned task of challenging royal complacence and popular corruption, and more freely in his protests against Yhwh's message of doom.

The second strategy of ordering the disorderly is simply through juxtaposing these diverse elements in a dramatic way. The shifting points of view contribute to a dramatic flow in which, despite the prophet's ongoing search for an appreciative audience, no perceptive thought emerges in his hearers. Doom inevitably follows.

To be more specific, Jer 1 opens in the usual way of prophetic books, with a superscription that dates the scenes in the book and the prophet's messages, and then explains his own background as one of the priests settled in Anathoth (Jer 1:1–3) during the late seventh and early sixth centuries BCE, though no oracle in the book seems to date to the reign of Josiah himself, despite the superscription. As part of the priestly clan that fled to the Benjaminite village north of Jerusalem after the destruction of the Shiloh sanctuary about four hundred years earlier (see 1 Kgs 2:26), Jeremiah had access to the ancient traditions of the people (hence his references to the destruction of Shiloh in Jer 7:12–14; 26:6–9). His work during the reigns of Josiah and his successors was an attempt to use ancient traditions as warnings about future calamities, at least in part.

The next pericope, Jer 1:4–10, reports his call to the prophet's work (cf. Exod 3–4; Isa 6; Ezek 1; Amos 7:14–15), setting it in his boyhood:

> Yhwh's word came to me, "Before I delivered you from your mother's belly, I knew you, and before you emerged from the womb, I consecrated you, making you a prophet for the nations." So I replied, "Lord Yhwh, I don't know how to speak because I am a boy." Whereupon Yhwh said to me, "Don't say 'I'm a boy' because you must go wherever I send you and say all I command you. Don't fear them for I am with you in order to rescue you—Yhwh's oracle." (Jer 1:4–8)

Like the Moses call narrative (Exod 3–4), the new prophet objects to the call by noting his inability to speak properly, indicating a deep awareness of the oral/aural nature of prophecy as well as its capacity for controversy (hence also Yhwh's charge not to fear).

The text goes on to explain Jeremiah's commission that first of all demands ritual purification of the lips (as with Isaiah in Isa 6:7). It then explains the prophet's mission as one involving "nations and kingdoms in order to uproot and demolish and destroy and damage [but also] to build up and to plant" (Jer 1:10). This two-sided mission of deconstruction and reconstruction well describes the ways in which the book of Jeremiah (and the prophet himself, no doubt) engaged its world.

In truth, the book returns to these themes of uprooting and demolishing several times. The words "uproot" (Hebrew: *nātaš*) and "demolish" (Hebrew: *nātaṣ*—note the pun!) appear several more times together or separately in the book, sometimes in obvious reference back to Jer 1. For example, Jer 12:14–17 announces that Yhwh will "uproot" all Israel's neighbors after uprooting Israel itself: that is, the oracle there explores Jeremiah's role as a prophet "regarding the nations" to imply that his job of warning people of divine indignation extends beyond Judah's borders.

Perhaps more importantly, Jer 18:7 warns that "in one moment I may speak about a nation or kingdom that [it is to be] *uprooted or demolished or destroyed,*" a clear echo of the call narrative and an elucidation of its international scope. Conversely, Jer 31:28 envisions a time after Judah's destruction, again echoing Jer 1: "It will be that, just as I watched [Hebrew: *šāqad,* also appearing in Jer 1:11] over them to uproot, demolish, destroy, damage, and inflict calamity, so shall I watch over them to build and plant—Yhwh's oracle." For this later text from the Book of Consolation, the mission for which Jeremiah is charged is fundamentally Yhwh's mission to be carried out over time.

In other words, a text that appears early in Jeremiah receives several layers of interpretation. Why? Because the charge to the prophet is a sort of thesis statement for the book as a whole.

This thesis statement is worked out in the remainder of chs 1–25 in several ways, as already noted. Jeremiah 1–6 contain a series of oracles introducing several themes, including idolatry, the wilderness period, the prophet as lamenter, and so on. Jeremiah 2, in particular, shows a strong influence from the book of Hosea, which it resembles in criticizing Israel and Judah's long-standing practice of committing sexual immorality (i.e., idolatry) "under every luxuriant tree" (Jer 2:20; cf. Hos 1–3 especially), and its dismay at polytheism as a breach of trust and a betrayal of the nation's foundational story. Jeremiah 3 continues the imagery of worshiping under trees and on hills (3:6, 13), that is, at the outdoor, unroofed sanctuaries closed by Josiah and other kings. The chapter also works out the marriage and family metaphors for the relationship between Yhwh and Israel/Judah, which Jeremiah derives from the book of Hosea (see the discussion in Chapter 29).

Jer 4, meanwhile, has Yhwh calling Israel to repent (Jer 4:1–8) and a lament for Jerusalem's suffering during warfare (Jer 4:11–31). Bridging these two sections, and offering another perspective on the whole theological exploration of history occurring in the book, is one of the most shocking lines in the Bible: "But I [Jeremiah?] said, 'Aha, Lord Yhwh, surely you have tricked this people and Jerusalem by saying "You will have peace" but the sword is bearing down on their throat'" (Jer 4:10). That is, the utterances of prophets who promised escape from invading hordes had proven to be a cruel lie. Whether they came from Yhwh or not, such words seem to carry divine sanction. Thus the book creates overwhelming cognitive dissonance and uncertainty as to how to evaluate competing claims from alleged prophets (a problem taken up also in Deuteronomy).

All the poetic material of Jer 1–6, which repeatedly alternates viewpoints to mimic the confusion and tragic nature of the times, gives way to prose in Jer 7, the famous "Temple sermon." The narrator of the book portrays Jeremiah as standing in the Temple courtyards denouncing an irrational attachment to the building as a token of God's presence when the behavior of the people belies their confession of loyalty to Yhwh. By exhorting his audience not to "oppress the alien, orphan, and widow nor shed innocent blood in this place [i.e., Jerusalem]" (Jer 7:6), this speech states clearly the basic moral commitments whose sustained violation prompts prophetic denunciations and leads inexorably to the death of the state.

This warning falling on deaf ears, the remainder of Jer 8–25 constructs the dialogue among Yhwh, Jeremiah, Judah as a whole, and several named leaders of the people. There are several large blocks of material here:

1. Details of the impending destruction of Judah (4:5–10:25)
2. Jeremiah's confrontation of doom (11:1–20:18)
3. Some supplementary material on similar themes (21:1–25:38)

Again, individual pericopes seem intelligible, whether they are poetry (especially laments) or prose narratives about Jeremiah's activities, but the overall flow is not as easy to discern.

The second large unit is particularly revealing because it highlights the prophet's reaction to his own task. For example, in response to the justification of the destruction as Yhwh's proper response to ungrateful generations of people (Jer 11:1–17), Jer 11:18–20 offers a poignant lament. The prophet plaintively says,

Yhwh made known to me so I know,
Yes you showed me their deeds.
But I am like a docile lamb led to the slaughter.
And I did not know that they schemed against me,
"Let us destroy the tree with its sap and cut him off from the land of the living, and let
　　his name never more be remembered."
But Yhwh of Hosts defends the righteous,
Testing kidneys and heart.[2]
I will see your retribution upon them,
For to you I have entrusted my defense.

In other words, the prophet admits underestimating the difficulties of his job, including physical danger, but still trusts Yhwh.

This trust does not hold up, however. Jeremiah 12 introduces charges of divine negligence in respect to evildoers, a claim that seems odd given the overall tone of the book, but makes sense as a rhetorical move justifying the final destruction of Jerusalem as a process of defending the innocent from their oppressors. Jeremiah 13 describes a prophetic sign act and further oracles that undercut the popular cliché "every jar will be filled with wine" (a promise whose meaning is obvious, and whose falsity is similarly clear).

Jeremiah 14:1–9 opens with an indictment of Judah but drifts into a penitential psalm asking Yhwh to intervene "for the sake of your reputation" (Jer 14:7) and save the people. Then the shocking command to Jeremiah, "Do not pray for this people's good" (Jer 14:11). Since ancient Israelite prophets functioned as mediators between the divine and human realms, ceasing his intercessions for the people resolves a tension in the prophet's life. And yet the resolution of the tension does not work because Jeremiah suffers with the people as the result of Yhwh's decision to allow the destruction of Jerusalem and Judah.

This failure to resolve tension becomes stronger in chs 15–19 as alternating oracles speak of judgment and the prophet's simultaneous moral innocence and distaste for his task (e.g., Jer 15:15–18) as well as oracles of salvation for the prophet but not his people (e.g., Jer 15:19–21).

This tension breaks out into the open in Jer 20:7–17, an accusatory critique of Yhwh's actions and motives. Part of the text, vv. 14–18, closely parallels Job 3:3–11 with Jeremiah probably serving as the model for the later wisdom text. Both lament the day of the singer's birth and therefore his place in the cosmic order.

JEREMIAH AND USES OF THE PAST

The book of Jeremiah frequently refers to the more or less distant past. For example, it notes that not even Moses or Samuel, two paragons of prophetic excellence, could save the present people (Jer 15:1). Interestingly, his near contemporary Ezekiel uses a similar rhetorical strategy to illustrate the hopelessness of the times by referring to the great intercessors Noah, Dan'el, and Job (Ezek 14:14–16), a fact that indicates a possibly widespread interest in the past prevalent during the sixth century BCE.

Also, the book mentions the ancestors on numerous occasions, usually with reference to their failings, which unfortunately their descendants have retained (see, e.g., Jer 3:24; 7:7, 14, 26; 11:5, 7, 10; 14:20; 16:3, 7, 12, 13, 15; 19:4; 23:39; 24:10; 25:5; 30:3; 31:32; 32:22; 34:5, 13; 35:14, 15; 44:3, 9, 17, 21; and 50:7).

However, the most searing aspect of this complaint is its opening, in which the prophet protests to Yhwh, "O Yhwh, you seduced me and I was seduced. You overpowered and subdued me. I am a laughingstock all day long. Everybody ridicules me" (Jer 20:7). Comparing himself to a victim of sexual abuse and group bullying, the prophet places his ministry in the worst possible light. In famous—and badly misunderstood—words, he speaks of a "fire in my bones" (Jer 20:9), that is, of chronic pain for which his religion provides no opiate. He cannot escape the mediatorial function of his role, nor can he distance himself from the suffering of the people. Rather, he must share in their suffering despite the justice of it as a punishment for sin.

Thus the text highlights the tension between two defensible understandings of Judah's suffering during the Babylonian invasions. On the one hand, the voices of Yhwh and of the prose narrator in Jer 1–25 insists that the events of these two decades were the just retribution on people who neglected the welfare of the vulnerable. Such a view of history arose out of a theological assumption that the divine realm caused events in the human realm and that since Yhwh was the only real occupant of the divine realm, Yhwh must be the ultimate cause of those events. On the other hand, a second view of these events comes to the surface, one that also appears in Lamentations and other biblical texts. The mayhem is not something to explain, much less defend, but something to acknowledge and protest against. Jeremiah 1–25 thus creates a dynamic theological discussion, which it does not resolve.

Yet to say that no final resolution comes from the text does not quite capture the full picture, for the last sections of the Book of Doom do allow for the possibility that "in days to come—Yhwh's oracle—I will raise up a righteous branch for David. A king will reign discerningly and execute justice and righteousness in the land" (Jer 23:5). This text and others like it owe something to the interpretation of the early parts of the book of Isaiah, which must have been available in some form to the creators of Jeremiah (just as they also knew of Micah, according to Jer 26:18–19).

This section of Jeremiah does not allow for the suspension of divine judgment because it must deal with events as they happened, not as they might have been. In the words of the great Lewis Carroll, "Contrariwise," continued Tweedledee, "if it was so, it might be; and if it were so, it would be; but as it isn't, it ain't. That's logic."[3]

Jeremiah's Stories and Words of (Deferred) Hope (Jer 26:1–29:32 and 37:1–45:5)

And yet some dreams of worlds that "ain't" do eventually come true. Following the conclusion of the Scroll of Doom, the book of Jeremiah contains a series of stories about Jeremiah's career before and after 586 BCE, most tragic in their outcome and all calculated to demonstrate both the prophet's fortitude and the profound unsettledness of the times. The stories apparently come from a single work, often attributed to Jeremiah's scribe Baruch, which was then inserted into the larger book of Jeremiah and perhaps rearranged (since they do not occur in chronological order). In other words, they are not in-the-moment bits of reportage but skillful literary productions.

Embedded within these stories, moreover, is the only stretch of hopeful poetry in the book, the Book of Consolation or Comfort in chs 30–33. These beautiful texts present a strong counteroption to the narrative: one describes only chaos, and the other peace, lifegiving order. Consider each group of material, then.

THE NARRATIVES OF JEREMIAH

The stories about the prophet in this material seem to fit together both thematically (his persecution by various bad leaders) and theologically (the perseverance of Yhwh's judgment on account of Judah's rejection of offers of salvation conditional on their repentance). Again, the stories do not appear in strictly chronological order, but there is a pattern:

1. The Temple Sermon revisited (26:1–24; set about 609 BCE)
2. Discussions about cooperation with Babylon (27:1–22; set in 609 BCE in the MT, undated in the LXX, and usually dated to about 597 BCE in English translations)

3. Conflict with the prophet Hananiah (28:1–17; set in 597 BCE)
4. A letter to the exile (29:1–32; 597–586 BCE, probably toward the earlier date)
5. Encounters during Jerusalem's siege (34:1–22; 586 BCE)
6. Events during the reign of Jehoiakim (35:1–36:32)
7. Events during and just after the siege of Jerusalem (37:1–39:18)
8. Events in the years following the destruction of Jerusalem (40:1–43:13)
9. Speech to the exiles in Egypt (44:1–30)
10. Baruch's Lament (45:1–5)

On the whole, the story moves forward in time, but Jer 35–36 seems out of order, apparently situated to fit the theme rather than the time.

This Jeremiah Narrative opens by returning to the scene of ch 7, Jeremiah's sermon in the Temple. Here, however, the emphasis does not lie on the sermon itself but on its aftermath. Facing possible lynching by the irritated mob, Jeremiah appeals to his calling by arguing "to all the leaders and all the people that 'Yhwh sent me to prophesy all the words you've heard about this house [i.e., the Temple] and this city'" (Jer 26:12). Strikingly, the audience accepts the argument, noting that, "This man does not deserve a death sentence because he spoke to us in the name of Yhwh our God" (Jer 26:16). They then cite similar incendiary words by Micah a century earlier and the accepting (or at least, not murderous) response of the then king Hezekiah (Jer 26:18–19).

It is difficult to capture all the nuances of this story, but at least two elements bear on the interpretation of Jeremiah's career and the development of the book about him. First, this story addresses the conflict between prophets and their hearers, and among prophets. While there is no reason to assume a fixed conflict among various social groups (e.g., prophets and priests were not irreconcilable foes), those who passed on the words of the prophets understood their heroes' messages to be a source of social conflict with a changing cast of characters. Interestingly, in this story, the prophetic conflict seems to revolve around the figure unnamed in the text, the king, for while other figures can accept Jeremiah's right to speak (if not necessarily his message), the text says nothing at all about royal response except that a past king got things right. This unstated criticism comes out in the open in ch 36.

Second, the leaders' appeal to older prophecy (Micah) demonstrates their awareness even when people question the words of individual prophets; here, they cannot question the validity of prophecy itself as a means of communication with the divine realm. This point will become more overt in ch 28.

In the meantime, ch 27 describes Jeremiah's speeches against resistance to Babylon, the new superpower of the Near East. Jeremiah apparently spoke openly of siding with the Babylonians, so much so that his hearers suspected him of outright collaboration with the enemy. (This sort of accusation still haunts religious thinkers who challenge the military-industrial complexes of their own time!) According to ch 28, the conflict over foreign policy (and its religious underpinnings) took concrete form in Jeremiah's dispute with another prophet, one Hananiah. This person had repeatedly and loudly prophesied the quick end to Babylonian rule and even carried out a prophetic sign act of breaking a yoke to signify impending liberation from foreign rule. To this, Jeremiah glumly replied:

> "For thus says Yhwh of Hosts, the God of Israel, 'I have placed an iron yoke on the neck of all nations to serve Nebuchadnezzar, the King of Babylon. They will serve him, and I have even given him the wild beasts." Jeremiah the prophet said further to Hananiah the prophet, "Listen, Hananiah. Yhwh did not send you and you have made these people trust lies. So, Yhwh says this: 'I am about to deport you from the land and within a year, you will die because you talked up abandoning Yhwh.'" (Jer 28:14–16)

In other words, one prophet promises hope and the other doom at a given moment. Sometimes this conflict between two prophets is understood as one between "true" and "false" prophecy or even between figures who always speak doom and those whose message consists entirely of false hopes. But neither of these understandings is satisfactory. To take the second one first, the interplay between doom and hope exists in all prophetic texts that have survived from ancient Israel, indicating that their creators understood legitimate prophecy to consist of both promise and criticism, dependent upon the circumstances of the time and therefore the attitudes and behaviors of human beings. And then again, the gap between "truth" and "falsity," while not in the eye of the beholder, becomes visible only with time and reflection. Here, time and reflection made a quick solution seem increasingly like a cruel joke, not a word of hope.

JEREMIAH AND THE MEDIA OF DIVINE COMMUNICATION

The book of Jeremiah describes several ways in which prophets communicate messages from Yhwh to human beings. These include prophetic sign acts, consultation ("inquiring") of God, dreams, reports of confessions and dialogues between the prophet and God, and most importantly oracles or what Becking calls "revelation-through-the-word." (See Bob Becking, "Means of Revelation in the Book of Jeremiah," in *Prophecy in the Book of Jeremiah* [ed. Hans M. Barstad and Reinhard G. Kratz; Berlin: de Gruyter, 2009, 33–47). As Deuteronomy points out (and as common sense would suggest), discernment of true words of prophecy take on urgency when the words in question address urgent concerns, and when the words of different prophets conflict. How does the hearer know the difference? Deuteronomy offers the tests of faithfulness to fulfillment (see Chapter 7), but more than one statement can claim Yhwh's authority, and verification takes time. Jer 26:8–9 notes that earlier spokespersons for the deity had "prophesied against many lands and great kingdoms about war and calamity and pestilence," a fact that puts the onus of proof on the one declaring good news. However, since the book of Jeremiah itself contains oracles of hope, the preference for bad news was not absolute. That is, the prophetic texts fear demagoguery, not salvation.

The next several chapters sort out the fate of the deportees and refugees. Thus chs 29 and 44 form a pairing addressing just such persons. Jeremiah 29 summarizes letters advising deportees to Babylonia itself to settle down in their new home, engage in normal careers and family life, and to pray on behalf of their captors. Jeremiah 29:7's warrant for continuing religion in the new land, "for your welfare (Hebrew: *šālôm*) lies in their welfare," reframes the old charges of collaboration against Jeremiah. Far from being a quisling, he has taken a broader view of the world, understanding even the most distant land as part of the realm of Yhwh's gracious activity. Exile is not the end, but simply a transitional phase.

Jeremiah 44 takes a different tack in addressing refugees who headed to Egypt. That community, of which Jeremiah himself was unwillingly a part according to Jer 42–43, adopted the religious practices of their new land (Jer 44:8) either alongside or in substitution for the worship of Yhwh.

It is often argued that the difference between chs 29 and 44 illustrates a postexilic preference for the community that returned from Babylonia to Israel, as in the books of Ezra and Nehemiah, and in distinction from the acceptance of Egypt as a place for worshiping Yhwh seen in parts of Isaiah (Isa 19:18–25). Perhaps so. Undoubtedly the various groups making up the postexilic population of Israel/Judah debated among themselves the proper understanding of their shared and separate histories. Yet the book of Jeremiah as a whole understands all these issues as theological ones, revolving around the worship of Yhwh alone (as in Deuteronomy), not as a political dispute.

The remainder of these narratives (34:1–43:13), in any case, explains how the Judahites became displaced persons in Egypt after their mad assassination of the conqueror's appointed governor Gedaliah. Clearly described are the destructiveness of the war of 586 BCE, and the ensuing chaos as a superpower more skilled at conquest than at governance tried to impose order on a region whose communication and economic system, and more importantly social structure, had been disrupted.

Yet these chapters do not merely tell gripping stories. They also, and more importantly, work out a theological understanding of those events. This theological understanding is stated succinctly at several points, two of which may serve to illustrate the whole.

Jeremiah 29:10–11 is a text widely cited (and almost as widely misunderstood and misrepresented). The oracle says:

For thus says Yhwh, "I will attend to you after Babylon's seventy years is completed. Then I will fulfill my good word about you, concerning bringing you back to this place. Indeed, I know the thoughts I have thought about you—Yhwh's oracle—thoughts of shalom, not calamity, to give you a future and a hope.

Contrary to popular modern piety, the text does not describe a micromanaging deity awarding the right people whatever their heart desires. Rather, the text (1) focuses on the entire community of Israel as a collective ("you" is plural throughout the text) with a shared destiny; (2) the period of deportations and displacement should be temporary, the roughly seventy years between the invasion of 605 BCE and the permission to return granted by Cyrus the Great in 539/8 BCE; and most importantly (3), Yhwh's providential care has a specific focus, the return of the people to their promised land. That is, this part of Jeremiah shares with Isa 40–55 a belief in a renewal of Israel's history, this time with deliverance and resettlement leading to greater faith in Yhwh (similar to Second Isaiah's new exodus).

A complementary text appears in ch 45, an answer to Baruch. As Jeremiah's scribe and possibly a creator of a large part of the book bearing his master's name, Baruch becomes in this text an individual experiencing the trials of war and exile, and thus a sort of stand-in for each individual survivor of Jerusalem's destruction. This chapter reports both his lament ("how awful for me, for Yhwh has added grief to my suffering. I have grown tired by my sighing, but have found no respite" [Jer 45:3]) and Yhwh's chilling response ("I am demolishing what I built and uprooting what I planted" [Jer 45:4]). The divine reply echoes Jeremiah's call in Jer 1 and thus forms an inclusio with the book's opening. The echo of the opening commission of the book invites the reader to interpret everything in between as part of the process of demolition and uprooting, with both the historical events Jeremiah comments on and his comments themselves (or rather the book's depiction of both) as the divine activity of disruption.

Yet, says the oracle to Baruch, faithful individuals may survive even the worst tragedy, and he will do so, like a figure in Greek drama who has seen the worst and must tell the tale.

THE BOOK OF CONSOLATION (JER 30:1–33:26)

Almost alone in the book, Jer 30–33 speaks of an alternative world in which the chaos and violence of the sixth century BCE give way to lives of peace and joy before a merciful God. By carefully piecing together oracles of hope, these chapters posit a world after the "seventy years" of ch 29.

The opening of the section in Jer 30:1–2 describes what follows as a "scroll" (Hebrew: *sēper*) recording a revelation, just as in Jer 36:8, 11, 32. That is, the book of Jeremiah presents itself as a written work deriving from prior written works and consisting of several texts woven together. Jeremiah 30–33 seem to stand together as a discrete unit within the larger book, differing not only in content from surrounding material but also in its self-identification.

The opening oracle of the book, beginning with "thus says Yhwh" in Jer 30:5, describes a painful (and embarrassing) scene in which men hold their loins like birthing women and turning "green" while doing so. Simultaneously depicting the great pain of the times and showing its unnaturalness (and thus avoidability), the text soon shifts to the alternative with v. 10's overture to the (potentially) penitent audience. By saying

As for you, my servant Jacob, do not fear nor be dismayed—Yhwh's oracle.
For I am rescuing you from afar, your offspring from the land of your captivity,
So Jacob will return, and be undisturbed, at ease, with no one troubling him.

This picture of restoration, similar to that of Isa 40–55, embraces a renewed Israelite people, returned to their land, defended from gentile oppression, and freed from the religious and moral failings that led, according to Jeremiah and his followers, to their deportation and the disruption of their culture.

Jeremiah 30–33 continues in this vein, with a series of oracles in several genres, whose key idea can be summarized in the words of Jer 31:1: "At that time—Yhwh's oracle—I shall be God for all the families of Israel, and they will be my people." Not just the returnees from Babylon nor the clans that remained in the land of their origin, but all of the people will be part of the renewed community. Jeremiah 31 continues with this sort of rehabilitation of the victims of the Babylonian invasion, persons who were the target of the rest of the book of Jeremiah's criticism. In order to recast the character of Israel/Judah as something other than victim or perpetrator, the poetry continues by saying that "the people surviving the sword found grace in the wilderness" (Jer 31:2) and "with an eternal love Yhwh loved you" (Jer 31:3). Evoking both the wilderness language of the older prophecies of Hosea and, behind them, the still older stories of the exodus, the Book of Consolation tries to return its audience to its theological roots.

This transformation of the old into something new and old at the same time, becomes clearest in the famous text that promises

Truly, days are coming—Yhwh's oracle—when I shall make a new covenant with the house of Israel and the house of Judah. It will not resemble the old covenant that I made with their ancestors when I grasped their hand to bring them from the land of Egypt inasmuch as they broke my covenant, though I acted like a husband to them—Yhwh's oracle. Rather, this is the covenant that I will make with the house of Israel and the house of Judah after those days—Yhwh's oracle. I will put my Torah in their innards and write it on their minds. Then I will be their God, and they my people. (Jer 31:31–33)

In other words, the envisioned "new covenant" does several things: (1) it includes all Israelites, whether northern or southern, irrespective of past political or social loyalties; (2) it draws its warrant from a new act of divine deliverance parallel to the exodus (again, as in Isa 40–55); and (3) it presents itself as an internal state to the covenant partners, not merely as an external set of rules (this last point does not really differ from Deuteronomy's viewpoint, as we have seen). In short, Jer 30–33 picks up some of the older Deuteronomic theology of covenant renewal and applies it to a new situation, after the disaster of 586 BCE.

THE BOOK OF CONSOLATION IN LATER INTERPRETATION

Readers of the New Testament are familiar with Jer 31's promise of the new covenant, especially from the eighth and tenth chapters of the Epistle to the Hebrews. For early Christians, the Jeremiah texts anticipated their own era, or rather the eschatological resolution of all things. Such a reappropriation of the texts for later eras also appears in such texts as Baruch and the Epistle of Jeremiah (see Chapter 30) and in the Qumran text (i.e., Dead Sea Scrolls) *Apocryphon of Jeremiah A*. Those latter texts also share with Daniel a particular interpretation of Jer 29:10's "seventy weeks" as "seventy weeks of years" (i.e., 490 years), thus moving the promise of Israel's ultimate deliverance into the future. In other words, all of these recognize that the promised utopia of Jer 30–33 did not fully arrive with the return of deportees from Babylonian exile. Or put more theologically, these texts underscore the belief that Yhwh's promises come to fruition in the realm of history, at many times in partial ways but in completeness only at the end. Jews and, later, Christians understood the eschatological, future-oriented horizon of the prophetic promises to speak of something always just beyond human grasp.

Making sense of such a tragic event requires multiple channels for reflection, even given the anticipation of a benign resolution. Thus the Book of Consolation follows the soaring promises of Jer 31 with a long reflection on the tragedy of Jerusalem and Judah's devastation. This event, according to Jer 32–33 came about because of the people's sins (just as 2 Kgs asserts, and there the Deuteronomic influence is very strong), but the cultural meltdown is not the final word. Rather, sorrow will give way to rejoicing (cf. Jer 33:18; Pss 100, 106, 107, 136).

Oracles Against the Nations (Jer 46:1–51:64)

A condition of this hopeful future is the elimination of oppression from foreign powers, the subject of Jer 45–51. In the MT edition, this section forms the climax of the book, whereas it lies nearer the center of the LXX version of Jeremiah. Moreover, the constituent oracles are themselves in different orders, with minor differences also appearing throughout the oracles. In other words, these texts show ongoing reflection on the fates of Israel's neighbors and more distant lands, allowing not merely for their destruction but also for their renewal (as for Elam in Jer 49:39, possibly because Elam was part of the heartland of the Persian Empire and thus a friendlier place than some other kingdoms). The variant orders can be mapped like this:

MT (and ET)	LXX
Egypt (46:1–28)	Elam (25:14–20)
Philistia (47:1–7)	Egypt (26:1–28)
Moab (48:1–47)	Babylon (27:1–28:64)
Ammon (49:1–6)	Mediterranean coastal cities (29:1–7)
Edom (49:7–22)	Idumaea/Edom (30:1–16)

Damascus/Aram (49:23–27)	Ammon (30:17–21 [or 22])
Kedar/Hazor (49:28–33)	Kedar (30:23–28)
Elam (49:34–39)	Damascus/Aram (30:29–33)
Babylon (50:1–51:58)	Moab (31:1–44)

It is difficult to discern an obvious pattern in the LXX sequence, while the MT order makes more sense. There, the two major powers of the sixth century, Egypt and especially Babylon, begin and end the list, thus creating a literary frame for the entire set of poems about foreign nations. Both nations will face defeat, in part because of the impotence of their gods.

This overtly theological understanding of political history appears most transparently in the criticism of Babylon. For those telling stories about Jeremiah, the fall of Babylon was inevitable because Yhwh willed it. The disasters of 586 BCE could not be the last word because Yhwh had an enduring commitment to Israel's survival. Suffering must, therefore, exercise a disciplinary function as an invitation to repentance.

While the narratives about Jeremiah, especially in the stories associated (at least in part) with Baruch in Jer 34–45, take pains to exonerate the prophet of charges of collaboration with the Mesopotamian invaders and even seems at times almost pro-Babylonian, Jer 50–51 presents a lengthy denunciation of that empire and especially its chief god, Marduk. As Jer 51:52 says, "Therefore, days are surely coming—Yhwh's oracle—during which I will punish its [Babylon's] images, and in all her land the pierced shall mourn." That is, the gods of the foreigners will be exposed as non-gods (cf. Pss 105; 135). Jeremiah 51 even evokes the Babylonian theology according to which Marduk created the world by defeating the forces of chaos. Here, however, the monsters defeated were the very gods who presented themselves as agents of order. The imperial order created by pillaging and raping and deportation now lies in ruins. Despite all appearances, Babylon does not have the final say.

An Appendix (Jer 52:1–34)

In truth, the MT climax in Jer 50–51 would have made a perfectly reasonable ending of the book, much like those of Isaiah and some of the Twelve Minor Prophets. However, both the MT and the LXX contain a final chapter (52), which closely follows 2 Kgs 24:18–25:30 (much as Isa 36–39 copies 2 Kgs 18:13–20:19). The fact that both prophetic books share material with the Deuteronomistic History can hardly be accidental. Apparently at least one stage of the creation of the two prophetic works involved significant influence by (or on) the creation of the DH as well.

Accordingly, the existence of Jer 52 reveals an important literary and theological point. By describing in detail the final denouement of the siege of 586 BCE and especially the destruction of the Temple in Jerusalem, this conclusion of the book wants to remind the reader that whatever joy may lie ahead, a tragedy has occurred. For the MT reader, ch 52 insists that hopes for the destruction of enemies cannot remove the pain of the present suffering (whether in the immediate aftermath of Judah's demise or during later periods of displacement and diaspora). For the LXX readers, for whom the preceding pericope is the promise to Baruch that his life will be spared while others die, ch 52 must have seemed an odd flashback, since the narrative had already moved forward in time a few years to Jeremiah's sojourn in Egypt. Either way, however, the book ends on a sobering note, barely softened by the news that Jehoiachin gained some help from his overlords even in captivity. Like the book of 2 Kgs, Jeremiah ends in uncertainty.

Implications

Uncertainty is not quite the right word because the book bears witness. As such, it cannot find full closure, no matter how much the book and its readers might desire it. Bearing witness to suffering, deserved or not, requires a willingness to suspend the drive to satisfy the innate human psychological need for pattern and purpose. The great English poet Lord Byron once wrote that

> All tragedies are finish'd by a death,
> All comedies are ended by a marriage;
> The future states of both are left to faith.[4]

Jeremiah certainly falls in the category of tragedy, yet one with the future open to faith. Israel dies, but it may be reborn.

Unlike the other great prophetic works, Isaiah, Ezekiel, and the Twelve Minor Prophets, Jeremiah includes a major element of biography of its hero, the prophet who must "uproot and demolish and destroy and damage but also build up and plant." The book's creators wished to emphasize the identity of the messenger of Yhwh with the message itself, since Jeremiah found himself uprooted and damaged as much as most. He was not replanted, but such is the fate of the prophet. This turn to biography allows the book to encapsulate the passions of the age in the experiences of one man, and one whose life is revealed to an extent unparalleled elsewhere in the Bible or in much of the rest of ancient Near Eastern literature.

Notes

1. Frank Kermode, *Pieces of My Mind: Essays and Criticism 1958–2002* (New York: Farrar, Straus and Giroux, 2003), 165.

2. In Hebrew, the kidneys stand in for the emotions, and the heart for logical thinking and sustained commitments.

3. Lewis Carroll, *Through the Looking Glass*, chap. 4.

4. George Gordon, Lord Byron, "Don Juan," Canto 3, Stanza 9, lines 65–67.

For Further Reading

Barstad, Hans M., and Reinhard G. Kratz, eds. *Prophecy in the Book of Jeremiah*. Berlin: de Gruyter, 2009.

Kessler, Martin. *Battle of the Gods: The God of Israel Versus Marduk of Babylon*. Groningen: Van Gorcum, 2003.

Lundbom, Jack R. *Jeremiah*, 3 vols. Anchor Bible. New York: Doubleday, 1999–2004.

26 Mourning a Lost World
THE BOOK OF LAMENTATIONS

Key Text: *O Yhwh, you always sit [as king], your throne lasts through every generation. Why will you always abandon us? Will you forsake us throughout time? O Yhwh, return us to your-self, and we shall return. Renew our days like olden times—unless you have completely rejected us. Has your anger burned against us totally?* (Lam 5:19–22)

Just before 2000 BCE, the Mesopotamian city of Ur fell to its enemies. This catastrophe soon found appropriate commemoration in a ballad that modern scholars call the "Lament over Sumer and Ur." One of five similar lamentation songs known to have been written in Sumerian in the late third or early second millennium BCE, this tragic song set the tone for a literary genre that comes down to us in a much later text, the biblical book of Lamentations.

The lament for Ur opens with a description of how the Sumerian gods, especially its chief god Nanna and his consort Ningal, have abandoned the city: "The lord of all the lands has abandoned it, his sheepfold became haunted." It ends over four hundred lines later with the plaintive cry to Nanna, which says, "O Nanna, may your restored city radiate before you. Like a bright heavenly star, may it never be destroyed . . . . O Nanna, in your city again restored, may (your) praise be sung."[1] The text assumes that the divine world has caused the devastation of an entire culture in the human world. It also assumes that memorializing that tragedy in the form of ritual and prayer may not only preserve the memory of the event but also undo it by convincing the gods to relent in their punishment. In other words, the text wrestles with a theological question of great existential importance.

The destruction of a city and its surrounding culture thus occupied the thinking of ancient people long before parts of the Bible were written. Unlike the ancient Sumerian city laments, Lamentations assumes the existence (or at least the relevance) of only one deity, Yhwh. Therefore, Yhwh must not only bear responsibility for the destruction of the city (here, Jerusalem) but Yhwh is also the only actor who can see to its rebuilding. Lamentations, therefore, has to face the problem of the nature of God's mercy and God's agency in history. It does not address this problem in a theoretical way through a philosophical exploration of theodicy, the defense of God's reputation, but in the more visceral, emotional form of songs of protest and grief. Lamentations is a book of dissent, a great objection to Yhwh's work in history, and a probing examination of the possibilities of faith in times of acute suffering. As such it speaks to contemporary issues in profound ways.

LAMENTATIONS AND THE PROPHET JEREMIAH

Ancient tradition assumes that Jeremiah was the author of Lamentations, and this view has survived to the present. Since neither Lamentations nor Jeremiah makes that claim, the oldest attestation of it seems to be introduction to the book in the LXX (second century BCE), which says, "After the humiliation desolation of Israel and Jerusalem, Jeremiah wept and lamented this lament over Jerusalem." The claim seems to rest, however, on a misunderstanding of 2 Chron 35:25's notice that Jeremiah had written a now lost lament for the death of King Josiah in 610 or 609 BCE.

The Poetry of Lamentations

How does it speak, and what does it say? These are the next questions to consider.

On the question of how, it is worth observing that the book of Lamentations consists of five tightly interwoven poems. They may have had the same author. At least the first two and perhaps all five come from a period almost just after the destruction of Jerusalem in 586 BCE, or at least memories of that siege reflect its immediate aftermath. However, the sequence of the poems is not chronological. One should be cautious about dating the poems singly or together because Lam 5 speaks of the sinful ancestors who brought about the calamity as now dead and gone, indicating a slightly later date at least for that text. The graphic content of the poems seem to reflect direct experience of the siege, even if the poems come from a few years later. The poems speak of starving parents who eat their children, and of priests who die at Yhwh's altar, among other horrors of war. And so the story underlying the poems and often rising to their surface is of the most dismal sort.

And yet, the poems do not reflect that disorder in their structures or the elegance of their language. Quite the contrary. The first four poems employ the acrostic form (as in some psalms), a rigid poetic structure in which each verse or group of verses begins with the letter of the alphabet next in the sequence. Lamentations 1–4 vary the ways in which they do this, with chs 1–2 writing three-line clusters in which only the first line follows the acrostic, ch 4 creating two-line clusters, and ch 3 taking the most challenging tack of all by having each line in the three-line cluster begin with the same letter. Lamentations 5 is not an acrostic, but it does have twenty-two lines, the number of letters in the Hebrew alphabet. The poetry thus writes about the most chaotic sort of human experience via the most tightly structured available poetic form.

Why place a story of chaos in such a literary straitjacket? Certainly poetry cannot fully imitate the disorder of life. Even in its most avant-garde forms, poetry must bring some sort of order to the phenomenon it describes. This was especially true of ancient poetry, which did not accept the nineteenth-century Romantic view that the interior state of the imagination "was part of the contemporary belief in the individual self."[2] The book searches for order by employing the only sort of order available to it, that of literature itself. Moreover, Lamentations does not speak so much of the poet's response to tragedy as about the shared experience of Jerusalem's loss and the ways in which a cast of characters face that loss.

The book has four major characters: Jerusalem, Yhwh, the implied narrator, and the implied audience. The opening lines introduce the first character and set the tone of loss and desolation:

A lament. How lonesome sits the city that once with people teemed.
Like a widow is the one once great among the nations,
The princess-like capital—now forced labor.
By night she weeps, her tears wet her cheeks.
Without one comforter among her friends,
And her neighbors betray her—now they are her foes. (Lam 1:1–2)

The book's opening lines create a mood of desolation and aloneness, which the poem reinforces by lining up images of betrayal (mental or social isolation) and of geographic separation. The city that once sat at the center of a network of social relationships now lies abandoned and in ruins.

Lamentations personifies Jerusalem (and satellite cities, called "daughters") in order to state the book's subject as the joint suffering of an entire people, not just individuals. By depicting Jerusalem as more than a pile of stones, but as a living character with an emotional life and a sense of loss, the poems (especially Lam 1 and 4) allow their audience to enter into the moral and spiritual complexity of the postsiege situation.

While the first poem introduces the character of Yhwh, the second poem focuses on that character more intensely by shifting the focus from lonesome Jerusalem to the God who has "become like an enemy, engulfed Israel, engulfed all her citadels, sacked his own fortified cities." (Lam 2:5). That is, the poem attributes the disaster of 586 BCE to Yhwh's opposition to Israel. And so the poem appeals to Yhwh's sense of honor by naming the implications of the divine decision to destroy the people, cannibalism among starving people and then, after the Babylonian breach of Jerusalem's walls, the murder of priests and prophets in the city. The complete collapse of all social norms and forms of meaning making has come about, says the poem, because of Yhwh's choice.

Yet Lam 2 also assumes that an appeal to divine honor remains the only recourse. The text does not reject a religious viewpoint but wrestles with the tensions of such an outlook from the inside. The second poem thus addresses Yhwh with a heartbreaking appeal:

> O Yhwh, look and think. To whom have you done this thing?
> Should women devour their offspring, the beautiful babies?
> Should priest and prophet be killed in the lord's Temple? (Lam 3:20)

That is, the poem holds out the hope that the destructive God will in time revert to a more pacific role.

A similar idea occurs in the third poem, which opens with another shift of focus, this time to the implied narrator:

> I am the person who has seen affliction with his rod used in anger.
> Me has he driven off, led away. Darkness—not light!
> Oh, he keeps a hand on me all day long. (Lam 3:1–3)

That is, the narrator's experience of the divine presence revolves around the punitive. The trials of the postsiege death march seem best to reveal Yhwh's intentions toward Israel.

Yet Lam 3 also contains another perspective, a faint hope that appeals to the old traditions of divine helpfulness. The poet appeals to the ancient language of the Temple, "Yhwh's steadfast love do not cease, nor his mercies end. New each morning, your faithful acts are numerous" (Lam 3:22–23). The speaker who "has seen affliction" must remind himself and the poem's wider audience of this more hopeful theology, but the immediate audience is Yhwh, Israel's God, whom the poem invites to "remember" this affirmation of faith as well. Again, the appeal to the divine honor comes through.

A number of scholars have argued that the recitation of hope, because it comes never the center of the entire book of Lamentations, in fact states the book's core idea. Far from being a work of despair, the argument goes, the book ultimately expects salvation. The idea is that ancient books often used the literary device of chiasmus or nesting patterns in which the core idea or image sat at the center. Rather than placing the conclusion at the end, ancient authors placed them in the middle. Since the affirmation of divine love comes near the book's center, that must be the book's point.

While certainly defensible, this view seems incorrect for several reasons. First, laments in the book of Psalms often include affirmations of trust in God, but they are still laments. Second, this particular affirmation of trust does not, strictly speaking, appear at the center of the book but just before its center. The exact center is the space between statements of trust and statements of despair. Third, the center of a chiasmus does not necessarily indicate the "point" of a literary unit, even if we can speak of its single main point (which often is not appropriate). The structure of a literary work contributes to its meaning, but not at the expense of content.

In short, it would be better to say that the book of Lamentations places side-by-side two almost contradictory ideas. It affirms both Yhwh's justice and compassion and then questions that affirmation. By doing so, the book invites the Israelite audience into a search for meaning in their inherited religious tradition without providing easy (and therefore, implausible) answers.

This careful balancing of concerns, stated in the plaintive words of chs 4 and 5 as was well as earlier in the book, surfaces the concerns of the final character, the people of Israel as a whole, that is, the audience of the entire collection of laments. As the book ends with a question, it states the uncertainty of those who sought to build a new life either in the land of Israel itself or outside it in Babylonia or Egypt. Since the location of the book's composition remains unknown, it is impossible to state precisely which part of the Israelite community it intends as its audience. Indeed, such precision is unnecessary because the poetry speaks to both the crisis of its time and the patterns of shared suffering that humans continue to experience.

Implications

Certain kinds of piety actively try to avoid unpleasantness, much less an unsettled state of questioning of the actions of God. Lamentations will have none of this sort of thing. Radically honest, painfully descriptive of pain, steadfastly committed to drawing Yhwh to the side of suffering humanity, this book sings of the siege and later deportations surrounding Judah's war with Babylon in the early 580s BCE. By considering the harrowing events of that era from different angles and by explicitly not adopting a god's-eye point of view that might allow for readers' escapism and denial of the brutal facts, the book makes way for a different sort of piety. In its theology, available to sufferers and their empathetic supporters, the reality of human sin may explain the pain of life only in part. Human fault is never a sufficient explanation, for Yhwh bears responsibility too. This book searches for a path toward the moment when both God and humanity take responsibility and thus find a new way of living together. As such, Lamentations challenges glib answers and offers language to express deep agonies. For this reason, it remains an indispensable biblical book.

Notes

1. The translation (slightly modified) is by Jacob Klein in *The Context of Scripture*, vol. 1: *Canonical Compositions from the Biblical World*, ed. William W. Hallo and K. Lawson Younger (Leiden: Brill, 2003), 535–539.

2. The phrase comes from the influential study of the English Romantics by C. M. Bowra, *The Poetic Imagination* (New York: Oxford University Press, 1961), 1.

For Further Reading

Faust, Avraham. *Judah in the Neo-Babylonian Period: The Archaeology of Desolation.* Atlanta: SBL, 2012.

Westermann, Claus. *Praise and Lament in the Psalms.* Atlanta: John Knox, 1981.

27 Ezekiel, the Prophet of the Rebuilt Temple

> **Key Text:** *The cherubim spread their wings and rose from the ground in front of me. They hovered at the east entrance of the gate of Yhwh's temple, and the glory of Israel's God was above them (Ezek 10:19). Then Yhwh's glory came to the temple by way of the gate facing east. The wind picked me up and brought me to the courtyard nearby, whereupon Yhwh's glory filled the temple.* (Ezek 43:4–5)

Strange, psychedelic, hallucinatory, parapsychological—these are the sorts of labels often attached to the book of Ezekiel. It's easy to see why, since the book opens with three chapters describing a vision that the prophet has of Yhwh enthroned in the heavenly temple surrounded by wild creatures, all bathed in lurid colors of green and yellow. Yes, psychedelic experience does come to mind for modern readers. And yet there is much more here.

Ezekiel was a contemporary of Jeremiah (but there is no way of knowing if the two ever met). The two books bearing their names deal with the fall of Jerusalem in 586 BCE and with the resulting crisis in confidence in the meaningfulness of Israel's past and vitality of its future. Therefore, references to the some of the same figures (Jehoiachin, Nebuchadnezzar) appear. Both books also include oracles against the nations. Whereas the book of Jeremiah blames the crisis on Judah's and Jerusalem's sinfulness, while also telling the story of the prophet (in the third person) as an innocent victim of official persecution and mob violence, Ezekiel presents its prophet through first-person narration of visions seen and conversations held with heavenly messengers. (The book may have invented the literary device, which traveled through time to Dante's *Inferno, Purgatorio*, and *Paradiso* and in much later works by other authors.) Perhaps even more significantly, Ezekiel frames the destruction of the kingdom of Judah as a cosmic event made possible by the flight of the cherubim from Jerusalem, ending divine protection of the city. Only when they return can the city be rebuilt. In other words, these two books share much in common, but their way of thinking about the world differs significantly.

Why do the books differ? Clearly part of the difference arose from the varying careers of the prophets themselves, as well as the ways in which their followers preserved their words. For example, while Jeremiah's work took place in Judah and, toward the end, Egypt, Ezekiel's prophecies are said to have occurred in Babylonia, even though he also had visions of life in Jerusalem before 586 BCE and apparently intimate knowledge of some of the political and religious players there. Moreover, the book of Jeremiah contains a great deal of biographical material about Jeremiah (not by him), while Ezekiel usually speaks in the first person and seems to have an overall literary conception that goes back to the prophet himself (even if someone may have revised the material later). In short, then, the books came together in different ways reflecting the separate histories of their heroes' words.

Yet literary history does not explain everything. Part of the literary difference comes from different theological visions. Ezekiel, a priest like Jeremiah but much more deeply enmeshed in the sort of theology that also appears in Leviticus, thought of the Temple as more central to Israelite identity than did his contemporary prophet. Thus his view of the postrestoration world centered upon a new, grander Temple, as we will see.

How does the book of Ezekiel move toward that vision? There is more than one way to outline the book, though it is clear that chs 1–24, 25–32, and 40–48 form identifiable large units. The question is how the remaining chapters fit together with them. Some possible arrangements are

Chapters 1–3, 4–24, 25–32, 33, 34–37, 38–39, and 40–48 or
Chapter 1–24, 25–32, and 33–48 or
in a chiastic pattern   1:1–11:25 (A)
                         12:1–24:27 (B)
                         25:1–32:32 (C)
                         33:1–39:29 (B′)
                         40:1–48:35 (C′)[1]

For convenience, the chiastic arrangement is being followed here, but in some ways the precise structure is less important than paying attention to the overall flow of the work. Like Isaiah and the Book of the Twelve, Ezekiel moves from an existentially rich (yet painful) exploration of the causes and results of the fall of Jerusalem to a renewed hope.

Visions of the Fall and the Fall of Visions (Ezek 1:1–11:25)

Ezekiel opens with a vision story reporting the prophet's encounter with Yhwh in the heavenly throne room (Ezek 1:1–28), followed by a series of speeches closely associated with the vision (Ezek 2:1–5:17) and another series more loosely connected but taking the form of a sort of commentary on the first set of speeches (6:1–7:27). Ezekiel 8:1 opens a new subsection (8:1–11:25), introducing a vision of the departure of the divine presence from Jerusalem to complement the opening vision of Yhwh's presence. In other words, the two opening visions supply a lens through which to view the whole book as an exploration of the relationship between Yhwh's presence and absence, a complex theological problem brought home by the destruction of the temple.

Ezekiel 1–11, and for the most part also chs 12–24, are organized around a series of introductory statements about divine communication. Major subsections begin with "Yhwh's word came to me" (Ezek 1:3; 3:17; 6:1; 7:1), while minor subsections typically begin with "and he said" or "thus says Yhwh." All of these transitional clauses serve as literary boundary markers. The text keeps flowing smoothly. Yet there is a deeper theological purpose, as well. The emphasis on Yhwh's speaking (and the prophet's hearing, by implication) places all of the often lurid descriptions of human failure and consequent calamity within the ongoing stream of interaction between heaven and earth. By situating the historical tragedy of war and deportation within a context of communication between the divine and human realms—by thinking of history in cosmic terms—the book of Ezekiel also seeks to find a moral underpinning for Yhwh's decision to allow Jerusalem's destruction. How does all of this work?

The opening vision, and indeed the book as a whole, is introduced with "in the thirtieth year's fourth month, on the fifth of the month, I was in the midst of the exilic community on the Kebar River. The heavens were opened and I saw visions of God" (Ezek 1:1). This book opening, unique in the prophetic collection of the Hebrew Bible, invites the reader of the work to understand it all as springing somehow from the experience of divine encounter.

The opening vision is dated further to 592 BCE, the fifth year of King Jehoiachin of Judah, and thus six years before the fall of Jerusalem, and is set in Babylonia (as is much of the rest of the book, if not all of it). The vision itself describes swirling winds, fire blazing around bluish or yellowish stones (depending on the meaning of the Hebrew word *ḥašmal*, apparently a loanword from Akkadian), four-headed human-animal hybrid beasts, and objects with pivoting wheels. These images all derive from the iconography and furniture of the Jerusalem Temple, with the wheeled objects drawing inspiration from the wheeled washbasins (Hebrew: *mĕkônôt*; see 1 Kgs 7:27–37) in the Temple's courtyard, and the creatures being embellishments of the pictures on the building's interior walls. In other words, the priest Ezekiel experiences the heavenly throne room of which the earthly Temple is a copy.

At the center of that room sits Yhwh, resplendent and awe-inspiring, yet willing to communicate with humanity through the medium of prophecy. This divine communication includes several elements: Ezekiel's call to prophethood, a description of his audience's obstreperous behavior, and a vision of their impending destruction. A nice summary of these elements appears in Ezek 2:3–4:

> Human being, I am sending you to Israel's children, to rebellious people who revolt against me—both they and their ancestors sinned against me until this very day. Children who are hard-faced and strong-willed—they're the ones I'm sending you to. And you should say to them, "thus says the Lord Yhwh."

The book sets the tone for the reader by portraying the prophet's audience (not the later readers!) as insurrectionaries (the phrase "rebellious people" appears repeatedly throughout the book in Ezek 2:5, 6, 7, 8; 3:9, 26, 27; 12:2, 3, 9, 25: 17:12; 24:3; and 44:6), and the prophet as a sort of sacrificial lamb who must speak truthfully to them so to invite their change of heart and action. The book of Ezekiel must thus be understood first of all as an exploration of the negative side of the divine-human relationship.

"NOW YOU/THEY WILL KNOW THAT I AM YHWH"

The phrase "now you [or they] will know that I am Yhwh" appears about sixty-five times in Ezekiel, usually as the climax of a fierce denunciation of evildoing. A typical example is Ezek 11:12, a climactic point in an oracle describing the destruction of Jerusalem: "Then you will know that I am Yhwh, whose statutes you did not follow, and whose customs you did not practice. Instead you practiced the customs of the nations around you." In all these cases, the prophet expects insight to come from suffering that he explains as the consequence of a community's choice to reject the divine path to a just and peaceful world.

As will also be clear in the Book of the Twelve Minor Prophets, Ezekiel shades the words of doom into words of hope as the book progresses. So both chs 20 and 36 contain extended discussions of how "knowing Yhwh" results from the restoration of the people to their land and lifeways after a period of suffering.

Why then, does the book use the language of "knowing Yhwh" to describe its audiences' reflection on historical events affecting them? Although neither Ezekiel nor any other biblical writer works out a full-blown epistemology, the prophet does believe that Yhwh's actions in history are at least partially discernible, that they relate to human actions and respond to human decisions, that they are available to both Israelites and foreigners (see, e.g., Ezek 12:16), and that proper reflection on them leads to religious insight.

Ezek 3 continues the vision report with a prophetic sign act during which Ezekiel, at divine insistence, eats a scroll. At least in his mouth, the scroll was "sweet as honey" (though how his digestion fared later is probably another question). By ingesting the divine words, Ezekiel creates a complex symbol: the prophetic words are both nourishing and inaccessible, both revealing and obscuring. The words do not merely address an audience—they take over a prophet. This later point becomes clearer at the end of the chapter, for after a series of visions of the divine presence, Ezekiel hears Yhwh say, "I will stick your tongue to the roof of your mouth so you will be silent, unable to upbraid them, for they are a rebellious house. But when I have you speak, I will open your mouth and you will say to them, 'thus says Yhwh.' Whoever listens will listen and whoever refuses will refuse, for they are a rebellious house" (Ezek 3:26–27). That is, through a series of visions and discussions, a prophet is made.

Ezek 4–7 continue the speeches, this time turning to specific indictments but retracing much of the same ground in order to create a comprehensive, unforgettable picture of Judah's impending doom. Most of the individual units are introduced by references to speaking ("and he said to me" or "and as for you, human being" or "therefore"), making the basic structure easy to discern, even if the progress of thought is less obvious.

However, a turn does occur with the beginning of ch 8, where another date formula (now the "sixth year" of Jehoiachin) introduces a new set of visions of the final departure from Jerusalem of Yhwh and the divine entourage. So Ezekiel "sees" "Yhwh's glory lifted up above the cherubs" (Ezek 9:3), that is, the departure of the manifestation of the divine reality that made the temple what it was. (Recall that in stories of the dedication of the Temple or the Tabernacle in 1 Kgs 8:10–11 and Exod 40:34–35, respectively, Yhwh's "glory" [Hebrew: *kābôd*] filled the sanctuary in question as a token of the divine "presence.") He then sees the heavenly throne room, complete with blue floor (as in Exod 24) and the ascent of the cherubs bearing the earthly divine throne that notionally existed in the temple (Ezek 10:15–22).

This vision may seem strange, but it embeds within it major aspects of the priests' theology. According to this theology, which appears throughout Ezekiel and Leviticus (not in identical forms, however), Yhwh's "presence" in the Temple was real and qualitatively different from Yhwh's presence elsewhere in the cosmos. But at the same time, not only could the Temple not fully "contain" God (a theme also in Deuteronomistic theology), but the divine "glory" could not fully equate to the deity. In other words, Yhwh's "glory" both reveals and hides the deity. A few human beings (Moses or Ezekiel, say) may experience the presence of the "glory," but even this sort of theophany reminds the viewer (or the one reading about the viewer) that no one can approach God with all the blinders off or understand God as God truly is. Moreover, as John Kutsko puts it, "the Priestly *kābôd* has been understood to emphasize the temporary quality of God's presence."[2] Or put differently, the vision that Ezekiel reports reminds the reader not just of the possibilities attendant upon Yhwh's presence but also of the tragedy of Yhwh's absence. Yhwh chooses the timing and extent of Yhwh's presence.

This sense of divine authority becomes still clearer in the final scene of this opening section of Ezekiel, ch 11. Here Ezekiel names Judahite political leaders who oppress their own people. He also reports Yhwh's judgment on the nation as evildoers. The prophet asks, however, an obvious question: "As I was prophesying, Peletiah son of Benaiah died. So I fell on my face [in prayer] and cried out in a loud voice, 'Oh, Lord Yhwh, are you going to finish off the remnant of Israel?' " (Ezek 11:13). In other words, the prophet wants to know just how far the destruction will go—since some persons must be punished for oppressing others, it hardly makes sense to slay the victims along with their abusers.

Accordingly, the response (vv. 14–25) imagines a new Israel that will "return [home] and rid itself of all its disgusting and abominable things [i.e., idols]" (Ezek 11:18) and then receive from Yhwh "one heart and a new spirit," replacing their "stone heart" with one of "flesh" (Ezek 11:19). Just as Jer 30 envisions a new, inward circumcision that symbolizes human bodies employed for their proper ends of praising Yhwh and treating other persons with dignity, Ezekiel concludes the opening section of the book with a hope oracle that holds out the possibility (or indeed, inevitability) that following an era of suffering, of deportation and dislocation on an international scale, a new era will follow.

BABYLON IN EZEKIEL

Although the book of Ezekiel presents itself as a set of visions occurring in Babylonia, it speaks very little about life in Mesopotamia or even Babylonian efforts outside their homeland. Rather, the references to Babylon and its king, Nebuchadnezzar, point more or less entirely to military activities against Judah (Ezek 12:13; 17:12, 20; 19:9; 23:15, 17, 23; 24:2), Tyre (Ezek 26:7; 29:18, 19), and Egypt (Ezek 30:10, 24, 25; 32:11). Unlike Isaiah and Jeremiah, Ezekiel does not speak directly of the end of the Babylonian Empire, though its reference to the new Jerusalem in chs 40–48 would certainly imply such a turn of events.

To summarize so far, the opening section of Ezekiel is framed by clusters of vision reports that graphically depict the cosmic machinery behind the calamities wrought upon Israelite bodies and buildings by Babylon. The prophet must report the visions so that his readers may gain a wider perspective.

While the idea that a deity might destroy his or her own city long predates Israel and appears in such ancient Mesopotamian texts as the "Lament over the Destruction of Sumer and Ur" (see the discussion in Chapter 26 on Lamentations), Ezekiel does more than repeat the old theology. He argues that not only does the fault in Jerusalem lie in its excess of worship (honoring too many gods), but also those who experience the tragedies of urban destruction are the very ones called upon to rethink their beliefs and the language for them. That rethinking is the concern of the next section.

Finding New Words for New Worlds (Ezek 12:1–24:27)

The second section of Ezekiel closely follows upon the first, so that it is arguable that, in reality, chs 1–24 constitute a single large unit. Both sections consist of many short oracles connected by deceptively simple transitions to create the appearance of an anthology that is nevertheless not jumpy. However, chs 12–24 do shade into an extended meditation on the divine word, on what it means for Yhwh to speak and for human beings to respond.

Indeed, it is possible to outline this entire part of the book by noting the repeated appearance of the phrase "Yhwh's word came to me" (12:1, 8, 17, 21, 26; 13:1; 14:2, 12; 15:1; 16:1; 17:1; 18:1; 20:2; 21:1, 23; 22:1, 23, 27; 23:1; 24:1), and the medieval scholars who created chapter divisions for the Bible already recognized this phrase as a marker of new subdivisions within the larger text.

These chapters also explore the ways in which language can speak accurately or otherwise about theology. Without offering a full-blown theory of apophasis—or speaking of how one cannot speak of something—Ezekiel does try to revamp the theological discussions of the time, an act obvious necessitated by the radical disruptions that everyone experienced. He does so, at least in part, by exploring the inherited literary form, the *māšāl*, a word often rendered "aphorism" or "proverb" but actually wider in scope than those English labels would indicate. The *māšāl* seems most at home in Wisdom literature, such as Proverbs or Ecclesiastes, but it also was part of the intellectual toolkit of some prophets, such as Balaam (Num 23:7, 18; 24:3, 15, 20, 23).[3] Ezekiel 12–24 is built largely around a consideration of sayings, either popular and pithy or more elaborate.

The popular and pithy sayings frame the section. So Ezek 12:21–23 reads:

> Yhwh's word came to me, "Human being, what is this *māšāl* you folks of yours [plural!] about the land of Israel: 'the days are prolonged, and every vision perishes'? Therefore, say to them, 'thus says Yhwh, I eliminate this *māšāl* so that they will no longer utter it in Israel. Rather, say to them that the days draw near when every vision will be spoken, except that there will be no lying vision, and divination will cease in the middle of Israel's house.'"

In other words, the prophet should correct a popular saying of unknown origin that implied a lack of divine communication about events. There will be communication enough for anyone's taste, with the book of Ezekiel itself being a refutation of the popular "wisdom."

EZEKIEL AS A CRYPTIC TEXT

During the Second Temple period and later, Jewish and (yet later) Christian interpreters often read Ezekiel as an apocalyptic text speaking of cosmic conflict at the end of the age (or even the end of time). For example, the Dead Sea sectarians who produced the Dead Sea Scrolls, curated or perhaps wrote a book that modern scholars call Pseudo-Ezekiel. It is attested in fragments of six ancient manuscripts (see *Discoveries in the Judaean Desert*, vol. 30 for the critical text). This text reworks the famous story of the dry bones (see p. 328) and other parts of the book to speak to a new age needing encouragement in adverse times.

The New Testament also cites Ezekiel directly or recycles imagery from it in some way dozens of time, especially in the book of Revelation. For example, Rev 11:11, as part of a depiction of the defeat of the Roman Empire and the revival of the pious, quotes Ezek 37:5, 10, combining two verses that refer to the resurrection of dead Israel. This process of recycling (discussed further in Chapter 28 on Daniel) is part of the ongoing life of the biblical texts as they serve communities of readers.

Moreover, in Ezek 18:2 the prophet considers another then famous saying, "The ancestors have eaten sour grapes, and the children's teeth are pained." The slogan seems to blame the ancestors' actions for present misfortunes, prompting the prophet's rejection of transmitted guilt and embrace of individual responsibility—"the person who sins will die" (Ezek 18:4). Whether the book intends such a statement to reject entirely the older theology of cross-generational retribution (see, e.g., Exod 20:5; 34:7) or simply blames the present difficulties on the present citizens of Judah and Jerusalem rather than their ancestors, the correction of the old *māšāl* does mark an important moment in Israel's ethical thinking. It questions the appropriateness of dodging responsibility by seeking longer-term explanations of unpleasant historical realities that simply pass the blame to someone else.

So much, then, for simple sayings. These chapters also create much more complex examples of *māšāls*. The most complex begins in Ezek 17, which says in part

The giant griffon with giant wings outspread,
Its pinions full and colorful, came to Lebanon
And took off the cedar's top.
It broke off its branches' crown,
Brought it to Canaan's land
And put it in the traders' town.
And it took the land's seed and put in a sowable field,
A slip near abundant water, putting it next a willow.
It sprouted, and it became a vine,
Spreading high and low.
Its limbs hung, its roots underslung it,
And it was a vine, putting out shoots and
Sending forth branches.

The giant bird turns out to be Babylon and the tree Israel itself, at first, but then later the bird becomes Yhwh, and later still (Ezek 19), the tree appears again in association with prides of lions. (A text similar to this appears in Ps 80.) In other words, the initial imagery can be refigured in several ways, and the elasticity of its meaning becomes a tool in the prophet's hands as he (or perhaps the creator of the book) tries to find memorable language suitable for the realities of the time.[4]

Beyond the use of the *māšāl* in either its simple or more elaborate (almost allegorical) forms, this section of Ezekiel also employs the language of sexuality in two of the most challenging passages of the book, Ezek 16:1–63 and 23:1–49. These similar texts frame the ongoing discussion of Israel's fate traced out through the ever-turning reflections on the griffon/eagle and tree/vine. The first one, ch 16, describes Israel's ongoing idolatry through the imagery of sexual immorality (adultery or prostitution—the precise register hardly matters!), with Yhwh figuring as an aggrieved husband whose spouse's "lust is poured out and nakedness uncovered in your sexing up your lovers, your abominable idols, and [whose] children's blood was given to them" (Ezek 16:36). That is, the text's prolonged, grotesque exploration of Israel's behavior works to shock the reader by placing side by side two different types of language: religious commitment to idols (along with the practice of child sacrifice for some of them), and extreme sexual promiscuity, or indeed nymphomania, by a married person. Since the text ordinarily sees Yhwh as male, in order to adopt the marriage metaphor Ezekiel (like Hosea and Jeremiah before him) must think of Israel as female.

The second sexualized description of Israel's life appears in Ezek 23, the famous extended parable of Oholah and Oholibah, Yhwh's two wives. While polygyny was a practice more or less well known in the ancient world (though not necessarily commonplace), and was even a custom attributed to deities, the idea of Yhwh as a bigamist certainly plays with a risky set of metaphors. While at least the Israelites worshiping in the later temple at Elephantine Island in Egypt about a century after Ezekiel thought of Yhwh as having two divine wives (and they probably inherited that view from their homeland), the prophetic text here thinks of the wives as human collectivities, not goddesses. Ezekiel 23 recasts Israel's story not as a grand drama of deliverance from slavery but as a squalid love affair in which two orphaned girls—the dual states of Israel and Judah—found their way to their rescuers marriage bed but then betrayed their benefactor in the grossest sorts of ways. One wonders how such a story would have sounded to Ezekiel's earliest audiences. Perhaps their disgust with the characters outweighed their dismay at the author's use of the imagery, and in this they undoubtedly differ from contemporary western readers.

At the same time, the use of such strong anthropomorphism should not distract the reader from the main point, which is to argue that Israel's behavior warrants severe consequences precisely because it is characterized by such deep ingratitude. Ezekiel allows the metaphor of cuckoldry to run away with itself, as in Hosea but with the added stickiness of multiple partners engaging in the betrayal. Certainly this is not a comfortable text.

Oracles Against the Nations (Ezek 25:1–32:32)

The prophetic attempt to speak of social disruption and political change through metaphor and symbol continues in the next major section of the book, the oracles against the nations. As in other prophetic works in the Old Testament, Ezekiel's list of nations to consider reflects the political interactions of Judah and the rest of the region during this time. The list of nations, moving in a clockwise circle around Israel, includes

Ammon (25:1–7)
Moab (25:8–11)
Edom (25:12–14)

Philistia (25:15–17)
Tyre (26:1–28:26)
Egypt (29:1–32:32)

The choices are interesting for three reasons. First, the first four receive only brief mention, doubtless because of their political insignificance on the world stage. Second, the latter two receive much greater attention, doubtless because of their greater importance as a trading center (Tyre) or a military-political great power (Egypt). And third, the conspicuous absence of Judah's chief enemy, Babylonia, signals more than just a reluctance to write about the nation in which the prophet operated for fear of a government crackdown. Instead, the absence of Babylon in this part of the book bespeaks a conception of the history of the times, according to which that empire must defeat other powers and then fall in its own time.

The most complex set of oracles are those against Tyre and Egypt. Each deserves some attention.

The oracles against Tyre focus upon the city itself (chs 26 and 27) and its king (ch 28). During the seventh and sixth century BCE, and even later, Tyre was the center of a trade network that extended through the Mediterranean world and the Near East, including northern Africa and parts of Europe as well as Asia. It was the ancient equivalent of Singapore today or Venice a few centuries ago. Every luxury item could be bought and sold there, and the wealth of many firms depended directly or indirectly on the business decisions of the Tyrians. The very name of the city (Hebrew: *ṣôr*) means "rock" or "ledge." Resting on an island just off the Lebanese coast, Tyre was impregnable. (Alexander the Great during his siege of Tyre built a mole, an enormous breakwater or pier, connecting it to the mainland and turning the ancient island into the peninsula it is today.) Capturing it proved a difficult challenge for several ancient empires.

In any case, Ezekiel describes this mercantile empire in a mock funeral poem or *qînâ* in 27:3–10 (with expanded material in the rest of the chapter). Here he lists a series of regions along the eastern coast of the Mediterranean, its major islands, and more distant regions such as Iran, Lydia (in Anatolia), and even Put (on the African Red Sea coast). From these places came timber, ivory, linen, dyed fabrics, mercenaries, silver, iron, precious stones, lead, horses, bronze, wine, and a wide assortment of agricultural products. In other words, Ezekiel describes through poetry and prose the economy of its time. This economy was no longer local, and not entirely subject to the age-old interaction of local custom and the vagaries of the weather. Rather, trade involved the movement of capital and the cultivation of taste and know-how across hundreds or even thousands of kilometers. And Tyre was the center of it all.

Yet, as Ezek 27:23 puts it,

You [Tyre] are full and very important in the midst of the seas.
On the many waters, the rowers bring you things,
But the storm wind will shatter you in the midst of the seas.

That is, not even the best-laid plans of astute business leaders and their governments can stave off ruin during times of political turnover, for the Babylonians had other interests than those of Tyre and behind them both, Yhwh worked.

It is tempting to think of the Tyre stories in light of the slightly later Greek tales of Atlantis—another maritime empire (imaginary, this time) that controlled the world. There is no known connection between the two, though Plato's idea of an island empire a century and a half after Ezekiel may conceivably have had a basis in the facts of the time when an island city-state extended its influence (but not political control) throughout the known world.

Whatever the value of such a speculation, Ezekiel's portrayal of Tyre would not be complete without its appeal to a genuinely ancient story, that of Eden. In the portrayal of the (unnamed) king of Tyre, ch 28 refers to the monarch as a ruler "full of wisdom and completely handsome," adding that "you were in Eden, God's garden, adorned with every precious stone" (which the text lists) and "a sphinx⁵ anointed" (Ezek 28:12–14).

So much for Tyre, then. Ezekiel 29:1–32:32 contains an even more developed exploration of Egypt's imminent demise, for the country fell to Nebuchadnezzar. Again, the addressees are the nation and the monarch (called "Pharaoh" without a personal name). And again, the prophet evokes the local color of the place, with references to the Nile (Ezek 29:3–10) and to Pharaoh as a serpentine river dweller, apparently a crocodile, a common and much feared creature in the Nile valley. By threatening the Pharaoh and his country with Babylonian conquest (a correct forecast of their fate), these chapters place Egyptian self-understandings of their political might within a larger theological context, according to which Yhwh (not human beings and not their gods) dictate the fortunes of entire peoples.

Within this assemblage of oracles about Egypt, two stand out in particular. Ezekiel 32:2b–9 is a taunt song of Pharaoh:

To whose will you liken your greatness?
Think of Assyria, a cedar of Lebanon
With a beautiful canopy, a shady wood, a lofty top.

Picking up in altered form the tree imagery of ch 17, ch 32 speaks of a recently extinguished empire, Assyria, and makes an argument that, while unstated, is clear enough: "if the greatest empire in the world collapsed, what makes you, Egypt, think you're invulnerable?"

Yet the interesting point is not the argument itself, but the poetic dress it wears. The book of Ezekiel seeks evocative—and provocative—language. Nor is its choice of "cedar of Lebanon" accidental, for Near Eastern kings since Sargon of Agade in the third millennium BCE had boasted of their prowess at cutting down those magnificent old trees and using them in their own buildings. Pointing out the ultimate emptiness of their claims helps Ezekiel argue for a view of the world as the zone of Yhwh's sovereignty.

The second fascinating text here appears in Ezek 32:18–32, which closes off the book's section of oracles against the nations (though other such speeches appear later). This chapter recounts the descent of Pharaoh to the underworld, where he encounters those "slain by the sword" and the "uncircumcised" from distant lands. The highly imaginative text reports that "Assyria is there," "Elam is there," "Meshek and Tubal are there," listing lands from Iraq to Iran to Anatolia or the Caucasus. An appendix to the main oracle adds Edom and Sidon/Phoenicia (Ezek 32:28–32). In short, then, the prophet offers a sort of map of the gloomy world of the dead as the home of defeated warriors (leaving aside all the other human beings residing there), now joined by one more failed empire, Egypt.

This poetic obituary for Pharaoh and his dreams of conquest draws on a long tradition, not only of Egypt meditations on life in the underworld (as seen in the various versions of the *Book of the Dead*, for example) but perhaps more fully on the Mesopotamian tradition. Most famously, the Standard Babylonian edition of the *Epic of Gilgamesh*, written six or seven centuries before Ezekiel, added to the prior versions of the story a previously separate long tale of the hero's friend Enkidu's descent to the underworld, Gilgamesh manages a séance with Enkidu's ghost and hears a description of that world:

Did you see the way things are in the netherworld?
If I tell you, my friend, if I tell you,
If I tell you the way things are in the netherworld,
You would sit down and weep, I would sit down and weep too.
My body you once touched, in which you rejoiced,
It will [never] come [back].
It is infested with lice, like an old garment,
It is filled with dust, like a crack (in parched ground).[6]

The text goes on to describe a series of persons whose lives ended tragically and who still experience that calamity in the afterlife. That is, the epic tradition views the next world as an undesirable place of residence, even for heroes—perhaps especially for them. Ezekiel may or may not have known the great Mesopotamian text—certainly the basic story was very widely circulated both before and after his era, well into Roman times—but the idea of a hero descending into the underworld was not his invention.

Ezek 32 brilliantly evokes that tradition and places it inside a larger theological context by making the descent the result of Yhwh's intervention in human history and even an odd sort of consolation to the defeated Egyptians themselves:

Pharaoh sees them and is comforted for the loss of his entire army—Pharaoh and all his army slain by the sword—Yhwh's oracle. For I [or he] placed his terror in the land of the living, but Pharaoh was laid out amid the uncircumcised, the ones slain by the sword, as was his entire army. This is Yhwh's oracle. (Ezek 32:31–32)

Poor consolation, this knowledge that many would-be heroes have failed before. Yet, Ezek 32 signals more than the death of a person but also the death of Judah's last hope of relief from Babylonian conquest: its alliance with the great power on the Nile.

Moving Toward Hope (Ezek 33:1–39:29)

While Ezekiel's oracles against the nations aim to eliminate false hopes as well as unworthy fears, then Ezek 33:1–39:29 concatenates oracles of both doom and hopefulness pointing toward Israel's deliverance from tragedy after exile. After the first thirty-two chapters have made clear Yhwh's refusal to protect Jerusalem from Babylonian invasion and the deity's clearance of that empire's invasion of the entire Levant, this new section must (1) announce the denouement that is Judah's destruction, (2) offer partial explanations of that destruction, and (3) invite the book's readers to imagine a future after the tragedy.

Ezek 33:1–33 accomplishes the first task, with Yhwh justifying both Ezekiel's role in warning the people and then Yhwh's judgment to allow their destruction as part of a system of communication with people. Comparing Ezekiel to a sentinel who must warn the people of impending danger, and characterizing the people's response to that warning as a series of denials, this oracle makes an important contribution to the reflection on the Babylonian invasions. The problem with correlating invasion with human sinfulness is the utter messiness of such a form of "punishment." Are not the innocent caught up with the guilty?

Whereas Lamentations argues that in fact such collateral damage does occur, Ezekiel takes pains to argue otherwise:

> The children of your people [i.e., your fellow Judahites] say, "the ways of the Lord Yhwh are not straightforward." But in fact, their ways are not straightforward. When the righteous person turns from his or her righteousness and does evil, then that person will die. But if the evil person turns from his or her evil and does justice and righteousness, then that person will live by them. But you folks say, "the Lord's way is not straightforward." Yet each person according to his or her ways—so shall I judge you Israel's house. (Ezek 33:17–20)

Here, then, is the logical consequence of combining the ideas of divine payment for sins and individual, rather than collective, responsibility. The world does not simply root out evil automatically, nor does evil win for long. Rather, Ezekiel argues, a just God superintends history to bring about social harmony. One should expect, special circumstances excepted, that survivors of the nation's destruction will be the righteous.

Yet things are not so simple, as Ezekiel recognizes. After all, many righteous people, including the prophet himself, suffered during the wars of the early sixth century BCE and every century thereafter! Ezekiel corrects possible misunderstandings by noting that not all human beings have the same level of responsibility or accountability because the prerequisites of personal agency (power, understanding, self-awareness, etc.) are unequally distributed. Hence ch 34.

This chapter explores the failure of the leadership of Judah before the Babylonian invasions. In an oracle against "Israel's shepherds" who have "eaten the fat and worn the wool and sacrificed the fat" of those entrusted to them (Ezek 34:3), the book underscores the malfeasance of the monarchy and nobility, placing the blame for the nation's fall on those who should have ensured its success. At the same time, the oracle inverts the leadership language, with Yhwh assuming responsibility for tending the flock (thus implying its survival, in spite of every calamity) and promising a new leader from the Davidic dynasty (Ezek 34:23). Without denying the responsibility of each individual for his or her fate, the prophet shifts ground slightly by passing blame to the leaders for the suffering of the others.

This parceling out of blame leads inevitably to the final condemnation in chs 35–36, which describe the utter devastation of the Babylonian invasions and then blesses the land itself. Far from being an uninhabitable place or an abattoir for one nation after another, the land will be "worked and planted" (Ezek 36:9) and then populated by all of Israel, complete with cities, farms, and all the other accouterments of civilization (Ezek 36:10–23). The reversal of fortune will come, just not yet, and not without suffering.

The reality of both the suffering and its undoing underlies the most famous, and arguably weirdest, of Ezekiel's vision reports, that of the resurrection of the "dry bones" in Ezek 37:1–28. The words speak for themselves:

> Yhwh's hand was on me, bringing me by Yhwh's spirit and depositing me in the middle of a valley that was full of bones. Wherever I passed by, in any direction, the valley was covered with bones completely dried out [i.e., with no flesh upon them]. Then he said to me, "Human being, can these bones live?" I said, "Lord Yhwh, you know." (Ezek 37:1–3)

The vision underscores the horrors of the wars of the period, symbolized by a valley covered with skeletons. The scene sounds like something out of a symbolist movie of a few decades ago, but the symbolism here is transparent enough. Israel is dead. Yhwh's question seems out of place, then. No, the bones ought not to live again. Hence Ezekiel's evasive answer—evasive because the question presupposes an answer that contradicts normal experience. That experience is the resurrection of a people.

Prior to the book's final move toward resolution in chs 40–48, however, comes the loosely organized and mysterious series of oracles about Gog and Magog (Ezek 38:1–39:29). The place name Magog appears elsewhere in the Bible in Gen 10:2 and 1 Chron 1:5 (which copies Genesis), as one of several ethnic groups in far north or northwest of Israel's world. Obscure, distant, and therefore potentially unsettling, the image of Magog invading the land serves Ezekiel as a symbol of the final defeat of the invading foes.

There is some debate about the identity of Ezekiel's Magog, but the best solution seems to be to see it as a code word for Babylon. By using a Caesar cipher, in which one substitutes letters farther down the alphabet for the real letters of the word in question, the prophet creates a mystery that the reader can easily solve. So by moving forward one letter from *bet-bet-lamedh* (Babel = Babylon) to the next letter in the alphabet in each slot *gimel-gimel-mem* (GGM) and then reversing their order (MGG), the text comes up with Magog, a word otherwise known. (This sort of cryptic writing appears elsewhere in the Bible when Jeremiah converts the same word Babel to Sheshak [Jer 25:26; 51:41].) Calling Babylon "Magog" reminds readers that the familiar can be exotic from a certain point of view.

Beyond the cryptology, the point of the Gog and Magog stories comes through in the description of their utter defeat and the aftermath:

> You will fall all over the field, for I have spoken—the Lord Yhwh's oracle. And I will send fire upon Magog and the "secure" island dwellers, so that they will know that I am Yhwh. Then shall I make known my among my people Israel, and I will no longer allow my holy name to be profaned. Thus will the nations know that I am Yhwh, the Holy One in Israel. (Ezek 39:5–7)

The text then reintroduces the idea of a valley full of bones, belonging this time not to Israel but to its enemies who came from the north. (Recall that because of the presence of the Arabian Desert, invaders from Mesopotamia also had to come from the north, not the more direct, but impassable, east-west route.) This time, the bones will be buried, and no resurrection will ensue. For after the climactic battle, Yhwh promises "never again to hide my face from them, but instead to pour out my spirit on Israel's house" (Ezek 39:29). Thus has doom transmuted into hope. While the text apparently intends this battle scene to remain in the realm of the symbolic (since no such battle occurred in antiquity), it opens the door to a restoration of Israel's fortunes that is tangible enough (see Ezra and Nehemiah for that part of the story).

The Rebuilt Community and its Magnificent Temple (Ezek 40:1–48:35)

The final section of the book asks the simple question: "What does the restoration look like?" The answer is far from simple because Ezekiel draws on old priestly conceptions of the presence of Yhwh to envision not just the return of the departed divine glory to its proper place in the Temple (in Ezek 43:1–5) but a reconstructed Temple fit for the divine presence. (That is, again, the book interprets the seemingly random happenings of history as cosmic events that can be expressed only in highly symbolic language.) Just as Exod 25–31 and 35–40 describe the Tabernacle as a fit sanctuary for the newly delivered exodus people, so too do the last chapters of Ezekiel speak of a gigantic Temple in which Yhwh's "throne and footstool" would never again be in a situation in which his royal neighbors would "defile my holy name" (Ezek 43:7). The Temple becomes a symbol of a new order of peace and justice within a profoundly religious context.

Throughout the ancient world, the building and rebuilding of temples occupied kings' attention as a way of cementing cosmic order and their place in it. Ezekiel's temple does the first without necessarily the second. While the book does expect the restoration of the monarchy in reduced form, the temple itself is the centerpiece, with its revised admission policies (no irreligious foreigners) and staffing (only descendants of Zadok as priests). A sacred precinct covering 500 million square cubits (about forty square miles) belongs to the temple proper with the income of the property providing basic operating expenses. More to the point, this new space was to be the center of the revived Israel, a visual reminder of the importance of following Yhwh.

The book closes with this vision and with more. Ezekiel 47 and 48 imagine a reconstituted nation with all the tribes restored, not to their old territories but to lands farther north and more expansive. Enlivening all this land will be a new hydrological feature, a river flowing from the temple as the divine throne. But ch 47 sets forth this image, which draws on much older ideas of the river flowing from the divine palace set in the heavenly garden. The new becomes, Ezekiel argues, the improvement of the old. The end time returns to the beginning, but this time, Israel gets it all right.

Implications

To conclude this treatment of Ezekiel, it is useful to remember that this strange and intriguing book addresses a major problem: how to explain in theological terms the destruction of Jerusalem and Judah by the Babylonians. On the one hand, the book affirms Yhwh's absolute justice, the accountability of human beings, the transience of political power, and the importance of worship. By understanding Israel's sin not as violations of rules but as sacrilege (even when committed against other human beings), Ezekiel offers a view that is consonant with, but different from, those of other prophetic books. It is more priesthood- and Temple-oriented than the book closest to it, Jeremiah.

Yet on the other hand, Ezekiel also affirms Yhwh's refusal to accept human failure as the guiding principle of history. For God to be sovereign in a meaningful sense, divine mercy must prevail in the end. In its own strange way, wheels and flying cherubim and all, Ezekiel affirms that such does, in fact, occur.

Notes

1. This last arrangement was proposed by John Kutsko, *Between Heaven and Earth: Divine Presence and Absence in the Book of Ezekiel* (Winona Lake, IN: Eisenbrauns, 2000), 1.

2. Ibid., *Between Heaven and Earth*, 84.

3. NRSV's rendering of the Hebrew phrase "lifted up his *māšāl*" as "uttered his oracle" is unfortunate because it obscures the variety of ways in which prophets spoke. ESV's "took up his discourse" or even KJV's "took up his parable" would be preferable.

4. For a more detailed discussion of this and related passages, see Mark W. Hamilton, "Riddles and Parables, Traditions and Texts: Ezekielian Perspectives on Wisdom Traditions," in *Is There a Wisdom Tradition? New Prospects in Israelite Wisdom Studies,* ed. Mark Sneed (Atlanta: SBL, 2015), 241–262.

5. Hebrew: *kĕrûb*, whence the English word "cherub."

6. The translation is by Douglas Frayne in Benjamin Foster, ed., *The Epic of Gilgamesh* (New York: W. W. Norton, 2001), 138.

For Further Reading

Kutsko, John. *Between Heaven and Earth: Divine Presence and Absence in the Book of Ezekiel.* Winona Lake, IN: Eisenbrauns, 2000.

Patmore, Hector M. "Adam or Satan? The Identity of the King of Tyre in Late Antiquity." In *After Ezekiel: Essays on the Reception of a Difficult Prophet,* edited by Andrew Mein and Paul M. Joyce, 59–69. New York/London: T. & T. Clark, 2011.

Petter, Donna Lee. *The Book of Ezekiel and Mesopotamian City Laments.* Fribourg: Academic Press/Göttingen: Vandenhoeck & Ruprecht, 2011.

28 Keeping Faith in a Distant Land
THE BOOK OF DANIEL

Key Texts: *Now you, Daniel, hide the words and seal the book until the end time. Many will run about, and evil [or knowledge?] will increase* (Dan 12:4).

Even if history does not consist solely of human failure, still, much of it is grim. So, how does one speak intelligently of unhappy times? Like the book of Ezekiel, Daniel speaks of such an age through the medium of vision and symbol. Daniel, however, takes this emphasis on visionary language a step further into the realm of apocalyptic, a literary genre and mode of thinking that emphasizes the radical disruption of the present social structure. Through story and vision, the book tries to articulate a hopeful message during a time of crisis.

What is that time? The book sets itself within the sixth century BCE, during the Babylonian and Persian empires. Its hero interacts with the monarchs of that period, with their stories serving as models for ongoing Jewish interaction with the gentile world.

At the same time, however, the book seems to have come together over time through the combination of materials from different sources, reaching its completion during the second century BCE. On the most obvious level, the book is written in two different languages, Hebrew in Dan 1:1–2:4a and 8:1–12:13, Aramaic in Dan 2:4b–7:28. That is, a bilingual Hebrew speaker wrote around older Aramaic-language sources to construct the larger story, switching literary genres (short court stories to vision reports) in midstream. Moreover, the book presupposes a historical development otherwise unknown, in which a "Mede" named "Darius" ruled Babylon after the overthrow of the native Chaldean dynasty and its last king Nabonidus and his regent Belshazzar. In fact, Cyrus of Persia annexed the Babylonian Empire into his own much larger state in 539 BCE. The book seems to be a work of historical fiction, which clearly signals its fictional character. It is therefore a mistake to understand Daniel as straight-up history in the manner of, say, 1–2 Kgs.

At the same time, the book tells its story for a deep and important purpose. The latest events described in the book are the rise of Alexander the Great and his successors. After Alexander the Great's death in 322 BCE, his generals fought over the empire he had seized from the Persians. In time, Ptolemy became ruler of Egypt and the south Levantine coast, including the land of Israel, and Seleucus became ruler of Syria and Mesopotamia (and, for awhile, lands farther east). For a century, Palestine was a border zone subject to invasion and finally conquest by the Seleucid dynasty (after 202 BCE). This dynasty eventually produced a particularly tyrannical ruler, Antiochus IV Epiphanes who desecrated the Jerusalem Temple and triggered a revolt against gentile rule by a priest named Mattathias and his four sons. His most influential son, Judas, took the nickname "Maccabee" or "the hammer" as he led the insurrection (165–163 BCE) resulted in Israel's independence. Daniel reflects upon this story as an example of God's protection of Israel and fulfillment of prophecy.

Although the book consists of stories understandable on their own, Daniel does reveal a clear structure, with three major sections (1, 2–7, and 8–12), and the second section consisting of a ring structure (ABCCBA).

A. Introduction (1:1–21)
B. Daniel vs. the foreign rulers (2:1–7:28)
   1. Nebuchadnezzar's vision (2:1–49) A
   2. Three men in a flaming furnace (3:1–33 [ET 3:1–4:3]) B
   3. Nebuchadnezzar's humiliation (4:1–34 [ET 4:4–37]) C
   4. Belshazzar's feast and the handwriting on the wall (5:1–6:1 [ET 5:1–31]) C'
   5. Daniel in the lion's den (6:2–29 [ET 6:1–28]) B'
   6. Visions of four beasts (7:1–28) A'
C. World crises and final renewal (8:1–12:13)

ADDITIONS TO DANIEL

The book of Daniel existed in two versions in antiquity. The Hebrew and Aramaic text was later expanded in the Greek translation by adding stories of Daniel as a detective in the temple of Bel and as the protector of a woman falsely accused of adultery (Susanna), and by a prayer ascribed to Shadrach, Meshach, and Abednego in the flaming furnace. English Bibles ordinarily print a translation of the Hebrew and Aramaic (shorter) version and include the added material as "Additions to Daniel."

Introduction (Dan 1:1–21)

The book opens by situating the young Daniel among the deportees shuttled off to Babylon after 605 BCE, prior to the destruction of Jerusalem (the dating in Dan 1:1 seems imprecise on this point). Daniel and his youthful friends preserve their Jewish identity in the royal court by declining to eat the nonkosher, but undoubtedly luxurious, food of the palace and proposing instead a test of nutritional efficacy. Their traditional food laws prove superior, vindicating both their own personal courage and the supreme wisdom of their God.

This opening story of Daniel sets the stage for the entire book by noting the risks that Jews face in diaspora, while also offering models of courage in the face of such danger. Like Esther and such (slightly) later books as Tobit and Judith, Daniel finds heroes faithful to Israel's religion.

At the same time, Dan 1 considers two possible methods of identity-making, encouraging one and ignoring the other. The first is food. Just as twenty-first-century Westerners have become increasingly aware of the moral dimensions of food production and consumption, ancient Israel defined the boundaries of the community, in part, by foods consumed or not (see the discussion of *kašrût* in Chapter 5 on Leviticus). The second possible strategy for building group identity revolves around practices of name giving. While medieval Christians assigned their children the names of saints, and modern Jews have often adopted biblical or Talmudic names as identity markers, the audience of Daniel has no such expectations. Thus Daniel assumes the Babylonian name Belteshazzar ("protect the king's health"), while his friends Hananiah, Mishael, and Azariah, changed their perfectly good Yahwistic names to Shadrach, Meshach, and Abednego. The first two new names are of uncertain etymology, but are probably Persian, while Abednego is a slight corruption of a good, polytheistic Babylonian name, Abed-Nabû ("servant of [the god] Nabû"). The text responds to the perennial question, "what's in a name?" by answering "not much." Their Babylonian names did not in any way signal the inferiority of Israel or its God.

JEWS IN BABYLONIA AFTER THE BABYLONIAN EMPIRE

Recently published cuneiform tablets from Babylonia, dating to the Neo-Babylonian and Persian periods (i.e., sixth-fifth centuries BCE), show many Israelite/Jewish names, as well as traditional Akkadian names, indicating the mixture of populations (and shifting of names) that Ezra-Nehemiah, Daniel, and Tobit would lead one to expect for that period and later centuries. So the sort of name-giving presupposed by Daniel 1, while colored by life at the royal court and thus unusual, fits into a larger period of the migration of names alongside the migration of peoples.

Stories of Daniel vs. the Foreign Rulers (Dan 2:1–7:28)

If names count for little, then faithfulness to Yhwh must come to light in some other way. For the book of Daniel, that way lies through passive resistance to imperial efforts to compel or at any rate encourage idolatry. The introduction of the characters in Dan 1 thus concludes with the claim that "in every instance of the king's seeking for insightful understanding from them [Daniel and friends], he found them to be ten times a match for all the soothsayers and diviners anywhere in his empire" (Dan 1:20). This superior insight, given by Yhwh through the men's adherence to Torah and thus the pursuit of wisdom, allowed them to survive. The book insists that similar actions will allow other Jews to survive as well.

Daniel 2–7 set forth six stories in a ring pattern that exemplify the superior wisdom, courage, and personal integrity of the book's heroes. To begin, then, Dan 2 tells the story of Nebuchadnezzar's dream. The emperor had dreamed of a giant four-metaled statue and sought the dream's meaning. He determined, however, to seek the interpretation from the usual assemblage of diviners and dream-sayers without revealing to them the content of the dream itself. Fortuitously, Daniel alone can perform such a feat, because he has received such power from

> The great God, blessed forever, who has wisdom and might.
> For he changes seasons and epochs, deposes kings and elevates kings . . . grants wisdom
>   to sages and knowledge to the insightful. (Dan 2:20–21)

Like Joseph in Genesis, on whose story the Daniel story is closely modeled, this Jewish wise man helps a king understand the unfolding of history more precisely through divine help.

The vision itself describes a statue with a gold head, silver shoulders and arms, a bronze gut, and iron legs resolving into iron mixed with clay. That is, the statue grew less valuable as one moved down it, with its base consisting of an unstable (and foolishly composed) base. This odd work of art turns out to represent a succession of four kingdoms through time, each progressively less precious or stable. Here, Dan 2 understands the history of the empires dominating Israel from Babylonia through the Hellenistic period to be a story of increasing tragedy and failure.

THE FOUR KINGDOMS OF DANIEL

Dan 2 combines ideas of long-lived consequence in the ancient Near East. The idea of a progression of ages, a divinely directed turning of epochs, goes far back in the Mesopotamian intellectual tradition. Daniel 2:20–22 accepts this tradition and places the responsibility for the turn of eras squarely on Yhwh, the God of Israel. The identification of the kingdoms could shift with time, but in Daniel the four kingdoms are Babylonia, Media (as in Herodotus), Persia, and the empires of Alexander and his successors (the last being the iron mixed with clay). Later texts such as Revelation and Josephus thought of Rome as the fourth kingdom, projecting the imagery forward into their own time (since Rome had absorbed the Ptolemaic and Seleucid dynasties in the first century BCE). Meanwhile, the idea of epochs of creation as metals of progressively less value seems to connect to the Greek idea of five ages (gold, silver, bronze, and iron, with the fourth age being unmetalized) that appears in Hesiod, *Works and Days*, 110–82 (composed ca. 700 BCE).

Speaking of statues, Dan 3 tells the story of Daniel's three friends (his absence seems odd, perhaps indicating a different origin for the story). Nebuchadnezzar commands all his subjects to bow to a giant figure 60 cubits (about 30 m) tall and 6 cubits (about 3 m) wide (a wobbly object, given its relative narrowness). This action surprises the reader because the previous story ends with Nebuchadnezzar's confession of Yhwh as "God of gods and Lord of kings" (Dan 2:47), but this apparent inconsistency reflects the episodic nature of the stories in the book. There is no attempt here to construct completely consistent characters, and indeed their inconsistency reflects the arbitrariness of the empires themselves, as Jews (and other subjects, no doubt) experienced them.

In any case, Shadrach, Meshach, and Abednego (and apparently they alone) refuse to pray to the idol, leading Nebuchadnezzar to toss them into a superheated furnace. Miraculously saved by angelic intervention, they survive unscathed, not even properly smoked by the experience. The story ends with a royal decree forbidding blasphemy of Israel's God because of that deity's unique power to rescue the oppressed. Again, the narrator of Daniel places his chief theological ideas in the mouth of the foreign ruler, who expresses proper wonderment at God's mercy to his Jewish worshipers.

The same basic theme appears in the third story, Dan 4:1–34 (ET 4:4–37), which recounts the madness of Nebuchadnezzar. Despite warnings in dreams of the folly of royal arrogance, the king extols his own city as "this great Babylon, which I built as a capital" (Dan 4:27 [ET 4:30]). He then meets the divinely ordained punishment of losing his mind, living as a hairy grazing beast with uncut nails and unwashed skin for a season. This story exposes the thin line between power and insanity, an interesting theme in its own right. But more importantly, it does so by evoking a theme common to folk literature (think of "Beauty and the Beast") according to which a human being becomes an animal for either good or bad reasons. Here, the story warns that all rulers must avoid pride if they wish also to avoid the loss of their humanity.

THE MAD KING IN THE DEAD SEA SCROLLS

The story of Nebuchadnezzar's madness finds a parallel in the Dead Sea Scrolls. *4QPrayer of Nabonidus* (4Q242) says that Nabonidus, the last emperor of the Neo-Babylonian Empire (reigned 556/555–539 BCE), had gone mad and could only be cured by a Jewish sage. That is, more than one version of the saga of the mad Babylonian king circulated in antiquity. The confusion between Nebuchadnezzar and his successor (after two intervening rulers) Nabonidus is otherwise attested in antiquity. The point of all these versions of the story remains the same: foreign rulers err grievously in elevating themselves or even their gods at the expense of Israel's God.

Paralleling the story of the mad king in ch 4, Dan 5 picks up the theme of royal feasting. As a depiction of excessive luxury and irresponsibility, such a literary type-scene also appears in the opening act of Esther and in Greek literature. With surprisingly contemporary resonance, the idea of a decadent royal court was apparently popular during the late first millennium BCE as a form of criticism of the powers that be. In this story, the imperial Babylonian regent Belshazzar throws a feast using the sacred vessels of the Jerusalem Temple as ordinary partyware. The answer to such sacrilege is not long in coming, for during the party Belshazzar sees a ghostly hand writing words in Aramaic on the wall. (The modern expression "to see the handwriting on the wall" comes from this story.) Only Daniel, whom the queen introduces as the best seer in the empire, can explain that the words "*mene, mene, tekel,* and *parsin*" refer to the fall of Babylonia and its replacement by the Persians (Dan 5:25–28). The story refers back to the earlier king Nebuchadnezzar as a brutal tyrant, helping cement his reputation for the next 2,500 years, and comparing the current ruler unfavorably even to him. The story ends by noting that the aftermath of the party was the fall of the city "that very night," indicating that Belshazzar's feast took place during a siege as an act of supreme irresponsibility.

Dan 6:1 (ET 5:30) introduces a new set of rulers, Median this time. Since no evidence for a Median king or governor of Babylonia exists, the historical location of such a story must remain doubtful. Again, it is a sort of parable rather than a factual account. However, its close parallelism to the persecution story in ch 3 signals its theological importance.

In this new story, Daniel disobeys a royal command obtained under false pretenses (much as in Esther), according to which all subjects of the new empire must pray to the king himself. For readers during the mid-second century BCE when Daniel became a complete work, such a vision of an egocentric ruler making himself out to be a god would have seemed more than pertinent, since Hellenistic kings often assumed divine titles and portrayed themselves on coinage and in statues as semidivine beings (in fact, the infamous Antiochus IV assumed the title "Epiphanes" or "divine manifestation"). Daniel prayed in the direction of Jerusalem, and found himself in a pit for domesticated lions as his reward. Since "domestication" is always a relative term with respect to lions, his escape from the creatures could only be a miracle, and the now penitent king sheepishly asks Daniel if he has survived. The affirmative answer prompts Darius, like Nebuchadnezzar in chs 2 and 3, to witness to Daniel's God as, "the living God, exalted forever, whose kingdom never ends, whose rule always endures" (Dan 6:27 [ET 6:26]).

This confession, then, leads to the last of the six core stories, set earlier during the regency of Belshazzar. In Dan 7, the book's hero reports an extended vision of creatures rising and falling, the divine throne set up, the fall of the fourth and final kingdom described in ch 2, and the final triumph of Israel. This chapter concludes the concentrically arranged stories of Daniel's encounters with gentile kings by citing Nebuchadnezzar's dreams in ch. 2. It also introduces the final section of the book, which consists entirely of dreams.

Dan 7 concludes the story cycle with an extended poem (Dan 7:23–27) on the fate of the final kingdom. Its ten kings give way to a final ruler, worse than all, who in turn loses the throne altogether. In the new reality, "empire and rule, indeed, the greatness of power under all of heaven, will be given to the holy people of the Most High, whose kingdom is an eternal kingdom" (Dan 7:27). That is, the Jewish people will escape their gentile masters and find independence, a dream that became reality during the rule of the family of Mattathias, the Hasmoneans, during the second and first centuries BCE.

WHO WERE THE TEN (OR ELEVEN) KINGS OF DAN 7?

After the death of Alexander the Great, his empire passed to his generals, who fought over it for an entire generation. The Ptolemaic and Seleucid dynasties ruled Israel/Palestine in turn. Assuming that Dan 7 intends the numbers "ten" or "eleven" to be taken literally, the rulers he has in mind might have been

Alexander and Regents for his Family
Alexander the Great
Perdiccas
Antipater

The Ptolemaic Dynasty (301–198 BCE)
Ptolemy I Soter
Ptolemy II Philadelphos
Ptolemy III Euergetes
Ptolemy IV (Philopator)
Ptolemy V Epiphanes

The Seleucid Dynasty (198–165 BCE)
Seleucus III the Great
Seleucus IV Philopator
Antiochus IV Epiphanes

Alternatively, Dan 7 may have in mind the entire Seleucid dynasty, or it may mean "ten" to be a round number. In any case, the identity of the last king as one who changes sacred law and the calendar itself fits Antiochus IV, the villain of the Maccabean revolt (see the discussion of 1–2 Macc in Chapter 30). Such a king ranges himself against God and the "holy ones," or angels, thus illustrating his utter folly. Speaking of mad kings!

The use of a vision report as the principal literary device here makes a nice segue to the vision reports of Dan 8–12. In both sections of the book, visions point to the idea of history as an esoteric mystery that must be illuminated by divinely designated interpreters for the understanding and self-preservation of the righteous insiders who accept that interpretation. This view presupposes that Yhwh controls history, explains it to some people, and thereby protects them from the world's worst tragedies. This view of things, characteristic of apocalyptic literature in ancient and more recent times, has the potent effect of encouraging Daniel's readers to persevere in the face of adversity, like the book's eponymous hero himself.

In summary, then, the stories of Dan 2–7 concentrate on a small number of repeated themes: the dangers of living in a gentile empire; the tyranny of kings, but also their conversion to respect for Israel's God; the intervention of angels; the use of dreams and inspired interpretation as a medium of divine communication; and the need for courage on the part of faithful people. While these chapters draw on older ideas, seen already in Genesis and Exodus, for example, they also explore themes of particular importance in an environment in which some Jews lived in the homeland and others in diaspora, but all experienced marginalization.

World Crises and Final Renewal (8:1–12:13)

The final section of Daniel, chs 8–12, breathes a more volatile and acrid atmosphere than the first seven chapters. On the whole, however, these chapters constitute an extended commentary on ch 7, with each element of the visions of that chapter receiving further development. At the same time, chs 8–12 are much more tightly integrated and carefully written than the earlier part of the book and follow a clearly defined plot.

Dan 8 opens with a vision report set in Susa, one of the capitals of the Persian Empire (and scene of the book of Esther). By placing the vision in a center crucial to one of his empires and the time period (the regency of Belshazzar) in an earlier one, Daniel signals the applicability of its theology to empires in general. There is a more specific context in mind, however, and that is the end of the Persian rule during the conquest of Alexander. A ram (Persia), though all-conquering, meets its match with the he-goat from the west (Alexander). The triumphant he-goat loses its horn (again, Alexander) only to have four horns grow in its place (the *Diadochi* or "successors" of Alexander).

The crux of the vision appears in vv. 11–12, which describe the end of sacrifices in Jerusalem, meaning Antiochus Epiphanes's desecration of the Temple. This period of turmoil and horror will last, the vision asserts, for 2,300 evening and morning sacrifices (therefore, 1,150 days, or almost the equivalent of the three and half years of Dan 7:25). In other words, the vision understands the history of the Hellenistic period as leading inexorably to the Temple's profanation.

Such a disaster cannot be the story's end, although Daniel cannot know that yet. Thus the vision scene ends with the visionary reporting himself "sick for days" (Dan 8:27) and seeking an explanation for things set in "the distant future" (8:26).

The book then returns to its theme of Daniel's piety, citing an extended penitential prayer of his (Dan 9:3–19). The text positions this cry for divine aid, which closely resembles such postexilic prayers as Neh 9 or Isa 63:7–64:11, as part of a larger attempt to understand history as God's theater of activity. As such, Dan 9 is highly typical of Second Temple Jewish theological reflection (see Chapter 30). Like many other texts, it draws upon the prophetic materials from earlier times, with Dan 9:2 explicitly referring to the "seventy years" of Jer 25:11–12; 29:10. The conundrum that Daniel and many other Second Temple period texts had to face was that the return from exile after about seventy years did not result in the full restoration of Israelite life. Quite the opposite, for the exile continued in some form, with varying degrees of suffering involved.

This delay of redemption leads Dan 9:24 to introduce an innovative interpretation: "seventy years" becomes "seventy weeks of years" or 490 years. The period will begin with a decree to return home (presumably Cyrus's decree of ca. 539 BCE), lead to the ordination of an "anointed one" (a high priest) after "seven weeks," and then reach a crisis after "sixty-two" further "weeks." The final resolution will occur during the seventieth week. While the text does not show the degree of chronological precision one might expect of a straight-up historical text (especially a modern one), the rough timeline of 490 years between the sixth-century crises leading to Jerusalem's fall and the second-century crisis leading to its restoration works well enough.

This detailed theological reflection on history rests upon prayer and vision. On the one hand, Daniel utters a prayer of penitence inviting God to consider the plight of Israel, justly punished as they are (a point underscored by references to the "Torah of Moses," i.e., Deut 28's covenant curses). The prayer names its dramatis personae: a merciful and just God who keeps covenant and a people who do evil and rebel. Yet it also asks the deity to rewrite the plotline:

Incline your ear and hear,
Open your eyes and see
Our ongoing humiliations
And the city over which your name is called. (Dan 9:18)

By calling upon the deity to identify with the people, the prayer seeks both to acknowledge human sinfulness as the trigger for exile and to put the onus for the continuation of the punishment back on God.

The response to this prayer is an angelic vision from Gabriel (called an archangel in later texts and most famous for appearing to the Virgin Mary in Luke 1:26–38). Gabriel offers Daniel the interpretation of the ancient texts (seventy years = seventy weeks of years) and thus the key to unlocking the secrets of the vision in ch 8. The sufferings of the present are simply part of the ancient prophets' expectations. No mystery here! Offering reassurance to the penitent, heartsick seer who piously seeks to understand history, the second half of the communication event closes the loop opened by the sorrowful prayer earlier in the chapter.

This closing of the loop becomes much more explicit in chs 10–12, which function as a single unit. In this final act of the book, Daniel has a vision just after Passover. He sees an angelic figure (Gabriel again?) appearing in the sort of shiny, metallic form attributed to Yhwh in Ezek 1; he calms the understandably nervous sage and promises him an appropriate interpretation of the various visions he has had, and thus of the history unfolding around him.

The rest of chs 10–11 cover much of the same ground as the visions in chs 7–8, just in greater detail. The unfolding of Persian- and especially Hellenistic-era history is described in forms of cosmic battles involving Michael and the guardian angel of Persian ("prince of Persia"), and then the king of the north (the Seleucids) and the king of the south (the Ptolemies), culminating in a final victory over the foes of Israel and Israel's God.

The text records a series of events such as the Roman intervention in the Near East (the Kittim in Dan 11:30), an intervention that prevented Antiochus (the "king of the north") from the destroying Egypt ("the king of the south"), but also led to the former's defilement of the Temple, Daniel's "abomination of desolation." By framing history in this pseudo-cryptic form (*pseudo*-cryptic because the reader understands the code), the book of Daniel highlights its understanding of human history as an arena of activity incomprehensible except to those possessing the secret of God's superintendence of it.

At last, the final movement of the book comes in ch 12. It opens with an announcement of the resurrection of the dead, the only explicit mention of this important Jewish and Christian doctrine in the Hebrew Bible:

> At that time, Michael the great prince shall stand,
> The one who stands over your people's children,
> Though it is a troubled time, unparalleled for any nation up to that time,
> And in that time your people, i.e., everyone written in the book, shall be rescued.
> And many of those asleep in the dusty ground will arise,
> some to eternal life and some to contempt and perpetual humiliation. (Dan 12:1–2)

This view of a differentiated afterlife, with different fates for different sorts of persons, functions here as part of an overall vision of the final defeat of evildoers. It is not an escapist idea (just as it is not in the New Testament, for that matter), but a natural outgrowth of the idea of God's justice. Since not everything works out well in this life, some of the injustice of the world must be solved through the miracle of resurrection.

The book ends by advising the character Daniel to seal the book until the proper time. By this literary device, the author points to the idea that long-held secrets of the divine realm are now revealed to the reader. In other words, the motif of secrecy is a paradoxical device by which the text advertises its transparency. The secret is not a secret except to the practitioners of evil, the oppressive gentile rulers. To the righteous who attend to the book, all of history now seems explainable and, more to the point, survivable.

Implications

So how does one talk about times of struggle? For Daniel, the method involves considering a series of alternatives:

- The power of God vs. the impotence of idols
- The justice of God vs. the complicity of idols in oppression
- God's wisdom vs. pagan wisdom

- Humility vs. arrogance
- Justice vs. injustice
- Faithfulness vs. accommodation
- The story of God vs. the story of the powers that be
- The permanence of the heavenly kingdom vs. the transience of human realms
- The complexity of living faithfully in a world of multiple value systems.

Yet the book does not easily reduce to such a list, for it considers these sets of oppositions in the form of story, and often stories within stories. By narrating the human struggle for spiritual integrity, as well as the revealed stories of God's struggle against evil forces much larger than individual human beings, the book of Daniel offers its readers a view of reality according to which human beings may act in accordance with the divine will, and for their own good. History, says this book, does not in the final analysis trap its participants in the ever-present patterns of oppression and suffering. Those patterns will collapse at last, but even in the meantime, by reconceiving of the story of faith and one's place in it, faithful Jews (or other believers, mutatis mutandis) may find a partial resolution even in the midst of evil empires and their all too human supporters. Far from being a book of suffering and doom, then, Daniel presents a profoundly hopeful picture of a dawning future far from the rule of tyrants, whether the Seleucids or their innumerable successors.

For Further Reading

Ballentine, Debra Scoggins. *The Conflict Myth and the Biblical Tradition*. Oxford: Oxford University Press, 2015.

Collins, John J. *The Apocalyptic Imagination*. 3rd ed. Grand Rapids: Eerdmans, 2016.

Levenson, Jon D. *Resurrection and the Restoration of Israel: The Ultimate Victory of the God of Life*. New Haven: Yale University Press, 2006.

Pearce, Laurie E., and Cornelia Wunsch. *Documents of Judean Exiles and West Semites in Babylonia in the Collection of David Sofer*, Cornell University Studies in Assyriology and Sumerology 28. Bethesda, MD: CDL, 2014.

29 The Twelve Minor Prophets

Key Text: *Who is wise and understands these things, insightful and knows them? For Yhwh's paths are straight, and the righteous walk in them. But sinners stumble in them.* (Hos 14:10 [ET 14:9])

Alongside the major prophetic scrolls of Isaiah, Jeremiah, and Ezekiel, a fourth prophetic work sits in the cabinet of ancient synagogues. That scroll contains words attributed not to one, but to twelve prophets. While all the prophetic books resulted from the work of multiple composers, the Book of the Twelve acknowledges that fact. It offers a kaleidoscope of perspectives on Israel's historical experiences, all with an aim toward helping the reader, as the last verse of the book of Hosea puts it, to "understand and know" the paths of Yhwh so as to order his or her life for a morally and spiritually vital future.

As it stands now, the Book of the Twelve includes material spanning the eighth to the fifth or fourth centuries BCE. The order of the books varies in extant Hebrew and Greek manuscripts, with most English Bibles following the order of the MT.[1] The original order remains unclear, if there was one. (For example, the Dead Sea Scrolls Hebrew manuscript 4QXII[a] apparently places Jonah last, a fact that may point to that book's late inclusion.)

Moreover, there is the problem of how carefully integrated the twelve booklets are. Is the collection a loose anthology of works that enjoyed circulation before being joined together, or did the editors who combined them also rework them to some extent so that they cohered more closely? (And if they did rework them, how much rewriting did they do?)

The answer to these questions is a matter of dispute because the clues in the text themselves seem to point in different directions. On the one hand, the beginnings and endings of the books are similar, pointing perhaps to an effort at tying them together more tightly. Also, in some cases, the ending of one book and beginning of the next one is similar, as is the case with the end of Joel and beginning of Amos. (Joel 4:16 [ET 3:16] and Amos 1:2 both say, "Yhwh roars from Zion," describing God as a metaphorical lion.) Or Amos 9:12 mentions Edom, and that nation is the primary subject of the next book, Obadiah. Or Mic 7:12 refers to Assyria, whose fate is the focus of Nahum. Or Haggai and Zechariah address the same issues because the two were contemporaries (and probably knew each other). And Jonah and Nahum seem to be in a sort of dialogue, with one celebrating the destruction of Nineveh and the other noting the possibility of its repentance. So the collection of twelve prophets is not completely haphazard or random.

BEGINNINGS OF THE MINOR PROPHETS

Hosea—word of Yhwh to X son of Y in days of Kings such-and-such
Joel—word of Yhwh to X son of Y
Amos—words of Amos which he saw in days of Kings such-and-such
Obadiah—the vision of Obadiah
Jonah—Yhwh's word was to X son of Y
Micah—word of Yhwh to X in days of Kings such-and-such
Nahum—an oracle about Nineveh; a vision book of X
Habaqquq—an oracle that X saw
Zephaniah—word of Yhwh to X son of Y (etc.) in days of King N
Haggai—on date, Yhwh's word was by X
Zechariah—on date, Yhwh's word was by X
Malachi—an oracle, a word of Yhwh to Israel by X

ENDINGS OF THE MINOR PROPHETS

Hosea—"who is wise?" plus oracle of salvation
Joel—oracle of salvation at the end
Amos—oracle of salvation
Obadiah—oracle of salvation

Jonah—question about salvation
Micah—"who is a God like you?" plus oracle of salvation
Nahum—oracle of doom for Assyria, which equals an oracle of salvation for Israel
Habakkuk—praise in response to acts of salvation
Zephaniah—promise of salvation
Haggai—oracle of salvation re Zerubbabel
Zechariah—oracle of salvation
Malachi—call to obey Torah of Moses and heed Elijah the prophet

On the other hand, it is possible to press the point of integration too far, for each book also has its own integrity. Each one speaks about a particular historical situation and invites its readers to weigh the implications of the experiences of the original hearers of the prophets' words.

So what should we conclude from this brief summary? Two things, at least: first, the Book of the Twelve is both a unified work and an anthology of smaller works. It both reuses certain themes and varies their meaning as occasion demands. Therefore, it must always be read at two levels: that of the particular book and that of the collection as a whole. And second, the scroll of the Twelve seeks to make available to successive audiences a view of Israel's history about which the reader must decide. Since history is never really past (as William Faulkner once said), the reader must decide whether the future will be characterized by doom or by hope. How precisely each book of the Minor Prophets carries on all this double-voiced work will be the concern of the rest of this chapter.

The Book of the Twelve assumes an underlying conception of history that is very similar to that of 1–2 Kings both in the events it reports and in its basic conception of Israel's as a story of disobedience to Yhwh. The books associated with eighth-century BCE prophets (Hosea, Amos, and Micah) coincide with the Assyrian invasion and so speak primarily of a pre-imperial era. As in the Deuteronomistic History, very little material overtly reflects the period of Assyrian occupation (although this gap may be more apparent than real), and prophets reappear at the end of the seventh century with Zephaniah and Nahum, just as 2 Kgs resumes detailed storytelling with the reign of Josiah. Several prophets are associated with the Babylonian invasions at the beginning of the sixth century BCE (Obadiah, Habakkuk). The final three clearly postdate the time period addressed in 1–2 Kgs, with Haggai and Zechariah anchored in the early reign of Darius the Great (r. 522–486 BCE), and Malachi coming sometime later. Joel and Jonah present special problems discussed later.

None of this is to say that all the material in each of these books dates to the years named in their superscriptions, only that the editors of the books concentrated on those times. But the Book of the Twelve as a whole rests upon a narrative substructure, a basic view of Israel's history as it unfolded over about three centuries. What is this view?

These prophetic works assume that Israel's tragic experiences with foreign invasion resulted from their sins, whether idolatry (as in Hosea) or social injustice (as in Micah and Amos). Yet, punishment was not the final word. The times of suffering gave way to redemption, the collapse of the great empires, and the return of healthy life under Yhwh's guidance. This basic historiographic construct is thus the same as that of the book of Isaiah. It is a theological interpretation of real historical events.

How do the shorter prophetic books tell this story of sin, punishment, and redemption? There are many ways, but one of the richest is the discussion of the "Day of the LORD" or "Yhwh's Day." Sometimes the phrase is highly negative, describing a catastrophe for Israel, as in Amos 5:18–20, which says,

> Alas for those who pine for Yhwh's Day. Why do you want Yhwh's Day? It is darkness, not light. It is like when somebody flees from a lion and meets a bear, and then he reaches the house, puts his hand on the wall and a snake bites him. Isn't Yhwh's Day darkness and not light, gloom in which nothing shines?

Things could hardly go worse! And this is the sort of idea that appears also in other texts describing military disaster (see also Amos 2:16; Zeph 1:7–2:3; Mal 3:19–20; similarly, Hos 9:5) or perhaps environmental catastrophe (Joel 2:1–11, in language very similar to Amos's).

Sometimes, however, the misfortune befalls Israel's enemies, and Yhwh's Day marks the salvation of Israel itself (Obad 15; Joel 4:14 [ET 3:14]), and more dramatically still, the "great and awe-inspiring day" follows immediately upon the outpouring of the divine spirit upon all Israelites (Joel 3:4 [ET 2:31]). In other words, these texts use the same phraseology to refer to different historical realities. By combining all these texts, the Book of the Twelve reminds its readers that the day of divine decision-making always remains near, and the human anticipation of, and response to, that day can shape lives in either positive or negative ways.

Hosea

Let us begin, then, with Hosea, which opens the Book of the Twelve. The text invites its readers, ancient or modern, to enter into the narrative and to choose among competing values, beliefs, actions, and relationships in order to fashion one of several possible lives—some of which end in disaster. Hosea opens with Yhwh's shocking instruction to the prophet to "go, take for yourself a whorish wife and whorish children, for the land is whoring away from Yhwh" (Hos 1:2). The prophets' tragically painful marriage thus becomes a parable for Israel's relationship with their God. (Or perhaps the other way around, for it is difficult to tell where biography ends and symbolism begins in this book.) Of all the personal lives of the prophets, his has most shaped how modern readers interpret the book bearing his name. The book's opening tale of cuckoldry and estrangement and tentative reconciliation triggers our deepest fears and fantasies, making this ancient work one of the Bible's best understood.

Or misunderstood. While the book seems at first glance to be about the life of one man in the mid-eighth century BCE, in truth it is more concerned with the story of God and Israel. Hosea's own marital woes serve merely as a parable for this larger story. To read Hosea as an overall work, we must know a few things about the book. To begin, it asks to be read through two overlapping frameworks. One is wisdom (if not perhaps in the technical sense of the wisdom literature of Job or Proverbs) and the other is narrative. The end of the book offers the "wisdom" framework by saying,

> Who is wise and understands these things, discerning and knows them?
> Yes, Yhwh's ways are right, and the righteous walk in them,
> But the iniquitous stumble in them. (14:10 [ET 14:9])

While the complex arrangement of the book defies easy interpretation, this last line casts the entire work as a book requiring careful thought. Reading such a work requires a level of intellectual and moral formation (as in Prov 1–9) that can be acquired only through discipline, study with a teacher, and piety. So this is the first frame for understanding the work.

The second is the narrative substructure. Put simply, the book tells a story, not just about the prophet and his agonizing marriage but about Israel's story with Yhwh. This story has some key plot points:

- The exodus (Hos 11:1; 12:9; 13:4–6)
- Systematic worship of the Baals (Hos 2:13, 16; 4:12–13; 8:4–7; 11:2)
- Prophetic announcements of doom (Hos 9:8–9; most of the rest of the book)
- The defeat of the nation at Assyrian hands (Hos 5:8–15; 7:11–13; 8:7–10; 10:3–15; 13:15–16)
- Return to Yhwh and repudiation of the Baals (Hos 2:17–18)
- Hard-won reconciliation (Hos 11:7–11; 14:1–9; but see 7:1–7)

(There are also allusions to the stories of the patriarchs and the matriarchs in Hos 2:20 and 12:2b–4, but these do not seem to factor in the overall storyline in important ways.) The overall storyline, then, is much the same as that in Deuteronomy–Kings or Amos.

The question is, what happens when these plot points work together? Like Deuteronomy, which tried to create a culture of memory that would help shape Israel's obedience to Yhwh, Hosea laments the people's tendency to "forget," their unwillingness to think of their own history of salvation as determinative of its present situation. Forgetting God's saving deeds leads to a misunderstanding of the divine-human relationship, so that Israel comes to think of the divine world merely as the road to prosperity in this world. In such a view, sacrifice becomes a means for persuading the deity to give human beings the things they identify as most needed, irrespective of the moral commitments of the humans in question. Like his contemporary Amos, Hosea insists that such a view of the world simply will not stand up to scrutiny. Rather, there is a deeper story—hence a deeper identity—in play.

At the same time, there is a curious interplay between remembering and forgetting in this book, for Israel is repeatedly said to "forget" God (Hos 2:15 [ET 2:13]; 4:6; 8:14; 13:6), while God "remembers" their evildoing (Hos 8:13). By thinking of sin as a cognitive failure to recognize past relationships and obligations, Hosea notifies Israel that attention to its past should be an important occupation for both them and God. Again, the past is never really gone.

Unlike its more linear cousin Amos, the book of Hosea is difficult to outline and sometimes hard to follow. In part, this jaggedness arises as the book builds its case through repetition of themes and images in order to create an overall effect.

The German scholar Jörg Jeremias divides the book into three major sections:

A. The prophet and his family as a symbol of the godless people of God (Hos 1:1–3:5)
B. A collection of prophetic oracles in a chronological sequence (Hos 4:1–11:12)
C. The last words (Hos 12:1–14:10 [ET 14:9])²

This arrangement makes sense for the most part, though it is debatable whether the oracles in chs 4–11 follow a chronological order. Rather, it is better to say that the three sections make the same moves. Each section opens with a discussion of Israel's sin and moves to the possibility of redemption. So chs 3, 11, and 14 are very similar. In the middle of the long central section, that is, in chs 6 and 7, the book raises the possibility of a swift resolution of Israel's problems, but then rejects this idea to turn back to the theme of doom. Only after a long, slogging discussion can the theme of salvation again appear in ch 11. The other two sections make the same sort of move, but more briefly.

The overall effect of this structure leaves the lingering impression that redemption for Israel will be a hard-won, closely run sort of undertaking. The problem does not lie with God's deep and abiding mercy but with Israel's recalcitrant spirit. In other words, the very structure of the book conveys its primary message, the one that the last verse tries to articulate as a choice between good and evil. Humans may decide their course of action with all its consequences. Meanwhile, God also remains free to choose mercy.

Joel

If Hosea confounds readers, Joel does so still more, for it is one of the strangest of the minor prophetic books, in part because of its heavy reliance on the imagery of the locust plague as a metaphor for the "Day of Yhwh," the moment of dramatic divine intervention in the life of Israel and its neighbors. The book follows a clear structure that can be outlined this way:

A. Superscription (Joel 1:1)
B. The current problem, the Day of Yhwh's discipline (Joel 1:2–2:27)

1. The locust plague and its consequences (Joel 1:2–12)
2. A call to repentance (Joel 1:13–20)
3. First call to the sound the shofar (Joel 2:1–14)
4. Second call to the sound the shofar (Joel 2:15–27)

C. The future solution, the Day of Yhwh's redemption (Joel 3:1–4:21 [ET 2:28–3:21])
1. The spreading prophetic gift (Joel 3:1–5 [ET 2:28–32])
2. A time of revenge on Phoenicia (Joel 4:1–8 [ET 3:1–8])
3. A time of final reckoning (Joel 4:9–17 [ET 3:9–17])
4. The renewal of Judah (Joel 4:18–21 [ET 3:18–21])

This straightforward structure moves the book from its opening warning about a catastrophic natural disaster (again either a real locust plague or a similarly destructive foreign invasion) to a sustained discussion of Yhwh's work to save Israel.

The date and occasion of the book remain obscure. It was probably written sometime in the early postexilic period, although the editors of the Book of the Twelve seemed to want to place it in the context of the eighth-century BCE books by squeezing it in between Hosea and Amos, two eighth-century prophets (or placing it after Hosea, Amos, and Micah in the LXX, with the same dating implied). They thus wanted to understand Joel as someone who expected the destruction of Israel before it happened. Yet nothing in the book locates it precisely in time.

If the date is unclear, still, the theological ideas give a sounder basis for interpreting the book. Perhaps the best known lines in Joel appear in Joel 3:1–5 (ET 3:28–32), which the New Testament cites in Peter's sermon on Pentecost in Acts 2:17–21 as a witness to the divine work in the early church. For Joel, however, the words seem to point to a renewal of Israel itself. The text says

> Later on, I will pour out my spirit upon all flesh, and your sons and your daughters will prophesy. Your elders will dream dreams, and your youths will see visions. Moreover, upon the male and female servants I will pour out my spirit in those days. And I will place marvels in the sky and on earth—blood, fire, and pillars of smoke. The sun will be darkened and the moon turned to blood before Yhwh's great and awe-inspiring Day comes. For in Mount Zion and in Jerusalem there will be redemption, just as Yhwh says, yes, among the fugitives whom Yhwh calls.

That is, Joel envisions the spread of the prophetic capacity to the entire nation of Israel. In that sense, his view of the ubiquity, commonplaceness of the prophetic "word" closely resembles the idea of the Second Isaiah that the old prophetic words will take on new life during a period of national renewal after the return from exile (see, e.g., Isa 40:8; 55:10–13). The miracle of Israel's renewal will accompany a revival of prophecy. (A similar, but different view of the reclamation of the old patterns of divine communication in new media informs Zechariah and Malachi as well.)

Joel's vision of a dramatic future uses a familiar phrase, "Yhwh's Day," a theme that appears earlier in the book. This expression appears in Joel 2:1 in the introduction to a long description of a terrible disaster befalling Zion/Jerusalem (perhaps its destruction by the Babylonians in 586 BCE, but this is unclear). Yet in ch 3 (ET 2:28–32, Yhwh's Day coincides with a period of revival, described at length in the following oracles in ch 4 (ET 3).

In other words, the book of Joel, like the other prophetic books around it, works with an assumed narrative timeline according to which a time of trial and devastation precedes a time of renewal. As Joel 4:1 (ET 3:1) puts it, "In those days and at that time, when I [i.e., Yhwh] restore the fortunes of Judah and Jerusalem." The book assumes that, following times of struggle, some revival of the people's fortunes will ensue.

An important element of the book's discourse is its use of quotations or allusions to other biblical books, especially Isaiah and Psalms, as well as other Minor Prophets. Two of these citations are especially interesting because they illustrate the book's balancing of prospects of doom and hope as part of its overall message requiring thoughtful engagement. First, Joel 2:12–14 reads

> So now—Yhwh's oracle—turn to me with all your heart, and in fasting and weeping and mourning. Tear your heart and not your clothes. And turn to Yhwh your God, for he is gracious (*ḥannûn*) and merciful (*raḥûm*), slow to anger, abundant in steadfast love, and forgiving of evil. Who knows? He may turn and forgive and leave a blessing behind him, a gift and a libation for Yhwh your God.

This text seems to merge two other biblical texts, Exod 34:6 ("gracious and merciful"; also paralleled in 2 Chron 30:9; Neh 9:17, 31; Pss 86:15–16; 111:4; 112:4; 145:8; and Jonah 4:2) and Jonah 3:9 ("who knows?"). That is, Joel draws on the prestigious texts known by its readers to point them to the depths of divine mercy. And second, Joel 4:10 (ET 3:10) calls upon Israelites to "beat your plowshares into swords and your pruning hooks into spears," a reversal of the famously pacific text found in Isa 2:4 and Micah 4:3 (and inscribed on a wall across from the United Nations building in New York). That is, the book invites its readers to prepare for a time of crisis that will lead to the people's restoration.

As in other minor prophetic books, Joel's message involves both struggle and resolution, both suffering and hope. The book invites its readers to move through crisis toward the moment when "Yhwh will dwell in Zion" (Joel 4:21 [ET 3:21], the book's final line).

Amos

The transition from Joel to Amos rests on repeated phrases:

> "Yhwh roars from Zion and gives his voice from Jerusalem." (Joel 4:16 [ET 3:16])
> "Yhwh roars from Zion and gives his voice from Jerusalem." (Amos 1:2)

By this simple device, the editor of the Book of the Twelve connects two works. And yet there is more here than repetition, for Joel's statement immediately precedes the book's concluding oracle of hope, while Amos's provides not only the theme statement of the book but an introduction to a devastating oracle of doom. The repetition is not mechanical, in other words.

After this transition, Amos itself forms a sort of drama in which three major characters speak: God, Israel, and Amos. The foreign nations constitute a fourth character, and the implied (postexilic) reader a fifth. Each of them stays in character, with Israel the rebellious one, Amos the pleading intermediary, and God the outraged judge. Even the final scene, a promise of renewed hope, does not take the characters out of their roles, though the effort at making God's actions internally consistent creates a theological problem. This problem, however, leads to the profoundest insights of the book.

The book is structured as follows

A. Superscription and motto (Amos 1:1–2)
B. Oracles against the nations, including Israel (Amos 1:3–2:16)
C. The divine witness against Israel (Amos 3:1–6:14)
   1. Judgment on Samaria (Amos 3:1–15)
   2. Judgment on elites (Amos 4:1–3)
   3. Judgment on idolatry (Amos 4:4–13)
   4. A funeral dirge (Amos 5:1–17)
   5. A response to the dirge, re: the "Day of the Lord" (Amos 5:18–20)
   6. Judgment on elites (Amos 6:1–7)
   7. Judgment on Samaria (Amos 6:8–14)
D. Amos's visions and pleas for Israel (Amos 7:1–9)
E. Israel's refusal to repent (played by Amaziah) (Amos 7:10–17)
F. The doom of Israel (Amos 8:1–9:10)
G. A promise of restoration (Amos 9:11–15)

Cutting across this dramatic structure is a series of five visions in chs 8–9. Note that part C takes the form of a chiasmus (ABBA pattern), with Part 1 = Part 7 and Part 2 = Part 6. Parts 3–5 interrogate the nature of Israelite religion.

The book opens with a series of oracles against the nations, comparable to those in Isaiah, Jeremiah, and Ezekiel. Here prophet uses a rhetoric technique called anaphora or the repetition of a word or phrase to create a sense of movement and connection:

"For three transgressions, yes four, of _____ I will not turn it away."

A succession of foreign powers fill the blank, creating at first a sense of outrage in the reader at the crimes of nation-states, but then turning back on the readers themselves as it turns out that their sins are the worst of all. The repetition creates a sort of mental spider-web encircling Israel on all sides this way, as illustrated by a glance at the map.

For the foreign nations, Amos espouses a norm according to which war crimes and other heinous acts are morally unacceptable. Thus he faults Aram/Damascus for destroying Israelite territory in Transjordan (Gilead) (Amos 1:3–5), Gaza and other Philistine cities for engaging in the slave trade (Amos 1:6–8), Tyre for the same offense (Amos 1:9–10), Edom for breaking long-standing alliances with Israel (Amos 1:11–12), Ammon for invading Gilead (Amos 1:13–15), and Moab for desecrating the body of a deceased Edomite king (Amos 2:1–3). This last item is telling, because it shows that Amos was not simply faulting Israel's enemies for violence against his own people—his concerns were moral, not merely nationalistic.

This fact becomes clear when he turns to Judah in Amos 2:4–5 (though his charges of "rejecting Yhwh's *torah*" offers less specificity than the prior charges against nations. And indeed, the real focus of Amos 1–2 lies neither on Judah nor on its gentile neighbors, but on Israel itself. As Amos 2:6–16 makes clear, Israel must follow a higher standard than merely avoiding crimes against humanity. The argument deserves consideration:

> They sell the righteous for silver and the poor for a pair of shoes.
> They trample the poor ones heads into the ground and push the poor off the road.
> In fact, a man and his father "go in" to the same young woman—to defile my holy name.
> They lie on collateralized clothing in front of every altar,
> And drink wine collected as a fine at their God's temple.
> (Amos 2:7)

Most of these infractions are self-explanatory, though the last two involve the use of other people's property taken as collateral for debt (clothing; see Exod 22:25–26 [ET 22:26–27], which forbids such practices) or as a fee exacted for some reason. The text interprets these moral failures (the financial and sexual oppression of the poor) as betrayals of the nation's central story, the exodus. Amos 2 does not see these cruel acts merely as violations of a law but as betrayals of Israel's core identity. Just as Yhwh punished the previous populations of Canaan, so too will Israel pay for its structure of oppression that favors the powerful over the weak.

The next several chapters of Amos work out this basic idea. The speeches in chs 3–6 catalogue a series of injustices in a society where dire poverty and gratuitous luxury coexist. Ch 6 perhaps says it most famously:

"Alas for those relaxing in Zion or trusting in Mount Samaria . . ."

These aristocrats expand their houses and farms, lie on ivory-inlaid furniture, drink wine to excess, and have private concerts "like David." Their kingly lives mask their lack of "care about Joseph's destruction" (Amos 6:6). That is, their luxury continues in spite of culturewide disruptions (in this case, probably the repeated Assyrian invasions of Israel during the 730s and 720s BCE).

The middle part of Amos does not confine itself to social criticism. However necessary any cold-eyed analysis of the structures of dominance and submission must be, it cannot rise to the level of prophetic speech unless also accompanied by something else—a call to an alternative pattern of life. Therefore, Amos 5:14 invites its readers to "seek good and not evil," and in a more famous text, the book contrasts an approach to God via sacrifices to one based on justice:

I hate, I detest your festivals and cannot abide your assemblies.
Quit bringing me your whole burnt offerings.
I do not enjoy your gifts and will not accept your sweet-smelling peace offerings . . .
But let justice roll down like water, and righteousness like an ever-flowing stream. (Amos 5:21–24)

The last line gained new fame from its appearance in Martin Luther King's "I Have a Dream" speech and is now inscribed on the north wall of his memorial in Washington, DC. As a Baptist preacher, King understood well the significance of Amos's vision of a society in which justice rested upon a sustained attempt of those who celebrated the exodus story to live out its truest values. He did not reject sacrifice or other religious acts but sought to penetrate to their central purposes, the restoration of lives and their healthy connections to one another.

This struggle for integrity appears throughout the last sections of the book, as well. Ch 7 portrays the prophet as mediator, allowing readers to hear the pain in Amos as he watches his nation destroy itself ("Adonai Yhwh, please forgive. Who of Jacob can survive? For he is so small"). Here we see the prophet both begging God to relent and venting indignation at other religious leaders besotted with comfort and status. Thus Amos 7:10–17 recounts a moment of opposition from the royally sponsored priesthood of Bethel. Accusing Amos of treason, the priest Amaziah seeks to deport Amos back to his homeland, Judah. The story illustrates the venality of the nation's leaders who sought to suppress legitimate prophetic dissent either by buying it off or silencing the troublemakers.

Chs 8 and 9 offer the wildest mood swing of all. Ch 8 opens with a vision of divine outrage, final this time, and the words of ch 9 seem like a description of hell itself. These lines are designed to hurt, and they do. In a most upsetting turn, the book denies the validity, or at least universal applicability of the foundational exodus story on which it has set so much stock in making moral arguments. Amos 9:7 says simply,

Aren't you like the Kushites [from Sudan] to me, o Israel's children? (Yhwh's oracle.)
Did I not bring Israel up from Egypt's land, but also the Philistines from Kaphtor [Cyprus] and Aram from Qir [Anatolia]?

In other words, the book asks, why would its readers imagine that its core story of deliverance was either unique or a guarantee of impunity from the vicissitudes of history? Shocking stuff, particularly as a sort of grand finale for the book, its final word.

Or almost final. The last pericope speaks of agricultural prosperity as a metaphor (harvesters and plowers getting their work entangled). It also employs the image of the repair and re-erection of "David's fallen booth," apparently a promise of the restoration of the Davidic dynasty. That is, the book of Amos ends with a word of hope (as in all the other Minor Prophets). Resoundingly, the prophetic book draws readers into future prospects, as if to hear the hope is to begin to make it a reality.

On a first reading, Amos seems emotionally limited, if intense. Outrage is the dominant passion. Yet, on closer examination, things become more complex. The book begins with a motto: "Yhwh has roared from Zion, given his voice from Jerusalem." At first, this seems to be a statement of national particularity, with Yhwh taking the side of Judah against Israel. But the next few verses quickly dissuade us from this view as they announce Yhwh's judgment on political iniquity, with the Israelite kingdoms coming in for the severest condemnation. By the end of the oracles against the nations, any sense of comfort has gone.

The next few chapters passionately dissect the anatomy of oppression in Israel. The prophet reasons with his hearers, mocks them, cajoles them, threatens them. Rhetorically sophisticated, these chapters try to construct an argument from pathos for the audience so that they will feel, as well as think, their way into repentance.

Obadiah

If Amos critiques Israel as part of its regionwide analysis of structures of oppression, then Obadiah focuses on a single foreign state, Israel's southern neighbor Edom. Apparently set soon after Jerusalem's destruction in 586 BCE, this shortest book in the Hebrew Bible denounces Edomite betrayal of "your brother Jacob through violence" (Obad 10). Like the Pentateuch, Obadiah assumes that the shared history of Edom and Israel/Judah implied an obligation of mutual help.

The book describes itself as a report of a vision about Edom's doom (Obad 1). The smoothly flowing poem in vv. 1–16 describes an impending day of reckoning, while vv. 19–21 seem to be a prose addition describing a more distant future in which the Israelite survivors ("the saved") will inhabit Zion again and will "judge" Edom. History, Obadiah asserts, will find its proper level.

The book uses several literary devices to describe Edom's arrogance and fall. First, it personifies the nation both as dwellers in rocky fastnesses whose arrogance will be their undoing ("who will bring us down to earth?" [Obad 3]) and as famously wise people whose best laid plans fail. Second, the poetry uses a number of puns to impress the Hebrew audience with its turns of phrase (much like a modern slam poet). Thus v. 5 speaks of *bōṣĕrîm* ("grape-pickers"), a word play on the major Edomite city Boṣrah, and v. 13 plays on the word "Edom" with the Hebrew *ʾēdām* ("their distress"). Such use of language implies a practice of oral performance for the text.

Finally, it is worth noting the close relationship between Obadiah and Jeremiah 49. Jeremiah 49:9–10 rearranges Obad 5–6 (or vice versa), while Jer 49:14–16 is almost identical to Obad 1–4. Which text came first? As elsewhere in the Old Testament with such synoptic relationships, a definite line of influence is hard to trace.

Jonah

Like Obadiah, Jonah concerns the relationship between Israel and a single nation, in this case Assyria. At the same time, this book about the misadventures of a reluctant prophet is an outlier in the Book of the Twelve because it is not a collection of oracles but a short story. Of course, some modern readers have tried to read Jonah as a literal report of an actual mission trip by the eighth-century BCE prophet bearing that name (who was also mentioned in 2 Kgs 14:25 as a prophet supporting Israel's territorial expansion). Yet there are many clues in the biblical text itself suggesting that it should be understood as a parable. The fish who serves as prophetic transportation, the sackcloth-wearing animals, the one-sentence sermon that converts everyone in a great city, the piety of sailors and impiety of the prophet—all of these elements suggest a different sort of literature than a strictly historical report.

And still, the book of Jonah explores important questions: What are the limits of Yhwh's mercy? Does human repentance cancel out the demands of justice? And if so, how? It carries out this exploration in the form of a story, and a comedic one at that.

Jonah opens with a divine command to the prophet to go to "Nineveh the great city . . . because their evil has gone up before me" (like Sodom and Gomorrah; see Gen 18:21). The prophet responds to this charge by fleeing in the opposite direction, taking a ship west for Tarshish (now Spain) rather than walking northeast to Assyria (now northern Iraq). This disobedience quickly leads to a storm at sea, during which Jonah fails to join the sailors in praying for help. Finally, he persuades them to appease the angry deity by throwing him into the sea. Yet surprisingly, they respond to this desperate solution with a prayer, "O Yhwh please don't let us perish for the sake of this man's life, and do not fault us for shedding innocent blood" (Jonah 1:14). Unlike Jonah, who boasted of serving "the God of heaven" but did not do so, the foreign, polytheistic sailors understand the proper approach to Yhwh as a God of mercy.

In any case, Jonah survives the storm after being swallowed by a large sea creature, which the text describes first as male (Hebrew: *dāg*), then female when Jonah is inside it (Hebrew: *dāgâ*) and then male again upon spitting Jonah out on the dry land. While inside this unusual form of transportation, he utters a lovely prayer (Jonah 2:3–10) thanking God for answering him when he "called from my distress . . . from the depths of the Underworld I cried and you heard my voice." This hymn of praise seems surprising in its context, but the text portrays Jonah's pleasure at not drowning, indicating that his interest in self-preservation had also survived.

His attachment to human life does not extend to the Assyrians. Although he does head to Nineveh and preach the sermon, "In forty days, Nineveh will be overthrown," his response to brilliant homiletical success is surprising. The dramatic repentance of the Assyrian king provokes in the prophet a deep emotional funk and then a protest against Yhwh's negligence in failing to punish an evil empire. His objection to divine mercy cites an oft-repeated text in the Bible. "I knew that you are a gracious and merciful God, slow to anger, abounding in kindness, and willing to acquit the wicked" (Jonah 4:2). This line or something close to it also appears in Exod 34:5–6; 2 Chron 30:9; Neh 9:17, 31; Pss 86:15–16; 111:4; 112:4; 145:8; and Joel 2:12–14. All of these texts emphasize God's mercy toward penitent sinners and therefore humankind's need to right its wrongs. For Jonah, this aspect of God's character seems most unwelcome, and so he objects to it.

The book ends, then, with an unresolved tension. In fact, its last line is a question, "Shouldn't I have concern for Nineveh the great city in which is a multitude of 120,000 people who don't know right from left, as well as many animals?" The book's author gives Yhwh the last word, but not a final resolution of the problem.

The author of Jonah deliberately created a puzzle by his choice of Nineveh as the prophet's destination based on knowledge of three things: (1) Nineveh was the capital of the Assyrian Empire, which eventually destroyed Israel; (2) it was a militarily oriented state that celebrated human suffering, including that of Israel; and yet (3) Nineveh itself was also destroyed by outside invaders in 612 BCE, long before the book of Jonah was written (probably in the fourth century BCE). In other words, this book has Yhwh sparing Israel's most feared enemy, an action that led eventually to Israel's own demise, just as Jonah feared. Now the reader is left with a problem: Can the sparing of the wicked lead to greater calamities? Must Yhwh always accept human repentance, and what might be the cost of doing so? There is no simple answer to that question, and in fact the Book of the Twelve keeps coming back to it. The book of Jonah, therefore, serves as a source of reflection even in its dark humor.

Micah

The organization of the book can be understood in several ways. One of the most common is to see in it three major sections:

Oracles of doom (Mic 1:1–3:12)
Oracles of hope and doom tangled together (Mic 4:1–5:14)
Calls to action (Mic 6:1–7:20)

According to this outline, the book moves toward a call to faith, the embrace of which would undo the oracles of doom. Thus the hearer can decide whether the threats of God become realities. As with all the prophetic books, Micah contains texts with widely different moods, often side by side. To read it properly, one must identify where a given section starts and stops, discern its overall tone, and then move to the next section in order to see how two different moods might work together to create something larger than either of them.

A brief conspectus of the book: ch 1 opens Micah with a description of God's appearance in judgment (Mic 1:1–4), the reasons for judgment (the sins of Jacob/Israel; Mic 1:5–9), and then a call to sinners to pay attention and consider turning from sin (Mic 1:10–16). The third section of the chapter is particularly difficult. It is full of Hebrew wordplays and obscure references, the overall tone of which is to point to the comprehensive nature of Israel's sinfulness—everyone is involved.

Ch 2 also contains three sections: vv. 1–5 talk about the reversal of fortune awaiting those who scheme to line their own pockets at the expense of others; vv. 6–11 describe the evildoers' response to the prophets: "Stop preaching," they say. Micah describes what prophets always experience, opposition and disbelief. It is difficult for us to face up to our own faults, and the same was true of his audience. Then vv. 12–13 put a bow around the chapter by describing exile and then the possibility of hope after that. The ones who are drawn through breaches in walls are victims of warfare, but their deliverance will come.

Ch 3 turns to the leaders of the people, accusing the government officials (Mic 3:1–4), the prophets (Mic 3:5–8), and the officials again (Mic 3:9–12) of misleading, swindling, neglecting, and otherwise oppressing the people. Some of the language of the prophet is very graphic, as when he describes the leaders as cannibals (Mic 3:3), surely an exaggeration, but one making the serious point that those who should have cared for the vulnerable exploit them instead. The failure of leadership has contributed to the social debasement that Micah criticizes.

Ch 4 opens in vv. 1–8 with a vision of the future, almost word-for-word to that in Isa 2:2–4. Micah uses the oracle differently than Isaiah, however. Rather than employing the hopeful vision as a sharp contrast to the audience's tendency to reject Yhwh's word, as in Isa, Micah 4 envisions a time of peace ("all will sit under their own vine or fig tree with no one to intimidate them . . . . For all the peoples will go, each in Yhwh's name."). This extraordinary vision imagines a time when the world will find hope in Israel's God. The chapter then turns to the hearer and answers his or her unstated objections, which must be something similar to those we see from other prophetic settings (e.g., Isa 49), in which people who have given up hope can no longer believe in the possibility of redemption. Micah 4:9–14 promises that the present calamity (predicted by chapter 3) is not the last word but merely an opportunity for God to save yet again.

Ch 5 continues the words of hope but sets them in the context of exile. Judah will not avoid tragedy, but after the catastrophe of invasion and loss will come a new dawn of hope. Sin will be punished, but punishment is not the last word. Rather, the oppressive foreign nations will be subject to God's rule, and thus peace will reign.

Ch 6 is a speech for a lawsuit (a similar speech appears in Isa 1). The prophet responds to Israel's complaints by reminding them of their history. It then states the prophetic ethic of individual and communal justice succinctly:

How should I approach Yhwh or draw near to God on high?
Should I approach [Yhwh] with whole burnt offerings? With year-old calves?
Will Yhwh be happy with thousands of rams or flooding streams of oil?
Should I give my firstborn for my transgression, my belly's fruit for my soul's sin?
[Yhwh] has told you, human being, what is good. What does Yhwh seek from you?
Just to do justice, love loyalty, and walk humbly with your God. (Mic 6:6–8)

The question lays out all the possibilities of the religious life based on the cult, only to reject them as substitutes for personal or group injustice. Sacrifice cannot bribe Yhwh. Micah's audience must renounce their sins.

Finally, ch 7 opens with Israel's (or perhaps the prophet's) lament for a lost world (7:1–7). The book ends on a note of hope, an appeal to divine mercy. Like the end of Hosea, Mic 7:18--20 poses a set of questions and calls upon the audience of the book to decide between a life of cruelty and oppression leading to death and one marked by care for the vulnerable fellow Israelite. But the end of Micah also marks an advance over Hosea, in that the audience in Micah does not consist simply of human beings but of Yhwh also. Micah 7:18's "Who is a God like you, lifting away iniquity?" appeals to the deity to decide to save a remnant of the people from the doom of the rest.

The sequence of oracles, again, may seem confusing, but the goal is to create a conversation between God and people about what makes a good community and good individuals in it.

Nahum

Like Jonah, Nahum concerns the fate of Nineveh and the Assyrian Empire. Unlike Jonah, however, Nahum celebrates the destruction of that city and state. The book of Nahum was apparently written shortly after the fall of Nineveh in 612 BCE, an event which it understands as the result of Yhwh's righteous judgment on a cruel and oppressive state. The book as it currently stands consists of two major parts plus the introductory superscription, but it is unclear whether Nah 2:2–11 (ET 2:1–10) fits better with the preceding or the succeeding succession. So one possible outline is

A. Superscription (Nah 1:1)
B. The work of the avenging God (Nah 1:2--2:11 [ET 1:2–2:10])
C. The final fate of Nineveh (Nah 2:12–3:19 [ET 2:11–3:19])

Each of these major sections consists of several shorter sections that create the same sort of effect one sees in other prophetic books: a careful balancing of announcements of doom with promises of salvation. Therefore, however one understands the overall structure of the book and its constituent parts, the careful analysis of history as the stage of Yhwh's activity shines through.

What history in particular? Not just the fall of Nineveh and the Assyrian Empire but also the implications of that fall for Judah, one of Assyria's vassals. Nahum seems intimately familiar with Assyrian propaganda, for he alludes to key ideas in it when using such phrases as "in a raging flood" (Nah 1:8) or in references to practices of military sieges in 3:14 or lion-breeding in 2:14 (ET 2:13).

The final chapter of the book is particularly striking, for it offers a mock lament for a city. As was already noted in the discussion of the book of Lamentations, a lament for a city was a popular (though not exactly enjoyable!) literary genre from the ancient world. Nahum adopts that form but transforms it, for he does not see the fall of Nineveh as a tragedy, but as an answer to prayers. This is why Nah 3:1 opens with the line "Woe to the city of blood, all of it treacherous, full of plunder—prey that never stops." That is, the prophetic book thinks of Assyria and its capital not as a great human artistic or governmental achievement (though it was those things) but as a brutal regime whose achievements rested upon human suffering.

In other words, the book is protest literature, carrying the prophetic criticism of social inequities to its logical conclusion. The reversal of fortune for which all the prophets call inevitably results in the overthrow of political systems, often by violence. And so in this sense, Nahum's message is a logical continuation of everything else in the prophetic books, however distasteful the celebration of a city's destruction might seem to readers who have not suffered from the decisions made in that locale.

JONAH AND NAHUM: A DIALOGUE

The views of Nineveh in Jonah and Nahum are obviously in tension with one another, since the former book emphasizes Yhwh's mercy toward a foreign power, while the latter underscores the justice of the divine judgment against it. This tension was noticed centuries ago. For example, in the preface to his lectures on Nahum, given shortly after his honeymoon in 1525, Martin Luther writes,

"Because they [the Ninevites who heard Jonah] turned to repentance, the punishment was deferred; but such are the hearts of men that when the punishment ceased, so did the repentance. They slipped back into the same wickedness under which they had labored before.... This has caused the ruin of all kingdoms, because they used success in their affairs immoderately." (Martin Luther, "Lectures on Nahum" [trans. Richard J. Dinda; Luther's Works 18; ed. Hilton C. Oswald; St. Louis: Concordia, 1975], 281)

Habakkuk

If Jonah explores the outer edges of divine mercy, Habakkuk must seek to find compassion's core. Following the collapse of Assyria, celebrated so exuberantly by the counter-Jonah book Nahum, Judah had borne the brunt of invasion by the successor empire of Babylonia, finally falling to Nebuchadnezzar's army in 586 BCE. Both Habakkuk and the following book, Zephaniah, respond to the events surrounding the Babylonian invasions and seek to find Yhwh's movements amid the vagaries of history.

The book of Habakkuk consists of three major sections following the superscription (Hab 1:1):

A. Laments and calls to observe the world (Hab 1:2–17)
B. The prophet's inquiry and Yhwh's reply (Hab 2:1–20)
C. A song mixing themes of victory and lamentation (Hab 3:1–19)

The three sections relate to the theme of Judah's fate and the prophet's questioning of its appropriateness. Accordingly Section A consists of two subdivisions of lamentation (Hab 1:2–4, 12–17) surrounding a call to the nation to return to consider the Babylonian threat realistically (1:5–11). Section B builds on this sense of foreboding by reporting a prophetic inquiry to Yhwh ("Let me stand on the watchtower." [Hab 2:1]) and then the divine response. Condemning those who "build a city on blood and establish a settlement on wickedness" (Hab 2:12), this middle section anatomizes the oppressive nature of Judahite society and its inevitable downfall owing to the work of a just God. Like the prophet Jeremiah, Zephaniah's contemporary, this book understands the Babylonian invasion to be a divine retribution for sin, yet also like Jeremiah, Zephaniah does not blindly accept the divine verdict in history but seeks a stay of execution.

Then comes the final section, a hymn appointed for performance in the Temple (hence the subscription, "for the director" [Hab 3:19]). Habakkuk 3 is either a hymn considerably older than the time of Habakkuk, or it deliberately uses archaizing language. Either way it uses old poetic themes such as Yhwh's conquest of the waters (derived from pre-Israelite Syro-Canaanite traditions as in the Ugaritic "Baal Epic" and seen in many psalms [e.g. Ps 24:2; 93:3]) and the idea of Yhwh's home as being in such southern locales as Teman (Hab 3:3; cf. Judg 5:4). This old liturgical language creates an impression: the book of Habakkuk makes a connection between the unsettled present, represented in the very troubled, jagged poetry of chs 1–2, and the primeval past, couched in ancient (or at least ancient-sounding) language familiar to worshipers in the Temple.

Meanwhile, the book's final lines,

I will exult in Yhwh, I will rejoice in my saving God.
Yhwh, my lord, is my strength. (Hab 3:18–19)

sound a final note of confidence even amid the turmoil of the early sixth century. This note also reverberates in the final placement of Habakkuk among the Twelve where it reminds later readers that Babylon also fell, and the tragedies of one era led to the victories of another.

HABAKKUK IN DEAD SEA SCROLLS AND THE NEW TESTAMENT

Perhaps the most famous text in Habakkuk is 2:4, which Paul quotes in Rom 1:17 as part of the thesis statement of his magnum opus. "The righteous shall live by faith" stands for Paul as a sharp alternative to justification through works (also in Gal 3:11). However, it was not always interpreted this way, for a few generations earlier, the Dead Sea community's work, the *Pesher of Habakkuk*, understood the line to refer to those who keep Torah according to the community's interpretations. And a generation or so after Paul, the early Christian author of the Epistle to the Hebrews connected Hab 2:4 to his plea for perseverance in the face of adversity (Heb 10:38). It seems that the meaning of "faith(fulness)" is always subject to continued reflection.

Zephaniah

A similar balancing of discordant themes, hope amid political and social turmoil, animates the following book. Addressing the situation in Judah and its neighbors during the last years of the Assyrian Empire and the transition to Babylonian rule, Zephaniah follows a straightforward outline:

A. Superscription (Zeph 1:1)
B. Oracles against Jerusalem and Judah (Zeph 1:2–18)
   1. Indictment of bad leaders and idolatrous people (Zeph 1:2–9)
   2. Description of the coming time of doom (Zeph 1:10–18)
C. Oracles against nations, including Judah (Zeph 2:1–15)
D. Woe oracle for the nations (Zeph 3:1–13)
E. Hope oracle for Israel (Zeph 3:14–20)

The four sections connect to form a dialogue about the fate of Judah. That is, Section B opens by describing the destruction of the human and animal inhabitants of the land during warfare, which it attributes to Yhwh's decision-making. This period of divine judgment will see not only the end of illicit forms of worship (Zeph 1:4–6) but also the disruption of the entire sociopolitical structure (Zeph 1:8). Section C reinforces this sense of doom by using the prophetic genre of the oracle against the nations (including Judah) to signal that the end of Assyrian rule did not lead to the thriving of the once-subjugated states, since the Babylonian Empire was at least as brutal in its techniques of rule. Section D makes the same point. In short, then, Zephaniah precludes an overly optimistic interpretation of prophecies such as those of Nahum.

Like all the other parts of the Twelve, Zephaniah ends with an announcement of divine salvation. Zephaniah 3:16–20 open with a phrase often used to introduce a hope oracle, "in that day" and then uses one of the most striking metaphors in all hope oracles:

In that day it will be said to Jerusalem, "Do not fear, O Zion.
Don't let your hands drop.
Yhwh your God is in your midst—a rescuing warrior.
He will sing over you with joy,
Renew you by his love,

Sing over you in song
As on a holiday. (Zeph 3:16–18a)

The idea of Yhwh as a balladeer for beloved Jerusalem, an image rare in the Hebrew Bible, charms both ancient and modern readers, especially as it reminds them of both the transience of tragedy and the faithfulness of God. Zephaniah resorts to a form of anthropomorphism that startles the reader out of the near despair caused by the previous chapters so as to anticipate a different future than the trends of the early sixth century would lead one to expect.

Read in the context of the Book of the Twelve, the end of Zephaniah points to the return of the exiles (or at least some of them) following the replacement of Babylonia with the Persian Empire in the 530s BCE. As elsewhere, the text assumes the historical sequence of deportation and restoration without laying out that narrative explicitly.

Haggai

If Nahum, Habakkuk, and Zephaniah presuppose the sweeping changes of the late seventh and early sixth centuries, the final three books of the Twelve assume a different time period, a few decades later, on the other side of the great divide called the Babylonian exile. Like Zechariah, the prophet Haggai was active during the early reign of Darius the Great (r. 522–486 BCE), a period of political unrest in much of the empire until Darius consolidated his power. The book of Haggai concerns primarily local problems, however, and in particular the failure of the Jerusalemite community to rebuild the Temple and reinstitute the Temple cult in a proper way. Also like the first part of the book of Zechariah, Haggai is arranged by the date on which the oracle was given, each dating to the early part of Darius's reign. The basic structure is

A. Superscription (Hag 1:1)
B. A call to rebuild the Temple (Hag 1:2–14)
   1. Criticism for not rebuilding the Temple (Hag 1:2–6)
   2. Criticism for stingy sacrifices (Hag 1:7–11)
   3. Comfort for the leaders Zerubbabel and Joshua (Hag 1:12–15)
C. Promises accompanying a rebuilt Temple (Hag 2:1–23)
   1. A vision of the new Temple (Hag 2:1–9)
   2. A legal argument for rebuilding the Temple (Hag 2:10–19)
   3. A final oracle encouraging Zerubbabel (Hag 2:20–23)

This structure, simple as it is, indicates the book's chief concerns, the practical need to rebuild the Jerusalem Temple as the center of communal life for the community of returnees from Babylonia.

It is tempting to denigrate Haggai as a politically-motivated work or even as one that focuses on narrow concerns, in contrast to the sweeping moral vision of an Amos or Micah. Certainly the concerns of the migrants from Babylonia differed from those of earlier generations. However, it would be a mistake to devalue Haggai in this way, for two reasons.

First, the Temple served as the symbolic center of the new community, not just during Haggai's lifetime but for centuries thereafter. Finishing its construction involved more than the practical problems of constructing a building or the priesthood's grasping of power. The cohesion of the group was at stake. The Temple provided a visible symbol of that solidarity, connecting the community's past, present, and future.

Second, the book of Haggai (as opposed to the prophet himself) exists as part of the larger Book of the Twelve, and so it serves a literary purpose distinct from that of the earlier units in the sequence. As will be clear with Zechariah, the book of Haggai pre-supposes the use of the prior works to form an audience in their worship of Yhwh and their morality with respect to communal life. Haggai underscores an idea that appears throughout the Twelve, the importance of honoring Yhwh in tangible ways as a key to the community's identity.

Zechariah

With Haggai and Malachi, the book of Zechariah forms a distinct part of the Book of the Twelve, a section commenting directly on life in Yehud (the name for Judah during the Persian period) in the first generation following the so-called Babylonian exile. Like Haggai, the first part of Zechariah dates to the early years of Darius the Great, and like Haggai's oracles, the first eight chapters of Zechariah are dated to events in that reign. The second section of Zechariah, chs 9–14, like Malachi, come from sometime later. This fact leads most scholars to assign the two parts of the book of Zechariah to different authors. Although this view is probably correct, Zech 9–14 offers an extended commentary on Zech 1–8 and on earlier texts in the Book of the Twelve, just as Zech 1–8 reflects at length on older prophecy. In other words, both parts of the book are part of a process of deep theological reexamination of prophecy that took place during the Persian period as the re-forming of the Israelite community (or what we might properly call practitioners of early Judaism) made sense of the older traditions that had survived the Babylonian holocaust.

The book of Zechariah is structured in this way:

A. Oracles of Zechariah During the Reign of Darius the Great (Zech 1:1–8:23)
 1. Introduction (year 2, month 8) (Zech 1:1–6)
 2. Seven visions and explanatory hope oracles (year 2, month 12, day 24) (Zech 1:7–6:15)
 3. Oracles about the end of exile (year 4, Kislev 4) (Zech 7:1–8:19)
 4. Summary oracle (Zech 8:20–23)

   B. The first "burden" (Zech 9:1–11:17)
   C. The second "burden" (Zech 12:1–14:21)

It not only a collection of visions about the restored community and its potential future, but also a commentary on both the past experiences of the people and on prior literary representations of that past. Consider each section, then.

THE VISIONS AND HOPE ORACLES (ZECH 1:2–8:23).

To begin, chs 1–8 consist of a series of seven visions, each followed with an explanatory section that offers the "plain" sense of the vision and seeks to persuade the audience of its value to their own self-understanding. The visions and comments on them acknowledge the conflicts of the moment but also hold out hope for a different future.

The opening subunit (Zech 1:2–6) lays out major themes of the book:

> Yhwh was extremely angry with your ancestors. So you should say to them [Zechariah's audience], "Thus says Yhwh of Hosts, 'Turn to me, and I will turn to you', says Yhwh of Hosts."
>
> "You should not be like your ancestors, to whom the first prophets announced, 'Thus says Yhwh of Hosts, please turn from your evil ways and evil deeds.' They neither listened nor thought about me. An oracle of Yhwh."
>
> Where are your ancestors? [implied answer: dead]. But the prophets live forever. Did not my commands, which I commanded my servants the prophets, overtake your ancestors?
>
> So they turned around and said, "Yhwh has done with us just as he planned to do to us in response to our ways and actions."

First, the author works with a tacit assumption about the flow of Israel's history: prior generations ignored Yhwh's warnings and suffered the consequences of sin, but then repentance came about. This historical reconstruction depends on the DH's viewpoint, shared by all the prophetic books, that Israel's history was a long saga of disobedience. However, Zech 1:2–6 marks an advance over the DH's viewpoint, because the implicit hope stated there (and in texts like Deut 30) had become a reality.

Second, this text states a view of the history of prophecy. Prior prophecy offered both an ongoing warning and a call for change. Its audience consistently ignored it (cf. Isa 6:9–11) until the threatened doom arrived. Yet, prophecy continues in a new key in the work of Zechariah, whom the book portrays as both heir to a long tradition of prophecy and an innovator in that tradition.

How does innovative continuity of tradition take place? The short answer: in the visions of the book. Therefore the reader's task is to understand how the visions work. A nice example appears in the first vision, Zech 1:8–13, which says,

One night, I saw a man riding on a roan horse, and he was standing next to a stand of myrtles in the hollow. Behind him were other horses—roan, sorrel, and white. So I said, "What are these things, sir?" The messenger speaking to me replied, " I will show you what these things are." Then the man standing next to the myrtles said, "These are the ones Yhwh sent to move around in the land." Then the one standing next to the myrtles said to Yhwh's messenger, "Let's move around in the land." (Now, all the land was undisturbed.) Then Yhwh's messenger prayed, "O Yhwh of Hosts, how long will you withhold mercy from Jerusalem and Judah's cities, at which you were angry for these seventy years?" Then Yhwh answered the messenger speaking to me good and compassionate words.

The text goes on to relate some of these divine words in a hopeful oracle about the future prosperity of Jerusalem and its environs.

What does the first vision report say about the use of visions in Zechariah? Several points deserve attention:

- Visions are not self-interpreting, or rather they are susceptible to any number of interpretations, including some quite far-fetched. The interpretation in Zechariah makes it clear that the vision is about the immediate past and the present of the book's audience, namely, their story of cultural death and rebirth following the Babylonian invasions.
- The prophet receives the explanation of the vision from an intermediary, a "messenger" or "angel" (the Hebrew word *malʾāk* can mean either). That is, the interpretation does not depend solely on the prophet's imagination.
- Not only does the interpretation receive authoritative confirmation from the heavenly realm, but it must also connect to previous prophetic speech. This is clearest here in Zech 1:12's reference to the "seventy years" of exile, a number that comes from Jeremiah (Jer 25:11; 29:10) and proved to be almost dead reckoning of the period of Babylonian rule (605–539 BCE). In other words, the visions comment on the previous generations of prophecy, to which the final books of the Twelve fell heir.

Zechariah strings together a series of visions about life in the postexilic community of Jerusalem and the surrounding subprovince of Yehud in order to provide its readers with ways of appropriating the older prophetic speech for a new, and more hopeful, day.

THE FINAL "BURDENS" OR ORACLES (ZECH 9:1–14:21).

A similar purpose also explains the last two sections of Zechariah, which are clearly demarcated with the introductory genre label "burden" or oracle (Hebrew: *massāʾ*). These chapters lack an obvious historical setting but rather consist of a series of hope oracles and comments on them.

This material seems to come from the final stages of the development of the Book of the Twelve and thus reflect what is sometimes called the early stages of apocalyptic, a form of literature that emphasizes a cosmic crisis and its resolution by divine intervention, as in Daniel. Zechariah 14, in particular, envisions just such a final defeat of all of Israel's foes.

The expectation of future resolution coexists with a focus upon past prophetic communication, and the recycling of images and ideas so common in later apocalyptic texts finds a complementary practice in the kind of reuse of nonapocalyptic material that is sometimes called inner-biblical interpretation. This label describes a phenomenon in which later biblical texts cite earlier ones in a variety of ways. (This practice is very familiar to students of the New Testament or of early Jewish midrash.) An example of this reinterpretive practice appears in the admittedly cryptic text of Zech 11:4–17. This section refers back to an image of leaders as (bad) shepherds and the people as a (mistreated) flock appearing in Jer 23:1–4 and Ezek 34. Without a reference to the earlier texts, the later one in Zech 11 would make little sense. Yet the later text does not simply refer to the past circumstances of the earlier texts but reappropriates them for its own time.

ZECHARIAH AND SOCIAL CONFLICT.

If Zechariah reuses old texts and fashions new ones for new situations, what sort of context gave rise to such a strange book? Many scholars have noted the language of conflict in the book, particularly conflicts among priests and prophets, and some have argued that the emerging apocalypticism seen here indicates a high degree of conflict among religious leaders in Jerusalem and Yehud. Of course, such a hypothesis is plausible, but the extent, nature, and depth of intragroup conflict is always difficult to gauge, especially after more than two millennia, especially when the literature of only one or a few sides of the conflict survive. Sometimes, of course, groups who share most viewpoints and assumptions fight more intensely than those with little in common, and such may be the case here as well. In any case, it does seem clear from Zechariah, as well as from Haggai and Malachi, the other latest additions to the group of the Twelve, that all was not harmonious in the generations following the rebuilding of the Temple in Jerusalem.

Malachi

How unwell those generations may appear can be read in Malachi, depending of course on how one interprets it. The concluding book of the Twelve Minor Prophets bears the name *malʾākî* or "my messenger" without any indication of the date of the work or even if its name coincides with that of an actual person. The book continues some of the themes of Haggai and Zechariah, especially the focus on the Temple and sacrifice. It offers a dramatic conversation about struggles both in the author's time and expectations of a happier future that resolves impending crises.

How the small units that make up the book fit together is debatable. Some scholars see two major divisions (Mal 1:6–2:16 and 2:17–3:21 [ET 2:17–4:3]) following the introduction in Mal 1:1–5 and preceding the conclusion in Mal 3:22–24 (ET 4:4–6). Other scholars see five panels of text following the introduction (Mal 1:6–2:9; 2:10–16; 2:17–3:5; 3:6–12; and 3:13–21 [ET 3:13–4:3]).[3] In other words, the boundaries of small units are clear enough, but how they fit together is not.

In any case, the Malachi opens with a sort of diatribe, a confrontation statement: "'I have loved you', says Yhwh. But you say, 'In what way have you loved us?'" In other words, the old relationship of mutual distrust described by Hos 1–3 at the beginning of the Book of the Twelve persists even after the tragedy of exile. For Malachi, this conflict revolves around a few issues, including the people acting as cheapskates in their approach to worship (Mal 1:6–14), the priests dishonoring Yhwh and failing to carry out their role as teachers of the people (Mal 2:1–9), and some persons disrespecting marriage (Mal 2:13–17). According to Malachi, a culture of contempt underlies all these behaviors, and this is why the first half of the book resorts to the language of family (especially parenthood, with God as parent and Israel as children, again as in Hos 1–3).

The second half of the book, beginning in Mal 3:1, offers a solution to the problems in the form of a reforming leader. "Behold, I am sending my messenger [Hebrew: *mal'ākî*]" introduces a promise to which the audience may react with either expectation or dread. The key to the reform lies in adherence to the old Israelite ethical ideal so often stated by the prophets and so often violated:

"Then I will draw near to you for judgment, and I will hurry up to testify against sorcerers, adulterers, oath-breakers, those who defraud day laborers of their wages or (mistreat) widows and orphans or shove aside the resident aliens, in short, all who disrespect me," says Yhwh of Hosts. (Mal 3:5)

Like most other prophetic texts, this one appeals to the past as a warning for the present. Utterly without nostalgia or sentimentality about the ancestors, Malachi joins the rest of the Book of the Twelve in regarding them as highly negative examples of human behavior. Yet in contrast to human sinfulness, Yhwh's faithfulness remains a constant. According to Mal 3:16, "It will be written in the book of memory before [Yhwh] about those who honor Yhwh and respect his name." Like the Mesopotamian idea of a divinely owned "book of destinies" that records the shape of both cosmic and human history, Yhwh's book records the plot lines of human lives. Unlike the ancient Near Eastern parallels, Malachi's conception of the book does not resort to an idea of fate or unconditional divine choice, but depends on Israel's chosen patterns of life.

Malachi ends, then, with a call to obedience to Torah, coupled with an appeal to the prophetic legacy:

Remember the Torah of Moses, my servant, to whom I gave commands for all Israel at Horeb—statutes and judgments.

Indeed, I am sending you Elijah the prophet before Yhwh's great and fearsome Day comes. He will turn the parents' heart to their children and the children's heart to their parents, so that I will not need to come and annihilate the land. (Mal 3:22–24 [ET 4:4–6])

That is, Malachi attempts to connect two major streams of Israelite theology (and two major parts of the biblical canon) by indicating that adhering to one equals honoring the other. Moses the lawgiver and Elijah the opponent of abusers of power speak with one voice. Those who heed that voice will find themselves united with one another. In this way, then, the family crisis involving Yhwh and Israel stated by Hos 1–3 and then explained by the succeeding parts of the Book of the Twelve will find a resolution.

MALACHI AS AN ENDING

In the Christian Bible, Malachi marks the end of the Old Testament, because early Christians understood its promise of a coming messenger in ch 3 as a foreshadowing of John the Baptist and the ministry of Jesus (see Matt 17:10; Mark 9:11). In the Hebrew Bible, on the other hand, Malachi merely ends the Former and Latter Prophets, while the Tanakh as a whole ends with 2 Chronicles, focusing on a different sort of promised renewal of Israel.

Perhaps most immediately fruitful for its interpretation, Malachi ends the Book of the Twelve. Why? One reason is simply chronological: it seems to come latest in the sequence of texts created, at least as an entire book. But since chronological concerns are not the only organizing principle for the Twelve, there must be another reason. Like Haggai and Zechariah, Malachi continues the legacy of the earlier prophets (from the eighth century BCE on) into a new era, both preserving the older sense of potential doom as the consequence of human evil and underscoring confidence in the future. Since Utopia did not arrive after the return from Babylonian Exile (a theme also in Isa 56–66), the latest known Israelite prophetic books sought to maintain hopefulness while dealing with the problems of the real world. Malachi reflects that attempt, and its placement at the end of the Twelve renders the desired balance as the lens through which to interpret the entire work and all twelve constituent parts.

Implications

Why twelve prophets collected together? Why not a single work or twelve separate works? While each of the twelve books here retains its integrity as a literary work and its own message, the collection of twelve voices reflects a desire for a complete witness. The number twelve coincides with the number of Israelite tribes and can hardly be accidental (even if at earlier stages, the prophetic assembly included four or six or eight or nine works, as it probably did). The final collector and editor of all this material wishes to speak to and for the entire people of Israel, not just parts of it. Certainly both the Northern Kingdom and the Southern Kingdom (Israel and Judah) must be represented, for they shared a common past and a common destiny. In seeking a communal solution, the Book of the Twelve reminds us that religious purity does not result from the perfectionism of individuals, even when courage is most required. The prophets and their disciples stand amid their own people and share their fate, whether tragic or joyous. Religion is not a zero sum game, nor a contest of human strength, nor an airing of grievances. It is, rather, a quest for a community to find its purpose in the work of God.

Notes

1. As observed recently by Mika S. Pajunen and Hanne von Weissenberg, "The Book of Malachi, Manuscript 4Q76 (4QXII[a]) and the Formation of the 'Book of the Twelve,'" *Journal of Biblical Literature* 134 (2015): 731–751. In the most ancient manuscripts, the order of the books can vary widely. For example, Malachi does not always come at the end.

2. Jörg Jeremias, *Der Prophet Hosea* (Göttingen: Vandenhoeck & Ruprecht, 1983).

3. For the first view, see Michael H. Floyd, *Minor Prophets, Part 2* (Grand Rapids: Eerdmans, 2000), 561–626; for the second, see esp. Rainer Kessler, *Maleachi* (Freiburg: Herder, 2011), 52–53.

For Further Reading

Birch, Bruce. *Let Justice Roll Down: The Old Testament, Ethics, and Christian Life.* Louisville: Westminster John Knox, 1991.

Edelman, Diana V., and Ehud Ben Zvi, eds. *The Production of Prophecy: Constructing Prophecy and Prophets in Yehud.* London: Equinox, 2009.

Floyd, Michael H. *Minor Prophets, Part 2.* Grand Rapids: Eerdmans, 2000.

Nogalski, James D., and Marvin A. Sweeney, eds. *Reading and Hearing the Book of the Twelve.* Atlanta: SBL, 2000.

Redditt, Paul L., and Aaron Schart, eds. *Thematic Threads in the Book of the Twelve.* Berlin: de Gruyter, 2003.

30 The Secondary Canon

Key Text: *O Lord, father and ruler of my life, do not forsake me to their company or allow me to walk among them. Who will set whips over my thoughts wise instruction over my heart, so that my stupidity may not overwhelm me or their sins overtake me? Otherwise, my ignorance will overwhelm me and my sins will be full and I will fall before the adversaries and the enemy will rejoice over me. O Lord, father and God of my life, do not give me haughty eyes nor let lust overtake me. Do not let a greedy belly or evil desire overwhelm me. Do not abandon me to a shameless spirit.* (Sir 23:1–6)

This book began with the memory of ancient synagogues housing cabinets of scrolls for use in worship and study, the earliest form of the canon of Scripture. It is noteworthy that the contents of those cabinets could vary, and as the technology of the scroll gave way to the newer technology of the codex or bound book (a device still with us) it became increasingly important to decide which texts to bind together in the Bible as it emerged in both Jewish and Christian circles. As different groups drew different theological conclusions even from the texts they shared, identifying the boundaries between texts that spoke with a prophetic voice and those that did not made an important difference. Christians and Jews shared (and share) all of the texts discussed earlier in this book.

Jews during the period between 400 BCE and 100 CE also wrote many texts of varying religious influence. Besides the New Testament, produced by Jewish followers of Jesus of Nazareth during the century after his death, these texts include 1 Enoch (quoted in the book of Jude), Jubilees, and the Testaments of the Twelve Patriarchs. Parts or all of these texts predate 200 BCE (although 1 Enoch in particular developed over several centuries, with the last parts coming from early Christians). The Dead Sea community (the Essenes) and groups predating them produced various community rules (e.g., the Damascus Document, the Community Rule or Serek ha-Yahad), biblical commentaries, wisdom texts, hymns, and such elaborate religio-political meditations as the Temple Scroll. Fragments of all this material survives in the Dead Sea Scrolls, and almost all of it predates the rise of Christianity. In addition, some parts of the Mishnah, the early comprehensive collection of Jewish laws from the third century CE, may date also to the Second Temple period, though in a form that must be reconstructed from the later texts in which they are embedded. Meanwhile, Greek-speaking Jews wrote meditations on political life (Aristeas), plays (Ezekiel the Tragedian), extensive biblical commentary (Philo), and the sources behind the late-first-century CE historian Josephus. In short, then, Jews under Persian, Hellenistic, and Roman rule produced a large and rich literature, much of which survives.

Some of these texts also became part of some forms of the Christian Bible. The Ethiopian church, for example, reveres 1 Enoch as part of a large and open-ended canon. Orthodox and Catholic Christians (and some Protestants), value a number of texts as Deuterocanonical, that is, not quite as central as the Old and New Testaments but more significant than any other texts. As the sixteenth-century Anglican document, the "Thirty-nine Articles of Religion" puts it, "And the other books (as Jerome saith) the church doth read for example of life and instruction of manners; but yet doth it not apply them to establish any doctrine." (Article 6). For the Anglican reformers and their successors (since the "Thirty-nine Articles" still appear in the *Book of Common Prayer*), these books include 3–4 Esdras, Tobit, Judith, Wisdom of Solomon, Sirach or Ecclesiasticus, Baruch and the Epistle of Jeremiah, expanded versions of Daniel and Esther, the Prayer of Manasseh, and 1–2 Maccabees. Other lists differ slightly. For now, a brief description of each of these works can be useful.

THE SECOND TEMPLE PERIOD IN OUTLINE (ALL DATES BCE)

Imperial History	Israelite/Jewish Leaders	Texts
Persian Empire (539–334) Hellenistic Empires (334–165)	Ezra, Nehemiah	Many biblical texts Core of Enoch, Sirach, Jubilees
The Hasmonean Period (Jewish Independence—165–63)	The Maccabees and their successors Judas (d. 160)	1–2 Maccabees, expanded Esther and Daniel, many

	Jonathan (d. 142)	DSS texts
	Simon (d. 135)	
	John Hyrkanos (d. 104)	
	Aristobulus I (d. 103)	
	Alexander Yamani (d. 76)	
	Hyrkanos II (d. 66)	
	Aristobulus II (deposed 63)	
Roman Domination (after 31)	Herod the Great and heirs	Wisdom of Solomon

Narrative Texts

The deuterocanonical books can be classified in various ways, but a useful division is to think of them as narratives, on the one hand, and prayers and wisdom texts, on the other. Each of these categories continues traditions already seen in the Hebrew Bible's primary canon itself.

The narrative texts retrace the stories in Ezra and Nehemiah and extend them well into the Second Temple period. Some of these narratives have a strong historical background (1–2 Macc), while others more closely resemble Greek novellas (Judith, Tobit). All of the narratives emphasize, however, the struggles of Jews either in the homeland or in diaspora as they confront the demands of gentiles powers controlling them.

1–2 ESDRAS

The texts most closely resembling the texts of the primary canon are 1 and 2 Esdras (Greek for Ezra). Despite their common name, the books actually have quite different origins, with 1 Esdras coming from ca. 100 BCE and 2 Esdras dating perhaps two hundred years later. Both books rework the stories of Ezra to fit new issues.

First Esdras (also known as 3 Esdras in the Vulgate) revises and condenses material in 2 Chronicles, Ezra, and Nehemiah (though some have argued for the reverse relationship).[1] It is thus an example of a well-known Hellenistic literary practice, the epitome or condensed book, which presents an older work in a new guise. The parallels (which are not identical in every detail because 1 Esdras revises its sources) are as follows:

1 Esdras	Older Works
1:1–55	2 Chron 35:1–36:21
2:1–15	Ezra 1:1–11
2:16–30	Ezra 4:7–24
3:1–5:6	no parallel
5:7–46	Ezra 2:1–70
5:47–71	Ezra 3:1–45
6:1–7:15	Ezra 4:24–6:22
8:1–9:55	Ezra 7:1–10:44 + Neh 7:73–8:12

The disjointed story of Ezra comes into a simpler (better?) order in 1 Esdras.

Perhaps the most interesting change occurs in the section that lacks a source in the older work, 1 Esdr 3:1–5:6. These chapters tell the story of a contest among courtiers of Darius the Great (r. 522–486 BCE). Three young men each face the challenge of coming up with the cleverest saying and its defense. The first proposes that the strongest thing in the world is wine since it can master anybody. The second offers the king as the strongest thing since all obey him. The third, who turns out to be Zerubbabel (the famous Jewish leader of the returnees from exile according to the books of Ezra and Haggai) wins the prize by arguing both that women overpower all other things in the human world, and that truth outranks even them. As a reward, he receives nothing less than a renewed commitment by the king to rebuild the Jerusalem temple and protect the city and its citizens. As in other books in the secondary canon, the story underscores Yhwh's concern for Jews in diaspora and their ultimately successful struggle to rebuild their lives in their ancestral land.

Second Esdras (parts of which are also called, confusingly, 5 Ezra, 4 Ezra, and 6 Ezra in that order), meanwhile, retains the tradition of Ezra's authorship but contains primarily apocalyptic material. The book, which is not always included in English versions of the Apocrypha or Deuterocanonical Books, was apparently composed in Hebrew, but it survives only in various translations (most of which derive from an earlier Greek translation), including those in Latin, Syriac (only chs 3–14 or 4 Ezra), Armenian, and Georgian. The book probably contains three originally separate works combined into a single, disjointed book.

Second Esdras 1:1–2:48, also called 5 Ezra, contains exchanges between God and Ezra in which the wise priest goes to Mount Horeb (Sinai) to receive divine instruction. The conversations between the two lays out Israel's history as one of potential threat but also divine salvation, complete with warnings to seek security away from evil forces. In this way, the book is reminiscent of such early Christian texts as Mark 13 (= Matt 24; Luke 21), during which Jesus anticipates the destruction of Jerusalem and warns disciples to escape the inferno of the Romano-Jewish war of 70–73 CE.

The middle section of the book, 2 Esdr 3:1–14:51, consists of seven visions of the conflagration of the Roman Empire and, after many trials, the triumph of the Jewish people. Again, the book's apocalypticism is reminiscent of both Zechariah and Daniel, on the one hand, and early Christian apocalyptic on the other. And finally, the last part of the book, 2 Esdr 15:1–16:78, continues the predictions of calamity ahead, as well as of supervening divine protection of the faithful.

Second Esdras, like other apocalyptic texts, speaks of the present or immediate past by using the popular fictional device of a vision by an already ancient figure (elsewhere Enoch or the sons of Jacob, but in this case Ezra). The narrative encourages the reader to persevere in the face of adversity, and in particular during a time of imperial oppression by the occupying power, Rome.

TOBIT

Long before 2 Esdras or even 1 Esdras, the book of Tobit (probably from the late third or early second century BCE) told the story of a family of exiles. Tobit, according to the story, experienced deportation during the late eighth century at the hands of Shalmaneser V. Taking up residence in Nineveh, he and his family manage to flourish, so much so that his relative Ahiqar becomes a key advisor to a later emperor. New trials await Tobit, including conflict with his wife and a tragic accident in which bird droppings fall into his eyes and blind him. He thus cries out to God, praying for death (Tob 3:1–6). At the same time, his relative Sarah, who has been exiled to Ecbatana in Media (Iran), prays for death after she has seen the seventh of her husbands die on their honeymoon thanks to a demon Asmodeus (Tob 3:7–15).

The archangel Raphael sets about answering both their prayers. In disguise, he leads Tobit's son Tobias from Nineveh to Ecbatana to collect some money owed his father. Along the way, the two travelers slay a giant fish from which they extract various fluids useful for expelling demons and curing blindness caused by bird droppings. This fairy-tale-like element allows the narrator to point toward God's protection of the family of Tobit (and Jewish exiles more generally). The magic realism of the text moves it into the realm of fantasy, but like all fantasy this tale can explore significant existential themes.

TOBIT AND OTHER TEXTS

Tobit refers to Ahiqar, the main character of another work also known from antiquity. The book of Ahiqar included a story about that figure, an advisor to Esarhaddon of Assyria during the mid-seventh century BCE (possibly with some historical basis), and then a long collection of proverbs. Written in Aramaic in the sixth century BCE and extant from at least one manuscript from the Persian era (that from Elephantine Island in Egypt), Ahiqar became popular among Jews even though it seems to have originated among gentiles. The story of Ahiqar and then his uncle Tobit remained popular for many centuries throughout the Middle East, especially among Christians from the Caucasus (Georgia and Armenia).

In time, Tobias marries Sarah, fashions a magic charm so foul-smelling that the demon flees from Iran to Africa never to bother anyone again, and returns home to heal his father. At that point, Raphael reveals his true identity, and Tobit addresses God and his fellow Israelites in a benedictory prayer (Tob 13:1–18) that reads in part (in the version in the Greek manuscript Codex Vaticanus):

Then Tobit wrote a prayer with joy:

Blessed be the living God and his Kingdom forever,
Because he afflicts and shows mercy,

Leading down to the underworld and back up,
And nothing escapes his grasp.
O children of Israel, confess him before the gentiles,
For he has scattered us among them.
There he has shown his greatness,
Exalted himself before all living things,
Inasmuch as he is our Lord and God.
He is our father forever.
Yes, he may afflict us because of our unrighteous deeds,
And then again he will have mercy and gather us from all the gentiles
Among whom you have been scattered.
If you turn to him with a whole heart,
And with a complete spirit do trustworthy things before him,
Then he will turn to you
And he will not hide his face from you.
Then you will see what he will do with you,
And you should confess him with all your mouth,
And bless the Righteous Lord
And exalt his eternal kingdom.
As for me, in the land of my captivity I will confess God,
And acknowledge God's strength and greatness among sinful nations.
Repent, O sinners, and do righteousness before him.
Who knows if he will wish to show mercy to you?
I will exalt my God,
And my spirit will extol Heaven's Kingdom,
So that God's greatness may be celebrated.
Let everything speak and confess him in Jerusalem,
Jerusalem the holy city . . .
Let my spirit bless God the Great King.
Because Jerusalem has been rebuilt with sapphire and emerald,
Your walls with precious stones,
And your towers and ramparts with pure gold,
And the streets of Jerusalem will be paved with beryl and antimony and stones
   from Oman.
Then all her gates will say "Hallelujah." They will praise and say, "Blessed be God, and
   may he be exalted forever."
Then Tobit stopped praying.

The last verses' references to the restoration of Jerusalem as a bejeweled city (anticipating
that same image for the heavenly city in the book of Revelation) reveals the period of the

book's composition as one that took place long after the time of the characters. Thus their story becomes a window onto both the fears and hopes of Jews for whom diaspora was a communal, if not always personal, reality.

JUDITH

A similar background also shapes the book of Judith, which tells the story of a beautiful widow whose very name means "Jewish woman" (*Yĕhûdît*) and who hails from the town of Bethuliah. The book comes from the mid-second century BCE, and it signals its fictional nature by making its principal villain one Holofernes, a general of Nebuchadnezzar the king of *Assyria* (the real Nebuchadnezzar being king of *Babylonia*). Judith saves her people by seducing Holofernes, or rather seeming to do so, since they never consummate their relationship. Instead, she insists on observing *kašrût* throughout her sojourn in the hostile invaders' camp. On the day when she has promised to let Holofernes have his way, and after he has drunk more wine than at any other time in order to steel himself to the task, she gracefully cuts off his head and carries it out of the camp in the very bag previously used for kosher food. A grisly touch, but one that artists have taken delight from for many centuries.

The book consists of three parts (1:1–3:10; 4:1–7:32; and 8:1–16:25), which tell the story in a meaningful progression. The book ends, as many of the novelistic works of the period do, with a prayer piously praising first Judith then God. As Jdt 16:1–6 puts it, the readers should

> Rejoice in my God with drums,
> Praise the Lord with cymbals,
> Sing to him a psalm and a hymn,
> Exalt and invoke his name,
> For God the Lord shatters armies.
> Among camps amid his people,
> He rescues me from my adversaries.
> Assyria came out of the mountains from the north,
> Came in its powerful hordes,
> With a multitude flowing like rivers,
> And their cavalry covered the hills.
> He promised to overspread my hills
> And slay my young people with the sword
> And dash my infants into the ground
> And seize my children as loot
> And violate my young women.
> The Lord Almighty has defeated them

By the hand of a woman.
For their leader did not fall by young men
Nor did the children of Titans cast him down,
Nor did towering giants hurl him down,
But Judith the daughter of Merari
With her beautiful face undid him.

Along with digs at Greek religious traditions ("children of Titans"), the text picks up older biblical themes to portray divine deliverance as the expected outcome of any crisis with hostile foreign powers. Such a message would no doubt have resonated with Jews of this period, when the struggle for political independence had led to the Maccabean revolt and its aftermath (see p. 379–81).

GREEK DANIEL

Some English Bibles print a text they call "Additions to Daniel," a practice that goes back at least to the Geneva Bible of 1560 (under the name of Dan 13 and 14). In antiquity, though, no such text existed. The Hebrew and Aramaic book of Daniel circulated in Jewish circles, while a longer Greek version circulated among Christians (though it had originated among Jews before the rise of Christianity). In other words, Greek Daniel minus Hebrew/Aramaic Daniel equals "Additions to Daniel."

The additions, which entered the book in the century or so after its composition, consists of three items: the stories of Bel and the Dragon, Susanna, and the Prayer of Azariah and the Three Men (whom Nebuchadnezzar attempted to roast for refusing to worship his idol).

The first two stories present Daniel as a detective. In "Bel and the Dragon," he proves that the Babylonian god Marduk or Bel (= "the lord") is no god. Since the priests of Bel argue that he eats the supper they leave for him each night behind closed doors, Daniel spreads flour on the floor unbeknown to them. When the temple doors are opened the next morning, footprints of the priest are visible all over the floor. The monotheistic Daniel shows the folly of polytheism.

In the Susanna story, a virtuous Jewish woman faces charges of sexual immorality lodged by two men who tried to force her to have sex with them. Daniel exposes the blatant injustice of this act of extortion, which perverts the law's assumption that two witnesses are necessary for conviction in a major crime.

In adding the third new text (Dan 3:26–90), the prayer from the superheated oven, the revisers of Daniel most closely resemble those recasting Esther and composing other books of this period. The heightened interest in personal piety seen in the prayer fitly reveals a major trend of the time. The intricate recasting of older themes of lament and praise, of national focus and individual concerns makes for a beautiful prayer:

Blessed are you, O Lord God of our ancestors,
And praiseworthy and glorified is your name forever,
Because you are righteous in all you do for us
And your works are true, and your roads are straight,
And all your judgments are true.
Yes, you execute true judgments
In all that you have done to us,
And to your holy city of our ancestors, Jerusalem,
Because in truth and justice you have done all these things on account of our sins.
(vv. 3–5)

Blessed are you, Lord God of our ancestors,
And praiseworthy and exalted is forever.
And your glorious, holy name is blessed forever,
Laudable and elevated forever.
Blessed are you in the holy temple of your glory. (vv. 29–31, inserted between Dan 3:23 and 3:24)

The prayer later calls the angels themselves to join in their prayer (cf. Pss 148–150). While it is hard to imagine men inside a fire praying so eloquently, no matter the extent of providential care for them, the composer of the prayer dares to consider just such a possibility. The prayer reclaims the threat of martyrdom from the realm of tragedy and makes it part of the fabric of Yhwh's care for Israel.

GREEK ESTHER

As with Daniel, so too with Esther: an expanded addition of that book appeared in the late Second Temple period. It included six additions to the Hebrew book: (A) an introduction, (B) an royal message positioned between Esth 3:13 and 3:14, (C) prayers by Esther and Mordecai after Esth 4:17, (D) a story about Esther's fears just after these prayers, (E) another royal edict between Esth 8:12 and 8:13, and finally (F) a dream by Mordecai. These sections do not seem to have come from the same hand, for Additions A, C, and D are translations, while Additions B and E were composed in Greek. The origins of F are less clear.[2] Each addition augments the earlier Hebrew text.

So, when the original text says that a character prays, the supplements add words of a prayer. Decrees are not merely mentioned but given a text. And most significantly, the actions of the major characters are connected to the work of God, whom the Hebrew original does not mention directly, if at all. In short, then, the Greek Esther makes the Hebrew work more coherent (explaining the motivations of the characters) while transforming the heroes Mordecai and Esther into models of religious faithfulness. Apparently, the various augmenters of the book felt that Esther deserved to survive but lacked certain important features that would render it more suitable "for example of life and instruction of manners" (to return to the phrasing of the BCP's Thirty-nine Articles).

BARUCH AND THE EPISTLE OF JEREMIAH

A different approach to the narrative of exile appears in Baruch (also called 1 Baruch to distinguish it from some later works) and the closely related Epistle of Jeremiah (sometimes presented as the sixth chapter of Baruch). These works speak in the voice of Jeremiah's scribe and sidekick Baruch and, of course, the prophet himself. The composition of the book occurred probably in the second century BCE (or possibly later), apparently in Hebrew; it survives today in Greek translation and in other versions made from the Greek.

Baruch has three major sections, a prose narrative (including prayers of penitence) about exile or a sort of fictional memoir by the book's eponymous hero (Bar 1:1–3:8), a more poetic set of instructions to "Israel" to "hear the commands of life" in their exile (Bar 3:9–4:4), and a second set of instructions to "my people" and "Jerusalem" along much the same lines (Bar 4:5–5:9). The book ends with an allusion to Isa 40 and possibly Isa 55:

> For God has commanded every high mountain to be leveled and every lofty hill to be lowered and every valley filled up to make a level surface, so that Israel may travel safely in God's glory. The forest will overshadow—every tree will shade Israel at God's instruction. For God will lead Israel with joy by his glorious light, with the mercy and righteousness that pertains to him. (Bar 5:7–9)

That is, just as the book of Daniel struggled with the prophetic promises of deliverance and their proper timing, given the ongoing struggle with gentile domination, Baruch anticipates the fulfillment of the ancient sayings in the near future and encourages its readers not to give up hope.

Similarly, the Epistle of Jeremiah addresses Jews living in pagan lands. It adopts the fiction of a message from the prophet to those in Babylonian exile, noting that they "see in Babylon gods of silver and gold and wood that people bear on their shoulders and that bring fear to the gentiles" (EpJer 3). This is a very nice description of the Babylonian custom of periodically parading statues of the deities during major festivals, even though it reduces foreign religion to its most objectionable elements from a Jewish point of view: the elevation of the material to the spiritual, the multiplication of deities, and the irrational behaviors that flow from worshiping nondeities. Noting that their exile may last as long as seven generations (EpJer 2) and thus justifying the delay of divine redemption as a due punishment, the book goes on to describe the utter impotence of idols as simply objects made by human beings. In contrast to the heavenly bodies, which while no gods, still obey the one God, the so-called gods of the nations lack the most basic abilities for self-care. Thus Jews have nothing to fear from them or their worshipers. The little book calls its readers to be resolute rather than allowing their minority status to dishearten them.

1–2 MACCABEES

The delay of deliverance cannot string along forever, and its arrival is the subject of the final two narrative texts to be considered here. Arguably some of the best known of the narrative texts in the secondary canon are 1 and 2 Maccabees. These two works, written by different authors during the late- and middle-second century BCE respectively, have in common only their basic story and their name. First Maccabees was written in Hebrew and then translated into Greek, while 2 Maccabees was in literary Greek from the beginning. The first book originated in Judea, while the second may have come from the diaspora (perhaps Alexandria or Antioch). They also differ in details, and 2 Maccabees is usually understood to be more historically reliable.

The basic storyline is this: on the death of Alexander the Great, his generals fought over the empire, finally reaching a long-term settlement after 301 BCE. The land of Israel fell to the Ptolemies, the rulers of Egypt. Syria and points east (originally all the way to Pakistan) fell to the Seleucids. Palestine was thus a border zone between the two successor states. After about a century, the Seleucids pushed the Ptolemies out of the southern Levant and occupied Samaria, Jerusalem, and neighboring zones.

After various mishaps, the Seleucid ruler Antiochus IV Epiphanes (r. 175–164 BCE), whose immodest title means "God manifest," desecrated the Temple in Jerusalem by offering on its altar a pig dedicated to Zeus Olympos. This act proved to be the match that lit a lot of powder lying about, that is, rising frustration among religious Jews at their "Hellenizing" neighbors and the government that supported them. The accoutrements of a Greek city-state present in Jerusalem itself created considerable resentment, and the porcine offering sparked a revolt whose causes lay deeper.

After much struggle, then, the Jews under the leadership of the priest Mattathias and especially his son Judas the Hammer ("Maccabee" means "hammer") managed to push the Seleucids out of Jerusalem. Over the next few decades, they succeeded in wrestling independence from the Hellenistic power, facilitating a century-long period of relative autonomy and prosperity.

HANUKKAH AND THE MACCABEAN REVOLT

To this day, Jews celebrate the Feast of Lights or Hanukkah during December. This festival, which does not appear in the Hebrew Bible, commemorates a miracle after the recapture of the Jerusalem temple from the Seleucid army. According to 1 Macc 4:36–61 and 2 Macc 10:1–8, Judas the Maccabee and his army cleaned up the wrecked Temple precinct and reconsecrated it on the 25th day of Kislev (roughly, mid-December). Among other things, they disassembled the old altar of burnt offering and stored it until a prophet could tell them what to do with it (one never did, apparently). Much later traditions from the Talmud tell a story of one-day's supply of oil for the lamps of the Temple stretching out for eight days, but this legend does not appear in the earliest sources. Still, the contemporary festival remembers a moment of courage and piety against state-sponsored terror.

In recounting this basic story, 1 and 2 Maccabees differ among themselves, but each contains an attractively told tale. First Maccabees contains six sections: an introduction (1 Macc 1:1–9), the period prior to the revolt (1 Macc 1:10–2:70), the battles of Judas the Maccabee (1 Macc 3:1–9:22), the battles of his brother Jonathan (1 Macc 9:23–12:53), the accomplishment of their youngest brother Simon (1 Macc 13:1–16:22), and a conclusion that refers to their successor John Hyrkanos (1 Macc 16:23–24). The book supports the Hasmonean dynasty founded by the brothers of Judas the Maccabee, emphasizing their prowess at gradually eliminating Seleucid domination of the land of Israel. The book highlights the brutality of Antiochus Epiphanes and his immediate successors, while also trying to situate their work in the larger political movements of the time. Since the Seleucids claimed overlordship of most of the Near East and Iran, and since the Romans had arrived to challenge their dominance, the potential for intractable foreign entanglements far beyond Palestine beset the Seleucid Empire. And, indeed, the morass in which they found themselves with the insurgents in Jerusalem was a relatively small concern in their geopolitical thinking.

Closer to home in Jerusalem, a significant theme in 1 Maccabees is the intra-Jewish strife between those who took a traditional view of Judaism and those who sought to accommodate Hellenistic practices, including even polytheism. While the Hellenizers eventually got their way to some extent (certainly the Jerusalem that Jesus of Nazareth knew was a heavily Hellenized place), the defense of monotheism and of ancestral religious practices did stick. First Maccabees describes the views it opposes variously as those of "evil" or "lawless" persons. Perhaps a window into the flashpoints of conflict comes from 1 Macc 1:14–15, which relates how, prior to the revolt, some Jews in Jerusalem fawned upon Antiochus and "built a gymnasium in Jerusalem according to gentile custom [i.e., they exercised naked] and hid their circumcision and deviated from the holy covenant. They joined the gentiles and did evil according to their practices." Circumcision became a boundary marker, not just a sign of membership in the group of one's birth. While it was acceptable to speak Greek or do business with gentiles, adopting their religious customs proved a deal-breaker.

Second Maccabees, meanwhile, tells roughly the same story in different ways. An abbreviated version of a now lost masterwork by Jason of Cyrene, with various supplements from other sources, 2 Maccabees places between an introduction (2 Macc 1:1–2:32) and a conclusion (2 Macc 15:37–39), a three-part story of the Maccabean revolt and its aftermath. Part 1 describes events before the insurrection (2 Macc 3:1–7:42), Part 2 the rebellion itself through the first successful settlement with Antiochus Epiphanes (2 Macc 8:1–11:38), and Part 3 the later continued struggle against Seleucid overlordship (2 Macc 12:1–15:36). Judas the Maccabee appears as an extraordinary guerilla leader who, against all odds, manages to secure both the religious integrity of the Jerusalem Temple and the people's ability to practice Judaism at home without fear.

Second Maccabees includes documents purporting to come from officials in the Seleucid Empire, other Hellenistic states, and the Roman Republic. This last power had begun to exert major influence in the Near East. According to 2 Macc 11:34–38, a letter from Titus Manius on behalf of the Roman Senate addressed the "people of the Jews," marking one of the first points of contact in the fateful history of the two peoples. Other texts embedded in the work reveal some of the inner workings of diplomacy of the period. While these quoted texts serve the overall narrative of 2 Maccabees, they offer an accurate picture of larger political realities, for history never happens inside an isolated system. The story of Judaism from this point on becomes part of the history of the entire Mediterranean world.

Wisdom and Liturgical Texts

While these narratives extended the biblical histories into the Second Temple period, emphasizing especially the resilience of Jews facing gentile opposition either in the land of Israel or in diaspora, other texts concentrate more upon the pursuit of piety and wisdom. These texts continue older biblical forms, particularly those of Proverbs and Psalms, but revitalize them for a new era.

SIRACH OR ECCLESIASTICUS

Perhaps another well-known work is the Wisdom of Joshua son of Sira(ch), or Ben Sira, a book also known in the Vulgate as Ecclesiasticus (the "church's book," not to be confused with Ecclesiastes). Writing a little after 200 BCE, Ben Sira wrote a four-part book (Sir 1:1–23:27; 24:1–43:33; 44:1–50:24; and 50:25–51:30). The first section contains extended praise for the value of wisdom, exhortations to young learners to acquire what knowledge they can, and strings of proverbs like those of the biblical book of Proverbs.

For example, consider these two clusters of proverbs:

> Do not hate hard work or agricultural labor, which comes from the Most High.
> Don't sign up for the crowd of sinners—remember that [divine] retribution does not tarry.

> Humble yourself fully because the punishment of the impious is fire and worms.
> Do not exchange a friend for cash, nor an intimate for the finest gold. (Sir 7:15–19)
> Don't get rid of a wise and good wife, for her grace is more valuable than gold.

Throughout this section, counsel against foolish and selfish actions leads the ideal reader into greater discernment.

The second major section continues this theme, opening with wisdom's self-praise in Sir 24. Ben Sira extends the conflation of wisdom and Torah that begins in such texts as Pss 1, 19, and 119, noting that wisdom has taken up residence in Israel (Sir 24:8). The text thus emphasizes the intimate connection between discernment of the world's ways and the need to pursue piety before the One God.

The third section is the most famous. Here Ben Sira shifts from the instructional mode so similar to Proverbs into the mode of "praising notable men, our ancestors from of old" (Sir 44:1). Like the later text in Heb 11, Sir 44–51 lists a series of prominent persons and praises virtues in their lives. The exemplars of the wise life, as Ben Sira sees them, are people who "rule through their understanding" (Sir 44:3). That is, they rise above their station in life to succeed at the things that matter most.

The list of heroes includes Enoch (Sir 44:16), Noah (Sir 44:17–18), Abraham (Sir 44:19–23), Moses (Sir 45:1–5), Aaron (Sir 44:6–22), his grandson Phineas (Sir 45:23–26), Joshua (Sir 46:1–6), Caleb (Sir 46:7–12), Samuel (Sir 46:13–20), Nathan the prophet and David (Sir 47:1–11), Solomon (Sir 47:12–25), Elijah (Sir 48:1–11), Elisha (Sir 48:12–16), Hezekiah (Sir 48:17–25), Josiah (Sir 49:1–10), Zerubbabel (Sir 49:11–13), and, after a summary of these worthies' achievements (Sir 49:14–16), Ben Sira's personal favorite, Simon the high priest (Sir 50:1–24). All his heroes are male, and all but the last one figure prominently in the Bible as models of piety if not necessarily wisdom. Simon was his older contemporary and role personal model. In all these examples, Ben Sira seeks practical models of leaders worthy of emulation.

THE LANGUAGE AND TEXT OF SIRACH

The book of Ecclesiasticus was written in Hebrew and translated a generation later into Greek by the author's grandson, a Jew living in Egypt. Over the next few centuries, the Hebrew text disappeared, but the Greek text remained popular among Christians, entering many Greek Bibles and being translated into Latin and other languages as well. Then in the nineteenth century, a partial copy of the Hebrew book came to light in the *genizah* (storeroom) of the old synagogue in Cairo. Much older Hebrew-language fragments of the book also surfaced during the mid-twentieth century as part of the Dead Sea Scrolls. This strange history reminds one of the importance of scholarship in the recovery of the past.

At last, then, the book ends with a prayer to God and an invitation to the reader to join him in "seeking wisdom openly in my prayer, asking for it before the temple and searching for it until the end" (Sir 51:14). Like other prayers interspersed throughout the book and still others in contemporary texts, the final prayer addresses God and seeks to situate the author's work with the divine care for the world. In writing "I extol you, O Lord the King, and I praise you, O God of my salvation" (Sir 51:1), Ben Sira invokes Yhwh's ongoing mercy. In the exhortation, similarly, he invites the reader to seek understanding from the God who gives such things.

WISDOM OF SOLOMON

Written in the late first century BCE or slightly later, the Wisdom of Solomon uses the ancient king's reputation as a sage and sponsor of learning to good effect. By pitching the book as the advice of one king to other rulers, the book ties into a Greco-Roman intellectual tradition of thinking of about human society through the lens of the ruler who models its highest values (*de monarchia* as the Romans would say). This text, written in Greek but steeped in the ideas of the Bible, counsels the rulers to "love righteousness, consider the Lord in goodness, and seek him with an honest heart" (Wisd 1:1). This exhortation to pursue understanding and morality operates throughout the first section of the book (Wisd 1:1–6:25). While the advice and encouragement could apply to any thoughtful person who sought a meaningful life in Judaism, the author particularly seeks to commend his faith to "kings" (Wisd 6:1). Whether any king read the book is another matter.

The second section (Wisd 7:1–10:21) extols the value of wisdom, connecting it especially to the great biblical heroes who lived by it (and villains who tragically did not). For example, in a take on the story of Adam that disagrees with the later Christian understanding of him as the vehicle for introducing sin into the world (cf. Rom 5:12–21), Wisd 10:1–2 claims that "She [i.e., Wisdom] guarded the first-formed father of the world [Adam] when he alone had been created and rescued him from his wrongdoing, giving him strength to govern all things." That is, the force of wisdom that guarded newly fashioned humankind in Paradise continued to do so after their expulsion from it. Alas, not all humans accepted its guidance, as seen in the stories of Cain (Wisd 10:3), the Flood (Wisd 10:4), and Sodom and Gomorrah (Wisd 10:6–8), among others. The character "Solomon" praises God for the grant of wisdom in a prayer (Wisd 9:1–18), connecting the life of an individual Israelite to the great story of the people.

This story continues in a more detailed form in Wisd 11:1–19:22, the third and last section of the book. Here the focus lies on the exodus and accompanying events. The text portrays the God of Israel as a savior, addressing the deity as "our God, faithful and true, patient and doing mercy toward all" (Wisd 16:1), in contrast to the gods of the nations, who have nonfunctioning body parts that merely underscore their lack of capacity to act (Wisd 16:15–16; cf. Ps 135 (LXX 134):15–18). Nonfunctioning eyes and ears do not make for a deity in whom one can trust. Israel's story, however, emplots the deeds of a God who has greater capacities.

As in other Deuterocanonical texts, then, Wisdom of Solomon connects elements that the older Israelite material left less tightly interrelated: the pursuit of wisdom, the remembrance of story (especially the foundation stories of Genesis and Exodus), and profound individual and communal piety. This rich and complex mix of ideas created Second Temple Judaism and the religions descending from it: rabbinic Judaism and Christianity.

THE PRAYER OF MANASSEH

In much the same vein but on a smaller scale, piety figures in the final work to be considered here. Like the prayers added to Esther and Daniel, the Prayer of Manasseh places in the mouth of a "biblical" figure a prayer suiting his life. According to 2 Chron 33:13, the wicked king Manasseh confronted his deportation to Babylon by repenting and seeking Yhwh's forgiveness. A much later writer composed (in Greek) a prayer of penitence suitable for the occasion. Indeed, the plaintive cry of the sinner speaks to a significant part of Jewish piety during the Second Temple period, extolling the beauty of the changed life. As the evil ruler puts it,

> Because of my numerous unrighteous acts.
> I am bound up by many iron bonds,
> So that I am rejected because of my sins
> And there is no relief for me,
> Because your wrath burns fiercely,
> And [my] evil works are before you,
> Abominations and multiple transgressions stand about.
> So now I bow the knees of my heart, entreating your compassion.
> I have sinned, Lord. I have sinned,
> And I know my lawless deeds.
> I ask, beg you,
> Forgive me, O Lord, forgive me.
> Do not release me together with my sins,
> Nor keep my evil deeds wrathfully (in mind) forever,
> Nor condemn me to the netherworld.
> Because you, O Lord, are the God of those who repent. (PrMan 10–13)

Such a prayer encourages the reader of the book to examine his or her own life too. The penitent ungodly person becomes a living demonstration of Yhwh's mercy to a penitent ungodly people.

Implications

Why read these texts, then? Many Christians accept them as part of the Bible, while others (going back to St. Jerome in the fourth century) argue that since they did not play a role in Jewish religious life, they ought to take a back seat for the church too. Even under this more modest approach, the Deuterocanonical texts (or Apocrypha) have an important historical value as witnesses to the piety that allowed the flourishing of Judaism before the rise of Christianity and far beyond. Since human beings frequently work out our concepts of values and commitments in the forms of story, wise sayings, and poetry, these texts represent important attempts to make sense of the world. Their legacy remains important no matter one's view of their use in a context of worship or doctrinal construction (the key purposes of the biblical canons for religious communities).

These texts, and others of less influence in Judaism and Christianity, exemplify the range of biblical interpretation occurring during the Second Temple period, the depth of individual and communal piety of Jews of that period, and the dangers that such a tight-knit community of believers faced in their adherence to monotheism and the ethical life inspired by Torah. Rich texts reveal rich lives whose profundity deserves study and appreciation even today.

Notes

1. On the complicated question of the relationships among these works, see the essays in *Was 1 Esdras First? An Investigation into the Priority and Nature of 1 Esdras*, ed. Lisbeth S. Fried (Atlanta: SBL, 2011).

2. See the discussion of the additions in Jon Levenson, *Esther* (Louisville: Westminster/John Knox, 1997), 27–34.

For Further Reading

Chyutin, Michael. *Tendentious Hagiographies: Jewish Propagandist Fiction BCE*. London: T. & T. Clark, 2011.

Feldman Louis H., James L. Kugel, and Lawrence H. Schiffman, eds. *Outside the Bible: Ancient Jewish Writings Related to Scripture*. 3 vols. Philadelphia: Jewish Publication Society, 2013.

Murphy, Frederick J. *Early Judaism: The Exile to the Time of Jesus*. Peabody, MA: Hendrickson, 2002.

31 What's It All About?

NOW WE REACH the conclusion and the inevitable question of what holds together all this diverse material called the Old Testament or Hebrew Bible. The ancient synagogue cabinets held works of different literary genres, theological interests and commitments, age of origin, method of composition, and purpose. Yet all of the texts worked together in some way as a canon of Scripture available to several interrelated religious communities. They still do. Today almost a third of the human population reveres them as divinely inspired words that comfort the dying and challenge the living. What are they about?

In his extraordinary book about gentiles who rescued Jews during the Holocaust, Sir Martin Gilbert records the story of David Prital, who found refuge among a small Ukrainian Baptist sect. He had sought them out on advice from a friendly German coachman. On meeting the poor Baptist farmer in his field, the two entered the farmer's house, each man knowing who the other was. Prital remembers:

> "God brought an important guest to our house," he said to his wife. "We should thank God for this blessing." They kneeled down and I heard a wonderful prayer coming out of their pure and simple hearts, not written in a single prayer book. I heard a song addressed to God, thanking God for the opportunity to meet a son of Israel in these crazy days . . . They stopped praying and we sat down at the table for a meal, which was enjoyable. The peasant's wife gave us milk and potatoes. Before the

meal, the master of the house read a chapter from the Bible. Here it is, I thought, this is the big secret. It is this eternal book that raised their morality to such unbelievable heights. It is this very book that filled their hearts with love for the Jews.[1]

Such a story, while risking mawkishness or sanctimony, says something about the history of the reception of the Bible as a central moral text of Western cultures. However often abused or neglected or fought against, it has been the indispensable work for two millennia. This historical fact deserves constant reflection.

To find what the Hebrew Bible is about, then, one must do more than analyze the text in terms of its central ideas. The history of twentieth-century scholarship has demonstrated this point repeatedly, as one brilliant reading after another has arisen based on the assumption that a central idea exists. For Gerhard von Rad, the center lay in the history of tradition-making of the story of Israel's salvation (*Heilsgeschichte*), while for his contemporary Walther Eichrodt, the key idea was covenant. More recently, for Walter Brueggemann, the various forms of imaginative testimony about divine activity forms a key to the Old Testament. There are many other proposals, all instructive, many dazzling, but too few willing to ask not just about what the biblical texts say but also about what they mean for particular religious communities to say these things.

Certainly we cannot solve this problem in a single book. But perhaps we can properly value a simple idea. The meanings of texts come in part from how they are used. That is, interpretation is a two-centered process (an ellipse rather than a circle) in which both the reader and the text must contribute something. On the one hand, a text does not mean any old thing that a reader imagines, for it has its own integrity. On the other hand, potential meanings latent within a text come out in the process of using just that text.

A survey of the acres of books interpreting the Bible written over the past two millennia reveals three basic ways in which these texts came to life in religious communities: in liturgy, moral formation, and theological reflection. In practice, the three ways intertwine at almost all times, for rabbis and bishops in all these communities confronted the daily challenge of planning worship, teaching children and adults basic lifestyle commitments, and thinking in detail about reasons behind the actions, beliefs, and values of their communities. The Bible thus has always fulfilled many tasks among Jews and Christians.

The texts that best serve those tasks have normally been most influential. The book of Psalms has inspired innumerable religious hymns and poems. Genesis or Samuel give model human beings living lives of moral integrity and piety. Song of Songs explores the depths of love, whether human or divine. And so on. These interpretations are not arbitrary or capricious but are often considered deeply and well. Liturgy could address the sorrows and joys of life. Moral reflection could avoid superficiality and probe the deepest corners of the mind and lifeways emerging from them. The theological reflection in its many forms could often land squarely in practicality, not just esoterica. But all of this is another story, for further reading another time.

What, then, is the Bible about? Yhwh and Israel, the nations and creation, sin and redemption, love and hate, fear and courage. Humankind in its quest for God and also, if the words mean what they say, the reverse. Through story, song, prophecy, and aphorism, the biblical texts consider the relationship between Yhwh and Israel and seek to foster a particular way of living into it. Their legacy lives on.

Note

1. Martin Gilbert, *The Righteous: The Unsung Heroes of the Holocaust* (New York: Holt, 2003), 13.

Index of Biblical References

Subject Index

Author's Note: *The index does not include topics or words that appear on the majority of pages of the book (e.g., Yhwh, Israel as a people).*